W9-DIG-727

On ribbon: "May it [he?] gleam with the greatest beauty."

THE TEN BOOKS OF ARCHITECTURE

The 1755 Leoni Edition

LEON BATTISTA ALBERTI

DOVER PUBLICATIONS, INC.
NEW YORK

Published in Canada by General Publishing Company, Ltd., 30 Lesmill Road, Don Mills, Toronto, Ontario.
Published in the United Kingdom by Constable and Company, Ltd., 10 Orange Street, London WC2H 7EG.

This Dover edition, first published in 1986, contains all the material on architecture from the work entitled *The Architecture of Leon Batista* [sic] *Alberti. In Ten Books. Of Painting. In Three Books. And of Statuary. In One Book. Translated into Italian By Cosimo Bartoli. And into English By James Leoni, Architect. Illustrated with Seventy-five Copper-plates, Engraved by Mr. Picart. In One Volume. London: Printed by Edward Owen, in Hand-Court, Holborn; For Robert Alfray, in the Hay-Market, St. James's. M.DCC.LV.* See the new Publisher's Note for further features of the present edition.

Manufactured in the United States of America
Dover Publications, Inc., 31 East 2nd Street, Mineola, N.Y. 11501

Library of Congress Cataloging-in-Publication Data

Alberti, Leon Battista, 1404–1472.
The ten books of architecture.

Translation of: De re aedificatoria.
Reprint. Originally published: The architecture of Leon Batista [sic] Alberti in ten books. London : Edward Owen, 1755.
1. Architecture—Early works to 1800. I. Bartoli, Cosimo, 1503–1572. II. Leoni, Giacomo, ca. 1686–1746. III. Title.
NA2515.A3513 1986 720 86-16230
ISBN 0-486-25239-6

PUBLISHER'S NOTE

THE vastly influential architectural treatise by Leon Battista Alberti (1404–1472), who foreshadowed Leonardo as a multitalented Renaissance man, was completed in manuscript in 1452. Composed in Latin, it bore the title *De re aedificatoria.* Although originally inspired by a wish to clarify Vitruvius, it goes far beyond the ancient Roman author. Alberti's work is a glorification of the architecture of antiquity as interpreted by a practicing architect of the Renaissance familiar with the latest advances in mathematics, engineering and aesthetic theory.

De re aedificatoria was first published in Florence in 1485, thirteen years after Alberti's death, by his brother Bernardo. The 1512 edition of the work published in Paris by Geoffroy Tory, the famous designer of lettering and typography, divided the book into chapters for the first time. The first Italian translation of the book, by Pietro Lauro, 1546, was superseded in 1550 by that of Cosimo Bartoli. Bartoli's edition of Alberti was the first to be illustrated.

The first English translation of the work was made from Bartoli's Italian version by Giacomo (James) Leoni (1686–1746) and appeared in London in 1726. Leoni, a Venetian architect, had come to London some time before 1715 and had published a lavish edition of Palladio in 1715–16. In Leoni's edition of Alberti, the engraving of the allegorical frontispiece and of the twenty most elaborate plates is attributed to the celebrated Amsterdam-based French artist Bernard Picart (1673–1733). Picart worked chiefly from Leoni's drawings, which in turn were based on the woodcuts in the 1550 Bartoli edition. In his volume Leoni also included translations of Alberti's works on painting and sculpture, and added a section of his own architectural drawings, entitled "Some Designs for Buildings both Public and Private." A second edition of Leoni appeared in 1739, and a third—the one reprinted here—in 1755. This latter was the first edition to print the English translation only; previous editions had run the English translation and Bartoli's

Italian version in parallel columns. This Dover volume includes only the *Ten Books of Architecture*.*

The present volume, while basically reproducing faithfully the architectural part of the 1755 Leoni, differs in a few ways. For one thing, many of the plates have been backed up and positioned in a slightly different place in the book (most were in the wrong position in the 1755 volume, anyway, as will shortly be explained). In order to keep two-page plates on facing pages, it has been necessary to place three plates slightly out of order. Thus, Plate 48 precedes Plate 47; 53 precedes 52; and 56 precedes 55.

In the 1755 edition (and presumably in the earlier English editions) the plates had inscribed references to the corresponding text passages. These references were *incorrect* (probably being based either on the text pages of some Italian edition—indeed, all the plates still bear only Italian legends—or else on an earlier English edition that had Italian and English parallel columns) and the plates were, to a large extent, placed near these incorrect text pages. In the present edition, not only are the plates as close as possible to the *correct* text pages, but also: (1) the correct references to the text have been added to the top of the plates; (2) the plates have been newly numbered 1 through 67 (exclusive of the frontispiece) for greater convenience; and (3) the text pages containing the matter which the plates illustrate have been newly furnished with cross-references of their own: an asterisk, dagger or double dagger in the margin alongside the line where the description corresponding to a plate begins, and a matching footnote indicating which plate is being referred to. Moreover, the Italian (and some Latin) plate legends have been newly translated at the foot of the plates.

On the other hand, no attempt has been made to correct minor flaws in the 1755 edition (such as the spelling "Batisti" in many running heads), which can create no confusion and indeed lend charm to the perusal of an old work.

---

* In actuality, only some seven of the above-mentioned 21 Picart plates in the *Ten Books of Architecture* part of the publication (at least speaking for the 1755 edition reprinted here) may have been engraved by Picart personally: the frontispiece and Plates 11–13, 53 and perhaps 65–67. The frontispiece and Plates 11, 12 and 53 bear the inscription "B. Picart sculpsit," Plate 13 merely states "B. Picart" but forms a clear pendant to 11 and 12, while 65–67 are credited to Picart as draftsman ("B. Picart del[ineavit]") and (to judge by their quality as well) were probably engraved by him. The rest of the Picart plates state "B. Picart sculp. direxit," implying that he merely supervised their engraving (and their quality is much more ordinary). Moreover, Plates 65–67, besides being based on drawings by Picart and not by Leoni, are dated 1727, and are thus later than the first edition of 1726. (Leoni's title page mentions 75 plates engraved by Picart, but these include the ones for the parts of the Leoni volume omitted here: painting, sculpture and Leoni's own buildings.) A final bibliographic note: Within the single physical volume that contains the 1755 edition of Leoni's translation of the three Alberti works (on architecture, painting and sculpture), Leoni's own section ("Some Designs for Buildings . . .") bears a separate date of 1758.

THE

P R E F A C E.

UR Anceſtors have left us many and various Arts tending to the Pleaſure and Conveniency of Life, acquired with the greateſt Induſtry and Diligence: Which Arts, though they all pretend, with a Kind of Emulation, to have in View the great End of being ſerviceable to Mankind; yet we know that each of them in particular has ſomething in it that ſeems to promiſe a diſtinct and ſeparate Fruit: Some Arts we follow for Neceſſity, ſome we approve for their Uſefulneſs, and ſome we eſteem becauſe they lead us to the Knowledge of Things that are delightful. What theſe Arts are, it is not neceſſary for me to enumerate; for they are obvious. But if you take a View of the whole Circle of Arts, you ſhall hardly find one but what, deſpiſing all others, regards and ſeeks only its own particular Ends: Or if you do meet with any of ſuch a Nature that you can in no wiſe do without it, and which yet brings along with it Profit at the ſame Time, conjoined with Pleaſure and Honour, you will, I believe, be convinced, that Architecture is not to be excluded from that Number. For it is certain, if you examine the Matter carefully, it is inexpreſſibly delightful, and of the greateſt Convenience to Mankind in all Reſpects, both publick and private; and in Dignity not inferior to the moſt excellent. But before I proceed further, it will not be improper to explain what he is that I allow to be an Architect: For it is not a Carpenter or a Joiner that I thus rank with the greateſt Maſters in other Sciences; the manual Operator being no more than an Inſtrument to the Architect. Him I call an Architect, who, by ſure and wonderful Art and Method, is able, both with Thought and Invention, to deviſe, and, with Execution, to compleat all thoſe Works, which, by means of the Movement of great Weights, and the Conjunction and Amaſſment of Bodies, can, with the greateſt Beauty, be adapted to the Uſes of Mankind: And to be able to do this, he muſt have a thorough Inſight into the nobleſt and moſt curious Sciences. Such muſt be the Architect. But to return.

Some have been of Opinion, that either Water or Fire were the principal Occaſions of bringing Men together into Societies; but to us, who conſider the Uſefulneſs and Neceſſity of Coverings and Walls, it ſeems evident, that they were the chief Cauſes of aſſembling Men together. But the only Obligation we have to the Architect is not for his providing us with ſafe and pleaſant Places, where we may ſhelter ourſelves from the Heat of the Sun, from Cold and Tempeſt, (though this is no ſmall Benefit); but for having beſides contrived many other Things, both of a private and publick Nature of the higheſt Uſe and Convenience to the Life of Man. How many noble Families, reduced by the Calamity of the Times, had been utterly loſt, both in our own native City, and in others, had not their paternal Habitations preſerved and cheriſhed them, as it were, in the Boſom of their Foreſathers. *Dædalus* in his Time was greatly eſteemed for having made the *Selinuntians* a Vault, which gathered ſo warm and kindly a Vapour, as provoked a plentiful Sweat, and thereby cured their Diſtempers with great Eaſe and Pleaſure. Why need I mention others who have contrived many Things of the like Sort conducive to Health; as Places for Exerciſe, for Swimming, Baths and the like? Or why ſhould I inſtance in Vehicles, Mills, Time-meaſures, and other ſuch minute Things, which neverthleſs are of great Uſe in Life? Why ſhould I inſiſt upon the great Plenty of Waters brought from the moſt remote and hidden Places, and employed to ſo many different and uſeful Purpoſes? Upon Trophies, Tabernacles, ſacred Edifices, Churches and the like, adapted to to divine Worſhip, and the Service of Poſterity? Or laſtly, why ſhould I mention the Rocks cut, Mountains bored through, Vallies filled up, Lakes confined, Marſhes diſcharged into the Sea, Ships built, Rivers turned, their Mouths cleared, Bridges laid over them, Harbours formed, not only ſerving to Men's immediate Conveniencies, but alſo opening them a Way to all Parts of the World; whereby Men have been enabled mutually to furniſh one another with Proviſions, Spices, Gems, and to communicate their Knowledge, and whatever elſe is healthful or pleaſurable. Add to theſe the Engines and Machines of War, Fortreſſes, and the like Inventions neceſſary to the Defending the Liberty of our Country, Maintaining the Honour, and Encreaſing the Greatneſs of a City, and to the Acquiſition and Eſtabliſhment of an Empire. I am really perſuaded, that if we were to enquire of all the Cities which, within the Memory of Man, have fallen by Siege into the Power of new Maſters, who it was that ſubjected and overcame them, they would tell you, the Architect; and that they were ſtrong enough to have deſpiſed the armed Enemy, but not to withſtand the Shocks of the Engines, the Violence of the Machines, and the Force of the other Inſtruments of War, with which the Architect diſtreſſed, demoliſhed and ruinated them. And the Beſieged, on the contrary, would inform you, that their greateſt Defence lay in the Art and Aſſiſtance of the Architect. And if you were to examine into the Expeditions that have been undertaken, you would go near to find that moſt of the Victories were gained more by the Art and Skill of the Architects, than by the Conduct or Fortune of the Generals; and that the Enemy was oftener overcome and conquered by the Architect's Wit, without the Captain's Arms, than by the Captain's Arms without the Architect's Wit: And what is of great Conſequence is, that the Architect conquers with a ſmall Number of Men, and without the Loſs of Troops. Let this ſuffice as to the Uſefulneſs of this Art.

But how much the Study and Subject of Building delights, and how firmly it is rooted in the Mind of Man, appears from ſeveral Inſtances, and particularly from this; that you ſhall find no body who has the Means but what has an Inclination to be building ſomething: And if a Man has happened to think of any Thing new in Architecture, he is fond of communicating and divulging it for the Uſe of others, as if conſtrained thereto by Nature. And how often does it fall out, that even when we are employed upon other Things, we cannot keep our Thoughts and Imaginations, from Projecting ſome Edifice? And when we ſee other Men's Houſes, we immediately ſet about a careful Examination of all the Proportions and Dimenſions, and, to the beſt of our Ability, conſider what might be added, retrenched or altered; and preſently give our Opinions how it might be made more compleat or beautiful. And if a Building be well laid out, and juſtly finiſhed, who is he that does not view it with the utmoſt Pleaſure and Delight? But why need I mention not only how much Benefit and Delight, but how much Glory to Architecture has brought to Nations, which have cultivated it both at home and abroad? Who that has built any publick Edifice does not think himſelf honoured by it, when it is reputable to a Man only to have built a handſome Habitation for himſelf? Men of publick Spirits approve and rejoice when you have raiſed a fine Wall or Portico, and adorned it with Portals, Columns, and a handſome Roof, knowing you have thereby not only ſerved yourſelf, but them too, having by this generous Uſe of your Wealth, gained an Addition of great Honour to yourſelf, your Family, your Deſcendants, and your City. The Sepulchre of *Jupiter* was the firſt Step to the ennobling the Iſland of *Crete*; and *Delos* was not ſo much reſpected for the Oracle of *Apollo*, as for the beautiful Structure of the City, and the Majeſty of the Temple. How much Authority accrued to the *Roman* Name and Empire from their Buildings, I ſhall dwell upon no further, than that the Sepulchres and other Remains of the ancient Magnificence, every where to be found, are a great Inducement and Argument with us for believing many Things related by Hiſtorians, which might otherwiſe have ſeemed incredible. *Thucydides* extreamly commends the Prudence of ſome Ancients, who had ſo adorned their City with all Sorts of fine Structures, that their Power thereby appeared to be much greater than it really was. And what potent or wiſe Prince can be named, that among his chief Projects for eternizing his Name and Poſterity, did not make Uſe of Architecture. But of this enough. The Concluſion is, that for the Service, Security, Honour and Ornament of the Publick, we are exceedingly obliged to the Architect; to whom, in Time of Leiſure, we are indebted for Tranquility,

Tranquility, Pleaſure and Health, in Time of Buſineſs for Aſſiſtance and Profit; and in both, for Security and Dignity. Let us not therefore deny that he ought to be praiſed and eſteemed, and to be allowed a Place, both for the wonderful and raviſhing Beauty of his Works, and for the Neceſſity, Serviceableneſs, and Strength of the Things which he has invented, among the Chief of thoſe who have deſerved Honour and Rewards from Mankind. The Conſideration of theſe Things induced me, for my Diverſion, to look a little further into this Art and its Operations, from what Principles it was derived, and of what Parts it conſiſted: And finding them of various Kinds, in Number almoſt infinite, in their Nature marvellous, of Uſe incredible, inſomuch that it was doubtful what Condition of Men, or what Part of the Commonwealth, or what Degree in the City, whether the Publick or Private, Things ſacred or profane, Repoſe or Labour, the Individual or the whole human Species, was moſt obliged to the Architect, or rather Inventor of all Conveniencies; I reſolved, for ſeveral Reaſons, too tedious here to repeat, to collect all thoſe Things which are contained in theſe Ten Books. In treating of which, we ſhall obſerve this Method: We conſider that an Edifice is a Kind of Body conſiſting, like all other Bodies, of Deſign and of Matter; the firſt is produced by the Thought, the other by Nature; ſo that the one is to be provided by the Application and Contrivance of the Mind, and the other by due Preparation and Choice. And we further reflected, that neither the one nor the other of itſelf was ſufficient, without the Hand of an experienced Artificer, that knew how to form his Materials after a juſt Deſign. And the Uſe of Edifices being various, it was neceſſary to enquire whether one and the ſame Kind of Deſign was fit for all Sorts of Buildings; upon which Account we have diſtinguiſhed the ſeveral Kinds of Buildings: Wherein perceiving that the main Point was the juſt Compoſition and Relation of the Lines among themſelves, from whence ariſes the Height of Beauty, I therefore began to examine what Beauty really was, and what Sort of Beauty was proper to each Edifice. And as we often meet with Faults in all theſe Reſpects, I conſidered how they might be altered or amended. Every Book therefore has its Title prefixed to it, according to the Variety of the Subject: The Firſt treats of Deſigns; the Second, of Materials; the Third, of the Work; the Fourth, of Works in general; the Fifth, of Works in particular; the Sixth, of Ornaments in general; the Seventh, of the Ornaments proper for ſacred Edifices; the Eighth, of thoſe for publick and profane ones; The Ninth, of thoſe for the Houſes of private Perſons; the Tenth, of Amendments and Alterations in Buildings: To which is added, a various Hiſtory of Waters, and how they are found, and what Uſe is to be made of the Architect in all theſe Works: As alſo Four other Books, Three of which treat of the Art of Painting; and the Fourth, of Sculpture.

The TABLE of CONTENTS.

BOOK I.

BOOK II.

BOOK III.

BOOK IV.

BOOK V.

BOOK VI.

CHAP.

CHAP.

BOOK X.

THE

ARCHITECTURE

OF

Leone Batista Alberti.

Book I. Chap. I.

Of Designs; their Value and Rules.

BEING to treat of the Designs of Edifices, we shall collect and transcribe into this our Work, all the most curious and useful Observations left us by the Ancients, and which they gathered in the actual Execution of these Works; and to these we shall join whatever we ourselves may have discovered by our Study, Application and Labour, that seems likely to be of Use. But as we desire, in the handling this difficult, knotty, and commonly obscure Subject, to be as clear and intelligible as possible; we shall, according to our Custom, explain what the Nature of our Subject is; which will shew the Origin of the important Matters that we are to write of, at their very Fountain-Head, and enable us to express the Things that follow, in a more easy and perspicuous Style. We shall therefore first lay down, that the whole Art of Building consists in the Design, and in the Structure. The whole Force and Rule of the Design, consists in a right and exact adapting and joining together the Lines and Angles which compose and form the Face of the Building. It is the Property and Business of the Design to appoint to the Edifice and all its Parts their proper Places, determinate Number, just Proportion and beautiful Order; so that the whole Form of the Structure be proportionable. Nor has this Design any thing that makes it in its Nature inseparable from Matter; for we see that the same Design is in a Multitude of Buildings, which have all the same Form, and are exactly alike as to the Situation of their Parts and the Disposition of their Lines and Angles; and we can in our Thought and Imagination contrive perfect Forms of Buildings entirely separate from Matter, by settling and regulating in a certain Order, the Disposition and Conjunction of the Lines and Angles. Which being

B granted,

granted, we ſhall call the Deſign a firm and graceful pre-ordering of the Lines and Angles, conceived in the Mind, and contrived by an ingenious Artiſt. But if we would enquire what a Building is in its own Nature, together with the Structure thereof, it may not be amiſs, to conſider from what Beginnings the Habitations of Men, which we call Edifices, took their Riſe, and the Progreſs of their Improvement: Which unleſs I am miſtaken, may be reſolved as follows.

Chap II.

Of the firſt Occaſion of erecting Edifices; of how many Parts the Art of Building conſiſts, and what is neceſſary to each of thoſe Parts.

IN the Beginning Men looked out for Settlements in ſome ſecure Country; and having found a convenient Spot ſuitable to their Occaſions, they there made themſelves a Habitation ſo contrived, that private and publick Matters might not be confounded together in the ſame Place; but that they might have one Part for Sleep, another for their Kitchen, and others for their other neceſſary Uſes. They then began to think of a Covering to defend them from Sun and Rain; and in order thereto, they erected Walls to place this Covering upon. By this means they knew they ſhould be the more compleatly ſheltered from piercing Colds, and ſtormy Winds. Laſtly, in the Sides of the Walls, from Top to Bottom, they opened Paſſages and Windows, for going in and out, and letting in Light and Air, and for the Conveniency of diſcharging any Wet, or any groſs Vapours, which might chance to get into the Houſe. And whoſoever it was, whether the Goddeſs *Veſta*, Daughter of *Saturn*, or *Euryalus* and *Hyperbius*, the two Brothers, or *Gellio*, or *Thraſo*, or the Cyclop *Typhinchius*, that firſt contrived theſe Things: I am perſuaded the firſt Beginnings of them were ſuch as I have deſcribed, and that Uſe and Arts have ſince improved them to ſuch a Pitch, that the various Kinds of Buildings are become almoſt infinite: Some are publick, ſome private, ſome ſacred, ſome profane, ſome ſerve for Uſe and Neceſſity, ſome for the Ornament of our Cities, or the Beauty of our Temples: But no body will therefore deny, that they were all derived from the Principles abovementioned: Which being ſo, it is evident, that the whole Art of Building conſiſts in ſix Things, which are theſe: The Region, the Seat or Platform, the Compartition, the Walling, the Covering and the Apertures; and if theſe Principles are firſt thoroughly conceived, that which is to follow will the more eaſily be underſtood. We ſhall therefore define them thus, the Region with us ſhall be the whole large open Place in which we are to build, and of which the Seat or Platform ſhall be only a Part: But the Platform ſhall be a determined Spot of the Region, circumſcribed by Walls for Uſe and Service. But under the Title of Platform, we ſhall likewiſe include all thoſe Spaces of the Buildings, which in walking we tread upon with our Feet. The Compartition is that which ſub-divides the whole Platform of the Houſe into ſmaller Platforms, ſo that the whole Edifice thus formed and conſtituted of theſe its Members, ſeems to be full of leſſer Edifices: By Walling we ſhall underſtand all that Structure, which is carried up from the Ground to the Top to ſupport the Weight of the Roof, and ſuch alſo as is raiſed on the Inſide of the Building, to ſeparate the Apartments; Covering we ſhall call not only that Part, which is laid over the Top of the Edifice to receive the Rain, but any Part too which is extended in length and breadth over the Heads of thoſe within; which includes all Ceilings, half-arched Roofs, Vaults, and the like. Apertures are all thoſe Outlets, which are in any Part of the Building, for the Convenience of Egreſs and Regreſs, or the Paſſage of Things neceſſary for the Inmates. Of theſe therefore we ſhall treat, and of all the Parts of each, having firſt premiſed ſome Things, which whether they are Principles, or neceſſary Concomitants of the Principles of this Work which we have undertaken, are certainly very much to our Purpoſe: For having conſidered, whether there was any Thing that might concern any of thoſe Parts which we have enumerated; we found three Things by no means to be neglected, which relate particularly to the Covering, the Walling, and the like: Namely, that each of them be adapted to ſome certain and determinate Conveniency, and above all, be wholeſome. That

That they be firm, ſolid, durable, in a Manner eternal, as to Stability: And as to Gracefulneſs and Beauty, delicately and juſtly adorned, and ſet off in all their Parts. Having laid down theſe Principles as the Foundations of what we are to write, we proceed to our Subject.

CHAP. III.

Of the Region, of the Climate or Air, of the Sun and Winds, which affect the Air.

THE Ancients uſed the utmoſt Caution to fix upon a Region that had in it nothing noxious, and was furniſhed with all Conveniences; and eſpecially they took particular Care that the Air was not unwholeſome or intemperate; in which they ſhewed a great Deal of Prudence; for they knew that if the Earth or Water had any Defect in them, Art and Induſtry might correct it; but they affirmed, that neither Contrivance nor Multitude of Hands was able ſufficiently to correct and amend the Air. And it muſt be allowed, that, as what we breathe is ſo conducive to the Nouriſhment and Support of Life, the purer it is, the more it muſt preſerve and maintain our Health. Beſides, how great an Influence the Air has in the Generation, Production, Aliment, and Preſervation of Things, is unknown to nobody. It is even obſerved, that they who draw a pure Air, have better Underſtandings than thoſe who breathe a heavy moiſt one: Which is ſuppoſed to be the Reaſon that the *Athenians* had much ſharper Wits than the *Thebans*. We know that the Air, according to the different Situation and Poſition of Places, affects us ſometimes in one Manner, and ſometimes in another. Some of the Cauſes of this Variety we imagine we underſtand; others by the Obſcurity of their Natures are altogether hidden and unknown to us. We ſhall firſt ſpeak of the manifeſt Cauſes, and conſider afterwards of the more occult; that we may know how to chuſe a Region commodious and healthful. The Ancient Theologiſts called the Air *Pallas*. *Homer* makes her a Goddeſs, and names her *Glaucopis*, which ſignifies an Air naturally clear and tranſparent. And it is certain, that Air is the moſt healthy, which is the moſt purged and purified, and which may moſt eaſily be pierced by the Sight, the cleareſt and lighteſt, and the leaſt Subject to Variations. And on the contrary we affirm the Air to be peſtiferous, where there is a continued Collection of thick Clouds and ſtinking Vapours, and which always hangs like a great Weight upon the Eyes, and obſtructs the Sight. The Occaſion of this Difference proceeds from ſeveral Cauſes, but chiefly I take it, from the Sun and Winds. But we are not here to ſpend Time in theſe phyſical Enquiries, how the Vapours by the Power of the Sun are raiſed from the moſt profound and hidden Parts of the Earth, and drawn up to the Sky, where gathering themſelves together in vaſt Bodies in the immenſe Spaces of the Air, either by their own huge Weight, or by receiving the Rays of the Sun upon their rarified Parts, they fall and thereby preſs upon the Air and occaſion the Winds; and being afterwards carried to the Ocean by their Drought, they plunge, and having bathed and impregnated themſelves with Moiſture from the Sea, they once more aſcend through the Air, where being preſſed by the Winds, and as it were ſqueezed like a Sponge, they diſcharge their Burthen of Water in Rains, which again create new Vapours. Whether theſe Conjectures be true, or whether the Wind be occaſioned by a dry Fumoſity of the Earth, or a hot Evaporation ſtirred by the Preſſure of the Cold; or that it be, as we may call it, the Breath of the Air; or nothing but the Air itſelf put into Agitation by the Motion of the World, or by the Courſe and Radiation of the Stars; or by the generating Spirit of all Things in its own Nature active, or ſomething elſe not of a ſeparate Exiſtence, but conſiſting in the Air itſelf acted upon and inflamed by the Heat of the higher Air; or whatever other Opinion or Way of accounting for theſe Things be truer or more ancient, I ſhall paſs it over as not making to my Purpoſe. However, unleſs I am miſtaken, we may conceive from what has been ſaid already, why ſome Countries in the World enjoy a pleaſant chearful Air, while others, cloſe adjoyning to them, and as it were laid by Nature in the ſame Lap, are ſtupified and afflicted with a heavy and diſmal Climate. For I ſuppoſe, that this happens from no other Cauſe, but their being ill diſpoſed for the Operation of the Sun and Winds. *Cicero* tells us, that *Syracuſe* was ſo placed, that the Inhabitants never miſſed ſeeing the Sun every Day in the Year; a Situation very ſeldom to be met with

with, but when Neceſſity or Opportunity will allow of it to be deſired above all Things. That Region therefore is to be choſen, which is moſt free from the Power of Clouds and all other heavy thick Vapours. Thoſe who apply themſelves to theſe Enquiries have obſerved, that the Rays and Heat of the Sun act with more Violence upon cloſe denſe Bodies, than upon thoſe of a looſer Contexture, upon Oil more than Water, Iron more than Wool; for which Reaſon they ſay the Air is moſt groſs and heavy in thoſe Places, which are moſt ſubject to great Heats. The *Ægyptians* contending for Nobility with all the other Nations in the World, boaſted, that the firſt Men were created in their Country, becauſe no Place was ſo fit to plant the firſt Race of Men in, as there, where they might live the moſt healthily; and that they were bleſſed by the Gods with a Kind of perpetual Spring, and a cónſtant unchangeable Diſpoſition of Air above all the Reſt of the Word. And *Herodotus* writes, that among the *Ægyptians*, thoſe chiefly who lived towards *Libia*, are the moſt healthy, becauſe they enjoy continual gentle Breezes. And to me the Reaſon why ſome Cities, both in *Italy* and in other Parts of the World, are perpetually unhealthy and peſtilential, ſeems plainly to be the ſudden Turns and Changes in the Air, from Hot to Cold, and from Cold to Hot. So that it very much concerns us to be extremely careful in our Obſervation, what and how much Sun the Region we pitch upon is expoſed to; that there be neither more Sun nor more Shade than is neceſſary. The *Garamantes* curſe the Sun, both at it's Riſing and it's Setting, becauſe they are ſcorched with the long Continuation of it's Beams. Other Nations look pale and wan, by living in a Kind of perpetual Night. And theſe Things happen not ſo much, becauſe ſuch Places have the Pole more depreſſed or oblique, tho' there is a great deal in that too, as becauſe they are aptly ſituated for receiving the Sun and Winds, or are ſkreened from them. I ſhould chuſe ſoft Breezes before Winds, but even Winds, though violent and bluſtering, before a Calm, motionleſs, and conſequently, a heavy Air. Water, ſays *Ovid*, corrupts, if not moved: And it is certain the Air, to uſe ſuch an Expreſſion, wonderfully exhilerated by Motion: For I am perſuaded, that thereby the Vapours which riſe from the Earth are either diſſipated, or elſe growing warm by Action are concocted as they ſhould be. But then I would have theſe Winds come to me, broken by the Oppoſition of Hills and Woods, or tired with a long Journey. I would take heed that they did not bring any ill Qualities along with them, gathered from any Places they paſſed through. And for this Reaſon we ſhould be careful to avoid all Neighbourhoods from which any noxious Particles may be brought: In the Number of which are all ill Smells, and all groſs Exhalations from Marſhes, and eſpecially from ſtagnating Waters and Ditches. The Naturaliſts lay it down for certain, that all Rivers that uſe to be ſupplied by Snows, bring cold ſoggy Winds: But no Water is ſo noiſome and pernicious, as that which rots and putrifies for want of Motion. And the Contagion of ſuch a Neighbourhood will be ſtill more miſchievous, according as it is more or leſs expoſed to unwholeſome Winds: For we are told, that the very Winds themſelves are in their own Natures ſome more wholeſome than others. Thus *Pliny* from *Theophraſtus* and *Hippocrates* informs us, that the *North* is the beſt for reſtoring and preſerving of Health; and all the Naturaliſts affirm, that the *South* is the moſt noxious of all to Mankind; nay further, that the very Beaſts may not ſafely be left in the Fields while that Wind blows; and they have obſerved, that at ſuch Times the Stork never flies, and that the Dolphins in a *North* Wind, if it ſtands fair towards them, can hear any Voice, but in a *South*, they are more ſlow in hearing it, and muſt have it brought to them oppoſite to the Wind. They ſay too, that in a *North* Wind an Eel will live ſix Days out of Water, but not ſo in a *South*, ſuch is the Groſſneſs and unwholeſome Property of that Wind; and that as the *South* Wind brings Catarrhs and Rheums, ſo the *North-Weſt* is apt to give Coughs. They likewiſe find Fault with the Neighbourhood of the *Mediterranean*, upon this Account chiefly, becauſe they ſuppoſe, that a Place expoſed to the Reflection of the Sun's Rays, does in effect ſuffer two Suns, one ſcorching them from the Heavens, and the other from the Water; and ſuch Places upon the Setting of the Sun feel the greateſt and moſt ſenſible Alterations in the Air when the cold Shadows of Night come on. And there are ſome who think, that the *Weſtern* Reverberations or Reflections of the Sun, either from the Sea or any other Water, or from the Mountains, moleſt us moſt of of all: Becaufe they double the Heat of a Place already fufficiently warmed by whole Day's Sun. And if it happens, that with all this Sun the heavy grofs Winds have free Accefs to you, what can be more annoying or intollerable? The early Morning Breezes too, which bring the Vapours crude juft as they are raifed, are certainly to be avoided. Thus we have briefly fpoken of the Sun and Winds, by which the Air is altered and made healthy and noxious, as much as we thought neceffary here: And in their Places we fhall difcourfe of them more diftinctly.

CHAP. IV.

Which Region is, and which is not commodious for Building.

IN chufing the Region it will be proper to have it fuch, that the Inhabitants may find it convenient in all Refpects, both as to its natural Properties, and as to the Neighbourhood and its Correfpondence with the reft of Mankind. For certainly I would never build a City upon a fteep inacceffible Cliff of the *Alps*, as *Caligula* intended; unlefs obliged by the utmoft Extremity: Nor in a folitary Defart, as *Varro* defcribes that Part of *France* to have been which was beyond the *Rhine*, and as *Cæfar* paints *England* in his Days. Neither fhould I be pleafed to live, as in *Ægina*, only upon the Eggs of Birds, or upon Acorns, as they did in fome Parts of *Spain* in *Pliny*'s Time. I would if poffible have nothing be wanting that could be of Ufe in Life. For this Reafon, more than any other, *Alexander* was perfectly in the right in not building a City upon Mount *Athos* (though the Invention and Defign of the Architect *Policrates* muft needs have been wonderful) becaufe the Inhabitants could never have been well fupplied with Conveniences. *Ariftotle* was indeed beft pleafed with a Region that was difficult of Accefs, and efpecially to build a City in: And we find there have been fome Nations, which have chofe to have their Confines quite ftript and laid into a Defart for a great Way together, only in order to diftrefs their Enemies. Whether this Method is to be approved or blamed, we fhall examine in another Place. If it is of Service in a publick Regard, I cannot find Fault with it: But for the Situation of other Buildings, I fhould much rather chufe a Region that had many and different Ways of Accefs, for the eafy bringing in all Manner of Neceffaries, both by Land-Carriage and Water-Carriage, as well in Winter as in Summer. The Region itfelf likewife fhould neither be too moift through too great abundance of Water, nor too much parched with Drought, but be kindly and temperate. And if we cannot find one exactly in all Refpects as we would have it, let us chufe it rather fomewhat cold and dry, than warm and moift: For our Houfes, our Cloaths, Fires, and Exercife, will eafily overcome the Cold; neither is it believed, that the Drynefs of a Soil can have any thing in it very noxious, either to the Bodies or Mind, only that by Drynefs Men's Bodies are hardened, and by Cold perhaps made fomewhat rougher: But it is held for certain, that all Bodies corrupt with too much Humidity, and are relaxed by Heat. And we find that Men either in cold Weather, or that live in cold Places, are more healthy and lefs fubject to Diftempers; though it is allowed, that in hot Climates Men have better Wits, as they have better Conftitutions in cold. I have read in *Appian* the Hiftorian, that the *Numidians* are very long lived, becaufe their Winters are never too cold. That Region therefore will be far the beft, which is juft moderately warm and moift, becaufe that will produce lufty handfome Men, and not fubject to Melancholy. Secondly, that Region will be moft eligible, which being placed among Countries liable to Snow, enjoys more Sun than its Neighbours; and among Countries burnt by the Sun, that which has moft Humidity and Shade. But no Building, let it be what it will, can be placed more unfightly or inconveniently, than in a Valley down between two Hills; becaufe, not to infift upon more manifeft Reafons, an Edifice fo placed has no Manner of Dignity, lying quite hid; and it's Profpect being interrupted can have neither Pleafure nor Beauty. But what is this to thofe greater Mifchiefs which will fhortly happen, when the Houfe is overwhelmed by Floods and filled with Waters that pour in upon it from the adjoining Hills; and imbibing continual Wet, rots and decays, and always exhales Vapours extreamly noxious to the Health of its Inhabitants. In ſuch a Place, the Underſtanding can never be clear, the Spirits being dampt and ſtupified; nor will any Kind of Bodies endure long. The Books will grow mouldy and rot; the Arms will ruſt, nothing in the Storehouſe will keep, and in ſhort, the Exceſs of Moiſture will ſpoil and deſtroy every Thing. If the Sun ſhines in, you will be ſcorched inſufferably by the frequent Reflection of his Rays, which will be beat back upon you from every Side, and if it does not, you will be dried and withered by the continual Shade. Add to this, that if the Winds gets in, being confined as it were in a Channel, it will rage there with greater Fury than in other Places; and if it never enters, the Air for want of Motion will grow thick and muddy; ſuch a Valley may not improperly be called a Puddle, or Bog of Air. The Form of the Place therefore in which we intend to build, ought to be graceful and pleaſant, not mean and low, as if it were buried below the reſt of the Earth, but lofty, and as it were a Hawk to look clear round about, and conſtantly refreſhed on every Side with delightful Breezes. Beſides this, let there be Plenty of every Thing neceſſary, either to the Convenience or Pleaſure of Life, as Water, Fire and Proviſions: But Care muſt be taken, that there is nothing in any of theſe Things prejudicial to the Health. The Springs muſt be opened and taſted, and the Water tried by Fire, that there be no Mixture in it of mucous, viſcous or crude Particles, that may affect the Conſtitutions of the Inhabitants. I omit the ill Effects that often proceed from Water, as breeding Wens in the Throat, and giving the Stone; as likewiſe thoſe other more wonderful Effects of Water, which *Vitruvius* the Architect has learnedly and elegantly ſummed up. It is the Opinion of the Phyſician *Hipocrates*, that they who drink Water not well purged, but heavy and ill-taſted, grow Cholicky, and to have large ſwelled Bellies, while the reſt of their Members, their Arms, their Shoulders and their Faces become thin and extenuated. Add to this, that though the Fault of the Spleen ill digeſting of the Blood, they fall into ſeveral Kinds of Diſtempers, ſome even peſtilential. In Summer, Fluxes of the Belly by the ſtirring of the Choler, and the diſſolving of the Humours waſte all their Strength; and all the Year round they are continually liable to heavy and tedious Infirmities, ſuch as the Dropſy, Aſthma and Pleuriſy. The young loſe their Senſes by melancholy Bile; the old are burnt by the Inflammation of the Humours; the Women with Difficulty conceive, and with more Difficulty bring forth: In a Word, every Age and every Sex will fall by early and untimely Deaths, deſtroyed and worn away by Diſeaſes; nor will they enjoy a ſingle Day while they live, without being tormented with Melancholy or black Humours, and fretted with Spleen and Vapours; ſo that their Minds will never be free from Vexation and Uneaſineſs. Many other Things might be ſaid of Water, which have been obſerved by the ancient Hiſtorians, very curious and remarkable, and of extream Efficacy to the Health of Mankind; but they are uncommon, and might ſeem rather intended to make a Shew of Knowledge than for actual Uſe; beſides that we ſhall ſpeak more copiouſly of Waters in their proper Place. Thus much certainly is not to be neglected, and is moſt manifeſt, namely, that Water gives Nouriſhment to all Plants, Seeds, and every Thing elſe that has the vegetative Life, with the Plenty of whoſe Fruits Men are refreſhed and ſupported. If all this be granted, certainly we ought very carefully to examine what Veins of Water the Country is furniſhed with, in which we intend to dwell. *Diodorus* tells us, that the *Indians* are generally luſty ſtrong Men, and very ſharp witted, which he imputes to their having a wholeſome Air and good Water. Now that Water we conceive to be the beſt taſted which has no Taſte, and that is beſt coloured which has no Colour at all. It is agreed, that the beſt Water is clear, tranſparent and light, ſuch as being poured upon a white Cloth leaves no Stain; and upon boiling has no Sediment, and which does not cover the Bed it flows in with Moſs or Slime, nor eſpecially the Stones which it runs over. A further Proof of the Goodneſs of Water is, when boiling any Kind of Pulſe in it makes them tender, and when it makes good Bread. Neither ſhould we be leſs careful to examine and note, whether the Region ingenders nothing peſtiferous or venemous, that the Inhabitants may be in no Danger. I paſs over ſome Things, which are recorded by the Ancients, to wit, that in *Colchos* there diſtills from the Leaves of the Trees a Honey, which whoſoever taſtes falls ſenſeleſs, and for a whole Day ſeems to be dead: As alſo what is ſaid to have happened in *Antony*'s Army, occaſioned by certain

certain Herbs, which the Soldiers eating for want of Bread, grew besotted, and employed themselves in nothing but digging Stones out of the Ground, till their Choler being stirred they fell down dead; nor was any Remedy found against this Plague, as we are informed by *Plutarch*, but drinking of Wine; these Things are commonly known. But good Heavens! what shall we say to what has happened in our own Days in *Apulia* in *Italy*; what incredible Effects of Poison have we seen there! the Bite of a small Earth Spider, commonly called a *Tarantula*, throwing Men into various Kinds of Madness, and even Fury; a Thing strange to be told. No Swelling, no livid Spot appearing in any Part of the Body from the sharp Bite or Sting of the venomous Beast; but suddenly losing their Senses, they fall piteously to bewail themselves, and if no Assistance is given them they die. They cure this Distemper with *Theophrastus*'s Remedy, who says, that Persons bit by Vipers used to be cured by the Sound of Pipes. The Musicians therefore with different Kinds of Harmony try to asswage the Pain, and when they hit upon the Kind proper to the Patient, immediately, as if he were suddenly awakened, he starts up, and transported with Joy, falls to bestirring himself to the Musick with all his Strength, in whatever his Fancy prompts him to. Some that are thus bit, you shall see exercise themselves in Dancing, others in Singing, and others stirring in other Motions, just as their Inclination or Madness guides them, till through mere Weariness they are forced to give over. And thus without giving themselves the least Rest, they will sweat themselves for some Days, and so recover their Health merely by their Madness having quite spent itself. We read too of something like this that happened among the *Albanians*, who fought against *Pompey* with such a Power of Horse; that there was a Sort of Cobweb among them, which whoever touched surely died, some Laughing, and others on the contrary Weeping.

CHAP. V.

By what Marks and Characters we are to know the Goodness of the Region.

NOR are those Things alone sufficient for the chusing of the Region, which are obvious and manifest of themselves; but we must weigh every Circumstance, and consider the most occult Tokens. Thus it will be a good Sign of an excellent Air and of good Water, if the Country produces Plenty of good Fruits, if it fosters a good Number of Men of a good old Age, if it abounds with lusty handsome Youth, if the People are fruitful, and if the Births are natural and never monstrous. I have myself seen some Cities, which out of Respect to the Times I forbear to name, where there is scarce a Woman, but what sees herself at the same Instant, the Mother both of a Man and of a Monster. Another City I know in *Italy*, where there are so many People Humpbacked, Squint-eyed, Crooked and Lame, that there is scarce a Family, but what has Somebody in it defective or distorted. And certainly, where we see such frequent and great Inequalities of Body to Body, and Member to Member; we may well conclude, that it proceeds from some Defect in the Climate or Air, or from some more hidden Cause of the Corruption of Nature. Nor is it foreign to our Purpose what has been observed, that in a gross Air we are more inclined to Hunger, and in a thin One to Thirst: and we may not improbably draw some Conjectures from the Shape and Looks of other Animals, what Constitutions the Men will have in the same Place; for if the Cattle look lively, fat and large, you may not unreasonably hope to have Children that will be so too. Neither will it be amiss to gather Notice of the Air and Winds, even from other Bodies not endued with animal Life; thus if the Walls of the neighbouring Buildings are grown rusty and rugged, it shews that some malignant Influence has Power there. The Trees too bending all one Way, as if by general Consent, shew that they have suffered the Force of high rough Winds; and the very Stones, whether growing in their native Seats, or placed in Buildings, if their Tops are any thing considerably rotted, shew the Intemperature of the Air, sometimes too hot and sometimes over cold. A Region so exposed to the furious Assaults of Tempests is to be avoided, as the very worst of all; for if the Bodies of Men are seized with too excessive Cold or Heat, the whole Frame and Contexture

ture of all the Parts is presently broken and diſſolved, and falls into dangerous Diſtempers and immature old Age. A City ſtanding at the Foot of a Hill, and looking towards the ſetting Sun, is accounted unhealthy, more for this Reaſon than any other, that it feels too ſuddenly the cold chilling Breezes of the Night. It may likewiſe be convenient by looking back into Times paſt, according to the Obſervations of the Wiſe, to examine into Properties yet more hidden, if there be ſuch in the Place: For there are Countries which have in their Nature ſome Secret undiſcovered Qualities, which confer Happineſs or Unhappineſs. *Locris* and *Crotona* are ſaid to have never been infected with any Plague. In the Iſle of *Candia* there is no miſchievous Creature. In *France* very few Monſters are born; in other Places the Naturaliſts ſay, that in the Middle either of Summer or Winter it never Thunders: But in *Campania*, according to *Pliny*, it Thunders at thoſe very Times over thoſe Cities that ſtand to the South; and the Mountains near *Albania* are ſaid to be called *Ceraunia*, from the frequent Lightnings that fall upon it. The Iſle of *Lemnos* too being very ſubject to Lightning, was the Reaſon, *Servius* informs us, of the Poets feigning that *Vulcan* fell there from Heaven. About the Streights of *Gallipoli* and the *Eſſedones*, it was never known either to Thunder or Lighten. If it Rains in *Ægypt* it is reckoned a Prodigy. Near the *Hydaſpes* in the Beginning of Summer it Rains continually. They ſay that in *Lybia* the Air is ſo ſeldom ſtirred by Winds, that it grows ſo thick, that ſeveral Kinds of Vapours are viſible in the Sky: And on the Contrary, in moſt Parts of *Galatia*, the Winds blow in Summer with ſo much Violence, that it drives along the very Stones like Sand. In *Spain* near the *Ebro*, they ſay the North-Weſt Wind blows ſo hard, that it overturns Carts heavy laden: In *Æthiopia* we are told the South never blows, and Hiſtorians write, that this Wind in *Arabia* and the Country of the *Troglodites* burns up every Thing that is green: And *Thucydides* affirms, that *Delos* was never troubled with Earthquakes, but always ſtood firm upon the ſame Rock, though the other Iſlands all about it were often laid in Ruins by Earthquakes, We ourſelves ſee, that the Part of *Italy*, which runs from the *Selva dell' Aglio* below *Rome*, all along the Ridge of Hills of the *Campagna di Roma* quite to *Capua*, is perpetually ſtript and almoſt quite laid waſte by Earthquakes. Some believe *Achaia* was ſo called from its frequent Inundations of Water. I find that *Rome* was always ſubject to Agues, and *Galen* takes thoſe Agues to be a new Kind of double Tertian, which muſt have varions and almoſt direct Remedies applied to it at different Seaſons. It is an old Fable among the Poets, that *Typho* the Giant being buried in the Iſland of *Prochyta*, often turns himſelf about, and with his turning ſhakes the whole Iſland from its very Foundation. The Reaſon of this Fiction of the Poets was, becauſe that Iſland was ſo tormented with Earthquakes and Eruptions, that the *Erythreans* and *Chalcidians*, who inhabited it, were forced to fly for it. And again, aftewards thoſe who were ſent by *Hiero* of *Syracuſe* to build a new City there, frightened with the continual Danger of Deſtruction, deſerted it too. Wherefore all Things of this Nature are to be ſifted out from long Obſervation, and examined and compared by other Places, in order to come at a clear and full Knowledge of every Particular.

CHAP. VI.

Of ſome more hidden Conveniencies and Inconveniencies of the Region which a wiſe Man ought to enquire into.

WE ought further to enquire carefully, whether the Region is uſed to be moleſted with any more hidden Inconveniency. *Plato* believed, that in ſome Places the Influence of Spirits often reigned, and was at ſometimes miſchievous, and at others propitious to the Inhabitants. It is certain there are ſome Places where Men are very ſubject to run mad, others where they are eaſily diſpoſed to do themſelves a Miſchief, and where they put an End to their own Lives by Halters or Precipices, Steel or Poiſon. It is therefore very neceſſary to examine by the moſt occult Traces of Nature, every Thing that can be attended with ſuch Effects. It was an ancient Cuſtom brought down even from *Demetrius*'s Time, not

not only in laying the Foundations of Cities and Towns, but alſo in marking out Camps for the Armies, to inſpect the Entrails of the Beaſt that grazed upon the Place, and to obſerve both their Condition and Colour. In which if they chanced to find any Defect, they avoided that Place as unhealthy. *Varro* informs us of his own Knowledge, that in ſome Places the Air was full of minute Animalcules as ſmall as Atoms, which being received together with the Breath into the Lungs, faſtened upon the Inteſtines, and gnawing upon them, cauſed dreadful raging Diſeaſes, and at length Plagues and Death. Nor ought we to forget that there are ſome Places, which, though in their own Nature, they are ſubject to no Inconvenience or Miſchief whatſoever, yet are ſo ſituated, that by the Arrival of Foreigners they will often be infected with peſtilential Diſtempers. And this ſhall happen, not only by Means of Armies of Enemies endeavouring to do you all the Miſchief they can, as befals thoſe Nations which are expoſed to inhuman Barbarians; but by a friendly Reception and Entertainment of them you ſhall expoſe yourſelf to extreme Calamities. Others by having Neighbours deſirous of Innovations, have by their Broils and Deſtruction fallen into great Dangers themſelves. *Pera* a City upon the *Pontus*, a Colony of the *Genoeſe*, is continually afflicted with the Plague, by their giving daily Admiſſion to Slaves, both infirm in Mind, and almoſt quste rotten and worn away with mere Filth and Naſtineſs. Some likewiſe will have it, that it is the Part of a prudent and wiſe Man to enquire by Augury and the Obſervation of the Heavens, what Fortune he ſhall have in ſuch a Place. Which Arts, provided they are not incompatiable with our Religion, I own I do not diſpiſe. Who can deny that what they call Fortune, whatever ſhe be, has a very great Power over human Affairs? Can we venture to affirm, that the publick Fortune of *Rome* had not a great Share in the Enlargement of the Empire? The City of *Iolaus* in *Sardinia*, built by a Grandſon of *Hercules*, though often attacked both by the *Carthaginians* and the *Romans*, yet as *Diodorus* writes, always preſerved its Liberty. Can we ſuppoſe that the Temple at *Delphos*, firſt burnt by *Flegias*, ſhould afterwards in *Sylla*'s Time be conſumed by Fire, the third Time, without the particular ill Fortune of that Place? What ſhall we ſay of the Capitol? How often has that been in Flames? The City of the *Sybarites*, after repeated Calamities, often deſerted and often reſtored, at length quite ruined, was utterly abandoned; nay, thoſe who fled from it were purſued by ill Fortune, nor could they, by removing their Dwellings and leaving the ancient Name of their City, ever ſave themſelves from Miſery and Deſtruction: For new Inhabitants coming in upon them, all their moſt ancient and principal Families, their ſacred Edifices and their whole City, were utterly laid waſte and deſtroyed with Fire and Sword. But we need not dwell upon theſe Things which Hiſtorians are full of. Our whole Deſign is to ſhew, that it is the Part of a wiſe Man to do every thing which may make him ſecure, that the Trouble and Expence of his Building ſhall not be in vain, and that his Work itſelf may be permanent. And certainly to omit no Precaution which may effect ſo great a Deſign, is the Buſineſs of every prudent Man. Or will you ſay, that it is not of the utmoſt Importance both to you and yours to execute an Undertaking, that brings with it Health, Dignity and Pleaſure, and recommends your Name with Reputation to Poſterity? Here you are to apply yourſelves to your Studies, here you are to breed your dear Children and live with your Family, here you are to ſpend your Days both of Labour and Reſt, here all the Schemes of your whole Life are to be executed; ſo that I do not think any Thing in the World can be named, except Virtue, which can deſerve more Care and Application, than to fix a good and convenient Habitation for yourſelf and Family. And who can be ſure of having ſuch a one, who deſpiſes the Precautions before-mentioned? but of theſe enough. Come we now to the Seat or Platform.

CHAP. VII.

Of the Seat or Platform, and of the ſeveral Sorts of Lines.

IN chuſing the Platform, we ought to obſerve all the ſame Rules that we have laid down about the Region; for as the Region is a determinate and ſelect Part of the whole

Country,

Country, ſo the Platform is a certain determinate Part of the Region taken up by the Building; and for this Reaſon, any Thing that may annoy or be of Service to the Region, may do the ſame to the Platform. But though this be ſo, yet our Diſcuſſion and Conſiderations here will offer us ſome Precepts, which ſeem particularly to regard the Platform only; and ſome again which do not ſeem ſo properly to belong to the Seat as in a great Meaſure to the Region; which are theſe. It is neceſſary to conſider what Work we are taking in Hand, publick or private, ſacred or profane, and ſo of the Reſt, which we ſhall treat of diſtinctly in their proper Places. For one Situation and one Space is to be allotted to an Exchange, another to a Theatre, another to a *Palæſtra*, or Place of Exerciſe, and another to a Temple; ſo that we muſt have regard to the Quality and Uſe of every Edifice in the Determining of its Situation and Form. But to proceed here only in a general Diſcuſſion of theſe Things as we began, we ſhall touch only upon thoſe Points which we judge neceſſary: Firſt ſaying ſomething of Lines, which may be of Service for underſtanding what follows. For being to treat of the Deſign of the Platform, it will not be inconvenient to explain thoſe Things firſt whereof that Deſign conſiſts. Every Deſign therefore is compoſed of Lines and Angles; the Lines are that extreme Deſign which includes the whole Space of the Platform. That Part of the Superficies of this Deſign, which is contained between two Lines touching at ſome certain Point, is called an Angle. The Interſection therefore or croſſing of two Lines over each other form four Angles. If each of theſe Angles be equal to all and each of the other three, they are called right Angles; if they are leſs, they are called acute, and the greater obtuſe. Of Lines too ſome are ſtrait and others curve; of involved winding Lines it is not neceſſary to ſpeak here. The ſtrait Line is a Line drawn from one Point to another, the ſhorteſt Way that poſſibly can be. The curve Line is Part of a Circle; a Circle is a Draught made from one of two Points, and turned upon the ſame Superficies in ſuch a Manner, that in its whole Circumference it is never nearer nor farther from that immoveable Point the Centre, than it was at the firſt Turn. But to this it is neceſſary to add, that the curve Line, which was ſaid to be Part of the Circle, among us Architects, for its Similitude, is called an Arch. And the ſtrait Line, which is drawn from the two extreme Points of the curve Line, for the ſame Reaſon is called a Chord. And that Line, which goes from the middle Point of the Chord up to the Arch, leaving equal Angles on each Side, is called the *Sagitta*. And that which is carried from the fixed immoveable Point within the Circle to the curve Line of the Circle, is called the *Radius*. And that immoveable Point in the Middle is called the Centre. And the Line which paſſes through the Centre and touches both Sides of the Circumference, is called the Diameter. Arches too are different, * for ſome are entire, ſome are imperfect, and ſome are compoſite. The entire is that which is the full Half of a Circle, or that whoſe Chord is the Diameter of the whole Circle. The Imperfect is that whoſe Chord is leſs than a Diameter, ſo that this imperfect Arch is Part of a Semi-circle. The compoſite Arch is formed of two imperfect Arches, and ſo the joyning of thoſe two Arches, interſecting each other, makes an Angle at Top, which never happens either in the entire or imperfect Arch. Theſe Things being premiſed, we proceed as follows.

Chap. VIII.

Of the Kinds of Platforms, their Forms and Figures, and which are the moſt ſerviceable and laſting.

Of Platforms, ſome are angular and others circular; of the angular, ſome conſiſt all of right Lines, and ſome of right Lines and curve mixed together. But I do not remember among the Buildings of the Ancients to have met with any angular Deſign, compoſed of ſeveral curve Lines, without any Mixture of ſtrait Lines at all: But in this we ſhould have regard to thoſe Things, which being wanting in all Parts of the Structure, are greatly blamed; and which, where they are, make the Edifice handſome and convenient. It

* *See Plate 1, facing page 12.*

It is that the Angles, the Lines and all the Parts have a certain Variety, but not too much nor too little of it, but ſo ordered both for Uſe and Beauty, that the entire Parts may anſwer to the entire, and like Parts to like. Right Angles are very convenient; the Acute are never uſed even in mean inconſiderable Platforms, unleſs upon abſolute Neceſſity, or the Conſtraint of the Nature and Manner of the Situation, or to make ſome other Part of the Platform more graceful. The obtuſe Angles, have been thought very convenient, but it has always been obſerved as a Rule never to place them any where in unequal Numbers. The circular Platform is eſteemed to be the moſt capacious of all, and the leaſt expenſive to encloſe either with Wall or Rampart. The neareſt to this is ſaid to be that which has ſeveral Sides, but then they muſt be all alike and anſwerable to each other, and equal throughout the whole Platform. But thoſe are commended moſt of all, which are moſt convenient for raiſing the Wall to the juſt Heighth of the Work, as are thoſe which have ſix and eight Sides. I have ſeen a Platform of ten Angles very commodious and majeſtick. You may make them very well of twelve, nay, ſixteen Angles. I myſelf have ſeen one of twenty-four; but theſe are very rare. The Side Lines ought to be ſo ordered, that thoſe which are oppoſite may be equal to them, nor ſhould we ever in any Work apply a long Line to correſpond to a ſhort one; but let there be a juſt and reaſonable Proportion, according to the Degree of the Thing, among all the Parts. We would have the Angles ſet towards that Side, which either any Weight of Earth, or the Violence and Aſſaults of Waters or Winds may threaten and endanger; to the Intent that the Force and Shock that beats upon the Edifice may be broken and ſplit into ſeveral Parts, reſiſting the Attack (to uſe ſuch an Expreſſion) with the ſtout Corner of the Wall, and not with one of the weak Sides. But if the other Lineaments of the Structure hinder you from diſpoſing of ſuch an Angle in ſuch a Part as you could deſire, at leaſt make uſe of a curve Line; that being a Part of a Circle, and the Circle itſelf according to the Philoſophers being all Angles. Further, the Seat muſt be either upon a Plain, or on the Side or Top of a Hill; if it is on a Plain, it is neceſſary to raiſe the Earth and make ſomething of an Eminence; for beſides that, ſuch a Situation in a Plain adds much of Dignity, if you neglect to do it, you will find very great Inconveniences. For the overflowing of Rivers and Rains generally leaves Mud upon level Grounds, which by degrees raiſes the Earth higher and higher, which ſtill increaſes, if through Negligence the Rubbiſh and Dirt, which gathers every Day be not removed. *Frontinus* the Architect uſed to ſay, that ſeveral Hills were riſen in *Rome* in his Time by the continual Fires. But we in our Days ſee it in a Manner quite buried under Ground with Filth and Rubbiſh. In the Dutchy of *Spoletto*, I have ſeen a ſmall ancient Temple, which at firſt was built in a Plain, that is now almoſt wholly buried by the raiſing of the Earth; that Plain reaching to the Foot of the Hills. But why ſhould I mention Buildings that ſtand under Mountains? That noble Temple by the Wall of *Ravenna*, which has for its Covering a Cup of Stone of one ſingle Piece, though it be near the Sea and far enough from the Hills, is above a fourth Part ſunk in the Earth, through the Injury of Time. But how high this Eminence ought to be raiſed for each Platform, ſhall be ſhewn in due Time, when we come to treat of that Subject more particularly, and not ſummarily as we do here. It is certain every Situation ſhould be made ſtrong, either by Nature or Art. And therefore it is not amiſs to follow their Method, who adviſe firſt to try the Goodneſs of the Earth by digging in ſeveral Places at ſome Diſtance the one from the other, whether it be firm or looſe, or ſoft, fit or unfit to bear the Weight of the Wall. For if it ſtands upon a Deſcent, we muſt have a Care that the upper Part does not lie too heavy and break down the lower; or that the lower Part, if any Accident ſhould ſhake it, does not pull the upper down along with it. I would have this Part of the Building, which is intended to be the Baſis of all the Reſt, particularly ſtrong and tightly knit together in all its Parts. If the Seat be upon the Summit of an Hill, either it ſhould be raiſed where it is not even, or elſe be made level by plaining away the Top. But here we are to conſider, that we ſhould always chuſe that Way (though ſtill with a due Regard to the Dignity of the Work) which is leaſt troubleſome and expenſive. Perhaps it may be proper to pare away ſome of the Top of the Hill, and enlarge and add to the Sides. For which Reaſon that Architect, whoever he was, ſhewed a great deal of Contrivance, that built *Alatro*, a Town of the *Campagna di Roma*, ſeated upon a Rocky Hill; for he ſo ordered it, it, that the Foundations of the Citadel or Temple (whatever it was) which are all that now remain, the Superſtructure being quite demoliſhed, ſhould be ſupported and fortified beneath by the Pieces of Stone cut off in plaining the Top of the Rock. And there is another Thing in that Work that I am extremely pleaſed with; namely, that he ſet the Angle of the Platform towards that Side on which the Rock has the moſt precipitate Deſcent, and fortified that Angle with huge Pieces of the Fragments piled up one upon the other, and contrived by the joyning of the Stones to make the Structure beautiful with a very little Expence. I am likewiſe very much pleaſed with the Contrivance of that other Architect, who not having a ſufficient Quantity of Stone, in order to keep up the Weight of the Hill, made a Fence of a great Number of Semi-circles, putting the Backs of the Curves within the Hill; which beſides that it looked handſome to the Eye, was extremely ſtrong and very cheap; for it makes a Wall, which though not ſolid, was as firm as if it had been ſolid, and of the Thickneſs of the *Sagitta* of thoſe Curves. I like *Vitruvius*'s Method too, which I find was obſerved by the ancient Architects all over *Rome*, and eſpecially in *Tarquin*'s Wall, of making uſe of Buttreſſes; though they did not every where mind to make the Diſtance between one Buttreſs and another, to be the ſame as the Heighth of the Wall; but as the Strength or Weakneſs of the Hill required it, they placed them ſometimes cloſer and ſometimes further off. I have taken Notice too, that the ancient Architects were not contented with making one Slope for their Platform, but raiſed ſeveral like ſo many Steps, which ſtrengthened and ſecured the Sides of the Hill quite down to the very Root of it. Nor can I diſapprove their Method herein. That Stream at *Perugia*, which runs under Mount *Lucino* and the Hill the Town ſtands upon, continually undermining and eating away the Root of the Mountain, by degrees brings down all the impending Weight; by which means a great Part of the Town drops and falls to Ruin. I am mightily pleaſed with that Number of little Chapels, which are fixed about the *Area* of the great Church in the Vatican; for of theſe, ſuch as are placed in the Hollows of the Mountains cloſe againſt the Wall of the Church, are of great Service both as to Strength and Convenience, in ſupporting the Weight of the Hill, which continually grows heavier and heavier, and in intercepting the Wet, which falls from the Top of the Cliff, and keeping it from getting into the Church; by which means the principal Wall of it keeps dry and ſound. And thoſe Chapels, which are placed on the other Side at the loweſt Decline of the Hill, ſerve with their Arches to cloſe the Plain, which is made above, and preventing the Earth from crumbling keeps it from falling in. And I have obſerved that the Architect, who built the Temple of *Latona* in *Rome*, contrived his Work and his Structure very ingeniouſly; for he ſo placed the Angle of the Platform within the impending Hill, that two upright Walls ſupported the incumbent Weight, and divided and broke the Preſſure by ſetting that Angle againſt it. But ſince we have begun to celebrate the Praiſes of the Ancients that contrived their Buildings prudently, I will not omit one Thing which I recollect, and which is very much to the preſent Purpoſe. In the Church of St. *Mark* at *Venice* is a very uſeful Precaution of the Architect, who having made the Foundation of the Temple very ſtrong, left every here and there a Hole, that if by chance any ſubterraneous Vapour or Wind ſhould be gathered there, it might eaſily find a Paſſage out. To conclude, all the Plains that you make which are to be under any Covering, muſt be laid exactly level, but thoſe which are to be left open, ſhould have juſt Slope enough for the Rain to run off; but of this we have ſaid enough, and perhaps more than was requiſite in this Place; becauſe moſt of theſe Things reſpect the Walling. But as they happened to fall naturally together, we did not think proper to ſeparate them in our Diſcourſe. It remains that we treat of the Compartition.

CHAP.

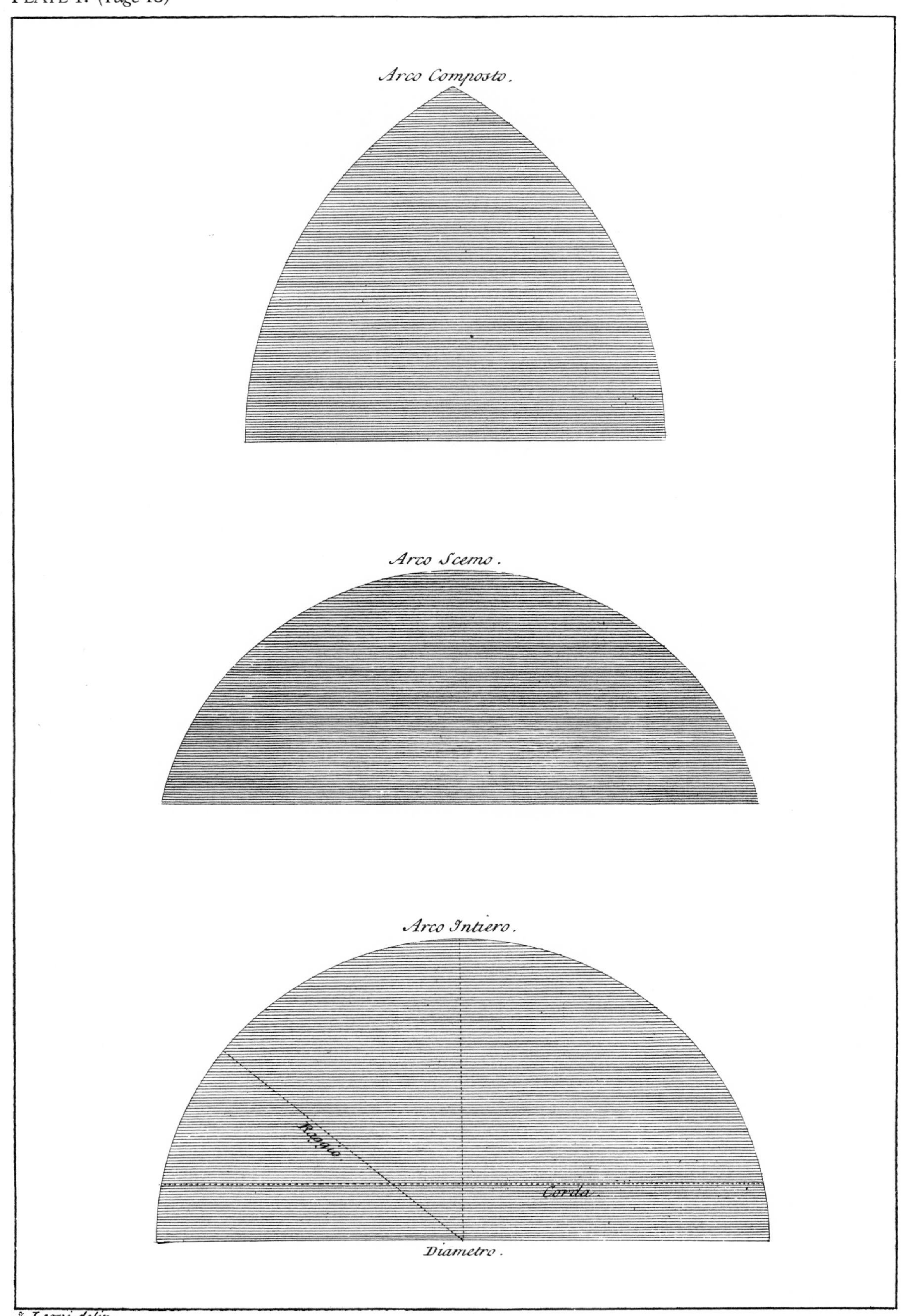

"Arco Composto" = composite arch. "Arco Scemo" = imperfect arch. "Arco Intiero" = entire arch. "Raggio" = radius. "Corda" = chord. "Diametro" = diameter.

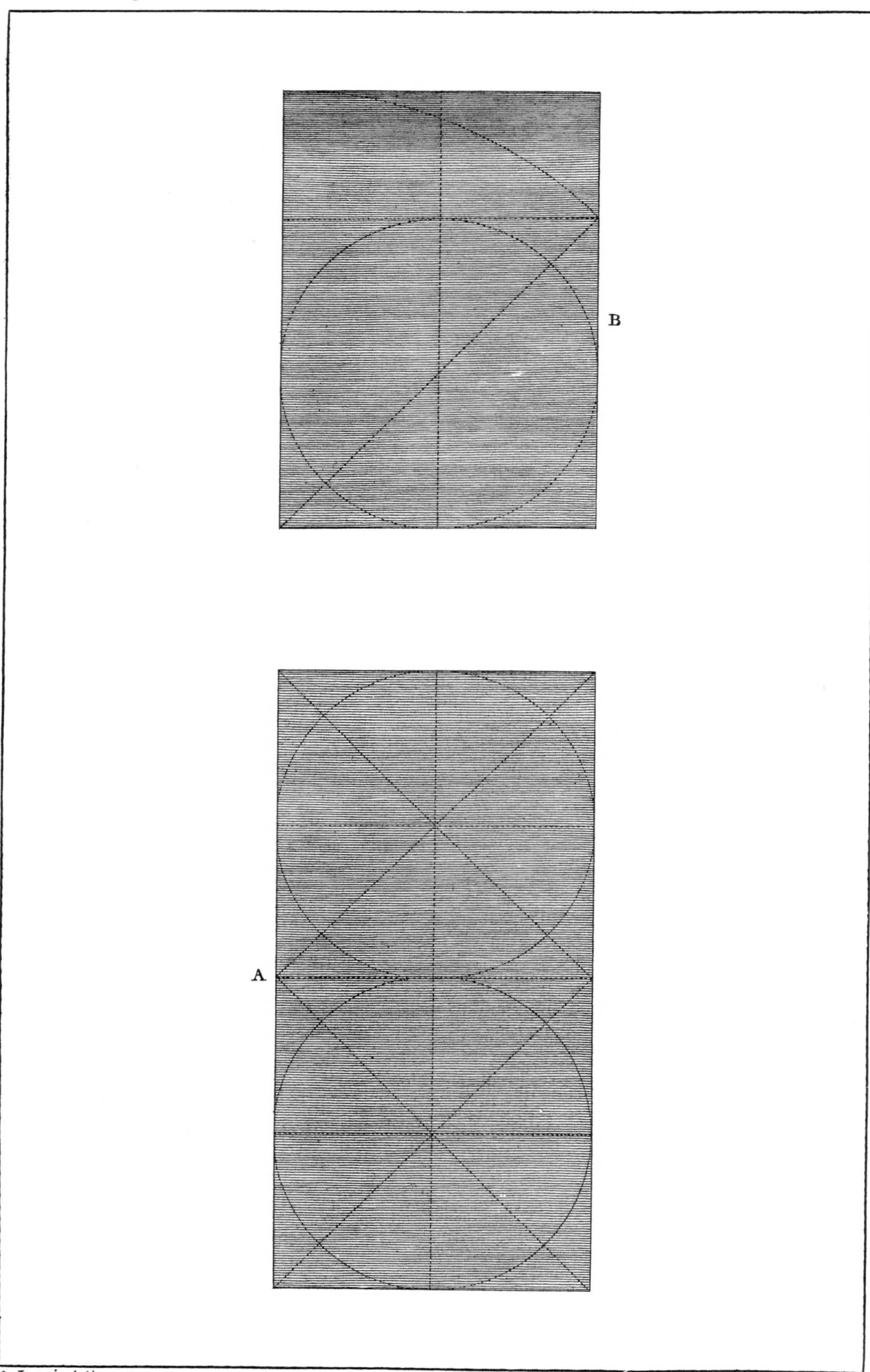

J. Leoni delin.

CHAP. IX.

Of the Compartition, and of the Origin of Building.

THE whole Force of the Invention and all our Skill and Knowledge in the Art of Building, is required in the Compartition: Becauſe the diſtinct Parts of the entire Building, and, to uſe ſuch a Word, the Entireneſs of each of thoſe Parts, and the Union and Agreement of all the Lines and Angles in the Work, duly ordered for Convenience, Pleaſure and Beauty, are diſpoſed and meaſured out by the Compartition alone: for if a City, according to the Opinion of Philoſophers, be no more than a great Houſe, and, on the other Hand, a Houſe be a little City; why may it not be ſaid, that the Members of that Houſe are ſo many little Houſes; ſuch as the Court-yard, the Hall, the Parlour, the Portico, and the like? And what is there in any of theſe, which, if omitted by Careleſſneſs or Negligence, will not greatly take from the Praiſe and Dignity of the Work. Great Care and Diligence therefore is to be uſed in well conſidering theſe Things, which ſo much concern the whole Building; and in ſo ordering it, that even the moſt inconſiderable Parts may not be uncomformable to the Rules of Art, and good Contrivance. What has been already ſaid above of the Region and Platform, may be of no ſmall uſe in doing of this aptly and conveniently; and as the Members of the Body are correſpondent to each other, ſo it is fit that one Part ſhould anſwer to another in a Building; whence we ſay, that great Edifices require great Members. Which indeed was ſo well obſerved by the Ancients, that they uſed much larger Bricks, as well as other Materials, about publick and large Buildings, than in private ones. To every Member therefore ought to be allotted its fit Place and proper Situation; not leſs than Dignity requires, not greater than Conveniency demands; not in an impertinent or indecent Place, but in a Situation ſo proper to itſelf, that it could be ſet no where elſe more fitly. Nor ſhould the Part of the Structure, that is to be of the greateſt Honour, be thrown into a remote Corner; nor that which ought to be the moſt publick, into a private Hole; nor that which ſhould be moſt private, be ſet in too conſpicuous a Place. We ſhould beſides have regard to the Seaſons of the Year, and make a great deal of Difference between hot Places and cold, both in Proportions and Situation. If Rooms for Summer are large and ſpacious, and thoſe for Winter more compact, it will not be at all amiſs; the Summer ones ſhady and open to the Air, and the Winter ones to the Sun. And here we ſhould provide, that the Inhabitants may not be obliged to paſs out of a cold Place into a hot one, without a Medium of temperate Air; or out of a warm one into one expoſed to Cold and Winds; becauſe nothing is ſo prejudicial to human Bodies. And theſe ought to agree one Member with another to perfect and compoſe the main Deſign and Beauty of the whole; that we may not ſo lay out our whole Study in adorning one Part, as to leave the reſt neglected and homely in Compariſon of it; but let them bear that Proportion among themſelves, that they may appear to be an entire and perfect Body, and not disjointed and unfiniſhed Members. Moreover in the forming of theſe Members too, we ought to imitate the Modeſty of Nature; becauſe in this, as well as in other Caſes, the World never commends a Moderation, ſo much as it blames an extravagant Intemperance in Building. Let the Members therefore be modeſtly proportioned, and neceſſary for your Uſes. For all Building in general, if you conſider it well, owes it's Birth to Neceſſity, was nurſed by Convenience, and embelliſhed by Uſe; Pleaſure was the laſt Thing conſulted in it, which is never truly obtained by Things that are immoderate. Let your Building therefore be ſuch, that it may not want any Members which it has not, and that thoſe which it has, may not in any Reſpect deſerve to be condemned. Nor would I have the Edifice terminated all the Way with even continued Lines void of all manner of Variety; for ſome pleaſe us by their Largeneſs, others with being little, and others moderate. One Part therefore ſhould be terminated with ſtrait Lines, another with curve, and another again with ſtrait and curve mixed together; provided you obſerve the Caution I have ſo often given you, to avoid falling into the Error of Exceſs, ſo as to ſeem to have made a Monſter with Limbs diſproportionable: Variety is without Diſpute a very great Beauty in every Thing, when it joins and brings together, in a regular manner, Things different, but proportionable to each other; but it is rather ſhocking, if they are unſuitable and incoherent. For as in Muſick, when the Baſe anſwers the Treble, and the Tenor agrees with both, there ariſes from that Variety of Sounds an harmonious and wonderful Union of Proportions which delights and enchants our Senſes; ſo the like happens in every thing elſe that ſtrikes and pleaſes our Fancy. Laſtly, theſe Things muſt be ſo executed, as Uſe or Conveniency requires, or according to the approved Practice of Men of Skill; becauſe deviating from eſtabliſhed Cuſtom, generally robs a Thing of its whole Beauty, as conforming to it, is applauded and attended with Succeſs. Neverthelefs, tho' other famous Architects ſeem, by their Practice, to have determined this or that Compartition, whether *Doric*, or *Ionic*, or *Corinthian*, or *Tuſcan*, to be the moſt convenient of any; yet they do not thereby tie us down to follow them ſo cloſely, as to tranſcribe their very Deſigns into this Work of ours; but only ſtir us up by their Inſtructions to produce ſomething of our own Invention, and to endeavour to acquire equal or greater Praiſe than they did. But of theſe Things we ſhall ſpeak more diſtinctly in their proper Places, when we come to conſider in what manner a City and its Members ought to be diſpoſed, and every thing neceſſary for the Convenience of each.

Chap. X.

Of the Columns and Walls, and ſome Obſervations relating to the Columns.

WE are now to treat ſummarily of the Diſpoſition of the Wall. But here I muſt not omit what I have obſerved among the Ancients; namely, that they conſtantly avoided drawing any of the outer Lines of the Platform quite ſtrait, ſo as to let any great Length go on without being interrupted by the Concavity of ſome curve Line, or the Interſection of ſome Angle; and the Reaſon why thoſe wiſe Men did this is plain, that the Wall, having, as it were, Props joined to it to reſt againſt, might be ſo much the ſtronger. In treating of the Walling, we ſhould begin with the moſt noble Parts of it. This Place therefore naturally leads us to ſpeak of the Columns, and of the Things belonging to them; a Row of Columns being indeed nothing elſe but a Wall open and diſcontinued in ſeveral Places. And having occaſion to define a Column, it would not be at all improper to ſay, that it is a certain ſtrong continued Part of the Wall, carried up perpendicular from the Foundation to the Top, for ſupporting the Covering. In the whole Compaſs of the Art of Building, you will find nothing, that either for Workmanſhip, Expence or Beauty, deſerves to be preferred before the Columns. But theſe Columns having ſome Particulars in which they differ from one another; in this Place we ſhall ſpeak only of their Agreement; becauſe that regards the Genus of them; but as to their Difference, which relates to their Species, we ſhall handle it in its proper Place. To begin therefore as we may ſay from the Root, every Column has its Foundation; this Foundation being brought up to a Level with the Plane of the *Area*, it was uſual to raiſe thereupon a kind of little Wall, which we ſhall call the Plinth, others perhaps may call it the Dye; upon the Plinth ſtood the Baſe, on the Baſe, the Column; and over the Column the Capital; their Proportion was, that from the middle downwards, they were ſomewhat bigger, and from thence upwards grew more and more taper, and that the Foot was ſomething larger than the Top of all. I make no doubt, that at firſt the Column was invented to ſupport the Covering. Afterwards Men's Thoughts being ſtirred up to worthy Attempts, they ſtudied, tho' themſelves were mortal, to make their Buildings in a Manner immortal and eternal; and for this Reaſon they made Columns, Architraves, Intablatures, and Coverings all of Marble. And in doing theſe Things, the ancient Architects always kept ſo cloſe to Nature, as to ſeem, if poſſible, never to have conſulted any Thing but mere Convenience in Building, and at the ſame Time made it their Care, that their Works ſhould be not only ſtrong and uſeful, but

but alſo pleaſant to the Sight. Nature at firſt certainly gave us Columns made of Wood, and of a round Figure, afterwards by Uſe they came in ſome Places to be cut ſquare. Thereupon, if I judge right, ſeeing in theſe wooden Columns certain Rings of Circles of Braſs or Iron, faſten'd about the Top and Bottom, that the continual Weight which they are made to bear, might not ſplit them; the Architects too left at the Foot of their Columns of Marble, a little Ring like a ſort of Binding; whereby they are defended from any Drops of Rain that might daſh up again upon them. And at the Top too they left another little Band, and over that an Aſtragal or Collar; with which helps they obſerv'd the Columns of Wood to be fortified. In the Baſes of their Columns it was their Rule, that the under Part ſhould conſiſt of ſtrait Lines and right Angles, but that their upper Superficies ſhould terminate circularly to anſwer to the Round of the Pillar; and they made this Baſe on every Side broader than high, and wider than the Column by a determinate Part of itſelf; and the under Superficies of the Baſe they made broader than the upper; the Plinth too they would have a certain Proportion broader than the Baſe, and the Foundation again a determinate Part wider than the Plinth. And all theſe Parts thus placed one upon the other, they erected perpendicular from the Center of the Foundation. On the other hand, the Capitals all agree in this, that their under Parts imitate their Columns, but their upper End in a Square; and conſequently the upper Part of the Capital muſt always be ſomewhat broader than the under. This may ſuffice here as to the Columns. The Wall ought to be raiſed with the ſame Proportions as the Columns; ſo that if it is to be as high as the Column and its Capital, its Thickneſs ought to be the ſame with that of the bottom of the Column. And they alſo obſerved this Rule, that there ſhou'd be neither Pillar, nor Baſe, nor Capital, nor Wall, but what ſhould in all reſpects correſpond with every thing elſe of the ſame Order, in Heighth, Thickneſs, Form and Dimenſion. But tho' both are Faults, either to make the Wall too thin or too thick, higher or lower than the Rule and Proportion requires; yet of the two I wou'd chuſe to offend on that Side, where we ſhou'd have occaſion to take away rather than to add. And here I think it will not be amiſs to take notice of ſome Errors in Buildings, that we our ſelves may be the more circumſpect: in as much as the chief Praiſe is to be exempt from Blame. I have obſerved therefore in St. *Peter*'s Church at *Rome* what indeed the thing itſelf demonſtrates, that it was ill adviſed to draw a very long and thick Wall over ſo many frequent and continued Apertures, without ſtrength'ning it with any curve Lines or any other Fortification whatſoever. And what more deſerves our Notice, all this Wing of Wall, under which are too frequent and continued Apertures, and which is raiſed to a great Heighth, is expoſed as a Butt to the impetuous Blaſts of the North-Eaſt: by which means already thro' the continual Violence of the Winds it is ſwerved from its Direction above two Yards: and I doubt not that in a ſhort time, ſome little accidental ſhock will throw it down into Ruins; and if it were not kept in by the Timber Frame of the Roof, it muſt infallibly have fallen down before now. But the Architect may not be ſo much in Fault, becauſe conſulting only the Neceſſity of his Situation, he might perhaps imagine that the Neighbourhood of the Mountain, which overlooks the Church, might be a ſufficient Shelter againſt the Winds. Neverthelefs it is certain, thoſe Wings ought to have been more ſtrengthned on both Sides.

Chap. XI.

Of the great Uſefulneſs of the Coverings both to the Inhabitants and the other Parts of the Building, and that being various in their Natures, they muſt be made of various Sorts.

THE Covering for Uſefulneſs far exceeds any other Part of the Building. It not only ſecures the Health of the Inhabitants by defending them from the Night, from the Rain, and eſpecially from the burning Rays of the Sun; but it alſo preſerves all the reſt of the Edifice. Take away the Covering and the Materials rot, the Wall moulders and ſplits, and

and in ſhort the whole Structure falls to Ruin. The very Foundations themſelves, which you will hardly believe, are ſecured by the Protection of the Covering: nor have ſo many Buildings been deſtroyed by Fire, Sword, War, by Multitude of Enemies, and all other Calamities put together, as have gone to Ruin by being left naked and uncovered thro Negligence. It is certain the Coverings are the defenſive Arms of the Building againſt the Aſſaults and Violence of Storms and Tempeſts. Wherefore our Anceſtors in this as in other things acted very laudably, in aſcribing ſo much Honour to the Covering, that they ſpent their whole Art and Study in adorning and beautifying it. For ſome of their Coverings we ſee of Braſs, others of Glaſs, ſome of Gold with gilded Beams and Rafters, and richly adorned with Corniſhes of Flowers and Statues. Of Coverings ſome are open to the Air, others not: the open are thoſe which are not for walking upon, but only for receiving the Rain. Thoſe not open to the Air, are the Roofs and Coves that are between the Covering and the Foundations, ſo that one Houſe ſeems to ſtand upon another. By this means it comes to paſs that the ſame Work, which is the Covering to the Apartments below, is the *Aréa* to thoſe above. Of theſe Coverings thoſe above our Heads we call Roofs, or Cielings; and thoſe which we tread upon with our Feet, *Areas*. Whether the uppermoſt Covering, which lies to the open Air, is to be reckoned as an *Area* or Pavement, we ſhall examine in another Place. But the Covering to the open Air, tho' it be of a plain Superficies, ought never to lie even with reſpect to the *Area* which it covers below; but ſhou'd always incline of one Side to throw off the Rain. But the Coverings within, that are of a plain Superficies, ſhould be in all Parts equally diſtant from the Floor. All Coverings muſt anſwer in Lines and Angles to the Form and Shape of the Platform and Wall which they are to cover: And as thoſe are various, ſome being all of curve Lines, others all of ſtrait, and others of both mixed together, the Coverings too are therefore various, and of ſeveral kinds. But tho' they have this natural Difference, and that ſome are hemiſpherical; others made up of four Arches; others vaulted; others conſiſting of Parts of ſeveral Arches; ſome ſloping or ridged like ordinary mean Houſes: yet which-ſoever of theſe Kinds we chuſe it is abſolutely neceſſary, that all Coverings ſhou'd be ſo diſpoſed as to ſhelter and ſhade the Pavement, and throw off all Water and Rain, defending the whole Edifice upon which it is placed for a Covering. For Rain is always prepared to do Miſchief, and wherever there is the leaſt Crack never fails to get in and do ſome Hurt or other: By its Subtility it penetrates and makes its way by its Humidity rots and deſtroys, by its Continuance looſens and unknits all the Nerves of the Building, and in the End ruins and lays Waſte the whole Structure to the very Foundations. And for this Reaſon prudent Architects have always taken care that the Rain ſhould have a free Slope to run off; and that the Water ſhould never be ſtop'd in any Place, or get into any Part where it cou'd do Hurt. And therefore they adviſed, that in Places ſubject to much Snow, the Coverings ſhould have a very ſteep Slope, riſing even to an acute Angle, that the Snow might never reſt and gather upon them, but fall off eaſily; but in more Summeriſh Climates (to uſe ſuch an Expreſſion) they laid their Covering leſs oblique. Laſtly we ſhould endeavour if poſſible, without Prejudice to the Lights or Wall, to have the whole Structure overlaid with one equal Covering in a manner all of one Piece, and ſo far jutting out, that the Water falling from the Gutters may not wet or ſoak into the Wall: and all the Coverings ſhould be ſo diſpoſed, where there are more than one, that one may not ſpout upon the other. The Space of Covering too that the Water is to run over ſhould never be too large, becauſe upon Rains the Water gathering in the Gutters in too great Abundance would waſh back again and flow into the Houſe; which would greatly prejudice the whole Work. Where the *Area* therefore is very large, the Covering ſhould be divided into ſeveral Slopes, and the Rain flow off in different Places; and this is not only attended with Convenience, but Beauty too. If you are obliged in any Place to have ſeveral Coverings, let them join one to another in ſuch a Manner, that when you are once under one, you may paſs from that to all the reſt always under ſhelter.

CHAP.

CHAP. XII.

Of the Apertures in the Building, that is to ſay of the Windows and Doors, and of thoſe which do not take up the whole Thickneſs of the Wall, and their Number and Sizes.

WE are now come to treat of the Apertures, which are of two Sorts, the one ſerving for the Admiſſion of Light and Air, and the other for the Entrance and Paſſage of the Inhabitants, and of all Manner of Conveniencies all thro' the Houſe. Thoſe for Light are the Windows; thoſe for Paſſage, the Doors, Stairs, and the Spaces between the Columns: Thoſe too which are for the carrying away of Water and Smoak, as Wells, Sinks, the Gullets, as we may call them of Chimneys, the Mouths of Ovens and Furnaces are alſo called Apertures. No Room ought to be without a Window, by which the incloſed Air may be let out and renew'd, becauſe elſe it will corrupt and grow unwholeſome. *Capitolinus* the Hiſtorian relates, that in the Temple of *Apollo* at *Babylon* there was found a little Gold Casket of very great Antiquity, upon opening of which there iſſued a Steam of Air, corrupted by Length of Time, and ſo poiſonous, that ſpreading itſelf abroad, it not only killed every body that was near, but infected all *Aſia* with a moſt dreadful Plague quite as far as *Parthia*. In the Hiſtory of *Ammianus Marcellinus*, we read, that in *Seleucia* in the Time of *Mark Anthony* and *Verus*, after the Plunder and Spoiling of the Temple, and carrying away the Image of the *Conic Apollo* to *Rome*, they diſcovered a little Hole which had been formerly ſtop'd up by the *Chaldean* Prieſts: Which being opened by the Soldiers, out of a greedy Deſire of Plunder, ſent forth a Vapour ſo dreadfully peſtilential and infectious, that from the Confines of *Perſia* quite to *Gaul*, the whole Country was tainted with a mortal and loathſome Diſtemper. Every Room therefore ſhould have Windows, not only to let in the Light, but to renew the Air; and they ought to be ſo accommodated to Convenience and the Thickneſs of the Wall, as not to admit more remote than Uſe and Neceſſity requires. Morevover we are to take notice what Winds our Windows are to ſtand open to; becauſe thoſe which look towards a healthy Air may be allow'd to be large every Way; and it will not be amiſs to open them in ſuch Manner that the Air may go clear round the Bodies of the Inhabitants; which may eaſily be contrived, if the Jambs of the Windows are made ſo low, that you may both ſee and be ſeen from the Inſide into the Street. But ſuch Windows as are expoſed to Winds not altogether ſo healthy, ought to be ſo proportion'd as to admit what Light is requiſite, but not any Thing larger than is juſt neceſſary for that Uſe; and they ſhould likewiſe be ſet high, that the Wall may break the Winds before they reach us: Becauſe by this means we ſhall have Wind enough to renew our Air, but ſo interrupted as to take off from the ill Effects of it. We ſhould alſo obſerve what Suns our Houſe ſtands to, and according to various Conveniencies make the Windows larger or ſmaller. In Summer Apartments, if the Windows are to the North, they ſhould be made large every Way; but if they are to the South Sun, it will be proper to make them low and ſmall; ſuch being beſt adapted for Reception of the Air, and leaſt liable to be offended by the Sun's Rays; and there is no Danger ſuch a Place ſhould ever want Light, when the Sun lies in a Manner continually upon it; ſo that Shade and not Light is what is to be conſulted there. On the contrary in Apartments for Winter, the Windows will be beſt contrived for admitting the Sun if they are made large, and yet we may avoid being troubled by the Winds at the ſame Time, if we place them high, ſo that the cold Air may not blow directly upon the People within. Laſtly from whatever Side we take in the Light, we ought to make ſuch an Opening for it, as may always give us a free Sight of the Sky, and the Top of that Opening ought never to be too low, becauſe we are to ſee the Light with our Eyes; and not with our Heels; beſides the Inconvenience, that if one Man gets between nother and the Window, the Light is intercepted, and all the reſt of the Room is darken'd, which never happens when the Light comes from above. The Doors ſhould imitate the Windows, that is, be larger or ſmaller, more or fewer, according to the Frequency or Neceſſity of the Place. But I obſerve, that the Ancients in their Publick Buildings always left a great many of both the afore-mention'd Kinds of Apertures. This appears from their Theatres, which if we obſerve are extremely full of Apertures, not only Stair-caſes, but Windows and Doors. And we ought ſo to order the Proportions of theſe Openings, as not to make very little ones in great Walls, nor too large in ſmall ones. In theſe Sorts of Apertures various Deſigns have been commended; but the beſt Architects have never made Uſe of any but Squares and ſtrait Lines. However all have agreed in this, that let them be of what Shape they will, they ſhould be acmodated to the Bigneſs and Form of the Building. *The Doors, then they ſay ſhould always be more high than broad; and the higheſt be ſuch as are capable of receiving two Circles [A] one upon t'other, and the loweſt ſhould be of the Heighth of the Diagonal of a Square [B] whereof the Groundſell is one of the Sides. It is alſo convenient to place the Doors in ſuch a Manner, that they may lead to as many Parts of the Edifice as poſſible: And in order to give Beauty to ſuch Apertures, Care muſt be taken that thoſe of like Dimenſions correſpond with each other both on the Right and Left. It was uſual to leave the Windows and Doors in odd Numbers, but ſo as for the Side ones to anſwer each other, and that in the Middle to be ſomewhat larger than the reſt. And particular Regard was always had to the Strength of the Building, for which Reaſon they contrived to ſet the Openings clear from the Corners and from the Columns, in the weakeſt Parts of the Wall, but not ſo weak as to be inſufficient to ſupport the Weight: It being their Cuſtom to raiſe as many Parts of the Wall as they could plum, and as it were of one Piece without any Interruption from the Foundation quite up to the Covering. There is a certain Kind of an Aperture, which in Form and Poſition imitates the Doors and Windows, but which does not penetrate the whole Thickneſs of the Wall, and ſo, as Niches leave very handſome and convenient Seats for Statues and Paintings. But in what Parts theſe are to be left, as alſo how frequent and large, will be ſhewn more diſtinctly when we come to treat of the Ornaments of Edifices. We ſhall only obſerve here, that they not only add to the Beauty of the Work, but alſo ſave ſome Expence, as they make leſs Stone and Lime to ſerve for the Walling. This chiefly is to be taken Care of, that you make theſe Niches in convenient Numbers, not too big, and of a juſt Form; and ſo as in their Order to imitate the Windows. And let them be as you will, I have remark'd in the Structures of the Ancients, that they never uſed to ſuffer them to take up above the ſeventh Part of the Front, nor leſs than the ninth. The Spaces between the Columns are to be reckoned among the principal Apertures, and are to be left variouſly according to the Variety of Buildings. But we ſhall ſpeak of theſe more clearly in their proper Place, and chiefly when we treat of Sacred Edifies. Let it be ſufficient to premiſe here, that thoſe Openings ſhould be left in ſuch a Manner, as to have particular Reſpect to the Nature of the Columns, which are deſign'd for the Support of the Covering; and firſt, that thoſe Columns be not too ſmall, nor ſtand too thin, ſo as not to be duly able to bear the Weight, nor too big, or ſet ſo thick as not to leave open convenient Spaces for Paſſage. Laſtly, the Apertures muſt be different, when the Columns are frequent from what they are when they ſtand thin, becauſe over frequent Columns we lay an Architrave, and over the others we turn an Arch. But in all Openings over which we make Arches, we ſhould contrive to have the Arch never leſs than a half Circle, with an Addition of the ſeventh Part of half its Diameter: The moſt experienced Workmen having found that Arch to be by much the beſt adapted for enduring in a Manner to Perpetuity; all other Arches being thought leſs ſtrong for ſupporting the Weight, and more liable to ruin. It is moreover imagined, that the half Circle is the only Arch which has no Occaſion either for Chain or any other Fortification; and all others, if you don't either chain them or place ſome Weight againſt them for a Counterpoiſe, are found by their own Weight to burſt out and fall to ruin. I will not omit here what I have taken Notice of among the Ancients, a Contrivance certainly very excellent and Praiſe-worthy: Their beſt Architects placed theſe Apertures and the Arches of the Roofs of their Temples in ſuch a Manner, that even tho' you took away every Column from under them, yet they would ſtill ſtand firm and not fall down, the Arches on which the Roof was placed being drawn quite down to the Foundation with wonderful Art, known but to few: So that the Work upheld itſelf by being only ſet upon Arches; for thoſe Arches having the ſolid Earth for their Chain, no Wonder they ſtood firm without any other Support.

**Plate* 2. *(facing page* 13*)*

Chap.

Chap. XIII.

Of the Stair cases, and their different Sorts, of the Steps of the Stairs which ought to be in odd Numbers, and how many. Of the resting Places, of the Tunnels for carrying away the Smoke. Of Pipes and Conduits for carrying off the Water, and of the proper Placing of Wells and Sinks.

THE placing of the Stairs is a Work of such Nicety, that without deliberate and mature Consideration you can never place them well: For in a Stair-case there meet three Apertures: One, the Door by which you enter upon the Stairs; another, the Window that supplies you with Light to see the Steps by, and the third, the Opening in the Ceiling which lets you into the *Area* above; and therefore it is said to be no Wonder, that the Stairs should perplex the Design of a Structure; but let him that is desirous to have the Stair not hinder him, take Caré not to hinder the Stair, but allow it a determinate and just Portion of the Platform, in order to give its free Course quite up to the Covering at the Top of all. And do not let us repine that the Stair-case should take up so much of the *Area*, for it furnishes us with very many Conveniencies, and is no Inconvenience to the other Parts of the Building. Add to this, that those little Vaults and Spaces under the Stairs are very serviceable for a great many Purposes. Our Stair-cases therefore are of two Sorts (for as to those Steps or Ladders which belong to military Expeditions, I shall not speak of them here.) The first is that which has no Steps, but is mounted by a sloping Ascent, and the other is that which is mounted by Steps. The Ancients used to make the sloping one as easy and as little steep as possible, and as I have observed from their Works, thought it a convenient Ascent when the highest Part of its Perpendicular was raised one sixth Part of the Line at Bottom. In making of Stair-cases with Steps, they recommend the making of the Steps in odd Numbers, and especially in their Temples: Because they said that by this Means we always set our right Foot into the Temple first; which was accounted a Point of Religion. And I have observed, that the best Architects never put above seven, or at most nine Steps together in one Flight; imitating I suppose, the Number either of the Planets or of the Heavens; but at the End of these seven or nine Steps, they very considerately made a Plain, that such as were weak or tired with the Fatigue of the Ascent, might have Leisure to rest themselves, and that if they should chance to stumble, there might be a Place to break their Fall, and give them Means to recover themselves. And I am thoroughly of Opinion, that the Stairs ought to be frequently interrupted by these landing Places, and that they should be well lighted, and be ample and spacious according to the Dignity of the Place. The Steps they never made higher than nine Inches, nor lower than six, and in Breadth never less than a Foot and a half, nor more than a Yard, The fewer Stair-cases that are in a House, and the less Room they take up, the more convenient they are esteem'd. The Issues for Smoak and Water ought to be as direct as possible, and so built, that they may not lie and gather within, or soil, or offend, or endanger the Building For this Reason too the Tunnels of the Chimnies should be carried quite clear from all Manner of Wood-work, for fear some Spark, or their meer Heat should set Fire to the Beams or Rafters that are near them. The Drains also for carrying off the Water should be so contrived, as to convey away all Superfluities, and in their Passage not to do any Harm to the House, either by sapping or dirtying it. For if any of these Things do Mischief, let it be ever so little, yet by Length of Time and continuation, they will in the End be of the utmost ill Consequence; and I have observed, that the best Architects have contrived either to throw off the Rain by Spouts, so as not to wet any body that is going into the House, or carried it thro Pipes into Cisterns to serve for Use, or else brought it together to some Place where it might wash away all the Filth, so that the Eyes and Noses of the Inhabitants might not be offended with it. Indeed they seem to have been particularly careful to throw the Rain Water clear away from the Building, that it might not sap the Foundations, as well

as

as for ſeveral other Reaſons. In a Word, they were very obſervant to make all their Apertures in the moſt convenient Places, and where they might be moſt ſerviceable. I am particularly for having the Wells ſet in the moſt publick and open Part of the Structure, ſo that they do not take off from the Dignity of the Work, by being ſet in a Place improper for them; and the Naturaliſts affirm, that Water moſt expoſed and open is beſt and moſt purified. But in whatever Part of the Building you make either Wells or Drains, or any other Conveyance for the Water, they ought to have ſuch Apertures, as to admit a good Quantity of Air, that the Pavement may be kept dry from the damp Exhalations, which will be purged and carried off by the Paſſage of the Winds, and the Motion of the Air. We have now taken a ſufficient Review of the Deſigns of Buildings, as far as they ſeem to relate to the Work in general, noting each Particular by itſelf that we intend to ſpeak of. We are now to treat of the Work itſelf and of the Structure of Edifies. But firſt we will conſider of the Materials, and of the Preparations neceſſary for the Materials.

End of the Firſt Book.

THE

THE

ARCHITECTURE

OF

Leone Batiſta Alberti.

BOOK II. CHAP. I.

Treating of the Materials. That no Man ought to begin a Building haſtily but ſhould firſt take a good deal of Time to conſider, and revolve in his Mind all the Qualities and Requiſites of ſuch a Work: And that he ſhould carefully review and examine, with the Advice of proper Judges, the whole Structure in itſelf, and the Proportions and Meaſures of every diſtinct Part, not only in Draughts or Paintings, but in actual Models of Wood or ſome other Subſtance, that when he has finiſh'd his Building, he may not repent of his Labour.

I Do not think the Labour and Expence of a Building to be enter'd upon in a hurry; as well for ſeveral other Reaſons, as alſo becauſe a Man's Honour and Reputation ſuffers by it. For as a Deſign well and compleatly finiſh'd brings Praiſe to him that has employ'd his Pains and Study in the Work; ſo if in any particular the Author ſeems to have been wanting, either of Art or Prudence, it detracts very much from that Praiſe, and from his Reputation. And indeed the Beauties or Faults of Edifices, eſpecially publick ones, are in a Manner clear and manifeſt to every body; and (I know not how it happens) any Thing amiſs ſooner draws Contempt, than any Thing handſome or well finiſh'd does Commendation. It is really wonderful, how, by a Kind of natural Inſtinct, all of us knowing or ignorant, immediately hit upon what is right or wrong in the Contrivance or Execution of Things, and what a ſhrewd Judgment the Eye has in Works of this Nature above all the other Senſes. Whence it happens, that if any Thing offers itſelf to us that is lame or too little, or unneceſſary, or ungraceful, we preſently find ourſelves moved and deſirous to have it handſomer. The Reaſons of thoſe Faults perhaps we may not all of us be acquainted with, and yet if we were to be ask'd, there is none of us but would readily ſay, that ſuch a Thing might be remedied and corrected. Indeed every one cannot propoſe the Remedy, but only ſuch as are well practiced and experienced that Way. It is therefore the Part of a wiſe Man to weigh and review every particular thoroughly in his Mind: That he may not afterwards be forced to ſay, either in the Middle or at the End of this Work, I wiſh this, or I wiſh that were otherwiſe. And it is really ſurprizing, what a hearty Puniſhment a Man ſuffers for a Work ill managed: For in Proceſs of Time, he himſelf at Length finds out the Miſtakes he fooliſhly made in the Beginning for want of due Reflection: And then, unleſs he pulls it to pieces and reforms it, he is continually repenting and fretting at the Eye-ſore; or if he pulls it down, he is blamed upon Account of the Loſs and Expence, and accuſed of Levity and Inſtability of Mind. *Suetonius* tells us, that *Julius Cæſar* having begun a Structure at the Lake *Nemorenſis* from the very Foundations, and compleated it at vaſt Expence, pull'd it all down again, becauſe it was not exactly in all reſpects to his Mind. For which he is certainly very much to be blamed, even by us his Poſterity, either for not ſufficiently conſidering what was requiſite at firſt, or elſe afterwards for diſliking thro' Levity what might really not be amiſs. I therefore always highly commend the ancient Cuſtom of Builders, who not only in Draughts and Paintings, but in real Models of Wood or other Subſtance, examin'd and weigh'd over and over again, with the Advice of Men of the beſt Experience, the whole Work and the Admeaſurements of all its Parts, before they put themſelves to the Expence or Trouble. By making a Model you will have an Opportunity, thoroughly to weigh and conſider the Form and Situation of your Platform with reſpect to the Region, what Extent is to be allow'd to it, the Number and Order of the Parts, how the Walls are to be made, and how ſtrong and firm the Covering; and in a Word all thoſe Particulars which we have ſpoken of in the preceding Book: And there you may eaſily and freely add, retrench, alter, renew, and in ſhort change every Thing from one End to t'other, till all and every one of the Parts are juſt as you would have them, and without Fault. Add likewiſe, that you may then examine and compute (what is by no means to be neglected) the Particulars and Sum of your future Expence, the Size, Heighth, Thickneſs, Number, Extent, Form, Species and Quality of all the Parts, how they are to be made, and by what Artificers; becauſe you will thereby have a clear and diſtinct Idea of the Numbers and Forms of your Columns, Capitals, Baſes, Corniſhes, Pediments, Incruſtations, Pavements, Statues and the like, that relates either to the Strength or Ornament. I muſt not omit to obſerve, that the making of curious, poliſh'd Models, with the Delicacy of Painting, is not required from an Architect that only deſigns to ſhew the real Thing itſelf; but is rather the Part of a vain Architect, that makes it his Buſineſs by charming the Eye and ſtriking the Fancy of the Beholder, to divert him from a rigorous Examination of the Parts which he ought to make, and to draw him into an Admiration of himſelf. For this Reaſon I would not have the Models too exactly finiſh'd, nor too delicate and neat, but plain and ſimple, more to be admired for the Contrivance of the Inventor, than the Hand of the Workman. Between the Deſign of the Painter and that of the Architect, there is this Difference, that the Painter by the Exactneſs of his Shades, Lines and Angles, endeavours to make the Parts ſeem to riſe from the Canvaſs, whereas the Architect, without any Regard to the Shades, makes his Relieves from the Deſign of his Platform, as one that would have his Work valued, not by the apparent Perſpective, but by the real Compartments founded upon Reaſon. In a Word, you ought to make ſuch Models, and conſider them by yourſelf, and with others ſo diligently, and examine them over and over ſo often, that there ſhall not be a ſingle Part in your whole Structure, but what you are thoroughly acquainted with, and know what Place and how much Room it is to poſſeſs, and to what Uſe to be applied. But above all, nothing requires our Attention ſo much as the Covering, which ſeems in its Nature, if I miſtake not, beyond any Thing elſe in Architecture to have been of the greateſt and firſt Convenience to Mankind; ſo that indeed it muſt be own'd, that it was upon the Account of this Covering that they invented not only the Wall and thoſe other Parts which are carried up with the Wall and neceſſarily accompany it, but alſo thoſe Parts which are made under Ground, ſuch as Conduits, Channels, Receptacles of Rain Water, Sewers and the like. For my Part, that have had no ſmall Experience in Things of this Nature, I indeed know the Difficulty of performing

performing a Work, wherein the Parts are join'd with Dignity, Convenience and Beauty, having not only other Things praiſe-worthy, but alſo a Variety of Ornaments, ſuch as Decency and Proportion requires; and this no Queſtion is a very great Matter; but to cover all theſe with a proper, convenient and apt Covering, is the Work of none but a very great Maſter. To conclude, when the whole Model and the Contrivance of all the Parts greatly pleaſes both yourſelf and others of good Experience, ſo that you have not the leaſt Doubt remaining within yourſelf, and do not know of any Thing that wants the leaſt Re-examination; even then I would adviſe you not to run furiouſly to the Execution out of a Paſſion for Building, demoliſhing old Structures, or laying mighty Foundations of the whole Work, which raſh and inconſiderate Men are apt to do; but if you will hearken to me, lay the Thoughts of it aſide for ſome Time, till this favourite Invention grows old. Then take a freſh Review of every Thing, when not being guided by a Fondneſs for your Invention, but by the Truth and Reaſon of Things you will be capable of judging more clearly. Becauſe in many Caſes Time will diſcover a great many Things to you, worth Conſideration and Reflection, which, be you ever ſo accurate, might before eſcape you.

CHAP. II.

That we ought to undertake nothing above our Abilities, nor ſtrive againſt Nature, and that we ought alſo not only to conſider what we can do, but what is fit for us to do, and in what Place it is that we are to build.

ON examining your Model, among other Points to be conſider'd, you muſt take Care not to forget theſe. Firſt, not to undertake a Thing, which is above the Power of Man to do, and not to pretend to ſtrive directly contrary to the Nature of Things. For Nature, if you force or wreſt her out of her Way, whatever Strength you may do it with, will yet in the End overcome and break thro' all Oppoſition and Hindrance; and the moſt obſtinate Violence (to uſe ſuch an Expreſſion) will at laſt be forced to yield to her daily and continual Perſeverence aſſiſted by Length of Time. How many of the mighty Works of Men do we read of, and know ourſelves to have been deſtroy'd by no other Cauſe than that they contended againſt Nature? Who does not laugh at him, that having made a Bridge upon Ships, intended to ride over the Sea? or rather, who does not hate him for his Folly and Inſolence? The Haven of *Claudius* below *Oſtia*, and that of *Hadrian* near *Terracina*, Works in all other Reſpects likely to laſt to Eternity, yet now having their Mouths ſtop'd with Sand, and their Beds quite choak'd up, they have been long ſince totally deſtroy'd by the continual Aſſaults of the Sea, which inceſſantly waſhing againſt it gains from it daily. What then think ye will happen in any Place, where you pretend to oppoſe or entirely repel the Violence of Water, or the enormous Weight of Rocks tumbling down on you in Ruins? This being conſider'd, we ought never to undertake any Thing that is not exactly agreeable to Nature; and moreover we ſhould take Care not to enter upon a Work in which we may be ſo much wanting to ourſelves as to be forced to leave it imperfect. Who would not have blamed *Tarquin*, King of the *Romans*, if the Gods had not favoured the Greatneſs of the City, and if by the Enlargement of the Empire he had not received an Acceſſion of Wealth ſufficient to compleat the Magnificence of his Beginning, for throwing away the whole Expence of his future Work in laying the Foundations of his Temple. Beſides it is not amiſs to conſider, and that not in the laſt Place, not only what you are able, but alſo what is decent for you to do. I do not commend *Rhodope* of *Thrace*, the famous Courtezan, and the Wonder of her Days, for building herſelf a Sepulcher of incredible Expence: For though ſhe might poſſibly by her Whoredom have acquired the Riches of a Queen, yet ſhe was by no means worthy of a Royal Sepulcher. But on the other Hand I do not blame *Artemiſia*, Queen of *Caria*, for having built her beloved and worthy Conſort a moſt ſtately

Mauſoleum

Mauſoleum: Though in Things of that Nature, I think Modeſty is beſt. *Horace* blamed *Mæcenas* for having too furious a Paſſion for Building. I commend him, who according to *Cornelius Tacitus*, built *Otho*'s Sepulcher, modeſt, but extremely durable. And though it be true that private Monuments require Modeſty and publick ones Magnificence; yet publick ones too are ſometimes praiſed for being as modeſt as the others. We admire *Pompey*'s Theatre for the ſurprizing Greatneſs and Dignity of the Work: A Work truly worthy of *Pompey* and of *Rome* in the Midſt of her Victories: but *Nero*'s unadviſedly Fondneſs for Building, and mad Paſſion for Undertaking immenſe Deſigns, is commended by nobody. And beſides, who would not rather have wiſh'd, that he who employ'd ſo many thouſand Men to bore through the Hill near *Pozzuolo*, had taken the ſame Pains, and beſtowed the ſame Expence upon ſome Work of greater Uſe? Who will not deteſt the monſtrous Folly and Vanity of *Heliogabalus*? who had Thoughts of erecting a huge Column with Stairs on the Inſide of it to mount to the Top, whereon *Heliogabalus* himſelf was to be ſet as a God, which he pretended to make himſelf. But not being able to find a Stone of that Bigneſs, tho' he ſought for it quite to *Thebais*, he deſiſted from his wild Deſign. Hereunto we may add, that we ought not to begin a Thing, which though in ſome Reſpects worthy and uſeful, and not altogether ſo difficult of Execution, ſome particular Opportunity or Means ſavouring it at that Time, that yet is of a Nature to fall ſoon to decay, either thro' the Neglience of Succeſſors, or Diſlike of the Inhabitants. I therefore find Fault with the Canal which *Nero* made navigable for Gallies with five Rows of Oars from *Avernus* to *Oſtia*, as well upon other Accounts, as becauſe the Maintaining of it ſeem'd to require perpetual and eternal Felicity of the Empire, and a Succeſſion of Princes all inclined to the ſame Works. Theſe Conſiderations being granted, we ought to reflect duly upon all the Particulars beforemention'd, that is to ſay, what Work we undertake, the Place we are to build in, and what the Perſon is that is to build; and to contrive every Thing according to his Dignity and Neceſſities, is the Part of a diſcreet and prudent Architect.

CHAP. XII.

That having conſider'd the whole Diſpoſition of the Building in all the Parts of the Model, we ought to take the Advice of prudent and underſtanding Men, and before we begin our Work, it will not only be proper to know how to raiſe Money for the Expence, but alſo long before hand to provide all the Materials for compleating ſuch an Undertaking.

HAVING weigh'd and conſider'd theſe Things you muſt proceed to the Examination of the Reſt, whether each of them be perfectly contrived and conveniently diſpoſed in its proper Place. And to do this effectually, it is neceſſary you ſhould be full of this Perſuaſion, all the while you are meditating upon theſe Things, that it will be a Scandal to you, if as far as in you lies, you ſuffer any other Building with the ſame Expence or Advantages to gain more Praiſe and Approbation than your own. Nor is it ſufficient in theſe Caſes to be only not deſpiſed, unleſs you are highly and principally commended, and then imitated. Therefore we ought to be as ſevere and diligent as poſſible in our Scrutiny of every Particular, as well to ſuffer nothing but what is excellent and elegant, as to have all Things mutually concur to make the whole Handſome and Beautiful, inſomuch that whatever you attempted to add, or retrench, or alter, ſhould be for the Worſe and make a Defect. But herein, I repeat my Advice, let your Moderator be the Prudence and Counſel of the moſt experienced Judges, whoſe Approbation is founded upon Knowledge and Sincerity: Becauſe by their Skill and Directions you will be much more likely, than by your own private Will and Opinion, to attain to Perfection or Something very near it. And beſides, the Praiſe of good Judges is the higheſt Satisfaction; and as for others they praiſe you ſufficiently, and indeed too much in not doing Something better themſelves. So that you will be ſure of the

the Pleaſure of having the Approbation of all that underſtand theſe Matters. And you may find your Advantage in hearkning to every Body; for ſometimes it happens, that Perſons of no Skill make Obſervations by no Means to be deſpiſed. When therefore you have well weigh'd, review'd, and examin'd all the Parts of your Model, and all the Proportions of the whole Building, ſo that there is not the leaſt Particular any where about it, which you have not conſider'd and reflected upon, and that you are fully reſolved to build in that Manner in every Reſpect, and can raiſe the Money conveniently for bearing the Expence; then prepare the other Things neceſſary for the Execution of your Work, that when you have begun, nothing may be wanting ſo as to prevent your finiſhing your Structure expeditiouſly. For as you will have Occaſion for a great Number of Things for carrying on the Buſineſs, and as if but one is unprovided, it may ſtop or ſpoil the whole Work, it is your Care to have every Thing at Hand that may be of Uſe to you, if provided, or a Detriment, if wanting. The Kings of *Judea*, *David* and *Solomon*, when they had undertaken to build the Temple of *Jeruſalem*, having amaſs'd great Quantities of Gold, Silver, Braſs, Timber, Stone and the like Materials, that they might want Nothing that could be ſerviceable in the eaſy and ſpeedy Execution of the Work (as *Euſebius Pamphilus* tells us) ſent to the neighbouring Kings for ſeveral Thouſands of Workmen and Architects. Which I highly commend: Becauſe it certainly adds Dignity to the Work, and encreaſes the Glory of the Author; and Structures that have been handſomely contrived and ſpeedily finiſh'd beſides, have been very much celebrated by ancient Writers. *Quintus Curtius* relates that *Alexander* the Great, in Building a City, and that no very ſmall one, near the *Tanais*, ſpent but ſeven Days; and *Joſephus* the Hiſtorian tells us, that *Nebuchadnezzer* built the Temple of *Belus* in fifteen, and in the ſame Space of Time girt the City of *Babylon* with three Circuits of Walls. That *Titus* made a Wall little leſs than five Miles long, and *Semiramis* near *Babylon* built the eighth Part of a Mile of a prodigious Wall every Day; and that ſhe erected another of above five and twenty Miles in Length, very High and Thick, to confine the Lake, and in no more than ſeven Days. But of theſe in another Place.

CHAP. VI.

What Materials are to be provided for the Building, what Workmen to be choſe, and in what Seaſons, according to the Opinions of the Ancients, to cut Timber.

THE Things to be prepared are theſe, Lime, Timber, Sand, Stone, as alſo Iron, Braſs, Lead, Glaſs and the like. But the Thing of greateſt Conſequence is to chuſe skilful Workmen, not light or inconſtant, whom you may truſt with the Care and Management of an Edifice well deſign'd, and who will compleat it with all Expedition. And in fixing upon all theſe, it will be of Uſe to you to be ſomewhat guided by the Conſideration of other Works already finiſh'd in your Neighbourhood, and by the Information you receive from them to determine what to do in your own Caſe. For by obſerving the Faults and Beauties in them, you will conſider that the ſame may happen in yours. *Nero* the Emperor having form'd a Deſign of dedicacating a huge Statue of an hundred and twenty Foot high in Honour of the Sun at *Rome*, exceeding any Thing that had been done before in Greatneſs and Magnificence, as *Pliny* relates, before he gave final Orders for the Work to *Zenodarus*, a famous and excellent Sculptor in thoſe Days, would firſt ſee his Capacity for ſuch a Work by a *Coloſſus* of extraordinary Weight, which he had made in the Country of *Auvergne* in *France*. Theſe Things duly conſider'd, we proceed to the others. We intend, then, in treating of the Materials neceſſary for Building, to repeat thoſe Things which have been taught us by the moſt learned among the Ancients, and particularly *Theophraſtus*, *Ariſtotle*, *Cato*, *Varro*, *Pliny* and *Virgil*, becauſe they have learned more from long Obſervation than from any Quickneſs of Genius; ſo that they are beſt gathered from thoſe who have obſerved them with the greateſt Diligence. We ſhall therefor fore go on to collect those Rules which the most approved Ancients have left us in many and various Places, and to these, according to our Custom, we shall add whatever we ourselves have deduced from antique Works, or the Instructions of most experienced Artificers, if we happen to know any Thing that may be serviceable to our Purpose. And I believe it will be the best Method, following Nature herself, to begin with those Things which were first in Use among Men in their Buildings; which, if we mistake not, were Timber Trees which they fell'd in the Woods: Though among Authors, I find, some are divided upon this very Subject. Some will have it, that Men at first dwelt in Caves, and that they and their Cattle were both sheltered under the same Roof; and therefore they believe what *Pliny* tells us, that one *Gellius Texius* was the first, that, in Imitation of Nature built himself a House of Mud. *Diodorus* says that *Vesta*, the Daughter of *Saturn*, was the first that invented Houses. *Eusebius Pamphilus*, an excellent Searcher into Antiquity, tells us from the Testimony of the Ancients, that the Grandsons of *Protogenes* first taught Men the Building of Houses, which they patch'd up of Reeds and Bullrushes: But to return to our Subject. The Ancients, then, and particularly *Theophrastus*, inform us, that most Trees, and especially the Fir, the Pitch-tree and the Pine, ought to be cut immediately, when they begin to put forth their young Shoots, when through their abundance of Sap you most easily strip off the Bark. But that there are some Trees, as the Maple, the Elm, the Ash, and the Linden, which are best cut after Vintage. The Oak if cut in Summer, they observe is apt to breed Worms; but if in Winter, it will keep sound and not split. And it is not foreign to our Purpose what they remark, that Wood which is cut in Winter, in a North Wind, though it be green, will nevertheless burn extremely well, and in a Manner without Smoak; which manifestly shews that their Juices are not crude, but well digested. *Vitruvius* is for cutting Timber from the beginning of Autumn, till such Time as the soft Westerly Winds begin to blow. And *Hesiod* says, that when the Sun darts his burning Rays directly upon our Heads, and turns Mens Complections to brown, then is the Time for Harvest, but that when the Trees drop their Leaves, then is the Season for cutting of Timber. *Cato* moderates the Matter thus; let the Oak, says he, be felled during the Solstice, because in Winter it is always out of Season; other Woods that bear Seed may be cut when that is mature; those that bear none, when you please. Those that have their Seeds green and ripe at the same Time, should be cut when that is fallen, but the Elm when the Leaves drop. And they say it is of very great Importance, what Age the Moon is of when you fell your Timber: For they are all of Opinion, and especially *Varro*, that the Influence of the Moon is so powerful over Things of this Nature, that even they who cut their Heir in the Wane of the Moon, shall soon grow bald; and for this Reason, they tell us, *Tiberius* observed certain Days for cutting his Hair. The Astrologers affirm, that your Spirits will always be oppressed with Melancholly, if you cut your Nails or Hair while the Moon is oppressed or ill dispposed. It is to our present Purpose what they say, that such Things as are designed in their Uses to be moveable, ought to be cut and wrought when the Moon is in *Libra* or *Cancer* ; but such as are to be fixed and immoveable, when she is in *Leo*, *Taurus*, or the like. But that Timber ought to be cut in the Wane of the Moon, all the Learned are agreed, because they hold that the flegmatick Moisture, so very liable to immediate Putrefaction, is then almost quite dried up, and it is certain, that when it is cut in such a Moon, it is never apt to breed Worms. Hence they say you ought to reap the Corn which you intend to sell, at full Moon; because then the Ears are full; but that which you intend to keep in the Wane. It is also evident, that the Leaves of Trees cropt in the Wane of the Moon do not rot. *Columella* thinks it best to fell Timber from the twentieth to the thirtieth Day of the Moon's Age; *Vegetius*, from the fifteenth to the two and twentieth; and hence he supposes the religious Ceremony to arise, of celebrating all Mysteries relating to Eternity only on those Days, because Wood cut then lasted in a Manner for ever. They add, that we should likewise observe the Setting of the Moon. But *Pliny* thinks it a proper Time to fell Trees when the Dog-star reigns, and when the Moon is in Conjunction with the Sun, which Day is called an *Interlunium*, and says it is good to wait for the Night of that Day too, till the Moon is set. The Astronomers say, the Reason of this is, because the Action of the Moon puts the Fluids of all Bodies into Motion; and that therefore when those Fluids are

are drawn down, or left by the Moon in the lowest Roots, the Rest of the Timber is clearer and sounder. Moreover they think that the Tree will be much more serviceable, if it is not cut quite down immediately, but chopt round about, and so left standing upon the Stump to dry. And they say, that if the Fir (which is not the most unapt to suffer by Moisture) be barked in the Wane of the Moon, it will never afterwards be liable to be rotted by Water. There are some who affirm that if the Oak, which is so heavy a Wood that naturally it sinks in the Water, be chopt round the Bottom in the Beginning of Spring, and cut down when it has lost its Leaves, it will have such an Effect upon it, that it will float for the Space of ninety Days and not sink. Others advise to chop the Trees which you leave thus upon their Stumps, half way through, that the Corruption and bad Juices may distil through, and be carried off. They add, that the Trees, which are designed to be sawed or planed, should not be cut down till they have brought their Fruits and ripened their Seeds; and that Trees so cut, especially Fruit-bearers, should be barked, because while they are covered with the Bark, Corruption is very apt to gather between the Rind and the Tree.

Chap. V.

Of preserving the Trees after they are cut, what to plaister or anoint them with, of the Remedies against their Infirmities, and of allotting them their proper Places in the Building.

AFTER the Timber is cut, it must be laid where the scorching Heat of the Sun or rude Blasts of Winds never come; and especially, that which falls of itself, ought to be very well protected with Shade. And for this Reason, the ancient Architects used to plaister it over with Ox-Dung; which *Theophrastus* says they did, because by that Means all the Pores being stopped up, the superfluous Flegm and Humidity concreting within, distils and vents itself by Degrees through the Heart, by which Means the Dryness of the other Parts of the Wood is condensed by its drying equally throughout. And they are of Opinion that Trees dry better, if set with their Heads downward. Moreover, they prescribe various Remedies against their decaying and other Infirmities. *Theophrastus* thinks that burying of Timber hardens it extremely. *Cato* advises to anoint it with Lees of Oil, to preserve it from all Manner of Worms; and we all know that Pitch is a Defence to it against Water. They say that Wood, which has been soaked in the Dregs of Oil, will burn without the Offence of Smoak. *Pliny* writes, that in the Labyrinth of *Egypt*, there are a great many Beams made of the *Egyptian* Thorn rubed over with Oil, and *Theophrastus* says, that Timber dawbed over with Glue will not burn. Nor will I omit what we read in *Aulus Gellius*, taken out of the Annals of *Quintus Claudius*, that *Archelaus*, *Mithridates*'s Præfect, having thoroughly debawbed a wooden Tower in the Piræum with Allum, when *Sylla* besieged it, it would not take Fire. Several Woods are hardened and strengthened against the Assaults of Storms in various Manners. They bury the Citron-wood under Ground, plaistered over with Wax, for seven Days, and after an Intermission of as many more, lay it under Heaps of Corn for the same Space of Time, whereby it becomes not only stronger but easier to be wrought, because it takes away a very considerable Part of its Weight; and they say too, that the same Wood thus dryed, being afterwards laid some time in the Sea, acquires a Hardness incredibly solid and incorruptible. It is certain the Chesnut Tree is purged by the Sea-water. *Pliny* writes, the *Ægyptian* Fig-tree is laid under Water to dry and grow lighter, for at first it will sink to the Bottom. We see that our Workmen lay their Timber under Water or Dung for thirty Days, especially such as they design for turning, by which Means they think it is better dried and more easily worked for all Manner of Uses. There are some who affirm, that all Manner of Woods agree in this, that if you bury them in some moist Place while they are green, they will endure for ever; but whether you preserve it in Woods, or bury, or anoint it, the Experienced are universally of this Opinion, that you must not meddle with it under three Months: The Timber must have Time

Time to harden and to get a Kind of Maturity of Strength before it is applied to Uſe. After it is thus prepared, *Cato* directs, that it muſt not be brought out into the Air but in the Wane of the Moon, and after Mid-day, and even in the Wane of the Moon he condemns the four Days next after the fifteenth, and precautions us againſt bringing it out in a South Wind. And when we bring it out, we muſt take Care not to draw it through the Dew, nor to ſaw or cut it when it is covered with Dew or Froſt, but only when it is perfectly dry in all Reſpects.

Chap. VI.

What Woods are moſt proper for Building, their Natures and Uſes, how they are to be employed, and what Part of the Edifice each Kind is moſt fit for.

Theophraſtus thinks that Timber is not dry enough for the making of Planks, eſpecially for Doors, in leſs than three Years. The Trees of moſt Uſe for Building were reckoned to be theſe; the Holm, and all other Sorts of Oaks, the Beech, the Poplar, the Linden, the Willow, the Alder, the Aſh, the Pine, the Cypreſs, the Olive, both Wild and Garden, the Cheſnut, the Larch Tree, the Box, the Cedar, the Ebony, and even the Vine: But all theſe are various in their Natures, and therefore muſt be applied to various Uſes. Some are better than others to be expoſed without Doors, others muſt be uſed within; ſome delight in the open Air, others harden in the Water, and will endure almoſt for ever under Ground; ſome are good to make nice Boards, and for Sculptures, and all Manner of Joyner's Work; ſome for Beams and Rafters; others are ſtronger for ſupporting open Terraſſes, and Coverings; and the Alder, for Piles to make a Foundation in a River or marſhy Ground, exceeds all other Trees, and bears the Wet incomparably well, but will not laſt at all in the Air or Sun. On the contrary, the Beech will not endure the Wet at all. The Elm, ſet in the open Air, hardens extremely; but elſe it ſplits and will not laſt. The Pitch Tree and Pine, if buried under Ground, are wonderfully durable. But the Oak, being hard, cloſe, and nervous, and of the ſmalleſt Pores, not admitting any Moiſture, is the propereſt of any for all Manner of Works under Ground, capable of ſupporting the greateſt Weights, and is the ſtrongeſt of Columns. But though Nature has endued it with ſo much Hardneſs that it cannot be bored unleſs it be ſoaked, yet above Ground it is reckoned inconſtant, and to warp and grow unmanageable, and in the Sea-water quickly rots; which does not happen to the Olive, nor Holm Oak, nor Wild Olive, though in other Things they agree with the Oak. The Maſt-Holm never conſumes with Age, becauſe it's Inſide is juicy, and as it were always green. The Beech likewiſe and the Cheſnut do not rot in the Water, and are reckoned among the principal Trees for Works under Ground. The Cork Tree alſo, and the wild Pine, the Mulberry, the Maple, and the Elm are not amiſs for Columns. *Theophraſtus* recommends the *Negropont* Nut Tree for Beams and Rafters, becauſe before it breaks it gives Notice by a Crack, which formerly ſaved the Lives of a great many People, who, upon the falling of the publick Baths at *Andros*, by Means of that Warning had Time to make their Eſcape. But the Fir is much the Beſt for that Uſe; for as it is one of the Biggeſt and Thickeſt of Trees, ſo it is endued with a natural Stiffneſs, that will not eaſily give way to the Weight that is laid upon it, but ſtands firm and never yields. Add beſides, that it is eaſy to work, and does not lie too heavy upon the Wall. In ſhort, many Perfections, and Uſes, and great Praiſes are aſcribed to this ſingle Wood; neverthеleſs we cannot diſown that it has one Fault, which is, that it is too apt to catch Fire. Not inferior to this for Roofs, is the Cypreſs, a Tree, in many other Reſpects ſo uſeful, that it claims a principal Rank among the moſt excellent. The Ancients reckoned it as one of the Beſt, and not inferior to Cedar or Ebony. In *India* the Cypreſs is valued almoſt equal with the Spice Trees, and with good Reaſon; for whatever Praiſes may be beſtowed upon the Ammony or Cirenaic Field Pine, which *Theophraſtus* ſays is everlaſting, yet if you conſult either Smell, Beauty, Strength, Bigneſs, Straitneſs, or Duration, or all theſe together, what Tree can you put in Competition with the Cypreſs? It is affirmed

affirmed that the Cypreſs never ſuffers either by Worms or Age, and never ſplits of its own accord. For this Reaſon *Plato* was of Opinion, that the publick Laws and Statutes ſhould be carved in ſacred Tables of Cypreſs, believing they would be more laſting than Tables of Braſs. This Topick naturally leads me to give an Account of what I myſelf remember to have read and obſerv'd of this Wood. It is related that the Gates of the Temple of *Diana*, at *Epheſus*, being of Cypreſs, laſted four hundred Years, and preſerved their Beauty in ſuch a Manner that they always ſeemed to be new. In the Church of St. *Peter* at *Rome*, upon the repairing of the Gates by Pope *Eugenius*, I found, that where they had not been injured by the Violence of the Enemy in ſtripping away the Silver with which they were formerly covered, they had continued whole and ſound above five hundred and fifty Years; for if we examing the Annals of the *Roman* Pontiffs, ſo long it is from the Time of *Hadrian* the Third, who ſet them up, to *Eugene* the Fourth. Therefore, though the Fir is very much commended for making Rafters, yet the Cypreſs is preferred before it, perhaps only upon this one Account, namely, that it is more laſting; but then it is heavier than the Fir. The Pine and Pitch Trees alſo are valued, for the Pine is ſuppoſed to have the ſame Quality as the Fir, of riſing againſt the Weight that is laid upon it: But between the Fir and the Pine there is this Difference, among others, that the Firs is leſs injured by Worms, becauſe the Pine is of a ſweeter Juice than the Fir. I do not know any Wood that is to be preferred to the Larch, or Turpentine Tree, which, within my Obſervation, has ſupported Buildings perfectly ſtrong, and to a very great Age, in many Places, and particularly in thoſe very ancient Structures in the Market-place at *Venice*, and indeed this one Tree is reckoned to be furniſhed with the Conveniences of all the Reſt; it is nervous, tenacious of its Strength, unmoveable in Storms, not moleſted with Worms; and it is an ancient Opinion, that againſt the Injuries of Fire it remains invincible, and in a Manner unhurt, inſomuch that they adviſe us, on whatever Side we are apprehenſive of Fire, to place Beams of Larch by Way of Security. It is true I have ſeen it take Fire and burn, but yet in ſuch a Manner that it ſeemed to diſdain the Flames, and to threaten to drive them away. It has indeed one Defect, which is, that in Sea-water it is very apt to breed Worms. For Beams the Oak and Olive are accounted improper, becauſe of their Heavineſs, and that they give Way beneath the Weight that is laid upon them, and are apt to warp even of themſelves; beſides, all Trees that are more inclinable to break into Shivers than to ſplit, are unfit for Beams; ſuch are the Olive, the Fig, the Linden, the Sallow, and the like. It is a ſurprizing Property which they relate of the Palm Tree, that it riſes againſt the Weight that is laid upon it, and bends upwards in ſpite of all Reſiſtance. For Beams and Coverings expoſed to the open Air, the Juniper is greatly commended; and *Pliny* ſays it has the ſame Properties as the Cedar, but is ſounder. The Olive too is reckoned extreamly durable, and the Box is eſteemed as one of the Beſt of all. Nor is the Cheſnut, though apt to cleave and ſplit, rejected for Works to the open Air. But the wild Olive they particularly eſteem for the ſame Reaſon as the Cypreſs, becauſe it never breeds Worms, which is the Advantage of all Trees that have oily and gummy Juices, eſpecially if thoſe Juices are bitter. The Worm never enters into ſuch Trees, and it is certain they exclude all Moiſture from without. Contrary to theſe are ſuppoſed to be all Woods that have Juices of a ſweet Taſte, and which eaſily take Fire; out of which, nevertheleſs, they except the ſweet as well as the wild Olive. *Vitruvius* ſays, that the Holm Oak and Beech are very weak in their Nature againſt Storms, and do not endure to a great Age. *Pliny* ſays, that the Maſt-holm ſoon rots. But the Fir, and particularly that which grows in the *Alps*, for Uſes within Doors, as for Bedſteads, Tables, Doors, Benches, and the like, is excellent; becauſe it is, in its Nature, very dry, and very tenacious of the Glue. The Pitch-Tree and Cypreſs alſo are very good for ſuch Uſes; the Beech for other Service is too brittle, but does mighty well for Coffers and Beds, and will ſaw into extreme thin Planks, as will likewiſe the Scarlet-Oak. The Cheſnut, on the Contrary, the Elm, and the Aſh are reckoned very unfit for Planks, becauſe they eaſily ſplit, and though they ſplit ſlowly, they are very inclinable to it; though elſe the Aſh is accounted very obedient in all Manner of Works. But I am ſurprized the Ancients have not celebrated the Nut Tree; which, as Experience ſhews us, is extremely tractable, and good for moſt Uſes, and eſpecially for Boards or Planks, They commend the Mulberry-Tree, both for its Durableneſs, and becauſe by Length of it grows blacker and handſomer. *Theophraſtus* tells us, that the Rich uſed to make their Doors of the Lote-Tree, the Scarlet-Oak, and of Box. The Elm, becauſe it firmly maintains its Strength, is ſaid to be very proper for Jambs of Doors, but it ſhould be ſet with its Head downwards. *Cato* ſays, that Levers ought to be made of Holly, Laurel, and Elm: For Bars and Bolts, they recommend the Cornel-Tree; for Stairs, the wild Aſh or the Maple. They hollowed the Pine, the Pitch-Tree and the Elm for Aqueducts, but they ſay unleſs they are buried under Ground they preſently decay. Laſtly, the Female Larch-Tree, which is almoſt of the Colour of Honey, for the Ornaments of Edifices and for Tables for Painting, they found to be in a Manner eternal and never crack or ſplit; and beſides, as its Veins run ſhort, not long, they uſed it for the Images of their Gods, as they did alſo the Lote, the Box, the Cedar, and the Cypreſs too, and the large Roots of the Olive, and the *Egyptian* Peach-Tree, which they ſay is like the Lote-Tree.

IF they had Occaſion to turn any Thing long and round, they uſed the Beech, the Mulberry, the Tree that yields the Turpentine, but eſpecially the moſt cloſe bodied Box, moſt excellent for Turning; and for very curious Works, the Ebony. Neither for Statues or Pictures did they deſpiſe the Poplar, both white and black, the Sallow, the Hornbeam, the Service-Tree, the Elder, and the Fig; which Woods, by their Dryneſs and Evenneſs, are not only good for receiving and preſerving the Gums and Colours of the Painter, but are wonderfully ſoft and eaſy under the Carver's Tool for expreſſing all Manner of Forms. Though it is certain that none of theſe for Tractableneſs can compare with the Linden. Some there are that for Statues chuſe the Jubol-Tree. Contrary to theſe is the Oak, which will never join either with itſelf or any other Wood of the ſame Nature, and deſpiſes all Manner of Glue: The ſame Defect is ſuppos'd to be in all Trees that are grained, and inclin'd to diſtil. Wood that is eaſily plain'd, and has a cloſe Body, is never well to be faſten'd with Glue; and thoſe alſo that are of different Natures, as the Ivy, the Laurel and the Linden, which are hot, if glued to thoſe that grow in moiſt Places, which are all in their Natures cold, never hold long together. The Elm, the Aſh, the Mulberry, and the Cherry-Tree, being dry, do not agree with the Plane Tree or the Alder, which are Moiſt. Nay, the Ancients were ſo far from joining together Woods different in their Natures, that they would not ſo much as place them near one another. And for this Reaſon *Vitruvius* adviſes us againſt joining Planks of Beech and Oak together.

CHAP. VII.

Of Trees more ſummarily.

BUT to ſpeak of all theſe more ſummarily. All Authors are agreed that Trees which do not bear Fruit are ſtronger and ſounder than thoſe which do; and that the wild ones, which are not cultivated either with Hand or Steel, are harder than the Domeſtick. *Theophraſtus* ſays, that the wild ones never fall into any Infirmities that kill them, whereas the Domeſtick and Fruit-bearers are ſubject to very conſiderable Infirmities; and among the Fruit-bearers thoſe which bear early are weaker than thoſe which bear late, and the Sweet than the Tart; and among the tart ones, ſuch are accounted the Firmeſt, that have the Sharpeſt and the leaſt Fruit. Thoſe that bear Fruit only once in two Years, and thoſe which are entirely barren, have more Knots in them than thoſe which bear every Year; the Shorteſt likewiſe are the Hardeſt, and the Barren grow faſter than the Fruitful. They ſay likewiſe that ſuch Trees as grow in an open Place, unſhelter'd either by Woods or Hills, but ſhaken by frequent Storms and Winds, are ſtronger and thicker, but at the ſame Time ſhorter and more knotty than ſuch as grow down in a Valley, or in any other Place defended from the Winds. They alſo believe that Trees which grow in moiſt ſhady Places are more tender than thoſe which grow in a dry open Situation, and that thoſe which ſtand expoſed to the North are more ſerviceable than thoſe which grow to the South. They reject, as abortive all Trees that grow in Places not agreeable to their Natures, and though ſuch as ſtand to the South

South are very hard, yet they are apt to warp in their Sap, so that they are not strait and even enough for Service, Moreover, those which are in their Natures dry and slow growers, are stronger than those which are moist and fruitful; wherefore *Varro* suppos'd that the one were Male and the other Female, and that white Timber was less close and more tractable than that which has any other Colour in it. It is certain that heavy Wood is harder and closer than light; and the Lighter it is, the more Brittle; and the more Knotty the stronger. Trees likewise which Nature has endu'd with the longest Life, she has always endu'd with the Property of keeping longest from Decay when cut down, and the less Sap they have, so much they are the Stronger and more Hardy. The Parts nearest to the Sap are indeed harder and closer than the rest; but those next the Bark have more binding Nerves, for it is suppos'd, in Trees just as in Animals, the Bark is the Skin, the Parts next under the Bark are the Flesh, and that which encloses the Sap, the Bone; and *Aristotle* thought the Knots in Plants were in the Nature of Nerves. Of all the Parts of the Tree, the worst is the Alburnum, or Juice, that nourishes it, both because it is very apt to breed Worms, and upon several other Accounts. To these Observations we may add, that the Part of the Tree which, while it was standing, was towards the South, will be dryer than the rest, and thinner, and more extenuated, but it will be firmer and closer; and the Sap will be nearer to the Bark on that Side than on the other. Those Parts also which are nearest to the Ground and to the Roots, will be heavier than any of the rest; a Proof whereof is that they will hardly float upon the Water; and the Middle of all Trees is the most knotty. The Veins too, the nearer they are to the Roots, the more they are wreath'd and contorted; nevertheless the lower Parts are reckoned always stronger and more useful than the Upper. But I find in good Authors some very remarkable Things of some Trees; they say that the Vine exceeds even the Eternity of Time itself. In *Popolonia*, near *Piombino*, there was a Statue of *Jupiter* made of that Wood to be seen in *Cæsar*'s Days, which had lasted for a vast Number of Years without the least Decay; and indeed it is universally allow'd that there is no Wood whatsoever more durable. In *Ariana*, a Province of *India*, there are Vines so large, as *Strabo* informs us, that two Men can hardly embrace its Trunk. They tell us of a Roof of Cedar in *Utica* that lasted twelve Hundred and seventy eight Years. In a Temple of *Diana* in *Spain* they speak of Rafters of Juniper, that lasted from two Hundred Years before the Siege of *Troy* quite to the Days of *Hanibal*. The Cedar too is of a most wonderful Nature, if as they say it is the only Wood that will not retain the Nails. In the Mountains near the Lake *Benacus*, or the *Lago di Garda*, grows a Kind of Fir, which, if you make Vessels of it, will not hold the Wine, unless you first anoint them with Oil. Thus much for Trees.

CHAP. VIII.

Of Stones in general, when they are to be dug, and when used; which are the softest and which the hardest, and which best and most durable.

WE must likewise make Provision of the Stone which is to be used in our Walls, and this is of two Sorts; the one proper only for making the Lime and the Cement, the other for erecting the Building. Of this latter we shall treat first, omitting many Particulars, both for the Sake of Brevity, and because they are already sufficiently known. Neither shall we spend any Time here in philosophical Enquiries about the Principle and Origin of Stones; as, whether their first Particles, made viscous by a Mixture of Earth and Water, harden first into Slime, and afterwards into Stone; or what is said of Gems, that they are collected and concreted by the Heat and Power of the Rays of the Sun, or rather that there is in the Bosom of the Earth certain natural Seeds as of other Things, so also of Stones: And whether their Colour is owing to a certain proper blending of the Particles of Water with very minute ones of Earth; or to some innate Quality of its own Seed, or to an Impression receiv'd from the Sun's Rays. And though these Disquisitions might perhaps help to to adorn our Work, I ſhall omit them, and proceed to treat of the Method of Building as addreſſing myſelf to Artificers approv'd for Skill and Experience, with more Freedom than perhaps would be allow'd by thoſe who are for more exact philoſophiſing. *Cato* adviſes to dig the Stone in Summer, to let it lie in the open Air, and not to uſe it under two Years: In Summer, to the Intent that it may grow accuſtom'd by Degrees to Wind, Rain, and Froſt, and other Inclemencies of the Weather, which it had not felt before. For if Stone, immediately upon its being dug out of the Quarry, while it is full of its native Juice and Humidity, is expos'd to ſevere Winds and ſudden Froſts, it will ſplit and break to Pieces. It ſhould be kept in the open Air, in order to prove the Goodneſs of each particular Stone, and how well it is able to reſiſt the Accidents that injure it, making Experiment by this ſmall Trial, how long they are likely to hold againſt the Aſſaults of Time. They ſhould not be uſed under two Years, to the Intent that you may have Time to find out ſuch among them as are weak in their Nature, and likely to damage the Work, and to ſeperate them from the good ones; for it is certain, in one and the ſame Kind of Stones there is a Difference in Goodneſs of any Sort of Stone, and its Fitneſs for this or that particular Situation, is beſt learnt from Uſe and Experience; and you may much ſooner come at their Values and Properties from old Buildings, than from the Writings and Precepts of Philoſophers. However, to ſay ſomething briefly of Stones in general, we will beg Leave to offer the following Obſervations.

All white Stone is ſofter than red, the clear is more eaſily wrought than the Cloudy, and the more like Salt it looks, the harder it is to work. Stone that looks as if it were ſtrew'd over with a bright ſhining Sand, is harſh; if little Sparks, as it were, of Gold are intermix'd, it will be ſtubborn; if it has a Kind of little black Points in it, it will be hard to get out of the Quarry: That which is ſpotted with angular Drops is ſtronger than that which has round ones, and the ſmaller thoſe Drops are, the harder it will be; and the finer and clearer the Colour is, the longer it will laſt. The Stone that has feweſt Veins, will be moſt entire, and when the Veins come neareſt in Colour to the adjoining Parts of the Stone, it will prove moſt equal throughout: The ſmaller the Veins, the handſomer; the more winding they run, the more untoward; and the more knotty, the worſe, Of theſe Veins that is moſt apt to ſplit which has in the Middle a reddiſh Streak, or of the Colour of rotten Oker. Much of the ſame Nature is that which is ſtain'd here and there with the Colour of faded Graſs, but the moſt difficult of all is ſuch as looks like a cloudy Piece of Ice. A Multitude of Veins ſhews the Stone to be deceitful and apt to crack; and the ſtraiter they are, the more unfaithful. Upon breaking a Stone, the more fine and poliſh'd the Fragments appear, the cloſer bodied it is; and that which when broken has its Outſide the leaſt rugged, will be more manageable than thoſe which are rough. Of the Rough ones, thoſe which are whiteſt will be worſt for working; whereas, on the Contrary, in brown Stones, thoſe of the ſmalleſt and fineſt Grain are leaſt obedient to the Tool. All mean ordinary Stones are the Harder for being ſpungy, and that which being ſprinkled with Water is longeſt in drying, is the moſt crude.

All heavy Stones are more ſolid and eaſier to poliſh than light ones, which upon rubbing is much more apt to come off in Flakes than ſuch as are heavy. That which upon being ſtruck gives the beſt Sound, is cloſer made than that which ſounds dull; and that which upon ſtrong Friction ſmells of Sulphur, is ſtronger than that which yields no Smell at all. Laſtly, that which makes the moſt Reſiſtance againſt the Chizzel will be moſt firm and rigid againſt the Violence of Storms. They ſay, that thoſe Stones which hold together in the largeſt Scantlings at the Mouth of the Quarry, are firmeſt againſt the Weather. All Stone too is ſofter when it is juſt dug up, than after it has been ſome Time in the Air, and when it is wetted, or ſoftened with Water, is more yielding to the Tool than when it is dry. Alſo ſuch Stones as are dug out of the moiſteſt Part of the Quarry, will be the cloſeſt when they come to be dry; and it is thought that Stones are eaſier wrought in a South-wind than in a North, and are more apt to ſplit in a North-wind than in a South. But if you have a Mind to make an Experiment how your Stone will hold out againſt Time, you may judge from hence: If a Piece of it, which you ſoak in Water, increaſes much of its Weight, it will be apt to be rotted by Moiſture; and that which flies to Pieces in Fire, will bear neither Sun nor Heat. Neither do I think that we ought to omit here ſome Things worthy Memorial, which the Ancients relate of ſome Stones.

Chap

CHAP. IX.

Some Things worthy Memorial, relating to Stones, left us by the Ancients.

IT will not be foreign to our Purpoſe to hear what a Variety there is in Stones, and what admirable Qualities ſome are endued with, that we may be able to apply each to its propereſt Uſe. In the Territory of *Bolſena* and *Stratone*, they tell us there is a Stone extremely proper for all Manner of Buildings, which neither Fire nor any Injuries of Weather ever affects, and which preſerves the Lineaments of Statues beyond any other. *Tacitus* writes, that when *Nero* repaired the City, which lay in Ruins by the Flames, he made uſe of the *Albanian* and *Gabinian* Stone for Beams, becauſe the Fire never hurts that Stone.

IN the Territory of the *Genoeſe* and of *Venice*, in the Dutchy of *Spoletto*, in the March of *Anconia*, and near *Burgundy*, they find a white Stone, which is eaſily cut with a Saw and poliſh'd, which if it were not for the Weakneſs and Brittleneſs of its Nature, would be uſed by every body; but any thing of Froſt or Wet rots and breaks it, and it is not ſtrong enough to reſiſt the Winds from the Sea. *Iſtria* produces a Stone very like Marble, but if touch'd either by Flame or Vapour, it immediately flies in Pieces, which indeed is ſaid to be the Caſe of all Stones, eſpecially of Flint both white and black, that they cannot endure Fire.

IN the *Campagna di Roma* is a Stone of the Colour of black Aſhes, in which there ſeems to be Coals mix'd and interſpers'd, which is beyond Imagination eaſy to be wrought with Iron, thoroughly ſound, and not weak againſt Fire or Weather; but it is ſo dry and thirſty, that it preſently drinks and burns up the Moiſture of the Cement, and reduces it perfectly into Powder, ſo that the Junctures opening, the Work preſently decays and falls to Ruins. But round Stones, and eſpecially thoſe which are found in Rivers, are of a Nature directly contrary; for being always moiſt, they never bind with the Cement. But what a ſurprizing Diſcovery is this which has been made, namely, that the Marble in the Quarry grows! in theſe our Days they have found at *Rome* under Ground a Number of ſmall Pieces of *Trevertine* Stone, very porous and ſpungy, which by the Nouriſhment (if we may ſo call it) given it by the Earth and by Time, are grown together into one Piece.

IN the Lake *di pie di Luco*, in that Part where the Water tumbles down a broken Precipice into the River *Nera*, you may perceive that the upper Edge of the Bank has grown continually, inſomuch that ſome have believ'd that this Encreaſe and Growth of the Stone has in Length of Time cloſed up the Mouth of the Valley and turn'd it into a Lake.

BELOW *la Baſilicata*, not far from the River *Silari*, on that Side where the Water flows from ſome high Rocks towards the Eaſt, there are daily ſeen to grow huge Pieces of hanging Stone, of ſuch a Magnitude, that any one of them would be a Load for ſeveral Carts. This Stone while it is freſh and moiſt with its natural Juices, is very ſoft; but when it is dry, it grows extremely hard, and very good for all Manner of Uſes. I have known the like happen in ancient Aqueducts, whoſe Mouths, having contracted a Kind of Gummineſs, have ſeem'd incruſted all over with Stone. There are two very remarkable Things to be ſeen at this Day in *Romania*: In the Country of *Imola* is a very ſteep Torrent, which daily throws out, ſometimes in one Place and ſometimes in another, a great Number of round Stones, generated within the Bowels of the Earth: In the Territory of *Faenza*, on the Banks of the River *Lamona*, there are found a great many Stones, naturally long and large, which continually throw out a conſiderable Quantity of Salt, which in Proceſs of Time is thought to grow into Stone too. In that of *Florence*, near the River *Chiane*, there is a Piece of Ground all ſtrew'd over with hard Stones, which every ſeven Years diſſolve into Clods of Earth.

Pliny relates, that near *Cizicus*, and about *Caſſandra*, the Clods of Earth turn into Stone. In *Pozzuolo* there is a Duſt which hardens into Stone, if mix'd with Sea-water. All the Way upon the Shore from *Oropus* to *Aulis*, every thing that is waſh'd by the Sea is petrified. *Diodorus* writes, that in *Arabia* the Clods dug out of the Ground have a ſweet Smell, and will melt in Fire like Metal, and run into Stone; and he adds, that this Stone is of ſuch a Nature, that when the Rain falls upon it in any Building, the Cement all diſſolves, and the Wall grows to be all of a Piece.

We are told, that they find in *Troas*, a Stone very apt to cleave, call'd the *Sarcophagus*, in which any dead Corpſe buried, is intirely conſum'd in leſs than forty Days, all but the Teeth; and which is moſt ſurprizing, all the Habits, and every Thing buryed with the Body, turns into Stone. Of a contrary Nature to this is the Stone called *Chernites*, in which *Darius* was buried, for that preſerves the Body entire for a long Time. But of this Subject enough.

Chap. X.

Of the Origin of the Uſe of Bricks, in what Seaſon they ought to be made, aud in what Shapes, their different Sorts, and the Uſefulneſs of triangular Ones; and briefly, of all other Works made of baked Earth.

It is certain the Ancients were very fond of uſing Bricks inſtead of Stone. I confeſs, I believe that at firſt Men were put upon making Bricks to ſupply the Place of Stone in their Buildings, thro' Scarcity and Want of it; but afterwards finding how ready they were in working, how well adapted both to Uſe and Beauty, how ſtrong and durable, they proceeded to make not only their ordinary Structures, but even their Palaces of Brick. At laſt, either by Accident or Induſtry, diſcovering what Uſe Fire was of in hardening and ſtrengthening them, they began in moſt Places to bake the Bricks they built with. And from my own Obſervations upon the ancient Structures, I will be bold to ſay, that there is not a better Material for any Sort of Edifice than Brick, not crude but baked; provided a right Method be uſed in baking them. But we will reſerve the Praiſes of Works make of Bricks for another Place.

Our Buſineſs is to obſerve here, that a whitiſh chalky Earth is very much recommended for making them. The reddiſh alſo is approved of, and that which is call'd male Sand. That which is abſolutely ſandy and gravelly is to be avoided, and the ſtony moſt of all; becauſe in baking it is ſubject to warp and crack, and if over baked will fret away of itſelf. We are adviſed not to make our Bricks of Earth freſh dug, but to dig it in the Autumn, and leave it to digeſt all Winter, and to make it into Brick early in the Spring; for if you make it in Winter, it is obvious that the Froſt will crack it, and if you make it in the Middle of Summer, the exceſſive Heat will make it ſcale off in drying. But if Neceſſity obliges you to make it in Winter, in extreme cold Weather, cover it immediately over with very dry Sand, and if in Summer, with wet Straw; for being ſo kept, it will neither crack nor warp. Some are for having their Bricks glazed; if ſo, you muſt take Care not to make them of Earth that is either ſandy, or too lean or dry; for theſe will ſuck and eat away the Glazing: But you muſt make them of a whitiſh fat Clay, and you muſt make them thin, for if they are too thick they will not bake thorowly, and it is a great Chance but they ſplit; if you are oblig'd to have them thick, you may in a great Meaſure prevent that Inconveniency, if you make one or more little Holes in them about half Way through, whereby the Damp and Vapour having proper Vents, they will both dry and bake the better.

The Potters rub their Veſſels over with Chalk, by which Means, the Glazing, when it is melted over it, makes an even Surface; the ſame Method may be uſed in making Bricks. I have obſerv'd in the Works of the Ancients, that their Bricks have a Mixture of a certain Proportion of Sand, and eſpecially of the red Sort, and I find they alſo mix'd them with red Earth, and even with Marble. I know by Experience that the very ſame Earth will make harder and ſtronger Brick, if we take the Pains to knead every Lump two or three Times over, as if we were making of Bread, till it grows like Wax, and is perfectly clear of the leaſt Particle of Stone. Theſe, when they have paſs'd the Fire will attain the Hardneſs even of a Flint, and whether owing to the Heat in baking, or the Air in drying, will get a Sort of a ſtrong Cruſt, as Bread does. It will therefore be beſt to make them thin, that they may have the more Cruſt and the leſs Crum: And

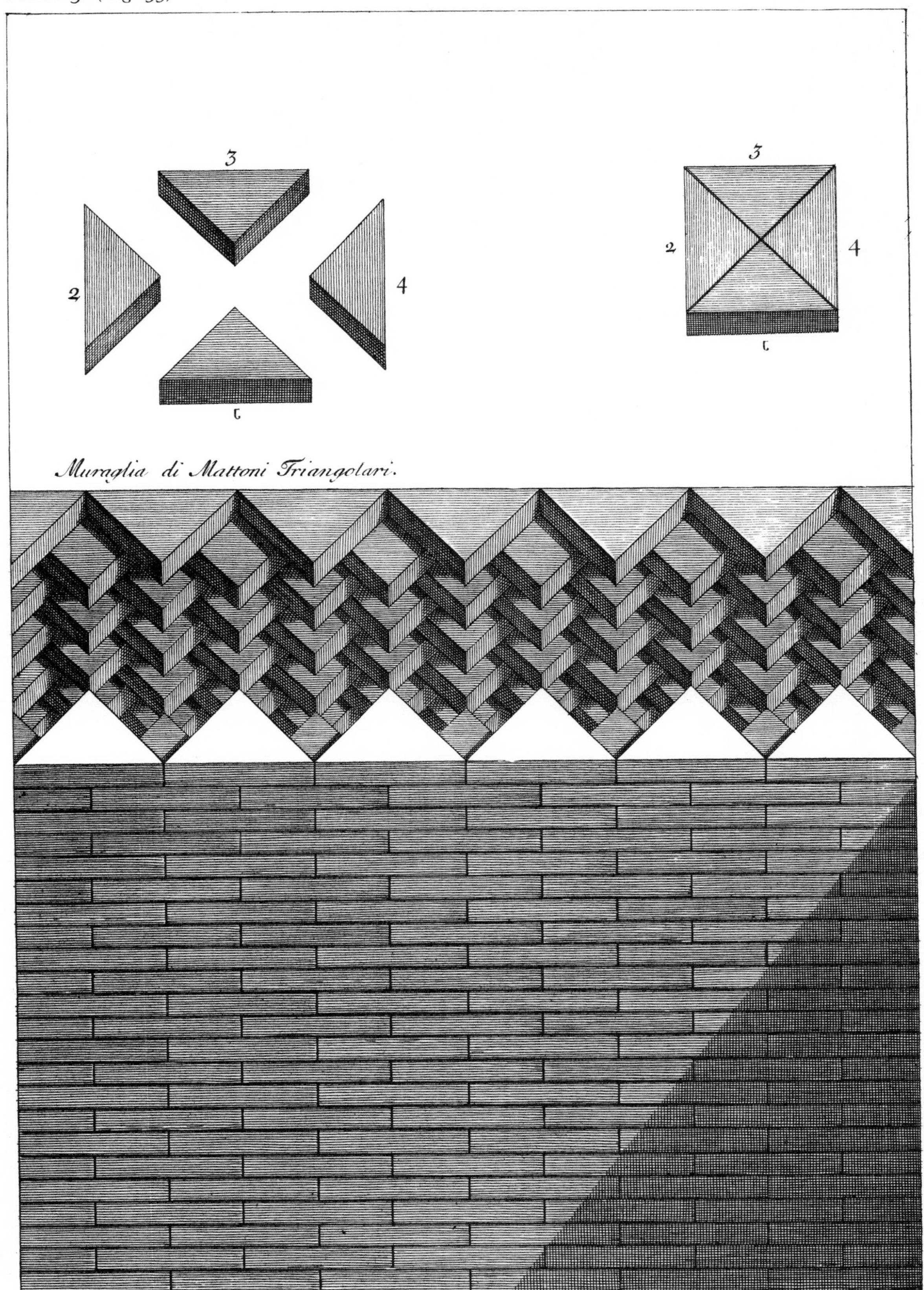

"Muraglia etc." = *wall of triangular bricks.*

And we ſhall find, that if they are well rubb'd and poliſhed, they will defy the Fury of the Weather. The ſame is true of Stones that are poliſhed, which thereby eſcape being eaten with Ruſt. And it is thought that Bricks ſhould be rubbed and ground either immediately upon their being taken out of the Kiln, before they are wetted; or when they have been wetted, before they are dry again; because when once they have been wetted and afterwards dryed, they grow ſo hard that they will turn and break the Edge of the Tool; but they are eaſier to grind when they are new, and hardly cold. There were three Sorts of Bricks among the Ancients; the Firſt was a Foot and an Half Long, and a Foot Broad, the Second fifteen Inches every Way, the Third a Foot. We ſee in ſome of their Buildings, and eſpecially in their Arches and *Moſaick* Works, Bricks two Foot every Way. We are told that the Ancients did not uſe the ſame Sort of Brick in their publick as in their private Edifices. I have obſerved in ſeveral of their Structures, and particularly in the *Appian* Way, ſeveral different Sorts of Bricks, ſome bigger, ſome ſmaller; ſo that I ſuppoſe they uſed them indifferently, and put in Practice not only what was abſolutely neceſſary for Uſe, but any Thing that came into their Fancy, or which they thought would conduce to the Beauty of the Work. But, not to mention others, I have ſeen ſome not longer than ſix Inches, and not thicker than one, nor broader than three; but theſe they chiefly uſed in their Pavements, * where they were laid edgeways. I am beſt pleaſed with their triangular ones, which they made in this Manner; they made one large Brick, a Foot Square, and an Inch and an Half Thick; and while it was freſh they cut it in two Lines croſſways from one Angle to the other, which divided it into four equal Triangles. Theſe Bricks had the following Advantages, they took up leſs Clay, they were eaſier to diſpoſe in the Kiln and to take out again, they were more convenient for working, becauſe the Bricklayer could hold four of them in one Hand, and with a ſmall Stroke divide the one from the other; when placed in the Wall, with their Fronts foremoſt and their Angles inward, they appeared like compleat Bricks of a Foot Long: This made the Expence leſs, the Work more graceful, and the Wall ſtronger; for as there ſeemed to be none but entire Bricks in the Wall, the Angles being ſet like Teeth in the Rubbiſh that was laid in the Middle, made it extremely ſtrong and durable. After the Bricks are moulded, they direct that they ſhould not be put into the Kiln till they are perfectly dry, and they ſay they never are ſo under two Years; and they are reckoned to dry better in the Shade than in the Sun: But of theſe too enough, unleſs we will add that in all this Sort of Works, which are called Plaſtick, they reckon excellent, among others, the Earth that is called *Samian*, the *Aretinian*, and the *Modeneze*; in *Spain*, the *Saguntan*; and the *Pergamean* in *Aſia*. Nor will I conſult Brevity ſo much as to omit, that whatever I have here ſaid of Bricks, will hold good of all Sorts of Tiles for Roofs of Houſes or Gutters, and in a Word, of all Manner of Works made of baked Earth. We have treated of Stone, let us now proceed to ſpeak of Lime.

CHAP. XI.

Of the Nature of Lime and Plaiſter of Paris, their Uſes and Kinds, wherein they agree and wherein they differ, and of ſome Things not unworthy of Memory.

CATO the Cenſor, condemns Lime made of different Sorts of Stone, and takes that which is made of Flint to be good for no Manner of Work whatſoever; beſides, in making of Lime all Stone is extremely improper that is dry and exhauſted, or rotten, and which in burning has nothing in it for the Fire to conſume, as all mouldering Stone, and the reddiſh and pale ones, which are found near *Rome* in the Country of the *Fidenates* and *Albanians*. The Lime commended by the beſt Judges, is that which loſes a third Part of its Weight by burning; beſides, Stone that is too moiſt in its Nature, is apt to vitrify in the Fire, ſo as to be of no Uſe for making of Lime. *Pliny* ſays, that the green, or *Serpentine*-ſtone mightily reſiſts the Fire; but we know very well that the *Porphiry* will not only not burn itſelf, but will

* See Plate 3, facing page 34.

will hinder the other Stones that are near it in the Kiln, from burning too. They also dislike all earthy Stone, because it makes the Lime foul. But the ancient Architects greatly praise the Lime made of very hard close Stone, especially white, which they say is not improper for any Sort of Work, and is extremely strong in Arches. In the second Place, they commend Lime made of Stone, not indeed light or rotten, but spungy; which they think for plaistering is better, and more tractable than any other, and gives the best Varnish to the Work; and I have observed the Architects in *France*, to use no other Sort of Lime but what was made of the common Stones they found in Rivers or Torrents, blackish, and so very hard, that you would take them for Flints; and yet it is certain, both in Stone and Brickwork, it has preserved an extraordinary Strength to a very great Age. We read in *Pliny*, that Lime made of the Stone of which they make Mill-stones, is excellent for all manner of Uses; but I find upon Experience, that such of them as seem spotted with Drops of Salt, being too rough and dry, will not do for this Use; but that which is not so spotted, but is closer, and when it is ground, makes a finer Dust, succeeds extremely well. However, let the Nature of the Stone be what it will, that of the Quarry will be much better for making of Lime, than that which we pick up; and that dug out of a shady, moist Quarry, better than out of a dry one; and made of white Stone, more tractable than of black. In *France*, near the Sea-shore about *Vannes*, for Want of Stone, they make their Lime of Oyster and Cockle-Shells. There is moreover a kind of Lime which we call Plaister of Paris, which too is made of burnt Stone; tho' we are told that in *Cyprus*, and about *Thebes*, this Sort of Plaister is dug out of the Surface of the Earth, ready baked by the Heat of the Sun. But the Stone that makes the Plaister of Paris, is different from that which makes the Lime; for it is very soft, and will easily rub to Pieces, except one found in *Syria*, which is very hard. It differs likewise in this, that the Plaister of Paris Stone requires but twenty Hours; and the Lime Stone takes threescore Hours in burning. I have observed, that in *Italy* there are four Sorts of Plaister of Paris, two of which are transparent, and two which are not: Of the transparent, one is like Lumps of Allum, or rather of Alabaster, and they called it the Scaly Sort, because it consists of extreme thin Scales, one over the other, like the Coats of an Onion. The other is scaly too, but is more like a blackish Salt than Allum. The Sorts that are not transparent are both like a very close Sort of Chalk, but one is pale and whitish, and the other with that Paleness has a Tincture of red; which last is firmer and closer than the first. Of the last, the reddest is the most tenacious. Of the first, that which is the clearest and whitest is used in Stuc Work for Figures and Cornishes.

Near *Rimini* they find a Plaister of Paris so solid that you would take it for Marble or Alabaster, which I had had cut with a Saw into large thin Pieces, extremely convenient for Incrustations. That I may omit nothing that is necessary, all Plaister of Paris must be broken and pounded with wooden Mallets, till it is reduced to Powder, and so kept in Heaps in some very dry Place, and as soon as ever it is brought out, it must be watered and used immediately.

But Lime on the Contrary need not be pounded, but may be soak'd in the Lumps, and must be plentifully soak'd with Water a good while before you use it, especially if it is for Plaistering; to the Intent that if there should be any Lumps not enough burnt, it may be dissolv'd and liquify'd by long lying in the Water: Because, when it is used too soon, before it is duly soak'd, there will be some small unconcocted Stones in it, which afterwards coming to rot, throw out little Pustules, which spoil the Neatness of the Work. Add hereunto, that you need not give your Lime a Flood, as I may call it, of Water at once, but wet it by little and little, sprinkling it several Times over, till it is in all Parts thoroughly impregnated with it; afterwards it must be kept in some shady Place, moderately moist, clear from all Mixture, and only cover'd over with a little Sand, till by Length of Time it is better fermented; and it has been found that Lime by this thorough Fermentation acquires inconceivable Virtue. I have known some found in an old neglected Ditch, that, as plainly appear'd by the strongest Conjectures, was left there above five hundred Years; which when it was discover'd was so moist and liquid, and, to use the Expression, so mature, that it far exceeded Honey or Marrow itself in Softness; and nothing in Nature can be imagin'd more serviceable for all Manner of Uses. It requires double the Sand if prepared thus, than

than if you mix it immediately. In this, therefore, Lime and Plaister of Paris do not agree; but in other Things they do. Carry your Lime, therefore, immediately out of the Kiln into a ſhady, dry Place, and water it; for if you keep it either in the Kiln itſelf, or any where elſe in the Air, or expos'd to the Moon or Sun, eſpecially in Summer, it would ſoon crumble to Powder, and be totally uſeleſs. But of this ſufficient. They adviſe us not to put our Stone into the Kiln till we have broken it into Pieces, not ſmaller than the Clods; for, not to mention that they will burn the eaſier, it has been obſerved that in the middle of ſome Stones, and eſpecially of round ones, there are ſometimes certain Concavities, in which the Air being incloſed often does a great deal of Miſchief: For when they come to feel the Fire in the Kiln, this Air is either compreſſed by the cold retiring inwards, or elſe when the Stone grows hot it turns to Vapour, which makes it ſwell till it burſts the Priſon wherein it is confined, and breaks out with a dreadful Noiſe and irreſiſtible Force, and blows up the whole Kiln. Some in the middle of ſuch Stones have ſeen living Creatures, of various kinds, and particularly Worms with a hairy Back, and a great Number of Feet, which do a great deal of Harm to the Kiln. And I will here add ſome Things worthy to be recorded, which have been ſeen in our Days, ſince I do not write only for the Uſe of Workmen, but alſo for all ſuch as are ſtudious of curious Enquiries; for which Reaſon, I ſhall not ſcruple, now and then, to intermix any thing that is delightful, provided it is not abſolutely foreign to my Purpoſe.

THERE was brought to Pope *Martin* V. a Serpent found by the Miners in a Quarry in *la Romagna*, which lived pent up in the Hollow of a great Stone, without the leaſt Crack or Hole in it for Admiſſion of Air; in like Manner Toads too have been found and Crabs, but dead. I myſelf have been Witneſs to the finding of the Leaves of Trees in the Middle of a very white Piece of Marble. All the Summit of Mount *Vellino*, one of thoſe which divide the Country of *Abruzzo* from *Marſi*, and is higher than any of the reſt, is covered over with a white Stone, ſo that the very Mountain looks white with it, among which, eſpecially on that Side, which looks towards *Abruzzo*, are a great many broken Pieces with Figures upon them, exactly like Sea-ſhells, not bigger than the Palm of a Man's Hand. But, what is more extraordinary, in the *Veroneze*, they daily find Stones upon the Ground marked with the Figure of the Cinquefoil, with every Line and Vein drawn ſo exactly and regularly, by the Hand of Nature, that the niceſt Artiſt cannot pretend to come up to it; and which is moſt curious of all, every one of theſe Stones are found with the Impreſſion turned downwards, and hid by the Stone, as if Nature had not been at the Pains of ſuch fine Sculptures to gain the Approbation of Men, but for her own Diverſion. But to return to our Subject.

I SHALL not ſpend Time here to ſhew how to make the Mouth of the Kiln, and its Covering, and the inward Seat of the Fire, and how to give Vent to the Flame when it grows hot, and to keep it, as it were, within its own Confines, ſo as to direct the whole united Strength and Power of the Fire to the burning of the Lime. Nor will I proceed to teach how the Fire is to be kindled by little and little, and never left till the Flame burns out at the Top of the Furnace perfectly clear, and without the leaſt Smoke, and till the very uppermoſt Stones are red hot; and that the Stone is not burnt enough, till the Kiln, which had been ſwelled and cracked by the Fire, afterwards ſettles and cloſes itſelf again. It is a ſurprizing Thing to obſerve the Nature of this Element; for if you take away the Fire, the Kiln will grow cooler and cooler by Degrees at the Bottom, while it continues burning hot at Top. But as in Building, we have Occaſion not only for Lime, but Sand, we will now ſay ſomething about that.

CHAP. XII.

Of the three different Kinds of Sands, and of the various Materials in Building, in different Places.

THERE are three Sorts of Sand, Pit-ſand, River-ſand, and Sea-ſand; the beſt of all theſe is the Pit-ſand; and this is of ſeveral Kinds; black, white, red, the carbuncly, and the gritty. But if any ſhould aſk what I take Sand to be, I might perhaps anſwer

ſwer, that it is nothing but a Compoſition of the ſmalleſt Stones, the large ones being all broken to Pieces; tho' it is *Vitruvius*'s Opinion, that Sand, eſpecially that which in *Tuſcany* they call the carbuncly Sort, is a Kind of Earth burnt by the Fire incloſed by Nature within the Hills, and made ſomewhat harder than Earth unburnt, but ſofter than any Stone. Of all theſe they moſt commend the carbuncly Sort. I have obſerved, that in the publick Buildings in *Rome*, they uſed the red as none of the worſt. Of all the Pit-ſand the white is the worſt. The gritty is of Uſe in filling up of Foundations; but among the beſt, they give the ſecond Place to the fineſt of the gritty, and eſpecially to the ſharp angular Sort, without the leaſt Mixture of Earth in it, as is that which they find in the Territory of the *Vilumbrians*. Next to this they eſteem the River Sand, which is dug after the uppermoſt Layer is taken off; and next to the River-ſand that of the Torrent, eſpecially of ſuch Torrents as run between Hills, where the Water has the greateſt Deſcent. In the laſt Place comes the Sea-ſand, and of this Sort, the blackeſt and moſt glazed is not wholly to be deſpiſed. In the Country, near *Salerno*, they eſteem their Sea-ſand not inferior to Pit-ſand, but they ſay it is not to be dug in all Parts of the Shore alike; for they find it worſt of all where it is expoſed to the South Wind; but it is not bad in thoſe Places which look to the South-weſt. But of Sea-ſands, it is certain the beſt is that which lies under Rocks, and which is of the coarſeſt Grain. There is a great deal of Difference in Sands, for that of the Sea is very ſlow in drying, and is continually moiſt and apt to diſſolve, by Reaſon of its Salt, and is therefore very improper and unfaithful in ſupporting of great Weights. That of the River too is ſomewhat moiſter than the Pit-ſand, and therefore is more tractable and better for Plaiſtering-work. The Pit-ſand, by means of its Fatneſs, is moſt tenacious, but is apt to crack, for which Reaſon they uſe it in Vault-work, but not in plaiſtering. But of each Sort, that is always beſt, which being rubbed with the Hand creeks the moſt, and being laid upon a white Cloth, makes the leaſt Soil, and leaves the leaſt Earth behind it. On the contrary, that is the worſt, which feels mealy inſtead of ſharp, and which in Smell and Colour reſembles red Earth, and being mixed with Water makes it foul and muddy, and if left abroad in the Air, preſently brings forth Graſs. Neither will that be good, which after it is dug, is left for any Time expoſed to the Sun, or Moon, or to Froſts; becauſe it turns it in a Manner to Earth, and makes it very apt to rot; or when it is inclined to bring forth Shrubs, or wild Figs, it is extremly bad for cementing of Walls. We have now treated of Timber, Stone, Lime, and Sand, ſuch as are approved of by the Ancients; but in all Places theſe Things are not to be found with all the Qualifications which we require. *Tully* ſays, that *Aſia*, by means of its Abundance of Marble, always flouriſhed in fine Buildings and Statues; but Marble is not to be got every where. In ſome Places there is either no Stone at all, or what there is, is good for no manner of Uſe. In all the Southern Parts of *Italy*, they ſay there is no Want of Sand-Pits, but on the other Side of the *Appenine* there are none. *Pliny* ſays, the *Babylonians* made Uſe of Slime, and the *Carthaginians* of Mud. In ſome Places, not having any Sort of Stone, they build with Hurdles and Potters Earth. *Herodotus* tells us, that the *Budini* make all their Structures, as well publick as private, of nothing but Wood, even to the Walls of their City, and the Statues of their Gods. *Mela* ſays, that the *Nervi* have no Wood at all; and that for Want of it they are obliged to make their Fires of Bones. In *Ægypt* their Fuel is the Dung of their Cattle. For this Reaſon, the Habitations of Men are different, according to the different Conveniencies of the Country. Among the *Ægyptians* there are Royal Palaces built of Ruſhes; and in *India*, of the Ribs of Whales. In *Carræ*, a Town in *Arabia*, they build with Lumps of Salt: But of theſe elſewhere. So that as we have already obſerved, there is not the ſame Plenty of Stone, Sand, and the like, every where, but in different Places there are different Accommodations and Conveniencies: Therefore we are to make Uſe of ſuch as offer themſelves; and out of thoſe we ſhould, in the firſt Place, make it our Buſineſs, always to ſelect and provide the beſt and propereſt, and, ſecondly, in building with them, we ſhould carefully allot to each its proper Place and Situation.

Chap.

CHAP. XIII.

Whether the Obſervation of Times and Seaſons is of any Uſe in beginning a Building; what Seaſon is moſt convenient; as alſo, with what Auguries or Prayers we ought to ſet out upon our Work.

HAVING got ready the Materials before ſpoken of, it remains now that we proceed to treat of the Work itſelf. For as to the providing of Iron, Braſs, Lead, Glaſs, and the like, it requires no Care, but merely the Buying, and having them in Readineſs, that your Building may not ſtand ſtill for them; tho' we ſhall in due Time lay down ſome Inſtructions about the Choice and Diſtribution of them, which is of Conſequence to the compleating and adorning the Work. And we ſhall take and conſider the Structure from the Foundation, in the ſame Manner as if we were actually about doing the Work ourſelves. But here I muſt again admoniſh you to conſider the Times, both with Relation to the Publick, and to yourſelf and Family, whether they are troubleſome or peaceable, proſperous or calamitous, leſt we expoſe ourſelves to Envy, if we go on with our Undertaking, or to Loſs if we give it over. We ſhould alſo have a particular Regard to the Seaſon of the Year; for we ſee that Buildings begun and proſecuted in Winter, eſpecially in a cold Climate, are taken with the Froſt, or in Summer, in a hot Climate, dry'd up with the Heat before ever they have faſten'd. For this Reaſon it was that *Frontinus*, the Architect, adviſ'd us never to undertake ſuch a Work but in a proper Seaſon of the Year, which is from the Beginning of *April* to the Beginning of *November*, reſting, however, in the greateſt Heat of Summer. But I am for haſtening or delaying the Work juſt according to the Difference of the Climate and of the Weather; and therefore if you are prepar'd with all the Things before recited, and your Convenience ſuits, you have nothing to do but to mark out the Area of your Structure in the Ground, with all its Lines, Angles and Dimenſions. But there are ſome who tell us that in Building we ſhould obſerve and wait for happy Auſpices, and that it is of the utmoſt Importance from what particular Point of Time the Structure is to date its Being. They relate, that *Lucius Tarutius* found out the exact Nativity of *Rome*, only by the Obſervation of the Turns in its Fortune. The wiſeſt Men among the Ancients had ſuch an Opinion of the Conſequence of the Moment of the Beginning a Thing might have as to its future Succeſs, that *Julius Fermicus Maturnus* tells us of ſome Mathematicians that pretended to have diſcover'd the very inſtant when the World had its Beginning, and that wrote very accurately about it: For *Æſculapius*, and *Anubius*, and *Petoſiris*, and *Necepſo*, who only wrote from them, ſay that it begun juſt at the Riſing of the *Crab*, when the Moon was fourteen Days old, the Sun being in *Leo*, *Saturn* in *Capricorn*, *Jupiter* in *Sagittary*, *Mars* in *Scorpio*, *Venus* in *Libra*, and *Mercury* in *Virgo*. And indeed, if we rightly conſider them, the Times may have a great Influence in Things. For how is it elſe, that in the ſhorteſt Day of the Year, the Penny-royal, tho' quite dry, ſprouts and flouriſhes; Bladders that are blown up burſt; the Leaves of Willows, and the Kernels of Apples turn and change Sides; and that the ſmall Fibres of a Shell-fiſh correſpond, increaſe and decreaſe with the Increaſe and Decreaſe of the Moon. I muſt confeſs, though I have not ſo much Faith in the Profeſſors of this Science, and the Obſervers of Times and Seaſons, as to believe their Art can influence the Fortune of any Thing, yet I think they are not to be deſpiſed when they argue for the Happineſs or Adverſity of ſuch ſtated Times as theſe from the Diſpoſition of the Heavens. But let this be as it will, the following their Inſtructions may be of great Service, if true; and can do little harm, if falſe. I might here add ſome ridiculous Circumſtances which the Ancients obſerved in the Beginning of their Undertakings; but I would not have them interpreted in a wrong Senſe; and indeed they deſerve only to be laughed at, who would perſwade us that the very Marking out of the Platform ought to be done under proper Auſpices. The Ancients were ſo governed by theſe Superſtitions, that in making out the Liſts of their Armies, obſerved they took great Care that the firſt Soldier had not an unlucky Name; which was a Rule they alſo obſerved in the Ceremony of purifying their Soldiers and their Colonies, wherein, the Perſon that was to lead the Beaſt to the Sacrifice muſt have a fortunate Name. And the Cenſors, in framing out the publick Revenues and Eſtates, always began with the Lake *Lucrinus*, becauſe of the Lucrativeneſs of its Name, So likewiſe, being terrified with the diſmal Name of *Epidamnus*, that ſuch as went thither might not be ſaid to be gone a damnable Voyage, they changed its Name into *Dyrrachium*; ſo likewiſe they ſerved *Beneventum*, which before was called *Maleventum*. Neither, on the other Hand, can I forbear laughing at their Conceit, that in beginning Undertakings of this Sort it was good to repeat certain favourable Words and Charms.

And there are ſome that affirm, that Men's Words are ſo powerful, that they are obey'd even by Beaſts and Things inanimate. I omit *Cato*'s Fancy, that Oxen when fatigued may be refreſh'd by certain Words. They tell us too, that they uſed with certain Prayers and Forms of Words to entreat and beſeech their Mother Earth to give Nouriſhment to foreign Trees, and ſuch as ſhe was not accuſtom'd to bear; and that the Trees alſo were to be humbly pray'd to ſuffer themſelves to be remov'd, and to thrive in another Ground. And ſince we are got into this fooliſh Strain of recording the Follies of other Men, I will alſo mention, for Diverſion Sake, what they tell us, that the Words of Mankind are of ſuch Effect, that Turnips will grow incredibly, if when we ſow them we at the ſame Time pray them to be gracious and lucky to us, our Families, and our Neighbourhood. But if theſe be ſo, I can't imagine why the Baſilico-root ſhould, as they ſay, grow the faſter for being curſt and abuſed when it is ſown. But let us leave this idle Subject. It is undoubtedly proper, omitting all theſe uncertain Superſtitions, to ſet about our Work with a holy and religious Preparation.

Ab Jove principium, Muſæ ;----
Jovis omnia plena.

We ought therefore to begin our Undertaking with a clean Heart, and with devout Oblations, and with Prayers to Almighty God to implore his Aſſiſtance, and Bleſſing upon the Beginnings of our Labours, that it may have a happy and proſperous Ending, with Strength and Happineſs to it and its Inhabitants, with Content of Mind, Encreaſe of Fortune, Succeſs of Induſtry, Acquiſition of Glory, and a Succeſſion and Continuance of all good Things. So much for our Preparation.

The End of Book II.

THE

THE

ARCHITECTURE

OF

Leone Batista Alberti.

Book III. Chap. I.

Of the Work. Wherein lies the Business of the Work; the different Parts of the Wall, and what they require. That the Foundation is no Part of the Wall; what Soil makes the best Foundation.

THE whole Business of the working Part of Building is this; by a regular and artful Conjunction of different Things, whether square Stone, or uneven Scantlings, or Timber, or any other strong Material, to form them as well as possible into a solid, regular, and consistent Structure. We call it regular and consistent when the Parts are not incongruous and disjointed, but are disposed in their proper Places, and are answerable one to the other, and conformable to a right Ordinance of Lines. We are therefore to consider what are the principal essential Parts in the Wall, and what are only the Lines and Disposition of those Parts. Nor are the Parts of the Wall any Thing difficult to find out; for the Top, the Bottom, the right Side, the Left, the remote Parts, the Near, the Middle are obvious of themselves; but the particular Nature of each of these, and wherein they differ, is not so easily known. For the raising a Building is not, as the Ignorant imagine, merely laying Stone upon Stone, or Brick upon Brick; but as there is a great Diversity of Parts, so there requires a great Diversity of Materials and Contrivance. For one Thing is proper in the Foundation, another in the naked Wall and in the Cornish, another for the Coins, and for the Lips of the Apertures, one for the outward Face of the Wall, another for the cramming and filling up the middle Parts: Our Business here is to shew what is requisite in each of these. In doing this, therefore, we shall begin at the Foundation, imitating, as we said before, those that are actually going to raise the Structure. The Foundation, if I mistake not, is not properly a Part of the Wall, but the Place and Seat on which the Wall is reared. For if we can find a Seat perfectly firm and solid, consisting perhaps of nothing but Stone, what Foundation are we obliged to make? None,

M certain-

certainly, but to begin immediately from thence to erect our Wall. At *Siena* there are huge Towers raised immediately from the naked Earth, because the Hill is lined with a solid Rock. Making a Foundation, that is to say, digging up the Ground, and making a Trench, is necessary in those Places, where you cannot find firm Ground without digging; which, indeed, is the Case almost every where, as will appear hereafter. The Marks of a good Soil for a Foundation are these; if it does not produce any kind of Herb that usually grows in moist Places; if it bears either no Tree at all, or only such as delight in a very hard, close Earth; if every Thing round about is extremely dry, and, as it were, quite parched up; if the Place is stony, not with small round Pebbles, but large sharp Stones, and especially Flints; if there are no Springs nor Veins of Water running under it; because the Nature of all Streams is either to be perpetually carrying away, or bringing something along with them: And therefore it is that in all flat Grounds, lying near any River, you can never meet with any firm Soil, till you dig below the Level of the Channel. Before you begin to dig your Foundations, you should once again carefully review and consider all the Lines and Angles of your Platform, what Dimensions they are to be of, and how they are to disposed. In making these Angles we must use a square Rule, not of a small but of a very large Size, that our strait Lines may be the truer. The Ancients made their square Rule of three strait ones joined together in a Triangle, whereof one was of three Cubits, the other of four, and the third of five. The Ignorant do not know how to make these Angles till they have first cleared away every Thing that incumbers the Area, and have it all perfectly open, almost level before them: For which Reason, laying furiously hold of their Tools, they fall like so many Ravagers to demolishing and levelling every Thing before them; which would become them much better in the Country of an Enemy. But the Error of these Men ought to be corrected; for a Change of Fortune, or the Adversity of the Times, or some unforeseen Accident, or Necessity, may possibly oblige you to lay aside the Thoughts of the Undertaking you have begun. And it is certainly very unseemly, in the mean while, to have no Regard to the Labours of your Ancestors, or to the Conveniencies which your Fellow-Citizens find in these paternal Habitations, which they have been long accustomed to; and as for pulling down and demolishing, that is in your Power at any Time. I am therefore for preserving the old Structures untouched, till such Time as it is absolutely necessary to remove them to make Way for the new.

Chap. II.

That the Foundation chiefly is to be marked out with Lines; and by what Tokens we may know the Goodness of the Ground.

IN marking out your Foundations, you are to remember, that the first Ground-work of your Wall, and the Soccles, which are called Foundations too, must be a determinate Proportion broader than the Wall that is to be erected upon it; in Imitation of those who walk over the Snow in the *Alps* of *Tuscany*, who wear upon their Feet Hurdles made of Twigs and small Ropes, plaited together for that very Purpose, the Broadness of which keeps them from sinking in the Snow. How to dispose the Angles, is not easy to teach clearly with Words alone; because the Method of drawing them, is borrowed from the Mathematicks, and stands in Need of the Example of Lines, a Thing foreign to our Design here, and which we have treated of in another Place, in our Mathematical Commentaries. However, I will endeavour, as far as is necessary here, to speak of them in such a Manner, that if you have any Share of Ingenuity, you may easily comprehend many Things, by Means of which you may afterwards make yourself Master of all the rest. Whatever may chance to seem more obscure, if you have a Mind to understand it thoroughly, you may apply to those Commentaries. My Method, then, in describing the Foundations, is to draw some Lines, which I call radical ones, in this Manner*. From the Middle of the Fore-front of the Work, I draw a Line quite thro' to the Back-front, in the Middle of

* Plate 4. (*facing page 44*)

of this Line I fix a Nail in the Ground, from which I raiſe, and let fall Perpendiculars, according to the Method of the Geometers; and to theſe two Lines I reduce every Thing that I have Occaſion to meaſure; which ſucceeds perfectly well in all Reſpects; for the Parallel Lines are obvious; you ſee exactly where to make your Angles correſpondent, and to diſpoſe every Part conſiſtently, and agreeably, with the others. But if it ſo happens, that any old Buildings obſtruct your Sight from diſcovering and fixing upon the exact Seat of every Angle; your Buſineſs then is to draw Lines, at equal Diſtances, in thoſe Places which are clear and free; then having marked the Point of Interſection, by the Aſſiſtance of the Diameter and Gnomon, and by drawing other Lines at equal Diſtances, fitted to the Square, we may compleatly effect our Purpoſe: And it will be of no ſmall Convenience to terminate the Ray of Sight with a Line in thoſe Places which lie higher than the reſt; whence letting fall a Perpendicular, we may find the right Direction and Production of our Lines. Having marked out the Lines and Angles of our Trenches, we ought to have, if poſſible, as ſharp and clear a Sight as a certain *Spaniard* in our Days was fabulouſly ſaid to have, who they tell us, could ſee the loweſt Veins of Water that run under Ground, as plainly as if they were above Ground. So the many Things happen under the Surface of Earth, which we know nothing of, as makes it unſafe to truſt the Weight and Expence of a Building to it. And, certainly, as in all the reſt of the Structure, ſo eſpecially in the Foundations, we ought to neglect no Precaution which it becomes an accurate and diligent Architect to take; for an Error in any other Part does leſs Miſchief, and is more eaſily remedied, or better borne, than in the Foundation; in which, a Miſtake is inexcuſable. But the Ancients uſed to ſay, dig on, and good Fortune attend you, till you find a ſolid Bottom; for the Earth has ſeveral Strata, and thoſe of different Natures; ſome ſandy, others gravelly, ſome ſtony, and the like; under which, at certain Depths, is a hard, firm Bank, fit to ſupport the heavieſt Structure. This alſo is various, and hardly like any thing of its own kind in any Particular; in ſome Places it is exceſſively hard, and ſcarce penetrable with Iron; in others, fatter and ſofter; in ſome Places blacker, in others whiter; which laſt is reckoned the weakeſt of all; in ſome Places chalky, in others, ſtony; in others, a Kind of Potters Clay mixed with Gravel; of all which, no other certain Judgment can be made, but that the beſt is reckoned to be that which is hardeſt to the Pick-axe, and which when wetted does not diſſolve. And for this Reaſon, none is thought firmer and ſtronger, or more durable, than that which ſerves as a Bottom to any Springs of Water in the Bowels of the Earth. But it is my Opinion, that the beſt Way is to take Counſel with diſcreet and experienced Men of the Country, and with the neighbouring Architects; who, both from the Example of old Structures, and from their daily Practice in actual Building, muſt be the beſt Judges of the Nature of the Soil, and what Weight it is able to bear. There are alſo Methods of proving the Firmneſs of the Soil. If you roll any great Weight along the Ground, or let it fall down from any Heighth, and it does not make the Earth ſhake, nor ſtir the Water ſet there on Purpoſe in a Baſon; you may ſafely promiſe yourſelf a good, ſound Foundation in that Place. But in ſome Countries there is no ſolid Bottom to be found any where; as near the *Adriatic*, and about *Venice*, where, generally, there is nothing to be met with but a looſe, ſoft Mud.

CHAP. III.

That the Nature of Places is various, and therefore we ought not to truſt any Place too haſtily, till we have firſt dug Wells, or Reſervoirs; but that in marſhy Places, we muſt make our Foundation with Piles burnt at the Ends, and driven in with their Heads downward with light Beetles, and many repeated Blows, till they are driven quite into the Head.

YOU muſt therefore uſe different Methods for your Foundations, according to the Diverſity of Places, whereof ſome are lofty, ſome low, others between both, as the Sides of Hills: Some again are parcht and dry, as generally the Summits and Ridges of Moun-

Mountains; others damp and washy, as are those which lie near Seas or Lakes, or in Bottoms between Hills. Others are so situated as to be neither always dry nor always wet, which is the Nature of easy Ascents, where the Water does not lie and soak, but runs gently off. We must never trust too hastily to any Ground, tho' it does resist the Pick-axe, for it may be in a Plain, and be infirm, the Consequence of which might be the Ruin of the whole Work. I have seen a Tower at *Mestri*, a Place belonging to the *Venetians*, which in a few Years after it was built, made its Way thro' the Ground it stood upon, which, as the Fact evinced, was a loose weak Soil, and bury'd itself in Earth, up to the very Battlements. For this Reason they are very much to be blamed, who not being provided by Nature with a Soil fit to support the Weight of an Edifice, and Lightning upon the Ruins or Remains of some old Structure, do not take the Pains to examine the Goodness of its Foundation, but inconsiderately raise great Piles of Building upon it, and out of the Avarice of saving a little Expence, throw away all the Money they lay out in the Work. It is therefore excellent Advice, the first Thing you do to dig Wells, for several Reasons, and especially in order to get acquainted with the Strata of the Earth, whether sound enough to bear the Superstructure, or likely to give way. Add, likewise, that the Water you find in them, and the Stuff you dig out, will be of great Service to you in several Parts of your Work; and moreover, that the Opening such Vents will be a great Security to the Firmness of the Building, and prevent its being injured by subterraneous Exhalations. Having therefore, either by digging a Well, or a Cistern, or a Shoar, or any other Hole of that Nature, made yourself thoroughly acquainted with the Veins or Layers of the Earth, you are to make Choice of that which you may most safely trust with your Superstructure. In Eminences, or wherever else the Water is running down washes away the Ground, the deeper you make your Trench, the better. And that the Hills are actually eaten and wash'd away, and wasted more and more daily by continual Rains, is evident from the Caverns and Rocks which every Day grow more visible, whereas at first they were so cover'd with Earth that we could hardly perceive them. Mount *Morello*, which is about *Florence*, in the Days of our Fathers was all over cover'd with Firs; and now it is quite wild and naked; occasion'd, as I suppose, by the Washing of the Rain In Situations upon Slopes, *Columella* directs us to begin our Foundations at the lowest Part of the Slope first; which is certainly very right, for besides that whatever you lay there will always stand firm and unmoveable in its Place, it will also serve as a Prop or Buttress, to whatever you add to the upper Parts, if you aftewards think fit to enlarge your Structure. You will also thereby discover and provide against those Defects which sometimes happen in such Trenches by the cracking or falling in of the Earth. In marshy Grounds, you should make your Trench very wide, and fortify both Sides of it with Stakes, Hurdles, Planks, Sea-weeds, and Clay, so strongly that no Water may get in; then you must draw off every drop of Water that happens to be left within your Frame-work, and dig out the Sand, and clear away the Mud from the Bottom till you have firm dry Ground to set your Foot upon. The same you are to do in sandy Ground, as far as Necessity requires. Moreover, the Bottom of the Trench must be laid exactly level, not sloping on either Side, that the Materials laid upon it may be equally balanced. There is a natural instinct in all heavy Bodies to lean and press upon the lowest Parts. There are other Things which they direct us to do in marshy Situations, but they belong rather to the Walling than to the Foundations. They order us to drive into the Ground a great Number of Stakes and Piles burnt at the End, and set with their Heads downwards, so as to have a Surface of twice the Breadth that we intend for our Wall; that these Piles should never be less in length than the eighth Part of the Heighth of the Wall to be built upon them, and for their Thickness, it should be the twelfth Part of their Length, and no less. Lastly they should be drove in so close that their is not room for one more. The Instrument we use for driving in these Piles, whatever Sort it it is of, should do its Business by a great many repeated Strokes; for when it is too heavy, coming down with an immense and intolerable Force, it breaks and splits the Timber; but the continual Repetition of gentle Strokes wearies and overcomes the greatest Hardness and Obstinacy of the Ground. You have an Instance of this when you go to drive a small Nail into a hard Piece of Timber; if you use a great heavy Hammer, it won't do; but if you work with a manageable light one, it penetrates immediately

PLATE 4. (*Pages 42–43*)

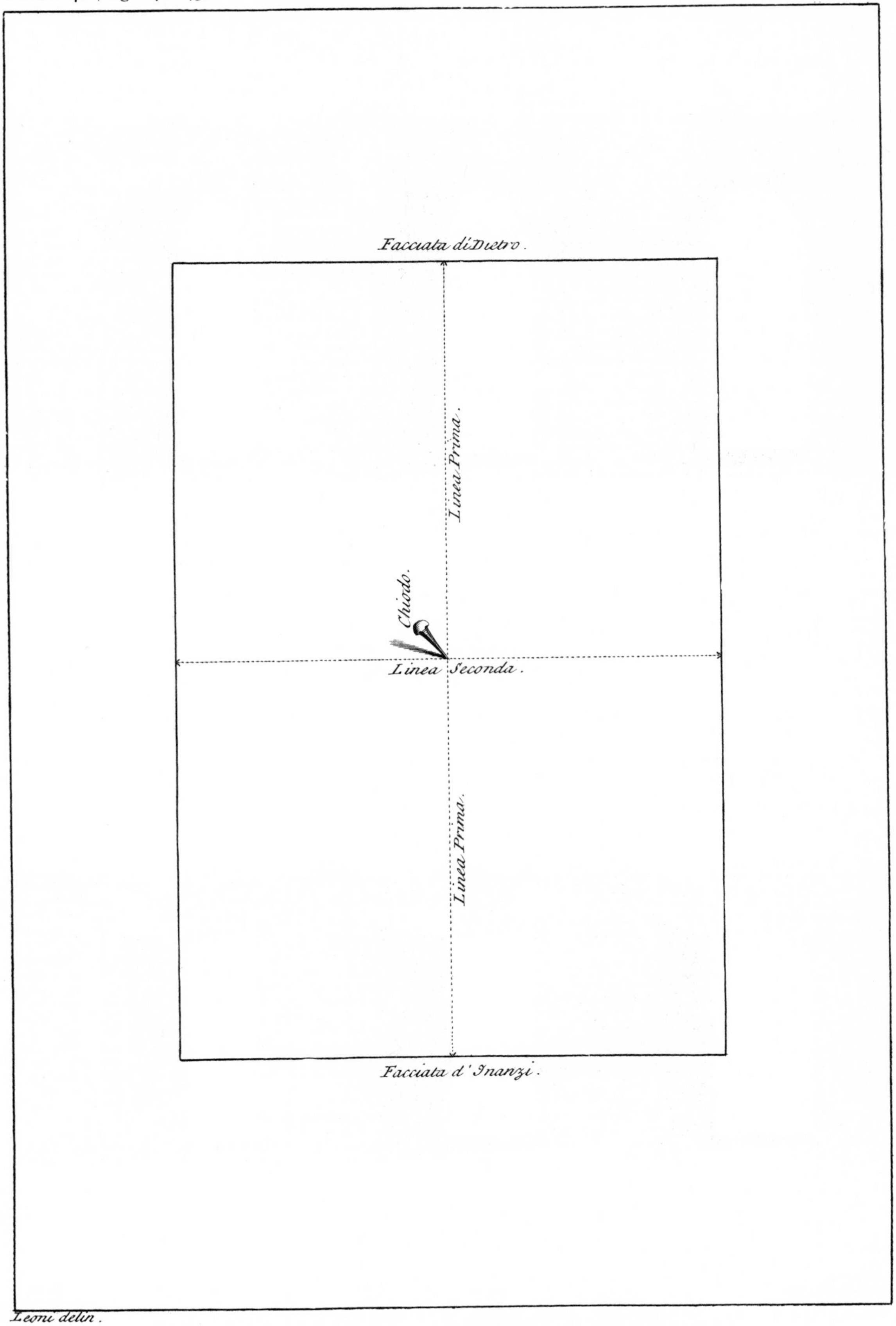

Facciata di Dietro.

Linea Prima.

Chiodo.

Linea Seconda.

Linea Prima.

Facciata d'Inanzi.

Leoni delin.

"Facciata di Dietro" = *back-front [rear facade]*. "Facciata d'Inanzi" = *fore-front*.
"Linea Prima" = *first line*. "Linea Seconda" = *second line*. "Chiodo" = *nail*.

PLATE 5. (A: *Page* 45; B: *Page* 47)

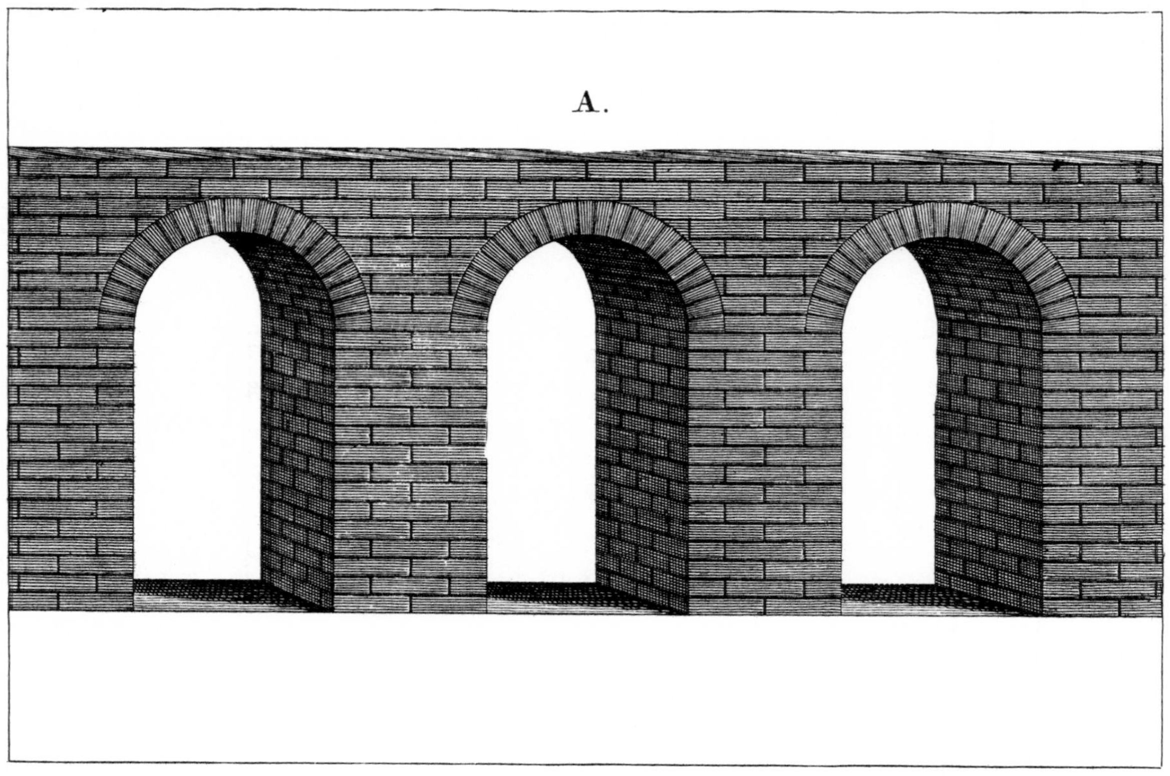

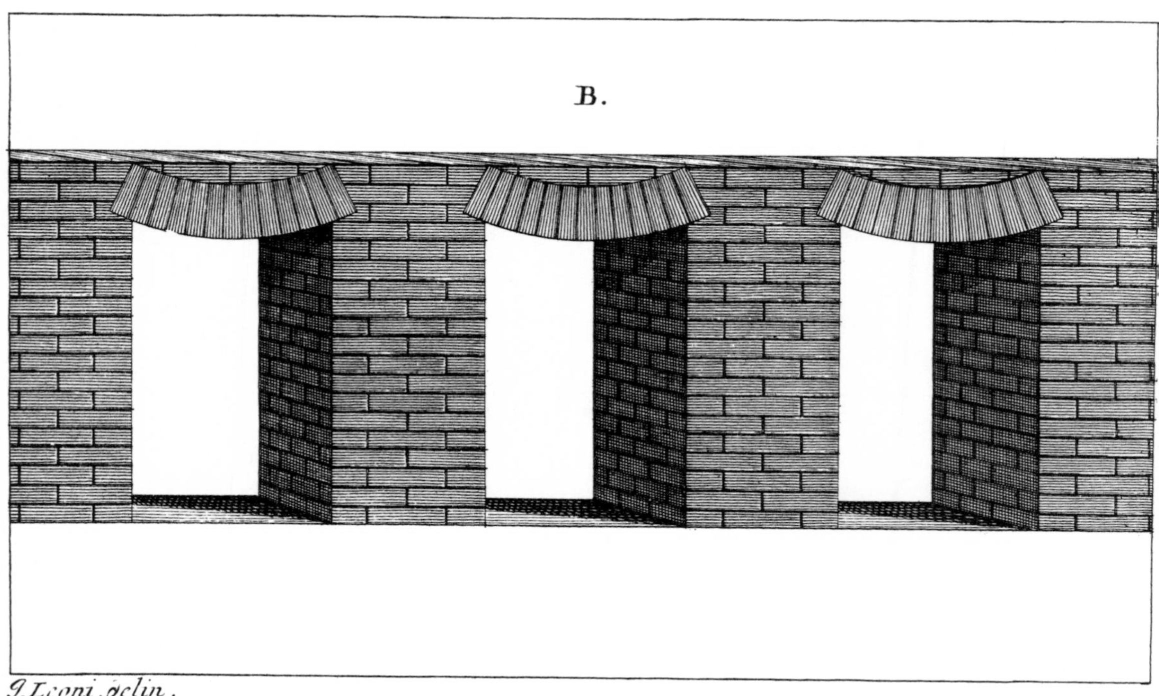

J. Leoni, delin.

What has been ſaid may ſuffice, with relation to our Trench, unleſs we would add, that ſometimes, either to ſave Money, or to avoid an intermediate Piece of rotten Ground, it may not be amiſs to make a Foundation not continued entire all the way, but with Intervals left between, as if we were only making Columns or Pilaſters, then turning Arches * from one Pilaſter to the other, to lay over them the reſt of the Wall In theſe we are to obſerve the ſame Directions as we gave before; but the greater Weight you are to raiſe upon them, the large. and ſtronger Pilaſters and Baſes you muſt make. But of theſe enough.

* A. Plate 5. (facing page 45)

CHAP. IV.

Of the Nature, Forms and Qualities of Stones, and of the Tempering of Mortar.

WE now come to begin our Wall; but as the Workman's Art and Manner of Building depends partly upon the Nature, Form and Quality of his Stone, and partly upon the Tempering of his Mortar, we are therefore firſt to treat briefly of theſe. Of Stones, ſome are living, juicy, and ſtrong, ſuch as Flint, Marble, and the like, which by Nature are heavy and ſonorous; others are exhauſted, light, and dead ſounding, as are all Stones that are ſoft and ſandy. Again, ſome have even Superficies, ſtrait Lines, and equal Angles, which are call'd Squared Stones; others have uneven Superficies, of various Lines, and unequal Angles, which we call Rough. Of Stones alſo, ſome are big and unweildy, ſo that a Man's Hand cannot manage them at Pleaſure, without the Aſſiſtance of Sleds, Leavers, Rowlers, Pullies, or the like Engines; others ſmall, ſo as you may raiſe and manage them with one ſingle Hand juſt as you pleaſe. The third Sort is between both, of a moderate Size and Weight, which are call'd ſizeable. All Stone ſhould be Entire, not Muddy, and well waſh'd; you may know whether it is Entire or Crack'd, by the Sound it gives when you Strike upon it. You can waſh them no where better than in a River; and it is certain that the Middling ſizeable Sort are not ſoak'd enough under nine Days, and the large ones under more. That which is freſh dug out of the Quarry is better than that which has been long kept; and that which has been once cemented with Mortar will not cement well again a ſecond Time. So much may ſuffice as to Stone. As for Lime, they condemn that which when it comes from the Kiln is not in entire Lumps, but in broken Pieces, and as it were in Powder, and they ſay it will never prove ſerviceable. They commend that which purges and grows white in the Fire, and which is light and ſonorous, and when you water it, burſts, and throws out a ſtrong thick Smoke high into the Air. The former, being weak, muſt of Courſe require leſs Sand; but this latter, being ſtrong, requires more. *Cato* directs, that to every two Foot of Work, we ſhould allow one Buſhel of Lime and two of Sand: Others preſcribe different Proportions. *Vitruvius* and *Pliny* are for mixing the Sand thus; namely to give to each Buſhel of Lime three of Pitſand, or two of River or Sea-ſand. Laſtly, when the Quality and Nature of your Stone requires your Mortar to be more liquid or tractable (which we ſhall ſpeak of more clearly below) your Sand muſt be ſifted through a Sieve; but when it is to be ſtiffer, then mix it with half Gravel and broken Fragments of Stone. All agree, that if you mix it with one third of broken Tile or Brick pounded, it will be much more tenacious. However, mix it as you will, you muſt ſtir it about often, till the ſmalleſt Pieces are incorparated; and ſome, for this Purpoſe, and that it may be well mingled together, ſtir it about and beat it a great while in a Mortar. But we ſhall ſay no more here of the Cement, only thus much, that Lime takes better hold with Stone of its own Kind, and eſpecially out of the ſame Quarry, than with a Stranger.

N

CHAP.

Chap. V.

Of the lower Courſes or Foundations, according to the Precepts and Example of the Ancients.

FOR making the lower Courſes, that is to ſay, raiſing the Foundations up to the Level of the Ground, I do not find any Precepts among the Ancients, except this one, that all Stones which, after being in the Air two Years, diſcover any Defect, muſt be baniſh'd into the Foundation. For as in an Army, the ſluggiſh and weak who cannot endure the Sun and Duſt, are ſent home with Marks of Infamy, ſo theſe ſoft enervated Stones ought to be rejected, and left to an inglorious Repoſe in their primitive Obſcurity. Indeed I find by Hiſtorians, that the Ancients took as much Care of the Strength and Soundneſs of their Foundation in all its Parts as of any other Part of the Wall. *Aſithis*, the Son of *Nicerinus*, King of *Ægypt*, (the Author of the Law, that whoever was ſued for Debt ſhould give the Corpſe of his Father in Pawn) when he built a Pyramid of Bricks to make his Foundations, drove Piles into the Marſh, and laid his Bricks upon them. And we are inform'd that *Cteſipho*, the excellent Architect that built the famous Temple of *Diana* at *Epheſus*, having made Choice of a level Piece of Ground, thoroughly drain'd, and likely to be free from Earthquakes; that he might not lay the Foundations of ſuch a huge Pile in ſo looſe and unfaithful a Soil without due Precautions, firſt made a Bottom of Coals pounded to Duſt; then drove in Piles with Fleeces and Coals wedged in between Pile and Pile; and over theſe a Courſe of Stone with very long Junctures.

We find that about *Jeruſalem*, in the Foundations of their Publick Works, they ſometimes uſed Stones thirty Feet long, and not leſs than fifteen high. But I have obſerved, that in other Places, the Ancients, who were wonderfully expert in managing of great Works, followed different Rules and Methods in filling up the Foundations. In the Sepulchre of the *Antonini* they filled them up with little Pieces of very hard Stone, each not bigger than a Handful, and which they perfectly drowned in Mortar. In the *Forum Argentarium*, with Fragments of all Sorts of broken Stones; in the *Comitia*, with Bits of the very worſt Sort of ſoft Stuff. But I am mightily pleaſed with thoſe who in the *Tarpeia* imitated Nature, in a Contrivance particularly well adapted to Hills; for as ſhe, in the Formation of Mountains, mixes the ſofteſt Materials with the hardeſt Stone, ſo theſe Workmen firſt laid a Courſe of ſquared Stone, as ſtrong as they could get, to the Heighth of two Feet; over theſe they made a Kind of Plaiſter of Mortar, and broken Fragments, then another Courſe of Stone, and with another of Plaiſter they finiſhed their Foundation. I have known other Inſtances, where the Ancients have made much the ſame Sort of Foundations and Structures too, of coarſe Pit-gravel, and common Stone that they have picked up by chance, which have laſted many Ages. Upon pulling down a very high and ſtrong Tower at *Bologna*, they diſcovered that the Foundations were filled with nothing but round Stones and Chalk, to the Heighth of nine Feet; the other Parts were built with Mortar. We find therefore that very different Methods have been uſed, and which to approve moſt I confeſs myſelf at a Loſs, all of them have ſo long endured firm and ſound. So that I think we ought to chuſe that which is leaſt expenſive, provided we do not throw in all manner of old Rubbiſh, and any thing apt to moulder. There are alſo other Sorts of Foundations; one belongs to Porticoes, and all other Places where Rows of Columns are to be ſet; the other to Maritime Places, where we cannot pick and chuſe the Goodneſs of our Bottom as we could wiſh. Of the Maritime we will conſider when we come to treat of making of Ports, and running Moles out into the Sea; becauſe theſe do not relate to the general Work of all manner of Buildings, which is the Subject of our Diſcourſe here, but only to one particular Part of the City, which we ſhall treat of together with other Things of the like Nature, when we give an Account of all Publick Works, Member by Member. In laying Foundations under Rows of Columns, there is no Occaſion to draw an even continued Line of Work all the Way without

without Interruption; but only first to strengthen the Places you intend for the Seats or Beds of your Columns, and then from one to the other draw Arches with their Backs downwards, so that the Plane or Level of the Area will be the Chord of those Arches; as * you may see by the Plate of the Page 41. let B. For standing thus, they will be less apt to force their Way into the Earth in any one Place, the Weight being counterpos'd and thrown equally on both Sides on the Props of the Arches. And how apt Columns are to drive into the Ground, by means of the great Pressure of the Weight laid upon them, is manifest from that Corner of the noble Temple of *Vespasian* that stands to the North-West. For being desirous to leave the publick Way, which was interrupted by that Angle, a free and open Passage underneath, they broke the Area of their Platform and turn'd an Arch against the Wall, leaving that Corner as a Sort of Plaister on the other Side of the Passage, and fortifying it, as well as possible, with stout Work, and with the Assistance of a Buttress. Yet this at last, by the vast Weight of so great a Building, and the giving Way of the Earth, became ruinous. But let this suffice upon this Head.

CHAP. VI.

That there ought to be Vents left open in thick Walls from the Bottom to the Top; the Difference between the Wall and the Foundation; the principal Parts of the Wall; the three Methods of Walling; the Materials and Form of the first Course or Layer.

THE Foundations being laid, we come next to the Wall. But I will not omit here a Precaution which belongs as well to the Compleating of the Foundation as to the Structure of the Wall. In large Buildings, where the Wall is to be very thick, we ought to leave Vents and Tunnels in the Body of the Wall, at moderate Distances one from the other, from the Foundation quite to the Top, through which any Vapour or Damp that may happen to engender or gather under Ground may have free Passage without damaging the Work. The Ancients in some of these Vents were used to make winding Stairs, as well for the Sake of the Beauty of the Contrivance itself, as for the Convenience of passing up to the Top of the Edifice, and perhaps too for the Saving of some Expence. But to return to our Subject; between the Foundation and the naked Wall there is this Difference, that the former having the Support of the Sides of the Trench, may be made of nothing but Rubbish, whereas the Latter consists of Variety of Parts, as we shall hereafter shew. The principal Parts of the Wall are these; first, the bottom Part, which begins immediately from the Level of the Foundations; this we call the first Course laid upon the Level, or the Course rising from the Ground: The middle Parts, which girt and surround the Wall, we shall call the second Course: The highest Parts, lastly, that is to say, those which support the top Roof, we call Cornices. Some of the principal Parts or rather the principal Parts of all are the Corners of the Wall, and the Pilasters, or Columns, or any thing else in their stead set in the Wall to support the Beams and Arches of the Covering; all which are comprized under the Name of Bones or Ribs. Likewise the Jambs on each Side of all Openings partake of the Nature both of Corners and of Columns. Moreover, the Coverings of Openings, that is to say, the Lintels or Transoms, whether strait or arched, are also reckoned among the Bones. And indeed I take an Arch to be nothing more than a Beam bent, and the Beam or Transom to be only a Column laid crossways. Those Parts which interfere or lie between these principal Parts, are very properly called Fillers up. There are some Things throughout the whole Wall which agree each with some one of the Parts we have here spoken of; that is to say, the filling up or cramming of the Middle of the Wall, and the two Barks or Shells of each Side, whereof that without is to bear the Sun and Weather, and that within is to give Shade and Shelter to the Inside of the Platform. The Rules for these Shells and for their stuffing are various, according to the Variety of Structures. The different Sorts of Structures are these; the ordinary Sort, the chequer Sort and the Irregular: And here it may not be amiss to take Notice

* *Refers to Part B of Plate 5, facing page 45.*

Notice of what *Varro* ſays, that the *Tuſcans* uſed to build their Country Houſes of Stone, but the *Gauls* of baked Brick, the *Sabines* of Brick unbaked, the *Spaniards* of Mud and little Stones mixed together. But of theſe we ſhall ſpeak elſewhere. The ordinary Sort of Structure, is that in which ſquared Stones, either the middling or rather the large Sort, are placed with their Fronts exactly anſwering to the ſquare level and plumb Line; which is the ſtrongeſt and moſt laſting Way of all. The chequered Way is when ſquared Stones, either the middle ſized, or rather very ſmall ones, are placed not on their Sides, but on their Corners, and lie with their Fronts anſwering to the ſquare and plumb Line. The irregular Way is where ordinary rough Stones are placed with their Sides anſwering, as well as the Inequality of their Forms will permit, one to the other; and this is the Method uſed in the Pavement of the publick Ways. But theſe Methods muſt be uſed differently in different Places; for in the Baſes, or firſt Courſe above the Ground, we muſt make our Shell of nothing but very large and very hard ſquare Stones; for as we ought to make the whole Wall as firm and entire as poſſible, ſo there is no Part of it that requires more Strength and Soundneſs than this; inſomuch that if it were poſſible for you to make it all of one ſingle Stone you ſhould do it, or at leaſt make it only of ſuch a Number as may come as near as may be to the Firmneſs and Durableneſs of one ſingle Stone. How theſe great Stones are to be mov'd and manag'd, belonging properly to the Article of Ornaments, we ſhall conſider of it in another Place.

Raise your Wall ſays *Cato*, of hard Stone and good Mortar to at leaſt a Foot high above the Ground, and it matters not if you build the reſt even of Brick unbak'd. His Reaſon for this Admonition is plainly becauſe the Rain-Water falling from the Roof might not rot this Part of the Wall. But when we examine the Works of the Ancients, and find that not only in our own Country the lower Parts of all good Buildings are compos'd of the hardeſt Stone, but that even among thoſe Nations which are under no Apprehenſions from Rain, as in *Ægypt*, they uſed to make the Baſes of their Pyramids of a black Stone of an extreme Hardneſs; we are obliged to look more nearly into this Matter. We ſhould therefore conſider that as Iron, Braſs, and the like hard Metals, if bent ſeveral Times firſt this way and then that, will at laſt crack and break; ſo other Bodies, if wearied with a repeated Change of Injuries, will ſpoil and corrupt inconceivably; which is what I have obſerved in Bridges, eſpecially of Wood: Thoſe Parts of them which ſtand all the Changes of Weather, ſometimes burnt with the Rays of the Sun, and ſharp Blaſts of Wind, at other Times ſoak'd with Night-dews or Rains, very ſoon decay and are quite eaten away by the Worms. The ſame holds good of thoſe Parts of the Wall which are near to the Ground, which by the alternate injuries of Duſt and Wet are very apt to moulder and rot. I therefore lay it down as an indiſpenſible Rule, that all the firſt Courſe of Work from the Level, ſhould be compos'd of the hardeſt, ſoundeſt, and largeſt Stones, to ſecure it againſt the frequent Aſſaults of contrary Injuries: Which Stone is hardeſt and beſt, we have ſhewn ſufficiently in the Second Book.

Chap. VII.

Of the Generation of Stones; how they are to be diſpos'd and join'd together, as alſo, which are the Strongeſt and which the Weakeſt.

It is certainly of very great Conſequence in what Manner we diſpoſe and join our Stone in the Work, either in this or any other Part; for as in Wood ſo alſo in Stone, there are Veins and Knots, and other Parts, of which ſome are weaker than others, inſomuch that Marble itſelf will warp and ſplit. There is in Stones a Kind of Impoſtumes, or Collections of putrid Matter, which in Time ſwell and grow, by means, as I ſuppoſe of the Humidity of the Air, which they ſuck in and imbibe which breeds larger Puſtules, and eats away the Building. For beſides what we have already ſaid of Stones in their proper Place, it is neceſſary to conſider here that they are created by Nature, lying flat as we ſee them in the Ground, of a liquid and fluxible Subſtance, which, as we are told, when it is afterwards harden'd and grown, reſerves in the Maſs the original Figure of its Parts. Hence it it proceeds, that the lower Part of Stones is of a more ſolid and weighty Conſiſtence than the Upper, and that they interrupted with Veins, juſt according as their Subſtances happened to unite and conglutinate. That Matter which is found within the Veins, whether it be the Scum of the firſt congealed Subſtance mix'd with the Dregs of the adventitious Matter, or whatever elſe it be, as it is plainly of ſo different a Conſiſtence, that Nature will not permit it to unite with the reſt, it is no Wonder that it is the Part in Stone which is apt to crack. And indeed, as Experience teaches us, the Devaſtations of Time too evidently demonſtrate, without ſearching into Cauſes more remote, that all vegetative and compound Bodies conſume and decay; ſo in Stones, the Parts expos'd to the Weather are ſooneſt rotted. This being the Caſe, we are adviſed in Placing our Stone to ſet thoſe Parts of it which are the ſtrongeſt, and leaſt apt to putrify, againſt the Violence of the alternate Injuries of the Weather, eſpecially in thoſe Parts of the Building where moſt Strength is requir'd. For this Reaſon we ſhould not ſet the Veins upright, leſt the Weather ſhould make the Stone crack and ſcale off; but they ſhould be laid flat downwards that the Preſſure of the incumbant Weight may hinder them from opening. The Side which in the Quarry lay moſt hid, ſhould be placed againſt the Air; becauſe it is always the ſtrongeſt and moſt unctious. But of all Stone, none will prove ſo hardy as that which has its Veins not running in parellel Lines with thoſe of the Quarry, but croſſway and directly tranſverſe. Moreover the Corners throughout the whole Building, as they require the greateſt Degree of Strength, ought to be particularly well fortify'd; and, if I miſtake not, each Corner is in effect the half of the whole Structure; for if one of them happens to fail, it occaſions the Ruin of both the Sides to which it anſwers. And if you will take the Pains to examine, I dare ſay you will find that hardly any Building ever begins to decay, but by the Fault of one of its Corners. It therefore ſhew'd great Diſcretion in the Ancients, to make their Corners much thicker than the reſt of the Wall, and in Porticoes of Columns to ſtrengthen their Angles in a particular Manner. This Strength in the Corners is not required upon Account of its Supporting the Covering (for that is rather the Buſineſs of the Columns) but only to keep the Wall up to its Duty, and hinder it from leaning any Way from its perpendicular. Let the Corners therefore be of the hardeſt and longeſt Stones, which may embrace both Sides of the Wall, as it were, like Arms; and let them be full as broad as the Wall, that there may be no need to ſtuff the Middle with Rubbiſh. It is alſo neceſſary, that the Ribs in the Wall and the Jambs or Sides of the Apertures, ſhould be fortify'd like the Corners, and made ſtrong in proportion to the Weight they are deſign'd to ſupport. And above all we ſhould leave Bits, that is to ſay, Stones left every other Row jutting out at the Ends of the Wall, like Teeth, for the Stones of the other Front of the Wall to faſten and catch into.

CHAP. VIII.

Of the Parts of the Finiſhing; of the Shells, the Stuffing, and their different Sorts.

THE Parts of the Finiſhing are thoſe which, as we ſaid before, are common to the whole Wall; that is, the Shell and the Stuffing; but there are two Shells, one outward and the other inward; if you make the outward of the hardeſt Stone you can get, the Building will be the more durable. And indeed in all Sorts of Finiſhing, let it be of what Kind of Work you will, either chequer'd, or of rough Stones, it is indifferent, provided you ſet againſt the continual miſchievous Violence either of Sun, or Wind, or of Fire, or Froſt, ſuch Stones as are in their Nature beſt fitted for reſiſting either Force, Weight, or Injuries; and we ſhould take Care to let our Materials be particularly Sound where-ever the Rain in its Fall from the Roof or Gutters is driven by the Wind againſt the Wall; ſince we often find in old Buildings, that ſuch Sprinklings will rot and eat into Marble itſelf. Though all prudent Architects, to provide againſt this Miſchief, have taken Care to bring all the Water on the Roof together into Gutters and Pipes, and ſo carry it clear away. Moreover, the Ancients obſerv'd that in Autumn the Leaves of Trees always began to fall to the South-ſide firſt; and in Buildings ruinated by Time, I have taken Notice that they always began to decay firſt towards the South. The Reaſon of this may perhaps be that the Heat and Force of the Sun lying upon the Work while it was ſtill in Hand might exhauſt the Strength of the Cement; and the Stone itſelf being frequently moiſten'd by the South-wind, and then again dry'd and burnt by the Rays of the Sun, rots and moulders. Againſt theſe and the like Injuries therefore, we ſhould oppoſe our beſt and ſtouteſt Materials. What I think too is principally to be obſerv'd, is to let every Row or Courſe of Stone throughout the Wall be even and equally proportion'd, not patch'd up of great Stones on the right Hand and little ones on the left; becauſe we are told that the Wall by the Addition of any new Weight is ſqueezed cloſer together, and the Mortar in drying is hinder'd by this Preſſure from taking due hold, which muſt of Courſe make Cracks and Defects in the Work. But you may be ſafely allow'd to make the inward Shell, and all the Front of the Wall of that Side, of a ſofter and weaker Stone; but whatever Shell you make, whether inward or outward, it muſt be always perpendicular, and its Line exactly even. Its Line muſt always anſwer juſtly to the Line of the Platform, ſo as not in any Part to ſwell out or ſink in, or to be wavy, or not exactly plum, and perfectly well compacted and finiſhed. If you rough Caſt your Wall as you build it, or while it is freſh, whatever Plaiſtering or Whitening you do it over with afterwards will laſt, in a Manner, for ever. There are two Sorts of Stuffing; the one is that with which we fill the Hollow that is left between the two Shells, conſiſting of Mortar and broken Fragments of Stone thrown in together without any Order; the other conſiſting of ordinary rough Stone, with which we may be ſaid rather to wall than only to fill up. Both plainly appears to have been invented by good-husbandry, becauſe any ſmall Coarſe Stuff is uſed in this Kind of Work. But if there was Plenty of large ſquare Stone eaſily to be had, who I wonder, would chooſe to make Uſe of ſmall Fragments? And indeed herein alone the Ribs of the Wall differ from what we call the Finiſhing, that between the two Shells of this latter we ſtuff in coarſe Rubbiſh or broken Pieces that come to Hand; whereas, in the Former we admit very few or no unequal Stones, but make thoſe Parts of the Wall quite through, of what we have call'd the *ordinary* Sort of Work. If I were to chooſe, I would have the Wall throughout made of nothing but regular Courſes of ſquared Stone, that it might be as laſting as poſſible; but whatever hollow you leave between the Shells to be filled up with Rubbiſh, you ſhould take Care to let the Courſes of each Side be as even as poſſible and it will be proper beſides to lay a good many large Stones, at convenient Diſtances, that may go quite through the Wall to both Shells, in order to bind and gird them together, that the Rubbiſh you ſtuff them with may not burſt them out. The Ancients made it a Rule in ſtuffing their Walls, not to continue the Stuffing uninterrupted to the Heigth of above five Foot, and then they laid over it a Courſe of whole Stone. This faſten'd and bound the Wall, as it were, with Nerves and Ligaments; ſo that if any Part of the Stuffing, either through the Fault of the Workman, or by Accident, happen'd to ſink, it could not pull every Thing elſe along with it, but the Weight above had in a Manner a new Baſis to reſt upon. Laſtly, we are taught what I find conſtantly obſerved among the Ancients, never to admit any Stone among our Stuffing that weighs above a Pound, becauſe they ſuppoſe that ſmall ones unite more eaſily, and knit bettter with the Cement than large ones.

It is not altogether foreign to our Purpoſe, what we read in *Plutarch* of King *Minos*, that he divided the Plebeans into ſeveral Claſſes, according to their ſeveral Profeſſions, upon this Principle, that the ſmaller the Parts are a Body is ſplit into, the more eaſily it may be governed and managed. It is alſo of no little Conſequence to have the Hollow completly fill'd up, and every the leaſt Crevice cloſe ſtopt, not only upon the Account of Strength, but likewiſe to hinder any Animals from getting in and making their Neſts there, and to prevent the Gathering of Dirt and Seeds, which might make Weeds grow in the Wall. It is almoſt incredible what huge Weights of Stone, and what vaſt Piles I have known moved and opened by the ſingle Root of one Plant. You muſt take Care therefore to let your whole Structure be girt and fill'd compleatly.

Chap.

CHAP. IX.

Of the Girders of Stone, of the Ligament and Fortification of the Cornices, and how to unite ſeveral Stones for the ſtrengthening of the Wall.

AMong the Girders we reckon thoſe Courſes of large Stone which tie the outward Shell to the Inward, and which bind the Ribs one into the other, ſuch as are thoſe which we ſaid in the laſt Chapter ought to be made every five Foot. But there are other Girders beſides, and thoſe principal ones, which run the whole Length of the Wall to embrace the Corners and ſtrengthen the whole Work: But theſe latter are not ſo frequent, and I do not remember ever to have ſeen above two, or at moſt three in one Wall. Their Place is the Summit of the Wall, to be as it were a Crown to the Whole, and to perform the ſame Service at the Top which the other more frequent Girders at the Diſtance of every five Foot do in the Middle, where ſmaller Stones are allow'd; but in theſe other Girders, which we call Cornices, as they are fewer and of more Importance, ſo much the larger and the ſtronger Stones they require. In both according to their different Offices, the beſt, the longeſt, and the thickeſt Stones are neceſſary. The ſmaller Girders are made to anſwer to the Rule and Plum-line with the reſt of the Shell of the Wall: but theſe great ones, like a Crown, project ſomewhat forwards. Theſe long, thick Stones muſt be laid exactly plum, and be well link'd with the under Courſes, ſo as to make a Kind of Pavement at Top to ſhadow and protect the Subſtructure. * The Way of placing theſe Stones one upon the other, is to let the Middle of the Stone above anſwer exactly to the Juncture of the two in the Courſe below, ſo that its Weight is equally pois'd upon them both; as (A.) Which way of Working, as it ought not indeed to be neglected in any Part of the Wall, ought to be particularly followed in the Girders. I have obſerved that the Ancients in their checquer'd Works uſed to make their Girders of five Courſes of Bricks, or at leaſt of three, and that all of them, or at leaſt one Courſe was of Stone, not thicker than the reſt, but longer and broader; as (B.) But in their ordinary Sort of Brick-work, I find they were content for Girders to make at every five Foot a Courſe of Bricks two Foot thick as (C)

I KNOW ſome too have interſpers'd Plates or Cramps of Lead of a conſiderable Length, and as broad as the Wall was thick, in order to bind the Work. But when they built with very large Stone, I find they were contented with fewer Girders, or even only with the Cornices. In making the Cornices, which are to girt in the Wall with the ſtrongeſt Ligature, we ought to neglect none of the Rules which we have laid down about the Girders; namely, we ſhould uſe in them none but the longeſt, thickeſt, and ſtrongeſt Stones, which we ſhould put together in the moſt exact and regular Order, each laid nicely even and level by the Square and Plum-line. And we ought to be more diligent and careful in this Part of the Work, becauſe it is to gird in the Whole Wall, which is more apt to ruinate in this Part than in any other. The Covering too has its Office with relation to the Wall; whence it is laid down as a Rule, that to a Wall of crude Bricks we are to make a Cornice of baked ones, to the Intent that if any Water ſhould chance to fall from the End of the Covering, or from the Gutters, it may be it may do no Miſchief, but that the Wall may be defended by the Projecting of the Cornice. For which Reaſon we ought to take Care that every Part of the Wall have a Cornice over it for a Covering to it, which ought to be firmly wrought and well ſtucco'd over to repel all the Injuries of the Weather. We are here again to conſider in what Manner we are to unite and conſolidate a Number of ſeperate Stones into one Body of Wall; and the principal Thing that offers itſelf to our Thoughts as neceſſary, is good Lime; though I do not take it to be the proper Cement for every Sort of Stone: Marble, for Inſtance, if touch'd with Lime, will not only looſe its Whiteneſs, but will contract foul bloody Spots. But Marble, is ſo delicate and ſo coy of its Whiteneſs, that it will hardly bear the Touch of any Thing but itſelf; it diſdains Smoke; ſmear'd with

* *See Plate 6, facing page 52.*

with Oil, it grows pale; waſh'd with Red Wine, it turns of a dirty brown; with Water, kept ſome time in Cheſſnut-wood, it changes quite thro' to black, and is ſo totally ſtain'd, that no ſcraping will fetch out the Spots. For this Reaſon the Ancients uſed Marble in their Works naked, and if poſſible without the leaſt Mortar: But of theſe hereafter.

Chap. X.

Of the true Manner of Working the Wall, and of the Agreement there is between Stone and Sand.

NOW as it is the Buſineſs of an expert Workman, not ſo much to make Choice of the fitteſt Materials, as to put thoſe which he is ſupplied with to the beſt and propereſt Uſes; we will proceed on our Subject in this Manner. Lime is well burnt, when after it has been water'd, and the Heat gone out of it, it riſes up like the Froth of Milk, and ſwells all the Clods. Its not having been long enough ſoak'd you may know by the little Stones you will find in it when you mix the Sand with it. If you put too much Sand to it, it will be too ſharp to cement well; if you put leſs than its Nature and Strength requires, it will be as ſtiff as Glue, and is not to be managed. Such as is not thoroughly ſoak'd, or that is weaker upon any other Account, may be uſed with leſs Danger in the Foundation than in the Wall, and in the Stuffing than in Shells. But the Corners, the Ribs, and the Band-ſtones muſt be entirely free from Mortar that has the leaſt Defect; and Arches eſpecially require the very beſt of all. The Corners, and Ribs, and the Band-ſtones, and Cornices require the fineſt, ſmalleſt and cleareſt Sand, particularly when they are built of poliſhed Stone. The Stuffing may be done with coarſer Stone.

Stone in its Nature dry and thirſty, agrees not ill with River-ſand. Stone in its Nature moiſt and watery, delights in Pit-ſand. I would not have Sea-ſand uſed towards the South; it may perhaps do better againſt the Northern Winds. For ſmall Stones, a thick lean Mortar is beſt; to a dry exhauſted Stone, we ſhould uſe a fat Sort; though the Ancients were of Opinion that in all Parts of the Walls the fattiſh Sort is more tenacious than the lean. Great Stones they always lay upon a very ſoft fluid Mortar, ſo that it rather ſeems deſign'd to lubricate and make the Bed they are laid upon ſlippery, to the Intent, that while they are fixing in their Places they may be eaſy to move with the Hand, then to cement and faſten them together. But it is certainly proper to lay a ſoft Stuff underneath in this Manner, like a Pillow, to prevent the Stones, which have a great Weight lying upon them, from breaking. There are ſome, who obſerving here and there in the Works of the Ancients, large Stones, which where they join ſeem dawb'd over with red Earth, imagine that the Ancients uſed that inſtead of Mortar. I do not think this probable, becauſe we never find both Sides, but only one of them, ſmear'd with this Sort of Stuff. There are ſome other Rules concerning the Working of our Walls, not to be neglected. We ought never to fall upon our Work with a violent Haſte, heaping one Stone upon another, in a Kind tumultuous Hurry, without the leaſt Reſpite: Neither ought we, after we have began to build, to delay it with a ſluggiſh Heavineſs, as if we had no Stomach to what we are about; but we ought to follow our Work with ſuch a reaſonable Diſpatch, that Speed and Conſideration may appear to go Hand in Hand together. Experienced Workmen forewarn us againſt raiſing the Structure too high, before what we have already done is thoroughly ſettled; becauſe the Work, while it is freſh and ſoft, is too weak and pliable to bear a Superſtructure. We may take Example from the Swallows, taught by Nature, which when they build their Neſts, firſt dawb or glue over the Beams which are to be the Foundation and Baſis of their Edifice, and then are not too haſty to lay the ſecond dawbing over this, but intermit the Work till the firſt is ſufficiently dry'd; after which they continue their Building reaſonably and properly. They ſay the Mortar has taken ſufficient hold when it puts forth a Kind of Moſs or little Flower well known to Maſons. At what Diſtances it is proper to reſpite the we may gather from the Thickneſs of the Wall itſelf, and from the Temperature of the Place

PLATE 6. *(Page 51)*

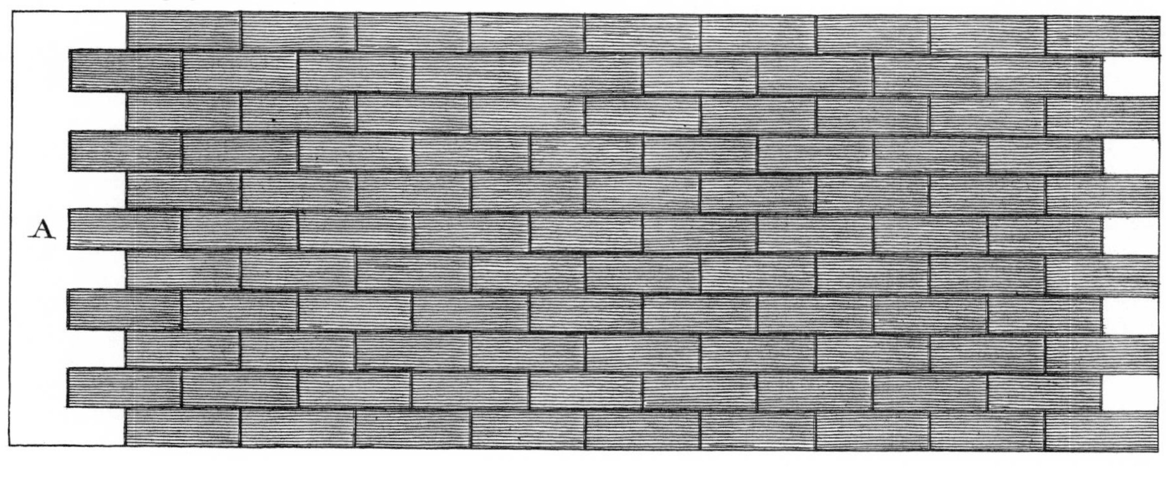

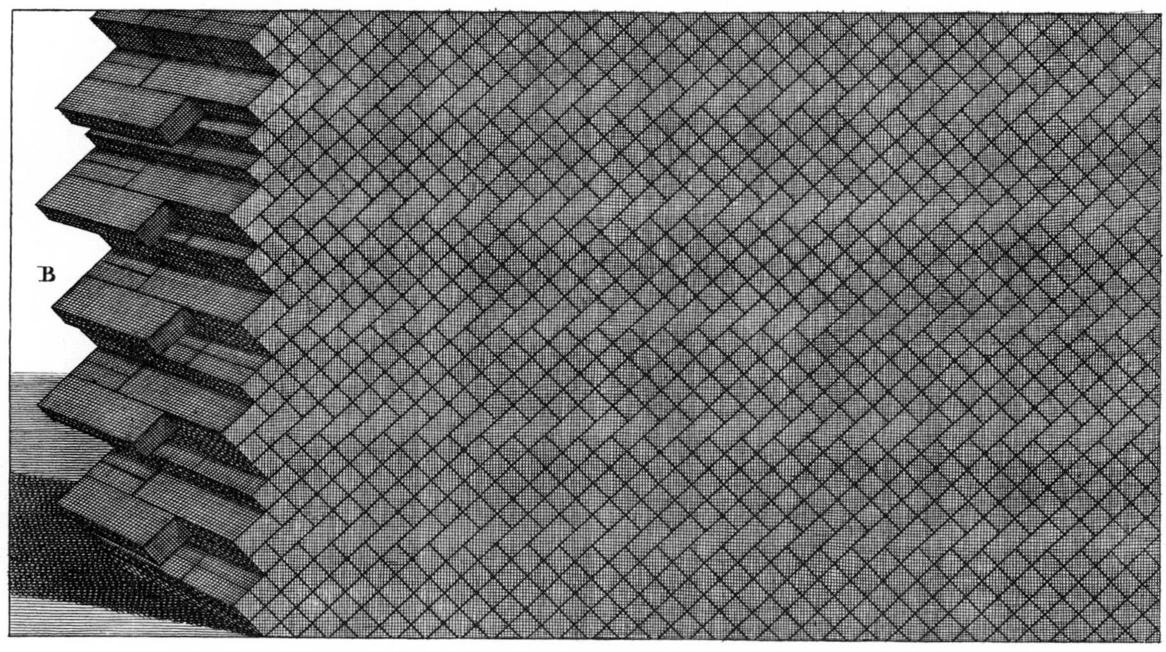

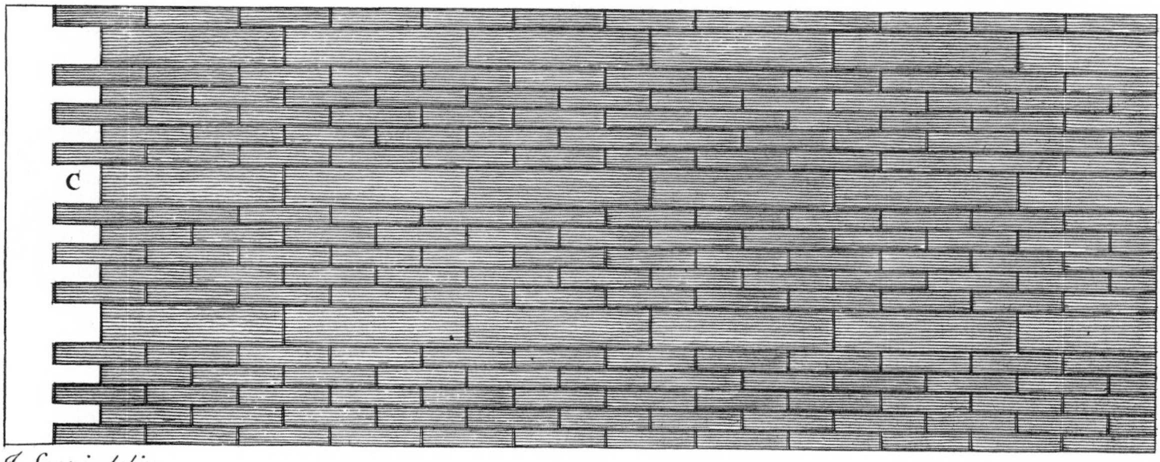

J. Leoni delin.

PLATE 7. *(Page 56)*

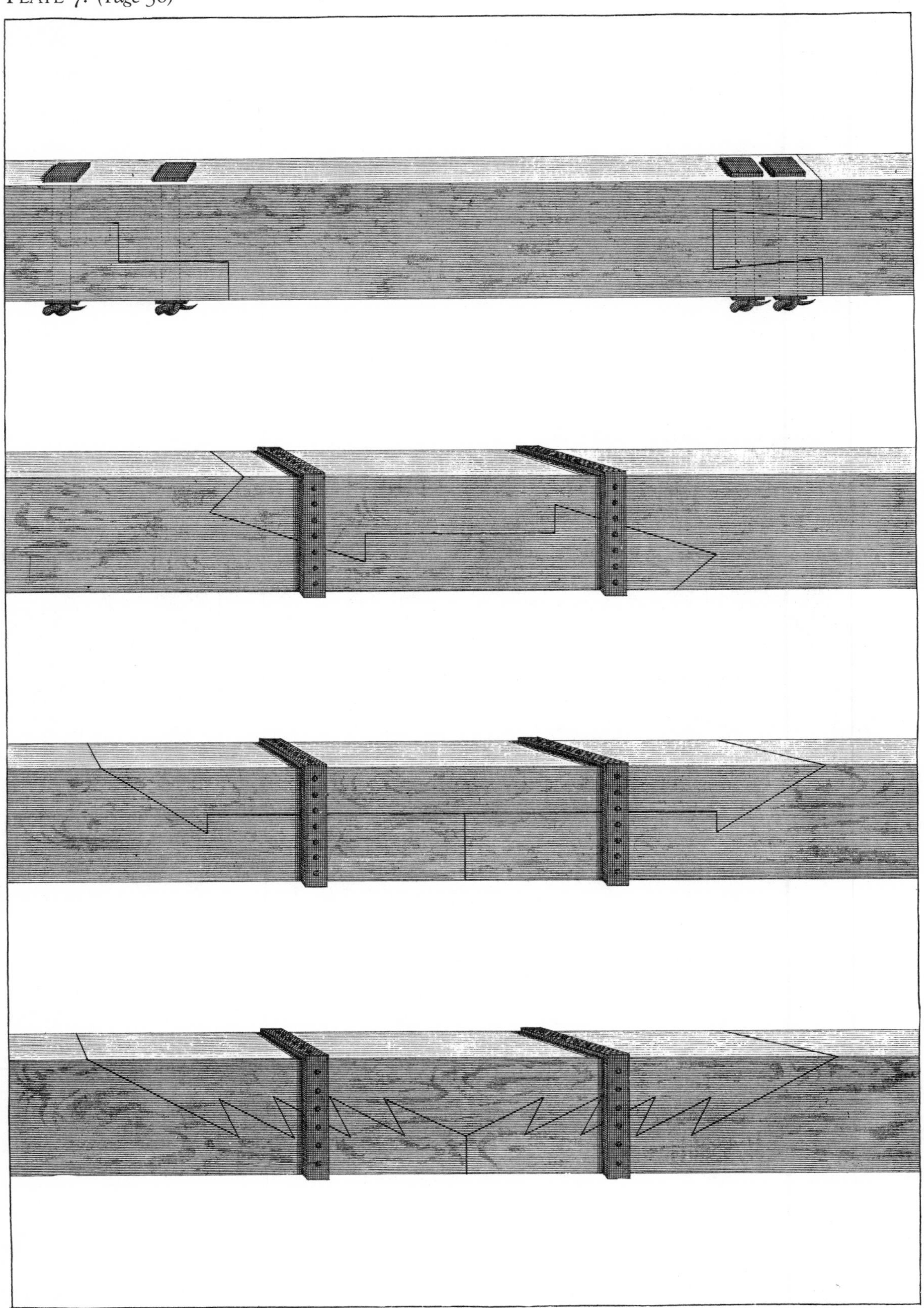

I. Leoni Delin

Place and of the Climate. When you think it Time for a Refpite, cover the Top of the Wall over with Straw, that the Wind and Sun may not exhauft the Strength of the Cement, and make it rather ufelefs than dry and binding. When you refume your Work, pour a confiderable Quantity of clean Water upon it, till it is thoroughly foak'd and wafh'd from all Manner of Dirt, that no Seeds may be left to engender Weeds. There is nothing that makes the Work ftronger and more durable than moiftening the Stone fufficiently with Water; and they fay the Stone is never foak'd as it fhould be, if upon breaking, the Infide all through is not moift and turned black. Add to what has been faid, that in erecting our Wall we ought, in fuch Places where it is poffible new Openings may afterwards be wanting either for Conveniency or Pleafure, to turn Arches in the Wall, that if you afterwards take out any of the Work from beneath thofe Arches, for the aforefaid Purpofes, the Wall may have a good Arch, built at the fame Time with itfelf, to reft upon. It is hardly to be conceiv'd how much the Strength of a Building is impair'd only by taking out one fingle Stone, be it ever fo little; and there is no fuch Thing as fetting a new Structure upon an old one, but that they will open and part one from the other; and how much fuch a Crack muft difpofe the Wall to ruin, need not be mention'd. A very thick Wall has no need of Scaffolding, becaufe it is broad enough for the Mafon to ftand upon the Wall itfelf.

CHAP. XI.

Of the Way of Working different Materials; of Plaiftering; of Cramps, and how to preferve them; the moft ancient Inftructions of Architects; and fome Methods to prevent the Mifchiefs of Lightening.

WE have treated of the beft Manner of Building, what Stone we are to choofe, and how we are to prepare our Mortar: But as we fhall fometimes be obliged to make ufe of other Sorts of Stone, whereof fome are not cemented with Mortar, but only with Slime; and others which are join'd without any Cement at all: And there are alfo Buildings confifting only of Stuffing, or rough Work, and others again only of the Shells; of all thefe we fhall fay fomething as briefly as poffible. Stones that are to be cemented with Slime, ought to be fquared, and very arid; and nothing is more proper for this than Bricks, either burnt, or rather crude, but very well dried. A Building made of crude Bricks is extremely healthy to the Inhabitants, very fecure againft Fire, and but little affected by Earthquakes; But then if it is not of a good Thicknefs, it will not fupport the Roof; for which Reafon *Cato* directs the Raifing of Pilafters of Stone to perform that Office. Some tell us, that the Slime which is ufed for Cement ought to be like Pitch, and that the beft is that which being fteep'd in Water is floweft in diffolving, and will not eafily rub off from one's Hand, and which condenfes moft in drying. Others commend the Sandy as beft, becaufe it is moft tractable. This Sort of Work ought to be cloathed with a Cruft of Mortar on the Outfide, and within, if you think fit, with Plaifter of *Paris*, or white Earth. And for the better Sticking thefe on, you muft in Building your Wall, fet little Pieces of Tile here and there in the Cracks of the Joining, jutting out like Teeth, for the Plaifter to cleave to. When the Structure is to be compofed of naked Stones, they ought to be fquared and much bigger than the other, and very found and ftrong; and in this Sort of Work we allow of no ftuffing; the Courfes muft be regular and even, the Junctures contrived with frequent Ligatures of Cramps and Pins. Cramps are what faften together with two Stones fideways that lie even with one another, and unite them into a Row: Pins are fix'd into an upper Stone and an under one, to prevent the Row from being by any Violence driven out from the reft. Cramps and Pins of Iron are not reckoned amifs; but I have obferved in the Works of the Ancients, that Iron rufts, and will not laft; But Brafs will almoft endure for ever. Befides, I find that Marble is tainted by the Ruft of the Iron, and breaks all round it. We likewife meet with Cramps made of Wood in very ancient Structures;

and indeed, I do not think them inferior to thoſe of Iron. The Cramps of Braſs and Iron are faſtened in with Lead: But thoſe of Wood are ſufficiently ſecured by their Shape, which is made in ſuch Manner, that for Reſemblance, they are called Swallow, or Dove-tailed. The Cramps muſt be ſo placed that no Drops of Rain may penetrate to them; and it is Thought that the Braſs ones are yet more ſtrengthened againſt old Age, if in Caſting they are mixed with one thirtieth Part of Tin: They will be leſs liable to ruſt if they are anointed with Pitch, or Oil. It is affirmed that Iron may be ſo tempered by White-lead, Plaiſter, and Liquid Pitch, as not to ruſt. Wooden Cramps done over with Maiden-wax and Lees of Oil, will never rot. I have known them pour ſo much Lead upon Cramps, and that ſo boyling Hot, that it has burſt the Stones. In ancient Structures we often meet with very ſtrong Walls made of nothing but Rubbiſh and broken Stuff; theſe are built like the Mud-Walls common in *Spain* and *Africa*, by faſtening on each Side Planks or Hurdles, inſtead of Shells, to keep the Stuff together till it is dry and ſettled: But herein they differ, that the Ancients filled up their Work with Mortar liquid, and in a Manner floating; whereas, the other only took a clammy Sort of Earth which they trod and rammed with their Feet, and with Beetles, after having firſt made it tractable by thorough wetting and kneading. The Ancients alſo in thoſe rough Works of theirs, at the Diſtance of every three Foot made a Kind of Band of Pieces of large Stone, eſpecially of the ordinary Sort, or at leaſt angular; becauſe round Stones, though they are very hardy againſt all Sorts of Injuries, yet if they are not ſurrounded with ſtrong Supports, are very unfaithful in any Wall. In theſe other Works, that is to ſay, in the *African* Buildings of Earth, they mixed with their Clay the *Spaniſh*-Broom, or Sea-Bullruſh, which made a Stuff admirably good for Working, and which remained unhurt either by Wind or Weather. In *Pliny*'s Time there was to be ſeen upon the Ridges of Mountains ſeveral little Towers for viewing the Country built of Earth, which had endured quite from the Days of *Hanibal*. We make this Sort of Cruſt (which is a fitter Name for it than Shell) with Hurdles and Mats, made of Reeds not freſh gathered; a Work indeed not very magnificent, but generally uſed by the Old *Plebeian Romans*. They rough Caſt the Hurdles over with Clay, beat up for three Days running with the Reeds, and then (as we ſaid before) cloath it with Mortar, or Plaiſter of *Paris*, which they afterwards adorn with Painting and Statues. If you mix your Plaiſter up with a third Part of broken Tile, or Brick pounded, it will be the leſs injured by wet: If you mix it with Lime, it will be the Stronger: But in damp Places, or ſuch as are expoſed to Cold and Froſt, Plaiſter of *Paris* is very unſerviceable. I will now, by Way of Epilogue, give you a Law of very great Antiquity among Architects, which in my Opinion ought no leſs to be obſerved than the Anſwers of Oracles: And it is this. Make your Foundation as ſtrong as poſſible: Let the Superſtructure lie exactly plum to its Centre: Fortify the Corners and Ribs of the Wall from the Bottom to the Top with the largeſt and the ſtrongeſt Stones: Soak your Lime well: Do not uſe your Stone till it is thoroughly watered: Set the hardeſt Sort to that Side which is moſt expoſed to Injuries: Raiſe your Wall exactly by the Square, Level and Plum-line: Let the Middle of the upper Stone lie directly upon the Meeting of the two below it: Lay the entire Stones in the Courſes, and fill up the Middle with the broken Pieces: Bind the inward and outſide Shells to one another by frequent Croſs or Band-ſtones. Let this ſuffice with Relation to the Wall; we come now to the Covering. But I will not paſs over one Thing which I find the Ancients obſerved very religiouſly. There are ſome Things in Nature which are endued with Properties by no means to be neglected; particularly, that the Lawrel-tree, the Eagle, and the Sea-calf, are never to be touched by Lightening. There are ſome therefore who ſuppoſe that if theſe are incloſed in the Wall, the Lightening will never hurt it. This I take to be juſt as probable as another wonderful Thing which we are told, that the Land-toad, or Rudduck, if ſhut up in an earthen Pot, and burned in a Field, will drive away the Birds from devouring the Seeds; and that the Tree *Oſtrys*, or *Oſtrya* brought into a Houſe, will obſtruct a Woman's Delivery; and that the Leaves of the Lesbian Oemony kept but under the Roof, will give a Flux of the Belly and an Evacuation that will certainly prove Mortal. Let us now return to our Subject, for the better underſtanding of which, it will be proper to look back to what we have formerly ſaid of the Lines of Building

Chap.

CHAP. XII.

Of Coverings of ſtrait Lines; of the Beams and Rafters, and of the uniting the Ribs.

OF Coverings, ſome are to the open Air, and ſome are within; ſome conſiſt of ſtrait Lines, others of curve, and ſome of both: We may add, not improperly, that ſome are of Wood, and ſome of Stone. We will firſt, according to our Cuſtom, mention one Obſervation which relates in general to all Sorts of Coverings; which is this: That all manner of Roofs, or Coverings have their Ribs, Nerves, Finiſhings, and Shells, or Cruſts, juſt the ſame as the Wall: Which will appear from the Conſideration of the Thing itſelf. To begin with thoſe of Wood, and conſiſting of ſtrait Lines; it is neceſſary for ſupporting the Cover to lay very ſtrong Beams acroſs from one Wall to the other; which, as we took Notice before, are Columns laid tranſverſe: Theſe Beams therefore, are a Sort of Ribs; and if it were not for the Expences, who would not wiſh to have the whole Building conſiſt, if we may uſe the Expreſſion, of nothing but Ribs and ſolid Work; that is to ſay, of continued Columns and Beams cloſe compacted? but we here conſult Oeconomy, and ſuppoſe every Thing to be ſuperfluous, that without Prejudice to the Strength of the Work, may be poſſibly retrenched; and for this Reaſon, we leave Spaces between the Beams. Between theſe we lay the Croſs-beams, Rafters, and the like; which may not at all improperly be reckoned the Ligatures: To theſe we fit and joyn Boards and Planks of greater Breadth, which there is no Reaſon why we ſhould not call the Finiſhing; and in the ſame Way of thinking, the Pavement and Tiling is the Outward Shell, and the Ceiling, or Roof, which is over our Head the Inward. If this be granted, let us conſider whether there is any Thing neceſſary to be obſerved with Relation to any of theſe Parts, that having duly examined it, we may the more eaſily underſtand what belongs to Coverings of Stone. We will ſpeak of them therefore as briefly as poſſible: Firſt, taking Notice of one Thing not foreign to our Purpoſe. There is a very vicious Practice among our modern Architects; which is, that in order to make their Ceilings, they leave great Holes in the very Ribs of the Building to let the Heads of the Beams into after the Wall is finiſhed; which not only weakens the Structure, but alſo makes it more expoſed to Fire; becauſe by theſe Holes the Flames find a Paſſage from one Apartment to another. For which Reaſon, I like the Method uſed among the Ancients, of ſetting in the Wall ſtrong Tables of Stone called Corbels, upon which they laid the Heads of their Beams. If you would bind the Wall, and the Beams together, you have Braſs Cramps, and Braces, and Catches or Notches in the Corbel itſelf, which will ſerve for that Purpoſe. The Beams ought to be perfectly ſound and clear; and eſpecially about the Middle of its Length it ought to be free from the leaſt Defect, placing your Ear at one End of it while the other is ſtruck, if the Sound come to you dead, and flat, it is a Sign of ſome private Infirmity. Beams that have Knots in them are abſolutely to be rejected, eſpecially if there are many, or if they are crouded together in a Cluſter. The Side of the Timber that lies neareſt the Heart, muſt be planed, and laid uppermoſt in the Building; but the Part that is to lie undermoſt, muſt be planed very ſuperficially, only the Bark, nay, and of that hardly any, or as little as poſſible. Which-ſoever Side has a Defect that runs croſſways of the Beam, lay uppermoſt; if there is a Crak longways, never venture it of the Side, but lay it either uppermoſt, or rather undermoſt. If you happen to have Occaſion to bore a Hole in it, or any Opening, never meddle with the Middle of its length, nor its lower Superficies. If, as in Churches, the Beams are to be laid in Couples; leave a Space of ſome Inches between them, that they may have Room to exhale, and not be ſpoyled by heating one another: And it will not be amiſs to lay the two Beams of the ſame Couple different Ways, that both their Heads may not lie upon the ſame Pillow; but where one has its Head, the other may have its Foot: For by this Means the Strength of the one's Foot will aſſiſt the Weakneſs of the other's Head; and ſo *vice verſa*. The Beams

Beams ought alſo to be related to one another; that is, they ſhould be of the ſame Kind of Timber, and raiſed in the ſame Wood, expoſed if poſſible to the ſame Winds, and fell'd the ſame Day; that being endued with the ſame natural Strength, they may bear their Shares equally in the Service. Let the Beds for the Beams be exactly level, and perfectly firm and ſtrong; and in laying them take care that the Timber does not touch any Lime, and let it have clear and open Vents all about it, that it may not be tainted by the Contact of any other Materials, nor decay by being too cloſe ſhut up. For a Bed for the Beams, ſpread under them either Fern, a very dry Kind of Herb, or Aſhes, or rather Lees of * Oil with the bruiſed Olives. But if your Timber is ſo ſhort, that you cannot make a Beam of one Piece, you muſt join two or more together, in ſuch a Manner as to give them the Strength of an Arch; that is to ſay, ſo that the upper Line of the compacted Beam, cannot poſſibly by any Preſſure become ſhorter; and on the contrary, that the lower Line cannot grow longer: And there muſt be a Sort of Cord to bind the two Beams together, which ſhove one another with their Heads, with a ſtrong Ligature. The Rafters, and all the reſt of the Wood-work, depend upon the Goodneſs and Soundneſs of the Beams; being nothing elſe but Beams ſplit. Boards or Planks are thought to be inconvenient if too thick, becauſe whenever they begin to warp they throw out the Nails; and thin Boards, eſpecially in Coverings expoſed to the Air, they ſay, muſt be faſtened with Nails in Pairs, ſo as to ſecure the Corners, the Sides and the Middle. They tell us, that ſuch Nails as are to bear any tranſverſe Weight, muſt be made thick; but as for others, it matters not if they are thinner; but then they muſt be longer, and have broader Heads.

BRASS Nails are moſt durable in the Air, or in wet; but I have found the Iron ones to be ſtronger under Cover. For faſtening of the Rafters together, wooden Pins are much uſed. Whatever we have here ſaid of Coverings of Wood, muſt be obſerved alſo with relation to thoſe of Stone; for ſuch Stones as have Veins, or Faults running croſſways, muſt be rejected for the making of Beams, and uſed in Columns; or if there are any ſmall inconſiderable Faults, the Side of the Stone in which it appears, when it is uſed, muſt be laid downwards, Veins running longways in Beams of any Sort, are more excuſable than tranſverſe ones. Tables, or Scantlings of Stones alſo, as well for other Reaſons, as upon Account of their Weight, muſt not be made too thick. Laſtly, the Beams, Rafters, and Planks that are uſed in Coverings, whether of Wood, or Stone, muſt be neither ſo thin, nor ſo few as not to be ſufficient for upholding themſelves, and their Burthens; nor ſo thick, or ſo crouded as to take from the Beauty, and Symmetry of the Work; but thoſe are things we ſhall ſpeak of elſewhere. And thus much for Coverings of ſtraight Lines; unleſs it may be proper to mention one Thing which is in my Opinion to be neglected in no Sort of Structure. The Philoſophers have obſerved, that Nature in forming the Bodies of Animals, always takes care to finiſh her Work in ſuch a Manner, that the Bones ſhould all communicate, and never be ſeperate one from the other: So we alſo ſhould connect the Ribs togther, and faſten them together well with Nerves and Ligatures; ſo that the Communication among the Ribs ſhould be ſo continued, that if all the reſt of the Structure failed, the Frame of the Work ſhould yet ſtand firm and ſtrong with all its Parts and Members.

CHAP. XIII.

Of Coverings, or Roofs of Curve Lines; of Arches, their Difference and Conſtruction, and how to ſet the Stones in an Arch.

WE come now to ſpeak of Roofs made of Curve Lines, and we are firſt to conſider thoſe Particulars wherein they exactly agree with Coverings of ſtrait Lines. A curvilinear Roof is compoſed of Arches; and we have already ſaid that an Arch is nothing but a Beam bent. We might alſo here mention the Ligatures, and thoſe Things which muſt be uſed for filling up the Vacuities; but I would be underſtood more clearly, by explaining what I take to be the Nature of an Arch, and of what Parts it conſiſts.

I SUPPOSE then, that Men learnt at firſt to turn Arches from this: They ſaw that two Beams ſet

* *See Plate 7, facing page 53.*

ſet with their Heads one againſt the other, and their Feet ſet wide, would, if faſtened at Top, ſtand, very firm, by means of the Equalneſs of their Weight: They were pleaſed with this Invention, and began to make their Roofs in the ſame Manner, to throw off the Rain, both Ways. Afterwards, perhaps, not being able to cover a wider Space for want of Beams long enough, they put between the Heads of theſe two Beams another croſſways at Top, ſo that they made a Figure much like that of the Greek Letter π, and this middle Beam they might call a Wedge; and as this ſucceeded very well, they multiplyed the Wedges, and thus made a Kind of Arch, whoſe Figure mightily delighted them. Then transferring the ſame Method to their Works of Stone, continuing to multiply the Wedges, they made an entire Arch, which muſt be allowed to be nothing elſe but a Conjunction of a Number of Wedges, whereof ſome ſtanding with their Heads below the Arch, are called the Foot of the Arch, thoſe in the Middle above, the Key of the Arch, and thoſe on the Sides, the Turn, or Ribs of the Arch. It will not be improper here to repeat what we ſaid in the firſt Book upon this Subject: There are different Sorts of Arches, the Entire, is the full half of a Circle, or that whoſe Chord runs through the Centre of the Circle; there is another which approaches more to the Nature of a Beam than of an Arch, which we call the Imperfect, or diminiſhed Arch, becauſe it is not a compleat Semi-circle; but a determinate Part leſs, having its Chord above the Centre, and at ſome Diſtance from it. There is alſo the Compoſite Arch, called by ſome the Angular, and by others an Arch compſed of two Arches leſs than Semi-circles; and its Chord has the two Centres of two Curve Lines, which mutually interſect each other. That the Entire Arch is the Strongeſt of all, appears not only from Experience, but Reaſon; for I do not ſee how it can poſſibly diſunite of itſelf, unleſs one Wedge ſhoves out another, which they are ſo far from doing, that they aſſiſt and ſupport one another. And indeed, if they were to go about any ſuch Violence, they would be prevented by the very Nature of Ponderoſity, by which they are preſſed downwards, either by ſome Superſtructure, or by that which is in the Wedges themſelves. This makes *Varro* ſay, that in Arches, the Work on the right Hand is keptup no leſs by that on the Left, than the Work on the Left is by that on the Right. And if we look only into the Thing itſelf; how i[s] it poſſible for the middle Wedge at Top, whic[h] is the Key-ſtone to the Whole, to thruſt ou[t] either of the two next Side Wedges, or how can that be driven out of its Place by them? The next Wedges alſo in the Turn of the Arch, being juſtly counterpoiſed, will ſurely ſtand to their Duty; and laſtly, how can the two Wedges under the two Feet of the Arch, ever be moved while the upper ones ſtand firm? Therefore we have no need of a Cord, or Bar in an entire Arch, becauſe it ſupports itſelf by its own Strength; but in diminiſh'd Arches there is Occaſion either for an Iron Chain or Bar, or for an Extenſion of Wall on both Sides, that may have the Effect of a Bar to ſupply the Want of Strength, that there is in the diminiſh'd Arch, and make it equal to the Entire. The ancient Architects always uſe theſe Precautions, and where-ever it was poſſible, conſtantly ſecured their diminiſh'd Arches, by ſetting them in a good Body of Wall. They alſo endeavour'd, if they had an Opportunity, to turn their imperfect Arches upon a ſtrait Beam; and over theſe imperfect ones, they uſed to turn entire Arches, which protected the diminiſhed ones which were within them, and took upon themſelves the Burthen of the Superſtructure. As for Compoſite Arches, we do not find any of them in the Buildings of the Ancients; ſome think them not amiſs for the Apertures in Towers; becauſe they ſuppoſe they will cleave the great Weight that is laid upon them, as the Prow of a Ship does the Water, and that they are rather ſtrengthened than oppreſs'd by it.

THE Stones uſed in Building an Arch, ſhould be every Way the biggeſt that can be got; becauſe the Parts of any Body that are united and compacted by Nature, are more inſeparable than thoſe which are join'd and cemented by Art. The Stones alſo ought to be equal on both Sides, as if they were balanced with reſpect to their Fronts, Sizes, Weight, and the like. If you are to make a Portico, and to draw ſeveral Arches over continued Apertures, from the Capitals of Columns, never let the Seat from which two or more Arches are to riſe, be made of two Pieces, or of as many as there are to be Arches, but only of one ſingle Stone, and that as ſtrong as may be, to hold together the Feet of all the Arches. The ſecond Stones in the Arch, which riſe next to theſe, if they are large Pieces, muſt be ſet with their Backs againſt each other, joining perpendicularly. The third Stone which is laid upon theſe ſecond ones, muſt be ſet by the Plum-lines, as we directed in raiſing the Wall, with even Joinings, ſo that they may ſerve both the Arches, and be a Binding to both their Wedges. Let the Lines of the Joinings of all the Stones in the Arch point exactly to the Centre of that Arch.

The moſt skillful Workmen always make the Key-ſtone of one ſingle Piece, very large and ſtrong; and if the Breadth of the Top is ſo great, that no one Stone will ſuffice, it will then be no longer only an Arch, but a vaulted Roof.

Chap. XIV.

Of the ſeveral Sorts of Vaults, and wherein they differ; of what Lines they are compoſed, and the Method of letting them ſettle.

There are ſeveral Sorts of Vaults; ſo that it is our Buſineſs here to enquire wherein they differ, and of what Lines they are compoſed; in doing of which, I ſhall be obliged to invent new Names, to make myſelf clear and perſpicuous, which is what I have principally ſtudied in theſe Books. I know *Ennius* the Poet calls the Arch of the Heavens the mighty Vaults; and *Servius* calls all Vaults made like the Keel of a Ship, Caverns: But I claim this Liberty; that whatever in this Work, is expreſſed aptly, clearly, and properly, ſhall be allowed to be expreſſed right. The different Sorts of Vaults are theſe, the plain Vault, the Camerated, or mixed Vault, and the hemiſpherical Vault, or Cupola; beſides thoſe others which partake of the Kind of ſome of theſe. The Cupola in its Nature is never placed but upon Walls that riſe from a circular Platform: The Camerated are proper for a ſquare one; the plain Vaults are made over any quadrangular Platform, whether long or ſhort, as we ſee in all ſubterraneous Porticoes. Thoſe Vaults too which are like a Hill bored through, we alſo call plain Vaults; the plain Vault therefore, is like a Number of Arches join'd together Sideways; or like a bent Beam extended out in Breadth, ſo as to make a Kind of a Wall turn'd with a Sweep over our Heads for a Covering. But if ſuch a Vault as this, running from North to South, happens to be croſs'd by another which runs from Eaſt to Weſt, and interſects it with equal Lines meeting at the Angles like crooked Horns, this will make a Vault of the Camerated Sort. But if a great Number of equal Arches meet at the Top exactly in the Centre, they conſtitute a Vault like the Sky, which therefore we call the Hemiſpherical, or compleat Cupola. The Vaults made of Part of theſe, are as follows: If Nature with an even and perpendicular Section, were to divide the Hemiſphere of the Heavens in two Parts, from Eaſt to Weſt, it would make two Vaults, which would be proper Coverings for any ſemi-circular Building. But if from the Angle at the Eaſt, to that at the South, and from the South to the Weſt, thence to the North, and ſo back again to the Eaſt, if Nature were to break and interrupt this Hemiſphere by ſo many Arches turn'd from Angle to Angle, ſhe would then leave a Vault in the Middle, which for its Reſemblance to a ſwelling Sail, we will venture to call a Velar Cupola. But that Vault which conſiſts of a Number of plain Vaults meeting in a Point at Top, we ſhall call an Angular Cupola.

In the Conſtruction of Vaults, we muſt obſerve the ſame Rules as in that of the Walls, carrying on the Ribs of the Wall clear up to the Summit of the Vault; and according to the Method preſcribed for the Former, obſerving the ſame Proportions and Diſtances: From Rib to Rib, we muſt draw Ligatures croſſways, and the Interſpaces we muſt fill up with Stuffing. But the Difference between the Working of a Vault and a Wall, lies in this; that in the Wall the Courſes of Stone are laid even and perpendicular by the Square and Plum-line; whereas, in the Vault the Courſes are laid by a curve Line, and the Joints all point to the Centre of their Arch.

The Ancients hardly ever made their Ribs of any but burnt Bricks, and thoſe generally about two Foot long, and adviſe to fill up the Interſpaces of our Vaults with the lighteſt Stone, that they might not oppreſs the Wall with too great a Weight. But I have obſerved that ſome have not always thought themſelves obliged to make continued ſolid Ribs, but in their ſtead, have at certain Diſtances, ſet Bricks lying Sideways, with their Heads jointing into each

PLATE 8. *(Page 59)*

each other, like the Teeth of a Comb; as a Man locks his right Hand Fingers into his left; and the Interſpaces they filled up with any common Stone, and eſpecially with Pumice Stone, which is univerſally agreed to be the propereſt of all, for the ſtuffing Work of Vaults. In building either Arches or Vaults, we muſt make uſe of Centres. Theſe are a Kind of Frames made with the Sweep of an Arch of any rough Boards juſt clapt together for a ſhort Service, and covered either with Hurdles, Ruſhes, or any ſuch common Stuff, in order to ſupport the Work till it is ſettled and hardened. Yet there is one ſort of Vault which ſtands in no Need of theſe Machines, and that is the *perfect Cupola*; becauſe it is compoſed not only of Arches, but alſo, in a Manner, of Cornices. And who can conceive the innumerable Ligatures that there are in theſe, which all wedge together, and interſect one another both with equal and unequal Angles? So that in whatſoever Part of the whole Cupola you lay a Stone, or a Brick, you may be ſaid at the ſame time to have laid a Key-ſtone to an infinite Number, both of Arches, and Cornices. And when theſe Cornices, or Arches are thus built one upon the other, if the Work were inclined to ruinate, where ſhould it begin, when the Joints of every Stone are directed to one Centre with equal Force and preſſure? Some of the Ancients truſted ſo much to the Firmneſs of this Sort of Structure, that they only made plain Cornices of Brick at ſtated Diſtances, and filled up the Interſpaces with Rubble. But I think, thoſe acted much more prudently, who in raiſing this Sort of Cupola, uſed the ſame Methods as in Walling, to cramp and faſten the under Cornices to the next above, and the Arches too in ſeveral Places, eſpecially if they had not plenty of Pit Sand to make very good Cement, or if the Building was expoſed to South Winds, or Blaſts from the Sea. You may likewiſe turn the Angular Cupolas without a Centre, if you make a perfect one in the Middle of the Thickneſs of the Work. But here you will have particular Occaſion for Ligatures to faſten the weaker Parts of the outer one tightly to the ſtronger Parts of that within. Yet it will be neceſſary when you have laid one or two Rows of Stone to make little light Stays, or Catchers jutting out, on which, when thoſe Rows are ſettled, you may ſet juſt Frame-work enough to ſupport the next Courſes above, to the Height of a few Feet, till they are ſufficiently hardened; and then you may remove theſe Frames, or Supports, higher and higher to the other Courſes till you have finiſh'd the whole Work. The other Vaults, both plain and * mixed, or camerated, muſt needs be turn'd upon Centres: But I would have the firſt Courſes, and the Heads of their Arches be placed upon very ſtrong Seats; nor can I approve the Method of thoſe who carry the Wall clear up firſt, only leaving ſome Mouldings, or Corbels, upon which, after a Time, they turn their Arches; which muſt be a very infirm and periſhable Sort of Work. The true Way is to turn the Arch immediately, and equally with the Courſes of the Wall which is to ſupport it, that the Work may have the ſtrongeſt Ligatures that is poſſible, and grow in a Manner all of one Piece. The Vacuities which are left between the Back of the Sweep of the Arch, and the Upright of the Wall it is turn'd from, call'd by Workmen, the *Hips* of the Arch, ſhould be fill'd up, not with Dirt, or old Rubbiſh, but rather with ſtrong ordinary Work, frequently knit and jointed into the Wall.

I AM pleaſed with thoſe who, to avoid overburthening the Arch, have ſtuffed up theſe Vacuities with earthen Pots, turn'd with their Mouths downwards, that they might not contain any wet, if it ſhould gather there, and over theſe thrown in Fragments of Stone not heavy, but perfectly ſound. Laſtly, in all Manner of Vaults, let them be of what Kind they will, we ought to imitate Nature, who, when ſhe has knit the Bones, faſtens the Fleſh with Nerves, interweaving it every where with Ligatures running in Breadth, Length, Height and circularly. This artful Contexture is what we ought to imitate in the joining of Stones in Vaults. Theſe Things being compleated, the next, and laſt Buſineſs is to cover them over; a Work of the greateſt Conſequence in Building, and no leſs difficult than neceſſary; in effecting, and compleating of which, the utmoſt Care and Study has been over and over employed. Of this we are to treat; but firſt, it will be proper to mention ſomething neceſſary to be obſerved in working of Vaults; for different Methods are to be taken in the Execution of different Sorts: Thoſe which are turn'd upon Centres muſt be finiſh'd out of hand, without Intermiſſion; but thoſe which are wrought without Centres muſt be diſcontinued, and left to ſettle Courſe by Courſe, leſt new Work being added to the firſt before it is dry, ſhould ruin the Whole. As to thoſe which

* *See Plate 8, facing page 58.*

which are turned upon Centres, when they are closed with their Key-stones, it will be proper immediately to ease the Props a little, that those Centres rest upon; not only to prevent the Stones fresh laid from floating in the Beds of Mortar they are set in, but that the whole Vault may sink and close by its own Weight epually, into its right Seat: Otherwise in drying, the Work would not compact itself as it ought, but would be apt to leave Cracks when it came afterwards to settle. And therefore you must not quite take away the Centre immediately, but let it down easily Day after Day, by little and little, for Fear, if you should take it away too soon, the Building should never duly cement. But after a certain Number of Days, according to the Greatness of the Work, ease it a little, and so go on gradually, till the Wedges all compact themselves in their Places, and are perfectly settled. The best Way of letting down the Frame is this: When you place your Centre upon the Pilasters, or whatever else it is to rest upon, put under each of its Feet two Wedges of Wood; aud when afterwards you want to let it down, you may with a Hammer safely drive out these Wedges by little and little, as you shall judge proper.

Lastly, it is my Opinion, that the Centres ought not to be taken away till after Winter, as well for other Reasons, as because the Washing of the Rains may weaken and demolish the whole Structure; though else we cannot do greater Service to a Vault than to give it Water enough, and to let it be thoroughly soak'd, that it may never feel Thirst. But of this Subject we have said enough.

Chap. XV.

Of the Shell of the Covering, and its Usefulness; the different Sorts and Shapes of Tiles, and what to make them of.

I Now come to cover the Roof. And certainly, if we weigh the Matter duly, there is no Convenience in the whole Building greater than the having Shelter from the burning Sun, and the inclement Seasons; and this is a Benefit which you owe the Continuance of, not to the Wall, nor to Area, nor any of these; but principally to the outward Shell of the Roof; which all the Art and Industry of Man, though they have tried all Means, has not yet been able to make so strong and impenetrable against the Weather as might be wish'd: Nor do I think, it will be an easy Matter to do it; for where, not only Rains, but Extremes of Heat and Cold, and above all, blustering Storms of Wind, are continually assaulting the same Place; what Materials are strong enough to resist such unwearied and powerful Adversaries? Hence it happens, that some Coverings presently rot, others open, others oppress the Wall, some crack, or break, others are washed away; insomuch, that even Metals, which are so hardy against the Weather, in other Places, are not here able to hold out against such frequent Assaults. But Men not despising such Materials as Nature furnished them with in their respective Countries, have provided against these Inconveniences as well as they were able; and hence arose various Methods of Covering in a Building. *Vitruvius* tells us, that the *Pyrgenses* covered their Houses with Reeds, and the People of *Marseilles* with Clay kneaded, and mixed with Straw. The *Chelonophagi*, near the *Garamantes*, *Pliny* tells us, cover'd theirs with the Shells of Tortoises. The greatest Part of *Germany* use Shingles. In *Flanders* and *Picardy*, they cut a white Sort of Stone which they have (which Saws easier than Wood itself) into their Scantlings, which they use instead of Tiles. The *Genoueze*, and *Florentines* use thin Pieces of a scaly Sort of Stone. Others have tried the Pargets, which we shall speak of by and by. But after having made Experiment of every Thing, the Wit and Invention of Man has found out nothing yet more convenient than Tiles of baked Clay. For all Sorts of Parget grow rugged in Frosts, and so crack and break: Lead is melted by the Sun's Heat: Brass, if laid in thick Plates, is very costly; and if it is thin, it is apt to warp, and to be eaten and consumed with Rust.

One *Grinias* of *Cyprus*, the Son of a Peasant, is said to be the Inventer of Tiles, which are of two Sorts, the one broad and flat, one Foot broad, and a Foot and a half long, with

with Rims of each Side, a ninth Part of its Breadth, which is call'd a Gutter-tile; the other round, like Greaves, (a Piece of Armour for the Legs,) which is called a Ridge-tile; both broader in that Part which is to receive the Rain, and narrower in that from which they are to difcharge it. But the Plain, or Gutter-tiles are the moft Commodius, provided they are laid exactly even, fo as not to lean of either Side, nor to make either Vallies or Hilocks to ftop the Current of the Water, or to let it fettle in, nor to leave any Cranny uncover'd. If the Superficies of the Roof is very large, it requires bigger Gutter-tiles, that the Rain may not overflow them for want of a fufficient Receptacle. To prevent the Fury of the Wind from ripping off the Tiles, I would have them all faftened with Mortar; efpecially in publick Buildings: But in private Ones, it will be enough if you fecure only the Gutter-tiles from that Violence, becaufe whatever Mifchief is done, is eafily repair'd. There is another very convenient Way of Tiling, in this Manner: If in Timber Roofs, inftead of Planks, you lay along the Girders Squares of baked Clay, faften'd with Plaifter of *Paris*, and over thefe Squares lay your Tiles with Mortar, it will be a Covering very fecure againft Fire, and very commodious to the Inhabitants; and it will be lefs expenfive, if, inftead of Squares, you underlay it with Reeds, bound with Mortar. I would not have you ufe your Tiles, and efpecially thofe which you lay with Mortar, in publick Works, till they have fupported the Froft and Sun two Years; becaufe, if you happen to ufe any bad ones, there is no taking them out again without a good deal of Trouble and Expence. It may not be amifs here to mention what I have read in *Diodorus* the Hiftorian, relating to the famous hanging Gardens in *Syria*, which were contrived with a new, and not unufeful Invention: For upon the Beams they laid Rufhes dawb'd over with Pitch, and on thefe two Rows of baked Bricks, one above the other, cemented with Mortar; and in the third Place, they laid Plates of Lead fo difpofed, and faften'd together, that not the leaft wet could penetrate to the Brick.

CHAP. XVI.

Of Pavements according to the Opinion of Pliny *and* Vitruvius, *and the Works of the Ancients; and of the proper Seafons for Beginning and Finifhing the feveral Parts of Building.*

WE come now to treat of Pavements, which alfo partake fomewhat of the Nature of Coverings. Of thefe, fome are open to the Air; others are laid upon Rafters and Boards, others not: All require for their Foundation a folid, and even Superficies, laid exactly according to their proper Lines. Thofe which are open to the Air ought to be raifed in fuch a Manner, that every ten Foot may have a Declivity of, at leaft, two Inches, to throw off the Water, which ought to be conveyed from thence either into Cifterns or Sinks. If from thefe Sinks you have not the Conveniency of a Drain, either into the Sea, or fome River, dig Pits for the Soil in convenient Places, fo deep as to come to fome Spring of Water, and then fill up thofe Pits with round Pebbles.

LASTLY, if you have no Opportunity to do this, make good large Sinks, and fling Coals into them, and then fill them up with Sand, which will fuck up, and dry away the fuperfluous Moifture. If the Superficies that your Pavement is to be laid upon, is a foft loofe Earth, ram it foundly, and lay it over with broken Fragments of Stone, well beat in with the Rammer alfo: But if the Pavement is to be upon Rafters, cover them over with Boards, and upon them lay your Rubbifh or Fragments of Stone a Foot high, and beaten together, and confolidated with the Rammer. Some are of Opinion, that under thefe we ought to lay Fern, or Spart, to keep the Mortar from rotting the Timber. If your Rubbifh is of new Stone, allow one Part of Mortar to three of Rubbifh; if it is of old, you muft allow two Parts in five; and when it is laid, the Way to ftiffen it, is to pound it heartily with the Rammer. Over thefe you lay a Plaifter fix Inches high, made of broken Tiles, or Bricks pounded, mix'd with one fourth Part of Mortar; and upon this, laftly, you lay your Pavement, of whatfoever Sort it is, whether of Brick or Tile, exactly by Rule and Level. The Work will be more ſecure ſtill, if between the Rubbiſh, and the Plaiſter you lay a Row of plain Tiles cemented with Mortar, mixed up with Oil. As for Pavements which are not to be expoſed to the open Air. *Varro* directs us to make them in the following Manner, which he tells us will be very ſerviceable by means of its extraordinary Dryneſs: Dig two Foot deep into the Ground, then ram the Bottom ſoundly, and lay a Pavement, either of Rubbiſh, or broken Brick, leaving Vent-holes for the Vapours to diſcharge themſelves; over this lay Coals well levell'd, and ramm'd down, and over all a Cruſt made of Sand, Mortar, and Aſhes. Theſe Things already mention'd, we have gathered from *Pliny* and *Vitruvius* eſpecially: I will now ſet down what I have with great Pains and Labour diſcovered relating to Pavements from the actual Works of the Ancients; from whence, I confeſs, I have learnt much more than from their Writings. We will begin with the Outward Shell, which it is very difficult to make, ſo as it ſhall not rot, or crack: For when once it has been thoroughly ſoak'd with wet, and comes to dry again, either by Sun, or Wind, it dries by Scales, and as we ſee in Mud left after Floods, the upper Coat ſhrinks, and leaves Cracks which cannot be filled up; for thoſe Parts which are dried and hardened, cannot be made to cohere again by any Art whatſoever, and thoſe which are ſtill moiſt, yield and give Way to the leaſt Violence. I find the Ancients made their Shell either of baked Earth, or of Stone; and where Mens Feet were not to tread, they made their Tiles ſometimes a Foot and a half every Way, cemented with Mortar mixed up with Oil; we alſo ſometimes meet with ſmall Bricks one Inch in Thickneſs, two in Breadth, and four in Length, join'd Sideways like a Fiſh's Backbone. We often find Pavements of very large Slabs of Marble, and others again of ſmaller Pieces, and little Squares. There are other Ancient Pavements made all of one Piece, which I ſuppoſe, was a Mixture of Lime, Sand, and pounded Brick, of each a third Part: which may be made more ſtrong and laſting yet, by the Addition of one fourth Part of *Tyber*-Stone, beat to Powder. Others in this Sort of Plaiſter mightily commend the Sand of *Pozzuolo*, which they call *Rapillo*. Plaiſter that is deſigned for Pavements muſt be tried by continual beating, whereby it will daily acquire greater Stiffneſs and Hardneſs, till it comes to be in a Manner firmer than Stone itſelf: And it is certain, that if this Plaiſter is ſprinkled with Lime-water, and Linſeed-oil, it will grow almoſt as hard as Glaſs, and defy all Manner of Weather. Mortar worked up with Oil, is ſaid in Pavements to keep out every Thing that is noxious. Under the Shell I obſerve they made a Layer of Mortar, and ſmall Pieces of broken Brick, of the Thickneſs of two or three Inches. Next to this we find a Courſe of Rubbiſh, of Bits of Bricks and Chippings of Stone, ſuch as the Maſons cut off with their Chizzel, and this is about a Foot in Thickneſs. In ſome Places betwixt theſe two Courſes, we find a regular one of baked Tile, or Brick, and at the Bottom of all a Layer of Stones, none bigger than a Man's Fiſt. The Stones found in Rivers, which are called Male ones, as for Inſtance, thoſe round ones which partake of the Nature of Flint, or Glaſs, grow dry immediately when they are taken out of the Water, whereas Brick and ordinary Stone retain Moiſture a long Time; for which Reaſon, many affirm that the Damps which ariſe out of the Earth will never be able to penetrate to the Shell of the Pavement, if it is underlaid with thoſe Stones. We ſometimes find that they made little ſquare Pilaſters a Foot and a half high next to the Ground, ſtanding about two Foot diſtance one from the other, upon which they laid baked Tiles, and upon theſe the Pavement abovemention'd. But this Kind of Pavement belongs chiefly to Baths; of which we ſhall treat in their proper Place. Pavements delight in Damps, and a wet Air, while they are making, and endure beſt and longeſt in moiſt and ſhady Places; and their chief Enemies are the Looſeneſs of the Earth, and ſudden Droughts. For as repeated Rains make the Ground cloſe and firm, ſo Pavements being heartily wetted, grow compact, and hard as Iron. That Part of the Pavement which is to receive the Water falling from the Gutters, ought to be made of the largeſt and ſoundeſt Stones, ſuch as will not eaſily be worn away by the continual Malice (if we may ſo call it) of the Spouts that fall upon them. In ſuch Pavements as are laid upon Timber-work, or Roofing, you muſt take Care that the Ribs upon which it reſts are ſufficiently ſtrong, and equal one to the other; for if it ſhould be otherwiſe, or one Wall, or Rafter which it lies upon, ſhould be ſtronger than another, the Pavement would decay and ſplit in that Part; for as Timber-work will not always keep exactly in the ſame Condition, but

but is affected and altered by the Variety of Weather, being ſwell'd by wet, and dried and ſhrunk by Heat, it is no Wonder that the weaker Parts ſhould ſink under the Weight, and ſo crack the Pavement. But of this we have ſaid enough.

HOWEVER, I will not paſs over one Thing which is not at all foreign to our Purpoſe, namely, that different Times and Seaſons, and Diſpoſitions of the Air, are proper for digging the Foundations, filling them up, raiſing the Wall, turning of Vaults, and finiſhing the Shells. The Foundations are beſt dug while the Sun is in *Leo*, and in *Autumn*, the Ground being then thoroughly dry, which will keep your Trench from being infeſted with Water. The Spring is very convenient for filling them up, eſpecially if they are pretty deep; becauſe they will be ſufficiently defended from the Heat of the Summer, by means of the Ground which ſtands about them as their Protector; though it will be ſtill more convenient to fill them up in the Beginning of Winter, unleſs in Countries near the Pole, or in ſuch cold Climates where they will be likely to freeze before they are dry. The Wall too abhors both exceſſive Heat, exceſſive Cold, and ſudden Froſts, and eſpecially Northerly Winds. Vaults, till they are dry and ſettled, require an equal and temperate Seaſon, more than any other Sort of Structure. The beſt Time for laying on the Coat is about the riſing of the Stars, call'd the *Pleiadas*, (which is in Spring) and particularly ſuch Days as have been ſufficiently moiſtened with ſoutherly Breezes; for if the Work which you are to plaiſter over, or white-waſh, is not extreamly moiſt, nothing that you lay on will ſtick to it, but it will part and crack, and always look rough and ſcandalous. But of Plaiſtering and Stuc-work we ſhall treat more largely in its proper Place. Having now gone through the general Conſideration of our Subject, it remains that we deſcend to Particulars; and accordingly we deſign to ſhew firſt the different Sorts of Buildings, and the Qualities requiſite in each of them; then their Ornaments; and laſtly, how to remedy ſuch Defects in them as are owing either to the Fault of the Workman, or the Injury of Time.

The End of Book III.

THE

ARCHITECTURE

OF

Leone Batista Alberti.

Book IV. Chap. I.

Of Works of a publick Nature. That all Buildings, whether contrived for Necessity, Conveniency or Pleasure, were intended for the Service of Mankind. Of the several Divisions of humane Conditions, whence arises the Diversity of Buildings.

IT is plain that Building was invented for the Service of Mankind; for if we consider the Matter ever so little, it is natural to suppose that their first Design was only to raise a Structure that might defend them and theirs from the ill Qualities of the Weather; afterwards they proceeded to make not only every Thing that was necessary to their Safety, but also every Thing that might be convenient or useful to them. At last, instructed and allured by the Opportunities that naturally offer'd themselves, they began to contrive how to make their Buildings subservient to their Pleasures and Recreations, and proceeded every Day further and further in so doing: So that if upon considering the various Sorts of Buildings, we should say, that some were contrived by Necessity, some by Convenience, and some by Pleasure, it might, perhaps, be no ill Definition of the Matter. Yet when we take a View of the great Plenty and Variety of Buildings all about us, we easily perceive that all were not erected merely upon those Accounts, or for one Occasion more than another, but that this great Variety and Difference among them, are owing principally to the Variety there is among Mankind. So that, if according to our Method we would make a careful Enquiry into their Sorts and Parts, it is here that we must begin our Disquisition, namely, from the Nature of Mankind, and wherein they differ from one another; since upon their Account it is that Buildings are erected, and for their Uses varied: So that having thoroughly considered these Things, we may treat of them more clearly. For this Purpose, it will not be amiss to recollect the Opinions of the wise Founders of ancient Republicks and Laws concerning

cerning the Divifion of the People into different Orders; in as much as they applied themfelves to the Confideration of thefe Things with the greateft Care, Diligence and Application, and have received the higheft Applaufes for their Difcoveries.

Plutarch tells us, that *Thefeus* divided the Commonwealth into two Ranks, one that made and expounded the Laws, both Humane and Divine, and the other that follow'd manual Occupations. *Solon* diftinguifh'd his Citizens according to their Wealth, and fuch as did not raife from their Poffeffions three hundred Bufhels of Grain every Year, he reckon'd fcarce worthy to be efteem'd a Citizen. The *Athenians* gave the firft Rank to Men of Learning and Wifdom; the fecond to the Orators, and the laft to Artificers. *Romulus* feparated the Knights and *Patricians* from the *Plebeians*; and *Numa* divided the *Plebeians* according to their refpective Employments. In *France* the *Plebeians* were in a Manner Slaves; the reft, fays *Cæfar*, were either Soldiers, or Profeffors of Religion, or the Study of Wifdom, whom they call'd *Druids*. Among the *Panchæi* the firft were the Priefts; the fecond, the Husbandmen, and the laft, the Soldiers, with whom were reckon'd the Shepherds, and Tenders of Herds. The *Britons* were divided into four Orders; the firft were thofe out of whofe Number they chofe their King; the fecond were the Priefts; the third, the Soldiers, and the laft the common People. The *Ægyptians* gave the firft Rank to their Priefts; the fecond to their King and Governours; the third to the Soldiers, and the reft of the People were fubdivided into Husbandmen, Shepherds, and Artificers, and further, as *Herodotus* informs us, into Mercenaries, and Seamen. We are told, that *Hipodamus* divided his Republic into three Parts, Artificers, Husbandmen, and Soldiers. *Ariftotle* feems not difpleafed with thofe who feparated from the Multitude fome Men of greateft Worth to manage their Counfels, and exercife their Office of Magiftracy and Judicature, and divided the Remainder of the People into Husbandmen, Artificers, Merchants, Mercenaries, Horfe, Foot and Seamen. Not much unlike this, according to *Diodorus* the Hiftorian, was the Commonwealth of the *Indians*, who were diftinguifhed into Priefts, Husbandmen, Shepherds, Artificers, Soldiers, Ephori, or Super-intendants, and thofe who prefided over the publick Counfels.

Plato obferves that a Nation is fometimes peaceable and defirous of Quiet and Repofe; and at other Times reftlefs and warlike, according to the Temper of thofe at the Helm; and therefore he divides the Body of the Citizens according to the Parts of the Mind of Man; one to moderate every Thing with Reafon and Counfel; another to refent and repel Injuries with Force; and a third to prepare and adminifter Nourifhment to all the reft. Thefe Things I have thus briefly recited out of numorous Writings of the Ancients; and the natural Refult feems to be this, that all thefe which I have mentioned are every one of them different Parts of the Republick, and confequently that each requires a particular Kind of Building. But that according to our Cuftom we may be able to treat of this Subject more diftinctly, it will not be amifs to reflect upon the following Confiderations: If any one were to feparate the whole Number of Mankind into different Parts, the firft Thing that would offer itfelf to his Thoughts would be this; that it is not the fame Thing to confider all the Inhabitants of any one Province all together collectively, and to confider them feparately according to their refpective Diftinctions; and the next Thing would be, that by a Contemplation of Nature itfelf, he would take Notice in what Particular they differ'd moft from one another, that from thence he might take Occafion to feparate them into their proper Divifions. Now there is nothing wherein Men differ more one from the other, than in the very particular wherein they differ from Brutes; namely, in Reafon, and the Knowledge of ufeful Arts, to which, if you pleafe, you may add Profperity of Fortune: In all which Gifts there are very few that excel at the fame Time. This then opens to us our firft Divifion, and inftructs us to felect from the Multitude, a fmall Number, whereof fome are illuftrious for their Wifdom, Experience and Capacity; others for their Progrefs, and Knowledge in ufeful Arts; and others, laftly, for their Riches, and Abundance in the Goods of Fortune. And who will deny that thefe are the moft fit to be intrufted with the principal Offices in the Commonwealth? The moft excellent Perfons, therefore, who are endued with the greateft Share of Wifdom, ought to be intrufted with the chief Care and Power of moderating in all Affairs. Such will order the ſacred Ceremonies with religious Minds, and frame Laws with Juſtice and Equity, and themſelves ſet the Example of Living orderly and happily. They will watch continually for the Defence and Enlargement of the Authority and Dignity of their Fellow-Citizens. And when they have determined upon any Thing convenient, uſeful, or neceſſary; being perhaps themſelves worn out with Years, and fitter for Contemplation than Action, they will commit the Execution of it to ſuch as they know to be well experienced, and brisk and courageous to bring the Matter to effect, to whom they will give an Opportunity of deſerving well of their Country, by the Proſecution of their Deſign. Then theſe others, having taken the Buſineſs upon themſelves, will faithfully perform their Parts at home with Study and Application, and abroad with Diligence and Labour, giving Judgment, leading Armies, and exerciſing their own Induſtry, and that of thoſe who are under them. And laſtly, as it is in vain to think of effecting any Thing without Means, the next in Place to thoſe already mentioned are ſuch as ſupply theſe with their Wealth, either by Husbandry or Merchandize. All the other Orders of Men ought in Reaſon to obey and be ſubſervient to theſe as chief. Now if any Thing is to be gather'd from all this to our Purpoſe, it is certainly that of the different Kinds of Building, one Sort belongs to the Publick, another to the principal Citizens, and another to the Commonality.

And again, among the principal Sort, one is proper for thoſe who bear the Weight of the publick Counſels and Deliberations, another for thoſe who are employ'd in the Execution, and another for ſuch as apply themſelves to the amaſſing of Wealth. Of all which one Part, as we obſerved before, having Relation to Neceſſity, and another to Convenience; it will be no Preſumption in us who are treating of Buildings to allow another Part to Pleaſure, while inſtead of claiming any Merit upon this Account to ourſelves, we confeſs that the Principles of this Diviſion are to be drawn from the firſt Rudiments of the Philoſophers.

Of this, therefore, we are now to treat, what belongs to a publick Building, what to thoſe of the principal Citizens, and what to thoſe of the common Sort. But where ſhall we begin ſuch great Matters? Shall we follow the gradual Courſe of Mankind in their procuring of all theſe, and ſo beginning with the mean Huts of poor People, go on by degrees to thoſe vaſt Structures which we ſee of Theatres, Baths, and Temples. It is certain it was a great while before Mankind encloſed their Cities with Walls. Hiſtorians tell us that when *Bacchus* made his Progreſs thro' *India*, he did not meet with one walled Town; and *Thucydides* writes, that formerly there were none in *Greece* itſelf: And in *Burgundy*, a Province of *Gaul*, even in *Cæſar*'s Time, there were no Towns encompaſs'd with Walls, but the People dwelt up and down in Villages. The firſt City I find any Mention of is *Biblus*, belonging to the *Phœnicians*, which *Saturn* girt in with a Wall drawn round all their Houſes: Whatever *Pomponius Mela* may ſay of *Joppa* built even before the Flood. *Herodotus* informs us, that while the *Æthiopians* had Poſſeſſion of *Ægypt*, they never puniſh'd any Criminal with Death, but obliged him to raiſe the Earth all round the Village he lived in; and this, they ſay, was the firſt Beginning of Cities in *Ægypt*. But we ſhall ſpeak of them in another Place. And though it muſt be confeſs'd that all humane Inventions take their Riſe from very ſmall Beginnings, yet I intend here to begin with the Works of the greateſt Perfection.

Chap. II.

Of the Region, Place, and Conveniencies and Inconveniencies of a Situation for a City, according to the Opinion of the Ancients, and that of the Author.

All the Citizens are concerned in every Thing of a publick Nature that makes Part of the City: And if we are convinced of what the Philoſophers teach, that the Occaſion and Reaſon of Building Cities is that the Inhabitants may dwell in them in Peace, and, as far as poſſibly may be, free from all Inconveniencies and Moleſtations, then certainly it requires

requires the moſt deliberate Conſideration in what Place or Situation, and with what Circuit of Lines it ought to be fix'd. Concerning theſe Things there have been various Opinions.

Cæſar writes, that the *Germans* accounted it the greateſt Glory to have vaſt uninhabited Deſarts for their Confines: Becauſe they thought theſe Deſarts ſecured them againſt ſudden Irruptions from their Enemies. The Hiſtorians ſuppoſe that the only Thing which deterr'd *Seſoſtris*, King of *Ægypt*, from leading his Army into *Æthiopia* was the Want of Proviſions, and the Difficulty of the Places through which he muſt march. The *Aſſyrians* being defended by their Deſarts and Marſhes, never fell under the Dominion of any foreign Prince. They ſay, that the *Arabians* too wanting both Water and Fruits, never felt the Aſſaults, or Injuries of any Enemies. *Pliny* ſays that *Italy* has been ſo often infeſted with Armies of Barbarians only for the Sake of her Wines and Figs: We may add that the too great Plenty of ſuch Things as ſerve only to Luxury, are very prejudicial, as *Crates* teaches, both to Young and Old; becauſe it is apt to make the Latter cruel, and the Former effeminate.

Livy tells us, that among the *Æmerici* there is a Region wonderfully fruitful, which as it generally happens in rich Soils, engenders a very cowardly weak Race of Men; whereas on the contrary the *Ligii*, who dwelt in a ſtony Country, being forced to conſtant Labour, and to live with great Frugality, were extremely robuſt and induſtrious. The State of Things being ſo, it is probable ſome may not diſlike theſe barren difficult Places for fixing a City in; tho' others again may be of a contrary Opinion, deſiring to enjoy all the Benefits and Gifts of Nature, and to want nothing that may contribute either to Neceſſity or Pleaſure; and for the right uſing of theſe Benefits, the Fathers may provide by Laws and Statutes. And they think the Conveniencies of Liſe are much more pleaſing when they may be had at home, than when they are obliged to fetch them from abroad: for which Reaſon, they deſire ſuch a Soil as *Varro* tells us is to be found near *Memphis*, which enjoys ſo favourable a Climate, that all the Trees even the Vines themſelves, never drop their Leaves the whole Year round: or ſuch a one as is under Mount *Taurus* in thoſe Parts which look to the North, where *Strabo* ſays the Bunches of Grapes are three Foot long, and that every ſingle Vine Tree yields half a Barrel of Wine, and one Fig Tree an hundred and forty Pound Weight of Figs; or ſuch a one as is in *India*, or the *Hyperborean* Iſland in the Ocean, where *Herodotus* tells us they gather their Fruits twice every Year; or like that of *Portugal*, where the Seeds that fall by chance yields ſeveral Harveſts, or rather like *Talge*, in the *Caſpian* Mountains, where the Earth brings forth Corn without Tillage. But theſe Things are uncommon, and rather to be wiſh'd for than had. And therefore the wiſe Ancients who have written upon this Subject, either from their own Obſervations, or the Books of others, are of Opinion, that a City ought to be ſo placed as to have all ſufficient Neceſſaries within its own Territory (as far as the Condition of human Affairs will permit) without being obliged to ſeek them abroad; and that the Circuit of its Confines ought to be fortified, that no Enemy can eaſily make an Irruption upon them, though at the ſame time they may ſend out Armies into the Countries of their Neighbours, whatever the Enemy can do to prevent it; which is a Situation that they tell us will enable a City not only to defend its Liberty, but alſo to enlarge the Bounds of its Dominion. But after all, what ſhall we ſay? No Place ever had thoſe Advantages more than *Ægypt*, which was ſo ſtrongly fortified in all its Parts, as to be in a Manner inacceſſible, having on one Side, the Sea, and on the other a vaſt Deſart; on the right Hand ſteep Mountains; and on the Left, huge Marſhes; beſides, the Fruitfulneſs of the Soil is ſo great, that the Ancients uſed to call *Egypt* the Granary of the World, and fabled that the Gods made it their common Retreat either for Safety or Pleaſure; and yet even this Country, though ſo ſtrong, and ſo abounding in all Manner of Plenty, that it could boaſt of feeding the Univerſe, and of entertaining and harbouring the Gods themſelves, could not, as *Joſephus* informs us, always preſerve its Liberty.

THOSE therefore are entirely in the Right, who teach us, though in Fables, that human Affairs are never perfectly ſecure though laid in the Lap of *Jupiter* himſelf. Upon which Occaſion we may not improperly make uſe of the ſame Anſwer that *Plato* made when he was ask'd where that perfect Commonwealth was to be found, which he had made ſo fine a Deſcription of; that, ſays he, was not the Thing

Thing I troubled myself about; all I studied was how to frame the best that possibly could be, and that which deviates least from a Resemblance of this, ought to be preferred above all the rest. So our Design is to describe and illustrate by Examples such a City as the wisest Men judge to be in all Respects the most convenient; and in other Respects accommodating ourselves to Time and Necessity, we shall follow the Opinion of *Socrates*, that whatever cannot be alter'd but for the worse, is really best. I lay it down therefore for granted, that our City ought to be contrived as to suffer none of the Inconveniencies spoken of in the first Book, nor to want any of the Necessaries of Life. Its Territory shall be healthy, wide, pleasant, various, fruitful, secure, and abounding with Plenty of Fruits, and great Quantities of Water. It must not want Rivers, Lakes, and an open Passage to the Sea for the convenient bringing in of such Things as are wanted, and carrying out such as may be spared. All Things, in a Word, must contribute to the establishing and improving all Affairs both civil and military, whereby the Commonwealth may be a Defence to its Subjects, an Ornament to itself, a Pleasure to its Friends, and a Terror to its Enemies. I take it to be a great Happiness to any City, to be able to cultivate a good handsome Part of its Territory, in Spite of any Enemy whatsoever. Moreover your City ought to stand in the Middle of its Territory, in a Place from whence it can have a View all round its Country, and watch its Opportunities, and be ready where-ever Necessity calls, which may lie convenient for the Farmer, and Ploughman to go out to his daily Labour, and return with Ease laden with Grain and Fruits. But the Situation is one of the Things of greatest Importance, whether it should be upon an open Plain, or upon the Shore, or on a Hill: because each of these have some particular Qualities that are useful, and others on the contrary that are not so agreeable.

When *Bacchus* led his Army through *India*, the excessive Heat bred Distempers among them; whereupon he carried them up to the Hills, where the Wholesomness of the Air immediately cured them. Those that first built Cites upon Hills, seem to have done it upon Account of the Security of such a Situation; but then they generally want Water. The Plains afford great Conveniencies of Water, and of Rivers; but the Air is more gross, which makes the Summer excessively hot, and the Winter as cold; besides, being less defended against any Violence.

The Sea-shore is mighty convenient for the Importation of Merchandizes; but all Sea-towns are reckoned too fond and greedy of Novelties, and to suffer perpetual Commotions from the too great Concourse, and the Broils of Strangers, and are exposed to very dangerous Insults and Revolutions from foreign Fleets. In which soever of these Situations therefore you build your City, you should endeavour to contrive that it may partake of all the Advantages, and be liable to none of the Disadvantages. Upon a Hill I would make the Ground level, and upon a Plain I would raise it to an Eminence in that Part where my City was to be placed. And if we cannot effect this just according to our Wish, by reason of the great Variety of Places, let us make use of the following Methods to obtain at least every Thing that is necessary: On a maritime Coast, if it is a Plain, do not let the City stand too near the Sea; nor too far from it, if it is hilly. We are told that the Shores of the Sea are liable to Alteration; and that several Towns, and particularly *Baiæ* in *Italy*, have been swallow'd up by the Waves.

Pharos in *Ægypt*, which anciently was surrounded by the Sea, is now become a *Chersonesus*, or Neck of Land. *Strabo* writes, that *Tyre* and *Clazomene* underwent the same Change: Nay they tell us that the Temple of *Jupiter Hammon* stood once upon the Sea-shore, though now the Sea has left it, and it stands far within the Land. They advise us to build our City either close to the Shore, or else at a pretty good Distance from the Sea: for we find that the Winds from the Sea are heavy and sharp, by reason of their Saltness: And therefore, when they arrive at some Place at a middling Distance from the Sea, especially if it is a Plain, you will find the Air there extremely moist through the dissolving of the Salt which it took from the Sea, which makes it thick and heavy, and perfectly ropy; so that in such Places you shall sometimes see a Sort of Strings flying about in the Air like Cobwebs; And they tell us, that a Mixture of Salt has the same Effect upon the Air as it has upon Water, which it will corrupt to such a Degree as to make it stink very offensively. The Ancients, and chiefly *Plato*, are for having a City stand at ten Miles Distance from

from the Sea; but if you cannot place it ſo far off, let it be at leaſt in ſome Situation where the above-mention'd Winds cannot reach it, otherwiſe than broken, tired and purified; placing it ſo, that between it and the Sea there may ſtand ſome Hill to interrupt any noxious Vapour from thence. A Proſpect of the Sea from the Shore is wonderfully pleaſant, and is generally attended with a wholeſome Air; and *Ariſtotle* thinks thoſe Countries are moſt healthy where the Winds keep the Atmoſphere in continual Motion: but then the Sea there muſt not be weedy, with a low Beach ſcarce covered with Water; but deep with a high bold Shore of a living craggy Rock. The placing a City upon the proud Shoulders of a Mountain (if we may be allowed ſo florid an Expreſſion) contributes greatly not only to Dignity and Pleaſure, but yet more to Health. In thoſe Places where the Hills overſhadow the Sea, the Water is always deep; beſides that if any groſs Vapours do ariſe from the Sea, they ſpend themſelves before they reach ſo high; and if any ſudden Attack is made upon you from an Enemy, you lie leſs liable to be ſurprized, and more advantageouſly for defending yourſelf. The Ancients commend a Situation upon the Eaſt Side of a Hill, and in hot Countries, that Side which lies open to Northern Winds. Others perhaps may rather chuſe the Weſt Side, from this Inducement, that manured Ground lying to that Aſpect is the moſt fruitful: And indeed it is certain Hiſtorians tell us, that under Mount *Taurus*, the Side which looks to the North, is much more healthy than the others, for the very ſame Reaſon that it is alſo more fruitful. Laſtly, if we build our City upon a Hill, we ſhould take particular Care that we are not expoſed to one great Inconvenience which generally happens in ſuch a Situation, eſpecially if there are other Hills near, which raiſe their Heads above us; namely, that there is not a ſettled heavy Body of Clouds to darken and eclipſe the Day and infect the Air. We ought, beſides, to have a Care that this Situation is not expoſed to the raging Fury and Violence of Winds, and eſpecially of the North-wind; which, as *Heſiod* tells us, ſhrinks up and bends every Body, and particularly old People. It will make the Situation very bad if there is any neighbouring Rock ſtanding above the City, ſo as to throw upon it the Vapours raiſed by the Sun, or any very deep Valley reaking with unwholeſome Steams. Others adviſe that the Circuit of the Town ſhould terminate in Clifts and Precipices; but that theſe are not always ſafe againſt Earthquakes, or Storms, is ſufficiently evident from very many Towns, and particularly *Voltera* in *Tuſcany*; for the very Ground itſelf falls away in ſuch Places, and brings down after it whatſoever is built upon it.

YOU ought alſo to take particular Care that ſuch a Situation has no Hill near that riſes above it, which falling into the Hands of an Enemy, may enable him to give you continual Trouble; nor any Plain laying under it big enough to conceal an Army in Safety, and give it Time to make Lodgments and open Trenches, or to range its Forces in Order of Battle to attack you. We read that *Dedalus* built the Town of *Agrigentum*, now called *Gergento*, upon a very ſteep Rock, with a very difficult Paſſage to it, inſomuch that only three Men were ſufficient to defend it; a Fortreſs certainly very convenient, provided your Paſſage out cannot be ſtopt by the ſame Number of Men that can ſecure the Paſſage in. Men of Experience in military Affairs greatly commend the Town of *Cingoli*, built by *Labienus* in the Mark of *Ancona*; becauſe, beſides ſeveral other Advantages that it has, it will not allow of one Thing common in mountainous Situations, which is that when once you have climbed up to the Top, you then can fight upon an equal Foot; for here you are repulſed by a very high ſteep Precipice: Neither can the Enemy here waſte and deſtroy the Country round with one ſingle Excurſion, nor ſecure all the Ways at one Time, nor make a ſecure Retreat to their Camp, nor ſend out to Forage, or to get Wood or Water without Danger; whereas thoſe in the Town enjoy all the contrary Advantages; for by Means of the Hills that lie beneath them all running one into another with a great Number of little Vallies between, they can at any Time iſſue out of a ſudden to attack the Enemy unawares, and ſurprize them whenever any immediate Opportunity offers itſelf. Nor are they leſs pleaſed with *Biſſeium*, a Town of the *Marſians*, prodigiouſly ſecured by the three Rivers which meet there from different Quarters, and very difficult of Acceſs thro' the narrow Paſſes of the Vallies guarded all round with ſteep and unpaſſable Mountains: ſo that the Enemy can find no Place to fix a Camp for a Siege, and can never guard all the Paſſes, which are vaſtly convenient to thoſe in the Place for bringing in Proviſions and Succours,

 and

and making Sallies. But let this suffice as to mountainous Situations. But if you build your City in a Plain, and according to the general Practice on the Banks of a River, so perhaps as to have the Stream run through the Middle of the Town, you must have a Care that this River does not come from the South, nor run towards that Point: Because on one Side the Damps, and on the other the Cold being encreased by the Vapours of the Water, will come to you with double Violence and Unwholesomeness. But if the River flows without the Compass of the Walls, you must take a View of the Country round about, and consider on which Side the Winds have the freest Passage, that you may there erect a sufficient Wall to restrain the River within its Limits. As for other Precautions, it may not be amiss to consider what the Mariners tell us; to wit, that the Winds are naturally inclined to follow the Sun and the Eastern Breezes, when the Physicians observe, that those of the Morning are the purest, and those of the Evening the most damp: Whereas on the Contrary when they blow from the West they are heaviest at Sun-rise, and lightest at Sun-set. For these Reasons the best Position for a City will be to have the River come in from the East, and go out towards the West; because then that Breeze or gentle Wind which rises with the Sun, will carry the Vapours out of the City, if any noxious ones should arise, or at least it will not encrease them itself: However, I would rather have a River, Lake, or any other Water extend to the North than to the South, provided the Town do not stand under the Shadow of a Mountain, which is the worst Situation in the World. I will not repeat what we have said before, and we know that the South Wind is very heavy and slow in its Nature, insomuch that when the Sails of a Ship are filled with it, the Vessel seems oppressed with its Weight, and draws more Water; whereas, the North Wind on the contrary seems to lighten the Ship and the Sea too: however, it is better to keep both these at a Distance, than to have them continually beating against the Wall. Nothing is more condemned than a River flowing under high steep Banks, with a very deep stony Channel, and always shaded; because its Water is unwholsome to drink, and the Air upon it dangerous: And to avoid settling near Bogs and Marshes, or standing muddy Waters is the Part of every prudent considerate Builder. I need not mention here the Diseases occasion'd by such Neighbourhoods: We need only observe of these Places, that besides the common Nuisances in Summer of ill Smells, Fleas and other nasty Vermin, they are liable to one great Inconvenience besides, when you imagine the Air to be wholesomest and clearest (which we also took Notice of in relation to all Plains) that they are Subject to excessive Colds in Winter and excessive Heats in Summer. Lastly, we must be very sure that none of these, whether Hill, Rock, Lake, Bog, River or Well, or the like, may be so disposed as to be likely to strengthen or support an Enemy, or to bring any Manner of Inconveniencies upon your own Citizens. And this is as much as is necessary with Regard to the Region and Situation.

Chap. III.

Of the Compass, Space and Bigness of the City, of the Form and Disposition of the Walls and Fortifications, and of the Customs and Ceremonies observed by the Ancients in marking them out.

It is certain the Form of the City and the Distribution of its Parts must be various according to the Variety of Places; since we see it is impossible upon a Hill to lay out an Area whether round or square, or of any other regular Form, with that Ease, that you may upon an open Plain. The ancient Architects in encompassing their Towns with Walls, condemn'd all Angles jutting out from the naked of the Wall, as thinking they help the Enemy more in their Assault than the Inhabitants in their Defence; and that they were very weak against the Shocks of military Engines; and indeed for Treacheries, and for the safer throwing their Darts they are of some Advantage to the Enemy, especially where they can run up to the Walls, and withdraw again immediately to their Camp; but yet they are sometimes of very great Service in Towns seated upon Hills, if they are set just answering to to the Streets. At the famous City *Perusia*, which has several little Towers placed here and there upon the Hills, like the Fingers of a Man's Hand extending out, if the Enemy offers to attack one of the Angles with a good Number of Men, he can find no Place to begin his Assault, and being obliged to march under those Towers, is not able to withstand the Weapons that will be cast, and the Sallies made upon him. So that the same Method for walling of Towns will not serve in all Places. Moreover the Ancients lay it down for a Rule, that Cities and Ships should by no means be either so big as to look empty, nor so little as to be crowded. Others are for having their Towns full and close, believing that it adds to their Safety: Others, feeding themselves with great Hopes of Times to come, delight in having a vast deal of Room: Others, perhaps, have an Eye to the Fame and Honour of Posterity. The City of the *Sun*, built by *Busiris*, and call'd *Thebes*, as Histories inform us, was twenty Miles in Circuit; *Memphis*, eighteen Miles, six Furlongs; *Babylon*, three and forty Miles, six Furlong; *Nineveh*, threescore Miles; and some Towns enclosed so much Ground, that even within the Walls they could raise Provisions for the whole Year. But, I think, there is a great deal of Wisdom in the old Proverb, which tells us, that we ought in all Things to avoid excess; though if I were to commit an Error of either Side, I should rather chuse that Proportion which would allow of an Encrease of Citizens, than that which is hardly sufficient to contain the present Inhabitants. Add to this, that a City is not built wholly for the Sake of Shelter, but ought to be so contrived, that besides mere civil Conveniencies there may be handsome Spaces left for Squares, Courses for Chariots, Gardens, Places to take the Air in, for Swimming, and the like, both for Ornament and Recreation.

WE read in the Ancients *Varro*, *Plutarch* and others, that their Forefathers us'd to design the Walls of their Town with abundance of religious Rites and Ceremonies. After the repeated taking of Auspices they yoked a Bull and a Cow together to draw a brazen Plough, with which they traced out the Line that was to be the Circuit of the Wall, the Cow being placed on the Inside, and the Bull without. The Fathers and Elders that were to dwell in the Town followed the Plough, laying all the Clods of Earth into the Furrow again inward, so that none might lie scattering outward, and when they came to those Places where the Gates were to be, they lifted up the Plough and carried it in their Hands, that the Groundsell of the Gates might remain untouch'd; and for this Reason they esteem'd the whole Circle of the Wall to be sacred, all except the Gates, which were by no means to be called so.

In the Days of *Romulus*, *Dionysius* of *Halicarnassus*, tells us, that the Fathers in Beginning their Towns, used, after performing a Sacrifice, to kindle Fires before their Tents, and to make the People pass through them, believing that they were purged and purified by the Flame; and they held it unlawful to admit any Body to this Ceremony that was polluted or unclean. This is what we find to have been the Custom of those Nations. In other Places they used to mark out the Foundation of their Walls by strowing all the Way a Dust made of white Earth, which they called *pure*; and *Alexander*, upon laying out the Town of *Pharos*, for want of this Earth made use of Meal. From these Ceremonies the Diviners took Occasion to foretell what should happen in Times to come; for noting the Nativity, as we may call it, of the City, and some Events that seemed to have some Connection with it, they imagined they might thence draw Predictions of its future Successes. The *Hetrurians* too in the Books of their Ceremonies taught this Art of foretelling the Fortune of Towns from the Day of their Nativities; and this not from the Observation of the Heavens, which we mentioned in the Second Book, but from Principles and Conjectures founded upon present Circumstances. *Censorinus* informs us, that the Method they taught was this: Such Men as happened to be born the very same Day that the City was begun, and lived the Longest of any one born on that Day, were reckoned by their Death to put a Period to the first Age of that City; next, the longest Liver of those that dwelt in the City; at that Time, when they died concluded the second Age; and so for the other Ages. Then they supposed that the Gods generally sent Omens to point out the Conclusion of each particular Age. These were the Superstitions which they taught; and they add that the *Hetrurians* by these Prognosticks could certainly fix every Age of their City, which they determined to to be as follows; their first four Ages they made an hundred Years each; the Fifth, an hundred and Twenty-three; the Sixth, an hundred and Twenty, and as many the Seventh;

Seventh; the Eighth was the Time they then lived in under the Emperors, and the Ninth was to come; and by theſe Prognoſticks they thought it no hard Matter to diſcover even the Events of future Ages. They conjectured that *Rome* ſhould come to be Miſtreſs of the World, from this Symptom, namely, becauſe a Man born on the Day of her Foundation became in Time her Maſter. And this Man, I find, was *Numa*: for *Plutarch* informs us, that on the Nineteenth of *April*, *Rome* was begun, and *Numa* born. But the *Spartans* gloried in having no Walls at all about their City; for confiding in the Valour and Fortitude of their Citizens, they thought there was no Occaſion for any Fortification beſides good Laws. The *Ægyptians* and *Perſians*, on the contrary, encloſed their Cities with the ſtrongeſt Walls; for not to mention others, *Nineveh* and *Semiramis* made the Walls of their Towns ſo thick, that two Chariots might paſs upon the Top abreaſt, and ſo high, that they were above an hundred Cubits. *Arrian* relates that the Walls of *Tyre* were an hundred and Fifty Foot high. Some again have not been ſatisfied with one Wall: The *Carthaginians* encloſed their City with Three; and *Herodotus* writes that *Deioces* fortified his Town of *Ecbatana*, though it was ſeated upon an Hill with Seven. Now as it is certain that Walls are a very powerful Defence both of our Perſons and Liberties, when the Enemy happens to be ſuperior either in Number or Fortune, I cannot join in with thoſe who are for having their City quite naked without any Wall, neither with ſuch as ſeem to place all their Hopes of Defence in their Wall alone. I agree with what *Plato* obſerves, that every City ſtands continually expoſed to the Danger of being brought under Subjection; ſince, whether it be owing to Nature or Cuſtom, neither publick Bodies nor private Perſons can ever ſet Bounds to their inſatiable Deſire of getting and poſſeſſing ſtill more and more; from which one Source ariſes all the Miſchiefs of War. So that what is there to be ſaid againſt adding Security to Security, and Fortification to Fortification? From what has been already ſaid, we may conclude that of all Cities, the moſt Capacious is the round One; and the moſt Secure, that which is encompaſſed with Walls broken here and there into Angles or Baſtions jutting out at certain Diſtances, as *Tacitus* informs us *Jeruſalem* was: Becauſe it is certain, the Enemy cannot come up to the Wall between two Angles jutting out, without expoſing themſelves to very great Danger; nor can their military Engines attack the Heads of thoſe Angles with any Hopes of Succeſs. But, however, we ſhould be ſure to make uſe of all the natural Advantages that offer themſelves for the Security of our Town or Fortification; as we may obſerve the Ancients did, according to the Opportunity or Neceſſity of the Situation. Thus *Antium*, an ancient City of the *Latins*, in order to embrace the Winding of the Shore, appears from the old Ruins which are left, to have been built of a very great Length. *Cairo*, upon the *Nile*, is ſaid alſo to be a very long City. *Palimbrota*, a City of *India*, belonging to the *Graſii*, as *Metaſthenes* informs us, was ſixteen Miles long, and three broad, running along the Side of the River. We read that the Walls of *Babylon* were ſquare; and thoſe of *Memphis* built in Shape of a D. But whatever Shape is choſen for the Walls, *Vegetius* thinks it ſufficient for Service, if they are ſo broad, that two armed Soldiers poſted there for Defence, may eaſily paſs without being in one anothers Way; and ſo high, that they cannot be ſcaled with Ladders; and built ſo firm and ſtrong, as not to yield to the battering Rams and other Engines. The military Engines are of two Sorts; one Sort are thoſe which break and demoliſh the Wall by Battery; the other are ſuch as attack and undermine the Foundation, and ſo bring down the Superſtructure. Now the greateſt Security againſt both theſe, is not ſo much a Wall as a good Ditch. The Wall is of no Uſe in the laſt Caſe, unleſs its Foundation lies under Water, or upon a ſolid Rock. The Ditch ought to be very broad and very deep; for then it will hinder the moveable Tortoiſe-ſhell, Towers, or other ſuch Machines from approaching the Wall; and when the Foundation is under Water, or on a Rock, it will be in vain to think of undermining it. It is a Diſpute among the military Men, whether it is beſt for the Ditch to be full of Water, or to be kept dry; but it is allow'd, that the firſt Thing to be conſulted is, which is moſt for the Health of the Inhabitants; and then ſome ſay thoſe Ditches are certainly beſt which are ſo contrived, that if by the Force of Battery any Part of the Wall is beaten into them, it may be ſoon removed, and the Ditch kept clear, that it may not be filled up, and ſo make a Path for the Enemy.

Chap.

CHAP. IV.

Of the Walls, Battlements, Towers, Cornishes and Gates, and the Timber-work belonging to them.

BUT to return to the Walls. The Ancients advise us to build them after this Manner. Raise two Walls one within the other, leaving between them a Space of twenty Foot, which Space is to be fill'd up with the Earth dug out of the Ditch, and well ramm'd in; and let these Walls be built in such a Manner, that you may mount from the Level of the City quite to the Top of the Battlements, by an easy Ascent, as it were by Steps. Others say, that the Earth which is dug out of the Ditch, ought to be thrown without the Wall, on the other Side of the Ditch, and there cast up into a Rampart, and from the Bottom of the Ditch a Wall should be run up, thick and strong enough to support the Weight of the aforesaid Earth which bears upon it. At a Distance from this another Wall should be raised in the Town, higher than the other, and as far from it, as to leave Space enough for the Soldiers to be drawn up, and to have Room to fight in. Besides this, you should between the principal Walls, and those within, erect other Walls crossways from one to the other, by the Help whereof, the principal Walls may unite with those behind, and more easily support the Weight of the Earth cast in between them. But indeed for my Part, I am best pleased with those Walls which are so situated, that if they happen to be at length demolished by the Force of Battery, they have somewhat of a Plain at the Foot of them, where they may lie and form a Kind of Rampart, and so be kept from filling up the Ditch with their Ruins. In other Respects I am very well pleased with *Vitruvius*, who says the Wall ought to be built thus: Within the Body of the Wall we should lay a good many Timbers of Olive-wood burnt, to the Intent that the two Sides of the Walls being fastened together by these wooden Bracers, the Work may be the more durable. Such a Wall as this, we are told by *Thucydides*, was made by the *Platæans*, to defend themselves against the People of the *Morea*, by whom they were besieged; inasmuch as they mixed Timbers among their Brick-work, and made a very stout Fortification of it. And *Cæsar* informs us, that in *France* most of their Walls were built in this Manner: They laid Beams within the Wall, and braced them together at equal Distances, filling up the Vacancies with huge Stones, so that one Beam never touched the other; and so proceeded with several Courses of Work in the same Method, till they raised a Wall of a good considerable Height. This Kind of Work was not unhandsome to the Sight, and was a very strong Fortification, because the Stones secured it against Fire, and the Timbers against the Battering Rams. But this mix'd Work others disapprove of; because they say the Lime and the Wood will not long agree together, for Timber is eaten and burnt up both by the Saltness and Heat of the Lime. Besides that, if the Wall should happen to be demolish'd by Battery, they say, that as it is thus made in a Manner all of one Piece, the whole Wall will be apt to go all together at once. In my Opinion one very good Way of Building a strong Wall, capable to stand the Shocks of Engines, is this: make triangular Projections out from the naked of the Wall, with one Angle facing the Enemy, at the Distance of every ten Cubits, and turn Arches from one Projection to the other; then fill up the Vacancies between them with Straw and Earth, well rammed down together. By this Means the Force and Violence of the Shocks of the Engines, will be deadened by the Softness of the Earth, and the Wall will not be weakned by the Battery, only here and there, and those small Breaches, or rather Holes, that are made in it, will presently be stopt up again. In *Sicily*, their Pumice-stones, which they have in great Plenty, will do extreamly well for this Kind of Work: But in other Places, for want of Pumice-stones and Earth, any soft Stone may be made use of; nor is Terrass amiss for this Purpose. Lastly, if any Part of such a Structure stands exposed to the most southerly Winds, or nocturnal Vapours, cloath and face it with a Shell of Stone. And particularly it will be of great Service to let the outer Bank of the Ditch have a good Slope, and lie a pretty deal higher than the Ground beyond it: For this will baulk the Aim of the military Engines, and make them throw over the Wall. And ſome think no Wall is ſo ſafe againſt Battery, as thoſe which are built in uneven Lines, like the Teeth of a Saw.

I am very well pleaſed with thoſe Walls in *Rome*, which at about half Way up to the Top have a Walk with little private Holes, out of which, the Archers may privately annoy the Enemy, as he moves about the Field in Security; and at the Diſtance of every fifty Cubits are Towers, adjoining to the Wall like Buttreſſes, projecting out in a round Figure forwards, and ſomewhat higher than the Wall itſelf; ſo that whoever offers to approach between theſe Towers, is expoſed to be taken in Flank and ſlain; and thus the Wall is defended by theſe Towers, and the Towers mutually by one another. The Back of the Towers, which look into the Town, ought to have no Wall, but ſhould be left quite open and naked; that if the Enemy ſhould get Poſſeſſion of them, they may not be ſafe in them from the Aſſaults of the Inhabitants.

The Corniſhes of the Towers and Walls, beſides that they add to their Beauty, and are a Ligature to ſtrengthen their Work, do alſo by their Projection hinder the getting into the Town from ſcaling Ladders. Some are for leaving Precipices of deep Holes here and there along the Side of the Wall, and eſpecially near the Towers, fortified with wooden Bridges which may be preſently raiſed or let down, as Occaſion requires.

The Ancients uſed on each Side of their Gates to erect two Towers, larger than the reſt, and ſtrongly fortified on all Sides, to ſecure and protect the Entrance into the Town. There ought to be no Rooms with vaulted Roofs in the Towers, but only wooden Floors, that upon any Emergency may eaſily be removed or burnt; and thoſe Floors ſhould not be faſtened with Nails, that if the Enemy gets the better, they may be taken away without Difficulty. All that is neceſſary is to have a Covering to ſhelter the Centinels from the Storms and Injuries of the Weather. The Battlements over the Gate ſhould have Holes through the Bottom of them, through which, Stones and Firebrands may be thrown down upon the Enemy's Heads, or even Water, if they have ſet Fire to the Gate; which for its Security againſt ſuch a Misfortune, they tell us ought to be covered over with Leather and Plates of Iron. But of this, enough.

Chap. V.

Of the Proportion, Faſhion and Conſtruction of great Ways, and private Ones.

In making our Gates we ſhould obſerve, that they ought to be juſt as many in Number as the Highways, or Streets; for ſome we ſhall call High Streets, and others, private ones. Not that I intend to trouble my ſelf about the Diſtinction of the Lawyers, who ſay that the Road for Beaſts, and the Way for Men, ought to be called by different Names: But by the Name of Way, I ſhall underſtand them all. The Highways are properly thoſe by which we go into the Provinces, with our Armies and all their Baggage; for which Reaſon the Highways ought to be much broader than others, and I find the Ancients ſeldom uſed to make them leſs than eight Cubits in any Part. By a Law in the twelve Tables it was ordained, that the Ways which ran ſtrait ſhould be twelve Foot broad, and thoſe which were crooked or winding, not leſs than ſixteen. The private Ways are thoſe which leaving the publick ones, lead us to ſome Town or Caſtle, or elſe into ſome other Highway, as Lanes in Cities, and croſs Roads in the Country. There are another Kind of publick Ways, which may not improperly be called High Streets, as are ſuch which are deſigned for ſome certain Purpoſe, eſpecially any publick one; as for Inſtance, thoſe which lead to ſome Temple, or to the Courſe for Races, or to a Place of Juſtice. The Ways are not to be made in the ſame Manner in the Country, that they are in the City. In the Country they ought to be ſpacious and open, ſo as a Man may ſee all about him; free and clear from all Manner of Impediments, either of Water or Ruins; without lurking Places or Retreats of any Sort for Rogues to hide themſelves in, nor too many croſs Roads to favour their Villanies: Laſtly, they ought to be as ſtrait, and as ſhort as poſſible: I do not reckon the ſhorteſt Way to be always

always that which is the ſtraiteſt, but that which is the ſafeſt: I would rather chuſe to have it ſomewhat the longer, than to have it inconvenient. Some think the Country of *Piperno* the moſt ſecure of any, becauſe it is cut through with deep Roads almoſt like Pits, doubtful at the Entrance, uncertain in their Paſſage, and unſafe upon Account of the Ground which lies above them, from whence any Enemy may be prodigiouſly infeſted.

THE Men of beſt Experience think that Way the moſt ſecure, which is carried over the Backs of ſmall Hills, made level. Next to this are ſuch as are made through the Fields upon a high raiſed Bank, according to the Manner of the Ancients, who indeed upon that Account gave them the Name of *Aggeres*, or *Highways*. And it is certain ſuch raiſed Cauſeys have a vaſt many Conveniences: It relieves the Traveller from the Fatigue and Vexation of his Journey, to enjoy a fine Proſpect from the Heighth of the Cauſey all the Way as he travels; beſides that, it is a great Convenience to be able to perceive an Enemy at a good Diſtance, and to have ſuch an Advantage as either to be able to repel them with a ſmall Force, or to retire without Loſs, if you find they are the ſtronger. There is a great Convenience, not at all foreign to our Purpoſe, which I have obſerved in the Road that goes to the Port of *Oſtia*. As there is a vaſt Concourſe of People, and great Quantities of Merchandize brought thither from *Ægypt*, *Africa*, *Lybia*, *Spain*, *Germany*, and the Iſlands, the Road is made double, and in the Middle of it is a Row of Stones, ſtanding up a Foot high like Terms to direct the Paſſengers to go on one Side, and return on the other, ſo to avoid the Inconvenience of meeting one another.

To conclude, ſuch ſhould be the Ways out of the City; ſhort, ſtrait, and ſecure. When they come to the Town, if the City is noble and powerful, the Streets ſhould be ſtrait and broad, which carries an Air of Greatneſs and Majeſty; but if it is only a ſmall Town or a Fortification, it will be better, and as ſafe, not for the Streets to run ſtrait to the Gates; but to have them wind about ſometimes to the Right, ſometimes to the Left, near the Wall, and eſpecially under the Towers upon the Wall; and within the Heart of the Town, it will be handſomer not to have them ſtrait, but winding about ſeveral Ways, backwards and forwards, like the Coarſe of a River. For thus, beſides that by appearing ſo much the longer, they will add to the Idea of the Greatneſs of the Town, they will likewiſe conduce very much to Beauty and Convenience, and be a greater Security againſt all Accidents and Emergencies. Moreover, this winding of the Streets will make the Paſſenger at every Step diſcover a new Structure, and the Front and Door of every Houſe will directly face the Middle of the Street; and whereas in larger Towns even too much Breadth is unhandſome and unhealthy, in a ſmall one it will be both healthy and pleaſant, to have ſuch an open View from every Houſe by Means of the Turn of the Street.

Cornelius Tacitus writes, that *Nero* having widened the Streets of *Rome*, thereby made the City hotter, and therefore leſs healthy; but in other Places, where the Streets are narrow, the Air is crude and raw, and there is a continual Shade even in Summer. But further; in our winding Streets there will be no Houſe but what, in ſome Part of the Day, will enjoy ſome Sun; nor will they ever be without gentle Breezes, which whatever Corner they come from, will never want a free and clear Paſſage; and yet they will not be moleſted by ſtormy Blaſts, becauſe ſuch will be broken by the turning of the Streets. Add to all theſe Advantages, that if the Enemy gets into the Town, he will be in Danger on every Side, in Front, in Flank, and in Rear, from Aſſaults from the Houſes. So much for the publick Streets. The private ones ſhould be like the publick; unleſs there be this Difference, that they be built exactly in ſtrait Lines, which will anſwer better to the Corners of the Building, and the Diviſions and Parts of the Houſes. The Ancients in all Towns were for having ſome intricate Ways and turn-again Streets, without any Paſſage through them, that if an Enemy comes into them, he may be at a Loſs, and be in Confuſion and Suſpence; or if he puſhes on daringly, may be eaſily deſtroyed. It is alſo proper to have ſmaller ſhort Streets, running croſs from one great Street to another; not to be as a direct publick Way, but only as a Paſſage to ſome Houſe that fronts it; which will both give Light to the Houſes, and make it more difficult for an Enemy to over-run all Parts of the Town.

Q. Curtius writes that *Babylon* was divided into a great Number of ſeparate Quarters, and that

that the Buildings there did not joyn one to ano her. *Plato*, on the contrary, is ſo far from approving of thoſe Separations, that he would have the Houſes all cloſe contiguous, and that the joyning together of their Walls ſhould make a Wall to the City.

Chap. VI.

Of Bridges both of Wood and Stone, their proper Situation, their Peers, Arches, Angles, Feet, Key-ſtones, Cramps, Pavements, and Slopes.

THE Bridge, no doubt, is a main Part of the Street; nor is every Part of the City proper for a Bridge; for beſides that it is inconvenient to place it in a remote Corner of the Town, where it can be of Uſe but to few, and that it ought to be in the very Heart of the City, to lie at hand for every body; it ought certainly to be contrived in a Place where it may eaſily be erected, and without too great an Expence, and where it is likely to be the moſt durable. We ſhould therefore chuſe a Ford where the Water is not too deep; where the Shore is not too ſteep; which is not uncertain and moveable, but conſtant and laſting. We ſhould avoid all Whirlpools, Eddies, Gulphs, and the like Inconveniences common in bad Rivers. We ſhould alſo moſt carefully avoid all Elbows, where the Water takes a Turn; for very many Reaſons; the Banks in ſuch Places being very liable to be broken, as we ſee by Experience, and becauſe Pieces of Timber, Trunks of Trees, and the like, brought down from the Country by Storms and Floods, cannot ſwim down ſuch Elbows in a ſtrait Line, but turn aſlant, meet and hinder one another, and lodging againſt the Piles grow into a great Heap, which ſtops up the Arches, and with the additional Weight of the Water at length quite breaks them down.

Of Bridges, ſome are of Stone, others of Wood. We ſhall ſpeak firſt of thoſe which are of Wood, as the moſt eaſy of Execution; next we ſhall treat of thoſe which are built of Stone. Both ought to be as ſtrong as poſſible; that therefore which is built of Wood, muſt be fortified with a good Quantity of the * ſtrongeſt Timbers. We cannot give a better Example of this Sort of Bridges than that built by *Julius Cæſar*, which he gives us a Deſcription of himſelf, as follows: He faſtened together two Timbers, leaving a Diſtance between them of two Foot; their Length was proportioned to the Depth of the River, and they were a Foot and an half thick, and cut ſharp at the Ends. Theſe he let down into the River with Cranes, and drove them well in with a Sort of Rammers, not perpendicularly down like Piles, but ſlanting upwards, and giving Way according to the Current of the River. Then, oppoſite to theſe, he drove in two others, faſtened together in the ſame Manner, with a Diſtance between them at Bottom of forty Foot, ſlanting contrary to the Force and Current of the Stream. When theſe were thus fixed, he laid acroſs from one to the other, Beams of the Thickneſs of two Foot, which was the Diſtance left between the Timbers drove down; and faſtened theſe Beams at the End, each with two Braces, which being bound round and faſtened of oppoſite Sides, the Strength of the whole Work was ſo great and of ſuch a Nature, that the greater the Force of Water was which bore againſt it, the cloſer and firmer the Beams united. Over theſe other Beams were laid acroſs and faſtened to them, and a Floor, as we may call it, made over them with Poles and Hurdles. At the ſame Time, in the lower Part of the River, below the Bridge, other Timbers, or ſloping Piles, were driven down, which being faſtened to the reſt of the Structure, ſhould be a Kind of Buttreſs to reſiſt the Force of the Stream; and other Piles were alſo driven in at a ſmall Diſtance above the Bridge, and ſtanding ſomewhat above the Water, that if the Enemy ſhould ſend Trunks of Trees, or Veſſels, down the Stream, in order to break the Bridge, thoſe Piles might receive and intercept their Violence, and prevent their doing any Prejudice to the Work. All this we learn from *Cæſar*. Nor is it foreign to our Purpoſe to take Notice of what is practiced at *Verona*, where they pave their wooden Bridges with Bars of Iron, eſpecially where the Wheels of Carts and Waggons are to paſs. It remains now that we treat

* *See Plate 9, facing.*

PLATE 9. *(Page 76)*

I. Leoni delin.

B. Picart sculp. direxit 1725.

treat of the Stone-Bridge, the Parts whereof are theſe: The Banks of the Shore, the Piers, the Arches, and the Pavement. Between the Banks of the Shore and the Piers, is this Difference, that the Banks ought to be by much the ſtrongeſt, inaſmuch as they are not only to ſupport the Weight of the Arches like the Piers, but are alſo to bear the Foot of the Bridge, and to bear againſt the Weight of the Arches, to keep them from opening in any Part. We ought therefore to be very careful in the Choice of our Shore, and to find out, if poſſible, a Rock of ſolid Stone, ſince nothing can be too ſtrong that we are to intruſt with the Feet of the Bridge; and as to the Piers, they muſt be more or leſs numerous in Proportion to the Breadth of the River. An odd Number of Arches is both moſt pleaſant to the Sight, and conduces alſo to Strength; for the farther the Current of the River lies from the Shore, the freer it is from Impediment, and the freer it is the ſwifter and eaſier it flows away; for this therefore we ought to leave a Paſſage perfectly free and open, that it may not ſhake and prejudice the Piers by ſtruggling with the Reſiſtance which it meets with from them. The Piers ought to be placed in thoſe Parts of the River, where the Water flows the moſt ſlowly, and (to uſe ſuch an Expreſſion) the moſt lazily: And thoſe Parts you may eaſily find out by means of the Tides: Otherwiſe you may diſcover them in the following Manner: Imitate thoſe who threw Nuts into a River, whereby the Inhabitants of a Town beſieged, gathering them up, were preſerved from ſtarving; ſtrew the whole Breadth of the River, about fifteen hundred Paces above the Place which you intend for your Bridge, and eſpecially when the River is fulleſt, with ſome ſuch light Stuff that will eaſily float: And in thoſe Places where the Things you have thrown in Cluſters thickeſt together, you may be ſure the Current is ſtrongeſt. In the Situation of your Piers therefore avoid thoſe Places, and chuſe thoſe others to which the Things you throw in come the ſloweſt and thinneſt.

King *Mina*, when he intended to build the Bridge of *Memphis*, turned the *Nile* out of its Channel, and carried it another Way among ſome Hills, and when he had finiſhed his Building brought it back again into its old Bed. *Nicore* Queen of the *Aſſyrians*, having prepared all the Materials for building a Bridge, dug a great Lake, and into that turned the River; and as the Channel grew dry as the Lake filled, ſhe took that Time to build her Piers. Theſe mighty Things were done by thoſe great Princes: As for us, we are to proceed in the following Manner: Make the Foundations of your Piers in Autumn, when the Water is loweſt, having firſt raiſed an Incloſure to keep off the Water, which you may do in this Manner: Drive in a double Row of Stakes, very cloſe and thick ſet, with their Heads above the Top of the Water, like a Trench; then put Hurdles within this double Row of Stakes, cloſe to that Side of the Row which is next the intended Pier, and fill up the Hollow between the two Rows with Ruſhes and Mud, ramming them together ſo hard that no Water can poſſibly get through. Then whatever you find within this Incloſure, Water, Mud, Sand, and whatever elſe is a Hindrance to you, throw out. For the reſt of your Work, you muſt obſerve the Rules we have laid down in the preceding Book. Dig till you come to a ſolid Foundation, or rather make one of Piles burnt at the End, and driven in as cloſe together as ever they can ſtick. And here I have obſerved that the beſt Architects uſed to make a continued Foundation of the whole Length of the Bridge, and not only under each Pier; and this they did, not by ſhutting out the whole River at once by one ſingle Incloſure, but by firſt making one Part, then another, and ſo joyning the whole together by degrees; for it would be impoſſible to withſtand and repulſe the whole Force of the Water at once; we muſt therefore, while we are at work with one Part, leave another Part open, for a Paſſage for the Stream.

You may leave theſe Paſſages either in the Channel itſelf, or if you think it more convenient, you may frame wooden Dams, or hanging Channels, by which the ſuperfluous Water may run off. But if you find the Expence of a continued Foundation for the whole Bridge too great, you may only make a ſeparate Foundation for every particular Pier, in the Form of a Ship with one Angle in the Stern, and another in the Head, lying directly even with the Current of the Water, that the Force of the Water may be broken by the Angle. We are to remember that the Water is much more dangerous to the Stern, than to the Head of the Piers, which appears from this, that at the Stern the Water is in a more violent Motion than at the Head, and forms Eddies, which turn up the Ground at the Bottom; while the Head ſtands firm and ſafe, being guarded and defended by the Banks of Sand thrown up before it by the Channel. Now this being fo, this Part ought of the whole Structure to be beft fortified againft the Violence of the Waters; and nothing will conduce more to this, than to make the Pile-work deep and broad every Way, and efpecially at the Stern, that if any Accidents fhould carry away any of the Piles, there may be enow left to fuftain the Weight of the Pier. It will be alfo extremely proper to begin your Foundation at the upper Part of the Channel, and to make it with an eafy Defcent, that the Water which runs over it may not fall upon it violently as into a Precipice, but glide over gently, with an eafy Slope; becaufe the Water that rufhes down precipitately, routs up the Bottom, and fo being made ftill rougher carries away every Thing that it can loofen, and is every Moment undermining the Work.

Build the Piers of the biggeft and longeft Stones, and of fuch as in their Nature are beft adapted for fupporting of Frofts, and as do not decay in Water, nor are eafily foftened by any Accident, and will not crack and fplit under a great Weight; and build them exactly according to the Square, Level and Plumline, omitting no Sort of Ligature Lengthways, and placing the Stones Breadth-ways in alternate Order, fo as to be a Binding one to another; abfolutely rejecting any ftuffing with fmall Pieces of Stone. You muft alfo faften your Work with a good Number of Brafs Cramps and Pins, fo well fitted in, that the Joynts of the Structure may not feparate, but be kept tight and firm. Raife both the Fronts of the Building angular, both Head and Stern, and let the Top of the Pier be fure to be higher than the fulleft Tide; and let the Thicknefs of the Pier be one fourth of the Heighth of the Bridge. There have been fome that have not terminated the Head and Stern of their Piers with an Angle, but with an half Circle; induced thereto, I fuppofe, by the Beautifulnefs of that Figure. But though I have faid elfewhere, that the Circle has the fame Strength as an Angle, yet here I approve better of an Angle, provided it be not fo fharp as to be broken and defaced by every little Accident: Nor am I altogether difpleafed with thofe which end in a Curve, provided it be very much lengthened out, and not left fo obtufe as to refift the Force and Weight of the Water. The Angle of the Pier is of a good Sharpnefs, if it is three Quarters of a Right Angle, or if you like it better, you may make it two thirds. And thus much may fuffice as to the Piers. If the Nature of your Situation is fuch, that the Sides or Banks of the Shore are not as you could wifh; make them good in the fome Manner as you build your Piers, and indeed make other Piers upon the Shore, and turn fome Arches even upon the dry Ground; to the Intent, that if in Procefs of Time, by the continual wafhing of the Water, and the Force of the Tides, any Part of the Bank fhould be carried away, your Paffage may ftill be preferved fafe, by the Production of the Bridge into the Land. The Arches ought upon all Accounts, and particularly becaufe of the continual violent fhaking and Concuffion of Carts and other Carriages, to be extreamly ftout and ftrong. Befides, as fometimes you may be obliged to draw immenfe Weights over them, fuch as a Coloffus, an Obelisk or the like; you fhould provide againft the Inconvenience which happened to *Scaurus*, who when he was removing that great Boundary Stone, alarmed all the publick Officers, upon Account of the Mifchief that might enfue. For thefe Reafons, a Bridge both in its Defign, and in its whole Execution, fhould be well fitted to bear the continual and violent Jars which it is to receive from Carriages. That Bridges ought to be built of very large and ftout Stones, is very manifeft by the Example of an Anvil, which, if is large and heavy, ftands the Blows of the Hammer unmoved; but if it is light, rebounds and trembles at every Stroke. We have already faid, that all vaulted Work confifts of Arches and Stuffing, and that the ftrongeft of all Arches is the Semi-circle. But if by the Difpofition of the Piers, the Semi-circle fhould rife fo high as to be inconvenient, we may make ufe of the Scheme Arch, only taking Care to make the laft Piers on the Shore the ftronger and thicker. But whatever Sort of Arch you vault your Bridge with, it muft be built of the hardeft and largeft Stones, fuch as you ufe in your Piers; and there fhould not be a fingle Stone in the Arch but what is in Thicknefs at leaft one tenth Part of the Chord of that Arch; nor fhould the Chord itfelf be longer than fix Times the Thicknefs of the Pier, nor fhorter than four Times. The Stones alfo fhould be ftrongly faftened together with Pins and Cramps of Brafs. And the laft Wedge, which is called the Key-ftone, fhould be cut according to the Lines of the other Wedges, but left a fmall Matter bigger at the Top, fo that it may not be got into its Place without fome Strokes of a light Beetle; which will drive

drive the lower Wedges closer together, and so keep them tight to their Duty. The filling up, or stuffing between the Arches should be wrought with the strongest Stone, and with the closest Joynts that can possibly be made, But if you have not a sufficient Plenty of strong Stone to make your Stuffing of it, you may in Case of Necessity make use of a weaker Sort; still provided that the whole Turn of the Arch, and the Course of Work behind both the Sides of it, be built entirely of strong Stone.

THE next Work it to pave the Bridge; and here we should observe, that we ought to make the Ground upon a Bridge as firm and solid as the most durable Roads; we should raise it with Gravel or coarse Sand, to the Heighth of a Cubit, and then pave it with Stone, filling up the Joints either with River or Sea-sand. Bnt the Substrature or Layer under the Pavement of a Bridge ought first to be levelled and raised quite to the Top of the Arches; with regular Masonry, and then the Pavement itself should be cemented with Mortar. In all other Respects we should observe the same Rules in paving a Bridge, as in paving a Road. The Sides should be made firm with the strongest Work, and the rest paved with Stones, neither so small as to be easily raised and thrown out upon the least Strain; nor so large, that the Beasts of Burden should slide upon them as upon Ice, and fall before they meet with any Catch for their Foot. And certainly we must own it to be of very great Importance what Kind of Stone we use in our Pavements, if we consider how much they must be worn by the continual grinding of the Wheels, and the Hoofs of all Manner of Cattle, when we see that even such small Animals as Ants, with constant passing up and down, will wear Traces even in Flints.

I HAVE observed that the Ancients in many Places, and particularly in the Way to *Tivoli*, paved the Middle of the Road with Flints, and only covered the Sides with small Gravel. This they did, that the Wheels might make the less Impression, and that the Horses Hoofs might not want sufficient Hold. In other Places, and especially over Bridges, there was a raised Way on each Side, with Stone Steps, for Foot Passengers; and the Middle of the Way was left for Beasts and Carriages. Lastly, the Ancients, for this Sort of Work greatly commend Flints, and especially those which are fullest of Holes; not because such are the strongest, but because they are the least slippery. But we may make use of any Sort of Stone, according to what we have in greatest Plenty, provided we only use the strongest we can get, and with those pave at least that Part of the Way which is most beaten by Cattle; and the Part most beaten by them is always most level, because they always avoid all sloping Ground as much as they can. Let the Middle and highest Part of the Way be laid with Flints, or whatever other Stone you use, of the Thickness of a Foot and an half, and the Breadth of at least a Foot, with the upper Face even, and so close compacted together that there are no Crevices left in order to throw off the Rain. There are three different Slopes for all Streets; either towards the Middle, which is proper for a broad Street, or to the Sides, which is least Hindrance to a narrow one; or else Lengthways. But in this we are to govern ourselves according to the Conveniences and Advantages of our Drains and Currents, whether into the Sea, Lake or River. A very good Rise for a Slope is half an Inch in every three Foot. I have observed that the Rise with which the Ancients used to build their Bridges, was one Foot in every thirty; and in some Parts, as particularly at the Summit of the Bridge, four Inches in every Cubit or Foot and an half; but this was only for so little a Way, that a Beast heavy loaden could get over it at one Strain.

CHAP. VII.

Of Drains or Sewers, their different Sorts and Uses; and of Rivers and Canals for Ships.

DRAINS or Sewers are look'd upon as a Part of the Street, inasmuch as they are to be made under the Street, thro' the Middle of it; and are of great Service, as well in the paving and levelling, as in cleaning the Streets; for which Reason they are by no means to be neglected here. And indeed, may we not very properly say that a Drain is a Bridge,

Bridge, or rather a very long Arch; ſo that in the Conſtruction of it we ought to obſerve all the ſame Rules that we have juſt now been laying down concerning Bridges. The Ancients had ſo high a Notion of the Serviceableneſs of Drains and Sewers, that they beſtowed no greater Care and Expence upon any Structure whatſoever, than they did upon them; and among all the wonderful Buildings in the City of *Rome*, the Drains are accounted the nobleſt. I ſhall not ſpend Time to ſhew how many Conveniences ariſe from good Drains; how clean they keep the City, and how neat all Buildings both publick and private, or how much they conduce to the Clearneſs and Healthineſs of the Air.

The City of *Smyrna*, where *Trebonius* was beſieged and relieved by *Dolabella*, is ſaid to have been extremely beautiful, both for the Straitneſs of the Streets, and its many noble Structures; but not having Drains to receive and carry away its own Filth, it offended the Inhabitants abominable with ill Smells. *Siena*, a City in *Tuſcany*, not having Drains wants a very great Help to Cleanlineſs; by which Means the Town not only ſtinks every Night and Morning, when People throw their Naſtineſs out of the Windows, but even in the Day Time it is ſeen lying about the Streets. Drains are of two Sorts; one carries away the Filth into ſome River, Lake or Sea; the other is a deep Hole dug in the Ground, where the Naſtineſs lies till it is conſumed in the Bowels of the Earth. That which carries it away, ought to have a ſmooth ſloping Pavement, ſtrong compacted, that the Ordure may run off freely, and that the Structure itſelf may not be rotted by the Moiſture lying continually ſoaking upon it. It ſhould alſo lie ſo high above the River, that no Floods or Tides may fill it with Mud and choak it up. A Drain that is to lie open and uncover'd to the Air, need have no other Pavement but the Ground itſelf; for the Poets call the Earth *Cerberus*, and the Philoſophers, the *Woolf of the Gods*, becauſe it devours and conſumes every Thing. So that whatever Filth and Naſtineſs is brought into it, the Earth rots and deſtroys it, and prevents its emitting ill Steams. Sinks for the Reception of Urine, ſhould be as far from the Houſe as poſſible; becauſe the Heat of the Sun makes it rot and ſmell intolerably. Moreover, I cannot help thinking that Rivers and Canals, eſpecially ſuch as are for the Paſſage of Ships, ought to be included under the Denomination of Roads; ſince many are of Opinion, that Ships are nothing but a Sort of Carriages, and the Sea itſelf no more than a huge Road. But there is no Neceſſity to ſay any thing more of theſe in this Place. And if it happens that the Conveniences we have here treated of, are not found ſufficient, our Buſineſs is to ſtudy how to mend the Faults, and make whatever other Additions are needful: The Method of doing which, we ſhall ſpeak of in due Time.

Chap. VIII.

Of the proper Structure for a Haven, and of making convenient Squares in the City.

NOW if there is any other Part of the City that falls in properly with the Subject of this Book, it is certainly the Haven, which may be defined a Goal or proper Place from whence you may begin a Voyage, or where having performed it you may put an End to the Fatigue of it, and take Repoſe. Others perhaps would ſay that a Haven is a Stable for Ships; but let it be what you will, either a Goal, a Stable, or a Receptacle, it is certain that if the Buſineſs of a Haven is to give a Reception to Ships out of the Violence of Storms, it ought to be made in ſuch a Manner as to be a ſufficient Shelter for that Purpoſe: Let its Sides be ſtrong and high, and let there be Room enough for large Veſſels heavy laden to come in and lie quiet in it. Which Conveniences, if they are offered to you by the natural Situation of the Place, you have nothing more to wiſh for; unleſs, as at *Athens* where *Thucidides* ſays there were three Havens made by Nature, it ſhould happen that you are doubtful among ſuch a Number, which to chuſe. But it is evident from what we have already ſaid in the firſt Book, that there are ſome Places where all the Winds cannot be, and others where ſome actually are continually troubleſome and dangerous. Let us therefore make

make Choice of that Haven into whoſe Mouth none blow but the moſt gentle and temperate Winds, and where you may enter or go out, with the moſt eaſy Breezes, without being forced to wait too long for them.

THEY ſay, that of all Winds the North is the gentleſt; and that when the Sea is diſturbed by this Wind, as ſoon as ever the Wind ceaſes, it is calm again: But if a South-wind raiſes a Storm, the Sea continues turbulent a long while. But as Places are various, our Buſineſs is to chuſe ſuch a one as is beſt provided with all Conveniencies for Shipping: we muſt be ſure to have ſuch a Depth, in the Mouth, Boſom and Sides of the Haven, as will nor refuſe Ships of Burthen, though ever ſo deep laden; the Bottom too ought to be clear, and not full of any Sort of Weeds: Though, ſometimes, thick entangled Weeds are of a good deal of Uſe in faſtening the Anchor. Yet I ſhould rather chuſe an Haven that does not produce any thing which can contaminate the Purity of the Air, or prejudice the Ships, as Ruſhes and Weeds which grow in the Water really do; for they engender a great many Kinds of Worms which get into the Timbers of the Veſſel, and the rotting of the Weeds raiſes unwholeſome Vapours. There is another Thing which makes an Haven noiſome and unhealthy, and that is a Mixture of freſh Water; eſpecially Rain-water that runs down from Hills: Though I would be ſure to have Streams and Springs in the Neighbourhood, from whence, freſh Water that will keep may be brought for the Uſe of the Veſſels. A Port alſo ought to have a clear, ſtrait and ſafe Paſſage outwards, with a Bottom not often ſhifting, free from all Impediments, and ſecure from the Ambuſhes of Enemies and Pirates. Moreover, I would have it covered with ſome high ſteep Hill, that may be ſeen a great Way off, and ſerve as a Land-mark for the Sailors to ſteer their Courſe by. Within the Port we ſhould make a Key and a Bridge for the more eaſy unlading of the Shipping. Theſe Works the Ancients raiſed in different Ways, which it is not yet our Time to ſpeak of; and we ſhall come to it more properly when we ſpeak of the Method of improving a Haven and running up a Pier. Beſides all this, a good Haven ſhould have Places to walk in, and a Portico and Temple, for the Reception of Perſons that are juſt landed; nor ſhould it want Pillars, Bars and Rings to faſten Ships to; and there ſhould alſo be a good Number of Warehouſes or Vaults for the laying up of Goods. We ſhould alſo at the Mouth erect high and ſtrong Towers, from the Lanterns of which we may ſpy what Sails approach, and by Fires give Directions to the Mariners, and which by their Fortifications may defend the Veſſels of our Friends, and lay Chains acroſs the Port to keep out an Enemy. And from the Port ſtrait thro' the Heart of the City ought to run a large Street, in which ſeveral other Quarters of the Town ſhould center, that the Inhabitants may preſently run thither from all Parts to repulſe any Inſult from an Enemy. Within the Boſom of the Haven likewiſe, ſhould be ſeveral ſmaller Docks, where battered Veſſels may refit. But there is one Thing which we ought not to omit, ſince it relates entirely to the Haven; which is, that there have been, and now are, many famous Cities, whoſe greateſt Security has lain in the unſafe and uncertain Entrance of their Harbours, and from the Variety of its Channels made almoſt hourly for the continual Alteration of the Bottom. Thus much we thought proper to ſay of publick Works in the univerſal Acceptation; and I cannot tell whether there is any Occaſion to add what ſome inſiſt upon, that there ought to be ſeveral Squares laid out in different Parts of the City, ſome for the expoſing of Merchandizes to ſale in Time of Peace; others for the Exerciſes proper for Youth; and others for laying up Stores in Time of War, of Timber, Forage, and the like Proviſions neceſſary for the ſuſtaining of a Siege. As for Temples, Chapels, Halls for the Adminiſtration of Juſtice, and Places for Shows, they are Buildings that, tho' for publick Uſe, are yet the Property of only a few Perſons; which are the Prieſts and Magiſtrates; and therefore we ſhall treat of them in their proper Places.

The End of Book IV.

THE

ARCHITECTURE

OF

Leone Batista Alberti.

Book V. Chap. I.

Of Buildings for particular Persons. Of the Castles or Habitations of a King or a Tyrant; their different Properties and Parts.

WE shewed in the last Book, that Buildings ought to be variously accommodated, both in City and Country, according to the Necessities of the Citizens and Inhabitants; and that some belong'd to the Citizens in common, others to those of greater Quality, and others to the meaner Sort; and finish'd our Account of those of the first Kind. The Design of this fifth Book is to consider of the supplying the Necessaries and Conveniencies for particular Persons. And in this copious and difficult Subject we shall make it our Study, to the utmost of our Ability and Industry, to omit nothing really material or instructive, and not to say any thing more for the Embellishment of our Discourse than for the necessary Explanation of our Subject. Let us begin therefore with the noblest. The noblest are certainly those who are entrusted with the supreme Authority and Moderation in publick Affairs. This is sometimes a single Person, and sometimes Many. If it is a single Person, that Person ought certainly to be him that has the greatest Merit. We shall therefore first consider what is necessary to be done for one that has the sole Power in himself. But we must previously enquire into one very material Difference; what Kind of a Governour this is; whether one that with Justice and Integrity rules over willing Subjects; one not guided so much by his own Interest, as the Good and Welfare of his People: or such a one as would have Things so contrived with Relation to his Subjects, that he may be able to continue his Dominion over them, let them be ever so uneasy under it. For the Generality of particular Buildings, and the City itself ought to be laid out differently for a Tyrant, from what they are for those who enjoy and protect a Government as if it were a Magistracy voluntarily put into their Hands. A good King takes Care to have his City strongly fortified in those Parts, which are most liable to be assaulted by a foreign Enemy: a Tyrant, having no less Danger to fear from his Subjects than from Strangers, must fortify his City no less against his own People, than against Foreigners: and his Fortifications must be so contrived, that upon Occasion he may employ the Assistance of Strangers against his own People, and of one Part of his People against the other. In the preceding Book, we shewed how a City ought to be fortified against foreign Enemies: Let us here consider how it is to be provided against the Inhabitants themselves.

Euripides thinks the Multitude is naturally a very powerful Enemy, and that if they added Cunning

Cunning and Fraud to their Strength, they would be irresistible. The politick Kings of *Cairo* in *Ægypt*, a City so populous that they thought it was extremely healthy and flourishing, when no more than a thousand People died in a Day, divided it by so many Cuts and Channels, that it seemed not to be one single City, but a great Number of small Towns lying together. This I suppose they did, not so much that the Conveniencies of the River might be equally distributed, as to secure themselves against the popular Commotions of a great Multitude, and that if any such should happen, they might the more easily suppress them: just as if a Man out of one huge Colossus, should make two or more Statues, that he might be better able to manage or remove them. The *Romans* never used to send a Senator into *Ægypt*, with Proconsular Authority, to govern the whole Province; but only some Knights, with Commission to govern separate Parts of it. And this they did, as we are informed by *Arrian*, to Intent that a Province so inclined to Tumults and Innovations, might not be under the Care of a single Person: and they observed that no City was more exempt from Discord, than those which were divided by Nature, either by a River flowing thro' the Middle of it, or by a Number of little separate Hills; or by being built one Part upon a Hill, and the other upon a Plain, with a Wall between them. And this Wall or Division, I think, ought not to be drawn like a Diameter clear thro' the Area, but ought rather to be made to enclose one Circle within another: for the richer Sort, desiring a more open Space and more Room, will easily consent to be shut out of the inner Circle, and will be very willing to leave the Middle of the Town, to Cooks, Victuallers and other such Trades; and all the scoundrel Rabble belonging to *Terence*'s Parasite, Cooks, Bakers, Butchers and the like, will be less dangerous there than if they were not to live separate from the nobler Citizens. Nor is it foreign to our Purpose what we read in *Festus*, that *Servius Tullius* commanded the *Patricians* to dwell in a certain Part of the Town, where if they offered at any Disturbance, he was immediately ready to quell them from a superior Situation. This Wall within the City ought to run thro' every District of the Town; and it should be built so strong and thick in all Respects, and be raised so high (as indeed so ought all the other City Walls) that it may overlook all the private Houses. It should also be fortified with Battlements and Towers; and a good Ditch on both Sides would not be amiss; that your Men may the more easily defend it on any Side. The Towers upon this Wall ought not to be open on the Inside, but walled up quite round; and they should be so seated as not only to repulse the Assaults of a foreign Enemy, but of Domestick one too upon Occasion; and particularly they ought to command the great Streets, and the Tops of all high Temples. I would have no Passage into these Towers but from off the Wall itself; nor any Way up to the Wall but what is entirely in the Power of the Prince. There should be no Arches nor Towers in the Streets that lead from the Fortress into the City; nor Leads or Terrasses from whence the Soldiers may be molested with Stones or Darts as they pass to their Duty. In a Word, the whole should be so contrived that every Place, which any Way commands the Town, should be in the Hands of the Prince; and that it should not be in the Power of any Person whatsoever, to prevent his Men from over-running the whole City as he pleases. And herein the City of a Tyrant differs from that of a King; and perhaps they differ too in this, that a Town in a Plain is most convenient for a free People; but one upon a Hill the safest for a Tyrant. The other Edifices for the Habitation both for King and Tyrant, are not only the same in most respects, but also differ very little from the Houses of private Persons: And in some Particulars they differ both from one another, and from these latter too. We shall speak first of those Things wherein they agree; and of their Peculiarities afterwards. This Sort of Buildings is said to have been invented only for Necessity: Yet there are some Parts of them which serve besides to Conveniency, that by Use and Habit seem to be grown as necessary as any: Such as Porticoes, Places for taking the Air in, and the like: Which, though Method may seem to require it, I shall not distinguish so nicely, as to divide what is convenient from what is necessary: But shall only say, that as in the City itself, so in these Particular Structures, some Parts belong to the whole Houshold, some to the Uses of a few, and others to that of a single Person.

CHAP.

Chap. II.

Of the Portico, Veſtibule, Court-yard, Hall, Stairs, Lobbies, Apertures, Back-doors, concealed Paſſages and private Apartments; and wherein the Houſes of Princes differ from thoſe of private Men; as alſo of the ſeparate and common Apartments for the Prince and his Spouſe.

I Do not think the Portico and Veſtibule were made only for the Conveniency of Servants, as *Diodorus* ſays; but rather for the common Uſe of the Citizens: But Places for walking in within the Houſe, the inner Court-yard, the Hall (which I believe took its Name from Dancing, becauſe Nuptials and Feaſts are celebrated in it) do not belong at all to the Publick, but entirely to the Inhabitants. Parlours for eating in are of two Sorts, ſome for the Maſter, and others for the Servants: Bedchambers are for the Matrons, Virgins, Gueſts, and are to be ſeparate for each. Of the univerſal Diviſion of theſe, we have already treated in our firſt Book of Deſigns, as far as was neceſſary under a general Title: We ſhall now proceed to ſhew the Number of all theſe, their Proportions, and proper Situations for the greateſt Convenience of the Inhabitants. The Portico and Veſtibule are adorned by the Nobleneſs of Entrance; the Entrance is adorned by the View which it has before it, and by the Magnificence of its Workmanſhip. Then the inner Rooms for eating, laying up all Manner of Neceſſaries, and the like, ought to be ſo contrived and ſituated, that the Things preſerved in them may be well kept, that there be no want of Sun or Air, and that they have all Manner of proper Conveniencies, and be kept diſtinct, ſo that too great Familiarity may not leſſen the Dignity, Conveniency or Pleaſure of Gueſts, nor encourage the Impertinence of Perſons that pay their Attendance to you. And indeed Veſtibules, Halls, and the like Places of publick Reception in Houſes, ought to be like Squares and other open Places in Cities; not in a remote private Corner, but in the Center and the moſt publick Place, where all the other Members may readily meet: For here all Lobbies and Stair-caſes are to terminate; here you meet and receive your Gueſts. Moreover, the Houſe ſhould not have above one Entrance, to the Intent that nobody may come in, nor any thing be carried out, without the Knowledge of the Porter. Take Care too, that the Windows and Doors do not lie handy for Thieves, nor be ſo open to the Neighbours that they can interrupt, or ſee or hear what is ſaid or done in the Houſe. The *Ægyptians* built their private Houſes without any Windows outwards. Some perhaps may be for having a Back-gate to which the Fruits of the Harveſt may be brought home, either in Carts or on Horſes, and not make a Naſtineſs before the principal Entrance; as alſo a ſmaller private Door, at which the Maſter of the Houſe, without the Knowledge of any of his Family, may receive any private Meſſages or Advices, and go out himſelf, as his Occaſions call him. I have nothing to ſay againſt theſe: And I am entirely for having concealed Paſſages and private and hidden Apartments, barely known to the Maſter himſelf; where, upon any Misfortune, he may hide his Plate and other Wealth, or by which, if need be, he may eſcape himſelf. In *David*'s Sepulchre there were ſeveral private Places made for concealing the King's Hereditary Treaſures; and they were contrived ſo cunningly, that it was hardly poſſible to find them out. Out of one of theſe Places, *Joſephus* informs us, that *Hircanus*, the High Prieſt, thirteen hundred Years afterwards. took three thouſand Talents of Gold (which makes eighteen hundred thouſand *Italian* Crowns) to free the City from *Antiochus*'s Siege: And out of another of them, *Herod*, a long Time after that, got a vaſt Quantity of Gold. In theſe Things therefore the Houſes of Princes agree with thoſe of private Perſons. The chief Difference between private Houſes and Palaces is, that there is a particular Air ſuitable to each: In the Latter the Rooms deſigned for the Reception of Company ſhould be more numerous and ſpacious; thoſe which are intended only for the Uſe of a Few, or only of one Perſon, ſhould be rather neat than large: But here again a Palace ſhould differ from the Houſe of a private Perſon, and even theſe private Apartments ſhould be made more ſpacious and large, becauſe all Parts of a Prince's Palace are generally

generally crowded. In private Houſes, thoſe Parts which are for the Reception of many, ſhould not be made at all different from thoſe of a Prince; and the Apartments ſhould be kept diſtinct for the Wife, for the Huſband, and for the Servants; and every thing is not to be contrived merely for Conveniency, but for Grandeur too, and ſo, that the Number of Servants may not breed any Confuſion. All this indeed is very difficult, and hardly poſſible to be done under a ſingle Roof: therefore every Member of the Houſe muſt have its particular Area and Platform, and have a diſtinct Covering and Wall of its own: but then all the Members ſhould be ſo joined together by the Roof and by Lobbies, that the Servants, when they are wanted about their Buſineſs, may not be called, as it were, out of another Houſe, but be always ready at Hand. Children and Maids, among whom there is an eternal Chattering, ſhould be entirely ſeparated from the Maſter's Apartment, and ſo ſhould the Dirtineſs of the Servants. The Apartments where Princes are to eat ſhould be in the nobleſt Part of the Palace; it ſhould ſtand high, and command a fine Proſpect of Sea, Hills, and wide Views, which gives it an Air of Greatneſs. The Houſe for his Spouſe ſhould be entirely ſeparated from that of the Prince her Husband, except only in the laſt Apartment or Bed-chamber, which ſhould be in common between both; but then a ſingle Gate, under the Care of the ſame Porter, ſhould ſerve both their Houſes. The other Particulars wherein the Houſes of Princes differ from thoſe of private Perſons, are ſuch as are in a Manner peculiar to theſe latter; and therefore we ſhall ſpeak of them in their Place. The Houſes of Princes agree with one another in another Reſpect; which is, that beſides thoſe Conveniencies which they ought to have for their private Uſe, they ſhould have an Entrance from the Maſter Way, and eſpecially from the Sea or River; and inſtead of a Veſtibule, they ſhould have a large open Area, big enough to receive the Train of an Ambaſſador, or any other Great Man, whether they come in Coaches, in Barks, or on Horſeback.

CHAP. III.

Of the Properties of the Portico, Lobby, Halls, both for Summer and Winter, Watch-Towers, and the Difference between the Caſtle for a Tyrant, and the Palace for a King.

I Would have the Portico be not only a convenient Covering for Men, but for Beaſts alſo, to ſhelter them from Sun or Rain. Juſt before the Veſtibule nothing can be nobler than a handſome Portico, where the Youth, waiting till their old Gentlemen return from tranſacting Buſineſs with the Prince, may employ themſelves in all Manner of Exerciſe, Leaping, Tennis, Throwing of Stones, or Wreſtling. Next within ſhould be a handſome Lobby, or a large Hall; where the Clients waiting for their Patrons, may converſe together; and where the Prince's Seat may be prepared for his giving his Decrees. Wherein this there muſt be another Hall, where the principal Men in the State may aſſemble themſelves together in order to ſalute their Prince, and to give their Thoughts concerning whatſoever he queſtions them about: Perhaps it may not be amiſs to have two of thoſe, one for Summer and another for Winter; and in the Contrivance of them, particular Regard muſt be had to the great Age of the Fathers that are to meet in them, that there be no Inconveniencies in them which may any way endanger their Health, and that they may ſtay in them as long as their Buſineſs requires, with Safety and Pleaſure. We are told by *Seneca*, that *Gracchus* firſt, and afterwards *Druſus*, contrived not to give Audience to every body in the ſame Place, but to make proper Diſtinctions among the Crowd, and to receive ſome in private, others in ſelect Numbers, and the Reſt in publick, to ſhew which had the firſt, and which only the ſecond Share in their Friendſhip. If you are in the ſame high Rank of Fortune, and this Manner of Proceeding either becomes or pleaſes you, the beſt Way will be to have ſeveral Doors to receive your Friends at, by which you may diſmiſs thoſe that have had Audience, and keep out ſuch as you don't care to grant it to, without giving them too much Offence. At the Top of the Houſe there ſhould be a high Watch-Tower, from whence you may at any

Time ſee any Commotion in the City. In theſe Particulars the Palace of a King and of a Tyrant agree; but then they differ in theſe other. The Palace of a King ſhould ſtand in the Heart of a City, it ſhould be eaſy of Acceſs, beautifully adorned, and rather delicate and polite than proud or ſtately: But a Tyrant ſhould have rather a Caſtle than a Palace, and it ſhould ſtand in a Manner out of the City and in it at the ſame Time. It looks noble to have the Palace of a King be near adjoyning to the Theatre, the Temple, and ſome Noblemens handſome Houſes: The Tyrant muſt have his Caſtle entirely ſeparated from all other Buildings. Both ſhould be built in a handſome and noble Manner, but yet ſo that the Palace may not be ſo large and rambling as to be not eaſily defended againſt any Inſult; nor the Caſtle ſo cloſe and ſo crampt up, as to look more like a Jail than the Reſidence of a great Prince. We ſhould not omit one Contrivance very convenient for a Tyrant, which is to have ſome private Pipes concealed within the Body of the Wall, by which he may ſecretly hear every Thing that is ſaid either by Strangers or Servants. But as a Royal Houſe is different from a Fortreſs in almoſt all Reſpects, and eſpecially in the main Ones, the beſt Way is to let the Palace join to the Fortreſs. The Ancients uſed to build their Fortreſs in the City, that to they or their King might have a Place to fly to in any Time of Adverſity, and where the Virtue of their Virgins and Matrons might be protected by the Holineſs of a Sanctuary: For *Feſtus* tells us, that the Ancients uſed to conſecrate their Fortreſſes to Religion, upon which Account they were called *Auguriales*, and that in them a certain Sacrifice uſed to be performed by Virgins, which was extremely ſecret and entirely remote from the Knowledge of the Vulgar. Accordingly you ſeldom meet with an ancient Fortreſs without its Temple. But Tyrants afterwards uſurped the Fortreſs to themſelves, and overthrew the Piety and Religion of the Place, converting it to their cruel and wicked Purpoſes, and ſo made what was deſigned as a Refuge to the Miſerable, a Source of Miſeries. But, to return. The Fortreſs belonging to the Temple of *Jupiter Hammon* was encompaſſed with three Walls; the firſt Fortification was for the Prince, the ſecond for his Spouſe and her Children, and the laſt was the Poſt of the Soldiers. A Stucture very well contrived, only that it was much better adapted for Defence than Offence. I muſt confeſs that as I cannot ſay much for the Valour of a Soldier that only knows how to repulſe an Enemy that aſſaults him, ſo I cannot much commend a Fort that, beſides being able to defend itſelf, is not alſo well diſpoſed for offending its Enemies. But yet you ſhould contrive the Matter ſo, that though you have both thoſe Advantages, you ſhould ſeem to have had an Eye only to one of them, namely, your own Defence; that it may be thought the other happened only from the Situation and Nature of the Building.

Chap. IV.

Of the proper Situation, Structure and Fortification of a Fortreſs, whether in a Plain, or upon a Hill, its Incloſure, Area, Walls, Ditches, Bridges, and Towers.

I Find that even Men of good Experience in military Affairs, are in Doubt which is the beſt and ſtrongeſt Manner of building a Fortreſs, either upon a Hill or Plain. There is ſcarce any Hill but what may be either attacked or undermined; nor any Plain but what may be ſo well fortified that it ſhall be impoſſible to aſſault it without great Danger. But I ſhall not diſpute about this Queſtion. Our Buſineſs is to contrive every Thing ſuitably to the Nature of the Place; and indeed all the Rules which we have laid down for the building a City, ſhould be obſerved in the building a Fortreſs. The Fortreſs particularly ſhould be ſure to have even and direct Streets, by which the Garriſon may march to attack an Enemy, or in Caſe of Sedition or Treachery, their own Citizens and Inhabitants, and bring in Succours, either out of their own Country or from Abroad, without Impediment, by Land, River, Lake, or Sea. One very good Form for the Area of a Fortreſs, is that of a C joining to all the City Walls as to a round O with bending Horns, but not encomcompaſſing them quite round; as is alſo that which is ſhaped like a Star with Rays running out to the Circumference; and thus the Fortreſs will be, as we before obſerved it ought, neither within nor without the City. If we were to give a brief Deſcription of the Fortreſs, or Citadel, it might perhaps be not amiſs to ſay that it is the Back-door to the City ſtrongly fortified on all Sides. But let it be what it will, whether the Crown of the Wall, or the Key to the City, it ought to look fierce, terrible, rugged, dangerous, and unconquerable; and the leſs it is, the ſtronger it will be. A ſmall one will require the Fidelity only of a few, but a large one that of a great many: And, as *Euripides* ſays, there never was a Multitude without a great many dangerous Spirits in it; ſo that in the Caſe before us, the Fewer we have occaſion to truſt, the Safer we ſhall be. The outward Wall, or Incloſure of the Fortreſs ſhould be built very ſtrong, of large Stone, with a good Slope on the Outſide, that the Ladders ſet againſt it may be weakened by their ſtanding too oblique; and that the Enemy who Aſſaults it and endeavours to ſcale it, may lie entirely open to the Stones thrown down upon him; and that Things caſt at the Wall by the military Engines may not ſtrike it full, but be thrown off aſlant. The Ground or Area on the Inſide ſhould be all paved with two or even three Layers of very large Stones, that the Beſiegers may not get in upon you by Mines run under the Wall. All the Reſt of the Walls ſhould be made very high, and very ſtrong and thick quite to the uppermoſt Corniſh, that they may ſtoutly reſiſt all Manner of Battery, and not eaſily be mounted by Ladders, nor commanded by Intrenchments caſt up on the Outſide. In other Reſpects the ſame Rules are to be obſerved that we have given for the Walls of the City. The greateſt Defence to the Walls either of a City or Fortreſs is to be ſo provided, that the Enemy cannot approach you on any Side without being expoſed to imminent Danger. This is done both by making very broad and deep Ditches, as we ſaid before; and alſo by leaving private Loop-Holes almoſt at the very Bottom of the Wall, by which, while the Enemy is covering himſelf with his Shield from the Beſieged above, he may be taken in his Flank which lies unguarded. And indeed, there is no Kind of Defence ſo ſerviceable as this. You gaul the Enemy from theſe Loop-Holes with the greateſt Safety to yourſelf, you have a nearer Aim at him, and you are ſure to do moſt Execution, ſince it is impoſſible he ſhould defend all Parts of his Body at the ſame Time: And if your Weapon paſſes by the firſt Man without hurting him, it meets another, and ſometimes wounds two or three at a Time. On the Contrary, when the beſieged throws Things down from the Top of the Wall, they muſt ſtand expoſed to a good Deal of Danger, and it is a great Chance whether they hit ſo much as one Man, who may eaſily ſee what is coming upon him, and avoid it, or turn it aſide with his Buckler. If the Fortreſs ſtands upon the Sea-ſide, you ſhould fix Piles and Heaps of Stone ſcattered up and down about the Coaſt to make it unſafe, and prevent any Batteries in Shipping from coming too near. If it is upon a Plain it ſhould be ſurrounded with a Ditch filled with Water; but then to prevent its ſtinking and infecting the Air, you ſhould dig for it till you come to a living Spring. If it is upon a Hill, it ſhould be encompaſſed with broken Precipices; and where we have an Opportunity we ſhould make uſe of all theſe Advantages together. Thoſe Parts which are expoſed to battery, ſhould be made Semi-circular, or rather with a ſharp Angle like the Head of a Ship. I am not to learn that ſome People of good Experience in military Matters, are of Opinion that very high Walls are dangerous in Caſe of Battery; becauſe their Ruins fill up the Ditch, and make a Way in it for the Enemy to approach and aſſault the Place. But we ſhall avoid this Inconvenience, if we obſerve all the Rules before laid down. But to return. Within the Fortreſs ought to be one principal Tower, built in the ſtouteſt Manner, and fortified as ſtrongly as poſſible, higher than any other Part of the Caſtle, and not acceſſible by more than one Way, to which there ſhould be no other Entrance but by a Draw-bridge. Draw-bridges are of two Sorts; one which is lifted up and ſtops up the Entrance; the other, which ſlides out and in, as you have occaſion for it. In a Place expoſed to boiſterous Winds, this laſt is the moſt Convenient. Any Tower that may poſſibly infeſt this principal One, ought to be left quite open and naked on that Side which ſtands towards it, or faced only with a very thin weak Wall.

Chap.

Chap. V.

Of those Parts of the Fortress where the Soldiers are to stand either to keep centinel, or to fight. Of the Covering or Roof of the Fortress, and in what Manner it is to be made strong, and of the other Conveniencies necessary in the Castle, either of a King or a Tyrant.

THE Place where the Soldiers are to stand to keep centinel, and to defend the Wall, should be so laid out, that some may guard the lower Parts of the Fortress, others the upper, thus being all distributed into various Posts and Employments. In a Word, the Entrance in, and Passage out, and every separate Part should be so contrived and secured, that it may be exposed neither to the Treachery of Friends, nor the Force or Fraud of Enemies. The Roofs in a Fortress should be built with an acute Angle, and very strong, that they may not easily be demolished by the Weight of what is thrown from the military Engines; the Rafters in them must stand very close together, and a Covering over them, and then lay the Gutters for carrying off the Rain, but entirely without Lime or Mortar. Then make a Covering over the Whole of Pieces of Tile, or rather of Pumice-stones, to the Heighth of three Foot: Thus it will neither be in Danger from any Weight falling upon it, nor from Fire. In short, a Fortress is to be built like a little Town: It should be fortified with the same Care and Art, and if possible, provided with all the Conveniencies that a Town should be. It must not want Water, nor sufficient room for lodging the Soldiers, and laying up Stores of Arms, Corn, Salted-meat, Vinegar, and particularly Wood. And within this Fortress too, that which we called the principal Tower, ought to be a little Fortress within itself, and should want none of the Conveniencies required in a great one. It should have its own Cisterns, and Store-rooms for all Provisions necessary, either for its Maintenance or Defence. It should have Passages, by which it may upon Occasion attack even its own Friends, and for the Admission of Succours. I will not omit one Circumstance, which is, that Castles have sometimes been defended by Means of their private Passages for Water, and Towns taken by Means of their Drains. Both these may be of Use for sending out private Messengers. But you should be sure to contrive them so, that they may do you more Service than Prejudice. Let them therefore be made but just big enough; let them run winding several Ways, and let them end in some very deep Place, that there may not be room enough for a Man with his Arms, and that even one unarmed may not get into the Castle without being permitted or called. The Mouths of them may end very conveniently in some common Drain, or rather in some unknown desart Place, or in a private Chapel, or a Tomb in some Church. We should likewise never be unprovided against human Accidents and Calamities; and therefore it will be very proper to have some Passage into the very Heart of the Fortress, known to nobody but yourself; by which if you should ever happen to be shut out, you may immediately get in with an armed Force: And perhaps one good Way to do this may be to have some very private Part of the Wall built only of Earth or Chalk, and not of Stone and Mortar. Thus much may suffice for what is necessary to be done for a single Person that is possessed of the Government, whether King or Tyrant.

Chap. VI.

Of the several Parts of which the Republick consists. The proper Situation and Building for the Houses of those that govern the Republick, and of the Priests. Of Temples, as well large as small, Chapels and Oratories.

WE are now to treat of those Things which are proper to such as are at the Head not of a Monarchy but of a Commonwealth; and here the Power is lodged either in the Hands of some one single Magistrate, or else is divided among a certain Number. The

The Republick consists of Things sacred, which appertain to the publick Worship: The Care of which is in the Priests; and of Things profane, which regard the Welfare and good of the Society; the Care of which is in the Senators and Judges at Home, and in the Generals of Armies and Fleets Abroad. To each of these belong two Kinds of Building, one upon account of the Person's Office, the other for the Use of his own private Family. Every Man's House should certainly be suited to the Condition of Life which he is in, whether he is a King, a Tyrant, or a private Person. There are some Circumstances which in a particular Manner become Men in high Stations. *Virgil* very judiciously makes *Anchises* have his House in a private Part of the City, and shaded with Trees; knowing very well that the Habitations of great Men, for the Dignity and Quiet both of themselves and Families, should be remote from the Concourse of the Vulgar, and from the Noise of Trades; and this not only for the Pleasure and Conveniency of having Room for Gardens, Groves, or the like, but also that so large a Family, consisting of different Sorts of People, may not lie in the Way to be corrupted and debauched by an ill Neighbourhood, since (as is rightly observed) more Mischief is done by Wine Abroad than at Home: And moreover, in order to avoid the eternal Torment of numerous Visitors and Attendants. I have indeed observed that wise Princes have not only placed themselves out of the Way of the Crowd, but even out of the City itself, that the common People might not be troublesome to them, but when they were in some particular Want of their Protection: And, in Reality, what signifies all their Wealth and Greatness, if they can never enjoy a few Hours of Repose and Leisure? However, their Houses, let them stand where they will, ought to have large spacious Apartments to receive those that come to attend them, and the Street which leads from them to the Places where the publick Affairs are transacted, should be of a good Breadth, that their Servants, Clients, Suitors and Followers crowding to attend their Patron, may not stop up the Way, and breed Confusion. The different Places where the Magistrates are to exercise their Offices, are known to every Body: The Business of the Senator, is in the Senate-house; of the Judge, in the Tribunal, or Court of Justice; of the General in the Army; of the Admiral on board the Fleet. But what shall we say of the Priests? to whom belongs not only the Temple, but also the Cloyster, which might be called a Lodgement, or Camp for Soldiers, since the chief Priests, and all his inferior Ministers, are employed in a stubborn and laborious Warfare, (as we have shewed in the Book called *The Priest*) namely, that of Virtue against Vice. Of Temples, some are principal, as is that wherein the chief Priest upon stated Seasons celebrates some solemn Rites and Sacrifices: Others are under the Guardianship of inferior Priests, as all Chapels in Town, and Oratories in the Country. Perhaps the most convenient Situation for the principal Temple may be in the Middle of the City; but it is more Decent to have it somewhat remote from the Crowd: A Hill gives it an Air of Dignity, but it is more secure from Earthquakes in a Plain. In a Word, the Temple is to be placed where it may appear with most Majesty and Reverence: For which Reason it should lie entirely out of the Way of all Filth and Indecency, to the Intent that Fathers, Matrons and Virgins, who come to offer up their Prayers, may not be shocked and offended, or perverted from their intended Devotions. *Nigrigeneus* the Architect, who wrote about the *Termini*, informs us, that the ancient Architects were for having the Fronts of their Temples facing the West: But this Custom was afterwards quite altered, and it was thought better to have the Temples and the *Termini* look to the East, that they might have a View of the rising Sun. But I have observed myself that the Ancients in the situating of their smaller Temples or Chapels, generally turned their Fronts so as they might be seen from the Sea, or some River or great Road. To conclude, a Structure of this Kind ought to be so built as to entice those who are absent to come and see it, and to charm and detain those that are present by the Beauty and Curiosity of its Workmanship. An arched Roof will secure it most against Fire, and a flat one against Earthquakes; but the former will be the least liable to Decay by the Injury of Time. And this may suffice as to the Temples, because many Things which seem necessary to be said here, belong more properly to their Ornament than to their real Use: And therefore of those we shall treat elsewhere. Smaller Temples and Chaples must imitate the Greater, according to the Dignity of their Situation and Uses.

Chap. VII.

That the Prieſt's Camp is the Cloyſter; the Duty of the Prieſt; the various Sorts of Cloyſters and their proper Situations.

THE Prieſt's Camp is the Cloyſter, in which a certain Number of Perſons ſhut themſelves up together in order to devote themſelves either to Religion or Virtue; ſuch are thoſe who have dedicated themſelves to the ſacred Functions, or who have taken upon themſelves a Vow of Chaſtity. Beſides this Cloyſter is a Place where Perſons of ſtudious Diſpoſitions employ themſelves about the Knowledge of Things as well Divine as Human; for as the Prieſt's Duty is as far as in him lies to lead Mankind into a Courſe of Life as near to Perfection as poſſible, this can never be done more effectually than by Philoſophy. For as there are two Things in the Nature of Man to which this muſt be owing, Virtue and Truth; when the former has taught us to calm and govern our Paſſions, and the latter to know the Principles and Secrets of Nature, which will purge the Mind from Ignorance and the Contagion of the Body; we may then be qualified to enter into a happy Courſe of Life, and to have ſome Reſemblance with the divine Nature itſelf. Add to this, that it is the Duty of all good Men, as the Prieſts ought and would be thought to be, to exerciſe themſelves in all thoſe Offices of Humanity which are due from every Man to his Neighbour, namely, to aſſiſt and relieve the Poor, the Diſtreſſed and the Infirm, to the utmoſt of their Power. Theſe are the Things in which the Prieſt is to employ himſelf and all thoſe under his Direction. Of the Structures proper for theſe Purpoſes, whether belonging to the ſuperior or inferior Rank of Prieſts, we are now to treat; and firſt we ſhall begin with the Cloyſter. Cloyſters are of ſeveral Sorts, either for ſuch Perſons as are to be ſo ſtrictly confined that they muſt never appear in publick at all, unleſs at Church or in Proceſſions; or for thoſe who are to be allowed a little more Liberty. Of theſe again ſome are for Men, others for Women. Thoſe for Women ſhould, in my Opinion, be neither too much in the City, nor too much out of it: For though in a Solitude they may not be ſo much ſrequented, yet any one that has a Deſign may have more Opportunity to execute any villanous Enterprize where there are ſo few Witneſſes, than where there are a great many both to ſhame and diſſwade him from ſuch an Attempt. It is our Buſineſs in both to take Care not that they have no Inclinations to be unchaſte, but no means. For this Purpoſe every Entrance muſt be ſo ſecured, that nobody can poſſibly get in; and ſo well watched, that nobody may loyter about in order to attempt it without inſtant Suſpicion and Shame. No Camp for an Army ſhould be ſo well guarded by Intrenchments and Paliſadoes, as a Monaſtery ought to be by high Walls, without either Doors or Windows in them, or the leaſt Hole by which not only no Violator of Chaſtity, but not ſo much as the leaſt Temptation either by the Eye or Ear, may poſſibly get in to diſorder, or pollute the Minds of the Recluſe. Let them receive their Light from an open Court on the Inſide. Round this Court the Portico, Cells, Refectory, Chapter-houſe and the like Conveniencies ſhould be diſpoſed according to their various Uſes, in the ſame Manner as in private Houſes. Nor ſhould Space be wanting for Gardens and Meadows, for the moderate Recreation of the Mind, but not for adminiſtring to Pleaſure. If all theſe Precautions are taken, it will be beſt to have them out of the Way of a Concourſe of People. The Cloyſters for both Sexes therefore cannot be better placed than without the City; that the Attention of their Thoughts which are entirely dedicated to Holineſs, and the calm and ſettled Religion of their Minds may not be diſturbed by too many Viſitors. But then I would have their Houſes, whether they are for Men or Women, ſituated in the moſt healthy Air that can be found out; that the Recluſe, while they are wholly intent upon the Care of their Souls, may not have their Bodies, already impared, by conſtant faſting and watching, oppreſſed likewiſe with Weakneſs and Diſeaſes. Thoſe who are without the City ſhould be placed in a Situation naturally ſtrong, that neither Robbers nor any plundering Enemy with a ſmall Force, may be able at every turn to ſack it; and I would have it moreover fortified with a Trench and a Wall,

Wall, nor would it be amiſs to add a Tower, which is not at all inconſiſtent with a religious Edifice. The Monaſtery for thoſe Recluſe who to Religion join the Study of the liberal Arts, that they may be the more ready to promote the Good of Mankind, according to the Obligation of their Character, ought to be neither within the Noiſe and Hurry of Tradeſmen, nor too far remote from the Acceſs of the Citizens. And as they are a great many in Family, and there is generally a great Concourſe of People to hear them Preach and Diſpute concerning ſacred Things; they require a very large Houſe. They can be placed no where better than among ſome publick Buildings, ſuch as Theatres, Circuſſes, or Squares, where the Multitude going for their Pleaſure may more eaſily by the Exhortations, Example and Admonition of the Religious, be drawn from Vice to Virtue, and from Ignorance to Knowledge.

Chap. VIII.

Of Places for Exerciſe, publick Schools, and Hoſpitals both for Men and Women.

The Ancients, and eſpecially the *Greeks*, uſed in the very Middle of their Cities to erect thoſe Edifices which they called *Palæſtræ*, where thoſe who applied themſelves to Philoſophy, attended publick Diſputations. They were large ſpacious Places full of Windows, with a free Proſpect on all Sides, and raiſed Seats, and Porticoes running round ſome green flowery Meadow. Such a Structure is extremely proper for theſe Perſons, who may be reckoned a Kind of Religious; and I would have thoſe who delight in the Study of Learning, be provided with every Thing that may induce them to ſtay with their Tutors with Pleaſure, and without Uneaſineſs or Satiety. For this Reaſon, I would have the Meadow, the Portico, and every Thing elſe ſo laid out, that nothing whatſoever could be better contrived for Recreation. In Winter let them receive the kindly Beams of the Sun, and in Summer be ſhady and open to gentle refreſhing Breezes. But of the Delicacies of this Kind of Structures we ſhall ſpeak more particularly in another Place. Only if you do reſolve to erect publick Schools, where the Learned may meet and converſe, place them in that Situation which may be moſt convenient and pleaſant for them. Let there be no Noiſes of working Trades, no noiſome ill Smells; and do not let it be a Place for idle People to loyter in; but let it have more the Air of a Solitude, ſuch as becomes Men of Gravity employed about the nobleſt and moſt curious Enquiries: In a Word, it ſhould have more of Majeſty than Nicety. As for Hoſpitals where the Prieſt is to exerciſe his Charity towards the Poor and Diſtreſſed, they are to be built with much Thought, and a good Deal of Variety; for one Place is proper for harbouring the Diſtreſſed, and another for curing and foſtering the Sick and Infirm: Among theſe laſt too we ſhould take Care to make a good Deal of Diſtinction, that while we are providing for a few uſeleſs People, we do not neglect more that might really be of Service. There have been ſome Princes in *Italy* that would never ſuffer any tattered Cripples to go about their Cities begging Charity from Door to Door; but as ſoon as ever they came, an Order was brought to them not to be ſeen in that City without working at ſome Trade above three Days: For there is hardly any ſo maimed but what may do ſome Work or other; and even a blind Man may turn a Rope-maker's Wheel, if he can do nothing elſe. As for thoſe who are entirely oppreſſed and diſabled by ſome heavier Infirmity, they were taken care of by Magiſtrates appointed on purpoſe to provide for ſick Strangers, and diſtributed regularly to inferior Hoſpitlers, to be looked after. And by this Means theſe poor Wretches did not wander about begging Relief, perhaps in vain; and the City was not offended by miſerable and filthy Objects. In *Tuſcany*, always famous for Religion and Piety, there are noble Hoſpitals, built at a vaſt Expence; where as well Strangers as Natives, are furniſhed plentifully with all Manner of Neceſſaries for their Cure. But as the Sick are of various Sorts, ſome afflicted with Leproſy or Plague, with which they might infect thoſe who are in Health, and others, if ſuch an Expreſſion may be allowed, with more wholſome

Diſtempers:

Diſtempers: They ought to have Places entirely ſeperate. The Ancients dedicated their Buildings of this Nature to *Æculapius*, *Apollo*, and *Health*, Gods among them to whom they aſcribed the Cure of Sickneſs and Preſervation Health, and ſituated them in the beſt Air they could find out, and near Plenty of the cleareſt Water, where the Sick might recover their Health, not ſo much by the Aſſiſtanc of thoſe Gods, as the natural Healthineſs of the Place: And certainly nothing can be more reaſonable than to carry the Sick, whether under a private or a publick Cure, into the moſt healthy Places; and perhaps none are more ſo, than thoſe which are very dry and ſtony, fanned with continual Breezes, not burnt up by the Sun, but cool and temperate: Since we find that all Moiſture is the Mother of Corruption. We ſee that Nature in every Thing loves a Medium; and even Health itſelf is nothing but a due Moderation of the Qualities of the Body; and indeed nothing that is in Extreams can pleaſe. For the Reſt, thoſe who are ſeized with Diſeaſes which are contagious, ſhould be taken Care of not only without the City, but remote even from any high Road; the others may be kept in the City. The Apartments for all theſe ſhould be ſo laid out and diſtributed, that there may be diſtinct Places for thoſe who are curable, and thoſe whom you take in rather to maintain them for the Remainder of their unhappy Days, than to cure them: Of this Sort are the Superannuated, and thoſe who want their Senſes. Add further, that the Men and Women, as well the Patients, as the Perſons that attend them, ſhould have Apartments ſeparate from one another; and as ſome Parts of the Building ſhould be for Particulars, others ſhould be in common, according as it ſhall be found neceſſary for the Management of the Patients, and the more eaſy cohabiting together: Of which there is no Occaſion to ſay more in this Place. We ſhall only obſerve that all theſe Conveniencies are to be contrived according to the Rules hereafter to be laid down for the Houſes of private Perſons. We ſhall therefore now proceed according to the Method which we have preſcribed to ourſelves.

Chap. IX.

Of the Senate-houſe, the Temple, and the Tribunals for the Adminiſtration of Juſtice.

HAVING already obſerved that the Republick conſiſts of two Parts, the Sacred and the Profane, and having treated of the Sacred as much as was requiſite, and in a good Meaſure too of the Profane, where we took Notice of the Place in the Palace of the Prince where the Senate was to meet, and where Cauſes were to be heard; we ſhall now very briefly ſpeak of thoſe Things which ſeem neceſſary to be further added, then proceed to Incampments and Fleets, and laſtly treat of Things relating to the Uſes of private Perſons. The Ancients uſed to call their Senates together in Temples, and afterwards it grew a Cuſtom for them to meet ſomewhere out of the City. But at length, both for greater Dignity and Conveniency in tranſacting the publick Affairs, it was found neceſſary to raiſe Structures for this Purpoſe only; where neither the Length of the Way, nor any Inconveniency in the Place itſelf, might deter the aged Fathers from meeting often, and continuing a good while together; and for this Reaſon they placed the Senate-houſe in the Middle of the City, with the Place for the Adminiſtration of Juſtice and the Temple near adjoining, that not only thoſe who made Intereſt for Offices, or were obliged to attend Law-ſuits, might with greater Convenience, and without loſing their Time or Opportunity, look after their Affairs of both Natures; but alſo that the Fathers (as Men are generally moſt devoted to Religion in their old Age) might firſt pay their Devotions in the Temple, and afterwards repair immediately to the Tranſaction of the publick Buſineſs. Add to all this, that when any Ambaſſador or foreign Prince deſires Audience of the Senate, it becomes the Republick to have a Place ſuitable to the Dignity both of the Stranger and of the City, to receive them in, while they wait for Introduction. Laſtly, in publick Buildings of this Sort, you muſt neglect none of thoſe Rules which belong to the convenient and honourable Reception of a Multitude of Citizens, and their eaſy Diſmiſſion: And above all you muſt take particular Care, that there is not the leaſt

Want

Want of ſufficient Paſſages, Lights, open Areas, and the like. But in the Hall for the Adminiſtration of Juſtice, where Numbers of People reſort about various Contentions, the Apertures muſt be more and larger, and more direct than either in the Temple or Senate-houſe. The Entrance into the Senate-houſe ought to be made no leſs ſtrong than handſome, for very many Reaſons, and particularly to the Intent that no fooliſh headſtrong Rabble, at the Inſtigation of any ſeditious Ringleader, may be able at any Time to attack and inſult the Senators: For which Reaſon, more than for any other, there ought to be Porticoes, Veſtibules, and the like, where Servants, Clients and Attendants, waiting for their Patrons, may be ready at Hand to defend them in Caſe of any ſudden Commotion. I will not omit one Obſervation, namely, that no Place where we are to hear the Voices of Perſons either ſpeaking, ſinging, or diſputing, ſhould ever be vaulted becauſe ſuch Roofs confound the Voice with Ecchoes: Whereas a flat Ceiling made of Timbers renders the Sound more clear and diſtinct.

CHAP. X.

That Incampments, or Lodgments for Soldiers by Land are of three Sorts; in what Manner they are to be fortified; and the various Methods uſed by different Nations.

IN laying down a Camp we ought to review and re-conſider all thoſe Rules which we gave in the laſt Book for the Situation of a City; for, indeed, Camps are as it were the Seeds of Cities, and you will find that not a few Cities have been built in thoſe very Places, where excellent Generals had before incamped with their Armies. In making a Camp, the chief Matter is to know to what Intent it is deſigned. There would not be the leaſt Occaſion for a Camp if it were not for unforeſeen Accidents in War, and for the Apprehenſion of Aſſaults from a ſuperior Force: And therefore we are to conſider the Nature of the Enemy. Of Enemies ſome are inferior as to Valour and Number; ſome equal, ſome ſuperior. For this Reaſon we ſhall determine the different Sorts of Incampments to be three; the Firſt is that which is made only for a Time, and is moveable every Moment, which is proper for withſtanding and managing an Enemy equal to yourſelf, and is deſigned partly for keeping the Soldier ſafe from ſudden Attacks, and partly for watching and obtaining Opportunities of effecting your Deſigns. The ſecond Sort of Incampment is ſtationary, in which you wait to oppreſs and ſubdue an Enemy, who, diſtruſting his own Forces, ſhuts himſelf up in ſome ſtrong Hold. The third Sort is that in which you ſhut up yourſelf, to receive and repulſe the Attacks of a ſuperior Force, ſo as to be able to ſend the Enemy away weary of the Fatigues and Loſs in beſieging you. In all theſe you muſt take great Care that every Thing be ſo ordered, that not the leaſt Particular be wanting which can be of Service to your own Security and Welfare, and to the ſuſtaining, repulſing and breaking the Enemy; and on the Contrary, that the Enemy, as far as lies in your Power, may have no Conveniency whatſoever, by means of which he may either hurt you, or ſecure himſelf. For this Reaſon, the firſt Thing to be conſulted, is the Nature of the Situation, that it be in a Country well furniſhed with all Manner of Proviſions, and lie convenient for the eaſy bringing in either of Convoys or Supplies upon all Occaſions. Let Water by no means be wanting, and let Wood and Paſture be not far off. Take care to have a free Communication with your own Territory, and an open Paſſage at pleaſure into the Enemy's. Let the Enemy on the Contrary, have nothing but Difficulties and Obſtacles. I am for having a Camp placed on a Situation ſo high, as to have an open View of the Enemy's Country all round; ſo that they may not begin or attempt any Thing whatſoever, without your being immediately aware of it. Let it be ſecured all round with ſteep Slopes, difficult Aſcents, and broken Precipices; that the Enemy may not be able to ſurround you with Multitudes, nor to attack you on any Side, without expoſing himſelf to imminent Danger; or that if he ſhould come cloſe up to you, he may not conveniently uſe his Engines, or make any ſecure Lodgments for himſelf near you.

If the Situation offers all theſe Advantages, be ſure to be the Firſt to lay hold of them; if not, we muſt then conſider what Sort of Camp, and what Kind of Situation will beſt anſwer your Purpoſe. A ſtationary Camp ought to be much better fortified than a Flying one: And a Plain requires more Art and Diligence to ſtrengthen it, than a Hill. We ſhall begin with the moveable, or flying Camp, becauſe it is much more frequently uſed than a ſtationary one: And indeed, the frequent moving the Camp, has very often conduced extremely to the Health of the Army. In placing a Camp, it is a Queſtion that naturally ariſes in the Mind, whether it is beſt to fix it upon our own Territory, or upon that of the Enemy. *Xenophon* ſays, that by frequent changing our Camp, our Enemy is oppreſſed, but our Friends eaſed. Without doubt, it is honourable and brave to lie upon the Enemy's Country; but it is convenient and ſafe to be upon our own. But indeed a Camp is, with regard to all the Territory which is ſubject to it, what a Citadel is to a City; which ought to have a ſhort and eaſy Retreat towards its Friends, and an open and ready Paſſage upon its Enemies. Laſtly, in the fortifying of Camps various Methods have been uſed. The *Britains* uſed to make a Fence round their Camps with Stakes ten foot long, ſharpened and burnt at the Ends, with one End fixed in the Ground, and the other ſtanding up to keep off the Enemy. *Cæſar* tells us, that the *Gauls* uſed to make a Rampart of their Waggons, as he ſays the *Thracians* alſo did againſt *Alexander*. The *Nervii* (or People of *Tournay*) uſed to cut down young Trees, and binding and interlacing the Boughs together made them into a ſtrong Hedge, which ſerved chiefly for keeping off the Horſe. *Arrian* relates that when *Neurchus*, *Alexander*'s Admiral, ſailed along the *Indian* Sea, having Occaſion to land, he ſurrounded his Camp with a Wall to ſecure himſelf againſt the *Barbarians*. The *Romans* were always ſo well provided, and had ſo much Foreſight, that whatever happened they took care it ſhould never be by their own Fault; and they uſed to exerciſe their Soldiers no leſs in making Incampments, than in the other Parts of the Military Duty. Nor did they think there was ſo much Merit in offending their Enemies, as in ſecuring their own Men; and they accounted it no ſmall Part of the Victory, to be able to withſtand the Enemy, and to repulſe him ſo ſtoutly as to make him Deſpair of Succeſs. For which Reaſon they never neglected any Means of Deſence that they could learn or invent for their own Safety: And if high Hills or Precipices were not to be had, they imitated them as well as they could with very deep Ditches and high Ramparts, emcompaſſed with ſtrong Fences of Stakes and Hurdles.

Chap. XI.

The moſt convenient Situation for a Camp, and its Size, Form and various Parts; together with the different Methods of attacking and defending a Camp or other Fortification.

We ſhall here proceed further upon this Subject of Camps according to the Methods of the aforementioned Ancients. We muſt take Care to pitch upon a Place not only convenient, but ſo well adapted for whatever Purpoſe we have in Hand, that none could be found more ſuitable. And beſides the other Advantages before recited, let the Soil be dry, not muddy nor liable at any Time to be overflowed; but let the Situation be ſuch that it may be always clear and free for your own Men, and unſafe for the Enemy. Let there be no foul Puddle in the Neighbourhood, and let there be good Water at an eaſy Diſtance. Contrive, if poſſible, to have ſome clear Springs within the Camp itſelf, or to have the Foſs filled with ſome River or running Stream. The Camp ought not to be ſo large, out of Proportion to the Number of your Soldiers, that they cannot be able to keep ſufficient Centry about it, ſo as to give the Watch-word round one to another; or to relieve one another ſo often as may be requiſite in defending the Ramparts: Nor, on the Contrary, ought it to be ſo crampt up and confined, as not to afford ſufficient room for all proper Conveniencies. *Lycurgus* was of Opinion that Angles were uſeleſs in a Camp, and therefore he always laid out his in a Circle, unleſs he had ſome Hill, River or Fortification at his Back. Others commend a ſquare

ſquare Area for Incampments: But indeed in ſituating a Camp we muſt accommodate ourſelves to the Neceſſity of the Time, and the Nature of the Place, according to the Purpoſe which we have in Hand, whether it be to oppreſs the Enemy or to reſiſt him. Let us make our Foſs ſo big, that it may not be filled up without great Labour, and a long Space of Time; or rather let us have two Foſſes, with ſome intermediate Space between them. The Ancients, in Works of this Nature alſo, held it a Point of Religion to make uſe of odd Numbers; for which Reaſon it was their Cuſtom to make their Ditches fifteent Foot wide, and nine deep. Let the Sides of the Ditch be Perpendicular, ſo that it may be as broad at the Bottom as the Top; but where the Soil is looſe, you may allow a ſmall Slope, running ſomewhat narrower towards the Bottom. In a Plain, or a low Situation, fill your Ditch with Water brought from ſome River, Lake, or Sea: But if this cannot be effected ſtrew all the Bottom with ſharp Points of Steel and Caltrops, and fix up and down a good Number of Stakes with their Ends ſmoothed and ſharpened, to keep off the Enemy. Having compleated your Ditch, make your Rampart ſo thick, that it may not be to be ſhaken by every little military Engine, and ſo high as to be above the Reach of the grappling Hooks, and even of Darts thrown by the Hand. The Earth dug out of the Foſs lies very convenient and ready at Hand for making up the Rampart. The Ancients for that Work very much commended Turfs dug out of the Meadows with the Graſs upon them, the Roots whereof faſten them very ſtrongly together. Others intermix them with Twigs of green Oziers, which ſtrike their Roots into the Rampart, and by the Contexture of their Fibres ſtrengthen the whole Work. Along the inward Edge of the Foſs and the Outſide of the Rampart ſet Thorns, Spikes, Tenter-hooks and the like, to retard the Enemy in his Aſcent. Let the Top of the Rampart be girt with a ſtrong Frame of Timbers joyned to one another croſſways like a Corniſh, with Hurdles and Earth well rammed in together between them; and upon theſe raiſe your Battlements, and ſtick in forked Paliſadoes like Stag's Horns. In a Word, let every Thing be ſo contrived in this Kind of Structure, as to make it difficult to be either undermined, thrown down, or mounted; and to protect the Soldier who is to defend it. Upon the Edge of this Rampart erect Towers at the Diſtance of every hundred Feet, and eſpecially in ſuch Parts as are moſt likely to be attacked, where they ought to ſtand cloſer and be built higher that they may the more effectually annoy the Enemy, when he attempts to make his Way into the Camp. Let the *Prætorium*, or General's Tent, and the Gate looking towards the Enemy, as alſo that in the Back of the Camp, which two Gates uſed formerly to be called the *porta Quintana*, and the *porta Decumana*, be placed in the ſtrongeſt Parts of the Camp, and lie convenient for making any ſudden Sally with the Army, or bringing in of Proviſions, or giving a ready Retreat to your own Men. All theſe Conveniencies belong more particularly to a ſtationary Camp, than to a flying one: But as we ought to be provided againſt all Accidents that either Fortune or the Calamity of the Times can produce, we ſhould not, even in a flying Camp, neglect any of thoſe Particulars which we have ſpoken of, as far as may be neceſſary. Thoſe Things which belong to a ſtationary Camp, eſpecially one that is to expect a Siege, are very nearly the ſame with thoſe which we ſpoke of with Relation to the Citadel of a Tyrant. A Citadel is a Structure purpoſely deſigned for the Suſtaining a Siege, ſince the Citizens always look upon it with an irreconcileable Hatred: And it is indeed the moſt cruel Kind of Siege that can be imagined, to be continually watching it, and to be always upon the Catch for an Opportunity that may offer, by Means of which you may ſatiſfy the ſtrong Deſire you have to deſtroy it: And for this Reaſon, as we obſerved before, we ſhould take the greateſt Care to make it ſtrong, ſtout, durable, well provided for its own Defence, and for weakening and repulſing the Enemy, and able to defy the moſt obſtinate and violent Attacks. On the other Hand in thoſe Camps, where you are to be ſhut up and moleſt an Enemy, all the ſame Things are to be obſerved with the ſame Care: For it is indeed a juſt Obſervation, that the Nature of War is ſuch, that he who beſieges is in a great Meaſure beſieged himſelf. For this Reaſon you are to conſider not only how you may take the Place, but alſo how you may keep yourſelf from being oppreſſed, either by the Boldneſs or Diligence of the Enemy, or by the Careleſſneſs of your own Men. In order to take the Place, you muſt proceed either by Siege or by Aſſault: And to keep yourſelf from being oppreſſed, there are alſo two Methods, which are, being ſtoutly fortified, and

and making a brave Defence. The whole Purpoſe of an Aſſault is to break in either upon a Town or a Fortification. I ſhall not ſpeak here either of Scaling-ladders, by Means whereof you mount the Wall in ſpite of the Enemy; nor of Mines, moveable Towers, Engines for Battery, nor of any other Methods of Offence either by Fire, Water, or any other Force: Inaſmuch as we intend to treat of theſe military Engines more clearly in another Place. Thus much it may be proper here to mention, that againſt the Violence of Battery we ſhould oppoſe Beams, Planks, Parapets of ſtrong Timber, Hurdles, Ropes, Faſcines, Sacks ſtuffed with Wool, Ruſhes, or Earth; and they ſhould be ſo contrived as to hang looſe and pliable. Againſt Fire theſe Things ought to be wetted, and eſpecially with Vinegar, or Mud, and covered with Brick unbaked; againſt Water, to prevent the Bricks from being waſhed away, they ſhould be covered over with the Hides of Beaſts; and laſtly, againſt Battery, that the Hides may not be broken through or torn away, add any coarſe Cloths or Tarpawlins thoroughly wetted and ſoaked. Circumvallations or Trenches round the Place beſieged, ought for ſeveral Reaſons to be drawn pretty near it; for by that Means their Circuit will be leſs, they will require fewer Hands, Expence and Materials, to finiſh them, and when finiſhed, the fewer Men will be neceſſary to defend them: But they muſt not run ſo cloſe under the Wall, that the Beſieged may annoy your Men within their Trenches by Engines upon the Wall. If the Circumvallation be only intended to cut off from the Beſieged all Manner of Supplies, either of Men or Proviſions from without; you may do this by ſtopping up all the Ways and Paſſages, either by barracading the Bridges, and Fords, and blocking up the Roads with ſtrong Fences of Wood or Stones; or by running up a continued Rampart to joyn together the Lakes, Bogs, Marſhes, Rivers and Hills; or if you can any Ways lay the Country under Water. To theſe Precautions we ſhould add thoſe which relate to the Defence of our own Camp: For the Trenches, Ramparts, Towers and the like ought to be ſo well fortified both towards the Place beſieged, and on the Side of any Country that might throw in Succours, that the former may not be able to annoy you by Sallies, nor the Latter by Incurſions. Moreover, in convenient Places erect Watch-towers and Forts, that your Men may go out to forage for Wood, Water and Proviſions with Safety and Freedom. But do not let your Troops be diſperſed up and down in Places ſo remote from one another, that they cannot obey the Orders of a ſingle General, nor fight with united Forces, nor be ready at Hand to aſſiſt one another upon any ſudden Emergency. It will not be foreign to our Purpoſe to ſet down here an Account of a Fortification out of *Appian*, well worthy to be remembered. He tells us, that when *Octavianus Auguſtus* beſieged *Lucius Antonius* in *Peruſia*, he made a Trench quite to the *Tyber*, ſeven Miles long, thirty Foot broad, and as many deep: Which he fortified with a high Wall, and with a thouſand and fifty wooden Towers ſtanding up, each threeſcore Foot above the Wall, and made the Whole ſo ſtrong, that the Beſieged were not more ſtraitened in by it, than they were excluded from annoying the Enemy in any Part. And thus much may ſuffice for Incampments or Stations by Land, unleſs it may be thought neceſſary to add, that we ought to chuſe out a Place of the greateſt Dignity and Honour, wherein to plant the Standard of the Commonwealth with befitting Majeſty, where the Rites of Religion may be performed with all due Reverence, and where the Generals and other chief Officers may meet either in Council or for the Adminiſtration of Juſtice.

Chap. XII.

Of Incampments or Stations at Sea, which are Fleets; of Ships and their Parts; as alſo of Havens and their proper Fortification.

SOME perhaps will not allow that Fleets are Sea Incampments; but will be rather for ſaying, that we uſe Ships like a Kind of Water Elephant, which we direct as we pleaſe by its Bridle; and that the Haven is much more like a Sea Incampment, than the Fleet. Others on the Contrary, will ſay, that a Ship is no other than a travelling Fortreſs. We ſhall paſs

paſs by theſe Diſputes, and proceed to ſhew that there are two Things by Means of which the Art of Building may contribute to the Safety and Victory of Generals of Fleets and their Forces: The Firſt conſiſts in the right Conſtruction and Rigging of the Veſſels, and the Second in the proper fortifying the Haven; whether you are to go to attack the Enemy, or to ſtay to defend yourſelf. The primary Uſe of Shipping is to convey you and yours: The Second, is to fight without Danger. The Danger muſt ariſe either from the Ships themſelves, in which Caſe it ſeems to be innate and incorporate with them; or elſe muſt happen to them from without. That from without, is from the Force and Violence of Winds and Waves, from Rocks and Shelves; all which are to be avoided by Experience in Sea-affairs, and a thorough Knowledge of Places and Winds: But the Danger incorporate and innate with the Veſſel itſelf, ariſes either from the Deſign, or the Timbers; againſt which Defects it falls under our Province to provide. We ſhould reject all Timber that is brittle, or apt to ſplit, too heavy or liable to rot ſoon. Nails and Pins of Braſs or Copper, are reckoned better than thoſe of Iron. I have obſerved by Means of *Trajan*'s Ship, which while I was writing this Treatiſe was dug up out of the *lago di Nemi*, where it had lain under Water above thirteen hundred Years, that the Pine and Cypreſs Wood which was in it had remained ſurprizingly ſound. It was covered on the Outſide with double Planks, done over with *Greek* Pitch, to which ſtuck a Coat of Linen Cloth, and that again was plated over with Sheets of Lead faſtened on with braſs Nails. The ancient Architects took the Model of their Ships from the Shape of a Fiſh; that Part which was the Back of the Fiſh, in the Ship was the Keel; that which in the Fiſh was the Head, in the Ship was the Prow; the Tail was the Helm, and inſtead of Fins and Gills, they made Oars. Ships are of two Sorts, and are built either for Burthen or for Speed: A long Veſſel cuts its Way quickeſt through the Water, eſpecially when it Sails before the Wind; but a ſhort one is moſt obedient to the Helm. I would not have the Length of a Veſſel of Burthen leſs than three Times its Breadth; nor that of a Veſſel for Speed, more than nine Times. We have treated more particularly of every Thing relating to a Veſſel in a Book intended wholly for that Purpoſe, called the Ship; and therefore ſhall have Occaſion to ſay no more of it here, than what is juſt neceſſary. The Parts of a Ship are theſe, the Keel, the Poop, the Prow, the two Sides, to which you may, if you pleaſe, add the Sail, the Helm, and the Reſt of the Parts that belong to the Courſe of the Ship. The Hollow of the Veſſel will bear any Weight that is equal to the Weight of Water that would fill it quite up to the Top. The Keel muſt be ſtraight, but all the other Parts made with curve Lines. The broader the Keel is, the greater Weight the Veſſel will carry, but then it will be the ſlower; the narrower the Keel is, the Swifter will be the Ship, but then it will be unſteady, unleſs you fill it with Ballaſt. The broad Keel is moſt convenient in ſhallow Water; but in deep Seas the narrow one will be more ſecure. The Sides and Prow built high will make the ſtouteſt Reſiſtance againſt the Waves, but then they are more expoſed to Danger from the Winds; the Sharper the Head is, the Swifter the Ship will make its Way; and the Thinner the Stern, the more Steady will be the Veſſel in its Courſe. The Sides of the Ship towards the Head ought to be very ſtout, and a little Swelling outwards to throw off the Waves when it ploughs through the Water both with Sails and Oars; but towards the Stern they ſhould grow narrower, in order to ſlip through the Waves with the more Eaſe. A Number of Helms adds Firmneſs to the Veſſel, but takes off from its Swiftneſs. The Maſt ſhould be as long as the whole Ship. We ſhall not here deſcend to other minute Particulars neceſſary both to the Way and Defence of the Veſſel, ſuch as Oars, Ropes, ſharp Beaks, Towers, Bridges and the like; but ſhall only obſerve, that the Planks and Timbers which hang down by the Sides and ſtick out by the Beak of the Veſſel, will ſerve inſtead of a Fortification againſt the Attacks of the Enemy as will Poles ſtuck upright, inſtead of Towers, and the Boom, or the Skiff laid over the Boom, inſtead of Bridges. The Ancients uſed in the Prow of their Ships to place a military Engine, which they called a *Corvus:* But our Mariners now in the Head and Stem of their Veſſels near the Maſts have learnt to ſet up Towers, which they fence round with old coarſe Cloths, Ropes, Sacks, and the like, to deaden the Force of any Violence that might attack them; and to keep off any Enemy that ſhould attempt to board them, they ſet up a Fence of Net-work. I have in another Place contrived and ſhewn how the Floor of the Ship

may

may in a Moment, in the midſt of an Engagement, be filled with ſharp Points ſticking up cloſe to one another, ſo that an Enemy can never ſet his Foot any where without a Wound; and on the other Hand when there is Occaſion, how all theſe may in leſs Space of Time be all removed and cleared away; but this is not a proper Place for repeating it again, and it is ſufficient to have given the Hint to an ingenious Mind. Moreover I have found a Way how, with a ſlight Stroke of a Hammer, to throw down the whole Floor, with all the Men that have boarded the Veſſel and ſtand upon it, and then again with very little Labour to replace it as it was before, whenever it is thought neceſſary ſo to do. Neither is this a proper Place to relate the Methods which I have invented to ſink and burn the Enemy's Ships and deſtroy their Crews by miſerable Deaths. We may perhaps ſpeak of them elſewhere. One Thing muſt not be omitted, namely, that Veſſels of different Heights and Sizes are requiſite in different Places. In the *Mare Maggiore*, in the Narrows among the Iſlands, a large Ship, that cannot be managed without a great Number of Hands, is very unſafe when the Winds are any thing boiſterous: On the Contrary out of the Strait's Mouth, in the wide Ocean, a little Veſſel will not be able to live. To this Head of maritime Affairs alſo belong the Defending and Blocking up a Haven. This may be done by ſinking any great Body, or by Moles, Piers, Chains and the like, whereof we have treated in the preceding Book. Drive in Piles, block the Port up with huge Stones, and ſink large hollow Frames made either of Planks or Oziers and filled with any heavy Stuff. But if the Nature of the Place, or the Greatneſs of the Expence will not allow of this, as for Inſtance, if the Bottom be a Sand or Mud continually moving, or the Water be of too great a Depth, you may then block up the Haven in the following Manner. Make a Float of great Barrels faſtened together, with Planks and Timbers joyned croſs-ways to one another, and with large Spikes and ſharp Beaks ſticking out from the Float, and Piles with Points of Iron, ſuch as are called ſhod Piles, to the Intent that none of the Enemy's light Ships may dare to drive againſt the Float with full Sails, in order to endeavour to break or paſs it. Dawb the Float over with Mud to ſecure it againſt Fire, and fortify it with a Paliſado of Hurdles or ſtrong Boards, and in convenient Places with wooden Towers, faſtening the whole Work againſt the Fury of the Waves with a good Number of Anchors concealed from the Enemy. It would not be amiſs to make ſuch a Work ſinuous or wavy, with the Backs of the Arches turned againſt the Streſs of the Weather, that the Float may bear the leſs upon its Anchors. But upon this Subject, thus much may ſuffice.

Chap. XIII.

Of the Commiſſaries, Chamberlains, publick Receivers and the like Magiſtrates, whoſe Buſineſs is to ſupply and preſide over the publick Granaries, Chambers of Accompts, Arſenals, Marts, Docks and Stables; as alſo of the three Sorts of Priſons, their Structures, Situations and Compartitions.

NOW as the Execution of all theſe Things requires good Store of Proviſions, and of Treaſures to ſupply the Expence; it will be neceſſary to ſay ſomething of the Magiſtrates who have the Care of this Part of the Buſineſs; as for Inſtance, Commiſſaries, Chamberlains, publick Receivers, and the like, for whom the following Structures muſt Be erected: The Granary, the Chamber for keeping the Treaſures, the Arſenal, the Mart or Place for the tranſacting Commerce, the Dock and the publick Stables for Horſes. We ſhall have but little to ſay here upon theſe Heads, but that little muſt not be neglected. It is evident to every Man's Reaſon, that the Granary, the Chamber of Accompts, and the Arſenal or Magazine for Arms ought to be placed in the Heart of the City, and in the Place of greateſt Honour, for the greater Security and Conveniency. The Docks or Arſenals for Shipping ſhould be placed at a Diſtance from the Houſes of the Citizens, for fear of Fire. We ſhould alſo be ſure, in this laſt Sort of Structure, to raiſe a good many entire Party-walls in in different Places, running from the Ground quite up above the Roof, to confine the Flame, if any ſhould happen, and prevent it catching from one Roof to another. Marts ought to be fixed by the Sea-ſide, upon the Mouths of Rivers, and the Meeting of ſeveral great Roads. The Docks or Arſenals for Shipping ſhould have large Baſons or Canals of Water, wherein to receive ſuch Veſſels as want refitting, and from which they may be conveniently launched out again to Sea; but we ſhould take Care that this Water be not a ſtanding one, but be kept in conſtant Motion. Shipping is very much rotted by ſoutherly Winds, and cracked by the mid-day Heat; but the Aſpect of the riſing Sun preſerves it. All Granaries, or other Structures built for the laying up of Stores, abſolutely require a Drineſs both of Air and Situation. But we ſhall ſpeak more fully of the Particulars, when we come to the Conveniencies belonging to private Perſons, to whoſe uſe they are indeed referred; only we ſhall ſay ſomething here of the Places for laying up Salt. A Storehouſe for Salt ought to be made in the following Manner. Make up the Ground with a Layer of Coal to the Height of one Cubit or Foot and an half, and ſtamp it down very tight; then ſtrew it with Sand pounded together with clean Chalk, to the Height of three Hands breadths, and lay it exactly level; and then pave it with ſquare Bricks baked till they are quite black. The Face of the Walls on the Inſide ought to be made of the ſame Sort of Bricks; but if you have not a ſufficient Quantity of them, you may build it with ſquare Stone, not either with ſoft Stone or Flint, but with ſome Stone of a middle Nature between thoſe two, only very hard; and let this Sort of Work go the Thickneſs of a Cubit into the Wall; and then let the whole Inſide be lined with Planks of Wood, faſtened with braſs Nails, or rather joynted together without any Nails at all, and fill up the intermediate Space between the Lining and the Wall, with Reeds. It would alſo have a mighty good Effect to dawb over the Planks with Chalk ſteeped in Lees of Oil, and mixed with Spart and Ruſhes ſhred ſmall. Laſtly, all publick Buildings of this Nature ought to be well fortified with ſtout Walls, Towers, and Ammunition, againſt all Manner of Force, Malice, or Fraud either of Robbers, Enemies or ſeditious Citizens. I think I have now ſaid enough of publick Structures, unleſs it may be thought neceſſary to conſider of one Particular more which concerns the Magiſtrate, and that not a little; namely, that it is neceſſary he ſhould have Places for the Confinement of ſuch as he has condemned either for Contumacy, Treachery or Villany. I obſerve that the Ancients had three Sorts of Priſons. The firſt was that wherein they kept the Diſorderly and the Ignorant, to the Intent that every Night they might be doctored and inſtructed by learned and able Profeſſors of the beſt Arts, in thoſe Points which related to good Manners and an honeſt Life. The Second was for the Confinement of Debtors, and for the Reformation of ſuch as were got into a licentious Way of Living. The laſt was for the moſt wicked Wretches and horrid Profligates, unworthy of the Light of the Sun or the Society of Mankind, and ſoon to be delivered over to capital Puniſhment or perpetual Impriſonment and Miſery. If any Man is of Opinion that this laſt Sort of Priſon ought to be made like ſome ſubterraneous Cavern, or frightful Sepulchre, he has certainly a greater Regard to the Puniſhment of the Criminal than is agreeable either to the Deſign of the Law or to Humanity; and though wicked Men do by their Crimes deſerve the higheſt Puniſhment, yet the Prince or Commonwealth ought never to forget Mercy in the Midſt of Juſtice. Therefore let it be ſufficient to make this Sort of Buildings very ſtrong and ſecure, with ſtout Walls, Roofs and Apertures, that the Perſon confined may have no Means of making his Eſcape; which may in a great Meaſure be obtained, by the Thickneſs, Depth and Height of the Walls, and their being built with very hard and large Stones, joyned together with Pins of Iron or Braſs. To this you may, if you pleaſe, add Windows grated with ſtrong Bars of Iron or Wood; though in reality nothing of this Sort whatſoever can fully ſecure a Priſoner always thoughtful of his Liberty and Safety, nor prevent his making his Eſcape, if you let him uſe the Strength which Nature and Cunning have beſtowed upon him, and on which Account there is an excellent Admonition contained in this Saying, that the vigilant Eye of a Goaler is a Priſon of Adamant. But in other Reſpects, let us follow the Method and Cuſtoms of the Ancients. We muſt remember that in a Priſon there muſt be Privies and Hearths for Fire, which ought to be contrived to be without either Smoake or ill Smells. the following Plan of an entire Priſon may anſwer all the aforementioned Purpoſes. Encloſe with very high and ſtrong Walls, without any Apertures, a Space a Space of Ground in ſome ſecure and not unfrequented Part of the City, and fortify it with Towers and Galleries. From this Wall inwards the Apartments where the Priſoners are to be confined, let there be an open Walk about four Foot and an half wide, where the Keepers may take their Rounds every Night to prevent any Eſcapes by Conſpiracy among the Priſoners. The Space remaining in the Middle of this Circuit divide in the following Manner. Inſtead of a Veſtibule make a good pleaſant Hall, where thoſe may be inſtructed who are ſent thither in order to be forced to learn how to demean themſelves. Next to this Hall, make Habitations for the Goalers and Places for them to keep guard in, within an Encloſure of Lattices and Croſs-bars. Next let there be an open Court, with Porticoes on each Side of it, with Windows in them, through which you may ſee into all the Cells within; in which Cells Bankrupts and Debtors are to be confined, not all together, but in different Apartments. In the Front of this Court there muſt be a cloſer Priſon, for ſuch as are guilty of ſmall Offences, and beyond that a Place where Priſoners for capital Crimes may be confined with yet greater Strictneſs and Privacy.

Chap. XIV.

Of private Houſes and their Differences; as alſo of the Country Houſe, and the Rules to be obſerved in its Situation and Structure.

I Now come to treat of private Edifices. I have already obſerved elſewhere, that a Houſe is a little City. We are therefore in the building of it, to have an Eye almoſt to every Thing that relates to the Building of a City; that it be healthy, furniſhed with all Manner of Neceſſaries, not defficient in any of the Conveniencies that conduce to the Repoſe, Tranquility or Delicacy of Life. What thoſe are and how they are to be obtained, I think I have already, in a great Meaſure, ſhewn in the preceding Books. However, as the Occaſion here is different, we ſhall conſider them over again in the following Manner. A private Houſe is manifeſtly deſigned for the Uſe of a Family, to which it ought to be a uſeful and convenient Abode. It will not be ſo convenient as it ought, if it has not every Thing within itſelf that the Family has Occaſion for. There is a great Number of Perſons and Things in a Family, which you cannot diſtribute as you would in a City ſo well as you can in the Country. In building a Houſe in Town, your Neighbour's Wall, a common Gutter, a publick Square or Street, and the like, ſhall all hinder you from contriving it juſt to your own Mind; which is not ſo in the Country, where you have as much Freedom as you have Obſtruction in Town. For this, and other Reaſons, therefore, I ſhall diſtinguiſh the Matter thus: That the Habitation for a private Perſon muſt be different in Town from what it is in the Country. In both theſe there muſt again be a Difference between thoſe which are for the meaner Sort of Citizens, and thoſe which are for the Rich. The meaner Sort build only for Neceſſity; but the Rich for Pleaſure and Delight. I ſhall ſet down ſuch Rules as the Modeſty of the wiſeſt Men may approve of in all Sorts of Buildings, and for that Purpoſe ſhall begin with thoſe which are moſt eaſy. Habitations in the Country are the freeſt from all Obſtructions, and therefore People are more inclined to beſtow their Expence in the Country than in Town. We ſhall therefore firſt take a Review of ſome Obſervations which we have already made, and which are very material with Relation to the chief Uſes of a Country Houſe. They are as follows: We ſhould carefully avoid a bad Air and an ill Soil. We ſhould build in the Middle of an open Champian, under the Shelter of ſome Hill, where there is Plenty of Water, and pleaſant Proſpects, and in the healthieſt Part of a healthy Country. A heavy unhealthy Air is ſaid to be occaſioned not only by thoſe Inconveniencies which we mentioned in the firſt Book, but alſo by thick Woods, eſpecially if they are full of Trees with bitter Leaves; becauſe the Air in ſuch Places being not kept in Motion either by Sun or Winds, wants its due Concoction; it is alſo occaſioned by a barren and unwholſome Soil, which will never produce any Thing but Woods. A Country Houſe ought to ſtand in ſuch a Place as may lie moſt convenient for the Owner's Houſe in Town. *Xenophon* would have a Man go go to his Country Houſe on Foot, for the Sake of Exerciſe, and return on Horſeback. It ought not therefore to lie far from the City, and the Way to it ſhould be both good and clear, ſo as he may go it either in Summer or Winter, either in a Coach, or on Foot, and if poſſible by Water. It will be alſo very convenient to have your Way to it lie through a Gate of the City that is not far from your Town Houſe, but as near it as may be, that you may go backwards and forwards from Town to Country, and from Country to Town, with your Wife and Family, as often as you pleaſe, without being too much obſerved by the People, or being obliged in the leaſt to conſult your Dreſs. It is not amiſs to have a Villa ſo placed, that when you go to it in a Morning the Rays of the riſing Sun may not be troubleſome to your Eyes, nor thoſe of the ſetting Sun in the Evening when you return to the City. Neither ſhould a Country Houſe ſtand in a remote, deſart, mean Corner, diſtant from a reaſonable Neighbourhood: but in a Situation where you may have People to converſe with, drawn to the ſame Place by the Fruitfulneſs of the Soil, the Pleaſantneſs of the Air, the Plentifulneſs of the Country, the Sweetneſs of the Fields, and the Security of the Neighbourhood. Nor ſhould a Villa be ſeated in a Place of too much Reſort, near adjoyning either to the City, or any great Road, or to a Port where great Numbers of Veſſels and Boats are continually putting in; but in ſuch a Situation, as though none of thoſe Pleaſures may be wanting, yet your Family may not be eternally moleſted with the Viſits of Strangers and Paſſengers. The Ancients ſay that in windy Places Things are never ſpoilt by Ruſt or Mildew; but in moiſt Places, and low Vallies, where the Winds have not a free Courſe, they are very much expoſed to them. I cannot approve of one general Rule which is laid down for all Places, namely, that a Country Houſe ought to be built ſo as to look towards the riſing of the Sun when it is in the Equinox: For nothing can be ſaid relating to the Sun and Winds but what muſt alter according to the Difference of the Climate, ſince the North Wind is not light and the South unhealthy in all Places. *Celſus*, the Phyſician, very well obſerved that all Winds which blow from the Sea, are groſſer than thoſe which blow over Land, which are always lighter. Upon this Account of the Winds we ought to avoid the Mouths of all Vallies, becauſe in ſuch Places the Winds are too cold if they come in the Night, or too hot, if in the Day, being over-heated by the too great Reflection of the Sun's Rays.

Chap. XV.

That Country Houſes are of two Sorts; the proper Diſpoſition of all their Members whether for the Lodging of Men, Animals, or Tools of Agriculture and other neceſſary Inſtruments.

But as of Habitations in the Country ſome are deſigned for Gentlemen, others for Huſbandmen, ſome invented for Uſe, others perhaps for Pleaſure; we ſhall begin with thoſe which belong to Husbandmen. The Habitations of theſe ought not to be far from their Maſter's Houſe, that he may be at Hand to over-look them every now and then, to ſee what they are doing, and what Orders it is neceſſary for him to give. The peculiar Buſineſs of theſe Structures is for the getting in, ordering and preſerving the Fruits of the Earth: Unleſs you will ſay that this laſt Office, namely, of preſerving the Grain, belongs rather to the Houſe of the Maſter, and even rather to his Houſe in the City than to that in the Country. This Buſineſs is to be done by a Number of Hands and a good Quantity of Tools, but moſt of all by the Diligence and Induſtry of the Farmer or Overſeer. The Ancients computed the neceſſary Family of a Farmer to be about fifteen Perſons; for theſe therefore you muſt have convenient Places where they may warm themſelves when they are cold, or retire for Shelter when they are driven from their Labour by foul Weather, where they may eat their Meals, reſt themſelves and prepare the Things they will want in their Buſineſs. Make therefore a large Kitchen, not obſcure, nor liable to Danger from Fire, with an Oven, Stove, Pump and Sink. Beyond the Kitchen let there be a Room where the better Sort among your People may lie, and a Larder for preſerving all Sorts of Proviſions for daily Uſe. Let all the other People be ſo diſtributed, that every one may be near thoſe Things which are under his particular Care. Let the Overſeer lie near the principal Gate, that nobody may paſs and repaſs or carry any Thing out in the Night without his Knowledge. Let thoſe who have the Care of the Cattle, lie near the Stable, that they may be always at Hand to keep every Thing in good Order. And this may be ſufficient with Relation to your People. Of Tools or Inſtruments, ſome are animate, as Cattle; and ſome inanimate, as Carts, all Sorts of iron Tools, and the like; for theſe erect on one Side of the Kitchen a large Shed under which you may ſet your Cart, Plough, Harrow, Yoke, Hay-baskets, and the like Utenſils; and let this Shed have a South Aſpect, that in Winter Time the Family may divert themſelves under it on Holydays. Make a very large and neat Place for your Preſſes both of Wine and Oil. Let there be alſo a Store-houſe for the laying up and preſerving your Meaſures, Hampers, Baskets, Cordage, Houghs, Pitchforks and ſo forth. Over the Rafters that run acroſs within the Shed, you may ſpread Hurdles, and upon them you may lay up Poles, Rods, Staves, Boughs, Leaves and Fodder for your Oxen, Hemp and Flax unwrought, and ſuch like Stores. Cattle is of two Sorts; one, for Labour; as Oxen and Horſes; the other, for Profit, as Hogs, Sheep, Goats, and all Sorts of Herds. We ſhall ſpeak firſt of the labouring Sort, becauſe they ſeem to come under the Head of Inſtruments; and afterwards we ſhall ſay ſomething of thoſe which are for Profit, which belong properly to the Induſtry of your Overſeer or Farmer. Let the Stables for Horſes, and for Oxen, and all other black Cattle, be warm in Winter, and let their Racks be ſtrong and well fenced, that they may not ſcatter their Meat. Let the Hay for the Horſes be above them, that they may not reach it without ſome Pains, and that they may be forced to raiſe their Heads high for it, which makes their Heads drier and their Shoulders lighter. On the Contrary, let their Oats and other Grain lie ſo as they may be forced to ſtoop low for it; which will prevent their taking too large Mouthfuls, and ſwallowing too much whole; beſides that it will ſtrengthen their Breaſt and Muſcles. But above all you muſt take particular Care that the Wall behind the Manger, againſt which the Horſe's Head is to ſtand, be not damp. The Bone which covers the Horſe's Brain is ſo thin, that it will bear neither Damp nor Cold; and therefore take Care alſo that the Moon's Beams do not come in at the Windows; which are very apt to make him Wall-eyed and to give him grievous Coughs; and indeed the Moon's Beams are as bad as a Peſtilence to any Cattle that are infirm. Let the Oxe's Manger be ſet lower, that he may eat as he lyes. If Horſes ſee the Fire, they are prodigiouſly frightened and will grow rugged. Oxen are pleaſed with the Sight of Men. If a Mule is ſet up in a hot or dark Place, ſhe runs Mad. Some think the Mule does not want ſo much as the leaſt Shelter for any other Part but her Head, and that it is not at all the Worſe if her other Parts are expoſed to Dews and Colds. Let the Ground under the Oxen be paved with Stone, that the Filth and Dung may not rot their Hoofs. Under Horſes, make a Trench in the Pavement, and cover it with Planks of Holm or Oak, that their Urine may not ſettle under them, and that by their pawing they may not ſpoil both their Hoofs and the Pavement.

Chap. XVI.

That the Induſtry of the Farmer or Overſeer ought to be employed as well about all Sorts of Animals, as about the Fruits of the Earth; as alſo of the Conſtruction of the Threſhing-floor.

We ſhall juſt briefly mention that the Induſtry of the Overſeer, is not only to be employed about gathering in the Fruits of the Earth, but alſo about the Management and Improvement of Cattle, Fowls, Fiſh and other Animals. Set the Stalls for Cattle in a dry Place, and never in a Damp one; clear away every little Stone from under them, and make them with a Slope, that you may eaſily ſweep and clean them; let one Part of them be covered, and the other open, and take Care that no ſoutherly or other moiſt Wind can affect the Cattle in the Night, and that they be ſheltered from all other troubleſome Blaſts. For

For a Place to keep Rabbits in, build a Wall of ſquare Stone, with its Foundations dug ſo low as to be in Water; within the Space encloſed make a Floor of male Sand, with little Hillocks here and there of Fuller's Earth. Let your Poultry have a Shed in the Yard facing the South, and thick ſtrewed with Aſhes, and over this Places for them to lay their Eggs, and Perches to rooſt upon in the Night. Some are for keeping their Poultry in large Coops in ſome handſome incloſed Area facing the Eaſt; but thoſe that are deſigned for laying and hatching of Eggs, as they are more cheerful, having their Liberty, ſo too they are more fruitful; whereas, thoſe which are kept in a dark confined Place, ſeldom bring their Eggs to any Thing. Place your Dove-houſe ſo as to be in View of Water, and do not make it too lofty, but of ſuch an eaſy Heigth, that the Pidgeons wearied with flying, or after ſporting about in the Air with one another, may gently glide down upon it with Eaſe and Pleaſure. Some there are who ſay that when the Pidgeon has found her Meat in the Field, the farther ſhe has it to carry to her Young, the Fatter ſhe makes them with it; and the Reaſon they give is, becauſe the Meat which they carry Home to feed their Young in their Crop, by ſtaying there a good While is half concocted; and upon this Account, they are for placing the Dove-houſe on ſome very high ſteep Situation. They think too, that it is beſt for the Dove-houſe to be at a pretty good Diſtance from its Water, that the Pidgeons may not chill their Eggs by coming to them with their Feet wet. If in one Corner of the Tower you encloſe a Kaſtrel, it will ſecure your Dove-houſe from Birds of Prey. If under the Door you bury the Head of a Wolf ſtrewed over with Cummin-ſeed, in an earthen Veſſel full of Holes for the Smell to get out, it will bring you an infinite Number of Pidgeons. If you make your Dove-houſe Floor of Chalk, and wet it thoroughly with Man's Urine, you will bring Multitudes of Pidgeons from the Seats of their Anceſtors, to take up their Abode with you. Before the Windows let there be Cornices of Stone, or of Olive-wood, projecting out a Cubit, for the Pidgeons to light upon at their coming Home, and to take their Flight from at their going Abroad. If the Young ones which are confined have a View of Trees and the Sky before they can fly, it will make them Droop and Pine away. Other ſmaller Birds which you have a Deſire to breed, ought to have their Neſts and Apartments made for them in ſome warm Place. Thoſe which walk more than they fly, ſhould have them low, and upon the Ground itſelf; for others they ſhould be made higher. Each ſhould have a ſeparate Apartment, divided by Partitions on each Side to keep their Eggs or Young from falling out of the Neſt. Clay is better to make the Neſts of than Lime, and Lime than Terraſs. All Sort of old Stone new cut is bad; Bricks are better than Turf, if not too much baked. The Wood either of Poplar or Fir is very uſeful. All the Apartments for Birds ought to be ſmooth, clean and ſweet, and eſpecially for Pidgeons. Even four footed Beaſts, if kept naſty, will grow Scabby. Let every Part, therefore, be well done over with Rough-caſt, and plaiſtered and white waſhed, not leaving the leaſt Cranny unſtopped, that Pole-cats, Weezels, Newts, or the like Vermin may not deſtroy the Eggs, or the Young, or prejudice the Wall; and be ſure to make convenient Places to keep their Meat and Water in. It will be very Convenient for this Purpoſe to have a Moat quite round your Houſe, wherein your Geeſe, Ducks, Hogs and Cows may water and waſh themſelves, and near which, in all Weathers, they may have as much Meat lying ready for them as they will eat. Let the Water and Meat for your ſmaller Fowls be kept in Tunnels along the Wall, ſo that they may not ſcatter or dirty it with their Feet; and you may have Pipes into theſe Tunnels from without, through which you may convey their Food into them. In the Middle, let there be a Place for them to waſh in, with a conſtant ſupply of clean Water. Make your Piſh-pond in a chalky Soil, and dig it ſo deep that the Water may neither be over heated by the Rays of the Sun, nor too eaſily frozen up by the Cold. Moreover, make ſome Caverns in the Sides, for the Fiſh to run into upon any ſudden Diſturbance of the Water, that they may not be waſted and worn away by continual Alarms. Fiſh are nouriſhed by the Juices of the Earth; great Heat torments them, and extreme Froſt kills them; but they are very much pleaſed and delighted by the Mid-day Sun. It is thought not amiſs to have the turbid Floods after Rains flow into the Pond ſometimes; but never upon the firſt Rain after the Dog-days; becauſe they then have a ſtrong Tincture of Lime, and will kill the Fiſh; and afterwards too they ſhould be admitted but rarely, becauſe their ſtinking Slime is apt to prejudice both the Fiſh and Water too; but ſtill

ſtill there ought to be a continual Flux and Reflux of Water, either from ſome Spring, River, Lake or Sea. But concerning Fiſh-ponds which are to be ſupplied by the Sea-water, the Ancients have given us fuller Inſtructions, in the following Manner. A muddy Soil affords the beſt Nouriſhment for flat Fiſh, ſuch as Soals and the like, and a ſandy is beſt for ſhell Fiſh. The Sea itſelf is beſt for others, as the Dory and Shark; and the Sea-thruſt and Whiting feed beſt among the Rocks where they are naturally bred. Laſtly, they ſay that there can be no better Pond for keeping Fiſh in, than one ſo ſituated that the Waves of the Sea which flow into it are continually removing thoſe which were in it before, not ſuffering the Water ever to ſtagnate, and that the ſlower the Water is in renewing, the leſs wholeſome it is. And thus much may ſuffice as to the Care and Induſtry of the Farmer or Overſeer, in the Affairs abovementioned. But we muſt not here omit the chief Thing needful with Relation to the gathering together and ſtoring up the Fruits of the Harveſt, and that is the Threſhing-floor which ought to lie open to the Sun and Air, and not far from the Shed mentioned before, that upon any ſudden Rain you may immediately remove both your Grain and Workmen into Shelter. In order to make your Floor, you need not give yourſelf the Trouble to lay the Ground exactly level; but only plain it pretty even, and then dig it up and throw a good Quantity of Lees of Oil upon it, and let it ſoak in thoroughly; then break the Clods very ſmall and lay them down even, either with a Roller or a Harrow, and beat it down cloſe with a Rammer; then pour ſome more Lees of Oil upon it, and when this is dried into it, neither Mice, nor Ants will come a-near it, neither will it ever grow poachy or produce Graſs or Weeds. Chalk likewiſe adds a good Deal of Firmneſs to a Work of this Nature. And thus much for the Habitation of the Labourers.

Chap. XVII.

Of the Country Houſe for a Gentleman; its various Parts, and the proper Diſpoſition of each of thoſe Parts.

SOME are of Opinion that a Gentleman's Country Houſe ſhould have quite different Conveniencies for Summer and for Winter; and the Rules they give for this Purpoſe are theſe: The Bed-chambers for the Winter ſhould look towards the Point at which the Sun riſes in Winter, and the Parlour, towards the Equinoctial Sun-ſetting; whereas the Bed-chambers for Summer ſhould look to the South, the Parlours, to the Winter Sun-riſing, and the Portico or Place for walking in, to the South. But, in my Opinion, all theſe Conveniencies ought to be varied according to the Difference of the Country and Climate, ſo as to temper Heat by Cold and Dry by Moiſt. I do not think it neceſſary for the Gentleman's Houſe to ſtand in the moſt fruitful Part of his whole Eſtate, but rather in the moſt Honourable, where he can uncontrolled enjoy all the Pleaſures and Conveniencies of Air, Sun, and fine Proſpects, go down eaſily at any Time into his Eſtate, receive Strangers handſomely and ſpaciouſly, be ſeen by Paſſengers for a good Way round, and have a View of ſome City, Towns, the Sea, an open Plain, and the Tops of ſome known Hills and Mountains. Let him have the Delights of Gardens, and the Diverſions of Fiſhing and Hunting cloſe under his Eye. We have in another Place obſerved, that of the different Members of a Houſe, ſome belong to the whole Family in general, other to a certain Number of Perſons in it, and others again only to one or more Perſons ſeparately. In our Country Houſe, with Regard to thoſe Members which belong to the whole Family in general, let us imitate the Prince's Palace. Before the Door let there be a large open Space, for the Exerciſes either of Chariot or Horſe Racing, much longer than a Youth can either draw a Bow or throw a Dart. Within the Houſe, with Regard to thoſe Conveniencies neceſſary for a Number of Perſons in the Family, let there not be wanting open Places for Walking, Swimming, and other Diverſions, Court-yards, Graſs-plots and Porticoes, where the old Men may chat together in the kindly Warmth of the Sun in Winter, and where the Family may divert themſelves and enjoy the Shade in Summer. It is manifeſt ſome Parts of the Houſe are for the Family themſelves, and others for the

the Things neceſſary and uſeful to the Family. The Family conſiſts of the following Perſons: The Husband, the Wife, their Children and Relations, and all the different Sorts of Servants attendant upon theſe; beſides which, Gueſts too are to be reckoned as Part of the Family. The Things uſeful to the Family are Proviſions and all Manner of Neceſſaries, ſuch as Cloths, Arms, Books, and Horſes alſo. The principal Member of the whole Building, is that which (whatever Names others may give it) I ſhall call the Court-yard with its Portico; next to this is the Parlour, within this the Bed-chambers, and laſtly, the private Rooms for the particular Uſes of each Perſon in the Family. The other Members of the Houſe are ſufficiently known by their Uſes. The Court-yard therefore is the principal Member, to which all the other ſmaller Members muſt correſpond, as being in a Manner a publick Market-place to the whole Houſe, which from this Court-yard derives all the Advantages of Communication and Light. For this Reaſon every one deſires to have his Court-yard as ſpacious, large, open, handſome and convenient as poſſible. Some content themſelves with one Court-yard, others are for having more, and for encloſing them all with very high Walls, or ſome with higher and ſome with lower; and they are for having them ſome covered and others open, and others again half covered and half uncovered; in ſome they would have a Portico only on one Side, in others on two or more, and in others all round; and theſe Porticoes, laſtly, ſome would build with flat, others with arched Roofs. Upon theſe Heads I have nothing more to ſay, but that Regard muſt be had to the Climate and Seaſon, and to Neceſſity and Convenience; ſo as in cold Countries to ward againſt the bleak North-wind, and the Severity of the Air and Soil; and in hot Climates, to avoid the troubleſome and ſcorching Rays of the Sun. Admit the pleaſanteſt Breezes on all Sides, and ſuch a grateful Quantity of Light as is neceſſary; but do not let your Court-yard be expoſed to any noxious Vapours exhaled from any damp Place, nor to frequent haſty Showers from ſome overlooking Hill in the Neighbourhood. Exactly anſwering the Middle of your Court-yard place your Entrance, with a handſome Veſtibule, neither narrow, difficult or obſcure. Let the firſt Room that offers itſelf be a Chapel dedicated to God, with its Altar, where Strangers and Gueſts may offer their Devotions, beginning their Friendſhip by Religion; and where the Father of the Family may put up his Prayers for the Peace of his Houſe and the Welfare of his Relations. Here let him embrace thoſe who come to viſit him, and if any Cauſe be referred to him by his Friends, or he has any other ſerious Buſineſs of that Nature to tranſact, let him do it in this Place. Nothing is handſomer in the Middle of the Portico, than Windows of Glaſs, through which you may receive the Pleaſure either of Sun or Air, according to the Seaſon. *Martial* ſays, that Windows looking to the South, receive a pure Sun and a clear Light; and the Ancients thought it beſt to place their Porticoes fronting the South, becauſe the Sun in Summer running his Courſe higher, did not throw in his Rays, where they would enter in Winter. The Proſpect of Hills to the South, when thoſe Hills, on the Side which you have a View of, are continually covered with Clouds and Vapours, is not very pleaſant, if they are at a great Diſtance; and if they are near, and in a Manner juſt over your Head, they will incommode you with chill Shadows and cold Rimes; but if they are at a convenient Diſtance, they are both pleaſant and convenient, becauſe they defend you from the ſouthern Winds. Hills towards the North reverberating the Rays of the Sun, encreaſe the Heat; but at a pretty good Diſtance, they are very delightful, becauſe the Clearneſs of the Air, which is always ſerene in ſuch a Situation, and the Brightneſs of the Sun, which it always enjoys, is extremely chearful to the Sight. Hills to the Eaſt and ſo likewiſe to the Weſt, will make your Mornings cold and the Dews plentiful, if they are near you; but both, if at ſome tolerable Diſtance, are wonderfully Pleaſant. So too, Rivers and Lakes are inconvenient if too near, and afford no Delight, if too far off: Whereas, on the Contrary, the Sea, if it is at a large Diſtance, makes both your Air and Sun unhealthy; but when it is cloſe to you, it does you leſs Harm, becauſe then you have always an Equality in your Air. Indeed there is this to be ſaid, that when it is at a great Diſtance, it encreaſes the Deſire we have to ſee it. There is a good Deal too in the Point to which we lie open to it: For if you are expoſed to the Sea towards the South, it ſcorches you; if towards the Eaſt, it infeſts you with Damps; if to the Weſt, it makes your Air cloudy and full of Vapours; and if to the North, it chills you with exceſſive Cold. From the Court-yard we proceed to the Parlours, which muſt be contrived for different Seasons, some to be used in Summer, others in Winter; and others as we may say in the middle Seasons. Parlours for Summer require Water and the Verdure of Gardens; those for Winter, must be warm and have good Fire-places. Both should be large, pleasant and delicate. There are many Arguments to convince us that Chimnies were in Use among the Ancients; but not such as ours are now. One of the Ancients says, the Tops of the Houses smoke, *Et fumant culmina tecti:* And we find it continues the same all over *Italy* to this Day, except in *Lombardy* and *Tuscany*, and that the Mouths of none of the Chimnies rise higher than the Tops of the Houses. *Vitruvius* says, that in Winter Parlours it is ridiculous to adorn the Ceiling with handsome Painting, because it will be presently spoilt by the constant Smoke and continual Fires; for which Reason the Ancients used to paint those Ceilings with Black, that it might seem to be done by the Smoke itself. I find too, that they made Use of a purified Sort of Wood, that was quite clear of Smoke, like our Charcoal, upon which Account it was a Dispute among the Lawyers, whether or no Coal was to come under the Denomination of Wood; and therefore it is probable they generally used moveable Hearths or Chafing-pans either of Brass or Iron, which they carried from Place to Place where-ever they had Occasion to make a Fire. And perhaps that warlike Race of Men, hardened by continual Incampments, did not make so much Use of Fire as we do now; and Physicians will not allow it wholesome, to be too much by the Fire-side. *Aristotle* says, that the Flesh of Animals gains its Firmness and Solidity from Cold; and those whose Business it is to take Notice of Things of this Nature have observed, that those working Men who are continually employed about the Furnace have generally dry wrinkled Skins; the Reason of which they say is, because the Juices, of which the Flesh is formed, are exhausted by the Fire, and evaporate in Steam. In *Germany*, *Colchos*, and other Places, where Fire is absolutely necessary against the extreme Cold, they make Use of Stoves; of which we shall speak elsewhere. Let us return to the Chimney, which may be best made serviceable in the following Manner. It must be as direct as possible, capacious, not too far from the Light, it must not draw the Wind too much, but enough however to carry up the Smoke, which else would not go up the Tunnel. For these Reasons do not make it just in a Corner, nor too far within the Wall, nor let it take up the best Part of the Room where your chief Guests ought to sit. Do not let it be incommoded by the Air either of Doors or Windows, nor should it project too far out into the Room. Let its Tunnel be very wide and carried up perpendicular, and let the Top of it rise above the highest Part of the whole Building; and this not only upon Account of the Danger of Fire, but also to prevent the Smoke from being driven down the Chimney again by any Eddy of Wind on the Top of the House. Smoke being hot naturally mounts, and the Heat of the Flame quickens its Ascent: When it comes therefore into the Tunnel of the Chimney, it is compressed and straitened as in a Channel, and being pushed on by the Heat of the Fire, is thrust out in the same Manner as the Sound is out of a Trumpet. And as a Trumpet, if it is too big, does not give a clear Sound, because the Air has Room to rowl about in it; the same will hold good with Relation to the Smoke in a Chimney. Let the Top of the Chimney be covered to keep out Rain, and all round the Sides let there be wide Holes for the Passage of the Smoke, with Breaks projecting out between each Hole to keep off the Violence of the Wind. Where this is not so convenient, erect an upright Pin, and on it hang a brass Cover broad enough to take in the whole Mouth of the Chimney, and let this Cover have a Vane at the Top like a Sort of Crest, which like a Helm may turn it round according to the Wind. Another very good Method also is to set on the Chimney Top some Spire like a Hunter's Horn, either of Brass or baked Earth, broader at one End than the other, with the broad End turned downwards to the Mouth of the Chimney; by which means the Smoke being received in at the broad End, will force its Way out at the Narrow, in Spite of the Wind. To the Parlours we must accommodate the Kitchen, and the Pantry for setting by what is left after Meals, together with all Manner of Vessels and Linen. The Kitchen ought to be neither just under the Noses of the Guests, nor at too great a Distance; but so that the Victuals may be brought in neither too hot nor too cold, and that the Noise of the Scullions, with the Clatter of their Pans, Dishes and other Utensils, may not be troublesome. The Passage through which the Victuals are to be carried, should be handsome and convenient, not open to the Weather, nor

nor dishonoured by any Filth that may offend the Stomachs of the Guests. From the Parlour the next Step is to the Bed-chamber; and for a Man of Figure and Elegance, there should be different ones of these latter, as well as of the former, for Summer and for Winter. This puts me in Mind of *Lucullus*'s Saying, that it is not fit a great Man should be worse lodged than a Swallow or a Crane. However I shall only set down such Rules, with Relation to these Apartments, as are compatible with the greatest Modesty and Moderation. I remember to have read in *Æmilius Probus* the Historian, that among the *Greeks* it was never usual for the Wife to appear at Table, if any body was there besides Relations; and that the Apartments for the Women, were Parts of the House where no Men ever set his Foot except the nearest Kindred. And indeed I must own I think the Apartments for the Ladies, ought to be sacred like Places dedicated to Religion and Chastity. I am besides for having the Rooms particularly designed for Virgins and young Ladies, fitted up in the neatest and most delicate Manner, that their tender Minds may pass their Time in them with less Regret and be as little weary of themselves as possible. The Mistress of the Family should have an Apartment, in which she may easily hear every Thing that is done in the House. However, in these Particulars, the Customs of every Country are always to be principally observed. The Husband and the Wife should each have a separate Chamber, not only that the Wife, either when she lies in, or in Case of any other Indisposition, may not be troublesome to her Husband; but also that in Summer Time, either of them may lie alone whenever they think fit. Each of these Chambers should have its separate Door, besides which there should be a common Passage between them both, that one may go to the other without being observed by any body. The Wife's Chamber should go into the Wardrobe; the Husband's into the Library. Their ancient Mother, who requires Tranquility and Repose, should have a warm Chamber, well secured against the Cold, and out of the Way of all Noises either from within or without. Be sure particularly to let it have a good Fire-place, and all other Conveniencies necessary for an infirm Person, to comfort and cheer both the Body and Mind. Out of this Chamber let there be a Passage to the Place where you keep your Treasure. Here place the Boys; and by the Wardrobe the Girls, and near them the Lodgings for the Nurses. Strangers and Guests should be lodged in Chambers near the Vestibule or Fore-gate; that they may have full Freedom both in their own Actions, and in receiving Visits from their Friends, without disturbing the Rest of the Family. The Sons of sixteen or seventeen Years old, should have Apartments opposite to the Guests, or at least not far from them, that they may have an Opportunity to converse and grow familiar with them. The Strangers too should have some Place to themselves, where they may lock up any Thing private or valuable, and take it out again whenever they think fit. Next to the Lodgings of the young Gentlemen, should be the Place where the Arms are kept. Stewards, Officers and Servants should be so lodged asunder from the Gentlemen, that each may have a convenient Place, suitable to his respective Business. The Maid-servants and Valets should always be within easy Call, to be ready upon any Occasion that they are wanted for. The Butler's Lodging should be near both to the Vault and Pantry. The Grooms should lie near the Stable. The Saddle-horses ought not to be kept in the same Place with those of Draught or Burthen; and they should be placed where they cannot offend the House with any Smells, nor prejudice it by their Kicking, and out of all Danger of Fire. Corn and all Manner of Grain is spoilt by Moisture, tarnished and turned pale by Heat, shrunk by Wind, and rotted by the Touch of Lime. Where-ever therefore you intend to lay it, whether in a Cave, Pit, Vault, or on an open Area, be sure that the Place be thoroughly dry and perfectly clean and new made. *Josephus* affirms, that there was Corn dug up near *Siboli* perfectly good and sound, though it had lain hid above an hundred Years. Some say, that Barley laid in a warm Place, will not spoil; but it will keep very little above a Year. The Philosophers tell us, that Bodies are prepared for Corruption by Moisture, but are afterwards actually corrupted by Heat. If you make a Floor in your Granary of Lees of Oil mixed with Potter's Clay and Spart or Straw chopt small, and beat well together, your Grain will keep sound upon it a great While, and be neither spoilt by Weevil nor stolen by the Ant. Granaries designed only for Seeds are best built of unbaked Bricks. The North-wind is less prejudicial than the South to all Stores of Seeds and Fruits; but any Wind whatsoever blowing from damp Places

Places will fill them with Maggots and Worms; and any conſtant impetuous Wind will make them ſhrivelled and withered. For Pulſe and eſpecially Beans make a Floor of Aſhes mixed with Lees and Oil. Keep Apples in ſome very cloſe, but cool boarded Room. *Ariſtotle* is of Opinion, that they will keep the whole Year round in Bladders blown up and tied cloſe. The Inconſtancy of the Air is what ſpoils every Thing; and therefore keep every Breath of it from your Apples, if poſſible; and particularly the North-wind, which is thought to ſhrivel them up. We are told that Vaults for Wine ſhould lie deep under Ground, and be very cloſe ſtopt up; and yet there are ſome Wines which decay in the Shade. Wine is ſpoilt by the Eaſtern, Southern and Weſtern Winds, and eſpecially in the Winter or the Spring. If it is touched even by the North-wind in the Dog-days, it will receive Injury. The Rays of the Sun make it heady; thoſe of the Moon, thick. If it is in the leaſt ſtirred, it loſes its Spirit and grows weak. Wine will take any Smell that is near it, and will grow dead near a Stink. When it is kept in a dry cool Place, always equally tempered, it will remain good for many Years. Wine, ſays *Columella*, ſo long as it is kept cool, ſo long it will keep good. Make your Vault for Wine therefore in a ſteady Place, never ſhaken by any Sort of Carriages; and its Sides and Lights ſhould be towards the North. All Manner of Filth and ill Smells, Damps, Vapours, Smoke, the Stinks of all Sorts of rotten Garden-ſtuff, Onions, Cabbage, wild or domeſtick Figs, ſhould by all Means be quite ſhut out. Let the Floor of your Vault be pargetted, and in the Middle make a little Trench, to ſave any Wine that may be ſpilt by the Fault of the Veſſels. Some make their Veſſels themſelves of Stuc or Stone. The bigger the Veſſel is, the more Spirit and Strength will be in the Wine. Oil delights in a warm Shade, and cannot endure any cold Wind; and is ſpoilt by Smoke or any other Steam. We ſhall not dwell upon coarſer Matters; namely, how there ought to be two Places for keeping Dung in, one for the Old, and another for the New; that it loves the Sun and Moiſture, and is dried up and exhauſted by the Wind; but ſhall only give this general Rule, that thoſe Places which are moſt liable to Danger by Fire, as Hay-lofts and the like, and thoſe which are unpleaſant either to the Sight or Smell, ought to be ſet out of the Way and ſeparated by themſelves. It may not be amiſs juſt to mention here, that the Dung of Oxen will not breed Serpents. But there is one filthy Practiſe which I cannot help taking Notice of. We take Care in the Country to ſet the Dunghill out of the Way in ſome remote Corner, that the Smell may not offend our Ploughmen; and yet in our own Houſes, in our beſt Chambers (where we ourſelves are to reſt) and as it were at our very Bolſters, we are ſo unpolite as to make ſecret Privies, or rather Store-rooms of Stink. If a Man is Sick, let him make uſe of a Cloſe-ſtool; but when he is in Health, ſurely ſuch Naſtineſs cannot be too far off. It is worth obſerving how careful Birds are, and particularly Swallows, to keep their Neſts clean and neat for their young ones. The Example Nature herein ſets us is wonderful. Even the young Swallows, as ſoon as ever Time has ſtrengthened their Limbs will never Mute, but out of the Neſt; and the old ones, to keep the Filth at a ſtill greater Diſtance, will catch it in their Bills as it is falling, to carry it further off from their own Neſt. Since Nature has given us this excellent Inſtruction, I think we ought by no means to neglect it.

Chap. XVIII.

The Difference between the Country Houſe and Town Houſe for the Rich. The Habitations of the middling Sort ought to reſemble thoſe of the Rich; at leaſt in Proportion to their Circumſtances. Buildings ſhould be contrived more for Summer, than for Winter.

THE Country Houſe and Town Houſe for the Rich differ in this Circumſtance; that they uſe their Country Houſe chiefly for a Habitation in the Summer, and their Town Houſe as a convenient Place of Shelter in the Winter. In their Country Houſe therefore they enjoy the Pleaſures of Light, Air, ſpacious Walks and fine Proſpects; in Town,

Town, there are but few Pleaſures, but thoſe of Luxury and the Night. It is ſufficient therefore if in Town they can have an Abode that does not want any Conveniencies for living with Health, Dignity and Politeneſs: But yet, as far as the Want of Room and Proſpect will admit, our Habitation in Town ſhould not be without any of the Delicacies of that in the Country. We ſhould be ſure to have a good Court-yard, Portico, Places for Exerciſe, and ſome Garden. If you are crampt for Room, and cannot make all your Conveniencies upon one Floor, make ſeveral Stories, by which means you may make the Members of your Houſe as large as is neceſſary; and if the Nature of your Foundation will allow it, dig Places under Ground for your Wines, Oil, Wood, and even ſome Part of your Family, and ſuch a Baſement will add Majeſty to your whole Structure. Thus you may build as many Stories as you pleaſe, till you have fully provided for all the Occaſions of your Family. The principal Parts may be allotted to the principal Occaſions; and the moſt Honourable, to the moſt Honourable. No Store-rooms ſhould be wanting for laying up Corn, Fruits, and all Manner of Tools, Implements and Houſhold-ſtuff; nor Places for divine Worſhip; nor Wardrobes for the Women. Nor muſt you be without convenient Store-rooms for laying up Cloaths deſigned for your Family to wear only on Holidays, and Arms both defenſive and offenſive, Implements for all Sorts of Works in Wool, Preparations for the Entertainment of Gueſts, and all Manner of Neceſſaries for any extraordinary Occaſions. There ſhould be different Places for thoſe Things that are not wanted above once a Month, or perhaps once a Year, and for thoſe that are in Uſe every Day. Every one of which, though they cannot be always kept lockt up in Store-rooms, ought however to be kept in ſome Place where they may be conſtantly in Sight; and eſpecially ſuch Things as are ſeldomeſt in Uſe; becauſe thoſe Things which are moſt in Sight, are leaſt in Danger of Thieves. The Habitations of middling People ought to reſemble the Delicacy of thoſe of the richer Sort, in Proportion to their Circumſtances; ſtill imitating them with ſuch Moderation, as not to run into a greater Expence than they can well ſupport. The Country Houſes for theſe, therefore, ſhould be contrived with little leſs Regard to their Flocks and Herds, than to their Wives. Their Dove-houſe, Fiſh-ponds, and the like ſhould be leſs for Pleaſure, than for Profit: But yet their Country Houſe ſhould be built in ſuch a Manner, that the Wife may like the Abode, and look after her Buſineſs in it with Pleaſure; nor ſhould we have our Eye ſo entirely upon Profit, as to neglect the Health of the Inhabitants. Whenever we have Occaſion for Change of Air, *Celſus* adviſes us to take it in Winter; for our Bodies will grow accuſtomed to Winter Colds, with leſs Danger of our Health than to Summer Heats. But we, on the Contrary, are fond of going to our Country Houſes chiefly in Summer; we ought therefore to take Care to have that the moſt Healthy. As for the Town Houſe for a Tradeſman, more Regard muſt be had to the Conveniency of his Shop, from whence his Gain and Livelihood is to ariſe than to the Beauty of his Parlour; the beſt Situation for this is, in Croſs-ways, at a Corner; in a Market-place or Square, in the Middle of the Place; in a High-ſtreet, ſome remarkable jutting out; inaſmuch as his chief Deſign is to draw the Eyes of Cuſtomers. In the middle Parts of his Houſe he need have no Partitions but of unbaked Bricks and common Plaiſter; but in the Front and Sides, as he cannot always be ſure of having honeſt Neighbours, he muſt make his Walls ſtronger againſt the Aſſaults both of Men and Weather. He ſhould alſo build his Houſe either at ſuch a proper Diſtance from his next Neighbour's, that there may be room for the Air to dry the Walls after any Rain; or ſo cloſe, that the Water may run off from both in the ſame Gutter; and let the Top of the Houſe, and the Gutters particularly, have a very good Slope, that the Rain may neither lie ſoaking too long, nor daſh back into the Houſe; but be carried away as quick and as clear as poſſible. There remains nothing now but to recollect ſome few Rules laid down in the firſt Book, and which ſeem to belong to this Head. Let thoſe Parts of the Building which are to be particularly ſecure againſt Fire, and the Injuries of the Weather, or which are to be cloſer or freer from Noiſe, be all vaulted; ſo likewiſe ſhould all Places under Ground: But for Rooms above Ground, flat Ceilings are wholeſomer. Thoſe which require the cleareſt Light, ſuch as the common Parlour, the Portico, and eſpecially the Library, ſhould be ſituated full Eaſt? Thoſe Things which are injured by Moths, Ruſt or Mildew, ſuch as Cloaths, Books, Arms, and all Manner

of

of Provisions, should be kept towards the South or West. If there be Occasion for an equal constant Light, such as is necessary for Painters, Writers, Sculptors and the like, let them have it from the North. Lastly, let all Summer Apartments stand open to the Northern Winds, all Winter ones to the South, and all those for Spring and Autumn to the East. Baths and supper Parlours for the Spring Season should be towards the West. And if you cannot possibly have all these exactly according to your Wish, at least chuse out the most convenient Places for your Summer Apartments: For indeed, in my Opinion, a wise Man should build rather for Summer than for Winter. We may easily arm ourselves against the Cold by making all close, and keeping good Fires; but many more Things are requisite against Heat, and even all will sometimes be no great Relief. Let Winter Rooms therefore be small, low and little Windows, and Summer ones, on the Contrary, large, spacious, and open to cool Breezes, but not to the Sun or the hot Air that comes from it. A great Quantity of Air inclosed in a large Room, is like a great Quantity of Water, not easily heated.

The End of Book V.

THE

THE ARCHITECTURE OF *Leone Batiſta Alberti.*

BOOK VI. CHAP. I.

Of the Reaſon and Difficulty of the Author's Undertaking, whereby it appears how much Pains, Study and Application he has employed in writing upon theſe Matters.

N the five preceding Books we have treated of the Deſigns, of the Materials for the Work, of the Workmen, and of every Thing elſe that appeared neceſſary to the Conſtruction of an Edifice, whether publick or private, ſacred or profane, ſo far as related to its being made ſtrong againſt all Injuries of Weather, and convenient for its reſpective Uſe, as to Times Places, Men and Things: With how much Care we have treated of all theſe Matters, you may ſee by the Books themſelves, from whence you may judge whether it was poſſible to do it with much greater. The Labour indeed was much more than I could have foreſeen at the Beginning of this Undertaking. Continual Difficulties every Moment aroſe either in explaining the Matter, or inventing Names, or methodizing the Subject, which perfectly confounded me, and diſheartened me from my Undertaking. On the other Hand, the ſame Reaſons which induced me to be begin this Work, preſſed and encouraged me to proceed. It grieved me that ſo many great and noble Inſtructions of ancient Authors ſhould be loſt by the Injury of Time, ſo that ſcarce any but *Vitruvius* has eſcaped this general Wreck: A Writer indeed of univerſal Knowledge, but ſo maimed by Age, that in many Places there are great Chaſms, and many Things imperfect in others. Beſides this, his Style is abſolutely void of all Ornaments, and he wrote in ſuch a Manner, that to the *Latins* he ſeems to write *Greek*, and to the *Greeks*, *Latin*: But indeed it is plain from the Book itſelf, that he wrote neither *Greek* nor *Latin*, and he might almoſt as well have never wrote at all, at leaſt with Regard to us, ſince we cannot underſtand him. There remained many Examples of the ancient Works, Temples and Theatres, from whence, as from the moſt skilful Maſters, a great deal was to be learned; but theſe I ſaw, and with Tears I ſaw it, mouldering away daily. I obſerved too that thoſe who in theſe Days happen to undertake any new Structure, generally ran after the Whims of the Moderns, inſtead of being delighted and directed by the Juſtneſs of more noble Works. By this Means it was plain, that this Part of Knowledge, and in a Manner of Life itſelf, was likely in a ſhort Time to be wholly loſt. In this unhappy State of Things, I could not help having it long, and often, in my Thoughts to write upon this Subject myſelf. At the ſame Time I conſidered that in the Examination of ſo many noble and uſeful Matters,

Matters, and so necessary to Mankind; it would be a Shame to neglect any of those Observations which voluntarily offered themselves to me; and I thought it the Duty of an honest and studious Mind, to endeavour to free this Science, for which the most Learned among the Ancients had always a very great Esteem, from its present Ruin and Oppression. Thus I stood doubtful, and knew not how to resolve, whether I should drop my Design, or go on. At length my Love and Inclination for these Studies prevailed; and what I wanted in Capacity, I made up in Diligence and Application. There was not the least Remain of any ancient Structure, that had any Merit in it, but what I went and examined, to see if any Thing was to be learned from it. Thus I was continually searching, considering, measuring and making Draughts of every Thing I could hear of, till such Time as I had made myself perfect Master of every Contrivance or Invention that had been used in those ancient Remains; and thus I alleviated the Fatigue of writing, by the Thirst and Pleasure of gaining Information. And indeed the Collecting together, rehearsing without Meanness, reducing into a just Method, writing in an accurate Style, and explaining perspicuously so many various Matters, so unequal, so dispersed, and so remote from the common Use and Knowledge of Mankind, certainly required a greater Genius, and more Learning than I can pretend to. But still I shall not repent of my Labour, if I have only effected what I chiefly proposed to myself, namely, to be clear and intelligible to the Reader, rather than Eloquent. How difficult a Thing this is, in handling Subjects of this Nature, is better known to those who have attempted it, then believed by those who never tried it. And I flatter myself, it will at least be allowed me, that I have wrote according to the Rules of this Language, and in no obscure Style. We shall endeavour to do the same in the remaining Parts of this Work. Of the three Properties required in all Manner of Buildings, namely, that they be accommodated to their respective Purposes, stout and strong for Duration, and pleasant and delightful to the Sight, we have dispatched the two first, and are now to treat of the third, which is by much the most Noble of all, and very necessary besides.

CHAP. II.

Of Beauty and Ornament, their Effects and Difference, that they are owing to Art and Exactness of Proportion; as also of the Birth and Progress of Arts.

IT is generally allowed, that the Pleasure and Delight which we feel on the View of any Building, arise from nothing else but Beauty and Ornament, since there is hardly any Man so melancholy or stupid, so rough or unpolished, but what is very much pleased with what is beautiful, and pursues those Things which are most adorned, and rejects the unadorned and neglected; and if in any Thing that he Views he perceives any Ornament is wanting, he declares that there is something deficient which would make the Work more delightful and noble. We should therefore consult Beauty as one of the main and principal Requisites in any Thing which we have a Mind should please others. How necessary our Forefathers, Men remarkable for their Wisdom, looked upon this to be, appears, as indeed from almost every thing they did, so particularly from their Laws, their Militia, their sacred and all other publick Ceremonies; which it is almost incredible what Pains they took to adorn; insomuch that one would almost imagine they had a Mind to have it thought, that all these Things (so absolutely necessary to the Life of Mankind) if stript of their Pomp and Ornament, would be somewhat stupid and insipid. When we lift up our Eyes to Heaven, and view the wonderful Works of God, we admire him more for the Beauties which we see, than for the Conveniencies which we feel and derive from them. But what Occasion is there to insist upon this? When we see that Nature consults Beauty in a Manner to excess, in every Thing she does, even in painting the Flowers of the Field. If Beauty therefore is necessary in any Thing, it is so particularly in Building, which can never be without it, without giving Offence both to the Skilful and the Ignorant. How are we moved by a huge shapeless ill-contrived Pile of of Stones? the greater it is, the more we blame the Folly of the Expence, and condemn the Builder's inconſiderate Luſt of heaping up Stone upon Stone without Contrivance. The having ſatisfied Neceſſity is a very ſmall Matter, and the having provided for Conveniency affords no Manner of Pleaſure, where you are ſhocked by the Deformity of the Work. Add to this, that the very Thing we ſpeak of is itſelf no ſmall help to Conveniency and Duration: For who will deny that it is much more convenient to be lodged in a neat handſome Structure, than in a naſty ill-contrived Hole? or can any Building be made ſo ſtrong by all the Contrivance of Art, as to be ſafe from Violence and Force? But Beauty will have ſuch an Effect even upon an enraged Enemy, that it will diſarm his Anger, and prevent him from offering it any Injury: Inſomuch that I will be bold to ſay, there can be no greater Security to any Work againſt Violence and Injury, than Beauty and Dignity. Your whole Care, Diligence and Expence, therefore ſhould all tend to this, that whatever you build may be not only uſeful and convenient, but alſo handſomely adorned, and by that means delightful to the Sight, that whoever views it may own the Expence could never have been better beſtowed. But what Beauty and Ornament are in themſelves, and what Difference there is between them, may perhaps be eaſier for the Reader to conceive in his Mind, than for me to explain by Words. In order therefore to be as brief as poſſible, I ſhall define Beauty to be a Harmony of all the Parts, in whatſoever Subject it appears, fitted together with ſuch Proportion and Connection, that nothing could be added, diminiſhed or altered, but for the Worſe. A Quality ſo Noble and Divine, that the whole Force of Wit and Art has been ſpent to procure it; and it is but very rarely granted to any one, or even to Nature herſelf, to produce any Thing every Way perfect and compleat. How extraordinary a Thing (ſays the Perſon introduced in *Tully*) is a handſome Youth in *Athens*! This Critick in Beauty found that there was ſomething deficient or ſuperfluous, in the Perſons he diſliked, which was not compatible with the Perfection of Beauty, which I imagine might have been obtained by Means of Ornament, by painting and concealing any Thing that was deformed, and trimming and poliſhing what was handſome; ſo that the unſightly Parts might have given leſs Offence, and the more lovely more Delight. If this be granted we may define Ornament to be a Kind of an auxiliary Brightneſs and Improvement to Beauty. So that then Beauty is ſomewhat lovely which is proper and innate, and diffuſed over the whole Body, and Ornament ſomewhat added or faſtened on, rather than proper and innate. To return therefore where we left off. Whoever would build ſo as to have their Building commended, which every reaſonable Man would deſire, muſt build according to a Juſtneſs of Proportion, and this Juſtneſs of Proportion muſt be owing to Art. Who therefore will affirm, that a handſome and juſt Structure can be raiſed any otherwiſe than by the Means of Art? and conſequently this Part of Building, which relates to Beauty and Ornament, being the Chief of all the Reſt, muſt without doubt be directed by ſome ſure Rules of Art and Proportion, which whoever neglects will make himſelf ridiculous. But there are ſome who will by no means allow of this, and ſay that Men are guided by a Variety of Opinions in their Judgment of Beauty and of Buildings; and that the Forms of Structures muſt vary according to every Man's particular Taſte and Fancy, and not be tied down to any Rules of Art. A common Thing with the Ignorant, to deſpiſe what they do not underſtand! It may not therefore be amiſs to confute this Error; not that I think it neceſſary to enter into a long Diſcuſſion about the Origin of Arts, from what Principles they were deduced, and by what Methods improved. I ſhall only take Notice that all Arts were begot by Chance and Obſervation, and nurſed by Uſe and Experience, and improved and perfected by Reaſon and Study. Thus we are told that Phyſick was invented in a thouſand Years by a thouſand thouſand Men; and ſo too the Art of Navigation; as, indeed, all other Arts have grown up by Degrees from the ſmalleſt Beginnings.

Chap. III.

That Architecture began in Asia, *flouriſhed in* Greece, *and was brought to Perfection in* Italy.

THE Art of Building, as far as I can gather from the Works of the Ancients, ſpent the firſt Vigour of its Youth (if I may be allowed that Expreſſion) in *Aſia:* It afterwards flouriſhed among the *Greeks*; and at laſt came to its full Maturity in *Italy.* And this Account ſeems very probable; for the Kings of *Aſia* abounding in Wealth and Leiſure, when they came to conſider themſelves, their own Riches, and the Greatneſs and Majeſty of their Empire, and found that they had Occaſion for larger and nobler Habitations, they began to ſearch out and collect every Thing that might ſerve to this Purpoſe; and in order to make their Buildings larger and handſomer, began perhaps with building their Roofs of larger Timbers, and their Walls of a better Sort of Stone. This ſhewed noble and great, and not unhandſome. Then finding that ſuch Works were admired for being very large, and imagining that a King was obliged to do ſomething which private Men could not effect, theſe great Monarchs began to be delighted with huge Works, which they fell to raiſing with a Kind of Emulation of one another, till they came to erecting thoſe wild immenſe Moles, the Pyramids. Hereupon I imagine that by frequent Building they began to find out the Difference that there was between a Structure built in one Manner, and one built in another, and ſo getting ſome Notion of Beauty and Proportion, began to neglect thoſe Things which wanted thoſe Qualities. *Greece* came next; which flouriſhing in excellent Geniuſſes and Men of Learning, paſſionately deſirous of adorning their Country, began to erect Temples and other publick Structures. They then thought fit to look abroad and take a more careful View of the Works of the *Aſſyrians* and *Ægyptians*, till at laſt they came to underſtand that in all Things of this Nature the Skill of the Workman was more admired than the Wealth of the Prince: For any one that is rich may raiſe a great Pile of Building; but to raiſe ſuch a one as may be commended by the Skilful, is the Part only of a ſuperior Genius. Hereupon *Greece* finding that in theſe Works ſhe could not equal thoſe Nations in Expence, reſolved to try if ſhe could not out-do them in Ingenuity. She began therefore to trace and deduce this Art of Building, as indeed ſhe did all others, from the very Lap of Nature itſelf, examining, weighing and conſidering it in all its Parts with the greateſt Diligence and Exactneſs: enquiring with the greateſt Strictneſs into the Difference between thoſe Buildings which were highly praiſed, and thoſe which were diſliked, without neglecting the leaſt Particular. She tried all Manner of Experiments, ſtill tracing and keeping cloſe to the Footſteps of Nature, mingling uneven Numbers with even, ſtrait Lines with Curves, Light with Shade, hoping that as it happens from the Conjunction of Male and Female, ſhe ſhould by the Mixture of theſe Oppoſites hit upon ſome third Thing that would anſwer her Purpoſe: Nor even in the moſt minute Particulars did ſhe neglect to weigh and conſider all the Parts over and over again, how thoſe on the right Hand agreed with thoſe on the left, the Upright with the Platform, the nearer with the more remote, adding, diminiſhing, proportioning the great Parts to the Small, the Similar to the Diſſimilar, the Laſt to the Firſt, till ſhe had clearly demonſtrated that different Rules were to be obſerved in thoſe Edifices which were intended for Duration, to ſtand as it were Monuments to Eternity, and thoſe which were deſigned chiefly for Beauty. Theſe were the Methods purſued by the *Greeks.* *Italy*, in her firſt Beginnings, having Regard wholly to Parſimony, concluded that the Members in Buildings ought to be contrived in the ſame Manner as in Animals; as, for Inſtance, in a Horſe, whoſe Limbs are generally moſt beautiful when they are moſt uſeful for Service: from whence they inferred that Beauty was never ſeparate and diſtinct from Conveniency. But afterwards when they had obtained the Empire of the World, being then no leſs inflamed than the *Greeks* with the Deſire of adorning their City and themſelves, in leſs than thirty Years that which before was the fineſt Houſe in the whole City of *Rome*, could not then

then be reckoned ſo by a hundred; and they abounded in ſuch an incredible Number of ingenious Men who exerciſe their Talent this Way, that we are told there was at one Time no leſs than ſeven hundred Architects at *Rome*, whoſe Works were ſo noble that the extraordinary Praiſe which is beſtowed upon them, is hardly equal to their Merit. And as the Wealth of the Empire was ſufficient to bear the Expence of the moſt ſtately Structures, ſo we are told that a private Man, by Name *Tatius*, at his own proper Charges built Baths for the People of *Oſtia* with an hundred Columns of *Numidian* Marble. But ſtill though the Condition of their State was thus flouriſhing, they thought it moſt laudable to join the Magnificence of the moſt profuſe Monarchs, to the ancient Parſimony and frugal Contrivance of their own Country: But ſtill in ſuch a Manner, that their Frugality ſhould not prejudice Conveniency, nor Conveniency be too cautious and fearful of Expence; but that both ſhould be embelliſhed by every thing that was delicate or beautiful. In a Word, being to the greateſt Degree careful and exact in all their Buildings, they became at laſt ſo excellent in this Art, that there was nothing in it ſo hiden or ſecret but what they traced out, diſcovered and brought to light, by the Favour of Heaven, and the Art itſelf not frowning upon their Endeavours: For the Art of Building having had her ancient Seat in *Italy*, and eſpecially among the *Hetrurians*, who beſides thoſe miraculous Structures which we read to have been erected by their Kings, of Labyrinths and Sepulchres, had among them ſome excellent ancient Writings, which taught the Manner of building Temples, according to the Practice of the Ancient *Tuſcans*: I ſay, this Art having had her ancient Seat in *Italy*, and knowing with how much Fervour ſhe was courted there, ſhe ſeems to have reſolved, that this Empire of the World, which was already adorned with all other Virtues, ſhould be made ſtill more admirable by her Embelliſhments. For this Reaſon ſhe gave herſelf to them to be throughly known and underſtood; thinking it a Shame that the Head of the Univerſe and the Glory of all Nations ſhould be equalled in Magnificence by thoſe whom ſhe had excelled in all Virtues and Sciences. Why ſhould I inſiſt here upon their Porticoes, Temples, Gates, Theatres, Baths, and other gigantick Structures; Works ſo amazing, that though they were actually executed, ſome very great foreign Architects thought them impracticable. In ſhort, I need ſay no more than that they could not bear to have even their common Drains void of Beauty, and were ſo delighted with Magnificence and Ornament, that they thought it no Profuſion to ſpend the Wealth of the State in Buildings that were hardly deſigned for any thing elſe. By the Examples therefore of the Ancients, and the Precepts of great Maſters, and conſtant Practice, a thorough Knowledge is to be gained of the Method of raiſing ſuch magnificent Structures; from this Knowledge ſound Rules are to be drawn, which are by no means to be neglected by thoſe who have not a Mind to make themſelves ridiculous by building, as I ſuppoſe nobody has. Theſe Rules it is our Buſineſs here to collect and explain, according to the beſt of our Capacity. Of theſe ſome regard the univerſal Beauty and Ornament of the whole Edifice; other the particular Parts and Members taken ſeparately. The former are taken immediately from Philoſophy and are intended to direct and regulate the Operations of this Art; the others from Experience, as we have ſhewn above, only filed and perfected by the Principles of Philoſophy. I ſhall ſpeak firſt of thoſe wherein this particular Art is moſt concerned; and as for the others, which relate to the Univerſality, they ſhall ſerve by Way of Epilogue.

Chap. IV.

That Beauty and Ornament in every Thing ariſe from Contrivance, or the Hand of the Artificer, or from Nature; and that though the Region indeed can hardly be improved by the Wit or Labour of Man, yet many other Things may be done highly worthy of Admiration, and ſcarcely credible.

THAT which delights us in Things that are either beautiful or finely adorned, muſt proceed either from the Contrivance and Invention of the Mind, or the Hand of the Artificer, or from ſomewhat derived immediately from Nature herſelf. To the Mind belong

long the Election, Distribution, Disposition, and other Things of the like Nature which give Dignity to the Work: To the Hand, the amassing, adding, diminishing, chipping, polishing, and the like, which make the Work delicate: The Qualities derived from Nature are Heaviness, Lightness, Thickness, Clearness, Durability, &c. which make the Work wonderful. These three Operations are to be adapted to the several Parts according to their various Uses and Offices. There are several Ways of dividing and considering the different Parts: But at present we shall divide all Buildings either according to the Parts in which they generally agree, or to those in which they generally differ. In the first Book we saw that all Edifices must have Region, Situation, Compartition, Walling, Covering, and Apertures; in these Particulars therefore they agree. But then in these others they differ, namely, that some are Sacred, others Profane, some Publick, others Private, some designed for Necessity, others for Pleasure, and so on. Let us begin with those Particulars wherein they agree. What the Hand or Wit of Man can add to the Region, either of Beauty or Dignity, is hardly discoverable; unless we would give into those miraculous and superstitious Accounts which we read of some Works. Nor are the Undertakers of such Works blamed by prudent Men, if their Designs answer any great Conveniency; but if they take Pains to do what there was no Necessity for, they are justly denied the Praise they hunt after. For who would be so daring as to undertake, like *Stasicrates*, (according to *Plutarch*) or *Dinocrates* (according to *Vitruvius*) to make Mount *Athos* into a Statue of *Alexander*, and in one of the Hands to build a City big enough to contain ten thousand Men? Indeed I should not discommend Queen *Nitocris* for having forced the River *Euphrates*, by making vast Cuts, to flow three Times round the City of the *Assyrians*, if she made the Region strong and secure by those Trenches, and fruitful by the overflowing of the Water. But let us leave it to mighty Kings to be delighted with such Undertakings: Let them join Sea to Sea by cutting the Land between them: Let them level Hills: Let them make new Islands, or join old ones to the Continent: Let them put it out of the Power of any others to imitate them, and so make their Names memorable to Posterity: Still all their wast Works will be commended not so much in Proportion to their Greatness as their Use. The Ancients sometimes added Dignity not only to particular Groves, but even to the whole Region, by Means of Religion. We read that all *Sicily* was consecrated to *Ceres*; but these are Things not now to be insisted upon. It will be of great and real Advantages, if the Region be possessed of some rare Quality, no less useful than extraordinary: As for Instance, if the Air be more temperate than in any other Place, and always equal and uniform, as we are told it is at *Moroe*, where Men live in a Manner as long as they please; or if the Region produces something not to be found elsewhere and very desirable and wholesome to Man, as that which produces Amber, Cinnamon, and Balsam; or if it has some divine Influence in it, as there is in the Soil of the Island *Eubœa*, where we are told nothing noxious is produced. The Situation, being a certain determinate Part of the Region, is adorned by all the same Particulars as beautify the Region itself. But Nature generally offers more Conveniencies, and those more ready at Hand, for adorning the Situation than the Region; for we very frequently meet with Circumstances extreamly noble and surprising, such as Promontories, Rocks, broken Hills vastly high and sharp, Grottoes, Caverns, Springs and the like; near which, if we would have our Situation strike the Beholders with Surprize, we may build to our Hearts desire. Nor should their be wanting in the Prospect Remains of Antiquity, on which we cannot turn our Eyes without considering the various Revolutions of Men and Things, and being filled with Wonder and Admiration. I need not mention the Place where *Troy* once stood, or the Plains of *Leuctra* stained with Blood, nor the Fields near *Trasumenus*, and a thousand other Places memorable for some great Event. How the Hand and Wit of Man may add to the Beauty of the Situation, is not so easily shewn. I pass over Things commonly done; such as Plane-trees brought by Sea to the Island of *Tremeti* to adorn the Situation, or Columns, Obelisks and Trees left by great Men in order to strike Posterity with Veneration; as for Instance, the Olive-tree planted by *Neptune* and *Minerva*, which flourished for so many Ages in the Citadel of *Athens*: I likewise pass over ancient Traditions handed down from Age to Age, as that of the Turpentine-tree near *Hebron*, which was reported to have stood from the Creation of the World to the Days of *Josephus* the Historian. Nothing can give

give a greater Air of Dignity and Awfulneſs to a Place than ſome artful Laws made by the Ancients; ſuch as theſe: That nothing Male ſhould preſume to ſet Foot in the Temple of the *Bona Dea*, nor in that of *Diana* in the Patrician Portico; and at *Tanagra*, that no Woman ſhould enter the ſacred Grove, nor the inner Parts of the Temple of *Jeruſalem*; and that no Perſon whatſoever, beſides the Prieſt, and he only in order to purify himſelf for Sacrifice, ſhould waſh in the Fountain near *Panthos*; and that nobody ſhould preſume to ſpit in the Place called *Doliola* near the great Drain at *Rome*, where the Bones of *Numa Pompilius* were depoſited; and upon ſome Chapels there have been Inſcriptions, ſtrictly forbidding any common Proſtitute to enter; in the Temple of *Diana* at *Crete*, none were admitted, except they were bare-footed; it was unlawful to bring a Bond-woman into the Temple of the Goddeſs *Matuta*; and all common Cryers were excluded from the Temple of *Orodio* at *Rhodes*, and all Fiddlers from that of *Temnius* at *Tenedos*. So again, it was unlawful to go out of the Temple of *Jupiter Alſiſtius* without ſacrificing, and to carry any Ivy into the Temple of *Minerva* at *Athens*, or into that of *Venus* at *Thebes*. In the Temple of *Fauna*, it was not lawful ſo much as to mention the Name of Wine. In the ſame Manner it was decreed, that the Gate *Janualis* at *Rome* ſhould never be ſhut, but in Time of War, nor the Temple of *Janus* ever opened in Time of Peace; and that the Temple of the Goddeſs *Hora* ſhould ſtand always open. If we were to imitate any of theſe Cuſtoms, perhaps it might not be amiſs to make it criminal for Women to enter the Temples of Martyrs; or Men, thoſe dedicated to Virgin Saints. Moreover there are ſome Advantages very deſirable, ſaid to be procured by Art, which when we read of, we could ſcarcely believe, unleſs we ſaw ſomething like it in ſome particular Places even at this Day. We are told that it was brought about by human Art, that in *Conſtantinople* Serpents will never hurt any body, and that no Daws will fly within the Walls; and that no Graſshoppers are ever heard in *Naples*, nor any Owls in *Candy*. In the Temple of *Achilles*, in the Iſland of *Boriſthenes* no Bird whatſoever will enter, nor any Dog or Fly of any Sort in the Temple of *Hercules* near the *Forum Boarium* at *Rome*. But what ſhall we ſay of this ſurprizing Particularity, that at *Venice*, even at this Day, no Kind of Fly ever enters the publick Palace of the *Cenſors*? And even in the Fleſh-market at *Toledo*, there is never more than one Fly ſeen throughout the Year, and that a remarkable one for its Whiteneſs. Theſe ſtrange Accounts which we find in Authors, are too numerous to be all inſerted here, and whether they are owing to Nature or Art, I ſhall not now pretend to decide. But then, again, how can we, either by Nature or Art, account for what they tell us of a Laurel-tree growing in the Sepulchre of *Bibrias* King of *Pontus*, from which if the leaſt Twig is broken, and put aboard a Ship, that Ship ſhall never be free from Mutinies and Tumults till the Twig is thrown out of it: Or for its never raining upon the *Altar* in *Venus*'s Temple at *Paphos*: Or for this, that whatever Part of the Sacrifice is left at *Minerva*'s Shrine in *Phrygia minor*, will never corrupt: Or this, if you break off any Part of *Anteus*'s Sepulchre, it immediately begins to rain, and never leaves off till it is made whole again? Some indeed affirm, that all theſe Things may be done by an Art, now loſt, by means of little conſtellated Images, which Aſtronomers pretend are not unknown to them. I remember to have read in the Author of the Life of *Apollonius Tyaneus*, that in the chief Apartments of the Royal Palace at *Babylon*, ſome Magicians faſtened to the Cieling four golden Birds, which they called the Tongues of the Gods, and that theſe were endued with the Virtue of conciliating the Affection of the Multitude towards their King: And *Joſephus*, a very grave Author, ſays that he himſelf ſaw a certain Man named *Eleazer*, who in the Preſence of the Emperor *Veſpaſian* and his Sons, immediately cured a Man that was poſſeſſed, by faſtening a Ring to his Noſe; and the ſame Author writes that *Solomon* compoſed certain Verſes, which would give Eaſe in Diſtempers; and *Euſebius Pamphilus* ſays, that the *Ægyptian* God *Serapis*, whom we call *Pluto*, invented certain Charms which would drive away evil Spirits, and taught the Methods by which *Dæmons* aſſumed the Shapes of brute Beaſts to do miſchief. *Servius* too ſays, that there were Men who uſed to carry Charms about them, by which they were ſecured againſt all unhappy Turns of Fortune; and that thoſe Charms were ſo powerful, that the Perſons who wore them could never die till they were taken from them. If theſe Things could be true, I ſhould eaſily believe what we read in *Plutarch*, that among the *Pelenei* there was an Image, which if it were brought out of the

Temple by the Prieſt, filled every Creature with Terror and Dread on whatever Side it was turned; and that no Eye durſt look towards it, for Fear. Theſe miraculous Accounts we have inſerted only by way of Amuſement. As to other Particulars which may help to make the Situation beautiful, conſidered in a general View, ſuch as the Circumference, the Space round about it, its Elevation, Levelling, Strengthening, and the like, I have nothing more to ſay here, but to refer you for Inſtructions to the firſt and third Books. The chief Qualities requiſite in a Situation or Platform (as we have there obſerved) are to be perfectly dry, even, and ſolid, as alſo convenient and ſuitable to the Purpoſe of the Building; and it will be a very great Help to it, to ſtrengthen it with a good Bottom made of baked Earth, in the Manner which we ſhall teach when we come to treat of the Wall. We muſt not here omit an Obſervation made by *Plato*, that it will be a great Addition to the Dignity of the Place, if you give it ſome great Name; and this we find the Emperor *Adrian* was very fond of doing, when he gave the Names of *Lycus*, *Canopeis*, *Academia*, *Tempe* and other great Titles to the ſeveral Parts of his *Villa* at *Tivoli*.

Chap. V.

A ſhort Recapitulation of the Compartition, and of the juſt Compoſition and adorning the Wall and Covering.

THOUGH we have already ſaid almoſt as much as was neceſſary of the Compartition in the firſt Book, yet we ſhall take a brief Review of it again here. The chief and firſt Ornament of any Thing is to be free from all Improprieties. It will therefore be a juſt and proper Compartition, if it is neither confuſed nor interrupted, neither too rambling nor compoſed of unſuitable Parts, and if the Members be neither too many nor too few, neither too ſmall nor too large, not miſ-matcht nor unſightly, nor as it were ſeparate and divided from the Reſt of the Body: But every Thing ſo diſpoſed according to Nature and Convenience, and the Uſes for which the Structure is intended, with ſuch Order, Number, Size, Situation and Form, that we may be ſatisfied there is nothing throughout the whole Fabrick, but what was contrived for ſome Uſe or Convenience, and with the handſomeſt Compactneſs of all the Parts. If the Compartition anſwers in all theſe Reſpects, the Beauty and Richneſs of any Ornaments will ſit well upon it; if not, it is impoſſible it ſhould have any Air of Dignity at all. The whole Compoſition of the Members therefore ſhould ſeem to be made and directed entirely by Neceſſity and Conveniency; ſo that you may not be ſo much pleaſed that there are ſuch or ſuch Parts in the Building, as that they are diſpoſed and laid out in ſuch a Situation, Order and Connection. In adorning the Wall and Covering, you will have ſufficient Room to diſplay the fineſt Materials produced by Nature, and the moſt curious Contrivance and Skill of the Artificer. If it were in your Power to imitate the ancient *Oſiris*, who, we are told, built two Temples of Gold, one to the Heavenly, the other to the Royal *Jupiter*; or if you could raiſe ſome vaſt Stone, almoſt beyond humane Belief, like that which *Semiramis* brought from the Mountains of *Arabia*, which was twenty Cubits broad every Way, and an hundred and fifty long; or if you had ſuch large Stone, that you could make ſome Part of the Work all of one Piece, like a Chapel in *Latona*'s Temple in *Ægypt*, forty Cubits wide in Front, and hollowed in one ſingle Stone, and ſo alſo covered with another: This no doubt would create a vaſt deal of Admiration in the Beholders, and eſpecially if the Stone was a foreign one, and brought through difficult Ways, like that which *Herodotus* relates to have been brought from the City of *Elephantis*, which was about twenty Cubits broad, and fifteen high, and was carried as far as *Suſa* in twenty Days. It will alſo add greatly to the Ornament and Wonder of the Work, if ſuch an extraordinary Stone be ſet in a remarkable and honourable Place. Thus the little Temple at *Chemmis*, an Iſland in *Ægypt*, is not ſo ſurprizing upon Account of being covered with one ſingle Stone, as upon Account of ſuch a huge Stone's being raiſed to ſo great a Height. The Rarity and Beauty of the Stone itſelf will alſo add greatly to the Ornament; as for Inſtance, if it is that ſort of Marble, with which

which we are told *Nero* built a Temple to *Fortune* in his golden Palace, which was ſo white, ſo clear and tranſparent, that even when all the Doors were ſhut the Light ſeemed to be encloſe within the Temple. All theſe Things are very Noble in themſelves; but they will make no Figure if there is not Care and Art uſed in their Compoſition or putting together: For every Thing muſt be reduced to exact Meaſure, ſo that all the Parts may correſpond with one another, the Right with the Left, the lower Parts with the Upper, with nothing interfering that may blemiſh either the Order or the Materials, but every Thing ſquared to exact Angles and ſimilar Lines. We may often obſerve that baſe Materials managed with Art, make a handſomer Shew than the Nobleſt heaped together in Confuſion. Who can imagine that the Wall of *Athens*, which *Thucydides* informs us was built ſo tumultuouſly that they even threw into it ſome of the Statues of their Sepulchres, could have any Beauty in it, or be any ways adorned by being full of broken Statues? On the Contrary, we are very much pleaſed with the Walls of ſome old Country-Houſes, though they are built of any Stone that the People could pick up; becauſe they are diſpoſed in even Rows, with an alternate Checquer of Black and White: ſo that conſidering the Meanneſs of the Structure, nothing can be deſired handſomer. But perhaps this Conſideration belongs rather to that Part of the Wall which is called the outward Coat, than to the Body of the Wall itſelf. To conclude, all your Materials ſhould be ſo diſtributed that nothing ſhould be begun, but according to ſome judicious Plan; nothing carried on but in purſuance of the ſame; and no Part of it left imperfect, but finiſhed and compleated with the utmoſt Care and Diligence. But the principal Ornament both of the Wall and Covering, and eſpecially of all vaulted Roofs (always excepted Columns) is the outward Coat: And this may be of ſeveral Sorts; either all white, or adorned with Figures and Stuc-work, or with Painting, or Pictures ſet in Pannels, or with *Moſaic* Work, or elſe a Mixture of all theſe together.

Chap. VI.

In what Manner great Weights and large Stones are moved from one Place to another or raiſed to any great Height.

Of thoſe Ornaments laſt mentioned we are to treat; and to ſhew what they are and how they are to be made; but having in the laſt Chapter mentioned the moving of vaſt Stones, it ſeems neceſſary here to give ſome Account in what Manner ſuch huge Bodies are moved, and how they are raiſed to ſuch high and difficult Places. *Plutarch* relates that *Archimedes*, the great Mathematician of *Syracuſe*, drew a Ship of Burthen with all its lading through the Middle of the Market Place, with his Hand, as if he had been only leading along a Horſe by the Bridle: But we ſhall here conſider only thoſe Things that are neceſſary in Practice; and then take Notice of ſome Points, by which Men of Learning and good Apprehenſions may fully and clearly underſtand the whole Buſineſs of themſelves. *Pliny* ſays, that the Obelisk brought from *Phœnicia* to *Thebes*, was brought down a Canal cut from the *Nile*, in Ships full of Bricks, ſo that by taking out ſome of the Bricks they could at any Time lighten the Veſſel of its Lading. We find in *Ammianus Marcellinus* the Hiſtorian, that an Obelisk was brought from the *Nile*, in a Veſſel of three hundred Oars, and laid upon Rollers at three Miles diſtance from *Rome*, and ſo drawn into the great *Circus* through the Gate that leads to *Oſtia:* And that ſeveral thouſand Men laboured hard at the erecting it, though the whole *Circus* was full of nothing but vaſt Engines and Ropes of a prodigious Thickneſs. We read in *Vitruvius* that *Cteſiphon* and his Son *Metagenes* brought his Columns and Architraves to *Epheſus* by a Method which they borrowed from thoſe Cylinders with which the Ancients uſed to level the Ground: For in each End of the Stone they fixed a Pin of Iron which they faſtened in with Lead, which Pin ſtood out and ſerved as an Axis, and at each End was let into a Wheel ſo large as for the Stone to hang upon its Pins above the Ground; and ſo by the Motion of the Wheels the Stones were carried along with a great deal of Eaſe. We are told that *Chemminus* the *Ægyptian*, when he built that vaſt Pyramid

Pyramid of above ſix Furlongs high, raiſed a Mound of Earth all the Way up along with the Building, by which he carried up thoſe huge Stones into their Places. *Herodotus* writes that *Cheops*, the Son of *Rhampſinites*, in the building of that Pyramid which employed an hundred thouſand Men for many Years, left Steps on the Outſide of it, by means of which the largeſt Stones might by proper Engines, be raiſed up into their Places without having Occaſion for very long Timbers. We read too of Architraves of vaſt Stones being laid upon huge Columns in the following Manner: Under the Middle of the Architrave they ſet two Bearers acroſs, pretty near each other. Then they loaded one End of the Architraves with a great Number of Baskets full of Sand, the Weight of which raiſed up the other End, on which there were no Baskets, and one of the Bearers was left without any Weight upon it: Then removing the Baskets to the other End ſo raiſed up, and putting under ſome higher Bearers in the Room of that which was left without Weight, the Stone by little and little roſe up as it were of its own accord. Theſe Things which we have here briefly collected together, we leave to be more clearly learnt from the Authors themſelves. But the Method of this Treatiſe requires, that we ſhould ſpeak ſuccinctly of ſome few Things that make to our Purpoſe. I ſhall not waſte Time in explaining any ſuch curious Principles, as that it is the Nature of all heavy Bodies to preſs continually downwards, and obſtinately to ſeek the loweſt Place; that they make the greateſt Reſiſtance they are able againſt being raiſed aloft, and never change their Place, but after the ſtouteſt Conflict, being either overcome by ſome greater Weight or ſome more powerful contrary Force. Nor ſhall I ſtand to obſerve that Motions are various, from high to low or from low to high, directly, or about a Curve; and that ſome Things are carried, ſome drawn, ſome puſhed on, and the like; of which Enquiries we ſhall treat more copiouſly in another Place. This we may lay down for certain, that a Weight is never moved with ſo much Eaſe as it is downwards; becauſe it then moves itſelf, nor ever with more Difficulty, than upwards; becauſe it naturally reſiſts that Direction; and that there is a Kind of middle Motion between theſe two, which perhaps partakes ſomewhat of the Nature of both the others, inaſmuch as it neither moves of itſelf, nor of itſelf reſiſts, as when a Weight is drawn upon an even Plain, free from all Rubs. All other Motions are eaſy or difficult in Proportion as they approach to either of the preceding. And indeed Nature herſelf ſeems in a good Meaſure to have ſhewn us in what Manner great Weights are to be moved: for we may obſerve, that if any conſiderable Weight is laid upon a Column ſtanding upright, the leaſt Shove will puſh it off, and when once it begins to fall, hardly any Force is ſufficient to ſtop it. We may alſo obſerve, that any round Column, or Wheel, or any other Body that turns about, is very eaſily moved, and very hard to ſtop when once it is ſet on going; and if it is draged along without rowling, it does not move with half the Eaſe. We further ſee, that the vaſt Weight of a Ship may be moved upon a ſtanding Water with a very ſmall Force, if you keep pulling continually; but if you ſtrike it with ever ſo great a Blow ſuddenly, it will not ſtir an Inch: On the Contrary, ſome Things will move with a ſudden Blow or a furious Puſh, which could not otherwiſe be ſtirred without a mighty Force or huge Engines. Upon Ice too the greateſt Weights make but a ſmall Reſiſtance, againſt one that tries to draw them. We likewiſe ſee that any Weight which hangs upon a long Rope, is very eaſily moved as far as a certain Point; but not ſo eaſily, further. The Conſideration of the Reaſons of theſe Things, and the Imitation of them, may be very uſeful to our Purpoſe; and therefore we ſhall briefly treat of them here. The Keel or Bottom of any Weight, that is to be drawn along, ſhould be even and ſolid; and the Broader it is, the leſs it will plough up the Ground all the Way under it, but then the Thinner it is, it will ſlip along the Quicker, only it will make the deeper Furrows, and be apter to ſtick: If there are any Angles or Inequalities in the Bottom of the Weight, it will uſe them as Claws to faſten itſelf in the Plain, and to reſiſt its own Motion. If the Plain be ſmooth, ſound, even, hard, not riſing or ſinking on any Side, the Weight will have nothing to hinder its Motion, or to make it refuſe to obey, but its own natural Love of Reſt, which makes it lazy and unwilling to be moved. Perhaps it was from a Conſideration of theſe Things, and from a deeper Examination of the Particulars we have here mentioned, and *Archimedes* was induced to ſay, that if he had only a Baſis for ſo immenſe a Weight, he would not doubt to turn the World itſelf about. The Preparation of the Bottom of the Weight and the

the Plain upon which it is to be drawn, which is what we are here to conſider, may be effected in the following Manner. Let ſuch a Number of Poles be laid along, and of ſuch a Strength and Thickneſs as may be ſufficient for the Weight; let them be ſound, even, ſmooth, and cloſe joined to one another: Between the Bottom of the Weight and this Plain which it is to ſlide upon, there ſhould be ſomething to make the Way more ſlippery; and this may be either Soap, or Tallow, or Lees of Oil, or perhaps Slime. There is another Way of making the Weight ſlip along, which is by underlaying it croſs-ways with Rollers: But theſe, though you have a ſufficient Number of them, are very hard to be kept even to their proper Lines and exact Direction; which it is abſolutely neceſſary they ſhould be, and that they ſhould all do Duty equally and at once, or elſe they will run together in Confuſion, and carry the Weight to one Side And if you have but few of them, being continually loaded, they will either be ſplit or flatted, and ſo be rendered uſeleſs; or elſe that ſingle Line with which they touch the Plain underneath, or that other with which they touch the Weight that is laid upon them, will ſtick faſt with their ſharp Points and be immoveable. A Cylinder or Roller is a Body conſiſting of a Number of Circles joined together; and the Mathematicians ſay that a Circle can never touch a right Line in more than one Point; for which Reaſon I call the ſingle Line which is preſſed by the Weight, the Point of the Roller. The only Way to provide againſt this Inconvenience, is to have the Roller made of the ſtrongeſt and ſoundeſt Stuff, and exactly according to Rule and Proportion.

CHAP. VII.

Of Wheels, Pins, Leavers, Pullies, their Parts, Sizes and Figures.

BUT as there are ſeveral other Things, beſides thoſe already mentioned, which are neceſſary for our Purpoſe, ſuch as Wheels, Pullies, Skrews and Leavers, we ſhall here treat of them more diſtinctly. Wheels in a great Meaſure are the ſame as Rollers, as they always preſs down perpendicularly upon one Point: But there is this Difference between them, namely, that Rollers are more expeditious, Wheels being hindered by the Friction of their Pins or Axis. The Parts of a Wheel are three: The large outer Circle, the Pin or Axis in the Middle, and the Hole or Circle into which the Pin is let. This Circle ſome perhaps would rather call the Pole; but becauſe in ſome Machines it ſtands ſtill, and in others moves about, we rather deſire Leave to call it the Axicle. If the Wheel turns upon a very thick Axis, it will go very hard; if upon too thin a one, it will not ſupport its Load; if the outer Circle of the Wheel be too ſmall, the ſame Inconvenience will happen that we obſerved of the Roller, that is, it will ſtick in the Plain; if it be too large, it will go along tottering from Side to Side, and it will never be ready or handy at turning one way or the other. If the Axicle or Circle in which the Axis turns, be too large, it will grind its Way out; if it be too narrow, it will hardly be able to turn. Between the Axis and the Circle in which it turns, there ſhould be ſomewhat to lubricate: Becauſe one of theſe is to be conſidered as the Plain, and the other as the Bottom or Keel of the Weights. Rollers and Wheels ſhould be made of Elm or Holm-Oak: The Axis of Holly or the Cornel-tree, or indeed rather of Iron: The Circle for the Wheel to turn in, is made beſt of Braſs with one third of Tin. Pullies are little Wheels. Leavers are of the Nature of the Radii or Spokes of a Wheel. But every Thing of this Sort, whether large Wheels which Men turn about by walking within them, or Cranes or Skrews, or any other Engine, working either by Leavers or Pullies; the Principles, I ſay, of all theſe are deduced from the Balance. They tell us, that *Mercury* was believed to be a God chiefly upon this Account, that without the leaſt Geſture with his Hand, he could make his Meaning perfectly clear and plain by his Words. This, though I am a little fearful of ſucceeding in it, I ſhall here endeavour to do to the utmoſt of my Power: For my Deſign is to ſpeak of theſe Things not like a Mathematician, but like a Workman; and to ſay no more than is abſolutely neceſſary. For the clearer underſtanding* therefore of this Matter, I will ſuppoſe that you have in your Hand, a Dart. In this Dart I

* *See Plate 10, facing page 122.*

would have you consider three Places, which I call Points; the two Ends, that is the Steel and the Feathers, and the third is the Loop in the Middle for throwing the Dart by; and the two Spaces between the two Ends and the Loop, I shall call the Radii. I shall not dispute about the Reasons of these Names, which will appear better from the Consideration of the Thing itself. If the Loop be placed exactly in the Middle of the Dart, and the Feather End be just equal in Weight to the Steel, both Ends of the Dart will certainly hang even and be equally poised; if the steel End be the Heaviest, the Feather will be thrown up, but yet there will be a certain Point in the Dart further towards the heavy End, to which if you slip the Loop, the Weight will be immediately brought to an equal Poise again; and this will be the Point by which the larger Radius exceeds the smaller just as much as the smaller Weight is exceeded by the larger. For those who apply themselves to the Study of these Matters, tell us, that unequal Radii may be made equal to unequal Weights, provided the Number of the Parts of the Radius and Weight of the right Side, multiplied together, be equal to the Number of those Parts on the opposite left Side: Thus if the Steel be three Parts, and the Feather two, the Radius between the Loop and the Steel must be two, and the other Radius between the Loop and the Feather must be three. By which Means, as this Number five will answer to the five on the opposite Side, the Radii and the Weights answering equally to one another, they will hang even and be equally poised. If the Number on each Side do not answer to one another, that Side will overcome on which that Inequality of Numbers lies. I will not omit one Observation, namely, that if equal Radii run out from both Sides of the Loop, and you give the Ends a twirl round in the Air they will describe equal Circles; but if the Radii be unequal, the Circles which they describe, will be unequal also. We have already said that a Wheel is made up of a Number of Circles: Whence it is evident, that if two Wheels let into the same Axis be turned by one and the same Motion, so as when one moves the other cannot stand still, or when one stands still the other cannot move; from the Length of the Radii or Spokes in each Wheel we may come at the Knowledge of the Force which is in that Wheel, remembring always to take the Length of the Radius from the very Center of the Axis. If these Principles are sufficiently understood, the whole Secret of all these Engines of which we are here treating, will be manifest; especially with Relation to Wheels and Leavers. In Pullies indeed we may consider some further Particulars: For both the Rope which runs in the Pully and the little Wheel in the Pully are as the Plain, whereon the Weight is to be carried with the middle Motion, which we observed in the last Chapter was between the most Easy and the most Difficult, inasmuch as it is neither to be raised up nor let down, but to be drawn along upon the Plain keeping always to one Center. But that you may understand the Reason of the Thing more clearly, take a Statue of a thousand Weight; if you hang this to the Trunk of a Tree by one single Rope, it is evident this Rope must bear the whole thousand Weight. Fasten a Pully to the Statue, and into this Pully let the Rope by which the Statue hangs, and bring this Rope up again to the Trunk of the Tree, so as the Statue may hang upon the double Rope, it is plain the Weight of the Statue is then divided between two Ropes, and that the Pully in the Middle divides the Weight equally between them. Let us go on yet further, and to the Trunk of the Tree fasten another Pully and bring the Rope up through this likewise. I ask you what Weight this Part of the Rope thus brought up and put through the Pully will take upon itself: You will say five hundred; do you not perceive from hence that no greater Weight can be thrown upon this second Pully by the Rope, than what the Rope has itself; and that is five hundred. I shall therefore go no farther, having, I think, demonstrated that a Weight is divided by Pullies, by which means a greater Weight may be moved by a smaller; and the more Pullies there are, the more still the Weight is divided; from whence it follows that the more Wheels there are in them, so many more Parts the Weight is split into and may so much the more easily be managed.

* *See Plates 11–13, following Plate 10.*

PLATE 10. *(Pages 121–22)*

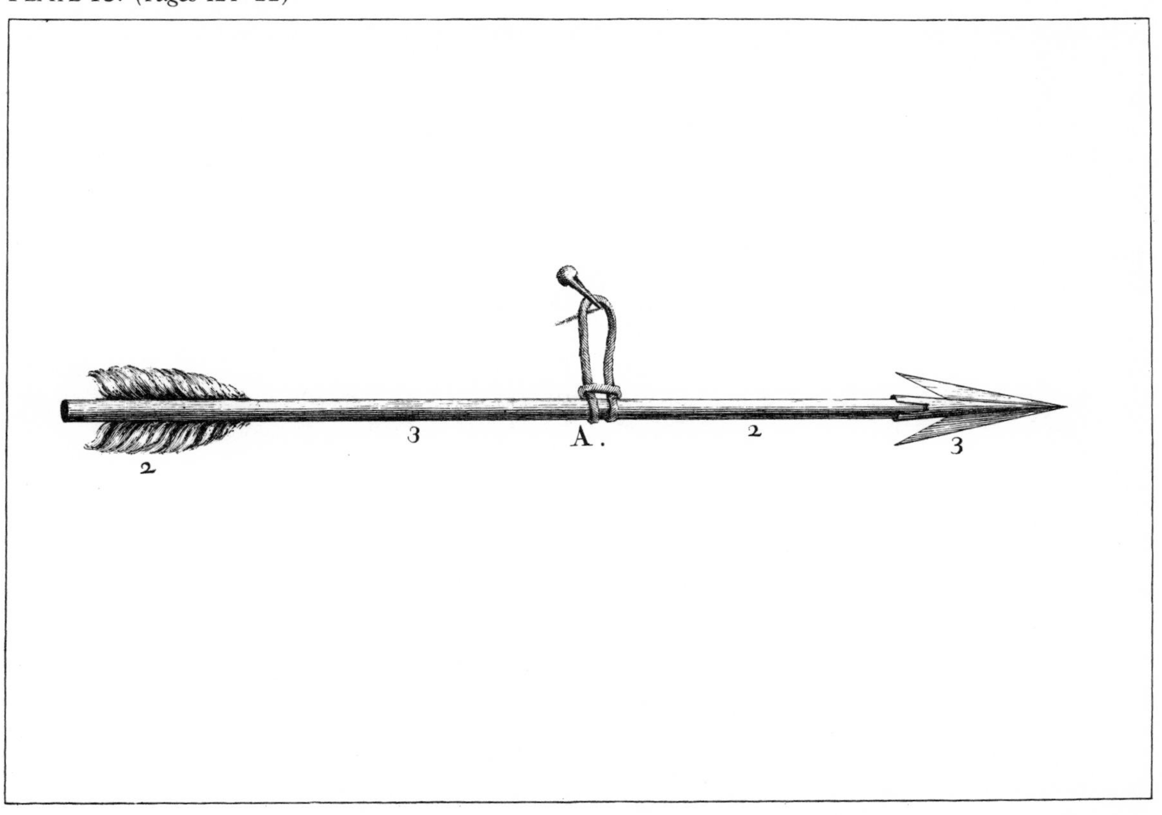

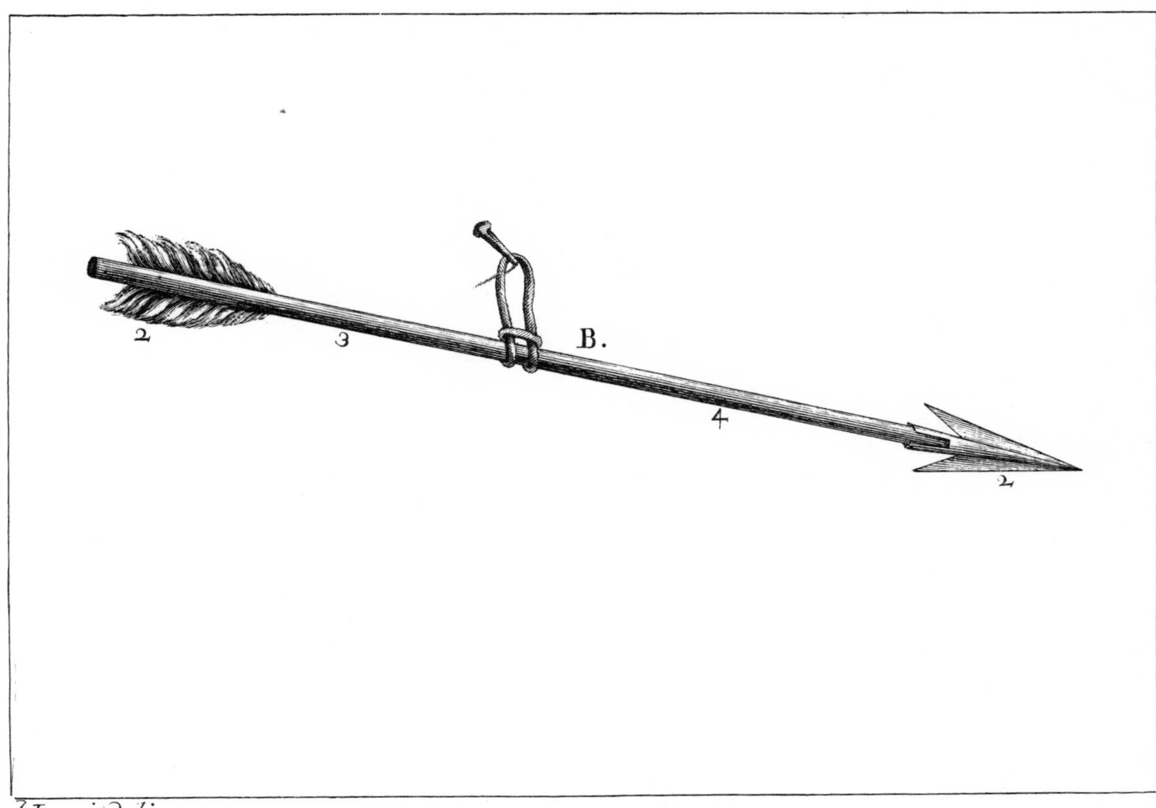

J. Leoni. delin.

PLATE 11. *(Page 122)*

B. Picart sculpsit, 1726.

PLATE 12. *(Page 122)*

PLATE 13. *(Page 122)*

Chap. VIII.

Of the Skrew and its Circles or Worm, and in what Manner great Weights are either drawn, carried or puſhed along.

WE have already treated of Wheels, Pullies and Leavers; we are now to proceed to the Skrew. A Skrew conſiſts of a Number of Circles like Rings, which take upon themſelves the Burthen of the Weight. If theſe Rings were entire, and not broken in ſuch a Manner, that the End of one of them is the Beginning of the other; it is certain the Weight which they ſupport, though it might be moved about, would neither go upwards nor downwards, but evenly round upon an equal Plain according to the Direction of the Rings: The Weight therefore is forced to ſlide either upwards or downwards along the Slope of the Rings, which act herein after the Manner of the Leaver. Again, if theſe Rings or this Worm be of a ſmall Circumference, or be cut in too near to the Center of the Skrew, the Weight will then be moved by ſhorter Leavers and with a ſmaller Force. I will not here omit one Thing which I did not think to have mentioned in this Place: Namely, that if you could ſo order it that the Bottom or Keel of any Weight which you would move might (as far as could be done by the Art and Skill of the Workman) be made no broader than a Point, and be moved in ſuch a Manner upon a firm and ſolid Plain as not in the leaſt to cut into it, I would engage you ſhould move *Archimedes*'s Ship, or effect any thing elſe of this Nature whatſoever. But of theſe Matters we ſhall treat in another Place. Each of theſe Forces in particular, of which we have already ſpoken, are of great Power for the moving of any Weight; but when they are all joined together, they are vaſtly ſtronger. In *Germany* you every where ſee the Youth ſporting upon the Ice with a ſort of wooden Pattens with a very fine thin Bottom of Steel, in which with a very ſmall Strain they ſlip over the Ice with ſo much Swiftneſs, that the quickeſt flying Bird can hardly out-go them. But as all Weights are either drawn, or puſhed along, or carried, we may diſtinguiſh them thus: That they are drawn by Ropes; puſhed along by Leavers; and carried by Wheels, Rollers and the like: And how all theſe Powers may be made uſe of at the ſame Time, is manifeſt. But in all theſe * Methods, there muſt of Neceſſity be ſome one Thing, which ſtanding firm and immoveable itſelf, may ſerve to move the Weight in Queſtion. If this Weight is to be drawn, there muſt be ſome greater Weight, to which you may faſten the Inſtruments you are to employ; and if no ſuch Weight can be had, fix a ſtrong iron Stake of the Length of three Cubits, deep into the Ground which muſt be rammed down tight all about it, or well ſtrengthened with Piles laid croſs-ways: And then faſten the Ropes of your Pullies or Cranes to the Head of the Stake which ſtands up out of the Ground. If the Ground be ſandy, lay long Poles all the Way for the Weight to ſlide upon, and at the Head of theſe Poles faſten your Inſtruments to a good ſtrong Stake. I will take Notice of one Thing which the Unexperienced will never allow, till they underſtand the Matter thoroughly; which is, that along a Plain it is more convenient to draw two Weights than one; and this is done in the following Manner: Having moved the firſt Weight to the End of the Timbers laid for it to ſlide upon, fix it there with Wedges in ſuch a Manner that nothing can ſtir it, and then faſten or tie to it the Engines, or Inſtruments with which you are to draw your other Weight; and thus the moveable Weight will be overcome and drawn along the ſame Plain by the other Weight, which is no more than equal to it, but only that it is fixed. If the Weight is to be drawn up on high, we may very conveniently make uſe of one ſingle Pole, or rather of the Maſt of a Ship; but it muſt be very ſtout and ſtrong. This Maſt we muſt ſet upright, faſtening the Foot of it to a Stake, or fixing it ſtrong in any other Manner that you pleaſe. To the upper End of it we muſt faſten no leſs than three Ropes, one on the right Side, another on the left, and the other running down directly even with the Maſt. Then at ſome Diſtance from the Foot of the Maſt fix your Capſtern and Pullies in the Ground, and putting this laſt Rope through the Pullies, let it run through them ſo as to draw the Head of the Maſt a little downwards, and

* *See Plate 14, facing page 124.*

and we may guide it which way we think proper by means of the two ſide Ropes, as with two Reins, making it either ſtand upright whenever we find it neceſſary, or ſtoop whichſoever way we Pleaſe to ſet down the Weight in the proper place. As to theſe two ſide Ropes, if you have no greater Weight to faſten them to, you may fix them in the following Manner: Dig a ſquare Pit in the Ground, and in it lay the Trunk of a Tree, to which faſten one or more Loops that may ſtand up out of the Ground; then lay ſome croſs Timbers over the Trunk, and fill up the Pit with Earth, ramming it down very cloſe, and if you wet it, it will be the heavier. In all the other Particulars, you may obſerve the Rules we have laid down as to the Plain on which the Weight is to ſlide: For you muſt faſten Pullies both to the Head of the Maſt and to the Weight which is to be raiſed, and near the Foot of the Maſt you muſt fix your Capſtern, or whatever other Inſtrument you uſe that acts with the Power of the Leaver. In all Engines of this Nature deſigned for the moving of great Weights, we ſhould take Care that none of the Parts of the Machine which are to have any Streſs upon them, be too ſmall, and that none of our Ropes, Spokes, or any other Medium which we uſe in the Movement be weak by means of their Length; for indeed long and thin are in a Manner ſynonimous Terms, and ſo, on the Contrary, are ſhort and thick. If the Ropes are ſmall let them run double in the Pullies; if they are very thick, you muſt get larger Pullies, that the Rope may not be cut by the Edges of the Pully-wheel. The Axis of the Pully ſhould be Iron, and not leſs in Thickneſs than the ſixth Part of the Semidiameter of the Pully itſelf, nor more than the eighth Part of the whole Diameter. If the Rope be wetted, it will be the more ſecure from taking Fire, which ſometimes happens by means of its Motion and Friction in the Pully; it will alſo turn the Pully round the better, and keep better within the Wheel. It is better to wet the Rope with Vinegar than with Water; but if you do it with Water, Sea-water is beſt. If you wet with freſh Water, and it is expoſed to the Heat of the Sun, it will rot preſently. Twiſting the Ropes together is much ſafer than tying them; and eſpecially you muſt take Care that one Rope does not cut the other. The Ancients uſed a Bar or Rule of Iron, to which they faſtened the firſt Knots of their Ropes, and their Pullies, and for taking up any Weight, and eſpecially of Stone, they had a Kind of Pincers or Forceps of Iron. The Shape of theſe Pincers or Forceps was taken from the Letter X, the lower Limbs of it being turned inwards like a Crab's Claw, by which means it faſtened itſelf to the Weight. The two upper Limbs had Holes at the Top, through which they put a Rope, which being tied, and ſtrained tight by the moving Force, made the Teeth of the Pincers keep cloſer to the Weight -A-. * In very large Stones, and eſpecially in the Middle of Columns, though perfectly ſmooth in all other Parts, I have ſeen little Knobs left jutting out, like Handles, againſt which the Ropes were hitched, to prevent their ſlipping. It is alſo common, eſpecially in Cornices, to make a Hole in the Stone like a Mortiſe, after this Manner; you make a Hole in the Stone like an empty Purſe, of a Bigneſs anſwerable to the Size of the Stone, narrower at the Mouth than at the Bottom. I have ſeen ſome of theſe Holes a Foot deep. You then fill it with iron Wedges, -B- the two ſide Wedges being ſhaped like the letter D, * which are put in firſt to fill up the Sides of the Hole, and the middle Wedge is put in laſt between theſe two. All theſe three Wedges have their Ears which project out beyond the Mortiſe, and theſe Ears have a Hole drilled in them, through which you put an iron Pin, which faſtens on a ſtrong Handle or Ring; and to this Ring you faſten the Rope which runs through the Pully that is to draw up the Weight. My way of faſtening my Ropes about Columns, Jambs of Doors, and other ſuch Stones which are to be ſet upright, is as follows. I make a Cincture or Hoop of Wood or Iron of a due Strength for bearing the Weight which I am to move, and with this Hoop I ſurround the Column or other Stone in ſome convenient Part, making it tight to the Stone with long thin Wedges drove in gently with a Hammer, then I faſten my Ligatures to this Hoop, and by this Means I neither ſpoil the Beauty of the Stone by making Mortiſes in it, nor break the Edges of the Jambs by the Rubbing of the Ropes againſt them: Beſides that it is the moſt expeditious, convenient and ſafeſt Way of faſtening the Ropes that has been thought of. In another Place I ſhall enlarge more particularly upon many Things relating to this Subject. All I ſhall obſerve further here is, that all Engines may be looked upon to be a Sort of Animals, with prodigious ſtrong Hands; and that they move Weights juſt in the ſame Manner as we Men

* *See Plate 15, facing page 125.*

J. Leoni Delin.

PLATE 15. *(Page 124)*

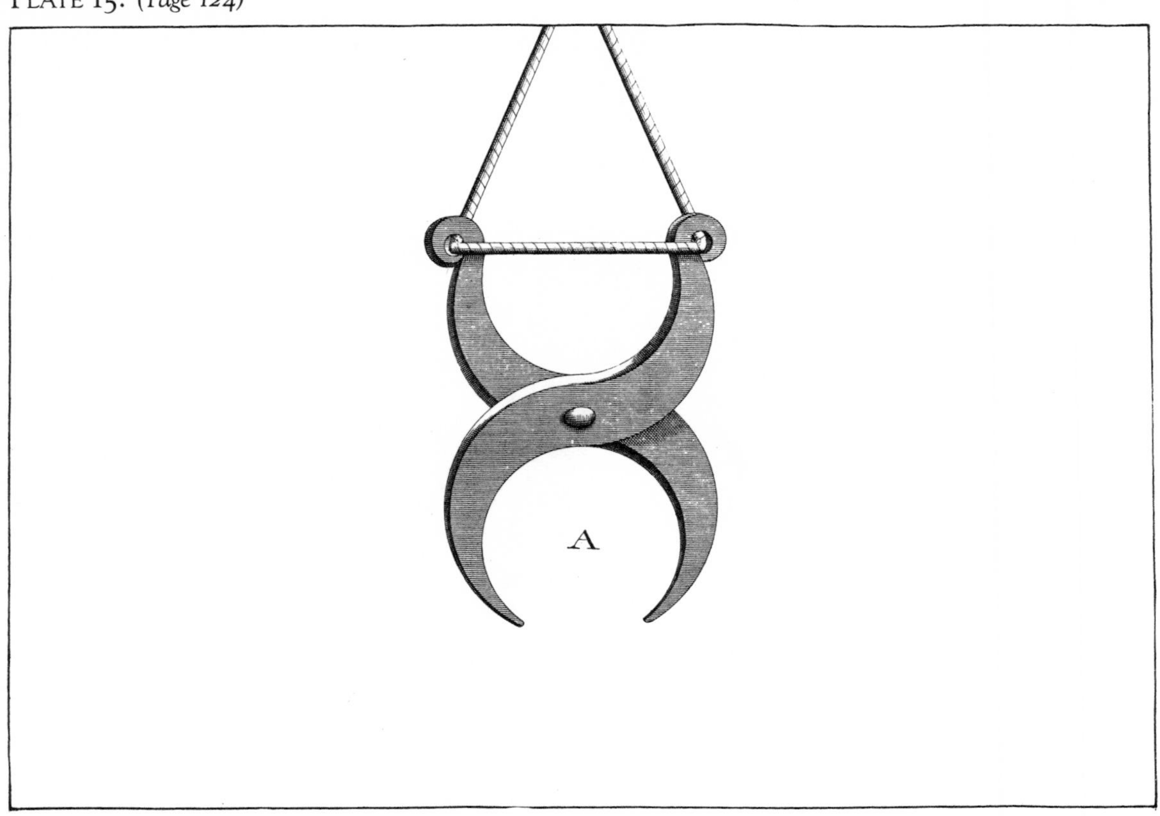

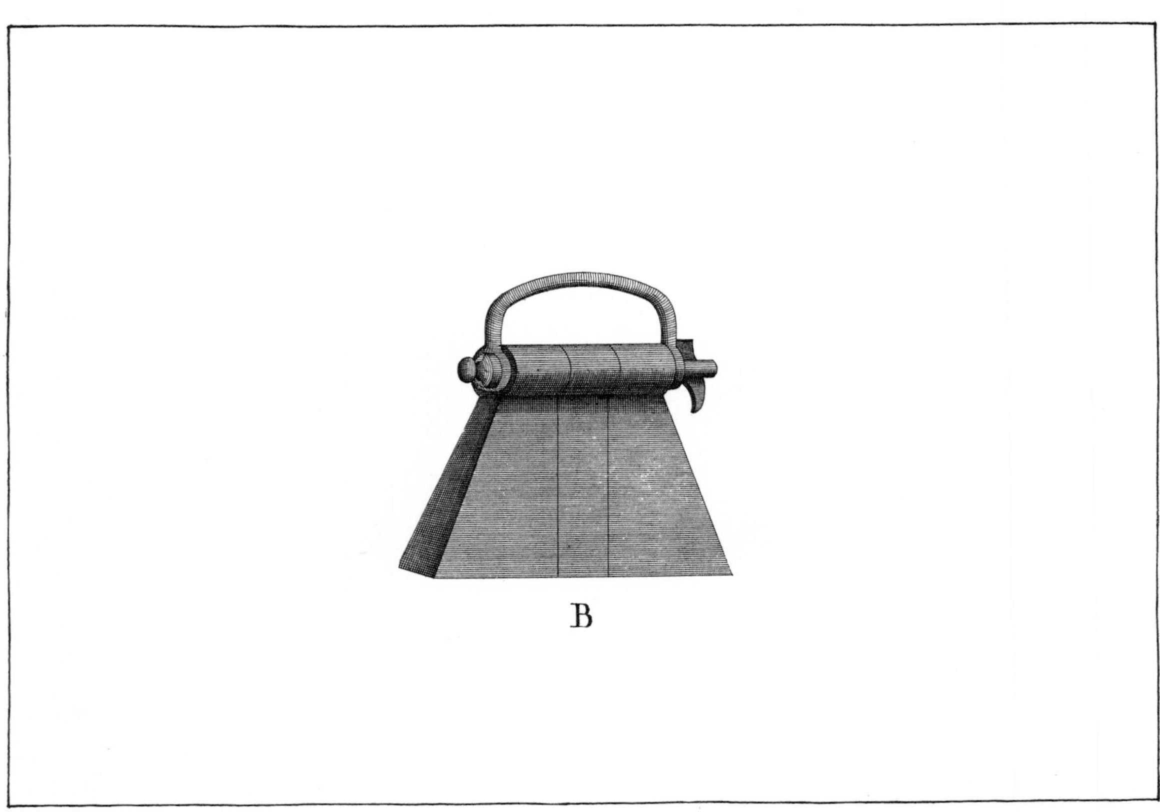

J. Leoni delin.

Men do with our Arms. For this Reaſon, the ſame Diſtention and Contraction of the Members and Nerves which we uſe in pulling, thruſting or lifting, we are to imitate in our Engines. I ſhall only add one Piece of Advice more, which is, that whenever you are to move any great Weight, in any Manner whatſoever, you would go about it carefully, cautiouſly and deliberately, remembering the many uncertain and irrecoverable Accidents and Dangers which ſometimes happen in Attempts of this Nature, even to the moſt experienced: For you will never get ſo much Honour and Reputation if what you undertake, ſucceeds, as you will incur Blame and the Imputation of Raſhneſs, if it fails. We ſhall now leave this Subject, to proceed to the outward Coat of the Wall.

CHAP. IX.

That the Incruſtations which are made upon the Wall with Mortar, muſt be three in Number: How they are to be made, and to what Purpoſes they are to ſerve. Of the ſeveral Sorts of Mortar, and in what Manner the Lime is to be prepared for making them: Of Baſs-relieves in Stuc-work and Paintings, with which the Wall may be adorned.

IN all Incruſtations there muſt be at leaſt three Coats of Mortar; the firſt is called Rough-caſting, and its Office is to ſtick as cloſe as poſſible to the Wall and to bind on the two outer Coats; the Office of the outer Coat, is to make the Work ſhew neat, ſmooth, and poliſhed; that of the middle Coat, which we call Plaiſtering, is to prevent any Faults or Defects in either of the other two. The Defects are theſe: If the two laſt, that is to ſay, the Plaiſtering and the outer Coat are ſharp, and to uſe ſuch an Expreſſion, tenacious of the Wall, as the Rough-caſt ought to be, their Acrimony will occaſion an infinite Number of Cracks in them in drying. And if the Rough-caſt be ſoft, as the outer Coat ſhould be, it will not take hold of the Wall as it ought, but will fall off in Pieces. The oftener we plaiſter the Wall over, the better we may poliſh it, and the longer it will endure the Injuries of Time. Among the ancient Buildings I have ſeen ſome which have been done over no leſs than nine Times. The firſt of theſe ſhould be very ſharp, and made of Pit-Sand and Brick beaten not too fine, but about the Size of ſmall Gravel, and laid on about the Thickneſs of three Inches. For the Plaiſtering, or middle Coat, River-Sand is better, and is leſs apt to crack. This Coat too ſhould be ſomewhat rough, becauſe to a ſmooth Surface nothing will ſtick that you lay on. The laſt of all ſhould be as white as Marble; for which Reaſon, inſtead of Sand you ſhould uſe the whiteſt Stone that can be got pounded ſmall; and it will be ſufficient if this Coat be laid on about half an Inch thick, for when it is much more, it will not eaſily dry. I know ſome that, out of good Huſbandry, make it no thicker than a Piece of Shoe-leather. The ſecond Coat, or Plaiſtering, ought to be ordered according to its Proximity to either of the other two. In Mountains where there are Stone-pits, you meet with certain Veins extremely like a tranſparent Alabaſter, which are neither Marble nor Tarres, but of a Kind of middle Nature between both, and very friable. If this be beat ſmall and mixed up inſtead of Sand, it will ſhew full of little Sparks that will ſhine like a fine Sort of Marble. In many Places we ſee Nails ſtuck into the Wall to keep on the Plaiſtering, and Time has proved to us that it is better to have them of Braſs than of Iron. I am very much pleaſed with thoſe who, inſtead of Nails, ſtick little Pieces of Flint in between the Joints of the Stone; which they drive in gently with a wooden Hammer. The freſher and rougher the Wall itſelf is, the faſter all your plaiſtering Work will cleave to it: For which Reaſon, if, as you build the Wall, and while the Work is Green, you rough-caſt it, though but ſlightly, the Plaiſtering and outer Coat will ſtick to it ſo faſt, as hardly ever to peel off. After ſoutherly Winds, it is very proper to do any of this Sort of Work; but if when a north Wind blows, or in any great Cold or Heat, you offer at any Sort of Plaiſtering, eſpecially at laying on the outer Coat, it will ſcale off preſently. Laſtly, all Incruſtations are of two Sorts; either ſpread on, or faſtened to the Work. Stuc and Plaiſter are ſpread on; but Stuc is never good but in very dry Places. The Moiſture trickling down from old Walls is extremely prejudicial to all Sorts of Incruſtations. Theſe Incruſtations which are faſtened to the Work are Stone, Glaſs and the like. The different Sorts of Incruſtations which are ſpread on are either flat White, Baſs-relieve, or painted in Freſco. Thoſe which are faſtened on, are either plain, pannelled or teſſelated. We ſhall ſpeak firſt of thoſe which are ſpread on, for which the Lime muſt be prepared in the following Manner: Quench it in a covered Pit with clear Water, and let there be much more Water than Lime; then with an Axe chop and cut it as if you were chopping of Wood, and you will know when it is ſufficiently ſoaked and diſſolved by the Axes not being offended by the leaſt Stone or Grit. It is thought not to be ſufficiently ſoaked under three Months. It is never good unleſs it be very glutinous and clammy; for if the Axe comes out of it dry, it is a Sign it has not had a ſufficient Quantity of Water to quench its Thirſt. When you mix it up with the Sand, or any other pounded Materials, beat it over and over again very heartily, till it perfectly foams again. That which was deſigned for the outer Coat the Ancients uſed to pound in a Mortar, and they tempered their Mixture ſo well, that it never ſtuck to the Trowel when they came to lay it on. Upon this firſt Coat, while it is ſtill wet and freſh, lay on the ſecond, and be ſure to let all the three be laid on ſo faſt as to dry together, beating them even and ſmooth while they are wet. The outer Coat of flat White, if you rub and ſmooth it well, will ſhine like a Looking-glaſs; and if when it is almoſt dry, you anoint it with Wax and Gum Maſtix diſſolved in a little Oil, and heat the Wall thus anointed with a Pan of Charcoal, ſo that it may imbibe that Ointment, it will out-do any Marble in Whiteneſs. I have found by Experience that this Coat will never ſcale off, if while you are working it, upon the firſt Appearance of any Crack, you make it good with a few Twigs of white Mallows or wild Spart. But if you are obliged to plaiſter in the Dog-days, or in any very hot Place, cut and beat ſome old Ropes very ſmall, and mix them with the Plaiſter. You may alſo give it a very fine Poliſh, by throwing in a little white Soap diſſolved in warm Water; but if you uſe too much of this, it will make your Work look pale. Figures in Stuc-work are eaſily made from a Mold; and the Mold itſelf is taken off from any Relieve, by pouring ſome liquid Plaiſter over it; and as it is drying, if it is anointed with the Compoſition above mentioned, it will get a Surface like Marble. Theſe Figures are of two Sorts, one alto Relieve and the other baſſo Relieve. In an upright Wall, the alto Relieve do extremely well: But on an arched Cieling the baſſo Relieve are better; becauſe thoſe of the high Relieve being to hang down from the Cieling, are very apt to break off by their own Weight, which may endanger the Perſons in the Room. It is a very good Admonition, that where there is likely to be much Duſt, we ſhould never make Ornaments of high Relieve; but flat and low, that they may be eaſily cleaned. Of painted Surfaces ſome are done while the Work is freſh, and others when it is dry. All natural Colours which proceed from the Earth, from Mines or the like, are proper for Paintings in Freſco: But all artificial Colours, and eſpecially thoſe which are altered by Means of Fire, require a very dry Surface, and abhor Lime, the Rays of the Moon, and ſouthern Winds. It has been newly found out that Colours mixed up with Linſeed Oil, will ſtand a vaſt While againſt all the Injuries of the Air and Seaſons, provided the Wall on which they are laid be perfectly dry, and quite clear of all Moiſture; though I have obſerved that the antient Painters, in painting the Poops of their Ships, make uſe of liquid Wax, inſtead of Size. I have alſo ſeen in the Works of the Ancients, ſome Colours of Gems laid on the Wall, if I judge rightly, with Wax, or perhaps with a white Sort of Terraſs, which was ſo hardened by Time, that it could not be got off either by Fire or Water, and you would have taken it for a hard Sort of Glaſs. I have known ſome too, that with the white milky Flower of Lime, have laid Colours upon the Wall, while it was ſtill freſh, that have looked as much like Glaſs as poſſible. But of this Subject, we need ſay no more.

CHAP.

CHAP. X.

Of the Method of cutting Marble into thin Scantlings, and what Sand is best for that Purpose; as also of the Difference and Agreement between Mosaic *Work in Relieve, and Flat, and of the Cement to be used in that Sort of Work.*

AS to those Incrustations which are fastened on to the Work, whether flat Facings, or pannelled Work, the same Method is to be used in both. It is very surprizing to consider the Diligence which the Antients used in sawing and polishing their Scantlings of Marble. I myself have seen some Pieces of Marble above six Foot long and three broad, and yet scarce half an Inch thick, and these have been joined together with a curve Line, that the Spectators might not easily find out where the Junctures were. *Pliny* tells us, that the Ancients commended the Sand of *Æthiopia* as the Best for sawing of Marble, and that the *Indian* came up the nearest to it: But that the *Ægyptian* was rather too soft, though even that was better than ours. They tell us that there is a Sort found in a certain Flat in the *Adriatic* Sea, which was much used by the Ancients. We dig a Sand about the Shore of *Pozzuolo*, which is not improper for this Purpose. The sharp Sand found in any Sort of Torrent is good, but the larger it is, the wider it cuts and the more it eats into the Stone; whereas the softer it goes through, the Smoother it leaves the Surface, and the more easily to be polished. The Polishing must be begun with chizzelling, but ended with the softest and smoothest rubbing. The *Theban* Sand is much commended for rubbing and polishing of Marble; so is the Whetstone, and the Emeril, whose Dust nothing can exceed for this Purpose. The Pumice-stone too, for giving the last Polish, is very useful. The Scum of calcined Tin, which we call Putty, white Lead burnt, the *Tripoli* Chalk in particular, and the like, if they are beat into the finest Dust that possibly can be, still retaining their Sharpness, are very good for this Work. For fastening on the Scantlings, if they are thick, fix into the Wall either Pins of Iron, or little Spars of Marble sticking out from the Wall, to which you may fasten your Scantling without any Thing of Cement. But if the Scantlings are thin, after the second Plaistering, instead of Mortar, take Wax, Pitch, Rosin, Gum Mastic, and a good Quantity of any other Sort of Gum whatsoever, all melted and mixed together, and warm your Piece of Marble by degrees, lest if you put it to the Fire at once of a Sudden, the Heat should make it crack. In fixing up your Scantlings, it will be very laudable if the Juncture and Order in which you place them, produce a beautiful Effect, by means of the Veins and Colours answering and setting off one another. I am mightily pleased with the Policy of the Ancients, who used to make those Parts which lay nearest to the Eye as neat and as exactly polished as was possible, but did not take so much Pains about those which stood at any Distance, or Heigth, and in some Places put them up without any polishing at all, where they knew the Eye of the most curious Examiner could not reach them. *Mosaic* Work in Relieve, and that which is flat, agree in this Particular, that both are designed to imitate Painting, by means of an artful Composition of various Colours of Stones, Glass, and Shells. *Nero* is said to have been the First that had Mother of Pearl cut and mixed in *Mosaic* Work. But herein they differ, that in *Mosaic* Work in Relieve we use the largest Pieces of Marble, *&c.* that we can get; whereas in the flat *Mosaic*, we put none but little square Pieces, no bigger than a Bean; and the smaller these Pieces are, the more Bright and Sparkling they make the Work, the Light by so many different Faces being broke into the more various Parts. They differ too in this, that in fastening on the former, Cement made of Gums is the Best; but in the flat Work, we should use Mortar made of Lime, with a Mixture of *Tyburtine* Stone, beat as small as Dust. There are some that, in flat Work *Mosaic* Work, are for steeping the Lime often in hot Water, in order to get out its Saltness and make it softer and more gluey. I have known some of the hardest Stone polished upon a Grind-stone, in order to be used in the *Mosaic* in Relieve. In the flat *Mosaic* Work you may fasten Gold to Glass with a Cement of Lead or Litharge, which may be made more liquid than any Sort of Glass whatsoever. All

that

that we have here ſaid of the outer Coat, or Surface of the Wall may likewiſe ſerve as to Pavements, of which we promiſed to ſpeak, only that on Pavements we never beſtow fine Painting nor ſuch good *Moſaic* Work, unleſs you will grant the Name of Painting to a Parget of various Colours poured into hollow little Spaces ſeparated from each other by thin Partitions of Marble in Imitation of Painting. This Parget may be made of red Oker burnt, with Brick, Stone and the Droſs of Iron; and when it is laid on and is thoroughly dry, it muſt be cleared and ground down ſmooth, which is done in the following Manner: Take a hard Stone, or rather a Piece of Lead of threeſcore Pound Weight, with its lower Surface perfectly ſmooth; to each End of this faſten a Rope, by which you muſt draw it backwards and forwards over your Pavement, ſtill keeping it ſupplied with Sand and Water, till it is rubbed exactly ſmooth, and is poliſhed as it ought, which it never is unleſs all the Lines and Angles of the Dies anſwer and fit one another to the greateſt Niceneſs. If this Parget be rubbed over with Oil, eſpecially that of Linſeed, it will get a Coat like Glaſs. It alſo does very well to anoint it with Lees of Oil, as alſo with Water in which Lime has been quenched, with which you ſhould rub it over often. In all our *Moſaic* Works we ſhould avoid uſing the ſame Colours too often in the ſame Places, as alſo too frequent Repetitions of the ſame Figures and Irregularity in the Compoſition of them. We ſhould likewiſe take Care that the Junctures are not too wide, but that every Thing be fitted together with the utmoſt Exactneſs, that equal Care may appear to have been uſed in all Parts of the Work.

Chap. XI.

Of the Ornaments of the Covering, which conſiſt in the Richneſs and Beauty of the Rafters, Vaults and open Terraſſes.

THE Coverings too have their Beauty and Gratefulneſs from the Contrivance of the Rafters, Vaults and open Terraſſes. There are Roofs yet to be ſeen in *Agrippa*'s Portico with Rafters of Braſs, forty Foot long; a Work wherein we know not which to admire moſt, the Greatneſs of the Expence, or the Skill of the Workmen. In the Temple of *Diana* at *Epheſus*, as we have taken Notice elſewhere, was a Roof of Cedar, which laſted a vaſt While. *Pliny* relates that *Salauces* King of *Colchos*, after he had overcome *Seſoſtris* King of *Ægypt*, made his Rafters of Gold and Silver. There are ſtill to be ſeen Temples covered with Slabs of Marble, as, we are told, was the Temple of *Jeruſalem* with prodigious large ones of ſuch wonderful Whiteneſs and Splendor, that at a Diſtance the whole Roof appeared like a Mountain of Snow. *Catulus* was the firſt that gilt the Braſs Tiles on the Capitol with Gold. I find too that the *Pantheon*, or *Rotonda* at *Rome*, was covered with Plates of Braſs gilt; and Pope *Honorius*, he in whoſe Time *Mahomet* taught *Ægypt* and *Africa* a new Religion and Worſhip, covered the Church of St. *Peter* all over with Plates of Braſs. *Germany* ſhines with Tiles glazed over. In many Places we cover our Roofs with Lead, which will endure a great While, ſhews very handſome, and is not very expenſive; but it is attended with this Inconvenience, that if it is laid upon a Stone Roof, not having room for Air under it, when the Stones come to be heated by the Rays of the Sun, it will melt. There is an Experiment which may convince us of the Truth of this. If you ſet a leaden Veſſel full of Water upon the Fire, it will not melt; but if you throw the leaſt Stone into it, where that touches it will immediately melt into a Hole. Beſides this, if it is not well cramped and pinned down in all Parts, it is eaſily ripped off by the Wind. Moreover it is preſently eat into and ſpoilt by the Saltneſs of Lime; ſo that it does much the beſt upon Timbers, if you are not afraid of Fire: But here again, there is a great Inconvenience ariſing from the Nails, eſpecially if they are of Iron, inaſmuch as they are more apt to grow hoter than Stone, and, beſides, eat away the Lead all about them with Ruſt. For this Reaſon the Cramps and Pins ought alſo to be all of Lead, and muſt be faſtened into the Sheets with hot Sodder. Under this Covering you ſhould make a thin Bed of Aſhes of Willow, waſhed and mixed with Chalk. Braſs Nails are not ſo apt to grow hot or to ruſt, as Iron

Iron ones. If Lead is daubed with any Sort of Filth, it quickly ſpoils; and for this Reaſon we ſhould take Care that our Roof be not a convenient Harbour for Birds; or if it is a likely Place for them to get together in, we ſhould make our Stuff thick where their Dung is to fall. *Euſebius* tells us, that all round the Top of *Solomon*'s Temple there was a great Number of Chains, to which hung four hundred little Bells continually vibrating, the Noiſe of which drove away the Birds. In the Covering we alſo adorn the Ridge, Gutters and Angles, by ſetting up Vaſes, Balls, Statues, Chariots and the like, each of which we ſhall ſpeak of in particular in its due Place. At preſent I do not call to Mind any thing further relating to this Sort of Ornaments in general, except that each be adapted to the Place to which it is moſt ſuitable.

CHAP. XII.

That the Ornaments of the Apertures are very pleaſing, but are attended with many and various Difficulties and Inconveniences; that the falſe Apertures are of two Sorts, and what is required in each.

THE Ornaments of the Aperture give no ſmall Beauty and Dignity to the Work, but they are attended with many great Difficulties, which cannot be provided againſt without a good deal of Skill in the Artificer, and a conſiderable Expence. They require very large Stones, ſound, equal, handſome and rare, which are Things not eaſily to be got, and when got not eaſily removed, poliſhed, or ſet up according to your Intention. *Cicero* ſays, that the Architects owned they could not ſet up a Column exactly perpendicular, which in all Apertures is abſolutely neceſſary both with Reſpect to Duration and Beauty. There are other Inconveniencies beſides; which, as far as lies in our Power, we ſhall endeavour to provide againſt. An Aperture naturally implies an Opening; but ſometimes behind this Opening we run up a Wall which makes a Kind of falſe Opening which is not pervious but cloſed up; which for this Reaſon we ſhall accordingly call a falſe Aperture. This Sort of Ornaments, as indeed were moſt of thoſe which ſerve either to ſtrengthen the Work or to ſave Expence, was firſt invented by the Carpenters, and afterwards imitated by the Maſons, who thereby gave no ſmall Beauty to their Structures. Any of theſe Apertures would be more beautiful if their Ribs were all of one Piece, made of one entire Stone; and next to this, is the having the Parts ſo nicely joined that the Joints cannot be ſeen. The Ancients uſed to erect their Columns and other Stones which ſerved as Ribs to theſe falſe Apertures, and fix them firm on their Baſes, before they carried up the Wall; and herein they did very wiſely; for by this Means they had more Room to uſe their Engines, and could take the Perpendicular more exactly. You may plant your Column perpendicular upon its Baſe in the following Manner: In the Baſe and at the Top and Bottom of the Column mark the exact Center of each Circle. Into the Center of the Baſe faſten an iron Pin, ſoddering it in with Lead, and make a Hole in the Center of the Bottom of the Column, juſt big enough to receive the Pin which ſticks up in the Center of the Baſe. In the Top of your Engine, or Scaffolding, make a Mark exactly perpendicular over the Pin which ſticks up in the Center of the Baſe, which you may find by letting fall Line from thence to that Pin. When you have thus prepared every Thing, it will be no hard Matter to move the Head of the Shaft till its Center anſwers exactly to the Mark which you have made above and is perpendicular to the Center of its Baſe. I have obſerved from the Works of the Ancients that the ſofter Sort of Marble may be ſmoothed with the very ſame Inſtruments with which we plane Wood. The Ancients alſo uſed to ſet up their Stones quite rough, only ſmoothing the Heads and Sides of them which were to join to other Stones, and afterwards when the Building was raiſed, they poliſhed the Faces of the Stones, which they had left rough before; and this I believe they did that they might leave the leaſt Expence that was poſſible to the Hazards of their Engines: For it would have been a much greater Loſs to them, if by Accident any Stone that was quite ſmoothed and poliſhed had been let fall and broke, than if

they

they broke one that was only half wrought. Besides that by this means they had the Advantage of doing their Work at different Times, according to the different Seasons which are requisite for building the Wall, and for cloathing and polishing it. * There are two Sorts of false Apertures: One is that where the Columns or Pilasters are so joined to the Wall, that one Part of them is hid within it, and only Part of them appears; the other is that wherein the whole Columns stand out of the Wall, somewhat imitating a Portico. The former therefore we may call the low Relieve, and the latter the whole Relieve. In the low Relieve we may use either half Columns or Pilasters. The half Columns must never stand more nor less out of the Wall than one half of their Diameter. Pilaster, never more than one fourth Part of its Breadth, nor less than a sixth. In the whole Relieve the Columns must never stand out from the Naked of the Wall more than with their whole Base and one fourth Part of the Breadth of their Base; and never less than with their whole Base and Shaft standing out clear from the Wall. But those which stand out from the Wall with their whole Base and one fourth Part more must have their Pilasters of the low Relieve, fixed against the Wall to answer to them. In the whole Relieve the Entablature must not run all along the Wall but be broke and project over the Head of each Column, as you may see in Plate 19. No. 4. But in the half Relieve you may do as you think fit, either carrying on your Entablature entire all the Length of the Wall, or breaking it over each Pilaster with a Sweep, after the Manner of the whole Relieve. We have now treated of those Ornaments wherein all Buildings agree: But of those wherein they differ, we shall speak in the following Book, this being already long enough. But as in this we undertook to treat of every Thing relating to Ornaments in general, we shall not pass by any Thing that may be serviceable under this Head.

A. *Plan of the Inter-space of the two half Columns, called* Basso Relievo.

CHAP. XIII.

Of Columns and their Ornaments, their Plans, Axes, Out-lines, Sweeps, Diminutions, Swells, Astragals and Fillets.

THE principal Ornament in all Architecture certainly lies in Columns; for many of them set together embellish Porticoes, Walls and all Manner of Apertures, and even a single one is handsome, and adorns the Meeting of several Streets, a Theatre, an open Square, serves for setting up Trophies, and preserving the Memory of great Events, and is so Beautiful and Noble that it is almost incredible what Expence the Ancients used to bestow in single Pillars, which they looked upon as a very stately Ornament: For oftentimes, not being content with making them of *Parian*, *Numidian* or other fine Marbles, they would also have them carved with Figures and Histories by the most excellent Sculptors; and of such Columns as these we are told there were above an Hundred and Twenty in the Temple of *Diana* at *Ephesus*. Others made their Capitals and Bases of gilt Brass, as we may see in the double Portico at *Rome*, which was built in the Consulship of that *Octavius* who triumphed over *Perseus*. Some made their whole Columns of Brass, and others plated them all over with Silver; but we shall not dwell upon such Things as those. Columns must be exactly round and perfectly smooth. We read that one *Theodorus* and one *Tholus*, Architects of *Lemnos*, contrived certain Wheels in their Workhouses, wherein they hung their Columns with so nice a Poise, that they could be turned about by a little Boy, and so polished smooth. But this is a *Greek* Story. We shall proceed to something more material. In all Columns we may consider two long Lines in the Shaft; one we may call the Axis of the Shaft, and the other the Out-lines; the short Lines that we are to consider are the several Diameters of those Circles which in different Places gird the Column about; and of those Circles, the principal are the two Superficies; one at the Top and the other at the Bottom of the Shaft. The Axis of the Shaft is a Line drawn through the very Center of the Column from the Center of the Circle which forms the flat Superficies at the Top, to the Center of the Circle which is the flat Superficies at the Bottom, and this Line may be also called the Perpendicular in the Middle of the Column. In this Line meet the Centers of all the Circles. But the out Line is one drawn from the Sweep of the Fillet at the Top along the Surface of the Column to the

* *See Plates 16–19, facing and following this page.*

PLATE 16. *(Page 130, No. 1)*

Mi: 34. Mi: 32. Mi: 30. Mi: 30.

7. 6. 5. 4. 3. 2. 1.

1.

6. 5. 4. 3. 2. 1.

Mi: 30.

Mi: 1

A.

I. Leoni delin.

PLATE 17. (*Page 130, No. 2*)

I. Leoni delin.

PLATE 18. *(Page 130, No. 3)*

J. Leoni Delin.

PLATE 19. *(Page 130, No. 4)*

J. Leoni delin.

PLATE 20. *(Page 131)*

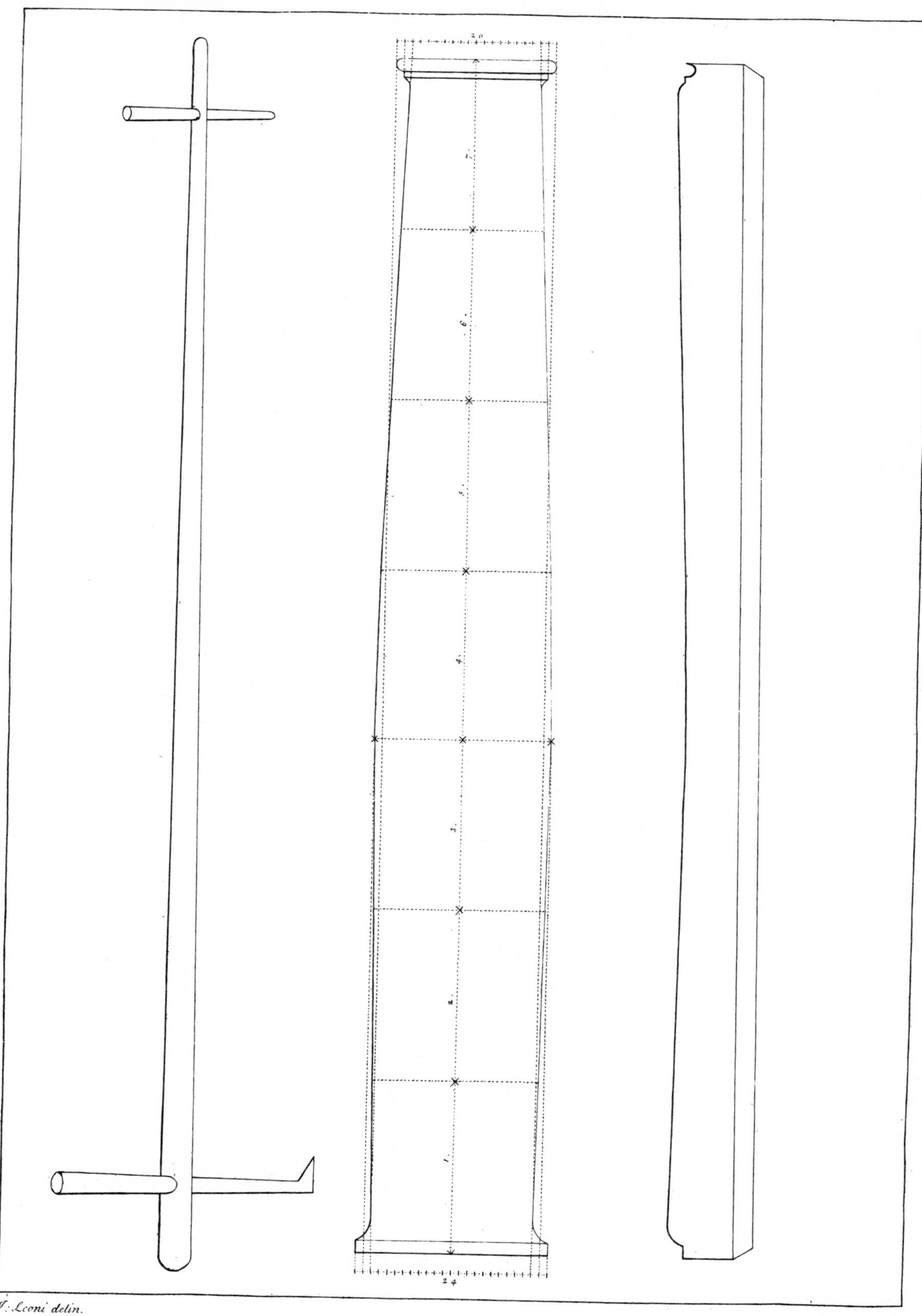

J. Leoni delin.

the Sweep of the Fillet at Bottom; and in this terminate all the Diameters that are in the Thickneſs of the Shaft, and it does not run ſtrait like the Axis, but is composed of a great Number of Lines, ſome ſtrait and ſome curve; as we ſhall ſhew hereafter. The ſeveral Diameters of Circles which we are to conſider in different Parts of the Column, are five; the Sweeps, the Diminutions, and the Swell or Belly of the Shaft. The Sweeps are two, one at the Top and the other at the Bottom of the Column, and are called Sweeps upon account of their running out a little beyond the Reſt of the Shaft, The Diminutions are likewiſe two, cloſe by the Sweeps at the Bottom and Top, and are ſo called becauſe in thoſe Parts the * Shaft diminiſhes inwards. The Diameter of the Swell or Belly of the Column is to be obſerved about the Middle of the Shaft, and is called the Belly, becauſe the Column ſeems to ſwell out juſt in that Part. Again, the Sweeps differ from one another, for that which is at the Bottom is formed by the Fillet and a ſmall Curve running from the Fillet to the Body of the Shaft; but the Sweep at the Top of the Shaft, beſides this Curve and its Fillet has likewiſe the Aſtragal. Laſtly, the Out-lines muſt be formed in the following Manner: On the Pavement, or upon the flat Side of a Wall, which is proper for the Drawing your Deſign, draw a ſtrait Line, of the Length which you intend to give the Column, which perhaps is as yet in the Quarry. This Line we call the Axis of the Shaft. Then divide this Axis into a certain Number of determinate Parts, according to the Nature of the Building, and of the various Sorts of Columns which you are to erect, of which Variety we ſhall ſpeak in due Time; and according to a due Proportion of theſe Parts you muſt make the Diameter of the Bottom of your Shaft, with a little Line drawn acroſs the Axis. The Diameter you divide into four-and-twenty Parts, one of which you give to the Height of the Fillet, which Height we mark upon the Wall with a ſmall Stroke; then take three more of thoſe Parts, and at that Height make a Mark in the Axis of the Shaft, which is to be the Center of the next Diminution, and through this Center draw a Line exactly parallel with the Diameter of the Bottom of the Shaft, which Line muſt be the Diameter of the lower Diminution, and be one ſeventh Part ſhorter than the Diameter of the Bottom of the Shaft. Having marked theſe two Lines, that is to ſay, the Diameter of the Diminution, and the Fillet, draw from the Point of the End of the Fillet to the Point of that Diameter in the Shaft of the Column a curve Line, as eaſy and neat as poſſible; the Beginning of this curve Line muſt be one Quarter of a little Circle, the Semi-diameter of which muſt be the Height of the Fillet. Then divide the whole Length of the Shaft into ſeven equal Parts, and mark thoſe Diviſions with little Dots. At the fourth Dot, counting from the Bottom, make the Center of the Belly of the Shaft, acroſs which draw its Diameter, whoſe Length muſt be equal to the Diameter of the Diminution at the Bottom. The Diminution and Sweep at the Top muſt be made as follows: According to the Species of the Column, of which we ſhall treat elſewhere, take the Diameter of the upper Superficies from the Diameter of the Bottom of the Shaft, and draw it at the Top of the Column in your Deſign; which Diameter ſo drawn muſt be divided into twelve Parts, one of which Parts muſt be allowed to the Projecture of the Fillet and Aſtragal, giving two thirds of it to the latter, and one third to the former. Then make the Center of your Diminution, at the Diſtance of one and a half of thoſe Parts from the Center of the upper Surface of the Shaft, and the Diameter of this Diminution a ninth Part leſs than the largeſt Diameter of that Surface. You muſt afterwards draw the Curve or Sweep in the ſame Manner as I taught you to draw that below. Laſtly, having thus marked in your Deſign the Sweeps, Diminutions, and all the other Particulars which we have here mentioned, draw a ſtrait Line from the Diminution at the Top, and another from the Diminution at the Bottom to the Diameter of the Belly or Swell of the Column, and this will make in your Deſign what we called the Outline of the Column, and by this Line you may make a Model of Wood by which your Maſons may ſhape and finiſh the Column itſelf. The Superficies of the Bottom of the Shaft, if the Column be exactly rounded, muſt make equal Angles on all Sides with the Axis in the Middle, and with the like Superficies at the Top of the Shaft. Theſe Things I do not find committed to writing by any of the Ancients, but I have gathered them by my own Induſtry and Application from the Works of the beſt Maſters. All that is to follow may be for the moſt Part referred to the Proportions of the Lines already treated of, and will be very delightful and of great Uſe, eſpecially to the Improvement of Painters.

The End of Book VI.

THE

* *See Plate 20, following Plate 19.*

THE

ARCHITECTURE

OF

Leone Batista Alberti.

Book VII. Chap. I.

Of the ORNAMENTS of Sacred EDIFICES.

That the Walls of Cities, the Temples, and Courts of Justice, used to be consecrated to the Gods; of the proper Region for the City, its Situation and principal Ornaments.

WE have already observed that all Buildings consist of several Parts, and that of these Parts some are those wherein all Manner of Buildings in general agree; such as Situation, Covering, and the like; and others, those wherein they differ. We have already treated of the Ornaments which belong to the former; we are now to speak of those which are proper to the latter. And this Discourse will be of so useful a Nature, that even Painters, those most accurate Searchers after every Thing that is beautiful, will confess, that they themselves have absolute Occasion for it. As for the Pleasantness of it, I shall only say, that I believe nobody will repent his having read it. But I must now desire not to be blamed, if, having proposed new Ends to myself, I begin to handle my Subject upon fresh Principles. The Principles and Steps to any Subject are found by the Division, Intent and Consideration of the Parts whereof that Subject consists. For as in a Statue made of Brass, Gold and Silver melted together, the Workman considers the Parts with regard to their Weight, the Statuary with regard to their Out-lines, and others perhaps as to other Respects; so, as we have observed before, the Parts of Architecture ought to be divided in such a Manner, that our Considerations upon each of them may be as clear and distinct as possible. We shall now therefore proceed upon that Division which regards the Beauty and Ornament of Buildings, more than either their Conveniency or Strength. Though indeed all these Qualifications have such a mutual Agreement with one another, that where any one of them is wanting, the others also lose their Commendation. All Buildings therefore are either publick or private; and both publick and private, are either sacred or profane. We shall first treat of publick Edifices. The Ancients used to found the Walls of their Cities with the greatest Religion, dedicating them to some God who was to be their Guardian: Nor did they think that it was possible for the publick Weal to be so perfectly secured by the Prudence of any Man whatsoever, but that it might be endangered by by the Insults and Treachery of those who were concerned with it; and they were of Opinion that a City, either through the Negligence of its own People, or the Envy of its Neighbours, was continually exposed to Dangers and Accidents; just as a Ship is which is tossed on the Sea. And upon this Account I suppose, they fabled that *Saturn*, out of his Care of human Affairs, appointed Semi-Gods and Heroes to be Guardians over Cities and to protect them by their Wisdom; since indeed we are not to trust wholly to Walls for our Defence, but stand in need besides of the Favour of Heaven. And the Reason they gave for *Saturn*'s so doing was this, that as we do not set one of the Beasts themselves to take Care of a Flock or Herd, but a Shepherd; so it was reasonable that the Guardians appointed over Men, should be some other Kind of Beings of superior Wisdom and greater Virtue than common Men; and therefore they dedicated their Walls to the Gods. Others say, that it is so ordered by the Providence of the great and good God, that as the Minds of Men have their fatal *Genii*, so have Cities also. It is no Wonder therefore that the Walls within which the Citizens were to be associated and defended, were accounted holy; and that the Ancients, whenever they were about to lay Siege to any Town, lest they should seem to offer any Insult to Religion, used to invoke, and with sacred Hymns endeavoured to appease the Gods that were Guardians of the Place, beseeching them to pass willingly over to them. As for the Temple, who can doubt that to be sacred, as well for other Reasons, as chiefly because we there pay the due Reverence and Honour to God for those infinite Obligations which Mankind has towards him? Piety is one of the Principal Parts of Justice, and who can doubt that Justice is a Present from Heaven? Another Part of Justice which has a very near Relation to the preceding, and is of the greatest Excellence and Dignity, and extremely grateful to the divine Being, and consequently highly sacred, it is that which is dispensed between Man and Man for the Maintenance of Peace and Tranquillity, and giving to every one his due Deserts: For this Reason the Places set apart for the Administration of Justice, should always be looked upon as sacred to Religion. What shall we say of the Monuments of great Actions and Events which are dedicated to Eternity, and left to future Ages? Surely we may venture to affirm, that all these have some Relation to Justice and Religion. We are now therefore to treat of the Walls, Temples, Places for the Administration of Justice, and Monuments of great Events; unless it may be first thought necessary to set down some Observations concerning Cities in general, which ought not to be omitted. A large Number of Edifices well distributed, and disposed in their proper Places, cannot fail of giving a City a great Air of Magnificence. *Plato* was for dividing the whole Area of a City into twelve Parts, allotting to each its particular Temples and Chapels, To these I would add particular Courts of Judicature for each District, together with Places for other inferior Magistrates, Fortresses, Spaces for publick Races, Exercises and Games, and every Thing else of this Nature, provided there be a sufficient Number of Houses to be allotted to every District: For of Cities, some are large, others small; such as are generally fortified Towns, and Places designed chiefly for Strength. The ancient Writers were of Opinion that the Cities which stood in Plains were not very ancient, and therefore could not pretend to much Authority; believing that such could not be built till long after the Deluge. But, indeed, Cities in large open Plains, and Castles in Places of steep and difficult Access, are best situated both for Pleasure and Convenience: But still in each of these I would always have this Difference, that the Town which stands in a Plain should rise upon a gentle Slope, for the Removal of Dirt and Filth; and that which is on a Hill, should be built upon a level and even Area, for the greater Beauty of the Streets and Buildings. *Cicero* was of Opinion, that *Capua* was preferable to *Rome*, because it neither hung upon Hills, nor was broken by Vallies, but lay open and level. *Alexander* desisted from compleating the Town he had begun to build in the Island of *Pharos*, though otherwise a Place of great Strength and many Conveniences, because he found it would not have Room enough to enlarge itself, as in all Probability it would have Occasion to do. Nor should we omit to take Notice here, that the greatest Ornament of a City is the Multitude of her Citizens. We read that *Tigranes*, when he built the City of *Tigranocerta*, constrained a vast Number of the Richest and most Honourable of his Subjects, to remove thither with all their Wealth to inhabit it, publishing an Edict, that whatever Effects they did not carry with them, but left elsewhere, should be forfeited to the publick

 Treasury.

Treafury. But this is no more than what the Neighbours all around, and other Strangers, will do willingly and of their own Accord, to a Place where they know they can live with Health, Pleafure and Plenty, and among a People of a fair and regular Behaviour. But the principal Ornament of the City will arife from the Difpofition of the Streets, Squares and publick Edifices, and their being all laid out and contrived beautifully and conveniently, according to their feveral Ufes; for without Order, there can be nothing Handfome, Convenient or Pleafing. In a well regulated City, *Plato* is of Opinion that the Laws fhould prevent the introducing of any foreign Delicacies or Corruptions; and, in order thereto fhould fuffer no Citizen to travel till full forty Years of Age; and that fuch Strangers as fhould be admitted into the City, in order to profecute their Studies, when they had fufficiently improved themfelves, fhould be fent Home again to their own Country. And this is neceffary, becaufe the Citizens, from the Contagion of Foreigners, are apt to fall off daily more and more from that Parfimony wherein they were educated by their Anceftors, and to defpife their own old Cuftoms and Ufages; which is the chief Reafon that Cities grow fo univerfally corrupted. *Plutarch* tells us, that the People of *Epidaurus* obferving that their Citizens grew vicious by their Intercourfe with the *Illyrians*, and knowing that a Depravity of Manners is always the Occafion of continual Innovations; in order to prevent it, elected one Citizen yearly out of their Number, who was always to be a Man of Gravity and Circumfpection, who fhould go among the *Illyrians*, and provide and bring them all fuch Things as any of thefe Citizens gave him Commiffion to procure them. In a Word, all the wifeft Men are agreed in this, that the greateft Care and Precaution ought to be ufed to keep the City from being corrupted by the Intercourfe of Strangers who come to it. Not that I am for imitating thofe who are againft granting Admiffion to any Strangers whatfoever. Among the *Greeks* it was the ancient Cuftom never to receive any People that were not in League with them, though not in Enmity neither, if they had Occafion to pafs through their Country in Arms: Neither would they drive them away; but they ufed to appoint a Market for all Neceffaries at fome little Diftance without the Walls, where the Strangers might refrefh themfelves with whatever Conveniencies they wanted, and the Citizens might not be expofed to any Danger. But I, for my Part, am beft pleafed with the *Carthaginians*, who, though they permitted Strangers to come among them, would not fuffer them to have every Thing in common with their own Citizens. The Streets which led to the Market or publick Place were open to all Strangers; but the more private Parts of the City, fuch as the Arfenal, and the like, they were not allowed fo much as to fee. Inftructed therefore by thefe Examples, let us lay out the Platform of our City in fuch a Manner, that not only Strangers may have their Habitations feparate, convenient for them, and not inconvenient to the Citizens; but alfo that the Citizens themfelves may converfe, negociate and dwell together commodioufly and honourably, according to their feveral Ranks and Occafions. It will add much to the Beauty of the City, if the Shops for particular Trades ftand in particular Streets and Diftricts in the moft convenient Parts of the Town. Goldfmiths, Silverfmiths and Painters may have their Shops in the publick Place, and fo may the Sellers of Drugs, of Habits, and other creditable Trades; but all nafty, ftinking Occupations fhould be removed out of the Way, efpecially the offenfive Smells of Tanners, which fhould be fet by themfelves and towards the North, becaufe the Winds feldom blow into the City from that Corner; or, if they do, they blow fo ftrong that they rather fly than pafs over it. There may perhaps be fome who would like better to have the Habitations of the Gentry feparate by themfelves, quite clear and free from all Mixture with the meaner Sort of People. Others are for having every Diftrict of the City fo laid out, that each Part might be fupplied at Hand with every Thing that it could have Occafion for, and for this Reafon they are not againft having the meaneft Trades in the Neighbourhood of the moft honourable Citizens. But of this Subject we have faid enough. Conveniency is one Thing, and Dignity another. Let us now return.

Chap. II.

Of how large and what Kind of Stone the Walls ought to be built, and who were the first that erected Temples.

THE Ancients, and particularly the *Hetrurians*, built their Walls of square Stones, and the Largest that could be got. The *Athenians*, as we are informed by *Themistocles*, did the same in their *Pireum*. There are some very ancient Castles still to be seen in *Tuscany*, and in the Territory of *Spoleto*, and near *Piperno* in *Campania*, built of huge unwrought Stone; which Sort of Work pleases me extremely, because it gives the Building a rugged Air of the antique Severity, which is a very great Ornament to a Town. I would have the Walls of a City built in such a Manner, that the Enemy at the bare Sight of them may be struck with Terror, and be sent away with a Distrust of his own Forces. There is a good deal of Majesty too in very broad deep Ditches close to the Foot of the Wall, with very steep Sides, like those which we are told were at *Babylon*, which were fifty royal Cubits broad and above an hundred deep. There is also much Majesty in the Height and Thickness of the Walls themselves, such as we are told were built by *Ninus*, *Semiramis* and *Tigranes*, and most of those whose Minds were inclined to Magnificence. In the Towers and Corridors of the Walls of *Rome*, I have seen Pavements of *Mosaic* Work, and Walls incrustated with the handsomest Materials; but all Ornaments are not suitable to all Cities alike. Delicate Cornices and Incrustations are not so proper for the Walls of a Town; but instead of a Cornice let there be a projecting Row of long Stones, somewhat more regularly wrought than the Rest, and set by the Level and Plum-line; and instead of Incrustations, tho' I would have the Front preserve its rugged and threatning Aspect, yet I would have the Stones so well fitted to one another, that there may be no Cracks in the Building. The best Way to fit such Stones together is by Means of the *Doric* Rule; like which *Aristotle* used to say, the Laws ought to be made; for it was of Lead and pliable; because having very hard Stones and difficult to be wrought, for the saving of Expence and Labour, they did not take the Pains to square them, but set them in the Wall without any certain Order and where-ever they would fit in; and finding it an endless Task to remove them from Place to Place till they could fit them in exactly, they invented this Rule which would bend any Way, which they moulded to the Sides and Corners of the Stone which they had already set, and to which they were to fit the next, and made use of the Rule thus moulded for chusing out such Stones as would fit the Vacancies they were to fill up, and answer best to the Stones which they had already set in the Wall. Moreover, for a still greater Addition of Reverence and Dignity, I would have a very handsome open Space left both within and without the Walls, and dedicated to the publick Liberty; which should not be cumbered up by any Person whatsoever, either with Trench, Wall, Hedge, or Shrub, under very great Penalties. Let us now proceed to the Temple. The first Builders of Temples I find to have been in *Italy*, Father *Janus*, and for that Reason the Ancients, in their Sacrifices, used always to begin with a Prayer to *Janus*. Some were of Opinion that *Jupiter* in *Crete* was the first that built Temples, and upon that Account thought him the first God to be adored. They say that in *Phenicia*, *Uso* was the first that erected Altars, and built Temples to Fire and Wind. Others tell us that *Dionysius*, another Name for *Bacchus*, in his Passage through *India*, finding no Cities in all that Region, after he had built Towns there, also erected Temples and established religious Rites. Others say that in *Achaia*, *Cecrops* was the first that built a Temple to the Goddess *Ops*, and the *Arcadians* the first that built one to *Jupiter*. Some write that *Isis*, who was also called the Law-giver, because she was the first Deity that commanded Men to live according to her Laws, was also the first that raised a Temple to *Jupiter* and *Juno* her Progenitors, and appointed Priests to attend their Worship. But what Manner of Temples any of these were, is not so well known. I am very much inclined to believe they were like that which was in the Citadel of *Athens*, or that in the Capitol at *Rome*; which, even when the

the City flouriſhed, was covered with Straw and Reeds, the *Romans* ſtill adhering to the ancient Parſimony of their Forefathers. But when the great Wealth of their Kings and of many of their Citizens brought them to think of honouring themſelves and their City by the Statelineſs of their Edifices, they looked upon it to be a Shame that the Habitations of the Gods ſhould not be made handſomer than the Houſes of Men; and this Humour in a ſhort Time made ſo great a Progreſs, that only in the Foundation of one ſingle Temple, while the City was yet extremely frugal, King *Numa* laid out four thouſand Pounds Weight of Silver: And I highly commend that Prince for this Act of Generoſity, as it was done out of Regard to the Dignity of the City, and to the Reverence which is due to the Gods, to whom we owe all Things: Though it has been the Opinion of ſome, who have had the Reputation of Wiſdom, that it is very improper to dedicate or build any Temples at all to the Gods, and we are told, that it was in this Perſuaſion that *Xerxes* burnt down the Temples in *Greece*, thinking it an impious Thing to ſhut up the Gods between Walls, to whom all Things ought to be open, and to whom the whole World ought to ſerve as a Temple. But let us return to our Subject.

Chap. III.

With how much Thought, Care and Diligence we ought to lay out and adorn our Temples; to what Gods and in what Places we ſhould build them, and of the various Kinds of Sacrifices.

IN the whole Compaſs of the Art of Building, there is nothing in which we ought to employ more Thought, Care and Diligence than in the laying out and adorning a Temple; becauſe, not to mention that a Temple well built and handſomely adorned is the greateſt and nobleſt Ornament a City can have; it is moreover the Habitation of the Gods: And if we adorn and beautify the Houſe where a King or any great Man is to dwell, with all the Art we are Maſters of, what ought we to do to thoſe of the immortal Gods? Whom we expect, when invoked, to be preſent at our Sacrifices, and to give Ear to our Prayers. And though the Gods may deſpiſe thoſe periſhable Things which we moſt highly value; yet Men are moved by the Purity of beautiful Materials, and raiſed by them to Reverence and Devotion for the Deity to which they are ſacred. It is certain that Temples may be of great Uſe for ſtirring up Men to Piety, by filling their Minds with Delight, and Entertaining them with Admiration of their Beauty. The Ancients were wont to ſay, that Piety was honoured when the Temples were frequented. For this Reaſon I would have the Temple made ſo beautiful, that the Imagination ſhould not be able to form an Idea of any Place more ſo; and I would have every Part ſo contrived and adorned, as to fill the Beholders with Awe and Amazement, at the Conſideration of ſo many noble and excellent Things, and almoſt force them to cry out with Aſtoniſhment: This Place is certainly worthy of God! *Strabo* ſays, that the *Mileſians* built their Temple ſo large, that they were not able to make a Roof to cover it; which I do not approve. The *Samians* boaſted of having the biggeſt Temple in the World. I am not againſt building them ſuch, that it ſhould be very hard to make any Addition to them. Ornaments are in a Manner infinite, and even in ſmall Temples there is always ſomething which we imagine might and ought to be added. I would have the Temple as large as the Bigneſs of the City requires, but not unmeaſurably huge. What I ſhould chiefly deſire in a Temple, would be this, that every Thing which you behold ſhould be ſuch; that you ſhould be at a Stand which moſt to commend, the Genius and Skill of the Workmen, or the Zeal and Generoſity of the Citizens in procuring and dedicating ſuch rare and beautiful Materials to this Service; and be doubtful whether thoſe very Materials conduce moſt to Beauty and Statelineſs, or to Duration, which, as in all other Buildings both publick and private, ſo chiefly in the Structure of Temples, ought to be very carefully conſulted; in as much as it is in the higheſt Degree reaſonable that ſuch a great Expence ſhould be well ſecured from being loſt by means of any Accidents, beſides that Antiquity gives no less Awfulness, than Ornaments do Beauty, to any Structure of this Nature. The Ancients, who had their Instructions from the *Etrurians*, thought the same Kind of Situation not proper for the Temples of different Gods: The Temples to the Gods that presided over Peace, Modesty and good Arts, they judged fit to be placed within the Compass of the Walls; but those Deities that were the Guardians of Pleasures, Feuds and Combustions, such as *Venus*, *Mars* and *Vulcan*, they placed somewhere without the City. *Vesta*, *Jupiter* and *Minerva*, whom *Plato* calls the Protectors of Cities, they seated in the Heart of the Town, or in the Citadel; *Pallas*, the Goddess of working Trades, and *Mercury*, to whom the Merchants sacrificed in the Month of *May*, and *Isis*, they set in the publick Market-place; *Neptune*, upon the Sea-shore, and *Janus* on the Summit of the highest Hills; the Temple of *Æsculapius* they built in the Island of the *Tiber*, being of Opinion that the chief Thing necessary to the Sick, was Water. In other Countries *Plutarch* tells us, that they used to place the Temple of this God out of the City, for the Sake of the Goodness of the Air. Further, they imagined that the Temples of various Gods ought to be built in various Forms. The Temple of the *Sun* and of *Bacchus* they thought should be round; and *Varro* says, that of *Jupiter* should be partly uncovered at the Top, because it was that God who opened the Seeds of all Things. The Temple of the Goddess *Vesta*, supposing her to be the Earth, they built as round as a Ball: Those of the other celestial Gods they raised somewhat above the Ground; those of the infernal Gods they built under Ground, and those of the terrestrial they set upon the Level. If I am not mistaken too, their various Sorts of Sacrifices made them invent different Sorts of Temples: For some washed their Altars with Blood, others sacrificed with Wine and a Cake; others were daily practising new Rites. *Posthumius* enacted a Law among the *Romans*, that no Wine should be sprinkled upon a funeral Pile; for which Reason the Ancients used to perform their Libations not with Wine but Milk. In the *Hyperborean* Island in the Ocean, where *Latona* was fabled to be born, the Metropolis was consecrated to *Apollo*; the Citizens of which, being used constantly every Day to sing the Praises of their Gods, were all good Masters of Musick. I find in *Theophrastus* the Sophist, that the People of the Isthmus, or the *Morea*, used to sacrifice an Ant to the Sun and to *Neptune*. It was not lawful for the *Ægyptians* to appease their Gods by any Thing but Prayers within their City; wherefore, that they might sacrifice Sheep to *Saturn* and *Serapis*, they built their Temples out of the Town. But our Countrymen by Degrees got into a Way of making use of Basiliques or Palaces for their Places of Worship; which was occasioned by their being accustomed from the Beginning to meet and get together in the Palaces of private Persons; besides, that the Altar had a very great Air of Dignity when set in the Place of the Tribunal, as had also the Choir when disposed about the Altar. The other Parts of the Structure, such as the Nave and the Portico, served the People either to walk about in, or to attend the religious Ceremonies. Add to this, that the Voice of the Pontiff, when he preached, might be more distinctly heard in a Basilique cieled with a Timber, than in a Temple with a vaulted Roof: But of these Things we shall treat in another Place. It may not be amiss to take Notice here of what the Ancients tell us, that the Temples dedicated to *Venus*, *Diana*, the *Muses*, the Nymphs and the more tender Goddesses, ought in their Structure to imitate that Virgin's Delicacy and smiling Gaiety of Youth, which is proper to them; but that *Hercules*, *Mars*, and the other greater Deities should have Temples which should rather fill the Beholders with Awe by their Gravity, than with Pleasure by their Beauty. Lastly, the Place where you intend to fix a Temple, ought to be noted, famous, and indeed stately, clear from all Contagion of secular Things, and, in order thereunto, it should have a spacious handsome Area in its Front, and be surrounded on every Side with great Streets, or rather with noble Squares, that you may have a beautiful View of it on every Side.

Chap. IV.

Of the Parts, Forms and Figures of Temples and their Chapels, and how these latter should be distributed.

THE Parts of the Temple are two; the Portico and the Inside: But they differ very much from one another in both these Respects; for some Temples are round, some square, and others, lastly, have many Sides. It is manifest that Nature delights principally in round Figures, since we find that most Things which are generated, made or directed by Nature, are round. Why need I instance in the Stars, Trees, Animals, the Nests of Birds, or the like Parts of the Creation, which she has chosen to make generally round? We find too that Nature is sometimes delighted with Figures of six Sides; for Bees, Hornets, and all other Kinds of Wasps have learnt no other Figure for building their Cells in their Hives, but the Hexagon. The Area for a round Temple should be marked out exactly circular. The Ancients, in almost all their quadrangular Temples made the Platform half as long again as it was broad. Some made it only a third Part of the Breadth longer; and others would have it full thrice the Breadth long. But in all these quadrangular Platforms the greatest Blemish is for the Corners to be not exactly rectangular. The Polygons used by the Ancients were either of six, eight, or sometimes * ten Sides. The Angles of such Platforms should all terminate within a Circle, and indeed from a Circle is the best Way of deducing them; for the Semidiameter of the Circle will make one of the six Sides which can be contained in that Circle. And if from the Center you draw Right-lines to cut each of those six Sides exactly in the Middle, you will plainly see what Method you are to take to draw a Platform of twelve Sides, and from that of twelve Sides you may make one of four, or eight, as in Fig. *B. C.* However here is another easier Way of drawing a Platform of eight Sides. Having drawn an equilateral and right-angled Square together with its Diagonals from Corner to Corner; from the Point where those Diagonals intersect each other in the Middle, I turn a Circle, opening the Compasses so wide as to take in all the Sides of the Square; then I divide one of those Sides into two equal Parts, and through the Point of that Division draw a Line from the Center to the Circumference of the Circle *D*, and thus from the Point where that Line touches the Circumference to the Angle of the Square, will be exactly one of the eight Sides which that Circle will contain. We may also draw a Platform of ten Sides by means of a Circle, in the following Manner: Draw two Diameters in the Circle, intersecting each other at Right-angles, and then divide the Half of either of those Diameters into two equal Parts, and from that Division draw a straight Line upwards aslant to the Head of the other Diameter; and if from this slant Line you take off the Quantity of the fourth Part of one of the Diameters, the Remainder of that Line will be one of the ten Sides which can be contained in that Circle, as you may see in Letter *E*. To Temples it is usual to joyn Chapels; to some, more; to others fewer. In quadrangular Temples it is very unusual to make above one, and that is placed at the Head, so as to be seen immediately by those that come in at the Door. If you have a Mind to make more Chapels on the Sides, they will not be amiss in those quadrangular Temples which are twice as long as broad; and there we should not make more than one in each Side: Though if you do make more, it will be better to make an odd Number on each Side than an even one. In round Platforms, and also in those of many Faces (if we may venture so to call them) we may very conveniently make a greater Number of Chapels, according to the Number of those Faces, one to each, or one with and one without alternately, answering to each other. In round Platforms six Chapels, or even eight will do extremely well. In Platforms of several Faces you must be sure to let the Corners be exactly answering and suiting to one another. The Chapels themselves must be made either Parts of a rectangled Square, or of a Circle. For the single Chapel at the Head of a Temple, the semicircular Form is much the handsomest; and next to that is the rectangular. But if you are to make a good Number of Chapels, it will certainly be much more pleasing

* *See Plate 21, facing.*

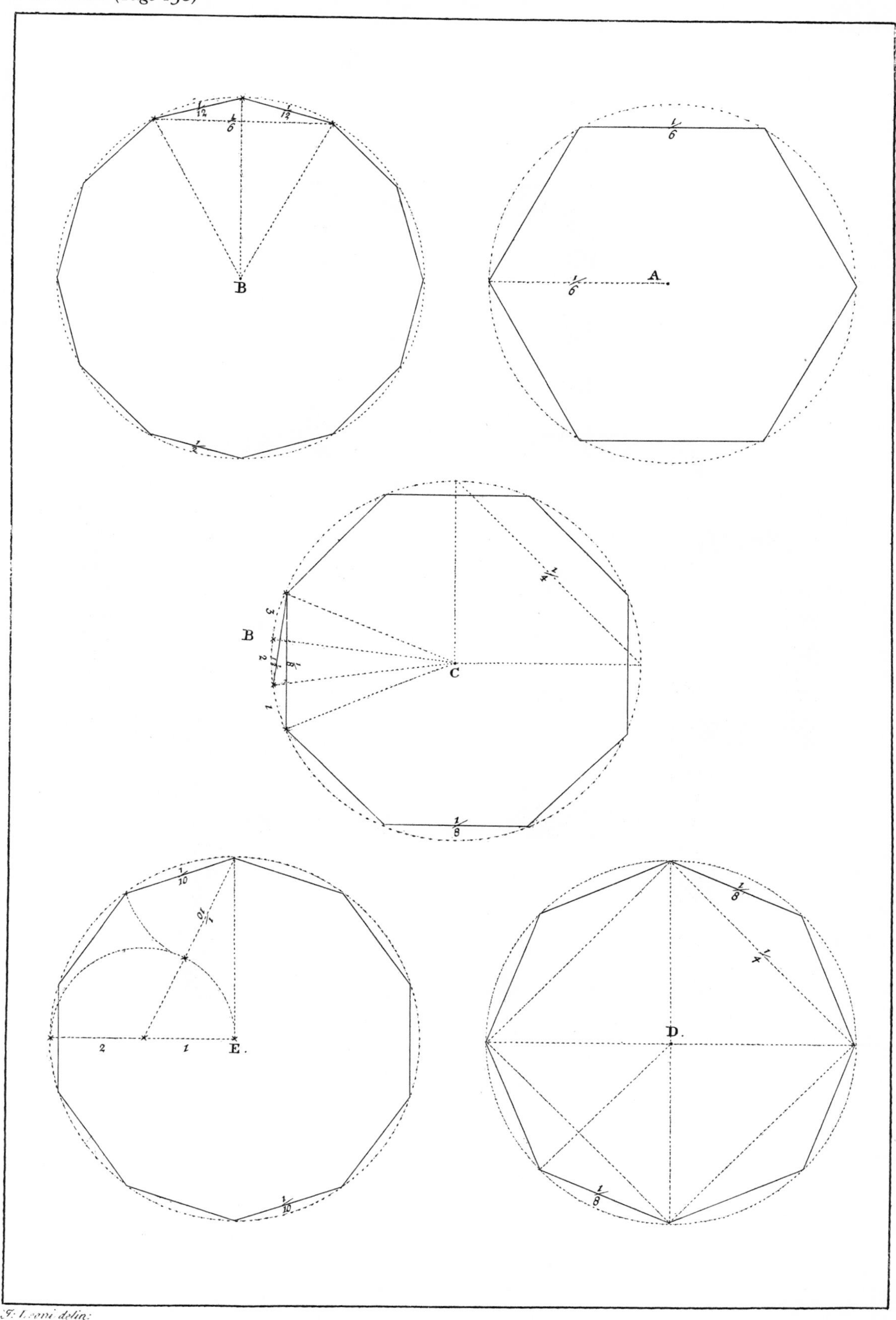

J: Leoni delin:

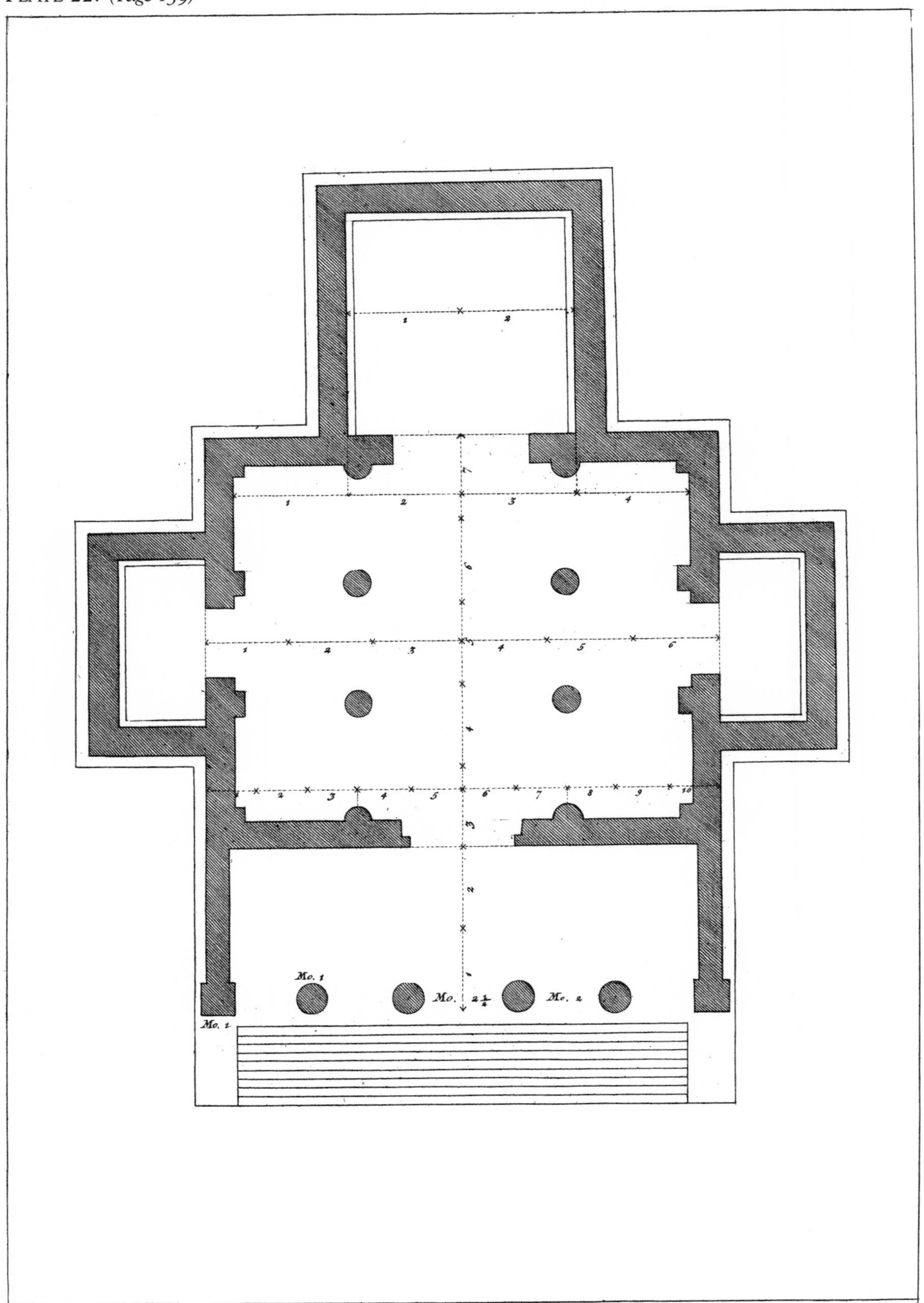

J. Leoni delin.

pleaſing to the Eye, to make Part of them ſquare and Part round alternately, and anſwering one to the other. For the Aperture of theſe Chapels obſerve the following Rule. When you are to make a ſingle Chapel in a quadrangular Temple, divide the Breadth of the Temple into four Parts, and give two of thoſe Parts to the Breadth of the Chapel. If you have a Mind to have it more ſpacious, divide that Breadth into ſix Parts, and give four of them to the Breadth of your Chapel. And thus the Ornaments and Columns which you are to add to them, the Windows, and the like, may be handſomely fitted in their proper Places. If you are to make a Number of Chapels about a round Platform, you may, if you pleaſe, make them all of the ſame Size with the principal one; but to give that the greater Air of Dignity, I ſhould rather chuſe to have it a twelfth Part bigger than the reſt. There is alſo this other Difference in quadrangular Temples, that if the principal Chapel is made of equal Lines, that is to ſay, in an exact Square, it may not be amiſs; but the other Chapels ought to be twice as broad as they are deep. The Solid of the Walls, or thoſe Ribs of the Building which in Temples ſeparate one Chapel from the other, ſhould never have leſs Thickneſs than the fifth Part of the Break which is left between them, nor more than the third; or, if you would have them extremely ſtrong, the half. But in round Platforms, if the Chapels are in Number ſix, let the Solid or Rib which is left between each Chapel, be one half of the Break; and if there be eight of thoſe Chapels, let the ſolid Wall between them, eſpecially in great Temples, be as thick as the whole Break for the Chapel: But if the Platform conſiſt of a great Number of Angles, let the Solid always be one third of the Break. In * ſome Temples, according to the Cuſtom of the ancient *Hetrurians*, it has been uſual to adorn the Sides not with Chapels, but with a ſmall Sort of Iſles, in the following Manner: They choſe a Platform, which was one ſixth Part longer than it was broad: Of this Length they aſſigned two of thoſe ſix Parts to the Depth of the Portico, which was to ſerve as a Veſtibule to the Temple; the reſt they divided into three Parts, which they gave to the three Breadths of the ſide Iſles. Again, they divided the Breadth of the Temple into ten Parts, three of which they aſſigned to the little Iſles on the right Hand, and as many to thoſe on the left, and the other four they gave to the Area in the Middle. At the Head of the Temple, and ſo fronting the Middle of each ſide Iſle, they placed Chapels, and the Walls which ſeparated the ſeveral Iſles they made in Thickneſs one fifth Part of the Interſpace.

CHAP. V.

Of the Porticoes and Entrance to the Temple, its Aſcent, and the Apertures and Interſpaces of the Portico.

HITHERTO we have ſpoken of the Platform for the Inſide. The Portico to a quadrangular Temple may be either only in Front, or on the Back of the Structure, or elſe both in the Front and the back Part at the ſame Time, or, laſtly, it may run quite round the Fabrick. Where-ever any Chapel projects out, there ſhould be no Portico. The Portico ſhould never be ſhorter, in quadrangular Temples, than the full Breadth of the Temple; and never broader than the third Part of its Length. In thoſe Porticoes which run along the Sides of the Temple, let the Columns be ſet as far from the Wall as they ſtand from one another. The back Portico may imitate which you pleaſe of the afore-mentioned. Circular Temples have either a Portico quite round them, or elſe have only one Portico, which muſt be in Front. In both, the ſame Proportions muſt be obſerved as in thoſe to quadrangular Platforms; nor indeed muſt ſuch Porticoes be ever made other than quadrangular. As to their Length, it muſt either be equal to the whole Breadth of the Inſide of the Platform, or an eighth Part leſs, or at the moſt a fourth Part, which is the ſhorteſt that is ever allowed. The *Hebrews*, according to the ancient Laws of their Forefathers, were to have one ſacred and chief City in a fit and convenient Place, and therein one ſingle Temple and one Altar built of Stones, not hewn by Men's Hands, but juſt ſuch as they could find, provided they were white and clean; and there was to be no Steps to aſcend to this Temple; inaſmuch

* *See Plate 22, facing.*

inasmuch as they were to be one People joyning in the Worship of one God, by whom alone they were defended and preserved. Now I cannot approve of either of these Particulars: For as to the First, it must be extremely inconvenient to the People, and especially to those who frequent the Temples most, as the old Folks and the Infirm; and the Second must take very much from the Majesty of the Structure. As to what I have observed in some sacred Edifices, built not long before our Time, to which you ascend by a few Steps on the Outside, and afterwards have as many to go down again within, I will not absolutely call it ridiculous; but why they should contrive it in this Manner, I cannot imagine. Indeed I would have the Plain of the Portico, and so of the whole Temple, somewhat raised above the Level of the rest of the Town, which gives the Fabrick a great Air of Dignity. But as in an Animal, the Head, the Feet, and every particular Member, should be exactly proportioned to all the other Members, and to all the rest of the Body; so in a Building, and especially in a Temple, all the Parts should be made to correspond so exactly, that let us consider which of them we please, it may bear its just Proportion to all the Rest. Thus I find that most of the best ancient Architects used to take their Elevation of the Plain of their Temple, from the Breadth of the Temple itself, which they divided into six Parts, giving one of those Parts to the Height of the Plain or Mound of the Structure. Others, in larger Temples, raised it only a seventh Part, and in the Biggest of all, only a ninth. The Portico, by its Nature, should have a continued Wall but of one Side, and all the other Sides should be full of large Apertures for Passage. Your Business therefore is to consider what Kind of Apertures you would make use of; for Colonades are of two Sorts; one where the Columns stand wide and at a great Distance from each other; and the other, where they stand close and thick. And neither of these Sorts is without its Inconveniencies; for in the wide Sort, the Apertures are so large, that if you would make use of an Architrave, it is apt to break in the Middle, and if you would carry Arches over it, it is no easy Matter to turn them upon the Heads of the Columns. Where the Columns stand close and thick, they intercept the View, the Light and the Passage, and upon this Account, a third Manner has been found out, in a Medium between the other two, which is called Elegant, and avoids the Defects of the others; is more convenient and much more approved. And with these three Sorts we might have been contented; but the Diligence of Architects have added two other Sorts, which I suppose may be accounted for as follows: Not having a sufficient Number of Columns for the Extensiveness of their Area, they deviated somewhat from the laudable Medium, and imitated the wider Apertures; and when they happen to have Plenty of Columns, they were fond of setting them closer together; whence arose five Sorts of Intercolumniations, which we may call by the Names of Wide, Close, Elegant, Less-wide, Less-close. I further suppose it to have happened, that the Architects being sometimes destitute of long Stones, were obliged to make their Columns shorter, knowing that this would take much from the Beauty of the Structure, they set a Plinth under their Columns, in order to give them their just Height; for they found by a careful View and Examination of other Buildings, that Columns had no Grace in a Portico, unless a right Proportion was observed both in their Height and Thickness. This induced them to lay down the following Rules for this Purpose. The Intercolumniation may be unequal; but the Columns themselves must always be exactly equal. Let the Apertures that answers to the Door be somewhat wider than the rest. Where the Intercolumniation is close, make use of thinner Columns; where it is wide, make use of thicker; thus always proportioning the Thickness of the Colums to the Interspaces, and the Interspaces to the Thickness of the Columns, which you may do by the following Rules. In the closest Sort of Colonades, let the Intercolumniation be never narrower than one Diameter and a Half of the Column; and in the widest, let it be never broader than three Diameters and three eighths. In the elegant Sort of Colonades you may allow two Diameters and a Quarter, in the Less-close, two; in the Less-wide, three. The middle Interspace in the Colonade should be somewhat wider than the rest, and the Ancients direct us to give it an Addition of one fourth Part: But by an Examination of old Buildings, I find that this middle Interspace was not always made according to this Rule; for in the wide Colonades, no good Architect ever made it a fourth Part wider, but only about a twelfth; and herein they acted very prudently, lest an unfaithful Architrave should not be able to bear even the Weight of its own Length, but

but crack in the Middle. Others indeed, in other Colonades, have allowed a ſixth Part; but moſt have made it only a twelfth, eſpecially in thoſe Colonades which we have called Elegant.

CHAP. VI.

Of Columns, and the different Sorts of Capitals.

WHEN we have reſolved upon our Intercolumniation, we are to erect our Columns which are to ſupport the Roof or Covering. But we are to make a great Difference between a Work that conſiſts of Pilaſters, and one that conſiſts of Columns, and between covering them with Arches, or with Architraves. Arches and Pilaſters are very proper in Theatres, and Arches are not amiſs in Baſiliques; but in the nobler Temples, we never ſee any Porticoes without Architraves. Of theſe Things we are now to treat. The Parts of the Column are theſe: The lower Plinth, upon that the Baſe, upon the Baſe the Column, then the Capital, next to that the Architrave, after which comes the Freeze, where the Ends of the Rafters either terminate or are concealed, and over all is the Cornice. I think it will be proper to begin with the Capitals, by which chiefly Columns are diſtinguiſhed from one another. And here I entreat thoſe who ſhall hereafter copy this Book, that they would take the Pains to write the Numbers which I ſet down, with Letters at length, in this Manner, twelve, twenty, forty, and not with numeral Characters, as XII. XX. XL. Neceſſity firſt taught Men to ſet Capitals upon their Columns, for the Heads of the Timbers of their Architraves to meet and reſt upon; but this being at firſt nothing but a ſquare Block of Wood, looked very mean and unhandſome. Some Artiſts therefore among the *Dorians* (if we may thus allow the *Greeks* the Honour of all Inventions) were the firſt that endeavoured to improve it by making it round, ſo as to look like a Cup covered with a ſquare Tile; and becauſe it ſeemed ſomewhat too ſquat, they raiſed it higher by lengthening the Neck. The *Ionians*, ſeeing the Invention of the *Dorians*, commended this Introduction of the Cup into the Capital; but they did not like to ſee it ſo naked, nor with ſo long a Neck, and therefore they added to it the Imitation of the Bark of a Tree hanging down on each Side, which by its Convolution inwards, or Volute, embraced the Sides of the Cup. Next came the *Corinthians*, among whom a certain Artiſt, named *Callimachus*, diſliking the ſquat Cup, made uſe of a high Vaſe covered with Leaves, in Imitation of one which he had ſeen on the Tomb of a young Maiden, all over-grown with the Leaves of an Acanthus, which had ſprung up quite round it, and which he thought looked very beautiful. Thus three Sorts of Capitals were now invented and received into Practice by the beſt Workmen in thoſe Days: The *Doric* (though I am convinced that this was in uſe before among the ancient *Etrurians*) the *Doric*, I ſay, the *Ionic* and the *Corinthian*. And what think you, was the Occaſion of that infinite Number of other Capitals which we ſee quite different the one from the other, but the Diligence and Application with which Men have been continually ſtudying to find out ſomething new? But yet there is none that deſerves to be preferred before thoſe already mentioned, except one which, that we may not own ourſelves obliged to Strangers for every thing, I call the *Italian*; for this Order to the Richneſs of the *Corinthian*, has added the Delicacy of the *Ionic*, and inſtead of thoſe Ears, has ſubſtituted Volutes, which are extremely admired and commended. But to return to the Ordonnance of Columns; the ancient Architects have left us the following Rules for their Proportions. They tell us that the *Doric* Capital requires a Shaft ſeven Times as long as its Diameter at Bottom; the *Ionic* muſt have eight, and the *Corinthian* ten of its own Diameters. The Baſes of all theſe Columns they made of the ſame Height; but they made them of different Lineaments and Deſigns: And indeed they differed as to the Lineaments of almoſt every particular Part, though they in a great Meaſure agreed as to the Proportions of Columns in general, and particularly as to thoſe Lineaments of Columns, whereof we treated in the laſt Book, all were of one accord, as well the *Dorians* and *Ionians*, as the *Corinthians*. In this Point too they agreed, from an Imitation of Nature, namely, that the Tops of the Shafts of all Columns ought to be thinner than they were at Bottom. Some laid it down as a Rule, that they ſhould be a fourth Part thicker at Bottom than at the Top. Others conſidering that Things always ſeem to loſe of their Bigneſs in Proportion to the Diſtance from which they are viewed, very prudently adviſe that ſuch Columns as were to be of a great Length, ſhould be made ſomewhat thicker at the Top than thoſe that were ſhorter; and for this Purpoſe they gave the following Directions. The Diameter of the Bottom of a Column of fifteen Foot high, ſhould be divided into ſix Parts, whereof five ſhould be given to the Diameter at the Top. Of all Columns from fifteen to twenty Foot high, the lower Diameter ſhould be divided into thirteen Parts, eleven whereof are to be allowed to the Thickneſs at the Top; all Columns from twenty to thirty Foot high, muſt have ſeven Parts at the Bottom, and ſix at the Top; thoſe from thirty to forty Foot, muſt have fifteen Parts Thickneſs below and thirteen above: Laſtly, thoſe amounting to fifty Foot height, muſt have eight Parts at the Bottom, and ſeven at the Top. According to the ſame Rule and Proportion, as the Column grows ſtill longer, the larger Diameter we muſt allow to the Top of its Shaft: So that in theſe Points all Columns agree. Not that I can ſay, upon thoſe Meaſurements which I have taken of ancient Structures, that theſe Rules were always ſtrictly obſerved among the *Romans*.

Chap. VII.

A neceſſary Rehearſal of the ſeveral Members of Columns, the Baſe, Torus, Scotia, Liſts, Die, and of the ſmaller Parts of thoſe Members, the Platband, Corona, Ovolo, ſmall Ogee, Cima-inverſa, and Cymatium, both upright and reverſed.

We ſhall here take a ſecond Review of the ſame Things relating to Columns, which we conſidered in the laſt Book; not indeed in the ſame Method, but in another no leſs uſeful. For this Purpoſe, out of thoſe Columns which the Ancients made uſe of in their publick Buildings, I ſhall take one of a middle Proportion between the Biggeſt and the Leaſt, which I ſuppoſe to be of about thirty Foot. The biggeſt Diameter of the Shaft of this Column, I ſhall divide into nine equal Parts, eight of which I ſhall aſſign to the biggeſt Diameter of its Cincture at the Top: Thus its Proportion will be as eight to nine, which the *Latins* call a Seſquioctave. In the ſame Proportion I ſhall make the Diameter of the Diminution at Bottom, to the largeſt Diameter of the Shaft, making the latter nine and the former eight. Again I ſhall make the Diameter of the Cincture at the Top to that of the upper Diminution, as ſeven to eight, or in the Proportion which the *Latins* call Seſquiſeptimal. I now proceed to the Deſcription of thoſe Members wherein they differ. Baſes conſiſt of theſe following; the Die, the Torus and the Scotia. The Die is that ſquare Member which is at the Bottom of all, and I call it by this Name, becauſe it is ſquare on every Side, like a flat Die; the Toruſſes are thoſe Cuſhions, upon one of which the Column reſts, and the other ſtands upon the Die; the Scotia is that circular Hollow which lies between two Toruſſes, like the Hollow in the Wheel of a Pully. All the Meaſures of theſe Members are taken from the Diameter of the Bottom of the Shaft; and firſt the *Dorians* gave the following Proportions for them. They made the Height * of the Baſe to be half the Diameter of the Bottom of the Shaft, and the Plinth or Die, as broad at moſt every Way as one Diameter and a Half of the Column, and as one Diameter and a Third at leaſt. They then divided the Height of the whole Baſe into three Parts, one of which they aſſigned to the Height of the Die. Thus the Height of the whole Baſe was three Times that of the Die, and the Breadth of the Die was three times the Height of the Baſe. Then excluſive of the Die they divided the Reſt of the Height of the Baſe into four Parts, the uppermoſt of which they gave to the upper Torus. Again, what remained between the upper Torus and the Die at Bottom, they divided into two Parts, one of which they allowed to the lower Torus, and the other they hollowed

* *See Plate 23, facing.*

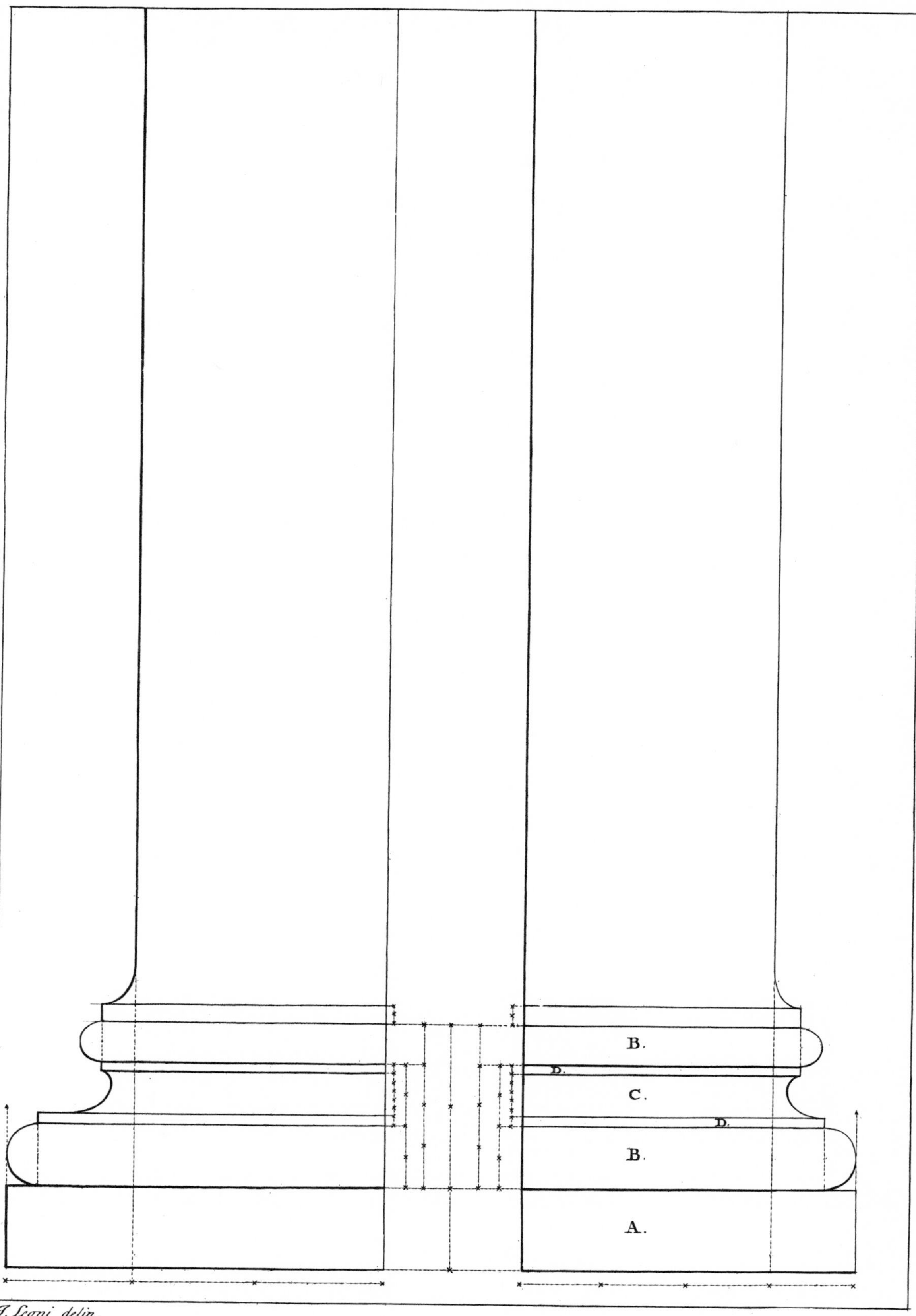

J. Leoni delin.

PLATE 24. *(Page 143)*

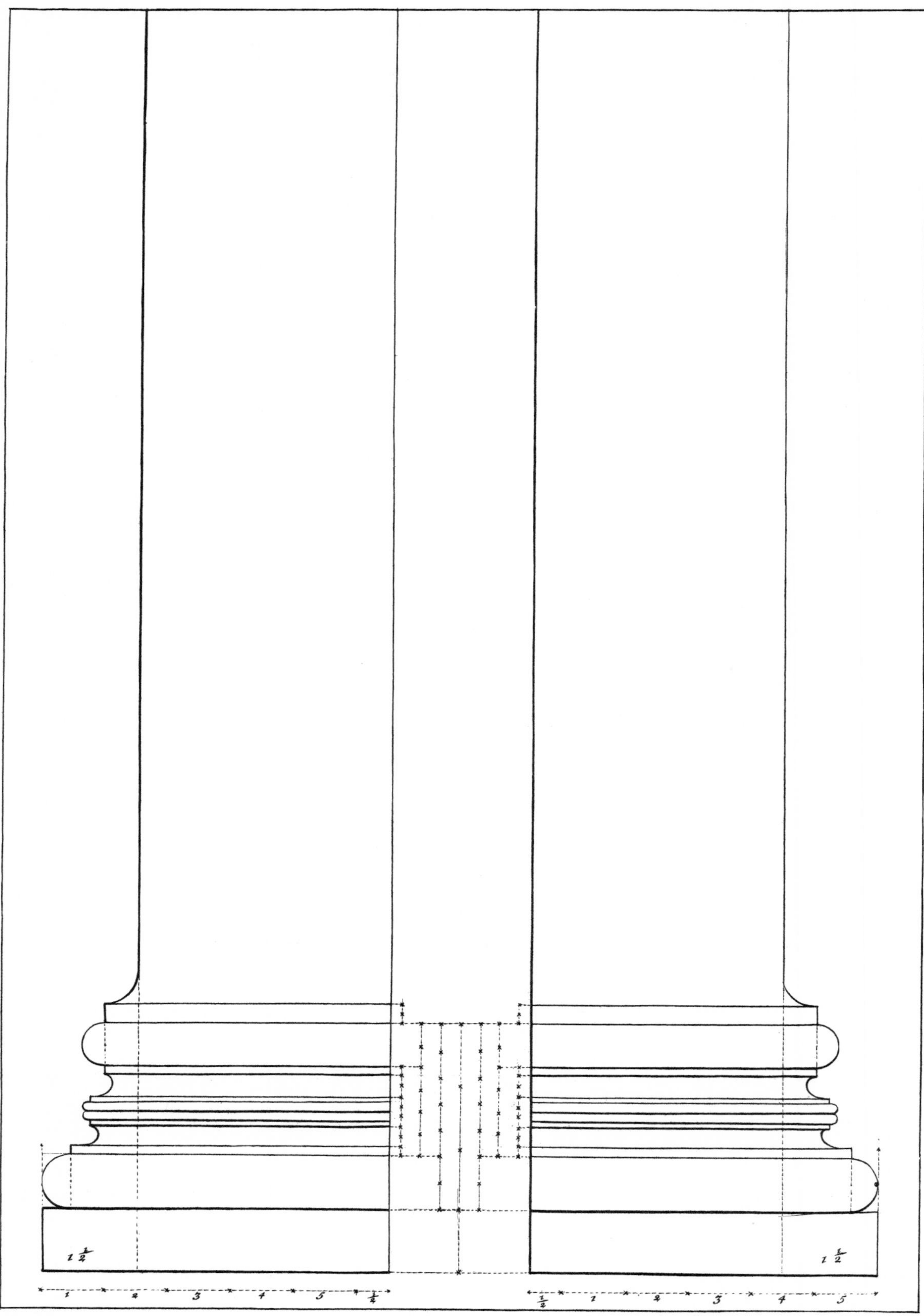

J. Leoni delin.

hollowed into a Scotia which lay between the two Toruſſes. A Scotia conſiſts of a hollow Channel edged on each Side with an Annulet; to each of thoſe Annulets they allowed one ſeventh Part of the Scotia, and the reſt they hollowed. We have formerly laid it down as a Rule, that in all Building particular Care muſt be taken that all the Work be ſet upon a perfect Solid. Now it would not be ſo, if a Perpendicular falling from the Edge of the upper Stone were to meet with any void Space or Hollow. For this Reaſon in cutting their Scotias, they took Care not to go in ſo far as to come within the Perpendicular of the Work above. The Toruſſes muſt project one Half and an Eighth of their Thickneſs, and the extremeſt Edge of the Circle of the biggeſt Torus muſt be exactly Perpendicular to the Die. This was the Method of the *Dorians*. The *Ionians* approved of the *Doric* Height, but they made two Scotias, and placed two Fillets between them.* Thus their Baſe was the Height of half the Diameter of the Bottom of the Shaft; and this Height they divided into four Parts, one of which they aſſigned to the Height of the Plinth, giving eleven of thoſe fourth Parts to its Breadth: So that the whole Height of the Baſe was as four, and the Breadth as eleven. Having thus deſigned their Plinth, they divided the reſt of the Height into ſeven Parts, two of which they gave to the Thickneſs of the lower Torus, and what remained beſides this Torus and the Plinth, they divided into three Parts, one of which they hollowed to the upper Torus, and the two middle Parts they gave to the two Scotias with their two Fillets, which ſeemed to be ſqueezed between the two Toruſſes. The Proportions of theſe Scotias and Fillets were as follows: They divided the Space between the two Toruſſes into ſeven Parts, one of which they gave to each Fillet, dividing the reſt equally between the two Scotias. As to the Projecture of the Toruſſes they obſerved the ſame Rules as the *Dorians*, and in hollowing their Scotias had regard to the Perpendicular Solid of the Stone that was to be laid over them; but they made their Annulets only an eighth Part of the Scotia. Others were of Opinion, that excluſive of the Plinth, the Baſe ought to be divided into ſixteen Parts, which we call Minutes; and of theſe they gave four to the lower Torus, and three to the upper, three and a half to the lower Scotia, and three and a half to the upper, and the other two they aſſigned to the Fillets between them. Theſe were the *Ionic* Proportions. The *Corinthians* liked both the *Ionic* and the *Doric* Baſe too, and made uſe indifferently of them both; ſo that indeed they added nothing to the Column, but a Capital. We are told that the *Etrurians* under their Columns (which we call the *Italian*) uſed to put not a ſquare but a round Plinth; but I never met with ſuch a Baſe among the Works of the Ancients. Indeed I have taken Notice, that in Porticoes which uſed to go clear round their circular Temples, the Ancients carved one continued Plinth quite round, which ſerved for all the Columns, and of the due Height which the Plinth of the Baſe ought to be of. This I doubt not they did, becauſe they were convinced that ſquare Members did not ſuit with a circular Structure. I have obſerved, that ſome have made even the Sides of the Abacus of their Capitals point to the Center of the Temple, which, if it were to be done in the Baſes, might not be altogether amiſs, though it would ſcarce be much commended. And here it may not be improper to ſay ſomething of the ſeveral Members of the Ornaments made uſe of in Architecture; and they are theſe; the Plat-band, the Corona, the Ovolo, or Quarter-round, the ſmall Ovolo, or Ogee, the Cima-inverſa, and the Cymatium, or Doucine, both upright and reverſed. All theſe particular Members have each a Projecture, but with different Lines. The Plat-band projects in a Square like the Letter L, and is indeed the ſame as a Liſt or Fillet, but ſomewhat broader. The Corona has a much greater Projecture than the Plat-band; the Ovolo, or Quarter-round, I was almoſt tempted to call the Ivy, becauſe it runs along and cleaves to another Member, and its Projecture is like a C placed under the Letter L, thus $\genfrac{}{}{0pt}{}{L}{C}$ and the ſmall Ovolo, or Ogee is only ſomewhat leſs. But if you place this Letter C reverſed under the Letter L, thus $\genfrac{}{}{0pt}{}{L}{Ↄ}$ it forms the Cima-inverſa. Again, if under the ſame Letter L you place an S in this Manner $\genfrac{}{}{0pt}{}{L}{S}$ it is called the Cymatium, or Gola from its Reſemblance to a Man's Throat; but if you place it inverted thus $\genfrac{}{}{0pt}{}{L}{\backsim}$ it is called Cima-inverſa, or by ſome from the Similitude of its Curve, the Onda, or Undula. Again, theſe Members are either plain, or elſe have ſome other Ornaments inſerted into them. In the Plat-band or Faſcia it is common to carve Cockle-ſhells, Birds, or Inſcriptions. In the Corona we frequently have Dentils, which are made in the following Proportions: Their Breadth

* *See Plate 24, facing.*

Breadth is one half of their Height, and the Interſpace between them is two thirds of their Breadth. The Ovolo, or Quarter-round, is ſometimes adorned with Eggs and ſometimes with Leaves, and theſe Eggs are ſometimes carved entire, and ſometimes ſheared off at the Top. The Ogee, or Baguette is make like a Row of Beads, ſtrung upon a Thread. The Cymatiums are never carved with any thing but Leaves. The Annulets are always left plain on every Side. In the putting theſe Members together, we muſt always keep to this Rule, that the upper ones have always more Projecture than thoſe below them. The Annulets are what ſeparate one Member from the other, and ſerve as a Kind of Cymaize to each Member; the Cymaize being any Liſt that is at the Top of any Member whatſoever. Theſe Cymaizes, or Annulets being always ſmooth and poliſhed, are alſo of Uſe in diſtinguiſhing the rough carved Members from each other, and their Breadth is a ſixth Part of the Member over which they are ſet, whether it be the Corona or Ovolo; but in the Cymatium their Breadth is one whole third.

Chap. VIII.

Of the Doric, Ionic, Corinthian and Compoſite Capitals.

* LET us now return to the Capitals. The *Dorians* made their Capital of the ſame Height as their Baſe, and divided that Height into three Parts: The Firſt they gave to the Abacus, the Second to the Ovolo which is unde rthe Abacus, and the Third they allow'd to the Gorgerin or Neck of the Capital which is under the Ovolo. The Breadth of the Abacus every Way was equal to one whole Diameter, and a twelfth of the Bottom of the Shaft. This Abacus is divided into two Members, an upright Cymatium and a Plinth, and the Cymatium is two fifth Parts of the whole Abacus. The upper Edge of the Ovolo joyned cloſe to the Bottom of the Abacus. At the Bottom of the Ovolo ſome made three little Annulets, and others a Cymatium as an Ornament, but theſe never took up above a third Part of the Ovolo. The Diameter of the Neck of the Capital, which was the loweſt Part of it, never exceeded the Thickneſs of the Top of the Shaft, which is to be obſerved in all Sorts of Capitals. Others, according to the Obſervations which I have made upon ancient Buildings, uſed to make the Height of the *Doric* Capital three Quarters of the Diameter of the Bottom of the Shaft, and divided this whole Height of the Capital into eleven Parts, of which they allowed four to the Abacus, four to the Ovolo, and three to the Neck of the Capital. Then they divided the Abacus into two Parts, the uppermoſt of which they gave to the Cymatium and the lowermoſt to the Plinth. The Ovolo alſo they divided into two Parts, aſſigning the lowermoſt either to the Annulets or to a Cymatium, which ſerved as an Edging to the Ovolo, and in the Neck of the Capital ſome cut Roſes, and others Leaves with a high Projecture. This was the Practice of the *Dorians*. Our Rules for the *Ionic* Capital are as follows. * Let the whole Height of the Capital be one half the Diameter of the Bottom of the Column. Let us divide this Height into nineteen Parts, or Minutes, three of which we muſt give to the Abacus, four to the Thickneſs of the Volute, ſix to the Ovolo, and the other ſix below we muſt leave for the Turn of the Volutes on each Side. The Breadth of the Abacus every Way muſt be equal to the Diameter of the Top of the Shafts; the Breadth of the Rind which is to terminate in the Scroll muſt both in the Front and Back of the Capital be equal to the Abacus. This Rind muſt fall down on each Side winding round like a Snail-ſhell. The Center of the Volute on the right Side muſt be diſtant from that on the Left two-and-thirty Minutes, and from the higheſt Point of the Abacus twelve Minutes. The Method of turning this Volute is as follows: About the Center of the Volute deſcribe a little Circle, the Semi-diameter of which muſt be one of the afore-mentioned Minutes. This is the Eye of the Volute. In the Circumference of this little Circle make two Points oppoſite to each other, one above and the other below. Then fix one Foot of your Compaſſes into the uppermoſt Point, and extend the other to the Line that divides the Abacus from the Rind, and turn it outwards from the Capital till you have made a perfect Semi-circle ending Perpendicular under the loweſt Point or Dot in the Eye of the Volute. Then contract your Compaſſes,

* *See Plate 25, facing, and Plate 26, following.*

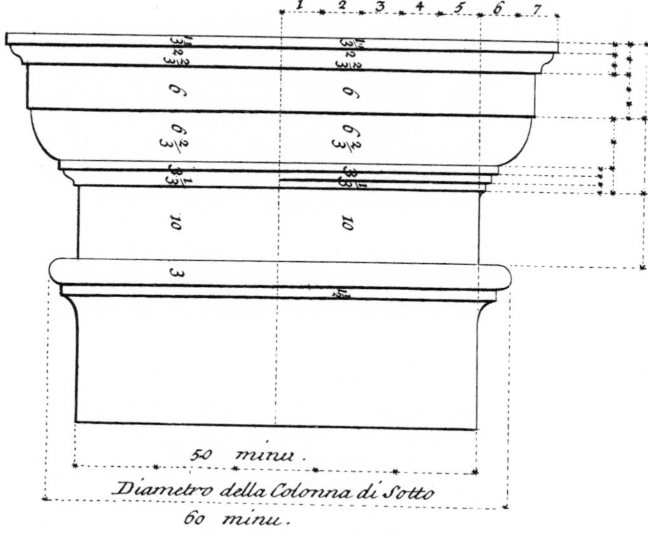

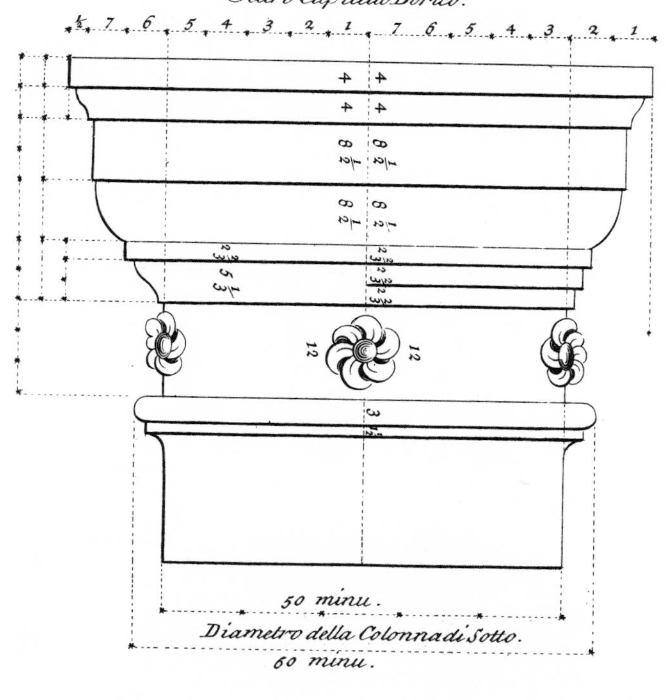

I. Leoni delin.

"(Altro) Capitello Dorico" = (another) Doric capital. "Diametro etc." = diameter of the column below. "minu." = minutes.

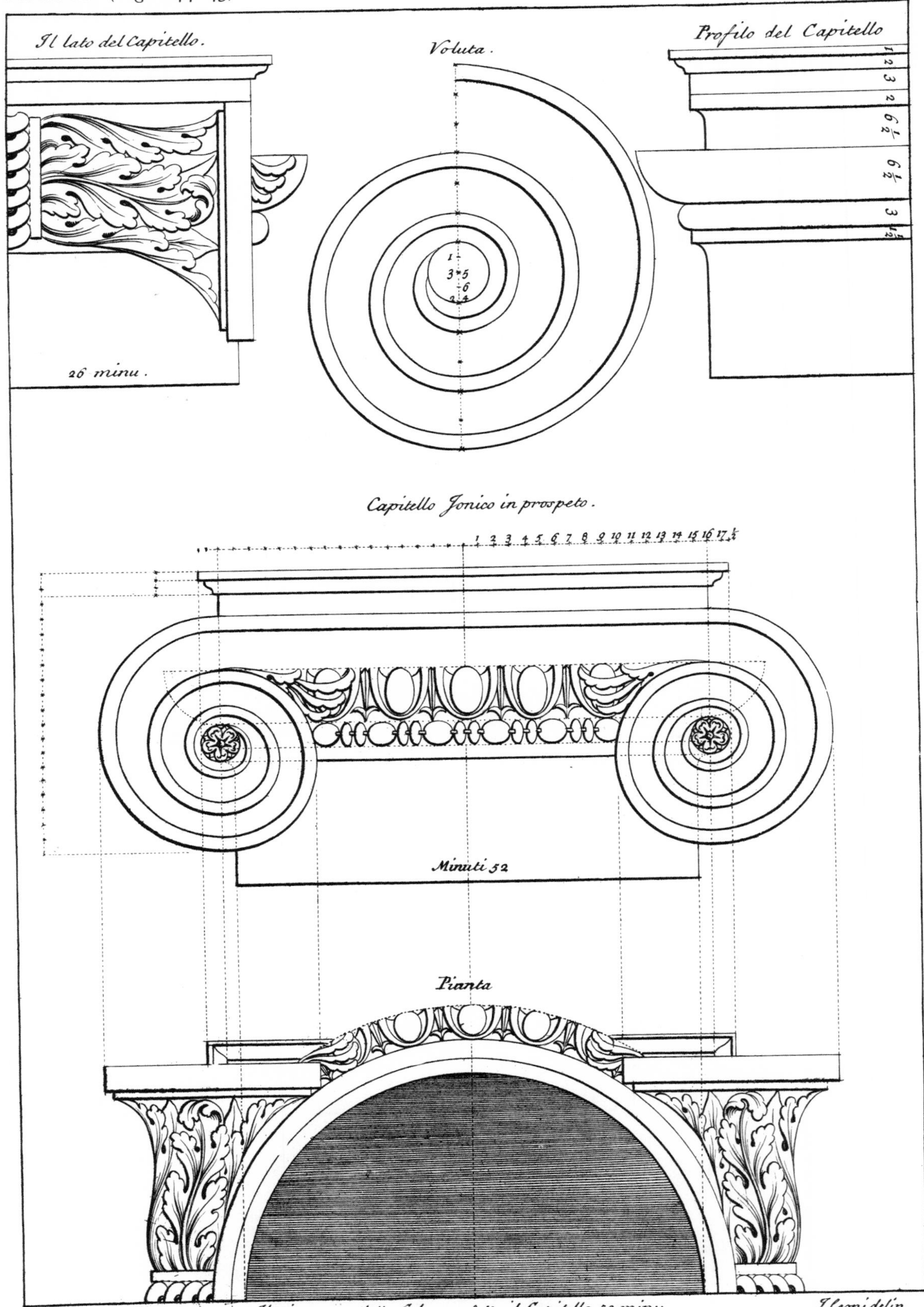

"Il lato del Capitello" = the side of the capital. "Voluta" = volute. "Profilo" = profile. "Pianta" = plan. "Capitello Ionico in prospeto" = Ionic capital in elevation.

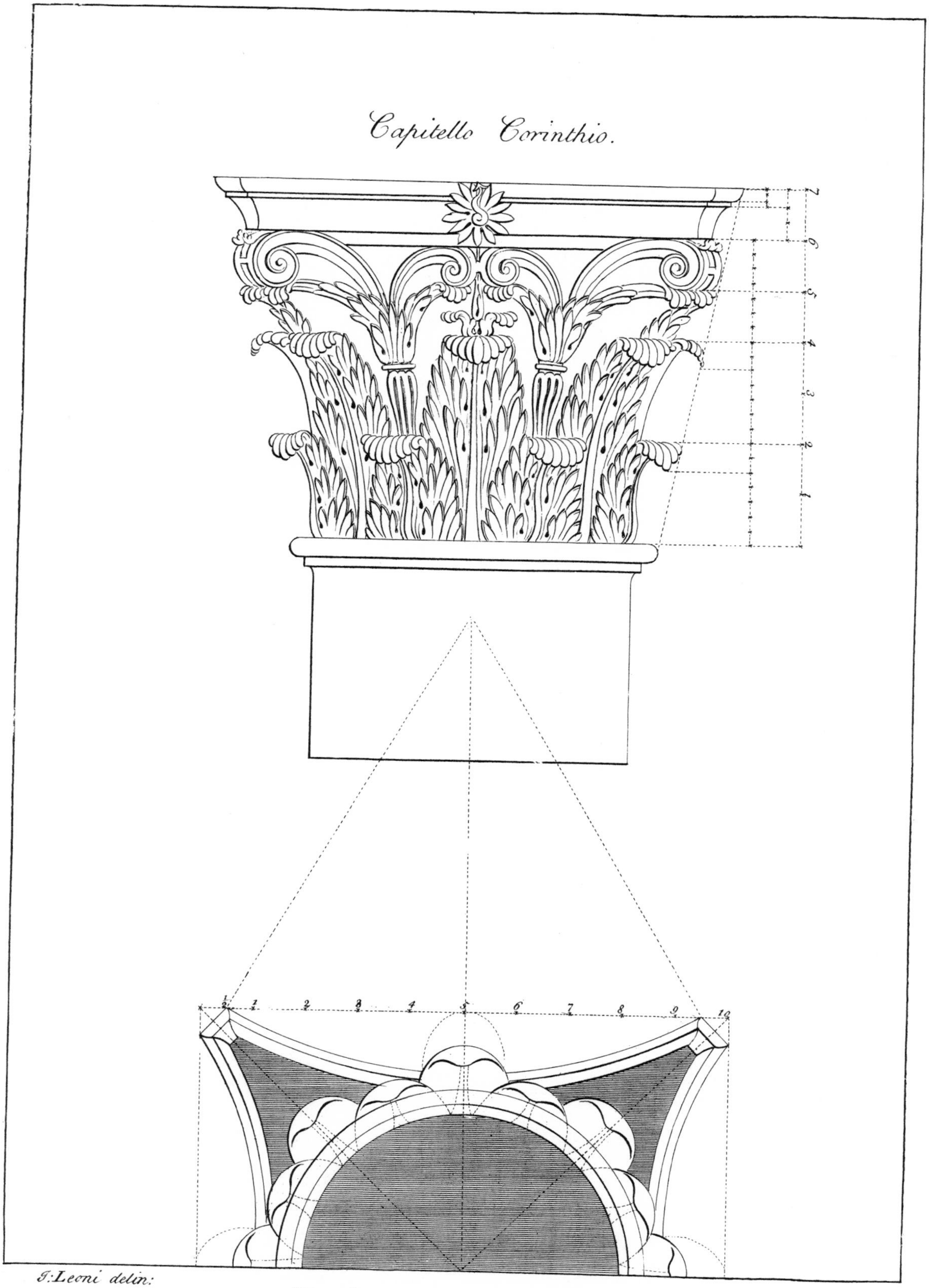

J: Leoni delin:

"Capitello Corinthio" = Corinthian capital.

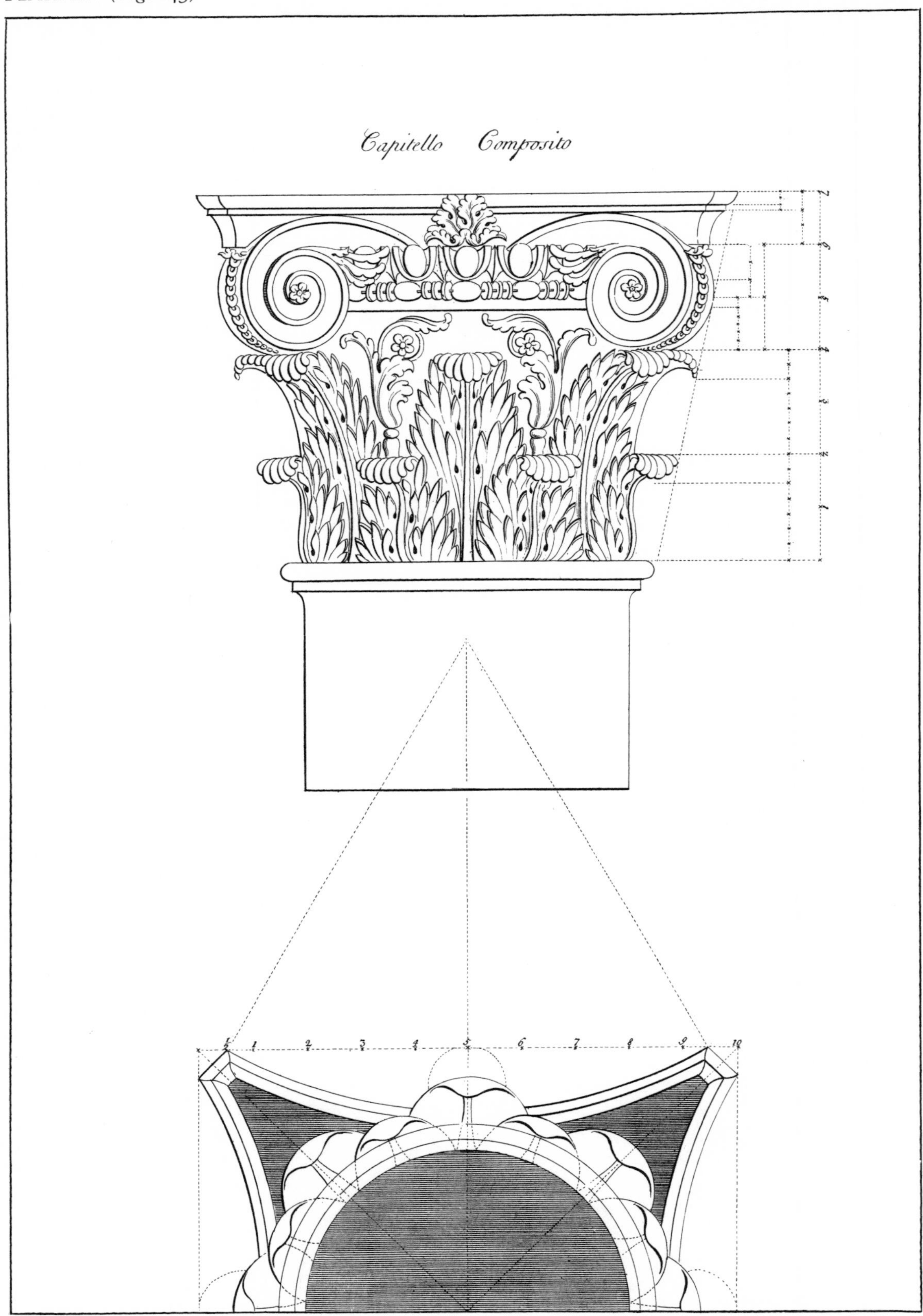

J. Leoni, delin:

"Capitello Composito" = *composite capital.*

Compaſſes, and fixing one Foot in the Point below the Eye, let the other reach to the End of the Line which you have already turned, that is to ſay, to the End of your Semi-circle, and turn it upwards till you touch the upper Edge of the Ovolo. Thus with two unequal Semi-circles, you will have made one entire Compaſs about the Eye of your Volute. Then go on with your Sweep in the ſame Manner, till you have turned it quite to the Eye of the Volute, or that little Circle in the Middle. The Top of the Ovolo in the Front muſt have a Projecture of two Minutes beyond the Rind, and the lower Part of it muſt be even with the Top of the Shaft. The Sides of the Volutes where the hindmoſt joins to the foremoſt on each Side of the Capital, muſt be contracted to the ſame Width as the Ovolo, with the Addition only of one half Minute. The Abacus muſt be adorned with an upright Cymatium of one Minute. The Back of the Volute muſt be adorned with a little Channel half a Minute deep, and the Annulets on the Side of this Channel muſt be one Fourth of its Breadth, and the Spaces on each Side the Channel muſt be filled with Leaves or Fruits. That Part of the Ovolo which appears forward in the Front of the Capital muſt be carved with Eggs, and under them with Berries. In the Void left on each Side by the Sweep of the Volute, carve Leaves or Scales. And thus much for the *Ionic* Capital. * The *Corinthian* Capital is in Height one whole Diameter of the Bottom of the Shaft. This Height muſt be divided into ſeven Parts or Minutes, of which the Abacus muſt be allowed one. The reſt is entirely taken up by the Bell or Vaſe, the Breadth of which at the Bottom muſt be exactly equal to that of the Top of the Shaft, without any of its Projectures, and the Breadth of the Top of the Vaſe muſt be equal to the largeſt Diameter of the Bottom of the Shaft. The Length of the Abacus on every Side muſt be equal to ten of the afore-mentioned Parts; but the Corners of it muſt be cut away to the Breadth of one half of thoſe Parts. The Abacus of the other Capitals conſiſts entirely of ſtraight Lines, but that of the *Corinthian* muſt go with a Sweep inwards to the Thickneſs of the Bottom of the Vaſe. The Thickneſs of the Abacus is divided into three Parts, the Uppermoſt of which muſt be made exactly as we adorn the Top of the Shaft, that is to ſay, with a Fillet and ſmall Baguette. The Vaſe muſt be covered with two Rows of Leaves ſtanding upright, each Row conſiſting of eight Leaves. Each Row muſt be in Height two of the afore-mentioned Parts, and the remaining Parts muſt be given to ſeveral little Shoots riſing out of the Leaves to the Top of the Vaſe. Theſe Shoots are in Number ſixteen, of which four are tied in each Front of the Capital, two on the left Hand in one Knot, and two on the right in another, ſpreading away from each Knot in ſuch a Manner, that the Tops of the two outward ones make a Sort of a Volute exactly under the Horns of the Abacus. The two Middle ones in each Front join together, winding alſo like Volutes, and exactly over the Middle of them is carved a beautiful Flower riſing out of the Vaſe, which muſt not exceed the Abacus in Breadth. The Breadth of thoſe Parts of the Lips of the Vaſe which thoſe Shoots do not conceal from us, is only one of the afore-mentioned ſeventh Parts. The Leaves muſt be divided into five Plumes, and never more than into ſeven. The Tops of the Leaves muſt project half a Minute. It looks handſome in the Leaves of this Capital, and all other Carving of the ſame Nature, to have all the Lines cut in deep and bold. This was the Capital of the *Corinthians*. The *Italians* brought into * their Capital all the Ornaments that they found in the others, and obſerved the ſame Method in making the Vaſe, Abacus, Leaves, and the Flower in the Abacus, as the *Corinthians*. But inſtead of Shoots they made uſe of a Sort of Volutes, under the four Horns of the Abacus, projecting two whole Minutes. The Front of the Capital, being otherwiſe naked, borrowed its Ornaments from the *Ionic*; for inſtead of Shoots it has Volutes, and the Lips of its Vaſe are carved full of Eggs with Berries underneath them, like an Ovolo. Beſides the Capitals here deſcribed, we up and down ſee a great many other Sorts made up of the Members of theſe, with either Additions or Diminutions: But I do not find that they are much approved. And thus much may ſuffice of Capitals, unleſs it be neceſſary juſt to mention one Practice; which is, that it is common over the Abacus to lay a very thick ſquare Piece of Stone, or Plinth, which ſeems as it were to give the Capital Breadth, and to prevent its being oppreſſed by the Architrave, and at the ſame Time is of Uſe to keep the niceſt and moſt delicate Parts of the Work from being injured in laying the Superſtructure.

* *See Plates 27 and 28, following Plate 26.*

Chap. IX.

Of the Entablature, the Architrave, Triglyphs, Dentils, Mutules, Cavetto, and Drip or Crona, as alſo of Flutings and ſome other Ornaments belonging to Columns.

HAVING fixed our Capitals, we upon them raiſe our Architraves, upon the Architrave the Freze, Cornice and other Members of the Covering. In moſt of theſe Members the *Ionians* and all others differ very much from the *Dorians*; though in ſome Particulars they agree. For Inſtance, it is a general Rule, that the Thickneſs of the Bottom of the Architrave ſhould be never greater than the Solid of the Top of the Shaft of the Column, nor ſhould the Breadth of the Top of the ſame Architrave be greater than the Diameter of the Bottom of the Shaft. The Cornice is that Member which lies upon the Freze, and projects over it. In this too they obſerved the Rule which we have already given, that the Projecture of all Members that ſtood out from the Naked of the Wall ought to be equal to their Height. It was alſo uſual with them to make their Cornice lean forwards about a twelfth Part of its Width, knowing that this Member would ſeem to be falling backwards, if it were ſet up at right Angles. I here again entreat thoſe who ſhall hereafter tranſcribe this Book, and I do it in the moſt earneſt Manner, that they would write the Numbers which I ſet down with Letters at Length, and not with numeral Characters, for the avoiding of more * numerous Errors. The *Dorians* then never made the Height of their Architrave leſs than half the Diameter of the Bottom of their Column, and this Architrave they divided into three Faſcias, under the uppermoſt of which ran ſome ſhort Mouldings, in each whereof ſtuck ſix Nails, which were fixed in thoſe Mouldings with their Heads downwards, and might at firſt be intended to keep the Freze from retiring backward. The whole Height of this Architrave they divided into twelve Parts or Minutes, by which we ſhall meaſure all the following Members. Four of theſe Minutes they gave to the lower Faſcia, ſix to the Middle one which is above it, and the other two they left for the upper Faſcia; and of the ſix Minutes given to the middle Faſcia, one was allowed to the Reglet or Moulding under the Tænia, and another to the Nails which ſtuck in that Moulding. The Length of theſe Reglets was twelves Minutes, and the Spaces from one Reglet to the other were eighteen. Over the Architrave for an Ornament they ſet the Triglyphs, the Front of which, being raiſed High and Perpendicular, projected over the Architrave half a Minute. The Breadth of the Triglyphs muſt be equal to the Thickneſs of the Architrave, and their Height or Length half as much more, ſo that this will be eighteen Minutes. Lengthways in the Face of theſe Triglyphs we cut three Furrows at equal Diſtance from each other, and hollowed at right Angles, allowing the Breadth of the opening one Minute. The Corners of theſe Furrows or Channels muſt be cut away to the Breadth of half a Minute. The Spaces or Metopes between the Triglyphs, where the Proportions are elegant, are flat Tables exactly ſquare, and the Triglyphs themſelves muſt be ſet perpendicularly over the Solid of their Columns. The Face of the Triglyphs project half a Minute out from the Metopes; but the Perpendicular of the Metopes muſt fall exactly upon the lower Faſcia of the Architrave. In theſe Metopes it is uſual to carve the Skulls of Oxen, Pateras, Wheels, and the like. Over each of theſe Triglyphs and Metopes, inſtead of a Cymatium, muſt run a Fillet of the Breadth of two Minutes, over theſe a Cima-inverſa of the Breadth of two Minutes, and above that a Platband of the Breadth of three Minutes, which is adorned with little Eggs, in Imitation, perhaps, of the ſmall Stones which ſometimes burſt out between the Joints of a Pavement through the too great Abundance of Mortar. In theſe we fix the Mutules of the ſame Breadth as the Triglyphs, and of the ſame Height as the Platband, placed directly over the Heads of the Triglyphs and projecting twelve Minutes. The Heads of the Mutules are cut Perpendicular, with a Cymaiſe over them. Over the Mutules runs a ſmall Cima of three Quarters of a Minute. In the Plat-fond of the Entablature between the Mutules we carve a Roſe or a Flower of

* *See Plate 29, facing.*

J. Leoni delin.

J. Leoni delin.

of the Branca Urfina. Upon the Mutules lies the Corona, which is allowed four Minutes, and this Corona confifts of a Plat-band or Drip and a Cima Recta, which laft takes up one Minute and a Half. If you are to have a Pediment over your Building, all the Members of the Cornice muft be transferred to that, and every Member in the Pediment muft correfpond with the fame in the Cornice, and anfwer to the fame Perpendiculars and Proportions. There is only this Difference between Pediments and the firft Cornices, that in Pediments the higheft Member of the Cornice is always the Drip, which in the *Doric* Order is a Cima-reverfa, four Minutes in Height, whereas this Drip or Cima has never Place in a Cornice that is to have a Pediment over it; but in thofe which are to have no Pediment it is conftantly ufed. But of Pediments we fhall fpeak by and by. This was the Entablature of the *Dorians*. The * *Ionians* were of Opinion, and not without Reafon, that the Proportion of the Architrave ought to encreafe according to the Bignefs of the Column; which muft certainly have a good Effect both here and in the *Doric* Order too. The Rules they gave for enlarging this Proportion were as follows: When the Column was twenty Foot high the Architrave ought to be the thirteenth Part of that Length; but when the Column was to be five-and-twenty Foot, the Architrave fhould be the twelfth Part of the Length of the Column. Laftly, if the Column was to be thirty Foot high, the Architrave was to be the eleventh Part, and for higher Columns in the fame Gradation. The *Ionic* Architrave, befides its Cymaife, confifted of three Fafcias, and the Whole was divided into nine Parts, two of which were allowed to the Cymaife, which was an upright one. The Remainder below the Cymaife they divided into twelve Parts, three of which went to the lower, four to the middle, and five to the upper Fafcia, which lies juft below the Cymaife. Some made thefe Fafcias without any Sort of Mouldings between them, but others made them with Mouldings, and thefe were fometimes a fmall Cima-inverfa, taking up a fifth Part of the Fafcia, and fometimes a Baguette taking up a feventh Part. We may obferve in the Works of the Ancients, that the Lineaments or Members of the feveral Orders were often mixed, one borrowing from another, and often with a very good Effect. But they feemed chiefly pleafed with an Architrave of only two Fafcias, which I take to be entirely *Doric* without its Reglets and Drops. Their Manner of defigning this Architrave was thus. They divided the whole Height into nine Parts, affigning one Part and two Thirds to the Cymaife. The upper Fafcia had four Parts and one Third, and the lower Fafcia the other three. Half the upper Part of this Cymaife was taken up with a Cima-inverfa and a Fillet, and the other half with a fmall Quarter-round. The upper Fafcia for its Cymaife had a Baguette, which took up an eighth Part of the Fafcia, and the lower Fafcia had a Cima-recta of the third Part of its whole Breadth. Upon the Architrave lay the Rafters; but their Heads did not appear out, as in the *Doric* Order, but were cut away Perpendicular to the Architrave, and were covered with a flat Pannel which I call the Freze, the Breadth of which was the fame as the Height of the Architrave which is under it. Upon this they ufed to carve Vafes and other Utenfils belonging to their Sacrifices, or Skulls of Oxen at certain ftated Diftances, with Feftoons of Flowers and Fruits hanging between their Horns. This Freze had over it a Cima-recta, which was never higher than four Parts of the Freze, nor lower than three. Over this ran the Denticle, four Parts high, fometimes carved and fometimes left quite plain. Above this was the Ovolo, out of which came the Mutules, three Parts in Height, and carved with Eggs, and from hence came the Mutules fupporting the Drip, which was four Parts high and fix Parts and a half Broad in its Soffit, or that Face underneath which lay over the Mutules. Over this Drip was a fmall Cima-recta, or elfe a Baguette two Parts in Height, and at the Top of all was a Cymaife or Cima-inverfa of three Parts, or if you pleafe of four. In this Cymaife both the *Ionians* and the *Dorians* ufed to carve the Mouths of Lyons, which ferved for Spouts to throw out the Water; but they took Care that they fhould neither fprinkle any Body that was going into the Temple, nor beat back into any Part of the Temple itfelf; and for this Reafon they ftopt up thofe Mouths that were over the Doors and Windows. The *Corinthians* * added nothing either to the Architrave, Freze or Cornice, that I can call to Mind, except only that they did not make their Mutules fquare like the *Dorians*, but with a Sort of Sweep like a Cymaife, and made the Diftances between them equal to their Projecture from the Naked of the Building. In all other Refpects they followed the *Ionians*. Thus much may

* *See Plate 30, facing, and Plate 31, facing page 148*

may ſuffice for thoſe Colonades which are to be covered with Architraves; of thoſe which are to ſupport Arches we ſhall ſpeak by and by, when we come to treat of the Baſilique. There are only ſome few Particulars more relating to Colonades of this Sort, which ought by no Means to be omitted. It is certain that a Column which ſtands in the open Air, always ſeems ſmaller than one that is under Cover, and the more Flutings there are in its Shaft, the Thicker it will appear. For this Reaſon we are adviſed either to make thoſe fluted Columns that ſtand in the open Air ſomewhat thicker, or elſe to encreaſe the Number of the * Channels. Theſe Channels are made either direct along the Shaft, or elſe run ſpiral about it. The *Dorians* made them direct along the Shaft. Theſe Channels are called by Architects Striæ, and among the *Dorians* they were in Number Twenty. Others made Twenty-four. Others ſeparated theſe Channels by ſmall Lifts, which were never more than a third, nor leſs than a fourth Part of the Groove of the Fluting, and theſe Flutings were a ſemi-circular Concave. In the *Doric* Order the Flutings are plain without any Lift, with very little hollow, or at moſt but the Quarter of a Circle, terminating the Channels in an Angle. For the lower third Part of the Shaft of the Column, they generally filled their Flutings with a Cable, to make the Column ſtronger, and leſs liable to Injuries. Thoſe Flutings which run direct along the Shaft, make the Column appear to the Eye of the Beholder thicker than it really is. Thoſe Channels that run ſpiral about the Shaft, vary it too; but the leſs they ſwerve from the Perpendicular of the Column, the Thicker the Column will appear. They muſt round clear round the Column never more than three Times, nor ever make leſs than one compleat Revolution. Whatever Flutings you make, they muſt always run from the Bottom to the Top of the Shaft in even and continued Lines, with an equal Hollow all the Way. The Sides of the Builder's Square will ſerve us as a Guide for making our Channels. There is a mathematical Line, which being drawn from any certain Point of the Circumference of a Semi-circle to the End of its Diameter is called a right Angle, which is the ſame as the Builder's Square. Having then marked out the Sides of your Flutings, ſink them ſo deep in the Middle, that the Angle of your Square may touch the Bottom and its two Sides of the Lips of them at the ſame Time. At each End of the Shaft of a fluted Column, you muſt leave a proper Diſtance plain between the Channels and the Cincture at one End, and the Aſtragal at the other. We are told, that all round the Temple of *Memphis*, inſtead of Columns, they made uſe of Coloſſal Statues eighteen Foot high. In other Places they had wreathed Columns twiſted round with Tendrils and Vine-leaves carved in Relief, and with the Figures of little Birds here and there interſperſed. But the plain Column is much more agreeable to the Majeſty of a Temple. There are certain Dimentions which are great Helps to the Workmen in the placing of their Columns, and theſe are taken from the Number of the Columns themſelves that are to be uſed in the Structure. Thus, for Inſtance, to * begin with the *Dorians*; when they had four Columns for the Front of their Building, they divided the Front of the Platform into ſeven-and-twenty Parts. If they had ſix Columns, they divided it into one-and-forty, and if eight into ſix-and-fifty, and of theſe Parts they allowed two for the Thickneſs of each Column. But in *Ionic* Structures where four Columns are * to be uſed, the Front of the Platform muſt be divided into eleven Parts and a half; where theſe are to be ſix, into eighteen, and where eight, into four-and-twenty and a half; whereof only one Part muſt be given to the Thickneſs of each Column.

Chap. X.

Of the Pavement of the Temple and its inner Area, of the Place for the Altar, and of the Walls and their Ornaments.

IT is the moſt approved Taſte to aſcend to the Floor of the Temple and to the inner Area by ſome Number of Steps, and to have the Place where the Altar is to be fixed, raiſed higher than the Reſt. The Apertures and Entrance to the Chapels on the Sides were ſometimes left quite open without any Incloſure whatſoever, and ſometimes ſhut in with two Columns,

* *See Plates 32–34, following Plate 31.*

PLATE 31. *(Pages 147–48)*

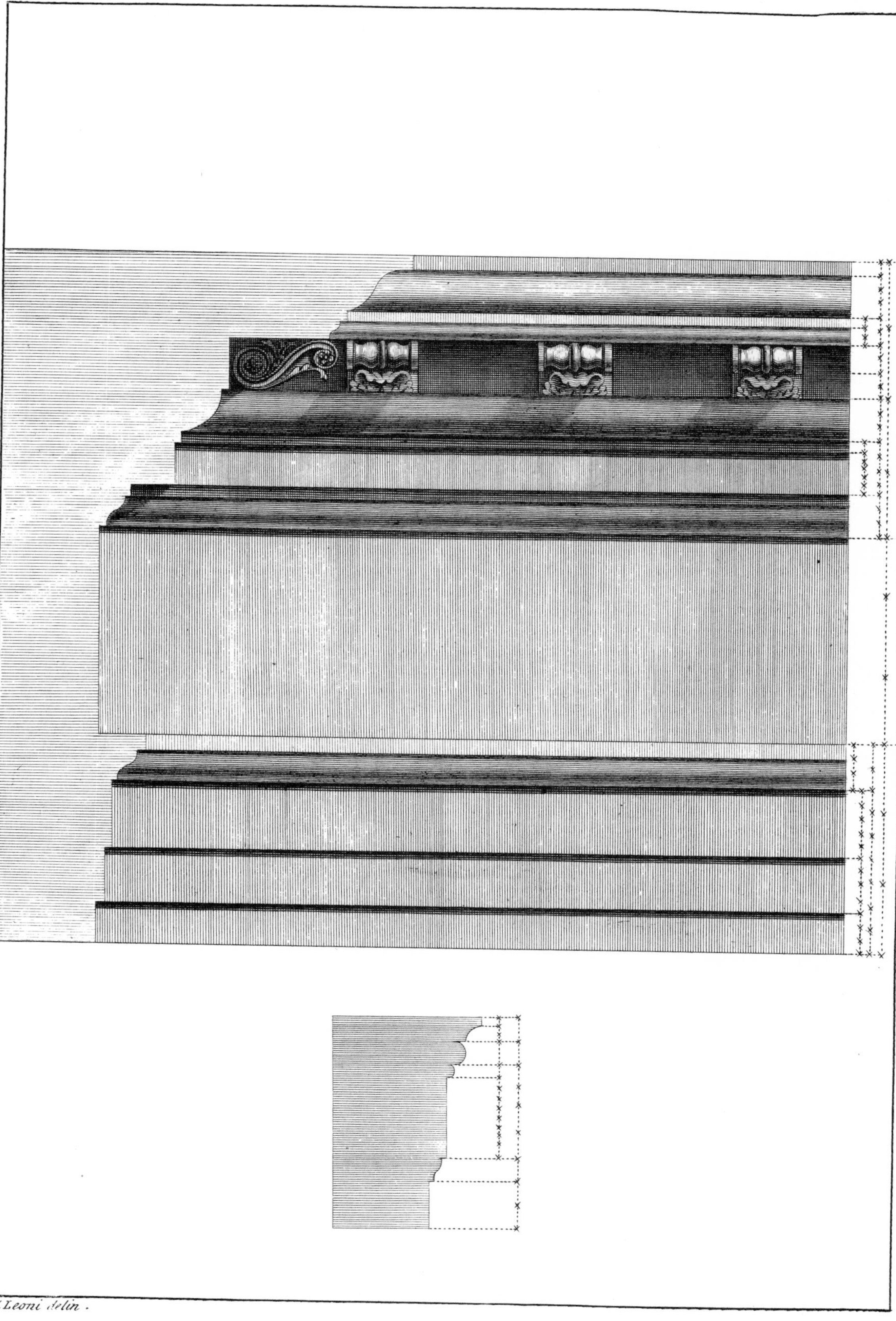

J. Leoni delin.

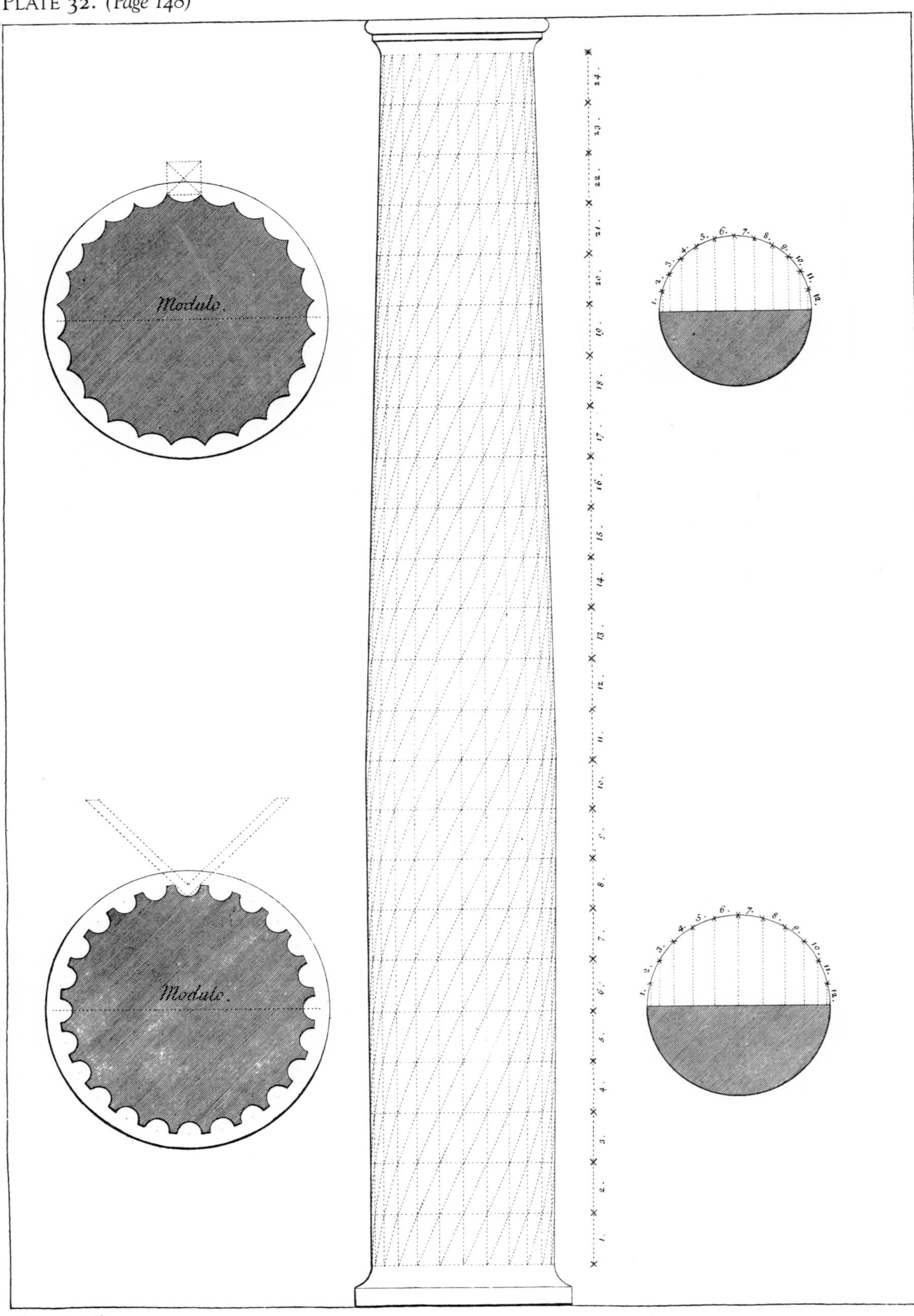

J. Leoni delin.

J. Leoni delin.

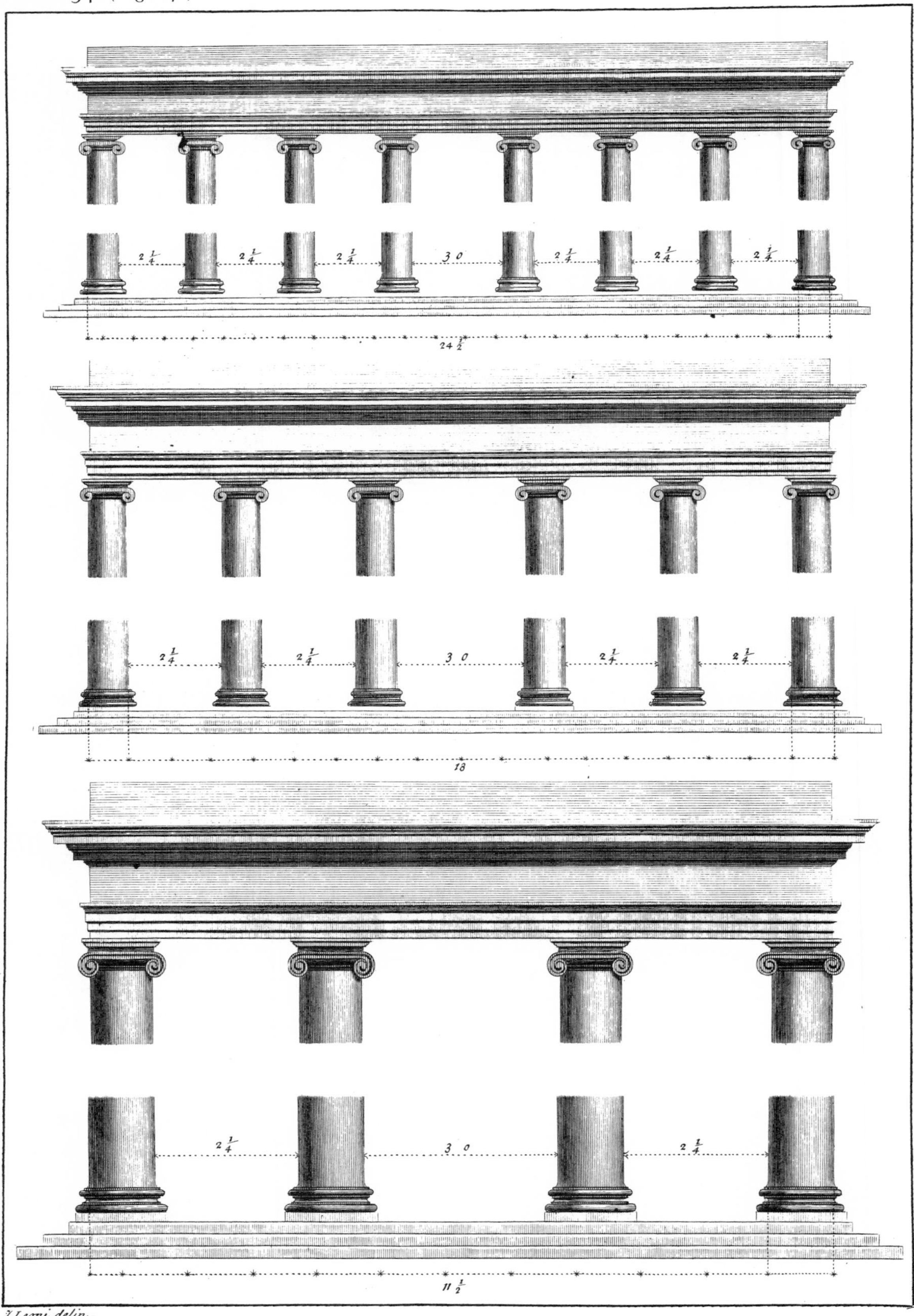

J. Leoni delin.

Columns, over which ran an Architrave, Freze and Cornice, according to the Rules just now laid down for Porticoes; and the rest of the Void above the Cornice was left quite open for setting of Statues or large Candlesticks. Others inclosed the Entrance into such Chapels with a Walls brought half Way on each Side. Those who imagine that the great Thickness of the Walls adds Dignity to a Temple, are greatly mistaken; for who is there that does not dislike a Body composed of gouty Limbs? besides that when the Walls are too thick, they always intercept the Light. In the *Rotonda* at *Rome*, the excellent Architect who had the Care of that great Work having in it Occasion for thick Walls, built the Ribs entirely of solid Work, without any Stuffing, and those Interspaces which a less skilful Artist would have stuffed, he employed in Niches and other Apertures, whereby he saved Expence, and made the Structure less heavy, and more beautiful. The Thickness of the Walls must be proportioned after the Manner of Columns; that is to say, their Thickness must correspond to their Height, as in those. I have observed that the Ancients, in building their Temples, used to divide the Front of their Platform into twelve Parts; or, when they would make them particularly strong, into nine, and one of those Parts was the Thickness of the Wall. In circular Temples the Wall was never less high than half the Diameter of its inner Area; many made it two Thirds of that Diameter, and some three Fourths, which was the Height to which they carried the Wall before they began the Sweep of the Cupola. But the more discreet Workmen divided the Circumference of this circular Platform into four Parts; and one of those fourth Parts being extended to a Line was equal to the inward Height of the Wall, which is as four to eleven: And this Practice has been also imitated in square Temples as well as round ones, and in many other Kinds of Structures that were to be covered with Arches. But where there were to be Chapels on each Side in the Wall, to make the Aperture seem the Larger they sometimes raised their Wall equal in Height to the whole Breadth of the Area. In round Temples the inward Height of the Wall will not be the same as the outward: Because within the Wall ends exactly where the Sweep of the Arch begins; but without, it is carried up straight to the Top of the Cornice. If the Cupola have a Cover on the Outside made with Degrees like Steps, the outward Wall will take up a third Part of it; but if the Cover be made with straight Lines and a common Slope, then the outward Wall will take up half. Nothing is more convenient for building the Walls of a Temple, than Brick; but then it must be cased with something handsomer. There have been many different Opinions with Relation to the Adorning of the Walls of Temples. At *Cyzicus* a Town in *Bythinia* there was a Temple which had its Walls adorned with a very beautiful Stone, and all the Joints pointed with massy Gold. In the Temple of *Minerva* at *Elis*, the Brother of *Phidias*, the celebrated Carver, made an Incrustation of Stuc tempered with Saffron and Milk. The Kings of *Ægypt* encompassed the Monument of *Simandes*, which was the Sepulchre for the Concubines of *Jupiter*, with a Circle of Gold no less than a Cubit or Foot and half broad, and three hundred sixty-five Cubits round, with a Day of the Year inscribed upon every Cubit. Others condemned this Excess of Ornament in Temples. *Cicero*, being guided by *Plato*'s Opinion, thought it necessary that the People should be admonished by the Laws to lay aside all Manner of Delicacy in the Adorning their Temples, and take Care only to have them perfectly clean and white. However, says he, let the Structure of them be beautiful. I confess, for my own Part, I am very ready to believe, that Purity and Simplicity of Colour, as of Life, must be most pleasing to the Divine Being; and that it is not proper to have any Thing in a Church that may be likely to draw off Men's Thoughts from Devotion and fix them upon the Pleasure and Delight of the Senses: But still I am of Opinion, that he is highly to be commended, who, as in other publick Structures, so also in Temples, without departing from the Gravity requisite in such Works, endeavours to have all the Parts, the Walls, Roof, and Pavement, as handsome and elegant as possible, still chiefly having it in his Eye to make all his Ornaments the most durable that may be. Thus nothing can be more proper for the Ornament of the Roof on the Inside than all Sorts of *Mosaic* Work made of Marble, Glass, and other lasting Materials. Stuc-work with Figures, according to the Practice of the Ancients, may be a very handsome Coat for the Outside. In both you must take the greatest Care to chuse proper Places as well for your Pictures as Figures. The Portico, for Instance, is the fittest Place for the Representation of great Actions in Pictures.

Indeed, within the Temple I think detached Pictures do much better than painting upon the Wall itself, and in my Mind Statues are handsomer than Pictures. unless they be such excellent ones as those two, for which *Cæsar* the Dictator gave ninety Talents, or fourteen hundred of our Crowns, in order to adorn the Temple of *Venus* his Progenitor; and I look upon a Picture with no less Pleasure (I mean a good one, for ill Painting is a Disgrace to the Wall) than I read a good History. They both indeed are Pictures, only the Historian paints with Words, and the Painter with his Pencil. All other Qualifications are common to them both, and they both require the greatest Genius and Application. But I would have nothing either on the Wall or Pavement of the Temple but what favours entirely of Philosophy. We read that in the Capitol there were Tables of Brass whereon were inscribed the Laws by which the Empire was to be governed; which, when the Temple was destroyed by Fire, were restored by the Emperor *Vespasian*, to the Number of three Thousand. We are told that at the Entrance of the Temple of *Apollo* at *Delos*, there were Verses engraved, containing several Compositions of Herbs proper to be used as Remedies against all Sorts of Poison. Thus I should think it would be proper among us, by Way of Inscription, to have such Precepts as may make us more just, more modest, more useful, more adorned with all Virtues, and more acceptable in the Sight of God; such as these, *Be what you would be thought*; *Love if you would be beloved*, and the like. And I would have the Composition of the Lines of the Pavement full of musical and geometrical Proportions; to the Intent that which-soever Way we may turn our Eyes, we may be sure to find Employment for our Minds. One Method which the Ancients took to adorn their Temples, was to fill them with Things that were uncommon and excellent; as in the Temple of *Hercules*, where were to be seen some Horns of Emmets brought from *India*; or like those Crowns made of Cinnamon which *Vespasian* gave to the Capitol; or like that great Root of Cinnamon which *Augusta* placed in the principal Temple of Mount *Palatine*, in a Cup of Gold. At *Thermus*, a Town in *Ætolia* plundered by *Philip*, we are told, that in the Porticoes of the Temple there were above fifteen thousand Suits of Armour, and to adorn the Temple itself above two thousand Statues; all which, according to *Polybius*'s Relation, were destroyed and broken by *Philip*, except those which were inscribed with the Name, or bore the Representation of some God; and perhaps Variety is more to be consulted in such Collections than Number. *Solinus* informs us, that in *Sicily* there were some Artificers who had the Secret of making Statues of Salt; and *Pliny* tells us, that there was one made of Glass. There is no Question but such Things must be exceeding rare, and very worthy to raise our Admiration of the Work both of Nature and Art. But of Statues we shall speak in another Place. The Walls and Apertures must be adorned with Columns; but not like a Portico. There is one Thing which I have observed in the Covering of some of the biggest Temples, which is, that not having Columns of Height sufficient to reach to the Spring of their Arches, they heightened the Sides of the Arches themselves in such a Manner that their Sagitta was a third Part longer than their Semi-diameter, which added not a little to the Clearness and Beauty of the Work itself. And here I must not omit one Precept, namely, that the Spring of the Arch should have at least so much Perpendicular, as to prevent the Projecture of the Cornices from taking away any Part of the Arch from the Sight of those that staid below in the Middle of the Temple.

Chap. XI.

Why the Roofs of Temples ought to be arched.

I Am entirely for having the Roofs of Temples arched, as well because it gives them the greater Dignity, as because it makes them more durable. And indeed I know not how it happens that we shall hardly meet any one Temple whatsoever that has not fallen into the Calamity of Fire. We read that *Cambyses* burnt all the Temples in *Ægypt* in general, and removed the Treasure and Ornaments belonging to them to *Persepolis*. *Eusebius* relates, that the Oracle of *Delphos* was burnt three Times by the *Thracians*, and another Time it took Fire of itself, and was rebuilt by *Amasis*, as we are informed by *Herodotus*. We read too that it was

was once burnt by *Phlegyas*, about the Time that *Phœnice* invented some Characters for the Use of his Citizens. It was also consumed by Fire in the Reign of *Cyrus*, a few Years before the Death of *Servius Tullus*, the King of *Rome*; and it is certain, that it was again burnt about the Time of the Birth of those three great Luminaries of Learning, *Catullus*, *Sallus* and *Varro*. The Temple of *Ephesus* was burnt by the *Amazons*, in the Reign of *Sylvius Posthumus*, as it was also about the Time that *Socrates* was condemned to drink Poison at *Athens*: and the Temple of the *Argives* was destroyed by Fire the same Year that *Plato* was born at *Athens*, at which Time *Tarquin* reigned at *Rome*. Why should I mention the sacred Porticoes of *Jerusalem*? Or the Temple of *Minerva* at *Miletus*? Or that of *Serapis* at *Alexandria*? Or at *Rome*, the *Pantheon*? And the Temple of the Goddess *Vesta*? And that of *Apollo*? In which last we are told the Sibyls Verses were destroyed. We indeed find, that scarce any Temple escaped the same Calamity. *Diadorus* writes, that there was none besides that dedicated to *Venus*, in the City of *Eryx* in *Sicily*, that had escaped to his Time unhurt by the Flames. *Cæsar* owned that *Alexandria* escaped being burnt, when he himself took it, because its Roofs were vaulted. Nor are vaulted Roofs destituted of their Ornaments. The Ancients transferred all the same Ornaments to their Cupolas, as the Goldsmiths used about the Pateras or Cups for the Sacrifices; and the same Sort of Work as was used in the Quilts of their Beds, they imitated in their vaulted Roofs, whether plain or camerated. Thus we see them divided into four, eight, or more Pannels, or crossed different Ways with equal Angles and with Circles, in the most beautiful Manner that can be imagined. And here it may be proper to observe, that the Ornaments of vaulted Roofs, which consist in the Forms of their Pannels or Excavations, are in many Places exceeding handsome, and particularly at the *Rotonda* at *Rome*; yet we have no where any Instruction left us in Writing how to make them. My Method of doing it, which is very easy and cheap, is as follows: I describe the Lineaments of the future Pannels or Excavations upon the Boards of the Scaffolding itself, whether they are to be Quadrangular, Sexangular, or Octangular. Then those Parts which I intended to excavate in my Roof, I raise to the stated Height with unbaked Bricks set in Clay instead of Mortar. Upon this Kind of Mount thus raised on the Back of the Scaffolding, I build my vaulted Roof of Brick and Mortar, taking great Care that the thinner Parts cohere firmly with the Thicker and Stronger. When the Vault is compleated and settled and the Scaffolding is taken away from under it, I clear the solid Building from those Mounts of Clay which I had raised at first; and thus the Shape of my Evcavations or Pannels are formed according to my original Design. But to return to our Subject. I am extremely delighted with an Ornament mentioned by *Varro*, who tells us of a Roof on which was painted a Sky with a moving Star in it, which by a Kind of Hand shewed at once the Hour of the Day and what Wind blew abroad. I should be wonderfully pleased with such a Contrivance. The Ancients were of Opinion that raising the Roof high and ending it with a Pedient gave such an Air of Greatness to a Building, that they used to say the House of *Jove* himself, though they never supposed it rained in Heaven, could not look handsome without it. The Rule for these Pediments is as follows. Take not more than the Fourth nor less than the Fifth of the Breadth of your Front along the Cornice, and let this be the Summit or upper Angle of your Pediment. Upon this Summit, as also at each End, you set Acroteria, or little Pedestals for Statues. The Height of the Acroteria or Pedestals at the Ends should be equal to that of the Freze and Cornice; but that which stands on the Summit, should be an eighth Part higher than the others. We are told that *Buccides* was the first that adorned his Pediments with Statues, which he made of Earth coloured red; but afterwards they came to be made of Marble, and the whole Covering too.

CHAP. XII.

Of the Apertures proper to Temples, namely, the Windows, Doors, and Valves; together with their Members, Proportions and Ornaments.

THE Windows in the Temple ought to be small and high, so that nothing but the Sky may be seen through them; to the Intent that both the Priests that are employed in the Performance of divine Offices, and those that assist upon Account of Devotion, may not

not have their Minds any Ways diverted by ſoreign Objects. That Horror with which a ſolemn Gloom is apt to fill the Mind naturally raiſes our Veneration, and there is always ſomewhat of an Auſterity in Majeſty: Beſides that thoſe Lights which ſhould be always burning in Temples, and than which nothing is more awful for the Honour and Ornament of Religion, look faint and languiſh, unleſs favoured by ſome Obſcurity. For this Reaſon the Ancients were very often contented without any other Aperture beſides the Gate. For my own Part, I am for having the Entrance into the Temple thoroughly well lighted, and thoſe Parts within, where People are to walk, not melancholy; but the Place where the Altar is to be ſeated, I think ſhould have more of Majeſty than Beauty. But to return to the Apertures themſelves. Let us here remember what has formerly been ſaid, namely, that Apertures conſiſt of three Parts, the Void, the Jambs and the Lintel, which two laſt we may call the Frame of the Door or Window. The Ancients never uſed to make either Doors or Windows otherwiſe than ſquare. We ſhall treat firſt of Doors. All the beſt Architects, whether *Dorians*, *Ionians* or *Corinthians*, always made their Doors narrower at the Top than at the Bottom by one fourteenth Part. To the Lintel they gave the ſame Thickneſs as they found at the Top of the Jamb, making the Lines of their Ornaments anſwer exactly to one another, and meet together in juſt Angles: And they raiſed the Cornice over the Door equal in Height to the Capital of the Columns in the Portico. Thus far they all agreed, but in other Particulars they differed * very much. And firſt the *Dorians* divided this whole Height, that is to ſay, from the Level of the Pavement up to the Roof, into ſixteen Parts, whereof they gave ten to the Height of the Void, which the Ancients uſed to call the Light; five to its Breadth, and one to the Breadth of the Frame. This was the *Doric* * Diviſion; but the *Ionians* divided the whole Height to the Top of the Columns, as aforementioned, into nineteen Parts, whereof they gave twelve to the Height of the Light, ſix to its Breadth, and one to the Frame. The *Corinthians* divided it into one-and-twenty Parts, aſſigning ſeven to the Breadth of the Light, and doubling that Breadth for its Length, and allowing for the Breadth of the Frame one ſeventh Part of the Breadth of the Light. In all theſe Doors the Frame was an Architrave. And, unleſs I am much miſtaken, the *Ionians* made uſe of their own Architrave, adorned with three Faſcias, as did the *Dorians* too of theirs, only leaving out the Reglets and Drops; and all adorned their Lintels with moſt of the Delicacies of their Cornice; only the *Dorians* left out their Triglyphs, and inſtead of them made uſe of a Freze as broad as the Jamb or Frame of the Door. Over the Freze they added an upright Cymatium; and over that a plain Dentil, and next an Ovolo; above that ran the Mutules with their Cymaiſe, and over them an inverted Cymatium; obſerving in all theſe Members the ſame Proportions as we have already ſet down for the *Doric* Entablature. The *Ionians*, on the contrary, did not make uſe of a plain Freze, as in their common Entablature; but inſtead of it made a ſwelling Freze, one third Part of the Breadth of the Architrave, adorned with Leaves bound about with a Kind of Swathes. Over this they made their Cymaſe, Dentil, Ovolo, Mutules, with their Cymaiſe, and above all the Drip and inverted Cymatium. Beſides this, at each End of the Entablature, on the Outſide of the Jamb, under the Drip, they made a Sort of Ears, as we may call them, from their Reſemblance to the handſome Ears of a fine Spaniel, by Architects called, *Conſoles.* Theſe Conſoles were turned like a great S. The Ends winding round in this Manner, ∽, and the Thickneſs of the Conſole at the Top was equal to the Breadth of the ſwelling Freze, and one fourth Part leſs at Bottom. The Length reached down to the Top of the Void or Light. The *Corinthians* applied to their * Doors all the Embelliſhments of a Collonade. And to avoid further Repetitions, we adorn a Door, eſpecially when it is to ſtand under the open Air with a Sort of little Portico, attached againſt the Wall, in this Manner. Having made the Frame of the Door, we place on each Side an entire Column, or if you will only an half Column, with their Baſes at ſuch a Diſtance from each other, as to leave the Jambs, or whole Antipagment clear. The Length of the whole Columns with their Capitals, muſt be equal to the Diſtance between the outward Edge of the left Baſe to the outward Edge of the Right. Over theſe Columns you make a regular Architrave, Freze, Cornice and Pediment, according to all the ſame Proportions as as we have above laid down for a Portico. Some on each Side of the Door, inſtead of a plain Jamb, made uſe of all the Ornaments of a Cornice,

* *See Plates 35–37, facing and following this page.*

PLATE 35. (*Page 152*)

PLATE 36. *(Page 152)*

J. Leoni delin.

PLATE 37. *(Pages 152–53)*

Cornice, ſo allowing the Open a greater Width; but this is a Delicacy much more ſuitable to the Houſe of a private Perſon, and eſpecially about Windows, than to the Door of a Temple. In very large Temples, and eſpecially in ſuch as have no other Apertures but the Door, the Height of the Open of that Door is divided into three Parts, the uppermoſt of which is left by Way of Window, and grated, the Remainder ſerves for the Door. The Door itſelf too, or Valve, conſiſts of different Members and Proportions. Of theſe Members the Chief is the Hinge, which is contrived after two Manners; either by an iron Staple fixed in the Door-caſe; or elſe by Pins coming out from the Top and Bottom of the Door itſelf, upon which it balances and turns, and ſo ſhuts and opens. The Doors of Temples, which for the Sake of Duration, are generally made of Braſs, and conſequently muſt be very heavy, are better truſted to Axles, in the later Manner, than to hang upon any Staples. I ſhall not here ſpend Time in giving an Account of thoſe Doors which we read of in Hiſtorians and Poets, enriched with Gold, Ivory, and Statues, and ſo heavy that they could never be opened without a Multitude of Hands, and ſuch a Noiſe as terrified the Hearers, I own Facility in opening and ſhutting them is more to my Mind. Under the Bottom therefore of the lower Pin or Axle, make a Box of Braſs mixed with Tin, and in this Box ſink a deep hollow Concave at the Bottom; let the Bottom of the Axle have alſo a Concavity in it, ſo that the Box and the Axle may contain between them a round Ball of Steel, perfectly ſmooth and well poliſhed. The upper Pin or Axle muſt alſo be let into a braſs Box made in the Lintel, and beſides muſt turn in a moveable iron Circle as ſmooth as it can be made; and by this Means the Door will never make the leaſt Reſiſtance in turning, but ſwing which Way you pleaſe with all the Eaſe imaginable. Every Door ſhould have two Valves or Leaves, one opening to one Side, and the other to the other. The Thickneſs of theſe Leaves ſhould be one twelfth Part of their Breadth. Their Ornament are Pannels or ſquare Mouldings applied lengthways down the Leaf, and you may have as many of them as you will, either two or three, one above the other, or only one. If you have two, they muſt lie like the Steps of a Stair, one above the other, and both muſt take up no more of the Breadth of the Leaf than a fourth, nor leſs than a ſixth Part; and let the laſt, which lies above the other, be one fifth Part broader than the under one. If you have three of theſe Mouldings, obſerve the ſame Proportions in them as in the Faces of the *Ionic* Architrave: But if you have only one Moulding, let it be not more than a fifth, nor leſs than a ſeventh Part of the Breadth of the Leaf. Theſe Mouldings muſt all fall inward to the Leaf with a Cimarecta. The Length of the Leaf ſhould alſo be divided by other Mouldings croſsways, giving the upper Pannel two fifth Parts of the whole Height of the Door. In Temples the Windows muſt be adorned in the ſame Manner as the Doors; but their Apertures, being near the higheſt Part of the Wall, and their Angles terminating near the Vault of the Roof, they are therefore made with an Arch, contrary to the Practice in Doors. Their Breadth is twice their Height; and this Breadth is divided by two little Columns, placed according to the ſame Rules as in a Portico; only that theſe Columns are generally ſquare. The Deſigns for Niches, Statues or other Repreſentations, are borrowed from thoſe of Doors; and their Height muſt take up one third Part of their Wall. The Ancients in the Windows of their Temples, inſtead of Panes of Glaſs, made uſe of thin tranſparent Scantlings of Alabaſter, to keep out Wind and Weather; or elſe made a Grate of Braſs or Marble, and filled up the Interſpaces of this Grate not with brittle Glaſs, but with a tranſparent Sort of Stone brought from *Segovia*, a Town in *Spain*, or from *Boulogne* in *Picardy*. The Scantlings are ſeldom above a Foot broad, and are of a bright tranſparent Sort of Plaiſter or Talk, endued by Nature with a particular Property, namely, that it never decays.

CHAP. XIII.

Of the Altar, Communion, Lights, Candleſticks, Holy Veſſels, and ſome other noble Ornaments of Temples.

THE next chief Point to be conſidered in the Temple, is fixing the Altar, where Divine Office is to be performed, which ſhould be in the moſt honourable Place, and this ſeems to be exactly in the Middle of the Tribune. The Ancients uſed to make their

Altar

Altar ſix Foot high and twelve Broad; and on it placed the Statue of their Deity. Whether or no it be proper to have more Altars for Sacrifice in a Temple, than one, I ſhall leave to the Judgment of others. Among our Forefathers, in the primitive Times of our Religion, the devout Chriſtians uſed to meet together at the Holy Supper, not to fill their Bodies with Food, but in order to ſoften and humanize their Manners by frequent Converſation and Communion with each other; and having filled their Minds with good Inſtructions, they returned every Man to his own Home, warmed and inflamed with the Love of Virtue. For having rather taſted than eat the moderate Portion that was ſet before them, they read and reaſoned upon all Sort of divine Subjects. Every one burnt with Charity towards his Neighbour, for their common Salvation, and for the Divine Worſhip. Laſtly, every Man, according to his Power, paid a Kind of Tax due to Piety, for the Maintenance of ſuch as truly deſerved it, and the Biſhop diſtributed theſe Contributions among ſuch as wanted. Thus all Things were common among them, as among loving Brethren. Afterwards when Princes conſented that theſe Duties ſhould be performed publickly, they did not indeed deviate much from the Inſtitution of their Forefathers; but as greater Numbers came in than before, the Supper was ſtill more moderate. The Sermons preached in thoſe Times by the learned Biſhops, are ſtill extant in the Writings of the Fathers. Thus in thoſe Ages they had but one Altar, where they uſed to meet to celebrate only one Sacrifice in a Day. Next ſucceeded theſe our Times, which I wiſh to God ſome worthy Man might ariſe to reform, and be this ſaid without Offence to our Popes, who, though to keep up their own Dignity, they hardly ſuffer themſelves to be ſeen by the People once in a Year, yet have ſo crowded every Place with Altars, and perhaps too with -------But I ſhall venture to ſay no more. This I may venture to affirm, that as there is nothing in Nature can be imagined more Holy or Noble than our Sacrifice, ſo I believe no Man of Senſe can be for having it debaſed by being made too common. There are other Sorts of Ornaments alſo, not fixed, which ſerve to adorn and grace the Sacrifice; and others of the ſame Nature that embelliſh the Temple itſelf, the Direction of which belongs likewiſe to the Architect. It has been a Queſtion which is the moſt beautiful Sight: A large Square full of Youth employed about their ſeveral Sports; or a Sea full of Ships; or a Field with a victorious Army drawn out in it; or a Senate-houſe full of venerable Magiſtrates; or a Temple illuminated with a great Number of chearful Lights? I would deſire that the Lights in a Temple ſhould have ſomewhat of a Majeſty in them which is not to be found in the blinking Tapers that we uſe now-a-days. They might, indeed, have a good Effect enough if they were ſet in Rows with any thing of a pretty Regularity, or ſtuck all along the Edge of the Cornice. But I am much better pleaſed with the Ancients, who on the Top of their Candleſticks fixed large Shells in which they lighted an odoriferous Flame. They divided the whole Length of the Candleſticks into ſeven Parts, two of which they gave to the Baſe, which was triangular, and longer than it was broad , and broader at Botton than at Top . The Shaft of the Candleſtick was divided by ſeveral little Pans placed one above the other, to catch the Drops that fell from the upper Shell; and at the Top of all was that Shell, full of Gums and odoriferous Woods. We have an Account how much ſweet Balm uſed to be burnt on every Holyday in the principal Churches by the Emperor's Order in *Rome*, at the publick Charge; and it was no leſs than five hundred and four ſcore Pounds Weight. And this may ſuffice as to Lamps: Let us now juſt mention ſome other Things, which are very noble Ornaments in Temples. We read that *Gyges* gave to the Temple of the *Pythian Apollo*, ſix great Cups of maſſy Gold, which weighed thirty thouſand Pound Weight; and that at *Delphos* there were Veſſels of ſolid Gold and Silver, each of which would contain ſix Amphoras, or about four-and-fifty of our Gallons, among which there were ſome that were more valued for the Invention and Workmanſhip than for the Metal. We are told that in the Temple of *Juno* at *Samos*, there was a Veſſel, carved all about with Figures in Steel, ſent by the *Spartans* as a Preſent to *Crœſus*, ſo large, that it would hold three hundred Amphoras, or two thouſand ſeven hundred Gallons. We read too that the *Samians* ſent as a Preſent to *Delphos* an iron Cauldron with the Heads of ſeveral Animals finely wrought upon it, and ſupported ſeveral kneeling coloſſal Statues ten Foot and a half high. It was a wonderful Contrivance of *Sanniticus* the *Ægyptian*, in the Temple of the God *Apis*, which was extremely rich in different

rent

rent Columns and Statues, in making an Image of that God which was continually turning round to face the Sun. And there was somewhat yet more wonderful than this in the Temple of *Diana* at *Ephesus*; which was, *Cupid's* Dart hanging upon nothing. For such kind of Ornaments no other certain Rule can be given, but that they be set in decent Places, where they may be viewed with Wonder and Reverence.

CHAP. XIV.

Of the first Original of Basiliques, their Porticoes and different Members, and wherein they differ from Temples.

IT is certain that at first Basiliques were nothing but Places where the Magistrates used to meet to administer Justice under Shelter, and the Tribunal was added to give the greater Air of Majesty to the Structure. Afterwards in order to enlarge them, the principal Roof being found not sufficient, Porticoes were added on each Side, first a single, and in Time a double one. Others across the Tribunal made a Nave, which we shall call the Justiciary Nave, as being the Place for the Concourse of the Notaries, Sollicitors and Advocates, and joined this Nave to the other Isles after the Manner of the Letter T. The Porticoes without were supposed to be added afterwards for the Convenience of Servants: So that the Basilique consists of Naves or Isles, and of Porticoes: But as the Basilique seems to partake of the Nature of the Temple, it has claimed most of the Ornaments belonging to the Temple, but still in such a Manner as to seem rather to imitate than to pretend to equal it in Embellishments. It is raised above the Level of the Ground, like the Temple, but an eighth Part less; that so it may yield to the Temple, as to the more honourable Structure: And indeed none of its other Ornaments must be allowed the same Solemnity as those used in a Temple. Moreover there is this further Difference between the Basilique and the Temple, that the Isles in the former must be clear and open, and its Windows perfectly lightsome, upon account of the sometimes tumultuous Crowd of Litigants, and for the Conveniency of examining and subscribing to Writings; and it would be very proper, if it could be so contrived, that such as came to seek either their Clients or their Patrons, might immediately find them out; For which Reason the Columns ought to be set at a greater Distance from each other; and therefore those that support Arches are the most proper, though such as bear Architraves are not to be wholly rejected. Thus we may define the Basilique to be a clear spacious Walk covered with a Roof, with Porticoes or Isles on the Inside; because that which is without Isles seems to me to have more in it of the Court of Justice or Senate-house, whereof we shall speak in due Time, than of the Basilique. The Platform of the Basilique should be twice as long as broad; and the chief Isle, which is that in the Middle, and the cross one, which we have called the Justiciary, should be entirely clear and free for Walkers. If it is to have only one single Isle on each Side, without the Justiciary Nave, you may order your Proportions as follows: Divide the Breadth of the Platform into nine Parts, whereof five of them must be allowed to the middle Isle, and two to each Portico or side Isle. The Length too must be divided into nine Parts, one of which must be given to the Sweep of the Tribunal, and two to the Breadth or Entrance into that Tribunal. But if besides the side Isle you would have a Justiciary Nave, then divide the Breadth of the Platform only into four Parts, giving two to the middle Isle, and one to each side Isle; and divide the Length as follows: Give one twelfth Part of it to the Sweep of the Tribunal, two twelfths and an half to the Breadth of its Entrance, and let the Breadth of the Justiciary Nave be the sixth Part of the Length of the whole Platform. But if you are to have not only the Justiciary Nave, but double Isles besides; then divide the Breadth of the Platform into ten Parts, giving four to the middle Isle, and three on each Side to be divided equally for the side Isles, and divide the Length into twenty Parts, giving one and a half to the Sweep of the Tribunal, and three and one third to its Entrance, and allowing only three Parts to the Breadth of the Justiciary Nave. The Walls of the Basilique need not be so thick as those of the Temple; because they

* See Plates 38 and 39, following page 156.
† See Plates 40 and 41, following page 156.
‡ See Plates 42 and 43, following page 156.

they are not designed to support the Weight of a vaulted Roof, but only a flat one of Summers and Rafters. Let their Thickness therefore be only one twentieth Part of their Height, and let their Height be only once the Breadth of the Front and an Half, and never more. At the Angles of the Isles come out Pilasters from the Naked of the Wall, running parallel with, and on a Line with, the Columns, not less than twice, nor more than three Times the Thickness of the Wall. Others, still more to strengthen the Building, make such a Pilaster in the Middle of the Row of Columns, in Breadth three of the Diameters of one the Columns, or at most four. The Columns themselves too must never have the same Solidity as those used in Temples; and therefore, if we make our Colonades with an Architrave over it, we may observe the following Rules. If the Columns are to be *Corinthian*, substract a twelfth Part from their Diameter; if *Ionic*, a tenth; if *Doric*, a ninth. As for the Composition of the other Members, the Capitals, Architrave, Freze, Cornice, and the like, you may proceed in the same Manner as in Temples.

Chap. XV.

Of Colonades both with Architraves and with Arches; what Sort of Columns are to be used in Basiliques, and what Cornices, and where they are to be placed; of the Height and Wedth of Windows and their Gratings; of the Roofs and Doors of Basiliques, and their Ornaments.

COLUMNS that are to have Arches over them, ought by rights to be square; for if they were round, the Work would not be true, because the Heads of the Arches would not lie plum upon the Solid of the Column underneath; but as much as their Squares exceeded a Circle, so much of them would hang over the Void. To remedy this Defect, the best ancient Masters placed over the Capitals of their Columns another Abacus or Plinth, in Thickness sometimes one fourth and sometimes one fifth Part of the Diameter of the Column; the upper Part of this Plinth, which went off with a Cima-recta, was equal to the greatest Breadth of the Top of the Capital, and its Projecture was equal to its Height, so that by this means the Heads and Angles of the Arches had a fuller and firmer Seat. Colonades with Arches, as well as those with Architraves, are various, some being thinner set, others closer, and so on. In the closer Sort the Height of the Void must be three Times and an half the Breadth of the Aperture; in the thin Set, the Height must be once the Breadth and two thirds; in the less thin, the Height must be twice the Breadth; in the closest of all, the Breadth must be one third of the Height. We have formerly observed, that an Arch is nothing else but a Beam bent. We may therefore give the same Ornaments to Arches as to Architraves, according to the different Sorts of Columns over which they are turned; besides which, if we would have our Structure very rich, over the Heads of our Arches we may run an Architrave, Freze, and Cornice in a straight Line, with the same Proportions as we should make them over Columns that should reach to that Height. But as the Basilique is sometimes encompassed only with one single Isle, and at other Times with two, the Place of the Cornice over the Columns and Arches must vary accordingly. In those which are encompassed only with one single Portico, having divided the Height of your Wall into nine Parts, the Cornice must go only to five; or if you divide it into seven, to four. But in those which are to have double Isles, the Cornice must be placed at one third of the Height of the Wall at least, and at never more than three eighths. We may also over the first Cornice, as well for the greater Ornament as for real Use, place other Columns, and especially Pilasters, directly plum over the Centers of the Columns which are below them. And this indeed is of great Service, as it maintains the Strength and Firmness of the Ribs of the Work, and adds Majesty to it, and at the same Time takes off much from the Weight and Expence of the Wall; and over this upper Colonade too we make a regular Entablature, according to the Order of the Columns. In Basiliques with double Side Isles, we may raise three Rows of Columns in this Manner one above another; but in others we should make but two. Where you

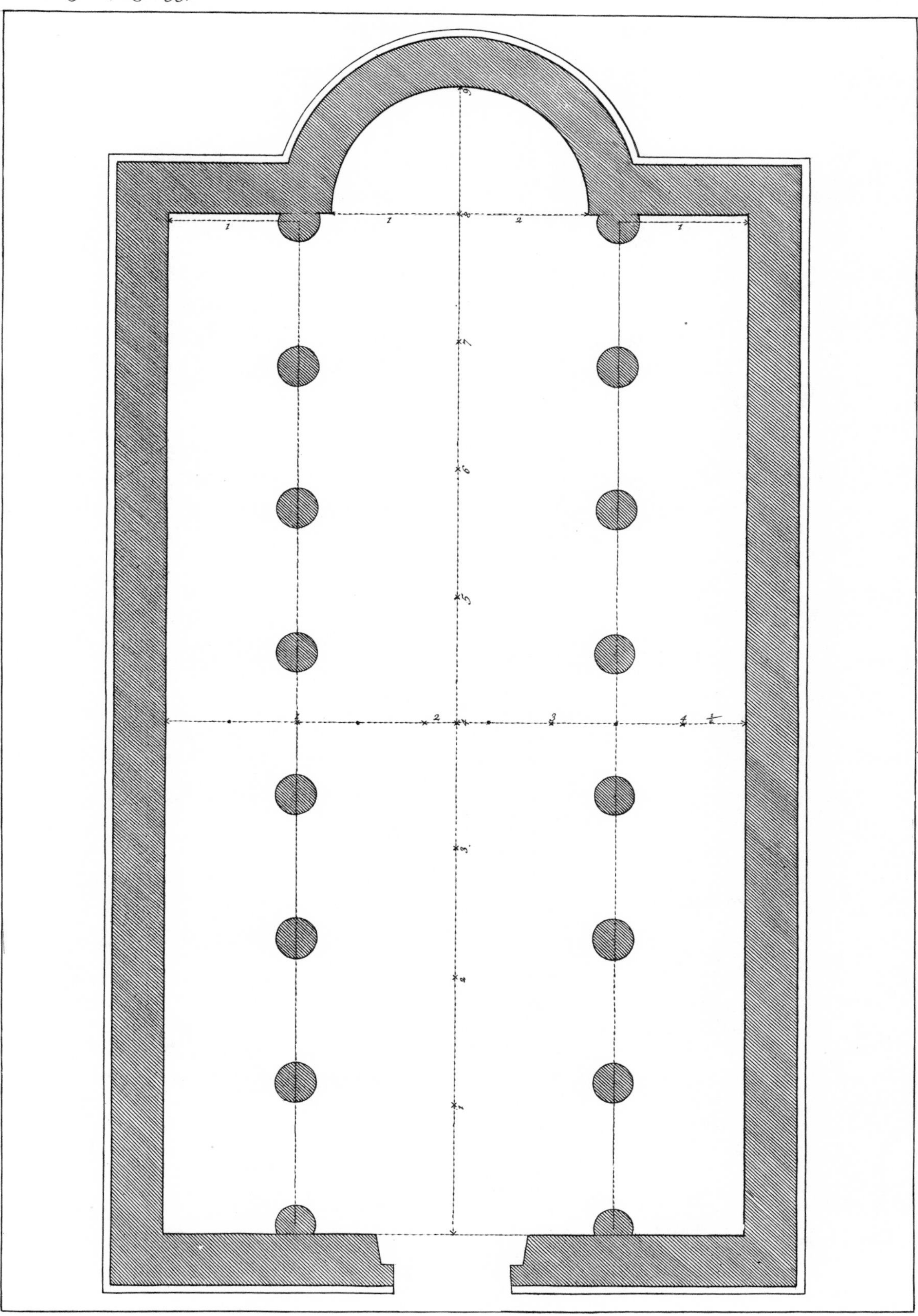

J. Leoni delin.

PLATE 39. *(Page 155)*

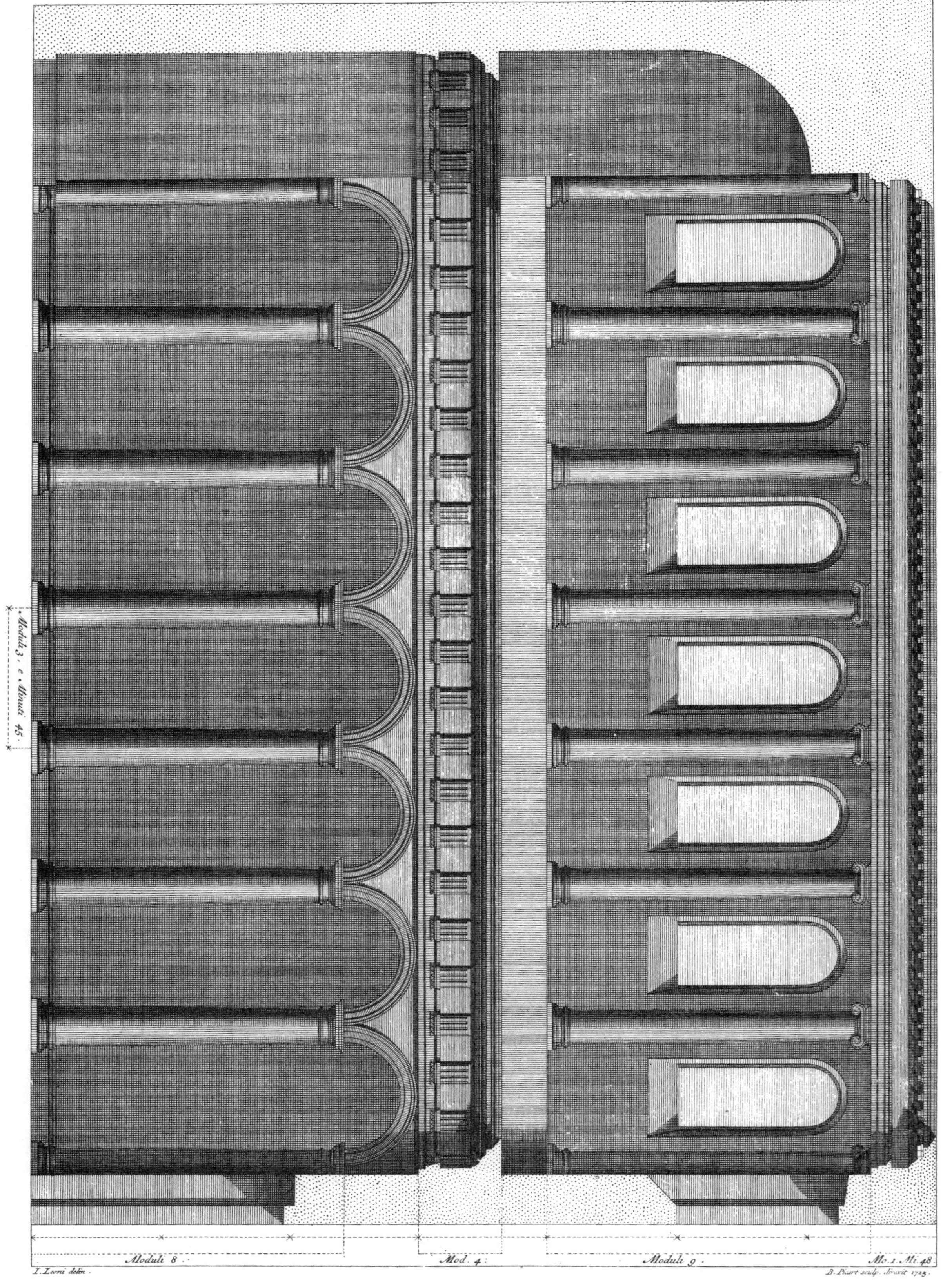

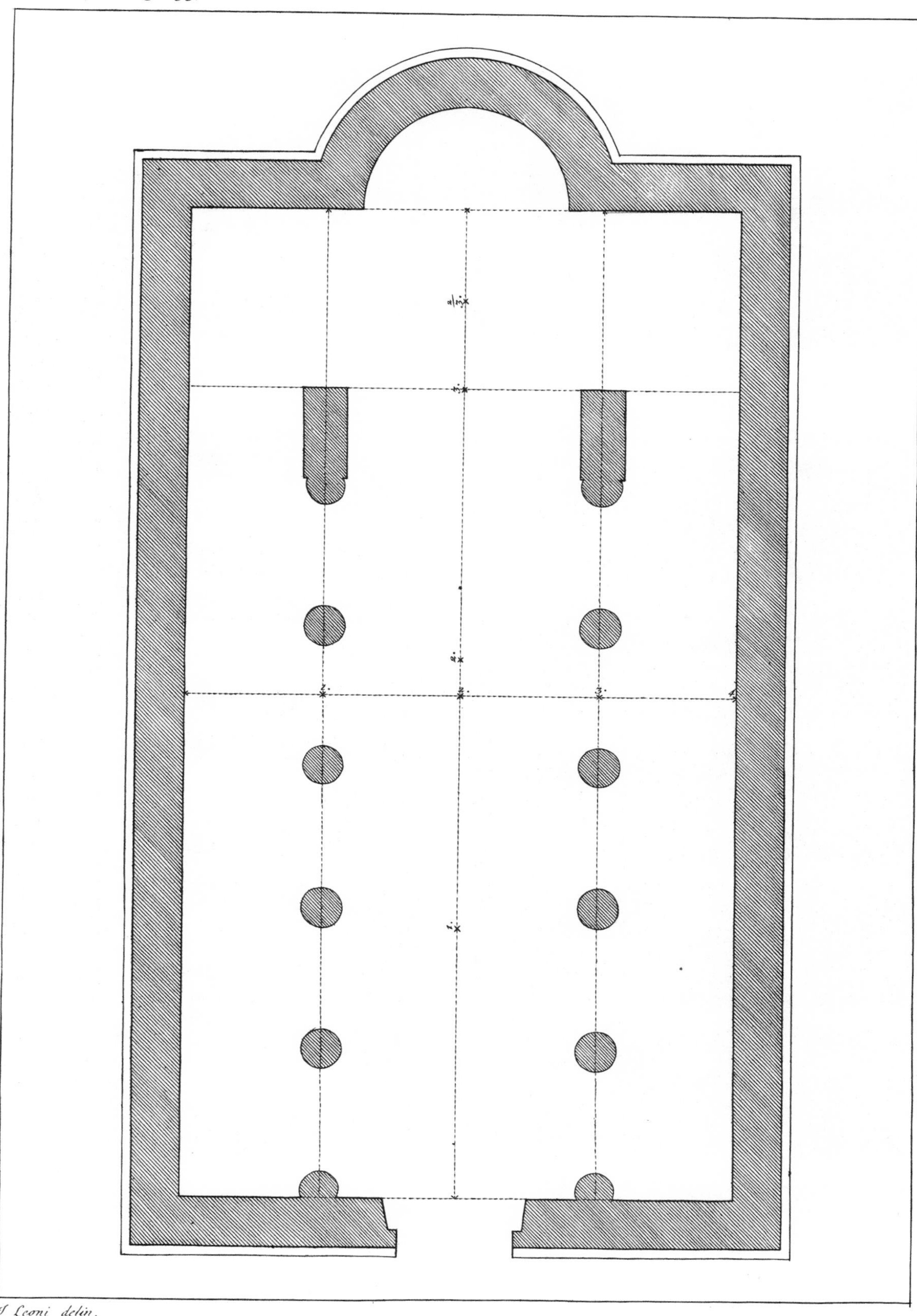

J. Leoni delin.

I. Leoni delin.

B. Picart sculp. direxit 1725.

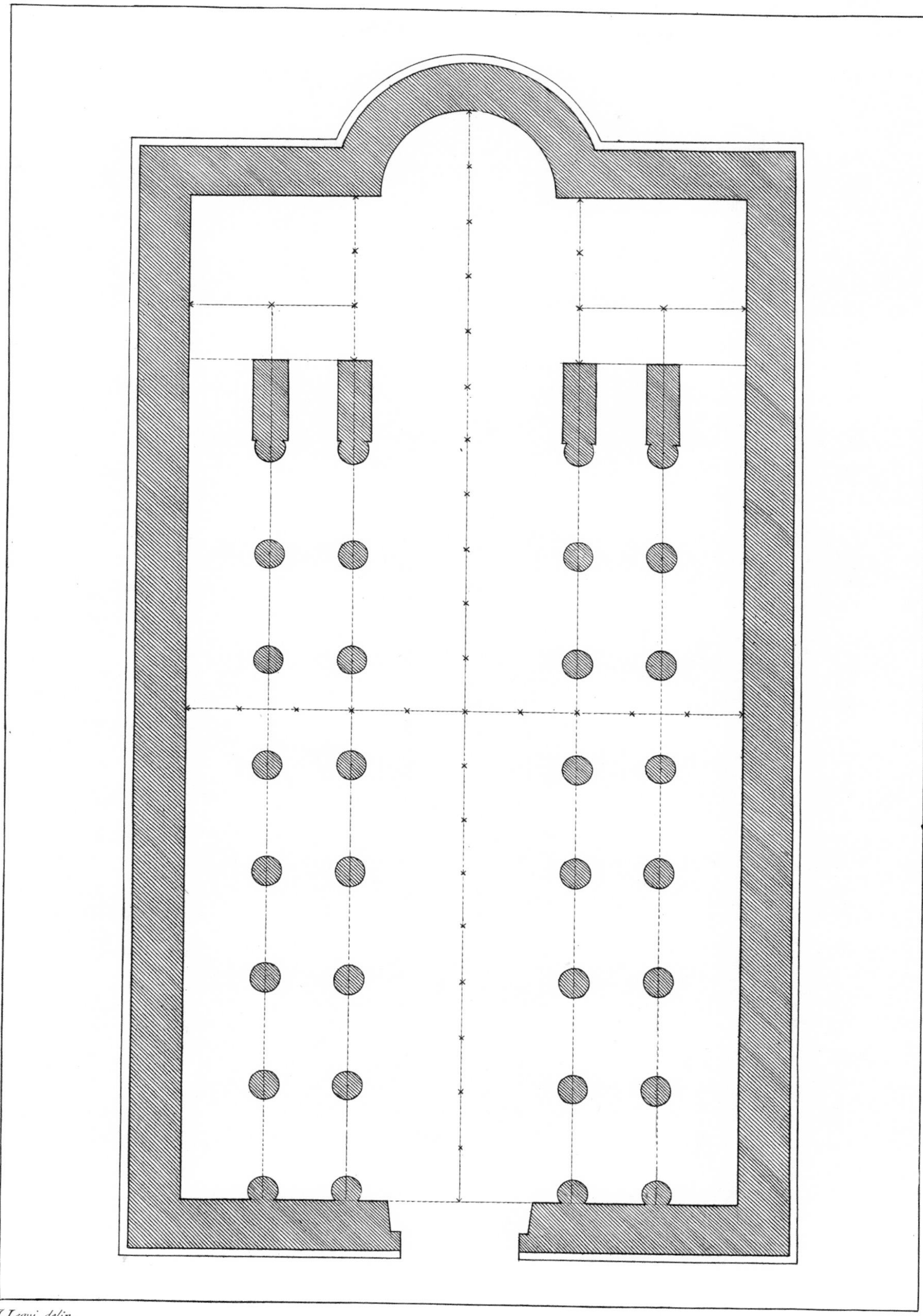

J. Leoni delin.

PLATE 43. *(Pages 155–56)*

you have three Rows of Columns, divide the Space that is between the first Row and the Roof into two Parts, and in that Division end the second Cornice. Between the first and second Cornices, let the Wall be preserved entire, and adorn it with some beautiful Sorts of Stuc-work; but in the Wall between the second and the third Cornices, you must make your Windows for lighting the whole Structure. The Windows in Basiliques must be set exactly over the Intercolumnations, and answer regularly to one another. The Breadth of these Windows must not be less than three Fourths of the Intercolumnation, and their Height may very conveniently be twice their Breadth. Their Head-piece may be upon a Line with the Top of the Columns, exclusive of the Capitals, if these Windows be made square; but if they are round, their Arch may come almost even with the Architrave, and so lower as you think fit to diminish the Arch; but they must never rise above the Tops of the Columns. At the Bottom of the Window must be a Plat-band for a Rest or Leaning Place, with a Cima-recta and an Ovolo. The Open of the Window must be grated, tho' not paned with scantling Tale like those of the Temple; but still they must have something to keep out Wind and Weather. On the other Hand, it is necessary to have a free Vent for the Air, that the Dust which is raised by the Peoples Feet may not injure their Eyes and Lungs; and therefore I think nothing does better here, than those fine Grates, either of Brass or Lead, with an infinite Number of small Holes disposed in a regular Order, almost like a Picture, which admit both Light and Air to refresh the Spirits. The Roof or Ceiling will be extreamly handsome, if it is composed of different Pannels nicely jointed together, with large Circles, in handsome Proportions, mixed with other Compartments and Angles, and if those Pannels are separated from each other with flying Cornices, with all their due Members, and with their Coffits adorned with carved Work of Gems in Relief, intermixed with beautiful Flowers, either of the Acanthus or any other, the Pannels being enriched with lively Colours, by the Hand of some ingenious Painter, which will add a singular Grace to the whole Work. *Pliny* tells us of an extraordinary Cement for laying Gold upon Wood-work; which may be made as follows. Mix together six Pounds of Sinoper, or Terra Pontica, and ten Pounds of red Oker, mixed with two Pounds of Terra Melina or White Lead, which must be all ground together, and the past kept full ten Days before it is used. Mastic steept in Linseed Oil, and mixed with Helbic Sinoper or Ruddle well burnt, makes a Cement or Glue that will hardly ever come off. The Height of the Door of the Basilique must be answerable to that of the Isles. If there be a Portico on the Outside, by Way of Vestibule, it must be of the same Height and Breadth as the Isle within. The Void Chambranle, and other Members of the Door must be made after the same Rules at the Door of the Temple; but in a Basilique the Leaf should never be of the Brass. But you may make it of Cypress, Cedar, or any other fine Wood, and enrich it with Bosses of Brass, contriving the Whole rather for Strength than Delicacy: Or if you would have it beautiful or noble, do not embelish it with any minute Ornaments in Imitation of Painting, but adorn it with some Relieve, not too high raised, that may make the Work look handsome, and not to be too liable to be injured. Some have of late begun to build Basiliques circular. In these the Height in the Middle must be equal to the Breadth of the whole Structure; but the Porticoes, Colonades, Doors and Windows must be in the same Proportions as in the square Basilique. Of this Subject sufficient has been said.

CHAP. XVI.

Of Monuments raised for preserving the Memory of publick Actions and Events.

I Come now to speak of Monuments erected for preserving the Memory of great Events; and here by Way of Relief I shall take the Liberty to unbend myself a little from that Intenseness and Dryness which is necessary in those Parts of this Work which turn altogether upon Numbers and Proportions: However, I shall take Care not to be too prolix. Our

Anceſtors, when, having overcome their Enemies, they were endeavouring with all their Power to enlarge the Confines of their Empire, uſed to ſet up Statues and Terms to mark the Courſe of their Victories, and to diſtinguiſh the Limits of their Conqueſts. This was the Origin of Pyramids, Obelisks, and the like Monuments for the Diſtinction of Limits. Afterwards being willing to make ſome Acknowledgment to the Gods for the Victories which they had gained, they dedicated Part of their Plunder to Heaven, and conſecrated the publick Rejoycings to Religion. This gave Riſe to Altars, Chapels, and other Monuments neceſſary for their Purpoſes. They were alſo deſirous of eternizing their Memory to Poſterity, and of making even their Perſons, as well as Virtues known to future Ages. This produced Trophies, Spoils, Statues, Inſcriptions, and the like Inventions for propagating the Fame of great Exploits. People of lower Rank too, tho' not eminent for any particular Service done their Country, but only for their Wealth or Proſperity, were fond of imitating the ſame Practice, in which many different Methods have been taken. The Terms erected by *Bacchus*, at the End of his Progreſs thro' *India*, were Stones ſet up at certain Diſtances, and great Trees with their Trunks encompaſſed with Ivy. At *Lyſimachia* was a very large Altar, which was ſet up by the *Argonauts*, when they paſſed by that Place in their Voyage. *Pauſanias*, on the Banks of the River *Hippanis*, near the Black Sea, fixed a huge Vaſe of Braſs, ſix Inches thick, which would contain ſix hundred * Amphoras. *Alexander*, near the River *Alceſtes*, which falls into the Ocean, erected twelve Altars of prodigious large ſquare Stones, and near the *Tanais* ſurrounded all the Space of Ground which his Army took up in its Encampment, with a Wall which was ſeven Miles and an half in Compaſs. *Darius*, having ſet down his Camp near *Othryſia*, upon the River *Arteſroe*, commanded his Soldiers to throw each of them one Stone in different Heaps, which being very large and numerous, might fill Poſterity with Aſtoniſhment. *Seſoſtris*, in his Wars, erected an Obelisk with handſome Inſcriptions, in Honour of thoſe who made a brave Reſiſtance againſt him; but thoſe who ſubmitted baſely he branded with Infamy, by ſetting up Obelisks and Columns with the Pudenda of a Woman carved upon them. *Jaſon*, in all the Countries thro' which he paſſed, erected Temples in his own Honour, which we are told were all demoliſhed by *Parmenio*, to the Intent, that no Memorial might any where remain but that of *Alexander*. Theſe were Monuments erected during the Expeditions themſelves; others, ſuch as follow, were raiſed after the Victory obtained, and the Conqueſt compleated. In the Temple of *Pallas*, *the Diligent* hung the Shackles with which the *Lacedemonians* had been fettered. The *Evians* not only preſerved in their Temple the Stone with which the *Phymian* King ſlew the King of *Machienſes*, but even worſhiped it as a God. The *Æginetæ* dedicated to their Temple the Beaks of the Ships which they took from their Enemies. In Imitation of them *Auguſtus*, having overcome the *Ægyptians*, erected four Trophies of the Beaks of their Ships; which were afterwards removed to the Capitol by the Emperor *Domitian*. *Julius Cæſar* had before raiſed two of the ſame Sort, one upon the Roſtrum, and the other before the Senate, upon defeating the *Carthaginians* in a naval Engagement. Why need I mention that infinite Number of Towers, Temples, Obelisks, Pyramids, Labyrinths, and the like Works which we read of in Hiſtorians? I ſhall only obſerve, that this Deſire of perpetuating their Names by ſuch Structures, roſe to ſuch a Pitch among the Heroes of old, that they even built Towns for no other Purpoſe, calling them by their own Names to deliver them down to Poſterity. *Alexander*, not to mention many others, beſides thoſe Cities which he built in Honour of his own Name, went ſo far as to build one after the Name of his Horſe *Bucephalus*. But in my Opinion, what *Pompey* did was much more decent; when having defeated *Mithridates* in the lower *Armenia*, he built the City *Nicopolis* (or of Victory) in the very Place where he had been Conqueror. But *Seleucus* ſeems to have far outſtript all theſe; for he built three Cities in Honour of his Wife, and called them *Apamia*; five in Honour of his Mother, by the Name of *Laodicea*; nine called *Seleucia*, in Honour of his own Name; and ten in Memory of his Father, which were called *Antiocha*. Others have made themſelves famous to Poſterity, not ſo much by Magnificence and Expence, as by ſome particular new Invention. *Cæſar*, with the Berries of the Laurel which he had worn in Triumph, planted a Grove which he conſecrated to future Triumphers. Near *Aſcalon* in *Syria*, was a famous

* An Amphora was about nine Gallons of our Meaſure.

a famous Temple, in which ſtood the Statue of *Dercetis* (the ſame that is called in Scripture *Dagon*) with his upper Parts like a Man, and his lower like a Fiſh; who was thus honoured, becauſe from that Place he threw himſelf into the Lake: And if any *Sytian* taſted of the Fiſh that was in it, he was looked upon as excommunicate. The *Mutinii*, or ancient *Modeneze*, near the Lake *Fucinus*, repreſented *Medea* the Serpent-killer, under the Shape of a Serpent, becauſe by her Means they fancied themſelves freed from thoſe Animals. Of the ſame Nature was *Hercules*'s *Lernæan Hydra*, *Io* changed into a Cow, and the other Fables related in the Verſes of the ancient Poets; with which Inventions I am very much delighted, provided ſome virtuous Precept be contained in them; as in that Symbol which was carved upon *Symandes*'s Sepulchre, in which was a Judge ſurrounded by ſome other chief Magiſtrates cloathed in the Habits of Prieſts, and from their Necks hung down upon their Breaſts the Image of Truth with her Eyes clos'd, and ſeeming to nod her Head towards them. In the Middle was a Heap of Books, with this Inſcription upon it: This is the true Phyſick of the Mind.

But the Invention of Statues was the moſt excellent of all, as they are a noble Ornament for all Sorts of Structures, whether ſacred or profane, publick or private, and preſerve a wonderful Repreſentation both of Perſons and Actions. Whatever great Genius it was that invented Statues, it is thought they owe their Beginning to the ſame Nation as the Religion of the ancient *Romans*; the firſt Statue being by ſome ſaid to be made by the *Etrurians*. Others are of Opinion, that the *Telchines* of *Rhodes*, were the firſt that made Statues of the Gods, which being formed according to certain magical Rules, had Power to bring up Clouds and Rain, and other Meteors, and to change themſelves into the Shapes of different Animals. Among the *Greeks*, *Cadmus*, the Son of *Agenor*, was the firſt that conſecrated Statues of the Gods to the Temple. We are informed by *Ariſtotle*, that the firſt Statues that were placed in the publick Forum of *Athens*, were thoſe of *Harmodius* and *Ariſtogiton*, who were the firſt Deliverers of the City from Tyranny; and *Arrian* the Hiſtorian tells us, that theſe very Statues were ſent back again to *Athens* by *Alexander* from *Suſa*, whither *Xerxes* had removed them. The Number of Statues was ſo great at *Rome*, that they were called a Marble People. *Rhapſinates*, a very ancient *Ægyptian* King, erected a Statue of Stone to *Vulcan* above ſeven-and-thirty Foot high. *Seſoſtris* made Statues of himſelf and his Wife of the Height of eight-and-forty Foot. *Amaſis* ſet up a Statue near *Memphis*, in a leaning Poſture, which was forty-ſeven Foot long, and in its Pedeſtal were two others, each twenty Foot high. In the Sepulchre of *Simandes* were three Statues of *Jupiter*, made by *Memnon*, of wonderful Workmanſhip, being all cut out of one ſingle Stone, whereof one, which was in a ſitting Poſture, was ſo large, that only its Foot was above ſeven Foot and an Half long; and what was extremely ſurprizing in it, beſides the Skill of the Artiſt, in all that huge Stone there was not the leaſt Spot or Flaw. Others afterwards, when they could not find Stones large enough to make Statues of the Size which they deſired, made uſe of Braſs, and formed ſome of no leſs than an hundred Cubits, or an hundred and fifty Foot high. But the greateſt Work we read of in this Kind, was that of *Semiramis*, who not being able to find any Stone large enough for her Purpoſe, and being reſolved to make ſomething much bigger than was poſſible to be done with Braſs, contrived near a Mountain in *Media* called *Bagiſtan*, to have her own Image carved out of a Rock of two Miles and a furlong in Length, with the Figures of an hundred Men offering Sacrifice to her, hewn out of the ſame Stone. There is one Particular relating to this Article of Statues, mentioned by *Diodorus*, by no means to be omitted; which is, that the *Ægyptian* Statuaries were arrived at ſuch a Pitch of Skill in their Art, that they would out of ſeveral Stones in ſeveral different Places make one Statue, which when put together ſhould ſeem to be all the Work of one Hand; in which ſurprizing Manner we are told the Statue of the *Pythian Apollo* at *Samos* was made, one half of it being wrought by *Theleſius*, and the other half by *Theodorus* at *Epheſus*. Theſe Things I thought it not amiſs to write here by way of Recreation, which, though very uſeful in themſelves, are here inſerted only as an Introduction to the following Book, where we ſhall treat of the Monuments raiſed by private Perſons; to which they properly belong. For as private Men have ſcarce ſuffered even Princes to outdo them in Greatneſs of Expence for perpetuating their Memories, but being equally fired with the Deſire of making their Names famous, have ſpared for no Coſt which their Fortunes would bear,

bear, to get the Aſſiſtance and Skill of the beſt Artiſts for their Purpoſe; they have accordingly rivalled the greateſt Kings in fine Deſigns and noble Compoſitions, ſo as, in my Opinion, to be very little, if at all, inferior to them. But thoſe Works are reſerved for the next Book, in which I dare promiſe the Reader he ſhall find ſome Entertainment worth his Pains. But firſt we are here to ſpeak of ſome few Particulars neceſſary to our preſent Subject.

Chap. XVII.

Whether Statues ought to be placed in Temples, and what Materials are the moſt proper for making them.

SOME are againſt placing any Statues in Temples; and we are told that *Numa*, being a Diſciple of *Pythagoras*, would allow of none: And *Seneca* rallies himſelf and his Countrymen upon this Account; we play with Babies, ſays he, like Children. The Ancients, who were of this Opinion, uſed to argue concerning the Gods in the following Manner: Who can be ſo weak as not to know, that every Thing relating to the Gods is to be conſidered with the Mind, and not with the Eyes, ſince it is impoſſible to give them any Form that can be in the leaſt Degree anſwerable to the Excellence of their Nature? And indeed they thought that the having no viſible Repreſentations of them made by Hands, muſt have a very good Effect, as it would put every Man upon forming ſuch an Idea of the firſt Mover, and of the ſupreme Intelligence, as beſt ſuited his own Capacity and Way of Thinking: By which he would be the more induced to revere the Majeſty of the Divine Name. Others thought quite differently, holding, that the Gods were repreſented under human Forms to a very wiſe End, and that they had a very good Influence upon the Minds and Morals of the Vulgar, who when they approached thoſe Statues, imagined they were in the Preſence of the Gods themſelves. Others eſpecially were for ſetting up to publick View in conſecrated Places, the Effigies of ſuch as had deſerved well of Mankind, and were therefore ſuppoſed to be admitted among the Gods, believing it muſt inſpire Poſterity, when they came to worſhip them, with a Love of Glory, and an Emulation of their Virtue. It is certainly a Point of great Importance what Statues we ſet up, eſpecially in Temples, as alſo whereabouts, in what Number, and of what Materials: For no ridiculous Figures are to be admitted here, as of the God *Priapus*, that is uſually ſet up in Gardens to ſcare away the Birds; nor of fighting Soldiers, as in Porticoes, or the like; neither do I think they ſhould be placed in cloſe Nooks and mean Corners. But firſt let us treat of the Materials with which they ſhould be made, and then proceed to the other Points. Of old, ſays *Plutarch*, they uſed to make their Images of Wood; as was that of *Apollo* at *Delos*; and at *Popolonia*, near *Piombino*, was one of *Jupiter* of Vine-tree, which many affirmed to have remained perfectly clear of the leaſt Corruption. Of the ſame Sort was that of the *Epheſian Diana*, which ſome ſaid was of Ebony, but *Muſianus* tells us it was of Vine-tree. *Peras*, who built the Temple of *Juno* the *Argive*, and dedicated his Daughter to be Prieſteſs of it, made a *Jupiter* out of the Trunk of a Pear-tree. Some would not allow the Statues of the Gods to be made of Stone, as thinking that Material had ſomething in it too rugged and cruel. They alſo diſapproved of Gold and Silver for this Uſe, becauſe thoſe Metals are produced of a barren ungrateful Soil, and have a wan ſickly Hue. The Poet ſays:

Great Jove *ſtood crampt beneath the lowly Roof,*
Scarce full erect; and in his mighty Hand
Brandiſh'd aloft a Thunderbolt of Clay.

Some among the *Ægyptians* were of Opinion, that the Subſtance of God was Fire, and that he dwelt in the elemental Flame, and could not be conceived by the Senſes of Mankind: For which Reaſon they made their Gods of Chriſtal. Others thought the Gods ought to be made of black Stone, in the Suppoſition of that Colour being incomprehenſible; and others laſtly of Gold, in Conformity with the Colour of the Stars. I own for my Part, I have been very much in Suſpenſe what Materials was moſt proper for making Images that are to be the Objects of Worſhip. You will ſay, no doubt, that whatever is to be made into

into the Repreſentation of God, ought to be the nobleſt Material that can be had. Next to the nobleſt is the rareſt; and yet I would not be for making them of Salt, as *Solinus* informs us the *Sicilians* uſed to do; nor of Glaſs, like ſome mentioned by *Pliny*; neither would I have them of maſſy Gold or Silver, not that I diſlike thoſe Materials for being produced of a barren Soil, or for their ſickly Hue; but for other Reaſons: Among which one is, that I think it ſhould be a Point of Religion with us that thoſe Repreſentations which we ſet up to be adored as Gods, ſhould bear as much Reſemblance to the Divine Nature as poſſible. For this Reaſon, I would have them made immortal in Duration, as far as it is in the Power of mortal Men to effect it. And here I cannot help enquiring, what ſhould be the Reaſon of a very whimſical, though very old Perſuaſion, which is firmly rooted in the Minds of the Vulgar, that a Picture of God, or of ſome Saint in one Place ſhall hear the Prayers of Votaries, when in another Place the Statue of the very ſame God or Saint ſhall be utterly deaf to them? Nay, and what is ſtill more nonſenſical, if you do but remove the very ſame Statue, for which the People uſed to have the higheſt Veneration, to ſome other Station, they ſeem to look upon it as a Bankrupt, and will neither truſt it with their Prayers, nor take the leaſt Notice of it. Such Statues ſhould therefore have Seats that are fixed, eminent and peculiar to themſelves. It is ſaid, that there never was any beautiful Piece of Workmanſhip known in the Memory of Man to be made of Gold, as if that Prince of Metals diſdained to owe any thing to the Skill of an Artificer. If this be true, we ſhould never uſe it in the Statues of our Gods, which we ſhould deſire to make ſuitable to the Subject. Beſides that, the Thirſt of the Gold might tempt ſome not only to rob our Statue of his Beard, but to melt him quite down. I ſhould chuſe Braſs, if the lovely Purity of fine white Marble did not oblige me to give that the Preference. Yet there is one Conſideration which weighs very much in Favour of Braſs, and that is its Duration, provided we make our Statue not ſo maſſy, but that the Odium and Deteſtation of ſpoiling it may be much greater than the Profit to be made by melting it down for other Purpoſes: I would have it indeed no more than if it were beat out with a Hammer, or run into a thin Plate, ſo as to ſeem no more than a Skin. We read of a Statue made of Ivory, ſo large that it would hardly ſtand under the Roof of the Temple. But that I diſlike, for there ought to be a due Proportion obſerved as well in Size, as in Form and Compoſition: Upon which Accounts too the Figures of the greater Deities, with their gruff Beards, and ſtern Countenances, do not ſuit well in the ſame Place with the ſoft Features of Virgins. I am likewiſe of Opinion, that the having but few Statues of Gods, may help to increaſe the People's Veneration and Reverence to them. Two, or at moſt three, may be placed properly enough upon the Altar. All the reſt may be diſpoſed in Niches in other convenient Places. In all ſuch Repreſentations of Gods and Heroes, the Sculptor ſhould endeavour as much as poſſible, to expreſs both by the Habit and Action of the Figure, the Character and Life of the Perſon. Not that I approve of thoſe extravagant Attitudes which make a Statue look like the Hero of a Droll, or a Prize-fighter; but I would have ſomewhat of a Dignity and Majeſty both in the Countenance, and all the reſt of the Body, that ſhould ſpeak the God, ſo that he may ſeem both by his Look and Poſture to be ready to hear and receive his Adorers. Such ſhould be the Statues in Temples. Let others be left to Theatres, and other profane Edifices.

THE

ARCHITECTURE

OF

Leone Batista Alberti.

BOOK VIII. CHAP. I.

Of the Ornaments of the great Ways eitherwithin or without the City, and of the proper Places for interring or burning the Bodies of the Dead.

WE have formerly obferved, that the Ornaments annexed to all Sorts of Buildings make an effential Part of Architecture, and it is manifeft that every Kind of Ornament is not proper for every Kind of Structure. Thus we are to endeavour, to the utmoft of our Power, to make our facred Works, efpecially if they are of a publick Nature, as compleatly adorned as poffible, as being intended for the Honour of the Gods; whereas profane Structures are defigned entirely for Men. The meaner therefore ought to yield to the more honourable; but yet they too may be embellifhed with fuch Ornaments as are fuitable to them. In what Manner facred Buildings of a publick Nature are to be adorned, we have fhewn in the laft Book: We now come to profane Structures, and to give an Account what Ornaments are proper to each diftinct Sort of them. And firft I fhall take Notice, that all Ways are publick Works, as being contrived for the Ufe of the Citizens, and the Convenience of Strangers: But as there are Travellers by Water as well as by Land, we fhall fay fomething of both. And here it will be proper to call to Mind what has been faid elfewhere, that of Ways fome are properly Highways, others in a Manner but private ones; as alfo, that there muft be a Difference between the Ways within the City, and thofe in the Country. Highways in the Country receive their greateft Beauty from the Country itfelf through which they lie, from its being rich, well cultivated, full of Houfes and Villages, affording delightful Profpects, now of the Sea, now of a fine Hill, now a River, now a Spring, now a barren Spot and a Rock, now a fine Plain, Wood, or Valley; nor will it be a fmall Addition to its Beauty, that it be not fteep, broken by Precipices, or deep with Dirt; but clear, fmooth, fpacious and open on all Sides: and what Pains were not the Ancients at to obtain thefe Advantages? I fhall not wafte the Reader's Time to relate how they paved their Highways for above an hundred Miles round their Capital with extreme hard Stones, raifing folid Caufeways under them with huge Stones all the Way. The *Appian* Way was paved from *Rome* quite to *Brundufium.* In many Places along their Highways we fee Rocks demolifhed, Mountains levelled, Vallies raifed, Hills cut through, with incredible Expence and miraculous Labour; Works of great Ufe and Glory. Another great Embellifhment to a Highway, is its furnifhing Travellers with frequent Occafion of Difcourfe, efpecially upon notable Subjects. A Friend or Companion that is not fparing of his Speech, fays *Laberius*, upon a Journey is as good as a Vehicle; and there is no doubt but Difcourfe takes of much from

from the Fatigue of Travelling. For which Reaſon, as I had always the higheſt Eſteem for the Prudence of our Anceſtors in all their Inſtitutions, ſo I particularly commend them for that Cuſtom of theirs, whereof we ſhall ſpeak immediately, by which, though in it they aimed at much greater Ends, they afforded ſo much Recreation to Travellers. It was a Law of the twelve Tables, that no dead Body ſhould be interred or burnt within the City, and it was a very ancient Law of the Senate that no Corpſe ſhould be interred within the Walls, except the Veſtal Virgins, and the Emperors, who were not included within this Prohibition. *Plutarch* tell us, that the *Valeri* and the *Fabricii*, as a Mark of Honour, had a Privilege to be buried in the Forum; but their Deſcendants, having only ſet their dead down in it, and juſt clapt a Torch to the Body, uſed immediately to take it up again to bury it elſewhere; thereby ſhewing that they had ſuch a Privilege, but that they did not think it decent to make uſe of it. The Ancients therefore choſe their Sepulchres in convenient and conſpicuous Places by the Side of Highways, and embelliſhed them, as far as their Abilities and the Skill of the Architect would reach, with a perfect Profuſion of Ornaments. They were built after the nobleſt Deſigns; no Columns or Pilaſters were ſpared for, nor did they want the richeſt Incruſtations, nor any Delicacies that Sculpture or Painting could afford; and they were generally adorned with Buſts of Braſs or marble finiſhed after the moſt exquiſite Taſte: By which Cuſtom how much that prudent People promoted the Service of the Commonwealth and good Manners, would be tedious now to recapitulate. I ſhall only juſt touch upon thoſe Points which make to our preſent Purpoſe. And how, think ye, muſt it delight Travellers as they paſſed along the *Appian* Way, or any other great Road, to find them full of a vaſt Number of Tombs of the moſt excellent Workmanſhip, and to be every Moment picking out ſome more beautiful than the reſt, and obſerving the Epitaphs and Effigies of their greateſt Men? Do you not think that from ſo many Monuments of ancient Story, they muſt of Neceſſity take continual Occaſion to diſcourſe of the noble Exploits performed by thoſe Heroes of old, thereby ſweetning the Tedious̄neſs of their Journey, and exalting the Honour of *Rome*, their native City? But this was the leaſt of the good Effects which they produced; and it was of much more Importance that they conduced not a little the Preſervation of the Commonwealth, and of the Fortunes of private Perſons. One of the chief Cauſes why the Rich rejected the *Agrarian* Law, as we are informed by the Hiſtorian *Appian*, was becauſe they looked upon it to be an Impiety to ſuffer the Property of the Tombs of their Forefathers to be transferred to others. How many great Inheritances may we therefore ſuppoſe them to have left untouched to their Poſterity, merely upon this Principle of Duty, Piety or Religion, which elſe would have been prodigally waſted in Riot and Gaming? Beſides that thoſe Monuments were a very great Honour to the Name of the City itſelf, and of a great Number of private Families, and was a conſtant Incitement to Poſterity to imitate the Virtues of thoſe whom they ſaw ſo highly revered. Then again, with what Eyes think you, whenever ſuch a Misfortune happened, muſt they behold a furious and inſolent Enemy ranſacking among the Sepulchres of their Anceſtors? And what Man could be ſo baſe and cowardly, as not to be immediately inflamed with Rage and Deſire of revenging ſuch an Inſult upon his Country and his Honour? And what Boldneſs and Courage muſt Shame, Piety and Grief ſtir up in the Hearts of Men upon ſuch an Occaſion? The Ancients therefore are greatly to be praiſed; not that I preſume to blame the preſent Practice of burying our Dead within the City, and in holy Places, provided we do not lay them in our Temples, where our Magiſtrates and great Men are to meet for the Celebration of holy Rites, ſo as to pollute the moſt ſacred Offices with the noiſome Vapours of a rotting Corpſe. The Cuſtom of burning the Dead was much more convenient.

CHAP. II.

Of Sepulchres, and the various Manner of Burial.

I Shall here take an Opportunity to inſert ſome Things, which in my Opinion, are by no means to be omitted, concerning the Structure of Sepulchres, ſince they ſeem to partake of the Nature of publick Works, as being dedicated to Religion. Let the Place where you inter

inter a dead Body, ſays the old Law, be ſacred; and we ſtill profeſs the ſame Belief, namely, that Sepulchres belong to Religion. As Religion therefore ought to be preferred before all Things, I ſhall treat of theſe, though intended for the Uſe of private Perſons, before I proceed to profane Works of a publick Nature. There ſcarce ever was a People ſo barbarous, as to be without the Uſe of Sepulchres, except, perhaps, thoſe wild *Ichthyophagi* in the remote Parts of *India*, who are ſaid to throw the Bodies of their Dead into the Sea, affirming that it mattered little whether they were conſumed by Fire, Earth, or Water. The *Albani* of *Scythia* too thought it to be a Crime to take any Care of the Dead. The *Sabæans* looked upon a Corpſe to be no better than ſo much Dung, and accordingly they caſt the Bodies, even of their Kings, upon the Dunghill. The *Troglodytes* uſed to tie the Head and Feet of their Dead together, and ſo hurried them away, with Scoffs and Flouts, to the firſt convenient Spot of Ground they could find, without more Regard to one Place than to another, where they threw them in, ſetting up a Goat's Horn at their Head. But no Man who has the leaſt Tincture of Humanity, will approve of theſe barbarous Cuſtoms. Others, as well among the *Ægyptians* as the *Greeks*, uſed to erect Sepulchres not only to the Bodies, but even to the Names of their Friends; which Piety muſt be univerſally commended. It was a very laudable Notion among the *Indians*, that the beſt Monument was to live in the Memory of Poſterity; and therefore they celebrated the Funerals of their greateſt Men no otherwiſe than by ſinging their Praiſes. However, it is my Opinion, that Care ought to be taken of the dead Body, for the Sake of the Living; and for the Preſervation of the Name to Poſterity, there can be no Means more effectual than Sepulchres. Our Anceſtors uſed to erect Statues and Sepulchres, at the publick Expence, in Honour of thoſe that had ſpilt their Blood and loſt their Lives for the Commonwealth, as a Reward of their Services, and an Incitement to others to emulate their Virtue: But perhaps they ſet up Statues to a great many, but Sepulchres to few, becauſe they knew that the former were defaced and conſumed by Age; whereas the Sanctity of Sepulchres, ſays *Cicero*, is ſo annexed to the very Ground itſelf, that nothing can either efface or remove it: For whereas other Things are deſtroyed, Tombs grow more ſacred by Age. And they dedicated theſe Sepulchres to Religion, as I imagine, with this View, that the Memory of the Perſon, which they truſted to the Protection of ſuch a Structure, and to the Stability of the Ground, might be defended by the Reverence and Fear of the Gods, from all Violence from the Hand of Man. Hence proceeded the Law of the twelve Tables, that the Veſtibule or Entrance of a Sepulchre ſhould not be employed to any Man's private Uſe, and there was moreover a Law which ordained the heavieſt Puniſhment upon any Man that ſhould violate an Urn, or throw down or break any of the Columns of a Tomb. In a Word, the Uſe of Sepulchres has been received by all the politeſt Nations, and the Care and Reſpect of them was ſo great among the *Athenians*, that if any of their Generals neglected to give honourable Burial to one of thoſe that were ſlain in War, he was liable to capital Puniſhment for it. There was a Law among the *Hebrews*, which injoined them to give Burial even to their Enemies. Many and various are the Methods of Burial and Sepulture which we read of; but they are entirely foreign to our Deſign: As for Inſtance, that which is related of the *Scythians*, who thought the greateſt Honour they could do their Dead, was to eat them at their Meals; and others kept Dogs to devour them when they died: But of this we need ſay no more. Moſt of the wiſeſt Legiſlators have been careful to prevent Exceſs in the Expence and Magnificence of Funerals and Tombs. *Pittacus* ordained, that the greateſt Ornament that ſhould be erected over any Perſon's Grave, ſhould be three little Columns, one ſingle Cubit high; for it was the Opinion, that it was ridiculous to make any Difference in a Thing that was common to the Nature of every Man, and therefore in this Point the Richeſt and the Pooreſt were ſet upon the ſame Foot, and all were covered with common Earth, according to the old Cuſtom; in doing which it was the received Notion, that as Man was originally formed of Earth, ſuch a Burial was only laying him once more in his Mother's Lap. We alſo find an ancient Regulation, that no Man ſhould have a more magnificent Tomb, than could be built by ten Men in the Space of three Days. The *Ægyptians*, on the contrary, were more curious about their Sepulchres than any other Nation whatſoever; and they uſed to ſay, that it was very ridiculous in Men to take ſo much Pains in the building of Houſes where they were to dwell but a very ſhort Space of Time, and to neglect the Structure of a Habitation where they were

were to dwell for ever. The moſt probable Account I can find of the firſt Original of theſe Structures, is as follows: The *Getæ*, in the moſt remote Antiquity, uſed at firſt, in the Place where they interred a dead Body, to ſet up a Stone for a Mark, or perhaps (as *Plato* in his Laws more approves) a Tree, and afterwards they uſed to raiſe ſomething of a Fence about it to keep off the Beaſts from routing it up, or moving it out of its Place; and when the ſame Seaſon of the Year came round again, and they ſaw that Field either chequered with Flowers, or laden with Grain as it was when the Perſon died, it was no wonder if it awakened in them the Love of their dear Friends whom they had loſt, and prompted them to go together to the Place where they lay, relating and ſinging their Actions and Sayings, and dreſſing up their Monuments with whatever they thought would embelliſh them. Hence perhaps aroſe the Cuſtom among ſeveral different Nations, and particularly among the *Greeks*, of adorning and offering Sacrifices upon the Tombs of thoſe to whom they were much obliged. They met, ſays *Thucydides*, upon the Place, in Habits ſuitable to the Occaſion, bringing with them the firſt Fruits of their Harveſt, thinking the publick Performance of theſe Rites to be an Act of the greateſt Piety and Devotion. From whence I proceed to conjecture, that beſides raiſing the Ground over the Place of Burial, and erecting little Columns for Marks, they uſed alſo to raiſe little Alars whereon to celebrate thoſe Sacrifices with the greateſt Decency, and conſequently they took care to make them as convenient and beautiful as was poſſible. The Places where theſe Tombs were erected, were various amongſt the Ancients. According to the Pontificial Law, it was not permitted to erect a Tomb in any publick Square. *Plato* was of Opinion, that a Man ought not to be in the leaſt offenſive to human Society either alive or dead; and for this Reaſon he ordained that the Dead ſhould be interred without the City, in ſome barren Place. In Imitation of this, others ſet apart a certain determined Place of Burial, under the open Air, and out of the Way of all Reſort; which I highly approve: Others, on the contrary, preſerved the Bodies of their Dead in their Houſes, incloſed either in Salt or Terraſs. *Mycerinus*, King of *Ægypt*, incloſed the dead Body of his Daughter within a wooden Figure of a Bull, and commanded the Sacrificers to perform Obſequies in her Honour every Day. *Servius* relates, that the Ancients uſed to place the Sepulchres of their Sons, that had the greateſt Stock of Merit and Nobility, upon the Top of very high Hills. The *Alexandrians*, in the Time of *Strabo* the Hiſtorian, had Gardens and Incloſures conſecrated wholly to the Burial of the Dead. Our more modern Anceſtors uſed to build little Chapels, along the Sides of their great Churches, on purpoſe for Tombs. All through the Country, which was once the ancient *Latium*, we find the Burial-places of whole Families, made under Ground, with Urns ſtanding in Rows along the Walls full of the Aſhes of the Deceaſed, with ſhort Inſcriptions, and the Names of the Baker, Barber, Cook, Surgeon, and other Officers and Servants that were reckoned Part of the Family; in thoſe Urns which incloſed the Aſhes of little Children, once the Joy of their Mothers, they made their Effigies in Stuc; but thoſe of grown Men, eſpecially if they were noble, were made of Marble. Theſe were the Cuſtoms of the Ancients: Nor do I blame the making uſe of any Place indifferently for burying the Body, provided ſome diſtinguiſhed Place be choſen for ſetting up an Inſcription in the Perſon's Honour. Now what chiefly delights us in all Tombs, is the Deſign of the Structure, and the Epitaph. What Sort of Deſign the Ancients approved moſt in theſe Works, I cannot ſo eaſily affirm. *Auguſtus*'s Sepulchre in *Rome* was built of ſquare Blocks of Marble, ſhaded with Ever-greens, and at the Top ſtood his Statue. In the Iſland of *Tyrina*, not far from *Carmania*, the Sepulchre of *Erythræa* was a great Mound of Earth planted with wild Palm-trees. The Sepulchre of *Zarina*, Queen of the *Saces*, was a Pyramid of three Sides, with a Statue of Gold on the Top. *Archatheus*, one of *Xerxes*'s Lieutenants, had a Tomb of Earth erected for him by the whole Army. But the main Point which all ſeem to have aimed at, was to have ſomething different from all others, not as to condemn the Sepulchres of others, but to draw the Eyes of Men to take the greater Notice of them: And from this general Uſe of Sepulchres, and theſe conſtant Endeavours to invent ſomething new in that Way, the Conſequence at laſt was, that it was impoſſible to think of any thing which had not already been put in Practice to a very great Perfection, and all were extremely beautiful in their ſeveral Kinds. From the Obſervation I have made of the numberleſs Works of this Nature, I find that ſome had nothing in their Eye, but adorning that which was to contain the Body, while others went farther, and raiſed ſuch a Superſtructure as was proper for placing Epitaphs and Inſcriptións of the Perſon's Exploits. The former were contented with a plain Caſe for the Body, or with adding ſomewhat of a little Chapel about it, according to the Religion of the Place. But the others erected either a Column, or a Pyramid, an Obelisk, or ſome other great Superſtructure, not principally for containing the Body, but rather for delivering down the Name with Glory to Poſterity. We have already taken Notice, that there is a Stone called *Sarcophagus*, found at *Aſon*, a Town of *Troas*, which conſumes a dead Body immediately; and in any made Ground, conſiſting chiefly of old Rubbiſh, the Moiſture is preſently dried up. But I ſhall inſiſt no longer upon theſe minute Particulars.

Chap. III.

Of little Chapels, by way of Sepulchres, Pyramids, Columns, Alars and Moles.

NOW ſince the Sepulchres of the Ancients are generally approved, and we find them in different Places built ſometimes after the Manner of little Chapels, ſometimes in Pyramids, ſometimes Columns, and in ſeveral other Forms, as Moles and the like, we ſhall ſay ſomething of each of theſe: And firſt of Chapels. Theſe little Chapels ſhould be like ſo many little Models of Temples; nor is it at all improper to add the Ornaments and Deſigns of any other Sort of Building, provided they be equally well adapted both for Beauty and Duration. Whether it be moſt adviſeable to build a Sepulchre which we would have, if poſſible, endure to Eternity, of noble or mean Materials, is not thoroughly determined, upon Account of the Danger of their being removed for their Value. But the Beauty of its Ornaments, as we have obſerved elſewhere, is extremely effectual to its Preſervation, and to ſecuring the Monument to Poſterity. Of the Sepulchres of thoſe great Princes *Caius Caligula*, and *Claudius Cæſar*, which no doubt muſt have been very noble, nothing now remains but ſome few ſmall ſquare Stones of two Cubits broad, on which their Names are inſcribed; and if thoſe Inſcriptions had been cut upon larger Stones, I doubt not they too would e'er now have been carried away with the other Ornaments. In other Places we ſee Sepulchres of very great Antiquity, which have never been injured by any body, becauſe they were built of common Chequerwork, or of Stone that would not adorn any other Building, ſo that they were never any Temptation to Greedineſs. From whence I draw this Admonition to thoſe who would have their Sepulchres remain to Perpetuity, that they build not indeed with a baſe Sort of Stone, but not with ſuch excellent, as to be a Temptation to every Man that beholds it, and to be in perpetual Danger of being ſtolen away. Beſides, in all Works of this Nature, a decent Modeſty ſhould be obſerved according to every Man's Quality and Degree; ſo that, I condemn a Profuſion of Expence in the Tombs even of Monarchs themſelves, nor can I help blaming thoſe huge Piles, built by the *Ægyptian* Kings for their Sepulchres, which ſeem to have been diſpleaſing to the Gods themſelves, ſince none of them were buried in thoſe proud Monuments. Others perhaps may praiſe our *Etrurians* for not coming ſhort even of the *Ægyptians* in the Magnificence of their Tombs, and particularly *Porſena*, who built himſelf a Sepulchre below the Town of *Cluſium*, all of ſquare Stone, in the Baſe whereof, which was fifty Foot high, was a Labyrinth which no Man could find his Way thro', and over this Baſe five Pyramids, one in the Middle, and one at each Corner, the Breadth of each whereof, at the Bottom was ſeventy-five Foot; at the Top of each hung a brazen Globe, to which ſeveral little Bells were faſtened by Chains, which being ſhaken by the Wind might be heard at a conſiderable Diſtance: Over all this were four other Pyramids, an hundred Foot high, and others again over theſe, aſtoniſhing no leſs for their Workmanſhip than for their Greatneſs. I cannot be pleaſed with theſe enormous Structures, ſerving to no good Purpoſe whatſoever. There is ſomething much more commendable in the Tomb of *Cyrus*, King of the *Perſians*, and there is more true Greatneſs in his Modeſty, than in the vain Glory of all thoſe haughtier Piles. Near the Town of *Paſargardæ*, in a little vaulted Temple built of ſquare Stone, with a Door ſcarce two Foot high, lay the Body of *Cyrus*, incloſed in a golden Urn, as the Royal Dignity required; round

round this little Chapel was a Grove of all Sorts of Fruit-trees, and a large green Meadow, full of Roſes and other Flowers and Herbs of grateful Scent, and of every Thing that could make the Place delightful and agreeable. The Epitaph was adapted to the Structure:

> Cyrus *am I that founded* Perſia'*s State,*
> *Then envy not this little Place of Reſt.*

BUT to return to Pyramids. Some few perhaps may have built their Pyramids with three Sides, but they have generally been made with four, and their Height has moſt commonly been made equal to their Breadth. Some have been particularly commended for making the Joints of the Stones in their Pyramids ſo cloſe, that the Shadow which they caſt was perfectly ſtraight without the leaſt Interruption. Pyramids have for the moſt Part been made of ſquare Stone, but ſome few have been built with Brick. As for theſe Columns which have been erected as Monuments; ſome have been ſuch as are uſed in other Structures; others have been ſo large as to be fit for no Edifice; but merely to ſerve as a Monument to Poſterity.

* OF this laſt Sort we are now to treat, and its Members are as follows: Inſtead of a Baſement there are ſeveral Steps riſing above the Level of the Platform, over theſe a ſquare Plinth, and above that another not leſs than the firſt. In the third Place came the Baſe of the Column, then the Column with its Capital, and laſt of all the Statue ſtanding upon a Plinth. Some between the firſt and ſecond Plinths under the Baſe placed a Sort of Die to raiſe the Work higher, and give it the greater Air of Majeſty. The Proportions of all theſe Members are taken from the Diameter of the Bottom of the Shaft, as we obſerved with Relation to the Columns of the Temples; but the Baſe, in this Caſe where the Superſtructure is to be ſo very large, muſt have but one Torus, and not ſeveral like common Columns. The whole Thickneſs of the Baſe therefore muſt be divided into five Parts, two of which muſt be given to the Torus, and three to the Plinth. The Meaſure of the Plinth every Way muſt be one Diameter and a Quarter of the Shaft of the Column. The Pedeſtal on which this Baſe lies muſt have the following Parts. The uppermoſt Member in this, and indeed all other Ornaments, muſt be a Cymatium, and the lowermoſt a Plinth, which, whether it be in the Nature of Steps, or of a Cyma either upright or reverſed, is properly the Baſe of each Member. But we have ſome few Things relating to Pedeſtals to take Notice of, which we purpoſely omitted in the laſt Book, in order to conſider them here. We obſerved that it was uſual to run up a continued low Wall under all the Columns, in order to ſupport them; but then to make the Paſſage more clear and open, it was common to remove that Part of this Wall which lay between the Columns, and to leave only that Part which was really neceſſary to the Support of the Column. This Part of the Wall thus left I call the Pedeſtal. The Ornament of this Pedeſtal at the Top was a Cymatium, either upright or reverſed, or ſomething of the ſame Nature, which was anſwerd at the Bottom by a Plinth. Theſe two Ornaments went clear round the Pedeſtal. The Cymatium was the fifth Part of the Height of the whole Pedeſtal, or elſe the ſixth; and the Body of the Pedeſtal was never leſs in Thickneſs than the Diameter of the Bottom of the Shaft, that the Plinth of the Baſe might not lie upon a Void. Some, in order to ſtrengthen the Work yet more, made the Pedeſtal broader than the Plinth of the Baſe, by an eighth Part of that Plinth. Laſtly, the Height of the Pedeſtal, beſides its Cymatium and Plinth, was either equal to its Breadth, or a fifth Part more: And this I find to have been the Ordonnance of the Pedeſtal under the Columns uſed by the moſt excellent Workmen. But to return to the Column. Under the Baſe of the Column we are to place the Pedeſtal, anſwering duly to the Proportions of the Baſe in the Manner juſt now mentioned. This Pedeſtal muſt be crowned with an entire Cornice, which is moſt uſually of the *Ionic* Order; the Members of which you may remember to be as follows: The firſt and loweſt Member is a Cymatium, then a Denticle, next an Ovolo, with a ſmall Baguette and a Fillet. Under this Pedeſtal is placed another anſwerable to the former in every Member, and of ſuch a Proportion that no Part of the Superſtructure may lie over a Void; but to this Pedeſtal we muſt aſcend from the Level of the Ground by three or five Steps, unequal both in their Height and Breadth; and theſe Stepts all together muſt not be higher than a fourth, nor lower than a ſixth Part of the Height of the Pedeſtal which ſtands upon them. In this lower Pedeſtal we make a Door dreſſed after the Manner of the *Doric* or *Ionic* Order, according to the Rules already laid down for the Doors of Temples. In the upper Pedeſtal we place our Inſcriptions or carve Trophies. If we make any

* *See Plate 44, facing page 170.*

any Thing of a Plinth between these two Pedestals, the Height of that Plinth must be a third Part of the Height of the Pedestal itself; and this Interspace must be filled up with the Figures of chearful Deities, such as Victory, Glory, Fame, Plenty, and the like. Some covered the upper Pedestal with Plates of Brass, gilt. The Pedestals and the Base being compleated, the next Work is to erect the Column upon them, and its Height is usually seven Times its Diameter. If the Column be very high, let its upper Diameter be no more than one tenth Part less than its lower; but in smaller Columns, observe the Rules given in the last Book. Some have erected Columns an hundred Foot high, and enriched all the Body of the Shaft with Figures and Stories in Relieve, leaving a Hollow within for a winding Stair to ascend to the Top of the Column. On such Columns they set a *Doric* Capital, but without any Gorgerine. Over the upper Cymaise of the Capital in smaller Columns they made a regular Architrave, Freze and Cornice, full of Ornaments on every Side; but in these great Columns those Members were omitted, it being no easy Matter to find Stones sufficiently large for such a Work, nor to set them in their Places when found. But at the Top of the Capital both of great and small, there was always something to serve as a Pedestal for the Statue to stand upon. If this Pedestal was a square Plinth, then none of its Angles ever exceeded the Solid of the Column: But if it was round, its Diameter was not to be more than one of the Sides of such a Square. The Height of the Statue was one third of the Column; and for this Sort of Columns thus much may suffice. The Structure of Moles among the Ancients was as follows: First they raised a square Basement as they did for the Platforms of their Temples. Then they carried up a Wall not less high than a sixth, nor higher than a fourth of the Length of the Platform. The whole Ornament of this Wall was either at the Top and Bottom, and sometimes at the Angles, or else consisted in a Kind of Colonade all along the Wall. If there were no Columns but only at the Angles, then the whole Height of the Wall, above the Basement, was divided into four Parts, three of which were given to the Column with its Base and Capital, and one to the other Ornaments at the Top, to wit, the Architrave, Freze and Cornice; and this last Part was again divided into sixteen Minutes, five of which were given to the Architrave, five to the Freze, and six to the Cornice and its Cymaise. The Space between the Architrave and the Basement was divided into five-and-twenty Parts; three whereof were given to the Height of the Capital, and two to the Height of the Base, and the Remainder to the Height of the Column, and there were always square Pilasters at the Angles according to this Proportion: The Base consisted of a single Torus, which was just half the Height of the Base itself. The Pilaster at the Bottom, instead of a Fillet, had just the same Projecture as at the Top of the Shaft. The Breadth of the Pilaster, in this Sort of Structure, was one fourth of its Height; but when the rest of the Wall was adorned with an Order of Columns, then the Pilasters at the Angles were in Breadth only a sixth Part of their Length, and the other Columns along the Wall borrowed all their Ornaments and Proportions from the Design of those used in Temples. There is only this Difference between this Sort of Colonades and the former, that in the first, as the Base is continued on from one Angle of the Wall to the other, at the Bottom, so also are the Fillet and Astragal at the Top of the Column under the Architrave, which is not practiced where there are a Number of Columns set against the Wall; though some are for carrying on the Base quite round the Structure here as well as in Temples. Over this square Structure which served for a Basement, rose a round one of excellent Workmanship, exceeding the Basement in Height not less than half its Diameter, nor more than two thirds, and the Breadth of this Rotunda was never less than half one of the Sides of the Basement, nor more than five sixths. Many took five thirds, and over this round Building raised another square one, with a second round over that, after the same Manner as the former, till the Edifice rose to four Stories, adorning them according to the foregoing Description. Neither within the Mole itself wanted there Stairs, or little Chapels for Devotion, or Columns rising from the Basement to the upper Stories, with Statues between them, and Inscriptions disposed in convenient Places.

Chap.

CHAP. IV.

Of the Inſcriptions and Symbols carved on Sepulchres

LET us now proceed to the Inſcriptions themſelves, the Uſe whereof was various, and almoſt infinite among the Ancients, being by them not only uſed in their Sepulchres, but alſo in their Temples, and even in their private Houſes. *Symmachus* tells us, that on the Pediments of their Temples they uſed to cut the Name of the God to whom they dedicated, and it is the Practice with our Countrymen to inſcribe upon their Churches the Name of the Saints, and the Year when they were conſecrated to them; which I highly approve. Nor is it foreign to our Subject to take Notice, that when *Crates* the Philoſopher came to *Cyzicus*, finding theſe Verſes wrote over the Door of almoſt every private Houſe:

The mighty Hercules, *the Son of* Jove,
The Sceurge of Monſters, dwells within theſe Walls.
Let nothing ill dare to approach the Place.

HE could not help laughing, and adviſed them rather to write over their Doors: *Here dwells Poverty*; thinking that would drive away all Sorts of Monſters muſt faſter than *Hercules* himſelf, though he were to live again. Epitaphs on Sepulchres are either written, which are properly Epigrams, or repreſented by Figures and Symbols. *Plato* would not have an Epitaph conſiſt of more than four Lines; and accordingly *Ovid* ſays:

On the rear'd Column be my Story wrote,
But brief, that every Paſſenger may read.

AND it is certain that Prolixity, though it is to be condemned every where, is worſe in this Caſe than any other: Or if the Inſcription be of any Length, it ought to be extremely elegant, and apt to raiſe Compaſſion, and ſo pleaſing that you may not regret the Trouble of reading it, but be fond of getting it by Heart, and repeating it often. That of *Omenea* has been much commended.

If cruel Fate allow'd the ſad Exchange
Of Life for Life, how chearfully for thee,
My beſt-lov'd Omenea *had I died!*
But ſince it muſt not be, theſe weeping Eyes
The hated Sun and painful Light ſhall fly,
To ſeek thee in the gloomy Realms below.

So this other:

Behold, O Citizens, the Buſt and Urn
Of ancient Ennius, *your old Bard, who ſung*
In lofty Notes your Fathers brave Exploits.
Let none with Tears or ſolemn funeral Pomp
Bewail my Death, for Ennius *ſtill ſurvives,*
Still honour'd lives upon the Tongue of Fame.

ON the Tombs of thoſe that were ſlain at *Thermopylæ*, was this Inſcription: *O Paſſenger, tell the* Spartans *that we lie here, obeying their Commands.* Nor is there any thing amiſs in throwing in a Stroke of Pleaſantry upon ſuch an Occaſion.

Thy Journey, Traveller, a Moment ſtay
To view a Wonder ſtrange and ſeldom ſeen:
A Man and Wife that lie for once at Peace.
Thou ask'ſt our Name. Ne'er ſhalt thou know
from me.
Mind not my ſtutt'ring Husband; come to me:
His Name is Balbus, Bebbra *mine. Ah Wife!*
Will nothing ſtop that drunken Tongue of thine!

I AM extremely delighted with ſuch Inſcriptions. The Ancients uſed to gild the Letters which they uſed in their Inſcriptions. The *Ægyptians* employed Symbols in the following Manner: They carved an Eye, by which they underſtood God; a Vulture for Nature; a Bee for King; a Circle for Time; an Ox for Peace, and the like. And their Reaſon for expreſſing their Senſe by theſe Symbols was, that Words were underſtood only by the reſpective Nations that talked the Language, and therefore Inſcriptions in common Characters muſt in a ſhort Time be loſt: As it has actually happened to our *Etrurian* Characters: For among the Ruins of ſeveral Towns, Caſtles and Burial-places, I have ſeen Tomb-ſtones dug up with Inſcriptions on them, as is generally believed, in *Etrurian* Characters, which are like both thoſe of the *Greeks* and *Latins*; but no body can underſtand them: And the ſame, the *Ægyptians* ſuppoſed, muſt be the Caſe with all Sorts of

Writing whatſoever; but the Manner of expreſſing their Senſe which they uſed upon theſe Occaſions, by Symbols, they thought muſt always be underſtood by ingenious Men of all Nations, to whom alone they were of Opinion, that Things of Moment were fit to be communicated. In Imitation of this Practice, various Symbols have been uſed upon Sepulchres. Over the Grave of *Diogenes* the *Cynic*, was a Column with a Dog upon the Top of it, cut in *Parian* Marble. *Cicero* glories, that he who was of *Arpinum*, was the Diſcoverer at *Syracuſe* of *Archimedes*'s Tomb, which was quite decayed and neglected, and all over-grown with Brambles, and not known, even to the Inhabitants of the Place, and which he found out by a Cylinder and ſmall Sphere which he ſaw cut upon a high Column that ſtood over it. On the Sepulchre of *Symandes*, King of *Ægypt*, the Figure of his Mother was cut out of a Piece of Marble twenty Cubits high, with three Royal Diadems upon her Head, denoting her to be the Daughter, Wife and Mother of a King. On the Tomb of *Sardanapalus*, King of the *Aſſyrians*, was a Statue which ſeemed to clap its Hands together by Way of Applauſe, with an Epitaph to this Effect: *In one ſingle Day I built* Tarſus *and* Archileum; *but do you, Friend, eat, drink and be merry*; *for there is nothing elſe among Men that is worthy of this Applauſe.* Such were the Inſcriptions and Symbols uſed in thoſe Nations. But our *Romans* recorded the Exploits of their great Men, by carving their Story in Marble. This gave riſe to Columns, Triumphal Arches, Porticoes enriched with memorable Events, preſerved both in Painting and Sculpture. But no Monument of this Nature ſhould be made, except for Actions that truly deſerve to be perpetuated. But we have now dwelt long enough upon this Subject. We have ſpoken of the publick Ways by Land; and the ſame Ornaments will ſerve thoſe by Water: But as high Watch-towers belong to both, it is neceſſary here to ſay ſomething of them.

Chap. V.

Of Towers and their Ornaments.

* THE greateſt Ornaments are lofty Towers placed in proper Situations, and built after handſome Deſigns: And when there are a good Number of them ſtrewed up and down the Country, they afford a moſt beautiful Proſpect: Not that I commend the Age about two hundred Years ago, when People ſeemed to be ſeized with a Kind of general Infection of building high Watch-towers, even in the meaneſt Villages, inſomuch that ſcarce a common Houſe-keeper thought he could not be without his Turret: By which means there aroſe a perfect Grove of Spires. Some are of Opinion, that the Minds of Men take particular Turns, at certain Seaſons, by the Influence of ſome Planet. Between three and four hundred Years ſince the Zeal for Religion was ſo warm, that Men ſeemed born for no other Employment but to build Churches and Chapels; for, to omit other Inſtances, in the ſingle City of *Rome* at this Day, though above half thoſe ſacred Structures are now ruinate, we ſee above two thouſand five hundred Churches ſtill remaining. And now again, what can be the Reaſon, that juſt at this Time all *Italy* ſhould be fired with a Kind of Emulation to put on quite a new Face? How many Towns, which when we were Children, were built of nothing but Wood, are now lately ſtarted up all of Marble? But to return to the Subject of Towers. I ſhall not here ſtay to repeat what we read in *Herodotus*, that in the Middle of the Temple at *Babylon* there was a Tower, the Baſe whereof was a whole Furlong, or the eighth Part of a Mile, on every Side, and which conſiſted of eight Stories built one above another; a Way of Building which I extremely commend in Towers, becauſe each Story growing leſs and leſs all the Way up, conduces both to Strength and Beauty, and by being well knit one into another, makes the whole Structure firm. Towers are either ſquare or round, and in both theſe the Height muſt anſwer in a certain Proportion to the Breadth. When they are deſigned to be very taper, ſquare ones ſhould be ſix Times as high as they are broad, and round ones ſhould have four Times the Height of their Diameter. Thoſe which are intended to be very thick, ſhould have in Height, if ſquare, but four Times their Breadth, and if round, but three Diameters. The Thickneſs of the Walls, if they are forty Cubits high, muſt

* *See Plates 45–48, facing and following this page. For reasons of page layout, 48 precedes 47 in the present edition.*

PLATE 44. *(Pages 167–68)*

"Colonn[a] Toscana" = Tuscan column. "Sei" = six.

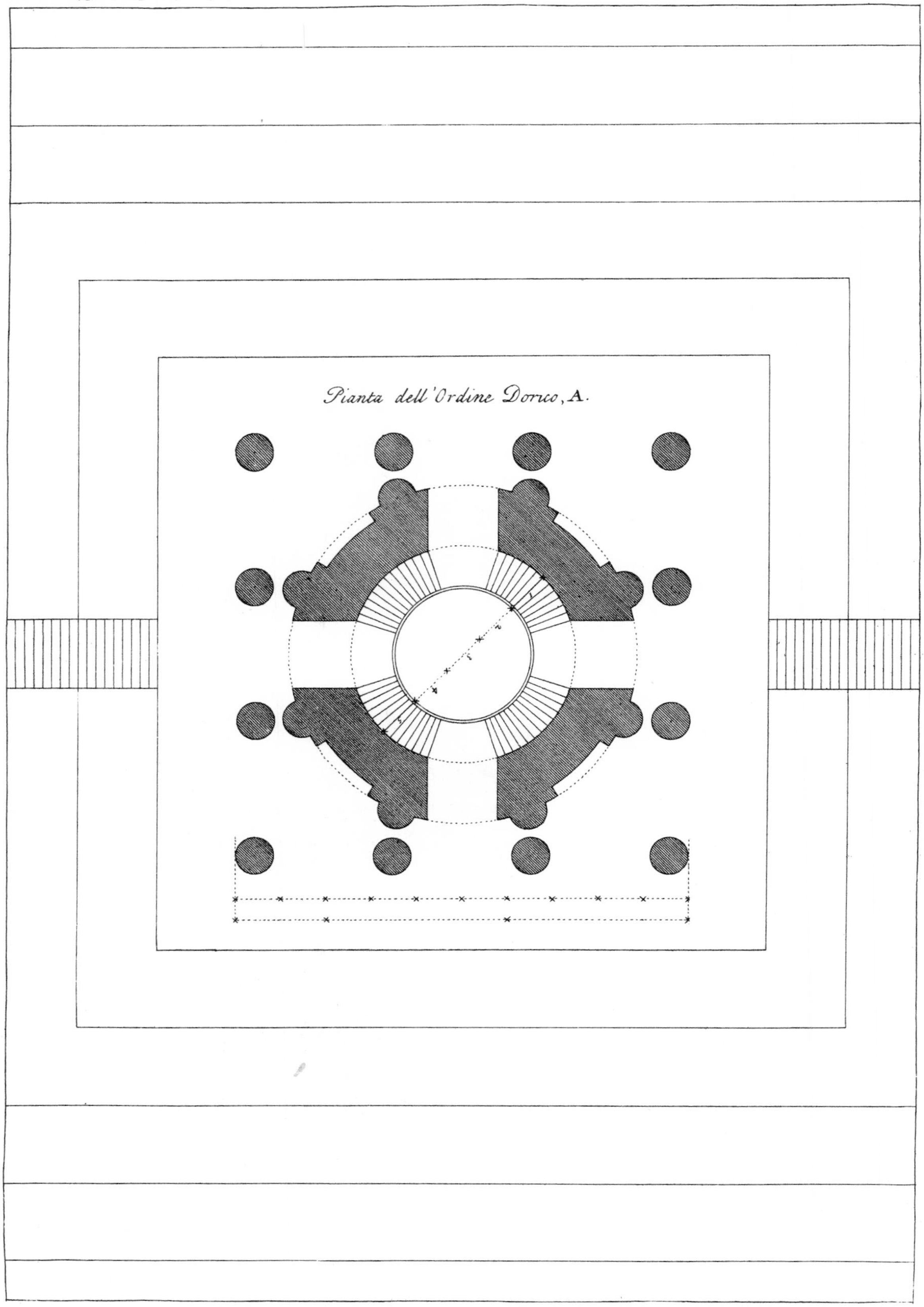

PLATE 45. *(Pages 170–71)*

Pianta dell' Ordine Dorico, A.

I. Leoni delin. & Inv.

"Pianta dell'Ordine Dorico" = *plan of the Doric order.*

Pianta dell Ordine Corinthio, C.

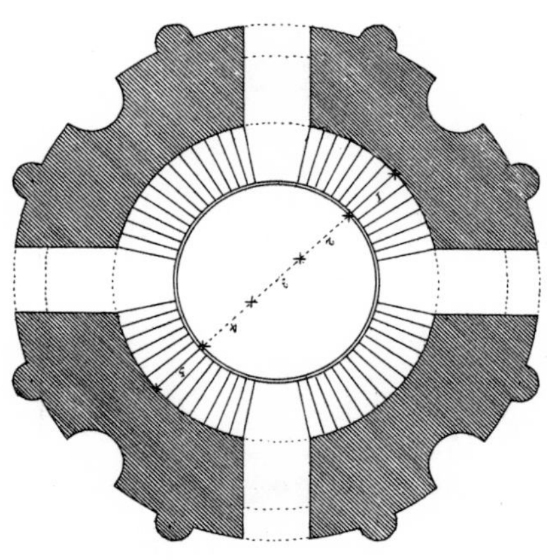

Pianta dell'Ordine Ionico, B.

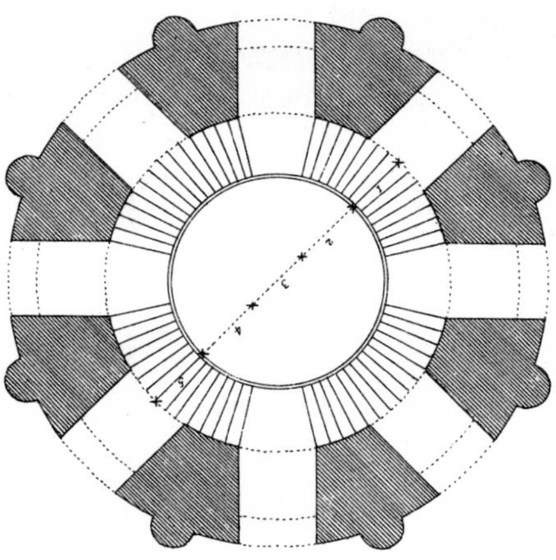

I. Leoni delin. & Inv

PLATE 48. *(Pages 170–71)*

Moduli 8.

Mo. 2.

Mo. 1

Moduli 9.

Mod. 2. Min. 15

Mod. 1.

A

B

I. Leoni delin.

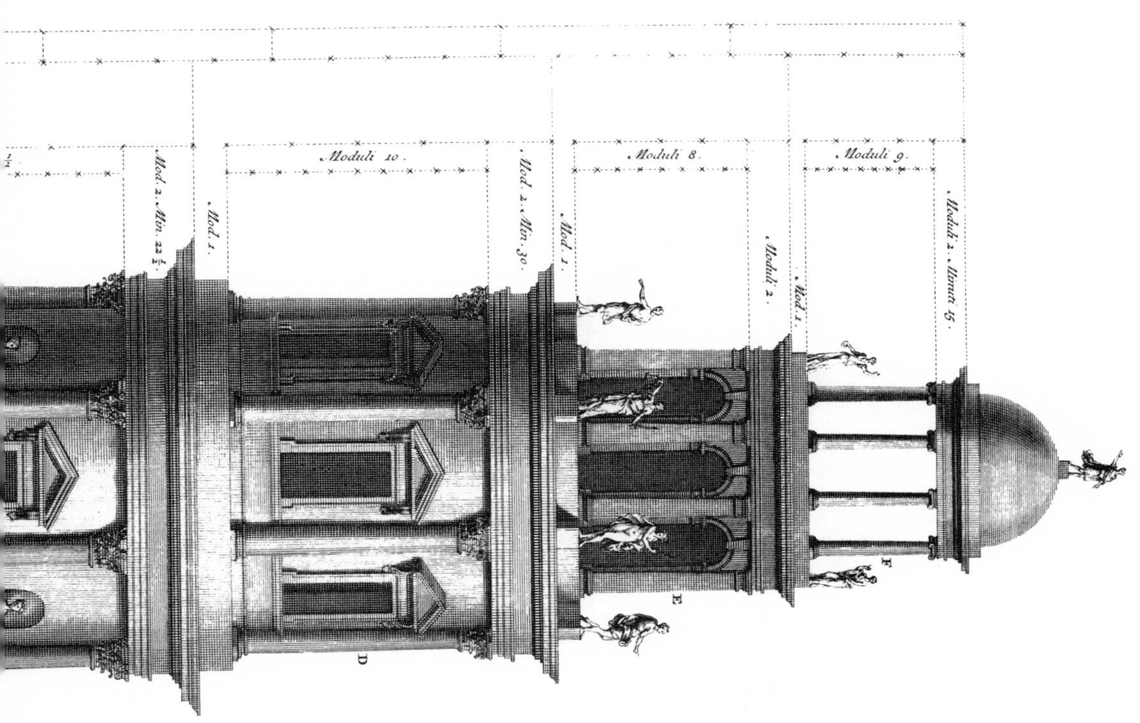

B. Picart sculp. direxit 1725.

Pianta dell' Ordine Ionico, F.

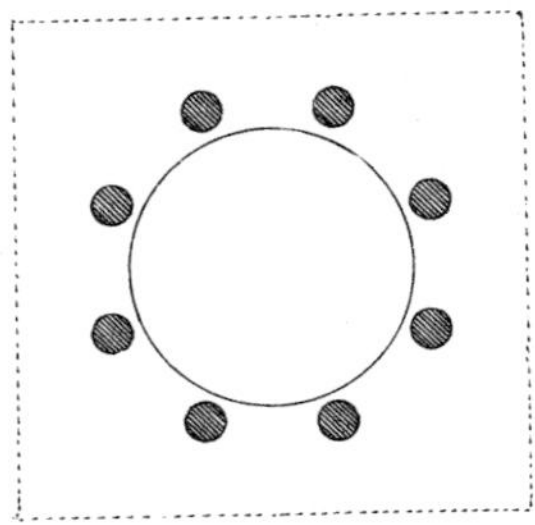

Pianta dell' Ordine Dorico, E.

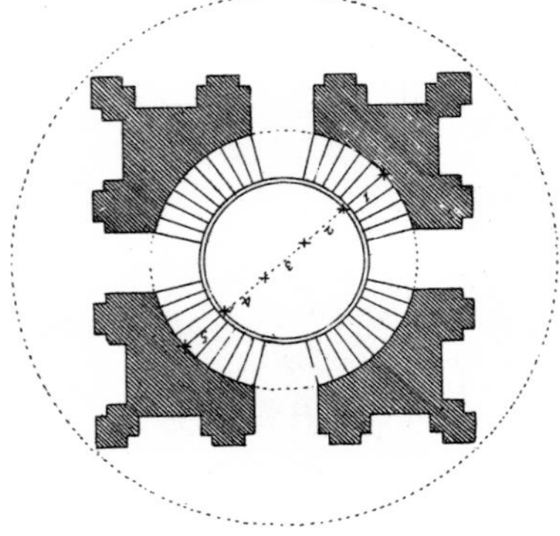

Pianta dell' Ordine Composito, D.

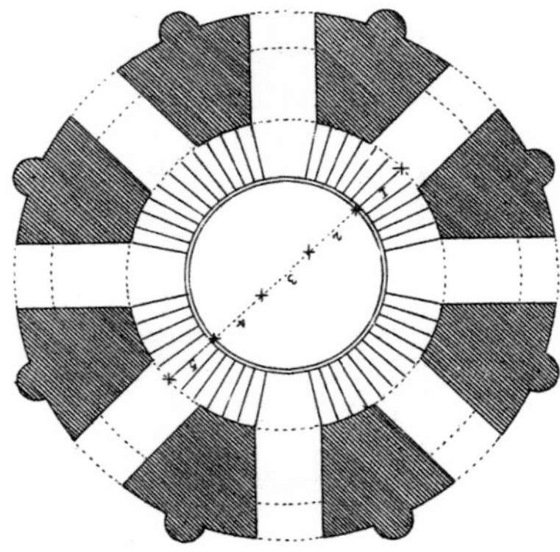

I. Leoni delin. & Inv.

muſt never be leſs than four Foot; if fifty Cubits, five Foot; if ſixty Cubits, ſix Foot, and ſo on in the ſame Proportion. Theſe Rules relate to Towers that are plain and ſimple: But ſome Architects, about half Way of the Height of the Tower, have adorned it with a Kind of Portico with inſulate Columns, others have made theſe Porticoes ſpiral all the Way up, others have ſurrounded it with ſeveral Porticoes like ſo many Coronets, and ſome have covered the whole Tower with Figures of Animals. The Rules for theſe Colonades are not different from thoſe for publick Edifices; only that we may be allowed to be rather more ſlender in all the Members, upon Account of the Weight of the Building. But whoever would erect a Tower beſt fitted for reſiſting the Injuries of Age, and at the ſame Time extremely delightful to behold, let him upon a ſquare Baſis, raiſe a round Superſtructure, and over that another ſquare one, and ſo on, making the Work leſs and leſs by Degrees, according to the Proportions obſerved in Columns. I will here deſcribe one which I think well worthy Imitation. Firſt from a ſquare Platform riſes a Baſement in Height one tenth Part of the whole Structure, and in Breadth one fourth Part of that whole Height. Againſt this Baſement, in the Middle of each Front ſtand two Columns, and one at each Angle, diſtinguiſhed by their ſeveral Ornaments, in the ſame Manner as we juſt now appointed for Sepulchres. Over this Baſement we raiſe a ſquare Superſtructure like a little Chapel, in Breadth twice the Height of the Baſement, and as high as broad, againſt which, we may ſet three, four or five Orders of Columns, in the ſame Manner as in Temples. Over this, we make our Rotondas, which may even be three in Number, and which from the Similitude of the ſeveral Shoots in a Cane or Ruſh, we ſhall call the Joints. The Height of each of theſe Joints ſhall be equal to its Breadth, with the Addition of one twelfth Part of that Breadth, which twelfth Part ſhall ſerve as a Baſement to each Joint. The Breadth ſhall be taken from that ſquare Chapel which we placed upon the firſt Baſement, in the following Manner: Dividing the Front of that ſquare Chapel into twelve Parts, give eleven of thoſe Parts to the firſt Joint; then dividing the Diameter of this firſt Joint into twelve Parts, give eleven of them to the ſecond Joint, and ſo make the third Joint a twelfth Part narrower than the ſecond, and thus the ſeveral Joints will have the Beauty which the beſt ancient Architects highly commended in Columns, namely, that the lower Part of the Shaft ſhould be one fourth Part thicker than the upper. Round theſe Joints we muſt raiſe Columns with their proper Ornaments, in Number not leſs than eight, nor more than ſix: Moreover, in each Joint, as alſo in the ſquare Chapel, we muſt open Lights in convenient Places, and Niches with the Ornaments ſuitable to them. The Lights muſt not take up above half the Aperture between Column and Column. The ſixth Story in this Tower, which riſes from the third Rotonda muſt be a ſquare Structure, and its Breadth and Height muſt not be allowed above two third Parts of that third Rotonda. Its Ornament muſt be only ſquare Pilaſters ſet againſt the Wall, with Arches turned over them, with their proper Dreſs of Capitals, Architraves and the like, and between Pilaſter and Pilaſter, half the Break may be left open for Paſſage. The ſeventh and laſt Story ſhall be a circular Portico of inſulate Columns, open for Paſſage every Way; the Length of theſe Columns, with their Intablature, ſhall be equal to the Diameter of this Portico itſelf, and that Diameter ſhall be three fourths of the ſquare Building, on which it ſtands. This circular Portico ſhall be covered with a Cupola. Upon the Angles of the ſquare Stories in theſe Towers we ſhould ſet Acroteria equal in Height to the Architrave, Freze and Cornice which are beneath them. In the lowermoſt ſquare Story, placed juſt above the Baſement, the open Area within may be five eighths of the outward Breadth. Among the ancient Works of this Nature, I am extremely well pleaſed with *Ptolomey*'s Tower in the Iſland of *Pharos*, on the Top of which, for the Direction of Mariners, he placed large Fires, which were hung in a continual Vibration, and kept always moving about from Place to Place, leſt at a Diſtance thoſe Fires ſhould be miſtaken for Stars; to which he added moveable Images, to ſhew from what Corner the Wind blew with others, to ſhew in what Part of the Heavens the Sun was at that Time, and the Hour of the Day: Inventions extremely proper in ſuch a Structure.

CHAP. VI.

Of the principle Ways belonging to the City, and the Methods of adorning the Haven, Gates, Bridges, Arches, Croſs-ways and Squares.

IT is now Time to make our Entrance into the City; but as there are ſome Ways both within and without the Town which are much more eminent than the common Sort, as thoſe which lead to the Temple, the Baſilique, or the Place for publick Spectacles, we ſhall firſt ſay ſomething of theſe. We read that *Heliogabalus* paved theſe broader and nobler Ways with *Macedonian* Marble and Porphiry. Hiſtorians ſay much in Praiſe of a noble Street in *Bubaſtus*, a City of *Ægypt*, which led to the Temple; for it ran thro' the Market-place, and was paved with very fine Stone, was four Jugera, or four hundred and eighty Foot broad, and bordered on each Side with ſtately Trees. *Ariſteas* tells us, that in *Jeruſalem* there were ſome very beautiful Streets, tho' narrow, thro' which the Magiſtrates and Nobles only were allowed to paſs, to the Intent chiefly that the ſacred Things which they carried, might not be polluted by the Touch of any Thing profane. *Plato* highly celebrates a Way all planted with Cypreſs Trees which led from *Gnoſſus* to the Cave and Temple of *Jupiter*. I find that the *Romans* had two Streets of this Sort, extremely noble and beautiful, one from the Gate to the Church of St. *Paul*, fifteen Stadia, or a Mile and ſeven Furlongs in Length, and the other from the Bridge to the Church of St. *Peter*, two thouſand five hundred Foot long, and all covered with a Portico of Columns of Marble, with a Roof of Lead. Such Ornaments are extremely proper for Ways of this Nature. But let us now return to the more common Highways. The principal Head and Boundary of all Highways, whether within or without the City, unleſs I am miſtaken, is the Gate for thoſe by Land, and the Haven for thoſe by Sea: Unleſs we will take notice of ſubterraneous Ways, of the Nature of thoſe which we are told were at *Thebes* in *Ægypt*, thro' which their Kings could lead an Army unknown to any of the Citizens, or thoſe which I find to have been pretty numerous near *Preneſte*, in the ancient *Latium*, dug under Ground from the Top of the Hill to the Level of the Plain, with wonderful Art; in one of which we are told, that *Marius* periſhed when cloſe preſſed by the Siege. We are told by the Author of the Life of *Apollonius*, of a very wonderful Paſſage made by a Lady of *Media* at *Babylon*, under the River, and arched with Stone and Bitumen, thro' which ſhe could go dryſhod from the Palace to a Country Houſe, on the other Side of the River. But we are not obliged to believe all that the *Greek* Writers tell us. To return to our Subject. The Gates are adorned in the ſame Manner as triumphal Arches, of which anon. The Haven is adorned by broad Porticoes, raiſed ſomewhat above the Level of the Ground, by a ſtately Temple, lofty and beautiful, with ſpacious Squares before it, and the Mouth of the Haven itſelf by huge Statues, ſuch as were formerly to be ſeen in ſeveral Places, and particularly at *Rhodes*, where *Herod* is ſaid to have erected three. Hiſtorians very much celebrate the Mole at *Samos*, which they ſay was an hundred and twenty Foot high, and ran out two Furlongs into the Sea. Doubtleſs ſuch Works muſt greatly adorn the Haven, eſpecially if they are maſterly wrought, and not of baſe Materials. The Streets within the City, beſides being handſomely paved and cleanly kept, will be rendered much more noble, if the Doors are built all after the ſame Model, and the Houſes on each Side ſtand in an even Line, and none higher than another. The Parts of the Street which are principally to be adorned, are theſe: The Bridge, the Croſs-ways, and the Place for publick Spectactles, which laſt is nothing elſe but an open Place, with Seats built about it. We will begin with the * Bridge, as being one of the chief Parts of the Street. The Parts of the Bridge are the Piers, the Arches and the Pavement, and alſo the Street in the Middle for the Paſſage of Cattle, and the raiſed Cauſeways on each Side for the better Sort of Citizens, and the Sides or Rail, and in ſome Places Houſes too, as in that moſt noble Bridge called *Adrian*'s *Mole*, a Work never to be forgotten, the very Skeleton whereof, if I may ſo call it, I can never behold without a Sort of Reverence and Awe. It was

* *See Plate* 49, *facing page* 174.

was covered with a Roof ſupported by two-and-forty Columns of Marble, with their Architrave, Freze and Cornice, the Roof plated with Braſs, and richly adorned. The Bridge muſt be made as broad as the Street which leads to it. The Piers muſt be equal to one another on each Side both in Number and Size, and be one third of the Aperture in Thickneſs. The Angles or Heads of the Piers that lie againſt the Stream muſt project in Length half the Breadth of the Bridge, and be built higher than the Water ever riſes. The Heads of the Piers that lie along with the Stream muſt have the ſame Projecture, but then it will not look amiſs to have them leſs acute, and as it were blunted. From the Heads of the Piers on each Side, it will be very proper to raiſe Butreſſes for the Support of the Bridge, in Thickneſs not leſs than two thirds of the Pier itſelf. The Crowns of all the Arches muſt ſtand quite clear above the Water: Their Dreſs may be taken from the *Ionic* or rather the *Doric* Architrave, and in large Bridges it muſt not be leſs in Breadth than the fifteenth Part of the whole Aperture of the Arch. To make the Rail or Side-wall of the Bridge the ſtronger, erect Pedeſtals at certain Diſtances by the Square and Plum-line, on which, if you pleaſe, you may raiſe Columns to ſupport a Roof or Portico. The Height of this Side-wall with its Zocle and Cornice muſt be four Foot. The Spaces between the Pedeſtals may be filled up with a ſlight Breaſt-wall. The Crown both of the Pedeſtals and Breaſt-wall may be an upright Cymatium, or rather a reverſed one, continued the whole Length of the Bridge, and the Plinth at Bottom muſt anſwer this Cymatium. The Cauſeway on each Side for Women and Foot Paſſengers muſt be raiſed a Foot or two higher than the Middle of the Bridge, which being intended chiefly for Beaſts of Carriage, may be paved only with Flints. The Height of the Columns, with their Intablature, muſt be equal to the Breadth of the Bridge. The Croſſways and Squares differ only in their Bigneſs, the Croſſway being indeed nothing elſe but a ſmall Square. *Plato* ordained that in all Croſſways there ſhould be Spaces left for Nurſes to meet in with their Children. His Deſign in this Regulation was, I ſuppoſe, not only that the Children might grow ſtrong by being in the Air, but alſo that the Nurſes themſelves, by ſeeing one another, might grow neater and more delicate, and be leſs liable to Negligence among ſo many careful Obſervers in the ſame Buſineſs. It is certain, one of the greateſt Ornaments either of a Square, or of a Croſſway, is a handſome Portico, under which the old Men may ſpend the Heat of the Day, or be mutually ſerviceable to each other; beſides that the Preſence of the Fathers may deter and reſtrain the Youth, who are ſporting and diverting themſelves in the other Part of the Place, from the Miſchievouſneſs and Folly natural to their Age. The Squares muſt be ſo many different Markets, one for Gold and Silver, another for Herbs, another for Cattle, another for Wood, and ſo on; each whereof ought to have its particular Place in the City, and its diſtinct Ornaments; but that where the Traffick of Gold and Silver is to be carried on, ought to be much the Nobleſt? The *Greeks* made their Forums or Markets exactly ſquare, and encompaſſed them with large double Porticoes, which they adorned with Columns and their Intablatures, all of Stone, with noble Terraſſes at the Top, for taking the Air upon. Among our Countrymen the *Italians*, the Forums uſed to be a third Part longer than they were broad: And becauſe in ancient Times they were the Places where the Shows of the *Gladiators* were exhibited, the Columns in the Porticoes were ſet at a greater Diſtance from each other, that they might not obſtruct the Sight of thoſe Diverſions. In the Porticoes were the Shows for the Goldſmiths, and over the firſt Story were Galleries projecting out for ſeeing the Shows in, and the publick Magazines. This was the Method among the Ancients. For my Part I * would have a Square twice as long as broad, and that the Porticoes and other Buildings about it ſhould anſwer in ſome Proportion to the open Area in the Middle, that it may not ſeem too large, by means of the Lowneſs of the Buildings, nor too ſmall, from their being too high. A proper Height for the Buildings about a Square is one third of the Breadth of the open Area, or one ſixth at the leaſt. I would alſo have the Porticoes raiſed above the Level of the Ground, one fifth Part of their Breadth, and that their Breadth ſhould be equal to half the Height of their Columns, including the Intablature. The Proportions of the Columns ſhould be taken from thoſe of the Baſilique, only with this Difference, that here the Architrave, Freze and Cornice together ſhould be one fifth of the Column in Height. If you would make a ſecond Row of Columns over this firſt, thoſe Columns ſhould be one fourth Part thinner and ſhorter than thoſe below, and

* *See Plates 50 and 51, following Plate 49.*

for a Basement to them you must make a Plinth half the Height of the Basement at the Bottom. But nothing can be a greater Ornament either to Squares or the Meeting of several Streets, than Arches at the Entrance of the Streets; an Arch being indeed nothing else but a Gate standing continually open. I am of Opinion, that the Invention of Arches were owing to those that first enlarged the Bounds of the Empire: For it was the ancient Custom with such, as we are informed by *Tacitus*, to enlarge the Pomoerium, or vacant Space left next the City Walls, as we find particularly that *Claudius* did. Now though they extended the Limits of the City, yet they thought it proper to preserve the old Gates, for several Reasons, and particularly because they might some Time or other happen to be a Safeguard against the Irruption of an Enemy. Afterwards as these Gates stood in the most conspicuous Places, they adorned them with the Spoils which they had won from their Enemies, and the Ensigns of their Victories. To these Beginnings it was that Arches owed their Trophies, Inscriptions, Statues and Relieves. A very proper Situation for an Arch is where a Street joins into a Square, and especially in the Royal Street, by which Name I understand the * most eminent in the City. An Arch, like a Bridge, should have no less than three open Passages: That in the Middle for the Soldiers to return through in Triumph to pay their Devotions to their paternal Gods, and the two Side ones for the Matrons and Citizens to go out to meet and welcome them Home. When you build one of these Triumphal Arches, let the Line of the Platform which runs lengthways with the Street be the Half of the Line that goes cross the Street from Right to Left, and the Length of this Cross-line should never be less than fifty Cubits. This Kind of Structures is very like that of a Bridge, only it never consists of more than four Piers and three Arches. Of the shortest Line of the Platform which runs lengthways with the Street, leaves one eighth Part towards the Square, and as much behind on the other Side, for the Platforms of Columns to be erected against the Piers. The other longer Line which crosses the Street must also be divided into eight Parts, two whereof must be given to the Aperture in the Middle, and one to each Pier and to each Side opening. The perpendicular Upright of the Piers that support the middle Arch, to the Spring of that Arch, must be two of the aforesaid Parts and a Third; and the Piers of the two Side Arches must bear the same Proportion to their respective Aperture. The Soffit of the Arches must be persect Vaults. The Crowns of the Piers beneath the Spring of the Arch, may be made in Imitation of the *Doric* Capital, only instead of the Ovolo and Abacus they may have a projecting Cornice either *Corinthian* or *Ionic*, and beneath the Cornice by Way of Gorgerine, a plain Freze, and below that an Astragal and a Fillet like those at the Top of the Shaft of a Column. All these Ornaments togther should take up the ninth Part of the Height of the Pier. This ninth Part must be again subdivided into nine smaller Parts, five whereof must be given to the Cornice, three to the Freze, and one to the Astragal and Fillet. The Architrave or Face of the Arch that turns from Pier to Pier must never be broader than the tenth Part of its Aperture, nor narrower than the twelfth. The Columns that are placed in Front against the Piers must be regular and insulate; they must be so raised that the Top of their Shafts may be equal to the Top of the Arch, and their Length must be equal to the Breadth of the middle Aperture. These Columns must have their Bases, Plinths and Pedestals as also their Capitals, either *Corinthian* or *Composite* together with Architrave, Freze and Cornice, either *Ionic* or *Corinthian*, according to the Proportions already prescribed for those several Members. Above these Columns must be a plain Wall, half as high as the whole Substructure from the lowest Basement to the Top of the Cornice, and the Height of this additional Wall must be divided into eleven Parts, one of which must be given to a plain Cornice at the Top, without either Freze or Architrave, and one and an Half to a Basement with a reversed Cymatium which must take up one third of the Height of that Basement. The Statues must be placed directly over the Intablature of the Columns, upon little Pedestals whose Height must be equal to the Thickness of the Top of the Shaft of the Columns. The Height of the Statues with their Pedestals must be eight of the eleven Parts to which we divided the upper Wall. At the Top of the whole Structure, especially towards the Square, must be placed larger Statues, triumphal Cars, Animals and other Trophies. The Base for these to stand upon, must be a Plinth three Times as high as the Cornice, which is immediately below it. These larger Statues which we thus place uppermost, must

* *See Plates 52 and 53, following Plates 49–51. These two plates appear in reverse order in the present edition.*

Plate 49. *(Pages 172–73)*

"Super[ficie] dell'Acqua" = *surface of the water.*

PLATE 50. (*Page 173*)

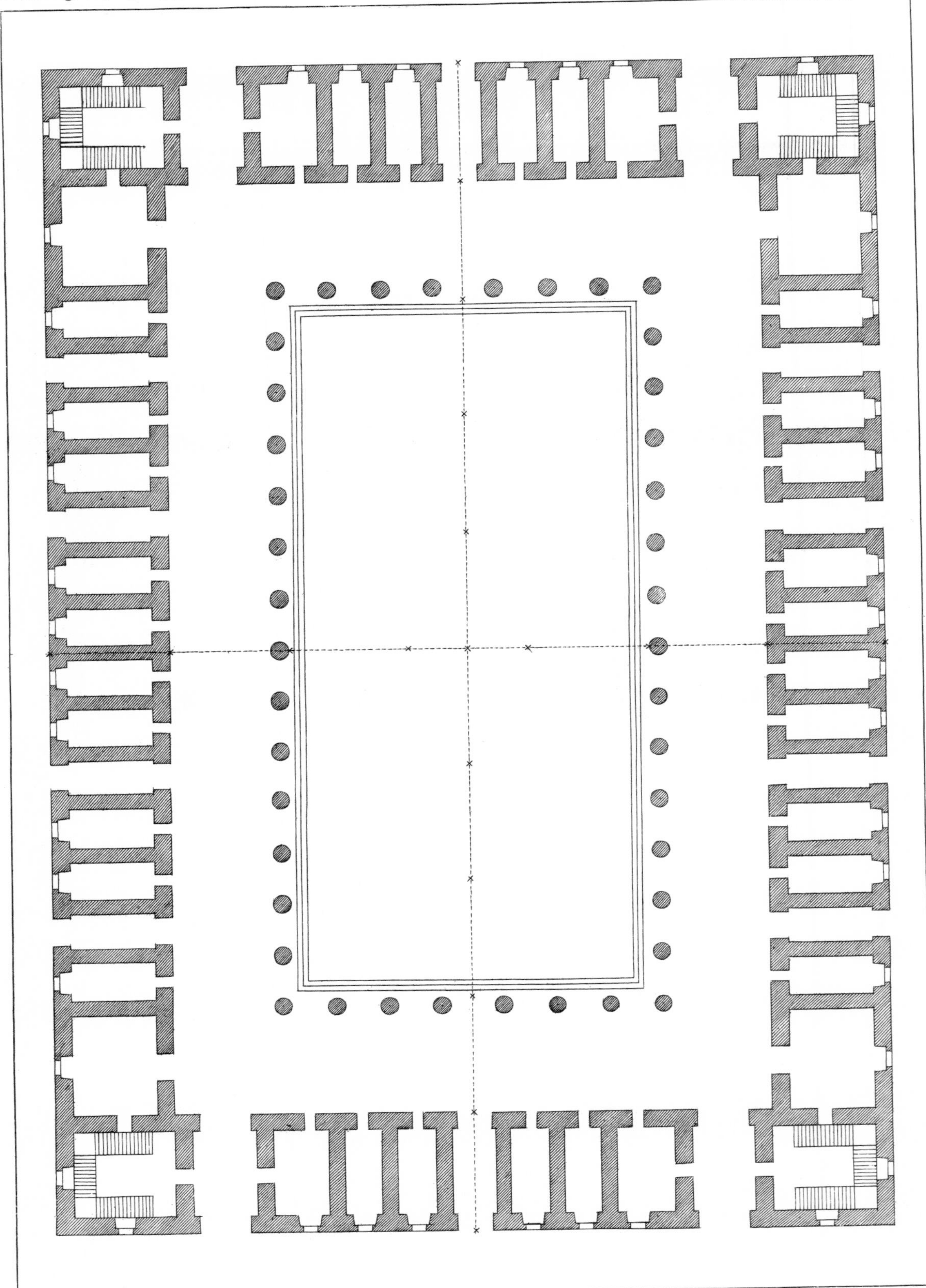

J. Leoni. delin.

PLATE 51. *(Page 173)*

Inscription: "To Great Britain, which holds the destinities of Europe in even balance."

ANNIAE
ATA
ONENTI.
Modu. 7 1/2.
Modu. 2 1/2.
Moduli 10.
Modu. 2 1/2.
8
50
30
40
50
B. Picart sculpsit 1725.

PLATE 52. *(Pages 174–75)*

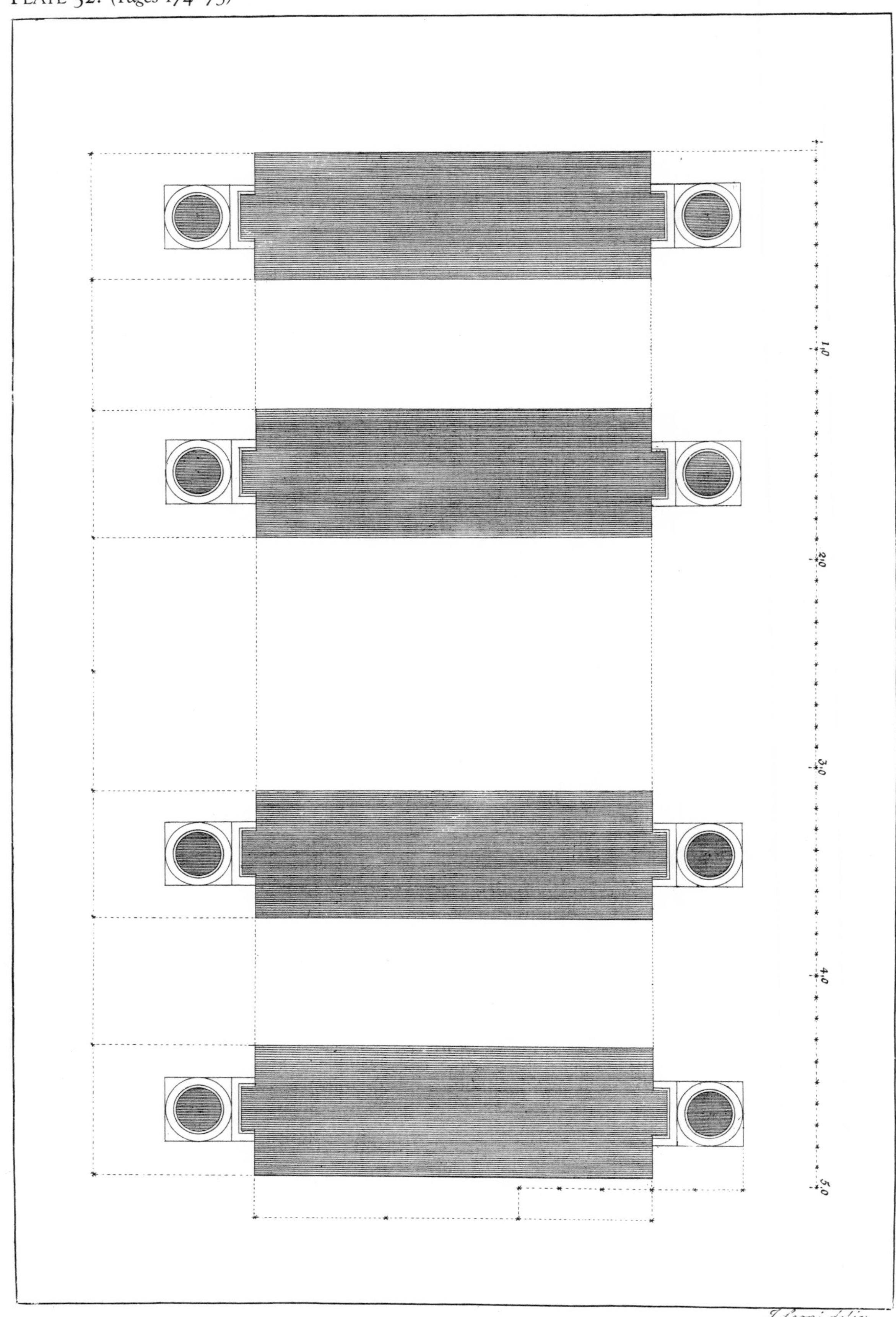

must in Height exceed those which stand below them over the Columns, not less than a sixth Part, nor more than two ninths. In convenient Places in the Front of the upper Wall we may cut Inscriptions or Stories in Relieve, in square or round Pannels. Beneath the Vault of the Arch the upper half of the Wall, upon which the Arch turns, is extremely proper for Stories in Relieve, but the lower Half being exposed to be spattered with Dirt, is very unfit for such Ornaments. For a Basement to the Piers we may make a Plinth not more than a Cubit and an Half high, and that its Angle may not be broke by the Brush of Wheels, we may carry it off into a Cima-reversa, which must take up one fourth of the Height of the Basement itself.

Chap. VII.

Of the adorning Theatres and other Places for publick Shows, and of their Usefulness.

We come now to Places for publick Shows. We are told that *Epimenides*, the same that slept fifty-seven Years in a Cave; when the *Athenians* were building a Place for publick Shows reproved them, telling them, you know not how much Mischief this Place shall occasion; if you did, you would pull it to Pieces with your Teeth. Neither dare I presume to find Fault with our Pontiffs, and those whose Business it is to set good Examples to others, for having, with good Cause no doubt, abolished the Use of publick Shows. Yet *Moses* was commended for ordaining, that all his People should upon certain solemn Days meet together in one Temple, and celebrate publick Festivals at stated Seasons. What may we suppose his View to have been in this Institution? Doubtless he hoped the People, by thus meeting frequently together at publick Feasts, might grow more humane, and be the closer linked in Friendship one with another. So I imagine our Ancestors instituted publick Shows in the City, not so much for the Sake of the Diversions themselves, as for their Usefulness. And indeed if we examine the Matter thoroughly, we shall find many Reasons to grieve that so excellent and so useful an Entertainment should have been so long disused: For as of these publick Diversions some were contrived for the Delight and Amusement of Peace and Leisure, others for an Exercise of War and Business; the one served wonderfully to revive and keep up the Vigour and Fire of the Mind, and the other to improve the Strength and Intrepidity of the Heart. It is indeed true that some certain and constant Medium should be observed, in order to make these Entertainments useful and ornamental to a Country. The *Arcadians*, we are told, were the first that invented publick Games, to civilize and polish the Minds of their People, who had been too much accustomed to a hard and severe Way of Life; and *Polybius* writes, that those who afterwards left off those Entertainments, grew so barbarous and cruel, that they became execrable to all *Greece*. But indeed the Memory of publick Games is extremely ancient, and the Invention of them is ascribed to various Persons. *Dionysius* is said to have been the first Inventor of Dances and Sports, as *Hercules* was of the Diversion of the Combate. We read that the Olympick Games were invented by the *Ætolians* and the *Eleans*, after their return from the Siege of *Troy*. We are told, that *Dionysius* of *Lemnos*, who was the Inventor of the Chorus in Tragedies, was also the first that built a Place on purpose for publick Shows. In *Italy*, *Lucius Mummius*, upon Occasion of his Triumph, first introduced theatrical Entertainments two hundred Years before the Emperor *Nero*'s Time, and the Actors were brought to *Rome* from *Etruria*. Horse-Races were brought from the *Tyrians*, and almost the whole Variety of publick Diversions came to *Italy* from *Asia*. I am inclined to believe that the ancient Race of Men, that first began to cut the Figure of *Janus* upon their brazen Coins, were content to stand to see these Sort of Games under some Beech or Elm, according to those Verses of *Ovid*, speaking of *Romulus*'s Show.

His Play-house, not of Parian *Marble made,*
Nor was it spread with purple Sails for shade.
The Stage with Rushes or with Leaves they strew'd:
No Scenes in Prospect, no machining God.

On

On Rows of homely Turf they ſat to ſee,
Crown'd with the Wreaths of every common Tree.
DRYDEN's Tranſlation.

HOWEVER, we read that *Jolaus*, the Son of *Iphiclus*, firſt contrived Seats for the Spectators in *Sardinia*, when he received the Theſpiad from *Hercules*. But at firſt Theatres were built only of Wood; and we find that *Pompey* was blamed for having made the Seats fixed and not moveable, as they uſed to be anciently: But Diverſions of this Nature were afterwards carried to ſuch a Height, that there were no leſs than three vaſt Theatres within the City of *Rome*, beſides ſeveral Amphitheatres, one of which was ſo large that it would hold above two hundred thouſand Perſons, beſides the *Circus Maximus*: All which were built of ſquare Stone and adorned with Columns of Marble. Nay, not content with all theſe, they erected Theatres, only for temporary Entertainments, prodigiouſly enriched with Marble, Glaſs, and great Numbers of Statues. The nobleſt Structure in thoſe Days, and the moſt capacious, which was at *Placentia*, a Town in *Lombardy*, was burnt in the Time of *Octavianus*'s War. But we ſhall dwell no longer upon this ancient Magnificence. Of publick Shows, ſome are proper to Peace and Leiſure, others to War and Buſineſs. Thoſe proper to Leiſure, belong to the Poets, Muſicians and Actors: Thoſe proper to War, are Wreſtling, Boxing, Fencing, Shooting, Running, and every Thing elſe relating to the Exerciſe of Arms. *Plato* ordained that Shows of this laſt Nature ſhould be exhibited every Year, as highly tending to the Welfare and Ornament of a City. Theſe Diverſions required various Buildings, which therefore have been called by various Names. Thoſe deſigned for the Uſe of the Poets, Comick, Tragick and the like, are called Theatres by way of Excellence. The Place where the noble Youth exerciſed themſelves in driving Races in Chariots with two or four Horſes, was called the *Circus*. That laſtly, where wild Beaſt were encloſed and baited, was called an Amphitheatre. Almoſt all the Structures for theſe different Sorts of Shows were built in Imitation of the Figure of an Army drawn up in Order of Battle, with its two Horns or Wings protending forwards, and conſiſted of an Area wherein the Actors, or Combatants, or Chariots are to exhibit the Spectacle, and of Rows of Seats around for the Spectators to ſit on: But then they differ as to the Form of the aforeſaid Area; for thoſe which have this Area in the Shape of a Moon in its Decreaſe are called Theatres, but when the Horns are protracted a great Way forwards, they are called *Circuſſes*, becauſe in them the Chariots make a Circle about the Goal. Some tell us, that the Ancients uſed to celebrate Games of this Kind in Rings between Rivers and Swords (*interenſes & flumina*) and that therefore they were called *Circenſes*, and that the Inventor of theſe Diverſions was one *Monagus* at *Elis* in *Aſia*. The Area incloſed between the Fronts of two Theatres joined together was called *Cavea*, or the Pit, and the whole Edifice an Amphitheatre. The Situation of a Building for publick Shows ought particularly to be choſen in a good Air, that the Spectators may not be incommoded either by Wind, Sun, or any of the other Inconveniences mentioned in the firſt Book, and the Theatre ought in an eſpecial Manner to be ſheltered from the Sun, becauſe it is in the Month of *Auguſt* chiefly, as *Horace* obſerves, that the People are fond of the Recitals of the Poets, and the lighter Recreations: And if the Rays of the Sun beat in, and were confined within any Part of the Theatre, the exceſſive Heat might be apt to throw the Spectators into Diſtempers. The Place ought alſo to be proper for Sound, and it is very convenient to have Porticoes, either adjoining to the Theatre, or at an eaſy Diſtance from it, for People to ſhelter themſelves under from ſudden Rains and Storms. *Plato* was for having the Theatre within the City, and the *Circus* ſomewhere out of it. The Parts of the ancient Theatres were as follows: The Area or open Space in the Middle, which was quite uncovered; about this Area, the Rows of Seats for the Spectators, and oppoſite to them the raiſed Floor or Stage for the Actors, and the Decorations proper to the Repreſentation, and at the Top of all, Colonades and Arches to receive the Actor's Voice, and make it more ſonorous. But the *Greek* Theatres differed from thoſe of the *Romans* in this Particular, that the *Greeks* brought their Choruſes and Actors within the Area, and by that Means had Occaſion for a ſmaller Stage, whereas the *Romans* having the whole Performance upon the *Pulpitum*, or Stage, beyond the Semicircle of the Seats, were obliged to make their Stage much larger. In this they all agreed, that at firſt in marking out the Platform for the Theatre, they made uſe of a Semicircle, only drawing out the Horns ſomewhat farther than to be exactly ſemicircular, with

with a Line which ſome made ſtrait, others curve. Thoſe who extended them with Strait-lines, drew them out beyond the Semicircle, parallel to each other, to the Addition of one fourth Part of the Diameter: But thoſe who extended them with Curve-lines, firſt mark'd out a compleat Circle, and then taking off one fourth Part of its Circumference, the Remainder was left for the Platform of the Theatre. The Limits of the Area being marked out and fixed, the next Work was to raiſe the Seats; and the firſt Thing to be done in order to this, was to reſolve how high the Seats ſhould be, and from their Height to calculate how much of the Platform they muſt take up. Moſt Architects made the Height of the Theatre equal to the Area in the Middle, knowing that in low Theatres the Voice was ſunk and loſt, but made ſtronger and clearer in high ones. Some of the beſt Artiſts made the Height of the Building to be four fifths of the Breadth of the Area. Of this whole Height the Seats never took up leſs than half, nor more than two thirds, and their Breadth was ſometimes equal to their Height, and ſometimes only two fifths of it. I ſhall here deſcribe one of theſe Structures which I think the moſt compleat and perfect of any. The outermoſt Foundations of the Seats, or rather of the Wall againſt which the higheſt Seat muſt terminate, muſt be laid diſtant from the Center of the Semicircle one whole Semidiameter of the Area, with the Addition of a third. The firſt or loweſt Seat muſt not be upon the very Level of the Area, but be raiſed upon a Wall, which in the larger Theatres muſt be in Height the ninth Part of the Semidiameter of the middle Area, from the Top of which Wall the Seats muſt take their firſt Flight: And in the ſmalleſt Theatres, this Wall muſt never be leſs than ſeven Foot high. The Benches themſelves muſt be a Foot and an half high, and two and an half broad. Among theſe Seats, Spaces muſt be left at certain Diſtances for Paſſages into the middle Area, and for Stairs to go up from thence to thoſe Seats, which Stair-caſes and Paſſages ſhould be with vaulted Roofs, and in Number proportionable to the Bigneſs of the Theatre. Of theſe Paſſages there ſhould be ſeven principal ones, all directed exactly to the Center of the Area, and perfectly clear and open, at equal Diſtances from each other; and of theſe ſeven, one ſhould be larger than the reſt, anſwering to the middle of the Semicircle, which I call the Maſter Entrance, becauſe it muſt anſwer to the high Street. Another Paſſage muſt be made at the Head of the Semicircle on the Right Hand; and ſo another on the Left to anſwer it, and between theſe and the Maſter Entrance four others, two on each Side. There may be as many other Openings and Paſſages as the Compaſs of the Theatre requires, and will admit of. The Ancients in their great Theatres divided the Rows of Seats into three Parts; and each of theſe Diviſions was diſtinguiſhed from the other by a Seat twice as broad as the others, which was a Kind of Landing-place, ſeparating the higher Seats from the lower; and at theſe Landing-places, the Stairs for coming up to the ſeveral Seats terminated. I have obſerved, that the beſt Architects, and the moſt ingenious Contrivers uſed at each great Entrance to make two different Stairs, one more upright and direct, for the Young and the Nimble, and another broader and eaſier, with more frequent Reſts, for the Matrons and old People. This may ſuffice as to the Seats. Oppoſite to the Front of the Theatre was raiſed the Stage for the Actors, and every thing belonging to the Repreſentation, and here ſate the Nobles in peculiar and honourable Seats, ſeparate from the common People, or perhaps in the middle Area in handſome Places erected for that Purpoſe. The *Pulpitum* or Stage, was made ſo large as to be fully ſufficient for every thing that was to be acted upon it. It came forward equal to the Center of the Semicircle, and was raiſed in Height not above five Foot, that the Nobles who ſate in the Area might from thence eaſily ſee every Geſture of the Actors. But when the middle Area was not reſerved for the Nobles to ſit in, but was allowed to the Actors and Muſicians: Then the Stage was made leſs, but raiſed higher, ſometimes to the Height of ſix Cubits. In both Kinds the Stage was adorned with Rows of Colonades one over another, in Imitation of Houſes, with their proper Doors and Windows, and in Front was one principal Door with all the Dreſs of the Door of a Temple, to repreſent a Royal Palace, with other Doors on each Side for the Actors to make their Entrances and Exits at, according to the Nature of the Drama. And as there are three Sorts of Poets concerned in theatrical Performances, the Tragick, who deſcribe the Misfortunes and Diſtreſſes of Princes; the Comick who repreſent the Lives and Manners of private Perſons, and the Paſtoral, who ſing the Delights of the Country, and the Loves of

Shepherds: There was a Contrivance upon the Stage of a Machine which turning upon a Pin, in an Inſtant changed the Scene to a Palace for Tragedy, an ordinary Houſe for Comedy, or a Grove for Paſtoral, as the Nature of the Fable required. Such was the Manner of the Middle, Area, Seats and Stage, Paſſages and the like. I have already ſaid in this Chapter, that one of the principal Parts of the Theatre was the Portico, which was deſigned for rendering the Sound of the Voice ſtronger and clearer. This was placed upon the higheſt Seat, and the Front of its Colonade looked to the middle Area of the Theatre. Of this we are now to give ſome Account.

The Ancients had learnt from the Philoſophers, that the Air, by the Percuſſion of the Voice, and the Force of Sound, was put into a circular Motion, in the ſame Manner as Water is when any thing is ſuddenly plunged into it, and that, as for Inſtance, in a Lute, or in a Valley, between two Hills, eſpecially if the Place be woody, the Sound and Voice are rendered much more clear and ſtrong, becauſe the ſwelling Circles of the Air meet with ſomething which beats back the Rays of the Voice that iſſue from the Center, in the ſame Manner as a Ball is beat back from a Wall againſt which it is thrown, by which means thoſe Circles are made cloſer and ſtronger: For this Reaſon the Ancients built their Theatres circular; and that the Voice might meet with no Obſtacle to ſtop its free Aſcent to the very higheſt Part of the Theatre, they placed their Seats in ſuch a Manner, that all the Angles of them lay in one exact Line, and upon the higheſt Seat, which was no ſmall Help, they raiſed Porticoes facing the middle Area of the Theatre, the Front of which Porticoes were as open and free as poſſible, but the Back of them was entirely ſhut up with a continued Wall. Under this Portico they raiſed a low Wall, which not only ſerved for a Pedeſtal to the Columns, but alſo helped to collect the ſwelling Orbs of the Voice, and to throw it gently into the Portico itſelf, where being received into a thicker Air, it was not reverberated from thence too violently, but returned clear and a little more ſtrengthened. And over all this, as a Cieling to the Theatre, both to keep off the Weather, and to retain the Voice, they ſpread a Sail all ſtrewed over with Stars, which they could remove at Pleaſure, and which ſhaded the middle Area, the Seats, and all the Spectators. The upper Portico was built with a great deal of Art; for in order to ſupport it, there were other Porticoes and Colonades at the Back of the Theatre, out to the Street, and in the larger Theatres, theſe Porticoes were made double, that if any violent Rain or Storm obliged the Spectators to fly for Shelter, it might not drive in upon them. Theſe Porticoes and Colonades, thus placed under the upper Portico, were not like thoſe which we have deſcribed for Temples or Baſiliques, but built of ſtrong Pilaſters, and in Imitation of triumphal Arches. We ſhall firſt therefore treat of theſe under Porticoes, as being built for the Sake of that above. The Rule for the Apertures of theſe Porticoes is, that to every Paſſage into the middle Area of the Theatre, there ought to be one of them, and each of theſe Apertures ſhould be accompanied with others in certain Proportions, anſwering exactly one to the other in Height, Breadth, Deſign and Ornaments. The Breadth of the Area for walking in theſe Porticoes, ſhould be equal to the Aperture between Pilaſter and Pilaſter, and the Breadth of each Pilaſter ſhould be equal to half that Aperture: All which Rules muſt be obſerved with the greateſt Care and Exactneſs. Laſtly, againſt theſe Pilaſters we muſt not ſet Columns entirely inſulate, as in triumphal Arches, but only three quarter Columns with Pedeſtals under them, in Height one ſixth of the Column itſelf. The other Ornaments muſt be the ſame as thoſe in Temples. The Height of theſe three quarter Columns, with their whole Entablature, muſt be equal to half the perpendicular Height of the Seats within, ſo that on the Outſide there muſt be two Orders of Columns one over the other, the ſecond of which muſt be juſt even with the Top of thoſe Seats, and over this we muſt lay the Pavement for the upper Portico, which as we ſhewed before, muſt look into the middle Area of the Theatre, in Shape reſembling a Horſe-ſhoe. This Subſtructure being laid, we are to raiſe our upper Portico, the Front and Colonade whereof is not to receive its Light from without, like thoſe before deſcribed, but is to be open to the Middle of the Theatre, as we have already obſerved. This Work being raiſed in order to prevent the Voice from being loſt and diſperſed, may be called the Circumvallation. Its Height ſhould be the whole Height of the outer Portico, with the Addition of one half, and its Parts are theſe. The low Wall under the Columns, which we may call a continued Pedeſtal. This Wall of the whole Height of the

the Circumvallation, from the upper Seat to the Top of the Entablature, muſt in great Theatres be allowed never more than a Third, and in ſmall ones, not leſs than a Fourth. Upon this continued Pedeſtal ſtand the Columns which with their Baſes and Capitals muſt be equal to half the Height of the whole Circumvallation. Over theſe Columns lies their Entablature, and over all a Plain Wall, ſuch as we deſcribed in Baſiliques, which Wall muſt be allowed the ſixth remaining Part of the Height of the Circumvallation. The Columns in this Circumvallation ſhall be inſulate, raiſed after the ſame Proportions as thoſe in the Baſiliques, and in Number juſt anſwering to thoſe of the three quarter Columns ſet againſt the Pilaſters of the outward Portico, and they ſhall be placed exactly in the ſame Rays, by which Name I underſtand Lines drawn from the Center of the Theatre to the outward Columns. In the low Wall, or continued Pedeſtal, ſet under the Columns of the inner Portico, muſt be certain Openings, juſt over the Paſſages below into the Theatre, which Openings muſt be in the Nature of Niches, wherein, if you think fit, you may place a Sort of Vaſes of Braſs, hung with their Mouths downwards, that the Voice reverberating in them, may be returned more ſonorous. I ſhall not here waſte Time in conſidering thoſe Inſtructions in *Vitruvius*, which he borrows from the Precepts of Compoſition in Muſick, according to the Rules of which he is for placing the juſt mentioned Vaſes in Theatres, ſo as to correſpond with the differerent Pitches of the ſeveral Voices: A Curioſity eaſily talked of, but how it is to be executed, let thoſe inform us, who know. Thus much I muſt readily aſſent to, and *Ariſtotle* himſelf is of the Opinion, that hollow Veſſels of any Sort, and Wells too, are of Service in ſtrengthening the Sound of the Voice. But to return to the Portico on the Inſide of the Theatre. The back Wall of this Portico muſt be quite cloſe and entire, and ſo ſhut in the whole Circumvallation, that the Voice arriving there, may not be loſt. On the Outſide of the Wall to the Street, we may apply Columns as Ornaments, in Number, Height, Proportions and Members, exactly anſwering to thoſe in the Porticoes under them, in the outward Front of the Theatre. From what has been ſaid, it is eaſy to collect in what Particulars the greater Theatres differ from the ſmaller. In the greater, the outward Portico below is double, in the ſmaller ſingle: In the former, there may be three Orders of Columns, one over the other; in the latter, not more than two. They alſo differ in this, that ſome ſmall Theatres have no Portico at all on the Inſide, but for their Circumvallation, have only a plain Wall and a Cornice, which is intended for the ſame Purpoſe of returning the Voice, as the Portico in great Theatres, and in ſome of the largeſt Theatres, even this inward Portico is double. Laſtly, the outward Covering of the Theatre muſt be well plaiſtered or coated, and made ſo ſloping that the Water may run into Pipes placed in the Angles of the Building, which muſt carry it off privately into proper Drains. Upon the upper Cornice on the Outſide of the Theatre, Mutules and Stays muſt be contrived to ſupport Poles, like the Maſts of Ships to which to faſten the Ropes for ſpreading the Vela or Covering of the Theatre upon any extraordinary Repreſentation. And as we are to raiſe ſo great a Pile of Building to a juſt Height, the Wall ought to be allowed a due Thickneſs for the ſupporting ſuch a Weight. Let the Thickneſs therefore of the outward Wall of the firſt Colonade be a fifteenth Part of the Height of the whole Structure. The middle Wall between the two Porticoes, when theſe are double, muſt want one fourth Part of the Thickneſs of the outward one. The next Story raiſed above this may be a twelfth Part thinner than the lower one.

Chap. VIII.

Of the Ornaments of the Amphitheatre, Circus, publick Walks, and Halls, and Courts for petty Judges.

HAVING ſaid thus much of Theatres, it is neceſſary to give ſome Account of the Circus and Amphitheatre which all owe their Original to the Theatre, for the Circus is indeed nothing elſe but a Theatre with its Horns ſtretched further on in Lines equi-diſtant one from the other, only that the Nature of this Building does not require Portices; and the

the Amphitheatre is formed of two Theatres with their Horns joined together, and the Rows of Seats continued quite round; and the chief Difference between them is, that a Theatre is properly an half Amphitheatre, with this further Variation too, that the Amphitheatre has its middle Area quite clear from any Thing of a Stage or Scenes; but in all other reſpects, and particularly in the Seats, Porticoes, Entrances and the like, they exactly * agree. I am inclined to believe, that the Amphitheatre was at firſt contrived chiefly for Hunting, and that for this Reaſon it was made round, to the Intent that the wild Beaſts which were encloſed and baited in it, not having any Nook or Corner to fly to, might be the ſooner obliged to defend themſelves againſt their Aſſailants, who were extremely bold and dextrous at engaging with the fierceſt wild Beaſts. Some armed only with a Javelin, would with the Help of that leap over a wild Bull that was making at him full Speed, and ſo elude his Blow. Others having put on a Kind of Armour, compoſed of nothing but thick Thorns and Prickles, would ſuffer themſelves to be rowled about and mumbled by a Bear. Others encloſed in a Kind of wooden Cage, teazed and provoked a Lion, and fome with nothing but a Cloak about their left Arm, and a ſmall Ax or Mallet in their right Hand would attack him openly. In a Word, if any Man had either Dexterity to deceive, or Courage and Strength to cope with wild Beaſts, he offered himſelf as a Champion, either merely for the Sake of Honour, or for Reward. We read too, that both in the Theatres and Amphitheatres, the great Men uſed to throw Apples, or let fly little Birds among the Mob, for the Pleaſure of ſeeing them ſcramble for them. The middle Area of the Amphitheatre, though it is ſurrounded by two Theatres joined together, yet muſt not be made ſo long as two compleat Theatres would make it, if their Horns both pretended to meet each other: But its Length muſt bear a certain Proportion to its Breadth. Some among the Ancients made the Length eight, and the Breadth ſeven Parts, and ſome made the Breadth three fourths of the Length. In other Particulars it agrees with the Theatre: It muſt have Porticoes on the Outſide, and one at the Top within, over the higheſt Seat, which we † have called the Circumvallation. We are next to treat of the Circus. Some tell us, that this was built in Imitation of the heavenly Bodies; for as the Heavens have twelve Houſes, ſo the Circus has twelve Gates for Entrance; and as there are ſeven Planets, ſo this has ſeven Goals, lying from Eaſt to Weſt at a good Diſtance one from the other, that through them the contending Chariots may hold their Courſe, as the Sun and Moon do through the Zodiac; which they did four-and-twenty Times, in Imitation of the four-and-twenty Hours. The Concurrents were alſo divided into four Squadrons, each of which was diſtinguiſhed by its particular Colour; the one was cloathed in Green, in Repreſentation of the verdant Spring; another to denote the flaming Summer in Red; the third in White, in Imitation of the pale Autumn; and the fourth in dusky Brown for the gloomy Winter. The middle Area of the Circus was neither clear nor open like the Amphitheatre, nor taken up with a Stage like the Theatre, but it was divided Lengthways into two Courſes by the Goals or Terms which were ſet up at proper Diſtances, about which the Horſes or Men performed their Races. Of theſe Goals there were three principal ones, whereof the Middlemoſt was the chief of all, and this was a Pile of Stone tapering up to the Top, upon account of which regular Diminution, it was called an Obelisk. The other two principal Goals were either coloſſal Statues, or lofty Piles of Stones in the Nature of Trophies, deſigned after the Workman's Fancy, ſo as they were only great and beautiful. Between theſe principal Goals were two others on each Side, either Columns or Obelisks leſs than the former, which made up the Number of Seven. We read in Hiſtorians, that the Circus Maximus at *Rome* was three Furlongs in Length, and one in Breadth. Now indeed it is entirely deſtroyed, and there are not the leaſt Footſteps remaining by which we can form a Judgment of its ancient Structure: But by an actual Survey of other Works of this Nature I find the Manner of them was as follows: The Ancients uſed to make the middle Area of the Circus in Breadth at leaſt threeſcore Cubits, or ninety Foot, and in Length ſeven Times that Breadth. The Breadth was divided into two equal Parts or Courſes by a Line drawn the Length of the Circus, on which Line the Goals or Terms were placed according to the following Method: The whole Length being divided into ſeven Parts, one of thoſe Parts was given to a Sweep at each End for the Concurrents to turn out of the right Courſe into the left, and the Remainder was allowed for the Goals, which ſtanding

* *See Plates 54–56, facing and following this page. Plate 56 precedes Plate 55.*

† *See Plate 57, following Plates 54–56.*

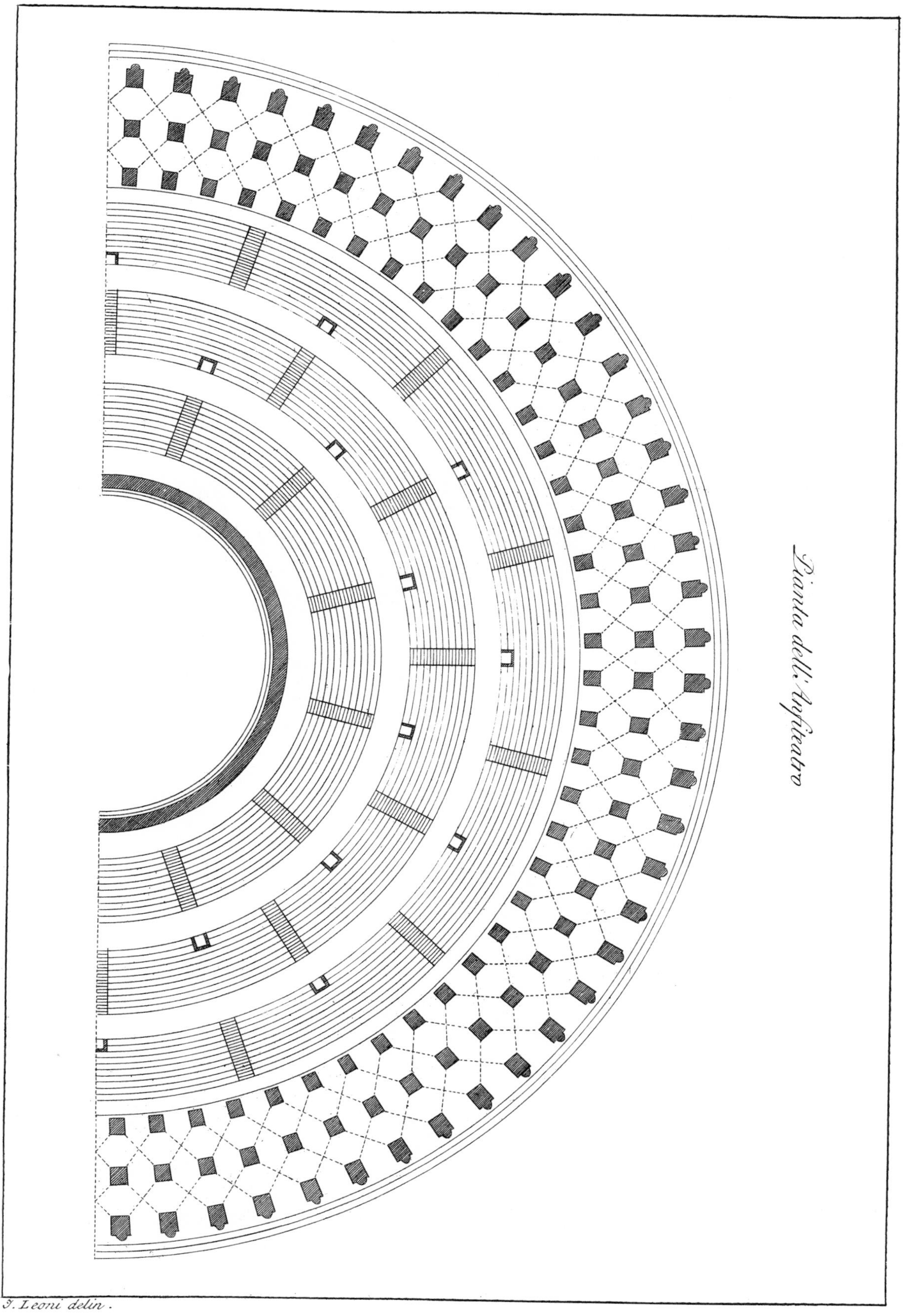

"*Pianta dell' Anfiteatro*" = *plan of the amphitheater.*

PLATE 56. *(Page 180)*

I. Leoni Inv. et delin.

Mo: 2.22½
Moduli 9 Minuti 30.
Corinthio
Mo: 2.15
Moduli 9
Jonico
Mod. 4
Moduli 17
Dorico.
B. Picart sculp. dir. 1726.

Mo: 2 Mi: 22½
Moduli 9 Minuti 30
Corinthio
Mo: 2 Mi: 15
Moduli 9
Jonico
Mod: 4
Mod: 4
Moduli 17
Moduli 17
Dorico
I. Leoni delin.
B. Picart sculp. direxit. 1726.

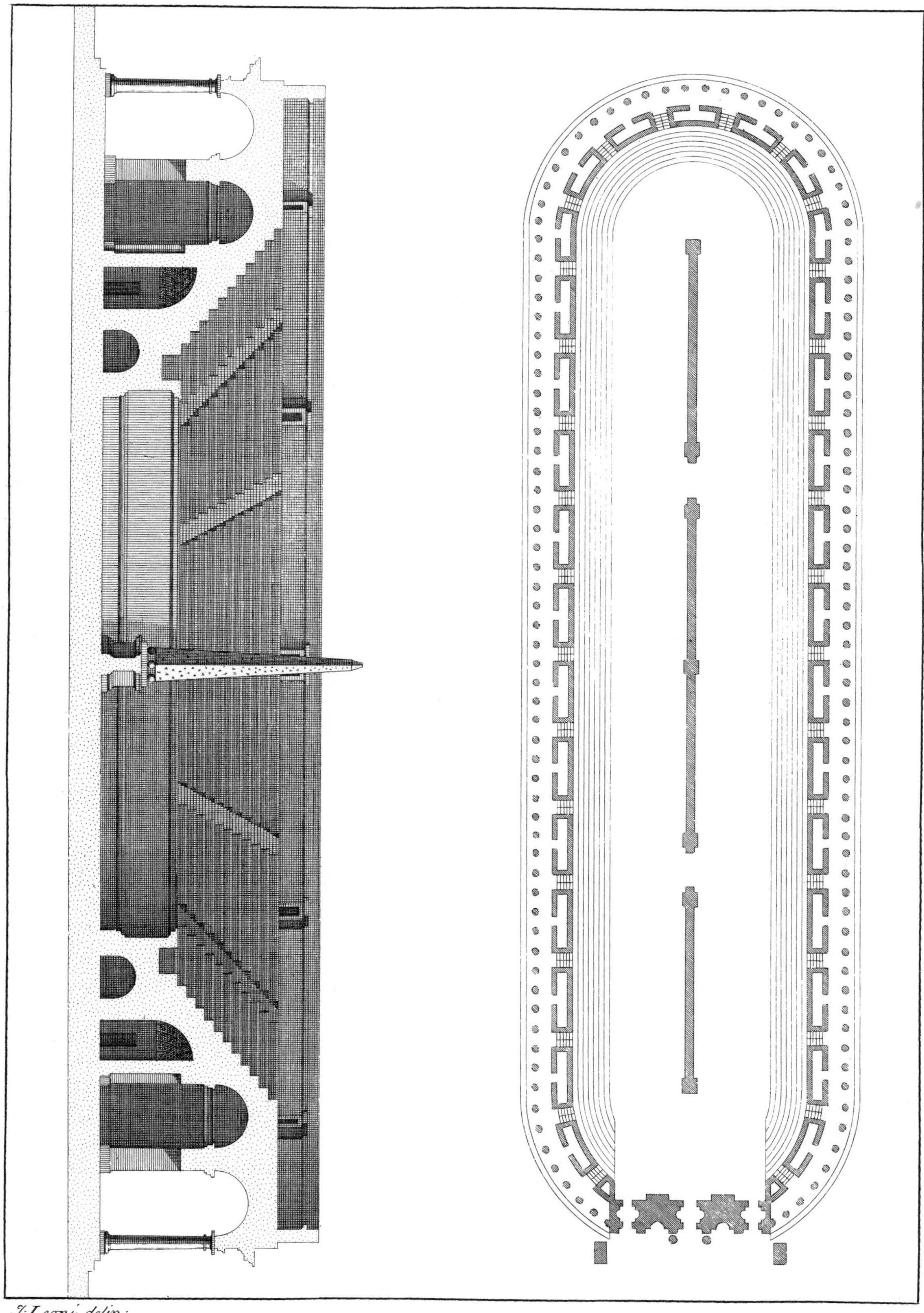

J. Leoni delin:

PLATE 58. *(Page 181)*

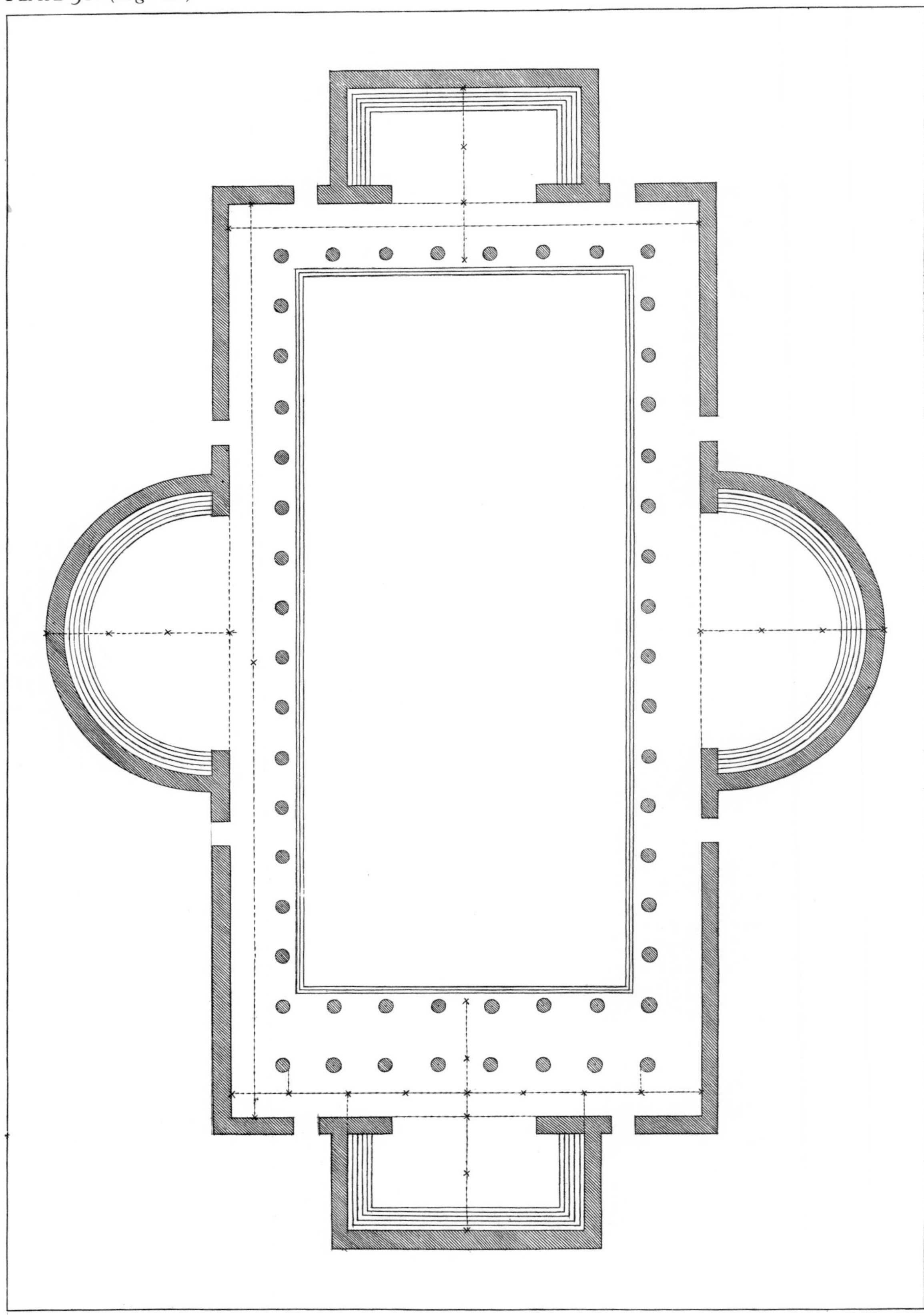

I. Leoni delin.

ſtanding at equal Diſtances from each other, took up the other five ſevenths of the whole Length of the Circus. One Goal was joined to the other by a Kind of Breaſt-wall which was never leſs than ſix Foot high, to keep the Horſes that were running from croſſing out of one Courſe into the other. On each Side of the Circus were Seats raiſed to the Height of never more than the fifth, nor leſs than the ſixth of the whole Breadth of the middle Area; and theſe Seats began from a Baſement, as in Amphitheatres, that the Spectators might not be within reach of any Hurt from the Beaſts. Among publick Works we may reckon thoſe publick Walks, in which the Youth exerciſe themſelves at Tennis, Leaping, or the Uſe of Arms, and where the old Men walk to take the Air, or if they are infirm, are carried about for the Recovery of their Health. *Celſus*, the Phyſician, ſays, that Exerciſe is much better in the open Air, than under Cover; but that they might exerciſe themſelves more commodiouſly even in the Shade, they added Porticoes which encloſed the whole Square. The Square itſelf was ſometimes paved with Marble and Moſaick Work, and ſometimes turfed with Graſs, and planted with Myrtles, Juniper, * Cypreſs and Cedar Trees. The Porticoes on three Sides were ſingle, and ſo large, that their Proportion was two ninth Parts greater than that of the Forum before treated of in this Book; but on the fourth Side, which fronted the South, the Portico was yet more ſpacious, and double. In Front it had *Doric* Columns, whoſe Height was equal to the Breadth of the Portico; the Columns behind, which divided the inner Portico from the outward, were higher than the former one fifth Part, for ſupporting the Cover, and giving a Slope to the Roof; and for this Reaſon they made them of the *Ionic* Order, *Ionic* Columns being in their very Nature taller than the *Doric*: Though I cannot ſee why the Cieling of theſe Porticoes ſhould not have been exactly level, which certainly muſt have been more beautiful to the Eye. In both theſe Colonades, the Diameters of the Columns were as follows: In the *Doric*, the lower Diameter of the Shaft was two fifteenths of the whole Height, including the Baſe and Capital; but in the *Ionic* and *Corinthian*, the lower Diameter of the Shaft was three ſixteenths of the Length of only the Shaft of the Column. In other Reſpects they were the ſame as thoſe uſed in Temples. To the back Walls of theſe Porticoes, they added handſome Walls or Rooms, where Philoſophers and Men of Knowledge might converſe and diſpute upon the nobleſt Subjects; and of theſe Rooms, ſome were proper for Winter, and others for Summer. Thoſe which lay any thing to the North, were for Summer, as thoſe to the South, and which were not expoſed to any ſharp Winds, were for Winter; beſides that thoſe for Winter were ſhut in with entire Walls, whereas thoſe for Summer were full of Windows, or rather were ſeparated only by a Colonade, and had an open View towards the North, with Proſpects of Sea, Hills, Lakes, or ſome other agreeable Landskip, and admitted as much Light as poſſible. The Porticoes on the Right and Left of theſe Squares, had the ſame Sort of back Rooms, ſhut in from Winds, but open to the Morning and to the Evening Sun, which ſhone in upon them from the middle Area. The Plan of theſe retiring Rooms was various, ſometimes they were ſemicircular, ſometimes rectangular, but always in a due Proportion to the Square itſelf, and to the Porticoes which encompaſſed it it. The Breadth of the whole Square with its Porticoes, was half its Length, and this Breadth was divided into eight Parts, ſix whereof were given to the open Square, and one to each Portico. When the back retiring Rooms were ſemicircular, their Diameter was two fifths of the open Area. In the back Wall of the Porticoes, were the Apertures for Entrance, and for Light into thoſe Rooms. The Height of the ſemicircular Retirements, in the greateſt Proportion, was only equal to their Breadth; but in ſmaller Works, it was one fifth Part more. Over the Top of the Roof of the Portico, Openings were broke for the Admiſſion of a ſtronger and more chearful Light into the Room. If theſe Withdrawing-rooms were ſquare, then their Breadth was twice the Breadth of the Porticoes, and their Length twice their own Breadth. That I call Length which runs along with the Portico, ſo that upon entering into thoſe Rooms from the Right, their Length lies to the Left, and entering them from the Left, to the Right. Among publick Works, we are alſo to include the Portico for the inferior Judges, which the Ancients uſed to build after the following Manner: Their Bigneſs was according to the Dignity of the City, but rather too large than too ſmall, and along them was a Row of Chambers, contiguous to each other, where petty Conteſts were heard and determined. Thoſe Works which I have hitherto deſcribed

* *See Plate 58, facing this page.*

ſeem to be truly publick, as they are deſigned for the Uſe of all the People in general, both noble and vulgar: But there are ſtill ſome other Works of a publick Nature, which are for the Uſe only of the principal Citizens, and of the Magiſtrates; as for Inſtance, the Senate-houſe and Council-chambers, whereof we are now to give ſome Account.

Chap. IX.

Of the proper Ornaments for the Senate-houſe and Council-chambers, as alſo of the adorning the City with Groves, Lakes for Swimming, Libraries, Schools, publick Stables, Arſenals and Mathematical Inſtruments.

PLATO appointed the Council to be held in a Temple, and the *Romans* had a determined Place for that Purpoſe, which they called their Comitium. At *Ceraunia* there was a thick Grove, conſecrated to *Jupiter*, in which the *Greeks* uſed to meet to conſult about the Affairs of their State, and many other Cities uſed to hold their Councils in the Middle of the publick Forum. It was not lawful for the *Roman* Senate to meet in any Place that was not appointed by Augury, and * they commonly choſe ſome Temple. Afterwards they erected *Curiæ*, or Courts for that particular Purpoſe, and *Varro* tells us, that theſe were of two Sorts: One in which the Prieſts conſulted about religious Matters; the other where the Senate regulated ſecular Affairs. Of the peculiar Properties of each of theſe I can find nothing certain; unleſs we may be allowed to conjecture, that the former had ſome Reſemblance to a Temple, the latter to a Baſilique. The Prieſts Court therefore may have a vaulted Roof, and that of the Senators a flat one. In both, the Members of the Council are to declare their Opinion, by ſpeaking; and therefore Regard is to be had in theſe Edifices to the Sound of the Voice. For this Reaſon there ought to be ſomething to prevent the Voice from aſcending too high and being loſt, and eſpecially in vaulted Roofs to prevent it from thundering in the Top of the Vault and deafening the Hearers: Upon which Account, as well for Beauty as for this neceſſary Uſe, the Wall ought to be crowned with a Cornice. I find from Obſervation of the Structures of this Sort left by the Ancients, that they uſed to make their Courts ſquare. The Height of their vaulted Courts was ſix ſevenths of the Breadth of the Front, and the Roof was a plain Arch. Juſt oppoſite to the Door the Beholder's Eye was ſtruck with the Tribunal, the Sagitta whereof was the Third of its Chord: The Breadth of the Aperture of the Door, was one ſeventh of the whole Front. At half the Height of the Wall, and one eighth Part of that half, projected an Architrave, Freze and Cornice upon an Order of Columns, either cloſe or thin ſet, as the Architect liked beſt, according to the Rules of the Colonades and Porticoes of a Temple. Over the Cornice on the right and left Sides, in certain Niches opened in the Wall, were Statues and other Figures of religious Veneration, but in the Front at the ſame Height with thoſe Niches, was a Window twice as broad as high, with two little Columns in the Middle of it, to ſupport the Tranſom. This was the Structure of the Prieſts Court. The Court for the Senators may be as follows: The Breadth of the Platform muſt be two thirds of its Length. The Height to the Rafters of the Roof muſt be equal to the Breadth of the Platform, with the Addition of one fourth Part of that Breadth. The Wall muſt be crowned with a Cornice, according to the following Rule. Having divided the whole clear Height into nine Parts, one of thoſe Parts muſt be given to the ſolid Baſement, or continued Pedeſtal of the Columns, and againſt this Baſement muſt be the Seats for the Senators. The Remainder muſt afterwards be divided into ſeven Parts, whereof four muſt be given to the firſt Row of Columns, over which you muſt raiſe another, both with their proper Baſes, Capitals, Architraves, Frezes and Cornices, in the Manner before preſcribed for a Baſilique. The Intervals between the Columns on each Side, muſt always be in an odd Number, and all equal to each other; but in Front, thoſe Intervals muſt be no more than three, the Middlemoſt whereof muſt be one fourth Part broader than the other two. In every Interval in the upper Row of Columns muſt be a Window, this Sort of Courts requiring as much Light as poſſible, and under each Window muſt be

* *For the* curia *and* senate house, *see Plates* 59–62, *facing and following this page.*

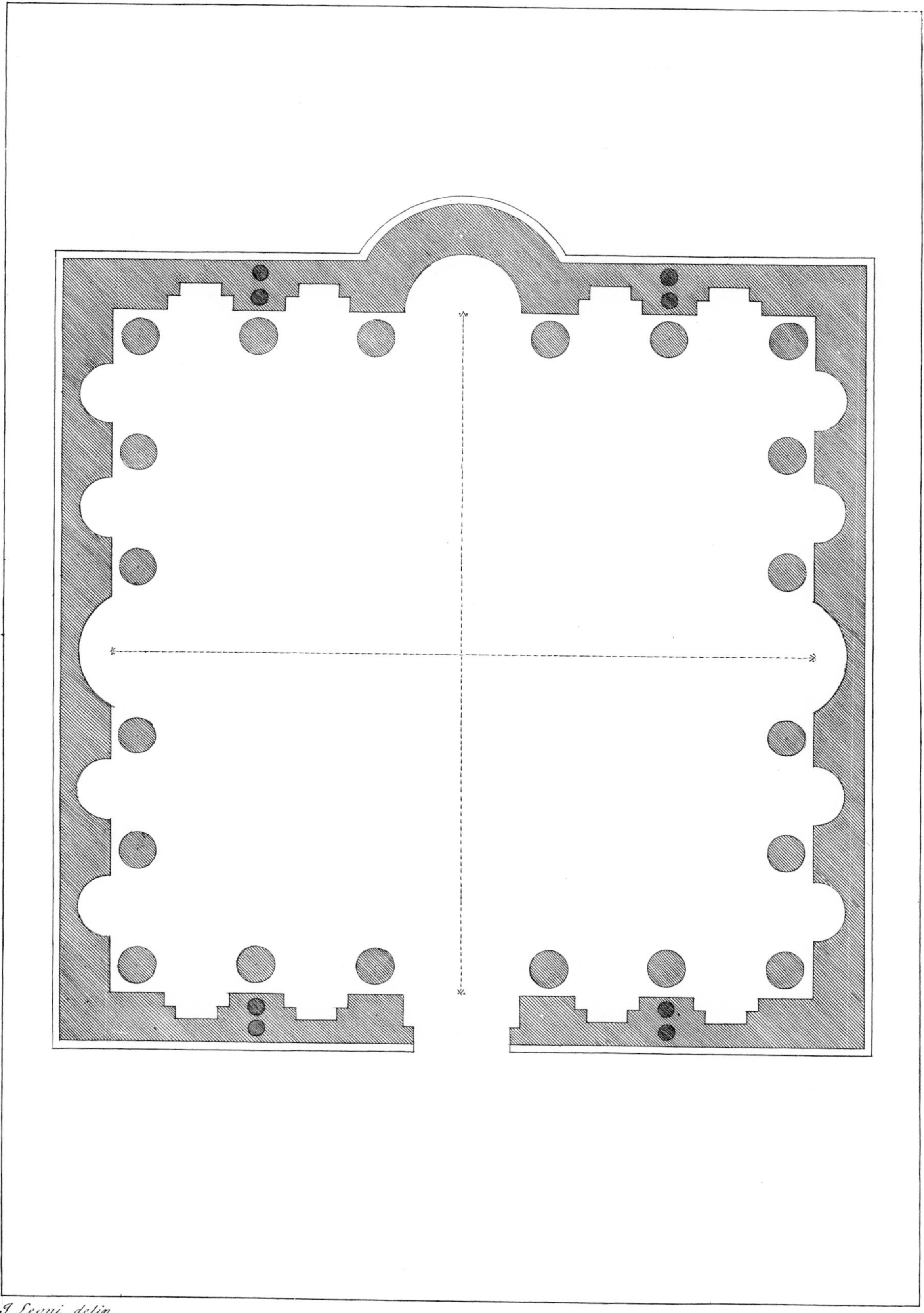

J. Leoni delin.

I. Leoni delin.

B. Picart sculp. direx. 1725.

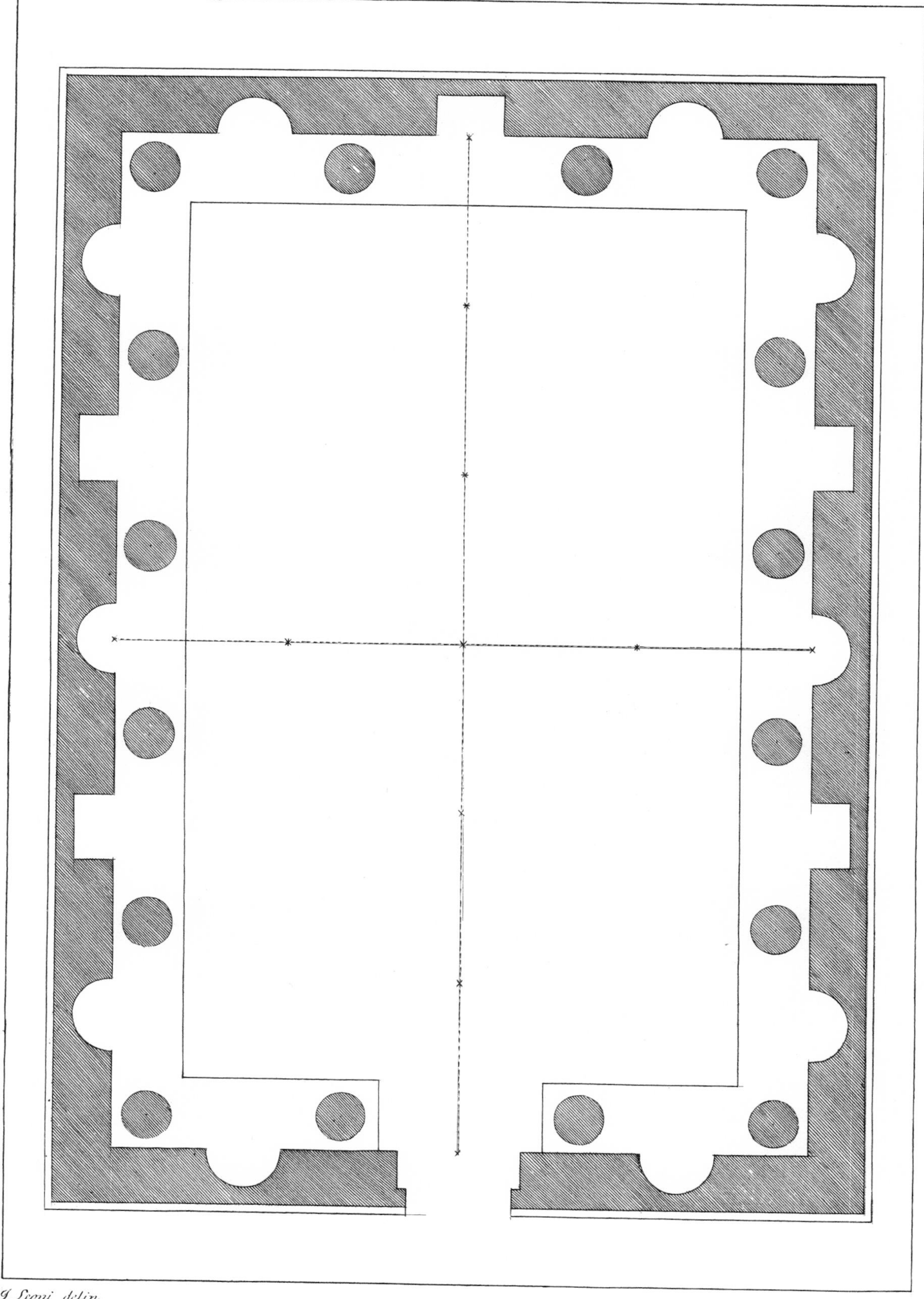

J. Leoni delin.

PLATE 62. *(Page 182)*

I. Leoni delin.

B. Picart sculp. direx. 1725.

be a Reſt, according to the Rules already given for the Baſilique, and no Part of the Dreſs of theſe Windows muſt riſe higher than the Shaft of the Columns between which they ſtand, excluſive of their Capitals. The Height of the Aperture of the Window being divided into eleven Parts, ſeven muſt be given to its Breadth. If you would have no upper Row of Columns at all, then you may ſupport the upper Cornice with Conſoles, inſtead of Capitals, according to the Method already given in the Deſcription of the *Ionic* Door. Then each Window will ſtand between two Conſoles made after the following Proportions. The Breadth of the Conſole muſt be the ſame as the Top of the naked Shaft of a Column in the ſame Place ought to be, excluſive of the Aſtragal and Fillet, and its Length equal to the Height of the *Corinthian* Capital without its Abacus. The Projecture of the Conſole muſt not exceed that of the Freze of its Entablature. The Ancients in a great many Places had ſeveral other Kinds of Structures and Inventions which admitted of Ornaments, and rendered the City more magnificent. We are told, that near the Academy of *Athens* there was a very fine Grove conſecrated to the Gods, which was cut down by *Sylla* in order for the caſting up an Intrenchment againſt *Athens*. *Alexander Severus* adorned his own Thermes, or Baths, with a pleaſant Grove, and added to thoſe of *Antoninus* ſeveral fine Lakes for Swimming in. The *Agrigentines*, upon *Zelo*'s Victory againſt the *Chalcedonians* made ſuch a Lake ſeven Furlongs long and twenty Cubits deep, from which they raiſed a conſiderable Income. We read, that at *Tivoli* there was a very famous publick Library. *Piſiſtratus* was the firſt that erected ſuch a Library at *Athens*, conſiſting of a great Number of Books, which were carried away by *Xerxes* into *Perſia*, and afterwards brought back again to *Athens* by *Seleucus*. The *Ptolomeys* King of *Ægypt* had a Library conſiſting of ſeven hundred thouſand Volumns; but why ſhould we wonder at ſuch a Number of Books in a publick Collection, when there was no leſs than ſixty-two thouſand Volumns in the particular Library of the *Gordians*? In the Country of *Laodicea*, beſides the Temple of *Nemeſis*, there was a noble Phyſick School, erected by *Zeuxis*, which was highly celebrated. *Appian* tells us, that at *Carthage* there was a Stable of three hundred Elephants, and another of hundred Horſes, an Arſenal for two hundred and twenty Ships, together with other Magazines both of Arms and Proviſions ſufficient to ſupply a whole Army. At *Thebes*, which was anciently called the City of the Sun, we read, that there were no leſs than an hundred publick Stables, each big enough to hold two hundred Horſes. In *Cizycus*, an Iſland of the *Propontis*, there were two Ports, and between them an Arſenal, the Roofs of which would give Shelter to two hundred Veſſels. Upon the *Pireum*, or Port of *Athens*, was a noble Station for no leſs than four hundred Ships, which was the celebrated Work of *Philo*. *Dionyſius*, at the Haven of *Syracuſe*, made an Arſenal divided into an hundred and ſixty Partitions, each whereof would contain two Veſſels, together with a Magazine, which in a few Days would furniſh above an hundred and twenty thouſand Shields, and an incredible Number of Swords. At *Sithicus* the *Spartans* had an Arſenal of above an hundred and ſixty Furlongs long. Thus we find Variety of Structures among various Nations: But as to their particular Forms, Deſigns and Contrivances, I have nothing certain to preſcribe, except that thoſe Parts of them which are for Uſe, muſt be borrowed from the Rules of private Edifices, and thoſe which are for Ornament and Magnificence, from thoſe of publick ones. I ſhall only obſerve, that the principal Ornament of a Library, is the Number and Variety of the Books contained in it, and chiefly their being collected from among the learned Remains of Antiquity. Another great Ornament, are curious mathematical Inſtruments of all Sorts, eſpecially if they are like that made by *Poſdonius*, in which all the ſeven Planets performed their proper Revolutions by their own Motion; or that of *Ariſtarchus*, who we are told deſcribed a Plan of the whole World, with all its ſeveral Provinces, upon a Table of Iron, to a moſt curious Exactneſs, and the Buſts of the ancient Poets, which *Tiberius* placed in his Library, were certainly a very proper and beautiful Ornament. I think I have now gone through with all the Ornaments that relate to publick Edifices. I have treated both of the Sacred and of the Profane, of Temples, Baſiliques, Porticoes, Sepulchres, Highways, Havens, Squares, Bridges, Triumphal Arches, Theatres, Circuſſes, Courts, Council-chambers, publick Places for Exerciſe, and the like, ſo that there ſeems nothing of this Nature now left for me to ſpeak of, except it be Thermes or publick Baths.

Chap.

Chap. X.

Of Thermes or publick Baths; their Conveniencies and Ornaments.

* SOME have condemned Baths, imagining they made Men effeminate, while others have had ſo great an Opinion of them, that they have waſhed in them ſeven Times a Day. The ancient Phyſicians, in order for the Cure of various Diſtempers by means of Bathing, erected a great Number of Thermes or publick Baths in the City of *Rome* at an incredible Expence. *Heliogabalus* particularly built *Thermæ* in a great many Places, but having waſhed once in each, he immediately ordered it to be demoliſhed, ſcorning ever to waſh twice in the ſame Bath. I am not thoroughly determined whether this Kind of Structure be of a publick or private Nature: And indeed I cannot help thinking that it partakes ſomewhat of both, ſince in many Particulars, it borrows from the Deſigns of private Edifices, and in many others from thoſe of publick ones. A publick Bath or Thermæ requiring a very large Area of Ground to ſtand upon, it is not proper to build it in the principal and moſt frequented Part of the City, neither ſhould it be placed too far out of the Way, becauſe both the chief Citizens and the Women muſt reſort thither to waſh themſelves. The Thermæ itſelf muſt have a large open Space clear round it, which muſt be encompaſſed with a high Wall, with proper Entrances at convenient Places. In the Middle of the Therme muſt be a large ſtately Hall, which muſt be as it were the Center of the whole Edifice, with Cells all round it after the Manner of the *Etrurian* Temple, which we have already deſcribed. Into this Hall we are to enter through a handſome Veſtibule, fronting to the South, from which we paſs into another ſmaller Veſtibule or Lobby, and ſo into the great Hall. From the Hall is a large Gate fronting to the North, which opens into a large open Square, on the Right and Left of which are ſpacious Porticoes, and immediately behind thoſe Porticoes are the cold Baths. Let us once more go back into the great Hall. On the right Side of this Hall, which lies to the Eaſt, is a broad ſpacious Lobby, with three Cells on each Side of it, lying oppoſite to each other. This Lobby carries us into another open Square, which I call the Xyſtus, which is encompaſſed with Porticoes on every Side. Of theſe Porticoes, that which fronts you as you come into the Square, has a handſome Withdrawing-room behind it. The Portico whoſe Front lies to the South has cold Baths behind it, in the ſame Manner as in the other Square, with convenient Dreſſing-rooms adjoining to them: And in the oppoſite Portico are the warm Baths, which receive the ſouth Sun by Windows broke out behind the Portico. In convenient Angles in the Porticoes of the Xyſtus are the other ſmaller Veſtibules, for Paſſages out into the open Space which encompaſſes the whole Thermæ. Theſe are the ſeveral Members of the Thermæ which lie on the right Side of the great Hall, and there muſt be juſt the ſame on the left which lies to the Weſt, anſwering to the former: The Lobby with three Cells on each Side, the open Square or Xyſtus with its Porticoes and Withdrawing-rooms, and the ſmaller Veſtibules in the Angles of the Xyſtus. Let us return once more to that principal Veſtibule of the whole Structure, which I ſaid fronted the South; on the right Hand of which, upon the Line which runs to the Eaſt are three Rooms, and as many on that which runs to the Weſt; the one for the Women, and the other for the Men. In the firſt Room they undreſſed; in the ſecond they anointed themſelves, and in the third they waſhed: And ſome for the greater Magnificence, added a fourth, for the Friends and Servants of thoſe that were bathing to wait for them in. Theſe Bathing-rooms received the Noon-day Sun at very large Windows. Between theſe Rooms and thoſe Cells which I told you lay along the Side of the inner Lobbies, which lead out of the great Hall into the open Square on the Side or Xyſtus, another open Area was left, which threw Light into the ſouth Side of thoſe inner Cells that lie along thoſe Lobbies from the great Hall. The whole Edifice of the Thermæ, as I before obſerved, was encompaſſed clear round with a broad open Space, which was even ſpacious enough for Races, nor were Goals wanting in proper Places of it for that Purpoſe. In the open Space on the ſouth Side in which is the principal Veſtibule of the whole Edifice,

was

* *See Plate 63, following this page.*

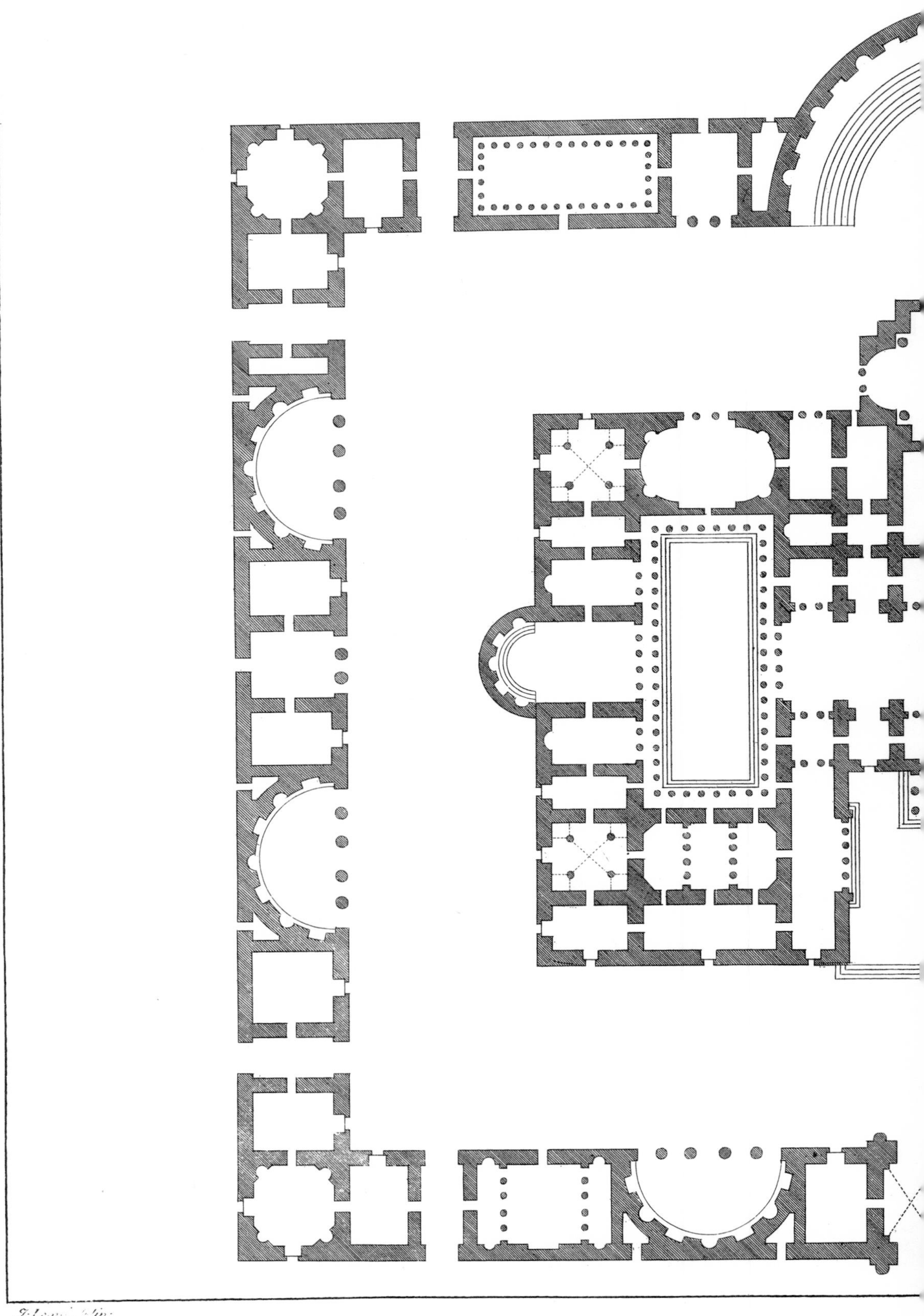

J. Leoni Delin.

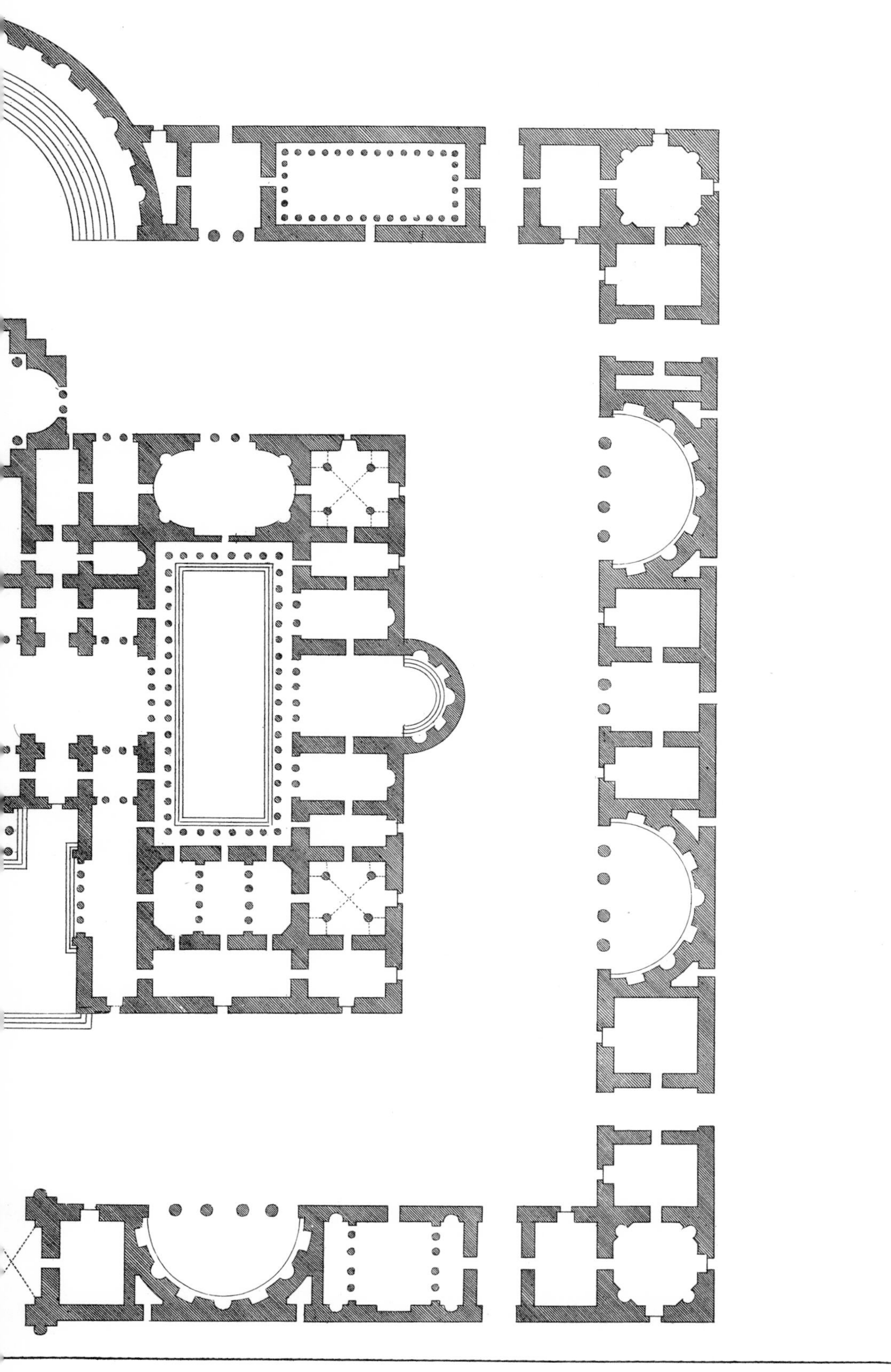

was a large ſemicircular Area verging to the South, in which ſeveral Rows of Seats were raiſed like thoſe in the Theatre, and the Wall was raiſed very high on that Side to keep off the ſouth Sun. All this open Space quite round the whole Thermæ was encloſed, like a Caſtle, with a continued Wall, and in this outward Wall were ſeveral handſome Rooms, either quadrangular or ſemicircular, which looked towards the Thermæ itſelf. In theſe Rooms the Citizens at Morning or Evening, or any Hour they liked beſt, enjoyed either Sun or Shade. Beſides all theſe, and eſpecially towards the North, behind the incloſing Wall were open Piazzas, of moderate Height, longer than broad, and drawn upon a curve Platform. Theſe Piazzas were ſurrounded by circular Porticoes, with a cloſe Wall at their Back, ſo that very little Sky was to be ſeen in theſe Piazzas, and between theſe Porticoes and the main Incloſure was a very good Refuge from the Heat in Summer, becauſe by means of the Narrowneſs of the Piazza itſelf, and the Height of the main Wall, the Sun, even in the Summer Solſtice could hardly ſtrike in upon it. In the Angles of the main Incloſure were Veſtibules and little Temples in which the Matrons, having cleanſed and purified themſelves, offered Oblations to their Gods. This is a brief Account of the ſeveral Members and Parts of the ancient Thermæ or Baths, and the Deſigns of the ſeveral Members were taken either from the Structures which we have already deſcribed, or from thoſe which we are ſtill to treat of, according as they had the greateſt Relation either to publick or to private Edifices; and the Platform of moſt of the ancient Edifices of this Sort contained above ten thouſand Foot ſquare.

The End of Book VIII.

THE

ARCHITECTURE

OF

Leone Batiſta Alberti.

Book IX. Chap. I.

That particular Regard muſt be had to Frugality and Parſimony, and of the adorning the Palaces or Houſes of the King and principal Magiſtrates.

WE are here to remember, that there are two Sorts of Houſes for private Men; ſome for the Town and others for the Country; and of theſe again ſome are intended for Citizens of meaner Rank, and others for thoſe of the higheſt Quality. We are now to treat of the proper Ornaments for each of theſe; but firſt I would premiſe ſome few neceſſary Precautions. We find that among the Ancients the Men of the greateſt Prudence and Modeſty were always beſt pleaſed with Temperance and Parſimony in all Things, both publick and private, and particularly in the Affair of Building, judging it neceſſary to prevent and reſtrain all Extravagance and Profuſion in their Citizens in theſe Points, which they did to the utmoſt of their Power both by Admonitions and Laws. For this Reaſon *Plato* commends thoſe who, as we have before obſerved, made a Decree, that no Man ſhould have in his Houſe any Picture that was finer than thoſe which had been ſet up in the Temples of their Gods by their Foreſathers, and that even the Temple itſelf ſhould be adorned with no other Painting but ſuch a ſingle Picture as one Painter could draw in one ſingle Day. He alſo ordained, that the Statues of the Gods themſelves ſhould be made only of Wood or Stone, and that Iron and Braſs ſhould be left for the Uſes of War, whereof they were the proper Inſtruments. *Demoſthenes* cried up the Manners of the ancient *Athenians*, much beyond thoſe of his Cotemporaries; for he tells us, they left an infinite Number of publick Edifices, and eſpecially of Temples, ſo magnificent and richly adorned that nothing could exceed them; but they were ſo modeſt in their private Buildings, that the Houſes of the very nobleſt Citizens differed very little from thoſe of the meaneſt; by which means they effected, what is very rarely known among Men, to overcome Envy by Glory. But the *Spartans* condemned even theſe, for having embelliſhed their City more with the Builder's Skill, than with the Splendor of their own Exploits, while they themſelves gloried, that they had adorned their own City more by their Virtue than by their fine Buildings. Among them it was one of *Lycurgus*'s Laws, that their Roofs ſhould be wrought with no nicer Tool than the Ax, and their Doors with the Saw. *Ageſilaus*, when he beheld ſquare Rafters in the Houſes in *Aſia*, laughed at them; and asked the People, whether if they had grown naturally ſquare, they would not have made them round? And doubtleſs he was in the Right; becauſe, according to the ancient Modeſty of his Nation, he was of Opinion, that the Houſes of private Perſons ought to be built only for Convenience, and not for Beauty or Magnificence. It was a Law in

Germany

Germany, in *Cæsar*'s Time, that no Man should build too delicately, and especially in the Country, to prevent Dissention among the People from a Desire of usurping each other's Possessions. *Valerious Poplicola* having built a stately House on that which is now the *Monte Cavallo* at *Rome*, pulled it down to avoid Envy, and built himself another in the Plain; and the same Modesty appeared in every Thing both Publick and Private in those ancient Times, while the Manners of the *Romans* continued uncorrupted: But afterwards, when the Empire was enlarged, the Luxury of Building ran so high in almost every Body (except in *Octavianus*, who had so great a Dislike to sumptuous Buildings, that he pulled down a Country-house only for its being too magnificent) I say, the Extravagance of Building ran so high in the City of *Rome*, that some of the *Gordian* Family, among others, built a House on the Road to *Preneste*, with two hundred Columns all of the same Bigness, and upon one Row, whereof fifty were of *Numidian*, fifty of *Claudian*, fifty of *Samian*, and fifty of *Titian* Marble, as I remember to have read. What a Piece of Magnificence was that which we read of in *Lucretius*, that in some Houses there were Statues of young Men all of Gold, holding lighted Torches in their right Hands, to light up their Feasts at Night? My Design in mentioning these Things is to confirm by the Comparison, what I said before, that the Magnificence of the Building should be adapted to the Dignity of the Owner; and if I may offer my Opinion, I should rather, in private Edifices, that the greatest Men fell rather a little short in Ornament, than they should be condemned for Luxury and Profusion by the more Discreet and Frugal. But since all agree, that we should endeavour to leave a Reputation behind us, not only for our Wisdom but our Power too; for this Reason, as *Thucydides* observes, we erect great Structures, that our Posterity may suppose us to have been great Persons. When therefore we adorn our Habitations not more for Delicacy than to procure Honour to our Country and our Families, who can deny this to be a Work well becoming the wisest Men? Accordingly I would have those Parts of the House which are chiefly in the publick View, and which are in a Manner to give the first Welcome to every Guest, as the Front, the Vestibule, and the like, be made as handsome as possible. And, though indeed I think those ought to be very much blamed that are guilty of too much Excess; yet I think those are much more to be condemned that lay out a great Expence upon a Building capable of no Ornament, than those that turn both their Thoughts and Money upon Ornament principally: Tho' I believe, I may venture to say, that whoever considers the true Nature of Ornament in Building will be convinced, that it is not Expence so much that is requisite,, as Taste and Contrivance. I think no prudent Man in building his private House should willingly differ too much from his Neighbours, or raise their Envy by his too great Expence and Ostentation; neither, on the other Hand, should he suffer himself to be out-done by any one whatsoever in the Ingenuity of Contrivance, or Elegance of Taste, to which the whole Beauty of the Composition, and Harmony of the several Members must be owing, which is indeed the highest and principal Ornament in all Building. But to return to our Subject.

The Royal Palace, or in a free City, the House of the Senator or chief Magistrate ought to be the first in Beauty and Magnificence. Of the Ornaments of those Parts of this Palace or House which bear any Relation to a publick Edifice, I have treated already. We are now to adorn those Parts which are intended only for private Use. I would have the Vestibule adorned in the most handsome and splendid Manner, according to the Quality of the Owner; besides which there should be stately Porticoes, and handsome Courts, with every Thing else in Imitation of a publick Edifice, that tends either to Dignity or Ornament, as far as the Nature of the Structure itself will bear, only using so much Moderation as to seem rather to aim at Beauty and Gracefulness, than at any Thing sumptuous: And as we observed in the last Book, with relation to Works of a publick Nature, that secular Buildings ought to yield in Dignity to the sacred, so here the Edifices of private Persons ought to give Way in Excellence and Number of Ornaments to those of the publick. A private House ought not to have Doors of Brass or Ivory, which was objected to *Camillus* as a Crime, nor Roofs fretted with great Quantities of Gold, or inlaid with Glass, nor should every Part be incrusted with *Hymettian* or *Parian* Marble; such Materials being proper only in Temples: But the Builder's chief Commendation in a private Structure, is to use moderate Materials elegantly, and elegant ones moderately. Let him be contented with Cypress, Larch and Box Wood;

Wood; let his Incruſtations or outward Coat be adorned with plain Figures in Stuc, or with ſome ſlight Painting, and his Cornices at moſt of common Marble. Not that he muſt abſolutely reject the moſt precious Materials; but he ſhould place them only in the moſt honourable Parts, like Gems in a Crown. But to give my Opinion of the whole Matter in one Word, I think that a ſacred Edifice ſhould be adorned in ſuch a Manner, that it ſhould be impoſſible to add any Thing that can conduce either to Majeſty, Beauty or Wonder: Whereas a private Structure ſhould be ſo contrived, that it ſhall be impoſſible to take any Thing from it, without leſſening its Dignity. Other Buildings, that is to ſay, the Profane of a publick Nature, ſhould obſerve the Medium between theſe two Extremes. Buildings of a private Sort ſhould keep ſtrictly to the Ornaments proper to them, only they may be made uſe of here with ſomewhat more Freedom. For Inſtance, if the Columns be of rather a ſmaller Diameter, or elſe more turgid, or if the Diminution of the Top of the Shaft be greater than the exact Proportions for publick Structures, they ought not here to be condemned, provided they do not look deformed or unſightly. And whereas in publick Works not the leaſt Deviation is allowed from the exacteſt Laws of Proportion, in private Works ſuch a Deviation is often handſome and commendable. Thus we may obſerve with what a beautiful Effect ſome of the more lively Architects uſed in the Doors of Halls, inſtead of Jambs to place huge Statues of Slaves, which ſupported the Lintel on their Heads; and to make Columns, eſpecially in the Porticoes of their Gardens, with Knots in the Shafts, in Imitation of Trees that had their Branches cut off, or girded round with a Cincture of Boughs, or with their whole Shaft wreathed and enriched with Leaves, Birds, and Channels: or where they would make the Work extremely ſtrong, we find them erecting ſquare Columns, fortified with a half Column on each Side; which inſtead of Capitals had either Baskets full of Vine Branches laden with Fruit, or the Head of a Palm-tree riſing up and full of Leaves, or a Knot of Serpents wreathed together, or an Eagle with its Wings expanded in Token of Pleaſure, or a *Meduſa*'s Head with the Snakes hiſſing at each other, or any other Fancy of the ſame Kind; to enumerate all which, would be endleſs. But in all theſe Liberties the Architect muſt be as careful as poſſible to keep the ſeveral Parts within the Terms of the regular Lines and Angles, and not ſuffer his Work to want a due Proportion in its ſeveral Members: So that the Beholder may immediately find, that his Deſign was to be wanton in theſe Particulars, and to indulge a Freedom of Invention. And as of the Parlours, Paſſages and Apartments, ſome are more publick, ſome more concealed, and as it were hidden; the former may be allowed ſomewhat more of the Splendor of a publick Structure, but yet ſo as not to create Envy; and in the latter we may allow ourſelves more Liberty in departing out of the common Road, and contriving ſomething new.

Chap. II.

Of the Adorning of private Houſes, both in City and Country.

BUT as of the Houſes of private Perſons, ſome are in the City, and ſome in the Country, we muſt ſay ſomething of the Ornaments proper to each of theſe. Between a Houſe in Town and a Houſe in the Country, there is this further Difference, beſides what we took notice of in the laſt Book, that the Ornaments, for that in Town ought to be much more grave than thoſe for a Houſe in the Country, where all the gayeſt and moſt licentious Embelliſhments are allowable. There is another Difference too between them, which is, that in Town you are obliged to moderate yourſelves in ſeveral Reſpects according to the Privileges of your Neighbour; whereas you have much more Liberty in the Country. In Town you muſt not raiſe your Platform or Baſement too high above your Neighbours, nor let your Portico project too far forwards from the Line of the adjacent Buildings. The Thickneſs and Height of the Walls at *Rome* anciently were not ſuffered to be according to every Man's particular Fancy, but by an old Law were all to be made according to a certain Standard; and *Julius Cæſar*, upon account of the Miſchiefs that might happen from bad Foundations,

ons, ordained that no Houſe ſhould be more than one Story high: To which Regulations a Country-houſe is not ſubject. It was reckoned one of the Glories of *Babylon*, that their Houſes had Inhabitants in the fourth Story. *Ælius Ariſtides*, the Orator, praiſing *Rome* in a publick Oration, cried it up as a miraculous Work of the *Romans* to have built upon great Houſes other Houſes as great: a handſome Piece of Flattery; but it ſhewed the Numerouſneſs of the People much more than the Magnificence of the Buildings themſelves. We are told that in Height of Houſes the City of *Rome* was outdone by *Tyre*, which by that means was formerly very near being wholly deſtroyed by Earthquakes. It is one very great Beauty and Convenience in a Building to have no more Aſcents and Deſcents in it than are abſolutely neceſſary; and it is certainly a very true Saying, that Stairs are nothing but Incumbrances to a Houſe, from which Incumbrances I find the Ancients were very ſtudious to keep clear. But in the Country there is no Manner of Neceſſity for ſetting one Houſe thus upon another: For only taking a larger Platform we may make whatever Conveniencies we think fit upon the ſame Floor; which I ſhould like extremely well in Town too, if it could be had. There is another Sort of private Houſes, in which the Dignity of the Town-houſe, and the Delights and Pleaſures of the Country-houſe are both required; of which we ſaid nothing in the former Books, reſerving it purpoſely for this very Place: And theſe are the Pleaſure-houſes juſt without the Town, or the Villa's which are by no means to be paſſed by without ſome Obſervations, though I ſhall be as brief in them as poſſible. Accordingly I ſhall here lay together all that I have to ſay of each of theſe three Sorts of Structures, and firſt of the Villa cloſe to the Town. The Saying among the Ancients, Let him that buys a Country-houſe ſell his Houſe in Town, and let him that has Buſineſs in Town, never think of a Houſe in the Country, ſeems to imply, that a Villa near Town is extremely convenient. The Phyſicians adviſe us to dwell in the cleareſt and openeſt Air that we can find; and there is no room to doubt but a Country-houſe ſeated upon an Eminence, muſt of Courſe be the Beſt: But then on the other Hand, the Maſter of a Family, upon account of his private Buſineſs, or the publick Affairs, may be obliged to be often in the City; for which Purpoſe a Houſe in Town ſeems neceſſary: But then as the former is inconvenient for Buſineſs, ſo the latter is prejudicial to the Health. It is a common Thing for the Generals of Armies to remove their Camps often, to avoid being incommoded by ill Smells: What can we think then of a great City, where ſuch vaſt Quantities of Filth, and ſo long kept, are continually exhaling their offenſive Steams? To reconcile this Dilemma therefore, I do not think that of all the Structures which are raiſed for the Conveniency of Mankind, there is any ſo commodious or ſo healthy as the Villa; which at the ſame Time as it lies in the Way for Buſineſs, is not wholly deſtitute of pure Air. *Cicero* deſired his Friend *Atticus* to build him a Villa in a Place of eminent Note: But I, for my Part, am not for having it in a Place of ſuch Reſort, that I muſt never venture to appear at my Door without being compleatly dreſſed. I would have it afford me the Pleaſure which the old Gentleman in *Terence* boaſts he enjoyed, *of being never tired either with the Town or Country*. *Martial* too gives a very juſt Deſcription of his Way of Living in ſuch a Villa.

You tell me, Friend, you much deſire to know,
What in my Villa I can find to do?
I eat, drink, ſing, play, bathe, ſleep, eat again,
Or read, or wanton in the Muſes Train.

There is certainly a vaſt deal of Satisfaction in a convenient Retreat near the Town, where a Man is at Liberty to do juſt what he pleaſes. The great Beauties of ſuch a Retreat, are being near the City, upon an open airy Road, and on a pleaſant Spot of Ground. The greateſt Commendation of the Houſe itſelf is its making a chearful Appearance to thoſe that go a little Way out of Town to take the Air, as if it ſeemed to invite every Beholder: And for this Reaſon I would have it ſtand pretty high, but upon ſo eaſy an Aſcent, that it ſhould hardly be perceptible to thoſe that go to it, till they find themſelves at the Top, and a large Proſpect opens itſelf to their View. Nor ſhould there be any Want of pleaſant Landskips, flowery Meads, open Champains, ſhady Groves, or limpid Brooks, or clear Streams and Lakes for ſwimming, with all other Delights of the ſame Sort, which we before obſerved to be neceſſary in a Country Retreat, both for Convenience and Pleaſure. Laſtly, what I have already ſaid conduces extremely to the Pleaſantneſs of all Buildings, I would have the Front and whole Body of the Houſe perfectly well

 lighted,

lighted, and that it be open to receive a great deal of Light and Sun, and a ſufficient Quantity of wholſome Air. Let nothing be within View that can offend the Eye with a melancholy Shade. Let all Things ſmile and ſeem to welcome the Arrival of your Gueſts. Let thoſe who are already entered be in Doubt whether they ſhall for Pleaſure continue where they are, or paſs on further to thoſe other Beauties which tempt them on. Let them be led from ſquare Rooms into round ones, and again from round into ſquare, and ſo into others of mixed Lines, neither all round nor all ſquare; and let the Paſſage into the very innermoſt Apartments be, if poſſible, without the leaſt Aſcent or Deſcent, but all be upon one even Floor, or at leaſt let the Aſcents be as eaſy as may be.

Chap. III.

That the Parts and Members of a Houſe are different both in Nature and Species, and that they are to be adorned in various Manners.

BUT as the Members or Parts of a Houſe are very different one from the other both in Nature and Species, it may now be proper to ſay ſomething of each, having indeed purpoſely reſerved them for this very Place: For there are many Parts which it matters very little whether you make round or ſquare, provided they are fit for the Purpoſes to which they are intended; but it is not equally indifferent what Number they are in, and how they are diſpoſed; and it is neceſſary that ſome ſhould be larger, as the inner Courts, while ſome require a ſmaller Area, as the Chambers and all the private Apartments. Some others muſt be in a Medium between the others, as Eating-parlours and the Veſtibule. We have already in another Place given our Thoughts of the apt Diſpoſition of each Member of a Houſe, and as to the reſpective Difference of their Areas, there is no Occaſion to ſpeak here, becauſe they are infinite both from the different Humours of Men, and the different Ways of Living in different Places. The Ancients, before their Houſes made either a Portico, or at leaſt a Porch, not always with ſtraight Lines, but ſometimes with curve, after the Manner of the Theatre. Next to the Portico lay the Veſtibule, which was almoſt conſtantly circular; behind that was the Paſſage into the inner Court, and thoſe other Parts of the Houſe which we have already ſpoken of in their proper Places, whereof to enter upon a freſh Deſcription would make us too prolix. The Things that we ought not to omit are theſe. Where the Area is round it muſt be proportioned according to the Deſign of the Temple; unleſs there be this Difference, that here the Height of the Walls muſt be greater than in the Temple, for Reaſons which you ſhall know ſhortly. If it be quadrangular, then in ſome Particulars it will differ from thoſe Inſtructions which we have given for ſacred Edifices, as alſo for profane ones of a publick Nature; but yet in ſome others it will agree with the Council-chambers and Courts. According to the general Cuſtom of the Ancients, the Breadth of the Porch was either two thirds of its Length, or elſe the Length was one whole Breadth and two thirds more, or elſe the Length was one whole Breadth with the Addition of two fifths. To each of theſe Proportions the Ancients ſeem always to have allowed the Height of the Wall to be equal to its whole Length, and one third more. By taking the actual Dimenſion of a great many Structures, I find that ſquare Platforms require a different Height of Wall where they are to be covered with vaulted Roofs, from what they do when their Roof is to be flat: As alſo that ſome Difference is to be made between the Proportions of a large Building and thoſe of a ſmall one: Which ariſes from the different Interval that there is from the Beholder's Eye, which muſt in this Caſe be conſidered as the Center, to the extreme Height which it ſurveys: But of thoſe Things we ſhall treat elſewhere. We muſt Proportion the Areas of our Apartments to our Roof, and our Roof to the Length of the Rafters with which it is to be covered in. I call that a moderate Roof which may be ſupported by a Piece of Timber of a moderate Length. But beſides the Proportions which I have already treated of, there are ſeveral other proper Dimenſions and Agreements of Lines which I ſhall here endeavour to explain as clearly and ſuccinctly as poſſible. If the Length of the Platform be twice its Breadth; then,

then, where the Roof is to be flat, the Height muſt be equal to the Breadth; where the Roof is to be vaulted, a third Part of that Breadth more muſt be added. This may ſerve for middling Buildings: In very large ones, if they are to have a vaulted Roof, the whole Height muſt be one whole Breadth, with the Addition of one fourth Part; but if the Roof is to be flat it muſt be one whole Breadth and two fifths. If the Length of the Platform be three Times its Breadth, and the Roof is to be flat, let the Height be one whole Breath and three quarters, if the Roof is to be vaulted, let the Height be one whole Breadth and an half. If the Length of the Platform be four Times its Breadth, and the Roof is to be vaulted, let the Height be half its Length; and if the Roof is to be flat, divide the Breadth into four Parts, and give one and three quarters of thoſe Parts to the Height. If the Length be five Times the Breadth, make the Height the ſame as where it is four Times, only with the Addition of one ſixth Part of that Height; and if it is ſix Times the Breadth, make it as before, adding not a ſixth as in the former, but a fifth. If the Platform be an exact Square with equal Sides, and the Roof is to be vaulted, let the Height exceed the Breadth as in the Platform of three Breadths; but if the Roof is to be flat, it muſt not exceed ſo much, and in the larger Platforms, it muſt not exceed this Breadth above one fourth Part. In thoſe Platforms where the Length exceeds the Breadth only one ninth Part, let the Height be exceeded by the Breadth one ninth Part too; but this muſt be only in a flat Roof. When the Length is to be one whole Breadth and a third, let the Height be one whole Breadth and a ſixth in flat Roofs; but in vaulted ones, let the Height be one whole Breadth and a ſixth of the Length. When the Length is one Breadth and an Half, let the Height be one Breadth and a ſeventh of that Breadth, in a flat Roof; but in a vaulted one, let the Height be one Breadth, and a ſeventh of the Length of the Platform. If the Platform conſiſt of Lines whereof one is as ſeven, and the other as five, or the Length be as five and the Breadth as three, or the like, according as the Neceſſity of the Place, or Variety of Invention, or the Nature of the Ornaments requires; add thoſe two Lines together, and allow one half of the Amount to the Height. I muſt not here omit one Precaution, namely, that the Veſtibule ought never to be above twice as long as broad, and the Apartments never leſs broad than two thirds of their Length. The Platforms which are in Length three or four Times their Breadth or more, belong only to Porticoes, and even they ought never to be above ſix Times their Breadth. In the Wall Apertures are to be left both for Windows and Doors. If the Window is broke in the Wall of the Breadth-line of the Platform, which in its very Nature is ſhorter than that of the Length, then there muſt be only a ſingle one; and this Window itſelf muſt either be higher than it is broad, or elſe on the contrary broader than it is high, which laſt Sort is called a reclining Window. If the Breadth is to be like that of the Door, ſomewhat leſs than the Length; then let the Breadth of the clear Opening be not more than a third, nor leſs than a fourth Part of the Inſide of the Wall in which it is made; and let the Reſt or Bottom of the Window be in Height from the Floor not more than four ninths of the whole Height, nor leſs than two. The Height of the clear Open of the Window muſt be one third more than its Breadth; and this is the Proportion, if the Window is to be higher than broad; but if the Window is to be broader then high, than of the whole inſide Length of the Wall in which it is made, you muſt not allow the Open of the Window leſs than one half, nor more than two thirds. In the ſame Manner its Height too muſt be made either half its Breadth, or two thirds, only it muſt have two little Columns to ſupport the Tranſom. If you are to make Windows in the longer Side, there muſt be more of them, and they ſhould be in an odd Number. I find the Ancients were beſt pleaſed with three, which were made in the following Manner: The whole longeſt Side of the Wall muſt be divided into never more than ſeven, nor leſs than five Parts, of which taking three, in each of them make a Window, making the Height of the Open one whole Breadth and three quarters, or one Breadth and four fifths. If you would make your Windows more numerous; as they will then partake of the Nature of a Portico, you may borrow the Dimenſions of your Openings from the Rules of the Portico itſelf, and eſpecially from that of the Theatre, as we laid them down in their proper Place. The Doors muſt be made after the Manner of thoſe which we deſcribed for the Court and Council-chamber. Let the Dreſs of the Windows be *Corinthian*; of the principal Door, *Ionic*; of the Doors of the Halls and Chambers, *Doric*. And thus much of the Lines, as far as they relate to this preſent Purpoſe.

Chap.

Chap. IV.

With what Paintings, Plants, and Statues, it is proper to adorn the Pavements, Porticoes, Apartments and Gardens of a private House.

THERE are some other Ornaments extremely proper for a private House, by no means to be omitted in this Place. The Ancients stained the Pavements of their Porticoes with Labyrinths, both square and circular, in which the Boys used to exercise themselves. I have myself seen Pavements stained in Imitation of the Bell-flower-weed, with its Branches twining about very beautifully. Other have paved their Chambers with a Sort of *Mosaic* Work of Marble, in Imitation of Carpets, others in Imitation of Garlands and Branches of Trees. It was a very ingenious Invention of *Osis*, who strewed the Pavement at *Pergamus* with inlaid Work, in Imitation of the Fragments that lie scattered about after Meals; an Ornament not ill suited to a Parlour. *Agrippa* was very right in making his Floors of common baked Earth. I, for my Part, hate every Thing that savours of Luxury or Profusion, and am best pleased with those Ornaments which arise principally from the Ingenuity and Beauty of the Contrivance. Upon side Walls no Sort of Painting shews handsomer than the Representation of Columns in Architecture. *Titius Cæsar* adorned the Walls of the Portico in which he used to walk, with a Sort of *Phœnician* Stone so finely polished, that it returned the Reflection of all the Objects like a Looking-glass. *Antoninus Caracalla*, the Emperor, painted his Portico with the memorable Exploits and Triumphs of his Father. *Severus* did the same; but *Agathocles* painted not his Father's Actions, but his own. Among the *Persians*, according to their ancient Laws, it was not permitted to paint or carve any other Story, but of the wild Beasts slain by their Kings. It is certain, the brave and memorable Actions of one's Countrymen, and their Effigies, are Ornaments extremely suitable both to Porticoes and Halls. *Caius Cæsar* embellished his Portico with the Statues of all those that had enlarged the Confines of the Republick, and he gained a general Approbation by so doing. I am as much pleased as any body with this Kind of Ornaments; but yet I would not have the Wall too much crowded with Statues or History Pieces. We may find by Gems, and especially by Pearls, that if they are set too thick together, they lose their Beauty. For this Reason, in some of the most convenient and most conspicuous Parts of the Wall, I am for making handsome Pannels of Stone, in which we may place either Statues, or Pictures; such as *Pompey* had carried along in his Triumph; Representing his Exploits both by Sea and Land in Picture. Or rather, I am for having Pictures of such Fictions of the Poets, as tend to the Promotion of good Manners; such as that of *Dædalus*, who painted the Gates of *Cumæ* with the Representation of *Icarus* flying. And as the Subjects both of Poetry and Painting are various, some expressing the memorable Actions of great Men; others Representing the Manners of private Persons; others describing the Life of Rusticks: The former, as the most Majestick, should be applied to publick Works, and the Buildings of Princes; and the latter, as the more chearful, should be set apart for Pleasure-houses and Gardens. Our Minds are delighted in a particular Manner with the Pictures of pleasant Landskips, of Havens, of Fishing, Hunting, Swimming, Country Sports, of flowery Fields and thick Groves. Neither is it foreign to our present Purpose just to mention, that *Octavianus*, the Emperor, adorned his Palace with the huge Bones of some extraordinary Animals. The Ancients used to dress the Walls of their Grottoes and Caverns with all Manner of rough Work, with little Chips of Pumice, or soft *Tyburtine* Stone, which *Ovid* calls the living Pumice; and some I have known dawb them over with green Wax, in Imitation of the mossy Slime which we always see in moist Grottoes. I was extremely pleased with an artificial Grotto which I have seen of this Sort, with a clear Spring of Water falling from it; the Walls were composed of various Sorts of Sea-shells, lying roughly together, some reversed, some with their Mouths outwards, their Colours being so artfully blended as to form a very beautiful Variety. In that Apartment which is peculiar to the Master of the Family and his Wife, we should take Care that nothing be be painted but the moſt comely and beautiful Faces; which we are told may be of no ſmall Conſequence to the Conception of the Lady, and the Beauty of the Children. Such as are tormented with a Fever are not a little refreſhed by the Sight of Pictures of Springs, Caſcades and Streams of Water, which any one may eaſily experience; for if at any Time you find it difficult to compoſe yourſelf to reſt in the Night, only turn your Imagination upon ſuch clear Waters as you can remember any where to have ſeen, either of Springs, Lakes or Streams, and that burning Drowth of the Mind, which kept you waking, ſhall preſently be moiſtened, and a pleaſant Forgetfulneſs ſhall creep upon you, till you fall into a fine Sleep. To theſe Delicacies we muſt add thoſe of well-diſpoſed Gardens and beautiful Trees, together with Porticoes in the Garden, where you may enjoy either Sun or Shade. To theſe add ſome little pleaſant Meadow, with fine Springs of Water burſting out in different Places where leaſt expected. Let the Walks be terminated by Trees that enjoy a perpetual Verdure, and particularly on that Side which is beſt ſheltered from Winds, let them be encloſed with Box, which is preſently injured and rotted by ſtrong Winds, and eſpecially by the leaſt Spray from the Sea. In open Places, moſt expoſed to the Sun, ſome ſet Myrtles, which will flouriſh extremely in the Summer: But *Theophraſtus* affirms, that the Myrtle, the Laurel, and the Ivy rejoyce in the Shade, and therefore directs us to plant them thick, that they may mutually ſhelter one another from the Sun by their own Shade: Nor let there be wanting Cypreſs-trees cloathed with Ivy. Let the Ground alſo be here and there thrown into thoſe Figures that are moſt commended in the Platforms of Houſes, Circles, Semicircles, and the like, and ſurrounded with Laurels, Cedars, Junipers with their Branches intermixed, and twining one into the other. *Phiteon* of *Agrigentum*, though but a private Man, had in his Houſe three hundred Vaſes of Stone, each whereof would hold an hundred Amphoras, or about fifteen of our Hogſheads. Such Vaſes are very fine Ornaments for Fountains in Gardens. The Ancients uſed to make their Walks into a Kind of Arbours by Means of Vines ſupported by Columns of Marble of the *Corinthian* Order, which were ten of their own Diameters in Height. The Trees ought to be planted in Rows exactly even, and anſwering to one another exactly upon ſtraight Lines; and the Gardens ſhould be enriched with rare Plants, and ſuch as are in moſt Eſteem among the Phyſicians. It was a good agreeable Piece of Flattery among the ancient Gardeners, to trace their Maſters Names in Box, or in ſweet-ſmeling Herbs, in Parterres. Roſe-trees, intermixed with Pomegranates and Cornels, are very beautiful in a Hedge: But the Poet ſays,

Your Hedge of Oak with Plums and Cornel made,
To yield the Cattle Food, the Maſter Shade.

BUT perhaps this may ſuit better with a Farm intended for Profit, than with a Villa calculated chiefly for taking the Air in: And indeed what we are told *Democritus* very much condemned, namely, the incloſing a Garden with any Sort of Wall, I ſhould not blame in the Caſe before us, but am rather of Opinion, that it is a very proper Defence againſt Malice or Rapine. Nor am I diſpleaſed with the placing ridiculous Statues in Gardens, provided they have nothing in them obſcene. Such ſhould be the Diſpoſition of the Villa. In Houſes in Town, the inner Apartments and Parlours ſhould not in the leaſt give way, either in Chearfulneſs or Beauty, to the Villa; but in the more publick Rooms, ſuch as the Hall and Veſtibule, you ſhould not aim ſo much at Delicacy, as to forget a decent Gravity. The Porticoes of the Houſes of the principal Citizens may have a compleat regular Entablature over the Columns; but thoſe of lower Degree, ſhould have only Arches. Vaulted Roofs are proper in both. The whole Entablature muſt be in Height one fourth Part of the Shaft. If there is to be a ſecond Order of Columns over the firſt, let that ſecond Order be one fourth Part ſhorter than the lower one; and if there is to be a third Order over this, let it be one fifth Part ſhorter than that below it. In each of theſe the Pedeſtal or Plinth under each Order of Columns, muſt be in Height one fourth Part of the Column which it ſupports; but where there is to be only one ſingle Row of Columns, the Proportions may be taken from thoſe of profane Works of a publick Nature. A private Houſe ſhould never have ſuch a Pediment as may ſeem to rival the Majeſty of a Temple. However, the Front of the Veſtibule may be raiſed ſomewhat above the reſt of the Building, and be adorned with a ſmaller Pediment. The reſt of the Front on each Side this Pediment may be adorned with a ſmall Plinth, which may riſe ſomewhat higher at the principal

pal Angles I cannot be pleaſed with thoſe who make Towers and Battlements to a private Houſe, which belong of right entirely to a Fortification, or to the Caſtle of a Tyrant, and are altogether inconſiſtent with the peaceable Aſpect of a well-governed City or Commonwealth, as they ſhew either a Diſtruſt of our Countrymen, or a Deſign to uſe Violence againſt them. Balconies in the Front of a Houſe are beautiful enough, provided they are not too large, heavy, and out of Proportion.

Chap. V.

That the Beauty of all Edifices ariſes principally from three Things, namely, the Number, Figure and Collocation of the ſeveral Members.

I Now come once more to thoſe Points which I before promiſed to enquire into, namely, wherein it is that Beauty and Ornament, univerſally conſidered, conſiſt, or rather whence they ariſe. An Enquiry of the utmoſt Difficulty; for whatever that Property be which is ſo gathered and collected from the whole Number and Nature of the ſeveral Parts, or to be imparted to each of them according to a certain and regular Order, or which muſt be contrived in ſuch a Manner as to join and unite a certain Number of Parts into one Body or Whole, by an orderly and ſure Coherence and Agreement of all thoſe Parts: Which Property is what we are here to diſcover; it is certain, ſuch a Property muſt have in itſelf ſomething of the Force and Spirit of all the Parts with which it is either united or mixed, otherwiſe they muſt jar and diſagree with each other, and by ſuch Diſcord deſtroy the Uniformity or Beauty of the Whole: The Diſcovery of which, as it is far from being eaſy or obvious in any other Caſe, ſo it is particularly difficult and uncertain here; the Art of Architecture conſiſting of ſo many various Parts, and each of thoſe Parts requiring ſo many various Ornaments as you have already ſeen. However, as it is neceſſary in the Proſecution of our Deſign, we ſhall uſe the utmoſt of our Abilities in clearing this obſcure Point, not going ſo far about as to ſhew how a compleat Knowledge of a Whole is to be gained by examining the ſeveral Parts diſtinct; but beginning immediately upon what is to our preſent Purpoſe, by enquiring what that Property is which in its Nature makes a Thing beautiful. The moſt expert Artiſts among the Ancients, as we have obſerved elſewhere, were of Opinion, that an Edifice was like an Animal, ſo that in the Formation of it we ought to imitate Nature. Let us therefore enquire how it happens that in the Bodies produced by Nature herſelf ſome are accounted more, others leſs beautiful, or even deformed. It is manifeſt, that in thoſe which are eſteemed beautiful, the Parts or Members are not conſtantly all the ſame, ſo as not to differ in any Reſpect: But we find, that even in thoſe Parts wherein they vary moſt, there is ſomething inherent and implanted which though they differ extremely from each other, makes each of them beautiful. I will make uſe of an Example to illuſtrate my Meaning. Some admire a Woman for being extremely ſlender and fine ſhaped; the young Gentleman in *Terence* prefered a Girl that was plump and fleſhy: You perhaps are for a Medium between theſe two Extremes, and would neither have her ſo thin as to ſeem waſted with Sickneſs, nor ſo ſtrong and robuſt as if ſhe were a Ploughman in Diſguiſe, and were fit for Boxing: In ſhort, you would have her ſuch a Beauty as might be formed by taking from the firſt what the ſecond might ſpare. But then becauſe, one of theſe pleaſes you more than the other, would you therefore affirm the other to be not at all handſome or graceful? By no means; but there may be ſome hidden Cauſe why one ſhould pleaſe you more than the other, into which I will not now pretend to enquire. But the Judgment which you make that a Thing is beautiful, does not proceed from mere Opinion, but from a ſecret Argument and Diſcourſe implanted in the Mind itſelf; which plainly appears to be ſo from this, that no Man beholds any Thing ugly or deformed, without an immediate Hatred and Abhorrence. Whence this Senſation of the Mind ariſes, and how it is formed, would be a Queſtion too ſubtle for this Place: However, let us conſider and examine it from thoſe Things which are obvious, and make more immediately to the Subject in Hand: For without Queſtion there is a certain Excellence and natural

natural Beauty in the Figures and Forms of Buildings, which immediately ſtrike the Mind with Pleaſure and Admiration. It is my Opinion, that Beauty, Majeſty, Gracefulneſs, and the like Charms, conſiſt in thoſe Particulars which if you alter or take away, the Whole would be made homely and diſagreeable. If we are convinced of this, it can be no very tedious Enquiry to conſider thoſe Things which may be taken away, encreaſed or altered, eſpecially in Figures and Forms: For every Body conſiſts of certain peculiar Parts, of which if you take away any one, or leſſen, or enlarge it, or remove it to an improper Place; that which before gave the Beauty and Grace to this Body will at once be lamed and ſpoild. From hence we may conclude, to avoid Prolixity in this Reſearch, that there are three Things principally in which the Whole of what we are looking into conſiſts: The Number, and that which I have called the Finiſhing, and the Collocation. But there is ſtill ſomething elſe beſides, which ariſes from the Conjunction and Connection of theſe other Parts, and gives the Beauty and Grace to the Whole: Which we will call Congruity, which we may conſider as the Original of all that is graceful and handſome. The Buſineſs and Office of Congruity is to put together Members differing from each other in their Natures, in ſuch a Manner, that they may conſpire to form a beautiful Whole: So that whenever ſuch a Compoſition offers itſelf to the Mind, either by the Conveyance of the Sight, Hearing, or any of the other Senſes, we immediately perceive this Congruity: For by Nature we deſire Things perfect, and adhere to them with Pleaſure when they are offered to us; nor does this Congruity ariſe ſo much from the Body in which it is found, or any of its Members, as from itſelf, and from Nature, ſo that its true Seat is in the Mind and in Reaſon; and accordingly it has a very large Field to exerciſe itſelf and flouriſh in, and runs through every Part and Action of Man's Life, and every Production of Nature herſelf, which are all directed by the Law of Congruity, nor does Nature ſtudy any Thing more than to make all her Works abſolute and perfect, which they could never be without this Congruity, ſince they would want that Conſent of Parts which is ſo neceſſary to Perfection. But we need not ſay more upon this Point, and if what we have here laid down appears to be true, we may conclude Beauty to be ſuch a Conſent and Agreement of the Parts of a Whole in which it is found, as to Number, Finiſhing and Collocation, as Congruity, that is to ſay, the principal Law of Nature requires. This is what Architecture chiefly aims at, and by this ſhe obtains her Beauty, Dignity and Value. The Ancients knowing from the Nature of Things, that the Matter was in Fact as I have here ſtated it, and being convinced, that if they neglected this main Point they ſhould never produce any Thing great or commendable, did in their Works propoſe to themſelves chiefly the Imitation of Nature, as the greateſt Artiſt at all Manner of Compoſitions; and for this Purpoſe they laboured, as far as the Induſtry of Man could reach, to diſcover the Laws upon which ſhe herſelf acted in the Production of her Works, in order to transfer them to the Buſineſs of Architecture. Reflecting therefore upon the Practice of Nature as well with Relation to an entire Body, as to its ſeveral Parts, they found from the very firſt Principles of Things, that Bodies were not always compoſed of equal Parts or Members; whence it happens, that of the Bodies produced by Nature, ſome are ſmaller, ſome larger, and ſome middling: And conſidering that one Building differed from another, upon account of the End for which it was raiſed, and the Purpoſe which it was to ſerve, as we have ſhewn in the foregoing Books, they found it neceſſary to make them of various Kinds. Thus from an Imitation of Nature they invented three Manners of adorning a Building, and gave them Names drawn from their firſt Inventors. One was better contrived for Strength and Duration: This they called *Doric*; another was more taper and beautiful, this they named *Corinthian*; another was a Kind of Medium compoſed from the other two, and this they called *Ionic*. Thus much related to the whole Body in general. Then obſerving, that thoſe three Things which we have already mentioned, namely, the Number, Finiſhing and Collocation, were what chiefly conduced to make the whole beautiful, they found how they were to make uſe of this from a thorough Examination of the Works of Nature, and, as I imagine, upon the following Principles. The firſt Thing they obſerved, as to Number, was that is was of two Sorts, even and uneven, and they made uſe of both, but in different Occaſions: For, from the Imitation of Nature, they never made the Ribs of their Structure, that is to ſay, the Columns, Angles and the like, in uneven Numbers; as you ſhall not find any Animal that ſtands or moves

moves upon an odd Number of Feet. On the contrary, they made their Apertures always in uneven Numbers, as Nature herſelf has done in ſome Inſtances, for tho' in Animals ſhe has placed an Ear, an Eye, and a Noſtril on each Side, yet the great Aperture, the Mouth, ſhe has ſet ſingly in the Middle. But among theſe Numbers, whether even or uneven, there are ſome which ſeem to be greater Favourites with Nature than others, and more celebrated among learned Men; which Architects have borrowed for the Compoſition of the Members of their Edifices, upon Account of their being endued with ſome Qualities which make them more valuable than any others.

Thus all the Philoſophers affirm, that Nature herſelf conſiſts in a ternary Principle; and ſo the Number five, when we conſider the many Things, and thoſe ſo admirable and various, which either follow this Number in themſelves, or are derived from thoſe Things which do, muſt be allowed to be divine in its Nature, and worthily dedicated to the Gods of the Arts, and particularly to *Mercury*. It is certain, that Almighty God himſelf, the Creator of all Things, takes particular Delight in the Number Seven, having placed ſeven Planets in the Skies, and having been pleaſed to ordain with Regard to Man, the Glory of his Creation, that Conception, Growth, Maturity and the like, ſhould all be reduceable to this Number Seven. *Ariſtotle* ſays, that the Ancients never uſed to give a Child a Name, till it was ſeven Days old, as not thinking it was deſtined to Life before; becauſe both the Seed in the Womb, and the Child after its Birth, is liable to very dangerous Accidents till the ſeventh Day is over. Among odd Numbers, that of Nine is highly celebrated, in which Number that great Artiſt, Nature, made the Spheres of Heaven; and the Philoſophers ſay, that Nature in many, and thoſe the greateſt Things, is contented with making uſe of the ninth Part of a Whole. Thus forty is about the Ninth Part of all the Days of the Year, according to the Revolution of the Sun, and *Hippocrates* tells us, that in forty Days the *Foetus* is formed in the Womb. Moreover we find, that in the Generality of acute Diſtempers, the Patient recovers at the End of forty Days. At the End of the ſame Time Women that are with Child of a Male, ceaſe their Purgations, which, if they are delivered of a Boy, after the ſame Term of forty Days, begin afreſh. They ſay further, that the Child itſelf for forty Days is never ſeen either to laugh or ſhed Tears while it is awake; tho' in its Sleep it will do both. And thus much of odd Numbers.

As to even Numbers, ſome Philoſophers teach, that the Number four is dedicated to the Deity, and for this Reaſon it was uſed in the Taking the moſt ſolemn Oaths, which were repeated four Times; and they tell us, that even among the moſt excellent Numbers, that of ſix is the moſt perfect, or conſiſting of all its own entire Parts, for Example:

$$\underbrace{1.1.1.1.1.1.}_{6.}\quad \underbrace{1.2.3.}_{6.}\quad \underbrace{1.5.}_{6.}\quad \underbrace{2.2.2.}_{6.}$$

$$\underbrace{2.4.}_{6.}\quad \underbrace{3.3.}_{6.}$$

And it is certain, that the Number eight has an extraordinary Power in the Nature of Things. Except in *Ægypt*, we never find, that any Child born in the eighth Month, lives long; nay, and even the Mother herſelf who is is ſo delivered in the eighth Month, when the Child is dead, will certainly, we are told, die ſoon afterwards. If the Father touches his Wife in the eighth Month, the Child will be full of foul Humours, and its Skin will be leprous and Scurfy, and nauſeous to the Sight. *Ariſtotle* was of Opinion, that the Number ten was the moſt perfect of all, which was probably becauſe its ſquare is compoſed of four continued Cubes put together. Upon theſe Accounts the Architects have moſt frequently made uſe of the foregoing Numbers; but in their Apertures they ſeldom have exceeded that of ten for an even, or nine for an odd Number, eſpecially in Temples. We are now to treat of the Finiſhing.

By the Finiſhing I underſtand a certain mutual Correſpondence of thoſe ſeveral Lines, by which the Proportions are meaſured, whereof one is the Length, the other the Breadth, and the other the Height.

The Rule of theſe Proportions is beſt gathered from thoſe Things in which we find Nature herſelf to be moſt compleat and admirable; and indeed I am every Day more and more convinced of the Truth of *Pythagoras*'s Saying, that Nature is ſure to act conſiſtently, and with a conſtant Analogy in all her Operations: From whence I conclude, that

that the same Numbers, by means of which the Agreement of Sounds affects our Ears with Delight, are the very same which please our Eyes and our Mind. We shall therefore borrow all our Rules for the finishing our Proportions, from the Musicians, who are the greatest Masters of this Sort of Numbers, and from those particular Things wherein Nature shews herself most excellent and compleat: Not that I shall look any further into these Matters than is necessary for the Purpose of the Architect. We shall not therefore pretend to say any thing of Modulation, or the particular Rules of any Instrument; but only speak of those Points which are immediately to our Subject, which are these. We have already observed, that Harmony is an Agreement of several Tones, delightful to the Ears. Of Tones, some are deep, some more acute. The deeper Tones proceed from a longer String; and the more acute, from a shorter: And from the mutual Connection of these Tones arises all the Variety of Harmony. This Harmony the Ancients gathered from interchangeable Concords of the Tones, by means of certain determinate Numbers; the Names of which Concords are as follows: *Diapente*, or the Fifth, which is also called *Sesquialtera: Diatessaron*, or the Fourth, called also, *Sesquitertia: Diapason*, or the Eighth, also called the double Tone; *Diapason Diapente*, the twelfth or triple Tone, and *Disdiapason*, the fifteenth or *Quadruple*. To these was added the Tonus, which was also called the *Sesquioctave*. These several Concords, compared with the Strings themselves, bore the following Proportions. The *Sesquialtera* was so called, because the String which produced it bore the same Proportion to that to which it is compared, as one and an half does to one; which was the Meaning of the Word *Sesqui*, among the Ancients. In the *Sesquialtera* therefore the longer String must be allowed three, and the shorter, two.

3 000
2 00 } *Sesquialtera.*

The *Sesquitertia* is where the longer String contains the shorter one and one third more: The longer therefore must be as four, and the shorter as three.

4 0000
3 000 } *Sesquitertia*

But in that Concord which was called *Diapason*, the Numbers answer to one another in a double Proportion, as two to one, or the Whole to the Half: And in the *Triple*, they answer as three to one, or as the Whole to one third of itself.

2 00
1 0 } *Diapason*, or double   3 000
1 0 } *Triple*

In the *Quadruple* the Proportions are as four to one, or as the Whole to its fourth Part.

4 0000
1 0 } *Quadruple*

Lastly, all these musical Numbers are as follows: One, two, three, four, and the Tone before-mentioned, wherein the long String compared to the shorter, exceeds it one eighth Part of that shorter String.

1. 2. 3. 4.
Musical Numbers { 8 00000000
9 00000000,0 } *Tone*

Of all these Numbers the Architects made very convenient Use, taking them sometimes two by two, as in planning out their Squares and open Areas, wherein only two Proportions were to be considered, namely, Length and Breadth; and sometimes taking them three by three, as in publick Halls, Council-chambers, and the like; wherein as the Length was to bear a Proportion to the Breadth, so they made the Height in a certain harmonious Proportion to them both.

Chap. VI.

Of the Proportions of Numbers in the Measuring of Areas, and the Rules for some other Proportions drawn neither from natural Bodies, nor from Harmony.

Of these Proportions we are now to treat more particularly, and first we shall say something of those Areas where only two are used. Of Areas, some are short, some long, and some between both. The shortest of all is the perfect Square, every Side whereof is of

 equal

equal Length, all correſponding with one another at Right Angles. The neareſt to this is the *Seſquialtera*, and the *Seſquitertian* alſo may be reckoned among the ſhorter Areas. Theſe three Proportions therefore, which we may alſo call ſimple, are proper for the ſmaller Platforms. There are likewiſe three others, which are proper for middling Platforms: The beſt of all is the Double, and the next beſt is that which is formed of the *Seſquialtera* doubled, which is produced as follows: Having ſet down the leaſt Number of the Area, as, for Inſtance, four, lengthen it to the firſt *Seſquialtera*, which will make ſix, and then add the *Seſquialtera* of this ſix, which will produce nine. Thus the Length will exceed the Breadth in a double Proportion, and one Tone more.

4 oooo } *Seſquialtera*
6 oooooo }
9 ooooooooo *Seſquialtera* doubled

For moderate Platforms alſo, we may uſe that Proportion which ariſes from the *Seſquitertian* doubled in the ſame Manner as the former; wherein the Length and Breadth will be as nine and ſixteen.

9 ooooooooo } *Seſquitertia*
12 oooooooooooo }
16 oooooooooooooooo *Seſquitertia* doubled

Here the longer Line contains the ſhorter twice, excluding one Tone of that ſhorter Line. In the longeſt Areas we either add the *Duple* to the *Seſquialtera*, which will produce the *Triple*; or add the *Seſquitertia* to the *Duple*, which will make the Proportion as three to eight; or laſtly make the Lines correſpond to each other in a *Quadruple* Proportion. We have now ſpoke of the ſhorter Platforms, wherein the Numbers anſwer to each other equally, as two to three, or three to four, and of the Middling, wherein they correſpond as two to four, or as four to nine, or as nine to ſixteen: And laſtly of the longeſt, wherein the Numbers anſwer in a *Triple* or *Quadruple* Proportion, or as three to eight. We may join together or compound all the three Lines of any Body whatſoever, by Means of theſe ſeveral Number, which are either innate with Harmony itſelf, or produced from other Proportions in a certain and regular Method. We find in Harmony thoſe Numbers from whoſe mutual Relations we may form their ſeveral Proporions, as in the *Duple*, the *Triple* and the *Quadruple*. For Inſtance, the *Duple* is formed of the ſimple *Seſquialtera*, with the Addition of the *Seſquitertia*, in the following Method. Let the leaſt Number of the *Duple* be two; the *Seſquialtera* of this is three, and the *Seſquitertia* of this Number three is four, which is juſt the Double of two before-mentioned.

oo
ooo The *Seſquialtera*
oooo The *Seſquitertia* or *Duple*

Or elſe the ſame is done in the following Manner: Let the ſmaller Number be, for Inſtance, three; I add one to make it a *Seſquitertia*, and it becomes four, to which adding a *Seſquialtera*, it makes it ſix, which, compared to three, is juſt in a double Proportion.

The *Duple* { ooo
oooo *Seſquitertia*
oooooo *Seſquialtera* }

The *Triple* is likewiſe made of the *Duple*, and of the *Seſquialtera* joined together: For Inſtance, let the ſmaller Number here be two; this being doubled, makes four; to which adding a *Seſquialtera*, it becomes ſix, which is the *Triple* of two.

The *Triple* { oo
oooo doubled
oooooo *Seſquialtera* }

Or the ſame Thing is done as follows; placing the ſame Number of two for the ſmaller Number, take the *Seſquialtera*, and you will have three, which being doubled, gives ſix, and ſo we ſhall have the *Triple* of two.

The *Triple* { oo
ooo *Seſquialtera*
oooooo doubled }

By Means of the ſame Extenſions we may produce the *Quadruple*, by compounding one *Duple* with another, ſince it is indeed nothing more than the *Duple* doubled, which is alſo called *Diſdiapaſon*, and is performed as follows: Let the ſmaller Number here, for Inſtance, be two; double this, and it makes the *Diapaſon*, that is to ſay four, which is the *Duple* of two, and doubling this four, it makes the *Diſdiapaſon*, which is as eight to two.

The *Quadruple*. { oo
oooo *Diapaſon.*
oooooooo *Diſdiapaſon.* }

This

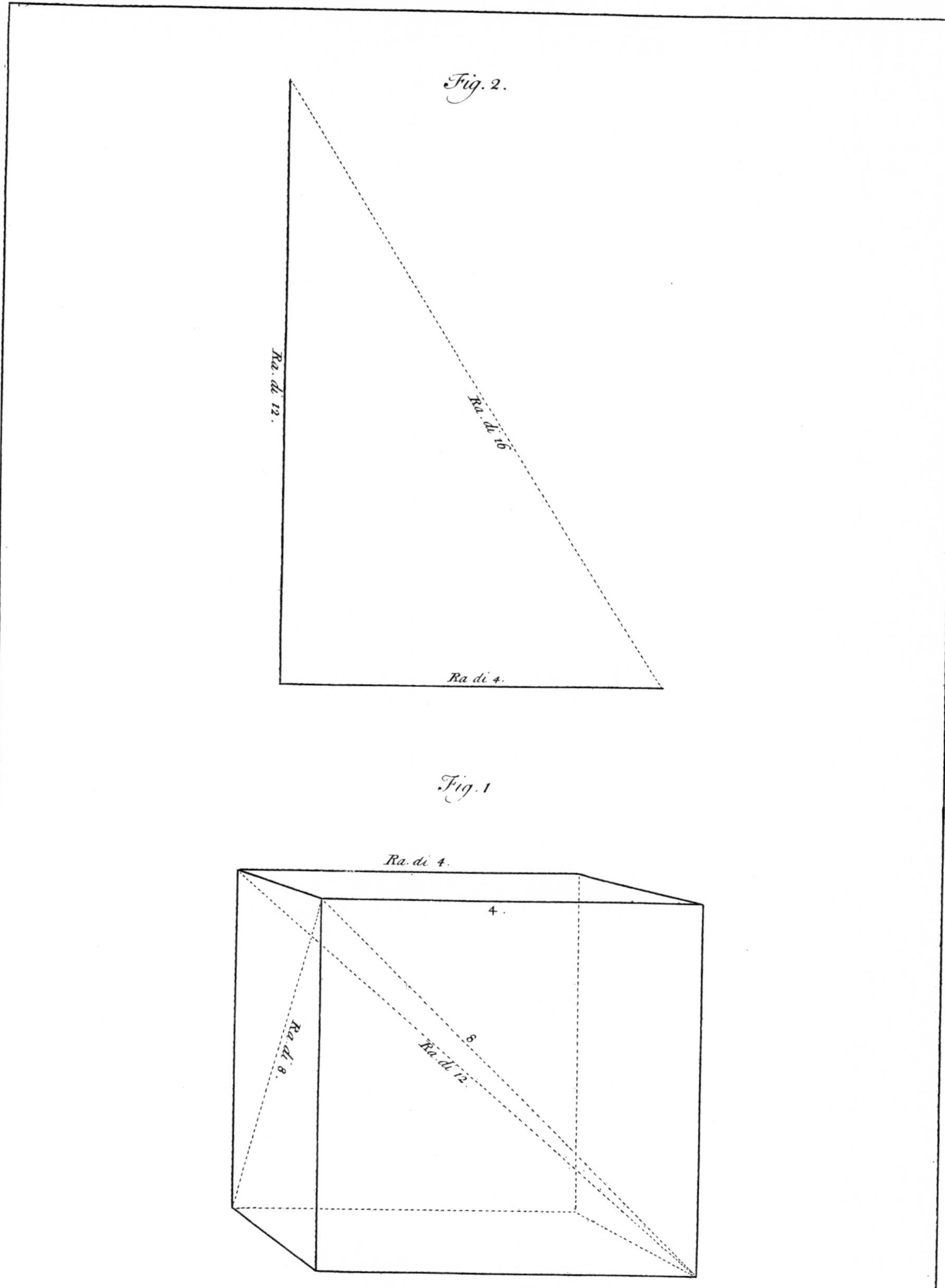

J. Leoni delin.

This *Quadruple* may be alſo formed by adding a *Seſquialtera* and a *Seſquitertia* to the *Duple*; and how this is done, is manifeſt by what we have ſaid above: But for its clearer Explanation, we ſhall give a further Inſtance of it here. The Number two, for Example, by Means of a *Seſquialtera* is made three, which by a *Seſquitertia* becomes four, which four being doubled makes eight.

The *Quadruple.*		
	oo	
	ooo	*Seſquialtera*
	oooo	*Seſquitertia*
	oooooooo	doubled

Or rather in the following Manner. Let us take the Number three; this being doubled makes ſix, to which adding another three, we have nine, and adding to this a third of itſelf, it produces twelve, which anſwers to three in a *Quadruple* Proportion.

The *Quadruple*		
	ooo	
	oooooo	doubled
	ooooooooo	a third added
	oooooooooooo	a third added

The Architects make uſe of all the ſeveral Proportions here ſet down, not confuſedly and indiſtinctly, but in ſuch Manner as to be conſtantly and every way agreeable to Harmony: As, for Inſtance, in the Elevation of a Room which is twice as long as broad, they make uſe, not of thoſe Numbers which compoſe the Triple, but of thoſe only which form the Duple; and the ſame in a Room whoſe Length is three Times its Breadth, employing only its own proper Proportions, and no foreign ones, that is to ſay, taking ſuch of the triple Progreſſions above ſet down, as is moſt agreeable to the Circumſtances of their Structure. There are ſome other natural Proportions for the Uſe of Structures, which are not borrowed from Numbers, but from the Roots and Powers of Squares. The Roots are the Sides of ſquare Numbers: The Powers are the Areas of thoſe Squares: The Multiplication of the Areas produce the Cubes. The firſt of all Cubes, whoſe Root is one, is conſecrated to the Deity, becauſe, as it is derived from One, So it is One every Way; to which we may add, that it is the moſt ſtable and conſtant of all Figures, and the very Baſis of all the reſt. But if, as ſome affirm, the Unite be no Number, but only the Source of all others, we may then ſuppoſe the firſt Number to be the Number two. Taking this Number two for the Root, the Areas will be four, which being raiſed up to a Height equal to its Root, will produce a Cube of eight; and from this Cube we may gather the Rules for our Proportions; for here in the firſt Place, we may conſider the Side of the Cube, which is called the Cube Root, whoſe Area will in Numbers be four, and the compleat or entire Cube be as eight. In the next Place we may conſider the Line drawn from one Angle of the Cube to that which is directly oppoſite to it, ſo as to divide the Area of the Square into two equal Parts, and this is called the Diagonal. What this amounts to in Numbers is not known: Only it appears to be the Root of an Area, which is as Eight on every Side; beſides which it is the Diagonal of a Cube which is on every Side, as twelve, *Fig.* 1. *

Lastly, In a Triangle whoſe two ſhorteſt Sides form a Right Angle, and one of them the Root of an Area, which is every Way as four, and the other of one, which is as twelve, the longeſt Side ſubtended oppoſite to that Right Angle, will be the Root of an Area, will be the Root of an Area, which is as ſixteen *Fig.* 2. *

These ſeveral Rules which we have here ſet down for the determining of Proportions, are the natural and proper Relations of Numbers and Quantities, and the general Method for the Practice of them all is, that the ſhorteſt Line be taken for the Breadth of the Area, the longeſt for the Length, and the middle Line for the Height, tho' ſometimes for the Convenience of the Structure, they are interchanged. We are now to ſay ſomething of the Rules of thoſe Proportions, which are not derived from Harmony or the natural Proportions of Bodies, but are borrowed elſewhere for determining the three Relations of an Apartment; and in order to this we are to obſerve, that there are very uſeful Conſiderations in Practice to be drawn from the Muſicians, Geometers, and even the Arithmeticians, of each of which we are now to ſpeak. Theſe the Philoſophers call *Mediocrates*, or *Means*, and the Rules for them are many and various; but there are three particularly which are the moſt eſteemed; of all which the Purpoſe is, that the two Extreams being given, the middle Mean or Number may correſpond with them in a certain detemined Manner, or to uſe ſuch an Expreſſion, with a regular Affinity. Our Buſineſs, in this Enquiry, is to conſider three Terms, whereof the two moſt remote are one the greateſt, and the other the leaſt; the third or mean Number muſt anſwer to theſe

* See Plate 64, facing page 198.

theſe other two in a juſt Relation or proportionate Interval, which Interval is the equal relative Diſtance which this Number ſtands from the other two. Of the three Methods moſt approved by the Philoſophers for finding this Mean, that which is called the arithmetical is the moſt eaſy, and is as follows. Taking the two extreme Numbers, as for Inſtance, eight for the greateſt, and four for the leaſt, you add them together, which produce twelve, which twelve being divided in two equal Parts, gives us ſix.

8 4
12
6

This Number ſix the Arithmeticians ſay, is the Mean, which ſtanding between four and eight, is at an equal Diſtance from each of them.

8. 6. 4.

The next Mean is that which is called the Geometrical, and is taken thus. Let the ſmalleſt Number, for Example, four, be multiplied by the greateſt, which we ſhall ſuppoſe to be nine; the Multiplication will produce 36: The Root of which Sum as it is called, or the Number of its Side being multiplied by itſelf muſt alſo produce 36. The Root therefore will be ſix, which multiplied by itſelf is 36, and this Number ſix, is the Mean.

4 Times 9 36
6 Times 6 36

This geometrical Mean is very difficult to find by Numbers, but it is very clear by Lines; but of thoſe it is not my Buſineſs to ſpeak here. The third Mean, which is called the Muſical, is ſomewhat more difficult to work than the Arithmetical; but, however, may be very well performed by Numbers. In this the Proportion between the leaſt Term and the greateſt, muſt be the ſame as the Diſtance between the leaſt and the Mean, and between the Mean and the greateſt, as in the following Example. Of the two given Numbers, let the leaſt be thirty, and the greateſt ſixty, which is juſt the Double of the other. I take ſuch Numbers as cannot be leſs to be double, and theſe are one, for the leaſt, and two, for the greateſt, which added together make three. I then divide the whole Interval which was between the greateſt Number, which was ſixty, and the leaſt, which was thirty, into three Parts, each of which Parts therefore will be ten, and one of theſe three Parts I add to the leaſt Number, which will make it forty; and this will be the muſical Mean deſired.

30 60
1 2
3
3 30
10
30
10
30 40 60

And this mean Number forty will be diſtant from the greateſt Number juſt double the Interval which the Number of the Mean is diſtant from the leaſt Number; and the Condition was, that the greateſt Number ſhould bear that Portion to the leaſt. By the Help of theſe Mediocrites the Architects have diſcovered many excellent Things, as well with Relation to the whole Structure, as to its ſeveral Parts; which we have not Time here to particularize. But the moſt common Uſe they have made of theſe Mediocrities, has been however for their Elevations.

Chap. VII.

Of the Invention of Columns, their Dimenſions and Collocation.

It will not be unpleaſant to conſider ſome further Particulars relating to the three Sorts of Columns which the Ancients invented, in three different Points of Time: And it is not at all improbable, that they borrowed the Proportions of their Columns from that of the Members of the human Body. Thus they found that from one Side of a Man to the other was a ſixth Part of his Height, and that from the Navel to the Reins was a tenth. From this Obſervation the Interpreters of our ſacred Books, are of Opinion, that *Noah*'s Ark for the Flood was built according to the Proportions of the human Body. By the ſame Proportions we may reaſonably conjecture, that the Ancients erected their Columns, making the Height in ſome ſix Times, and in others ten Times, the Diameter of the Bottom of the Shaft.

Shaft. But from that natural Inſtinct or Senſe in the Mind by which, as we have already obſerved, we judge of Beauty and Gracefulneſs, they found, that one of theſe was too thick and the other too ſlight; for which Reaſon they altered them both, rightly ſuppoſing that the Truth muſt lie in ſome Medium between theſe two vitious Extremes. Accordingly, with the Help of the Rules of the Arithmeticians, they joined their two Numbers together, and divided the Total in half, and then they found that the mean Number between ſix and ten was eight: Whereupon they made the Height of their Column eight Times the Diameter of the Bottom of the Shaft; and this they called the *Ionic*. They alſo formed their *Doric* Column, which is proper for Buildings of greater Solidity, by the ſame Rules. For Example, they joined the ſmaller Number before-mentioned, which was ſix, with the *Ionic* mean, which was eight, whereof the Total was fourteen; this Total they divided into two equal Parts, and this gave them the Number ſeven, which they took for their *Doric* Column, making its Length ſeven Times the Diameter of the Bottom of the Shaft. Laſtly, they made their thinneſt Order, which they called the *Corinthian*, from the *Ionic* mean Number joined to the greateſt of the former Numbers, and ſo taking the Half as before; for the *Ionic* mean Number was eight, and the greateſt Number was ten, which added together made eighteen, the Half whereof was nine, whence they made the Height of their *Corinthian* Column nine Times the Diameter of the Bottom of its Shaft, as they did the *Ionic* eight, and the *Doric* ſeven: Of which we need ſay no more in this Place. We are now to ſay ſomething of the Collocation, which relates to the Situation of the ſeveral Parts; and this is much eaſier to conceive where it is ill done, than it is to lay down exact Rules for the doing it: Becauſe indeed it is chiefly to be referred to the natural Judgment which we have formerly obſerved to be innate in the Mind of Man, though it may in ſome Meaſure be derived from the foregoing Rules for the Finiſhing. However, we ſhall juſt mention a few general Remarks upon this Head. The very ſmalleſt Parts or Members of the Work, if they are ſet in their right Places, add to the Beauty of the whole; if they are placed in mean or improper Situations, though excellent in themſelves, they become mean. We ſee the very ſame Thing in the Works of Nature: As for Inſtance, if a Dog had one Ear like that of an Aſs, or if a Man had one Foot bigger than the other, or one Hand very large, and the other very ſmall, we ſhould immediately pronounce ſuch a one deformed; or to ſee even an Horſe with one Eye grey, and the other black, is very offenſive: So agreeable it is to Nature, that the Members on the right Side ſhould exactly anſwer the left: Wherefore the very firſt Thing we are to take Care of muſt be, that every Part, even the moſt Inconſiderable, lie duly to the Level and Plum-line, and be diſpoſed with an exact Correſpondence as to the Number, Form and Appearance; ſo that the Right may anſwer to the Left, the High to the Low, the Similar to the Similar, ſo as to form a correſpondent Ornament in that Body whereof they are Parts. Even Statues, Pictures, or any other Ornaments of that Sort with which we embelliſh our Work, muſt be ſo diſpoſed as to ſeem to have ſprung up naturally in their propereſt Places, and to be Twins. The Ancients were ſo punctual in this mutual Correſpondence of the Parts, that even in fixing up their Scantlings of Marble, they uſed to make them anſwer each other exactly to a Size, Quality, Angles, Situation and Colour: And eſpecially in thoſe moſt beautiful Ornaments, Statues, wherein the Ancients were ſuch great Maſters, and in which I ſo much admire the Excellence of Art, they were careful in fixing them up, as well on Pediments of their Temples, as elſewhere, that thoſe on one Side ſhould not differ from thoſe on the other, in the ſmalleſt Particular either of Deſign or Material. We ſee Statues of two or four Horſes, and of their Drivers and Lookers on ſo exactly like to each other, that Art in them may be ſaid to have exceeded Nature, in whoſe Works we hardly ever ſee one Feature ſo exactly like the other. Thus we have ſhewn what is Beauty, and wherein it conſiſts, and with what Numbers and Finiſhing the Ancients uſed to erect their Structures.

Chap. VIII.

Some ſhort, but general Obſervations which may be looked upon as Laws in the Buſineſs of Building and Ornament.

I Shall here put together ſome ſhort and general Admonitions, which are abſolutely neceſſary to be obſerved as ſo many Laws, as well in Point of Ornament or Embelliſhment, as in all the other Parts of Architecture. And this may ſerve to acquit us of the Promiſe which we made of taking a ſhort Review of the whole Work by Way of Epilogue. Firſt therefore, as we laid it down for a Rule at the Beginning, that all Errors which any Ways deform the Structure were to be avoided principally: We will now ſpeak in the firſt Place of ſuch Errors, and eſpecially of the greateſt. Errors ariſe either from the Judgement, and lie either in the Deſign or Election; or from the Hand, and lie in the Workmen's Execution. The Errors of the Judgment are both in Time and in their Nature of much the greateſt Importance, and when committed, leſs capable of being remedied. With theſe therefore we ſhall begin. The firſt Error is to chuſe for your Structure a Region which is unhealthy, not peaceable, barren, unfortunate, melancholy, or afflicted with Calamities, either apparent or concealed. The next Errors to this are chuſing a Platform not proper or convenient; adding one Member to another, without conſtant Regard to the Accommodation of the Inhabitants, and not providing fit and ſuitable Conveniencies for every Rank and Degree of them, as well Maſters as Servants, Citizens as Ruſticks, Inmates as Viſitants: Making your Building either too large and ſpacious, or too ſmall and narrow; too open and naked, or too much ſhut in and confined; too much crowded, or too rambling with too many Apartments, or too few: If there be a Want of Rooms where you may ſecure yourſelf againſt exceſſive Heats, or exceſſive Colds, of Places where you may exerciſe and divert yourſelf when you are in Health, and of others where you may be ſufficiently ſheltered againſt any Inclemency of Air when you are ſick: To which add the Structures not being ſufficiently ſtrong, and as we may ſay, fortified to be ſafe againſt any ſudden Attack: If the Wall be either ſo ſlight as not to be ſufficiently ſtrong to ſupport itſelf and the Roof, or much thicker than Neceſſity requires, if the different Roofs beſpatter each other with their Waters, or throw them againſt any Part of the Wall, or near the Entrances: If they be either too low, or too high: If your Windows be too wide, and admit unwholeſome Winds, noxious Dews, or too much burning Sun; or, on the other Hand, if they be ſo narrow as to occaſion a melancholy Gloom: If they break into any of the Ribs of the Building: If the Paſſages are any Ways obſtructed, or lead us to any Object that is offenſive: Or, in ſhort, if any of thoſe other Inſtructions are neglected, which we have given in the preceding Books. Among the Errors in Ornament, the Principal, in Architecture as in Nature, is making any Thing prepoſterous, maimed, exceſſive, or any other Ways unſightly: For if theſe Things are reckoned defective and monſtrous in Nature herſelf, what muſt we ſay of an Architect that throws the Parts of his Structures into ſuch improper Forms? And as the Parts whereof thoſe Forms conſiſt, are Lines, Angles, Extenſion, and the like, it is certainly true, that there can be no Error or Deformity more abſurd and ſhocking, than the mixing together either Angles or Lines, or Superficies which are not in Number, Size and Situation equal to each other, and which are not blended together with the greateſt Care and Accuracy. And indeed who can avoid blaming a Man extremely, that without being forced to it by any Manner of Neceſſity, draws his Wall crooked and askew, winding this way and that like a Worm crawling upon the Ground, without any Rule or Method, with one Side long, and another ſhort, without any Equality of Angles, or the leaſt Connection with Regard to each other; making his Platform with an obtuſe Angle on one Side, and an acute one on the other, and doing every Thing with Confuſion, Abſurdity and at a Venture: It is another great Error to have raiſed your Structure in ſuch a Manner, that, though indeed with Relation to its Platform, it is not amiſs, yet, notwithſtanding it may be in very great Want of Ornament, it may be utterly incapable of any

Sort

Sort of Embellishment as if all you consulted in raising your Wall, was to sustain the Roof, not leaving any Space where you can afterwards conveniently or distinctly add either the Dignity of Columns, the Embellishment of Statues, the Majesty of Picture, or the Delicacy of any Incrustation. An Error of much the same Nature as this is, the Building with so little Consideration, that though the same Expence might make our Structure beautiful and graceful, yet we neglect the Pains and Contrivance of effecting it: For it is undeniable that there may be in the mere Form or Figure of a Building, an innate Excellence and Beauty, which strikes and delights the Mind, and is immediately perceived where it is, as much as it is missed where it is not; for, indeed, the Eye is naturally a Judge and Lover of Beauty and Gracefulness, and is very critical and hard to please in it; neither can I give any Account why it should always happen, that we should be much more offended at what is wanting, than ready to commend what is done well; for still we are continually thinking what further might be added to make the Object still more splendid, and are naturally displeased if any thing is omitted, which the most accurate, ingenious, and diligent Artist might possibly have procured: So that indeed we are often at a Loss to say what it is offends us, unless it be that there is not wherewithal fully to satisfy our immoderate Desire of Perfection. This being the true State of the Case, we should certainly endeavour, as much as in us lies, by the greatest Study and Care, to make whatever Structure we raise as handsome, and as compleatly adorned as possibly, especially if it be such a one as every body expects to see in the utmost Perfection, as, for Instance, a publick Structure, and particularly a sacred one, which no Man can bear to see naked of Ornament. It is another Error to apply the Ornaments peculiar to a publick Structure, to a private one; or, on the other Hand, those peculiar to private Edifices to one of a publick Nature: Especially if such Ornaments are any thing petty, or not durable, as, for Instance, to dish up a publick Structure with slight or paultry Painting; for every Thing used about a publick Edifice ought, if possible, to be eternal. It is another gross Error, which we see some ridiculous People run into, who e'er they have well begun their Building, fall to painting it, and decking it with Statues and other Embellishments without Number; all which are sure to be spoiled and demolished before the Building is finished. We should erect our Building naked, and let it be quite compleated before we begin to dress it with Ornaments, which should always be our last Work, being best done at leasure, when we can do it without any Impediment, and can take the Advantage of such Opportunities as may offer for that Purpose. I would have the Ornaments which you affix to your Structure, to be the Work of various Hands, and those moderate Masters; but if you can procure any rare Pieces of greater Excellence and Perfection, Statues and Pictuaes like those of a *Phidias* or a *Zeuxis*, let them be fixed only in Places of peculiar Dignity and Honour. I cannot commend *Dejoces* the King of *Media*, who encompassed his City of *Ecbatana* with seven Walls, and made each of them of different Colours, one Purple, another Blue, another gilt with Silver, and one even with Gold; nor can I help blaming *Caligula*, who made his Stable of Marble, and the Manger of Ivory. All that *Nero* built was covered with Gold and enriched with Gems. *Heliogabalus* was still more extravagantly profuse, for he paved his Apartments with Gold, and grieved that he could not do it with Amber. Contempt is the best Reward for these wild Prodigals who are ostentatious of such Vain-glories, or rather Follies, and who are thus profuse of the Labours and Sweat of Mankind, about Things which are of no Manner of Use or Advantage to the main Structure, nor capable of raising the least Admiration either for Ingenuity or Contrivance.

I THEREFORE over and over again advise you to avoid these Errors; and before you begin your Work, thoroughly consider the whole Design your self, and take the Advice of Men of Skill upon it; be sure to have a compleat Model of the Whole, by which examine every minute Part of your future Structure eight, nine, ten Times over, and again, after different Intermissions of Times; till there be not the least Member from the Foundation to the Roof of your whole Building, within or without, great or small, but what you have throughly and long weighed and considered, and determined of what Materials it shall be made, where placed, in what Order and Proportions, and to what it shall answer and bear Relation.

CHAP.

Chap. IX.

The Business and Duty of a good Architect, and wherein the Excellence of the Ornaments consists.

A Prudent Architect will proceed in the Method which we have been just laying down. He will never set about his Work without proper Caution and Advice. He will study the Nature and Strength of the Soil where he is to build, and observe, as well from a Survey of Structures in the Neighbourhood, as from the Practice and Use of the Inhabitants, what Materials, what Sort of Stone, Sand, Lime or Timber, whether found on the Place, or brought from other Parts, will best stand against the Injuries of the Weather. He will set out the exact Breadth and Depth of the Foundations, and of the Basement of the whole Wall, and take an Account of every Thing that is necessary for the Building, whether for the outward Coat or the filling up, for the Ligatures, the Ribs, or the Apertures, the Roof, the Incrustation, for Pavements abroad, or Floors within; he will direct which Way, and by what Method every thing superfluous, noxious or offensive shall be carried off by Drains for conveying away the rain Water, and keeping the Foundations dry, and by proper Defences against any moist Vapours, or even against any unexpected Floods or Violence from Winds or Storms. In a Word, he will give Directions for every single Part, and not suffer any thing to escape his Notice and Decree. And tho' all these Particulars seem chiefly to relate to Convenience and Stability, yet they carry this along with them, that if neglected they destroy all the Beauty and Ornament of the Edifice. Now the Rules which give the Ornaments themselves their main Excellence, are as follows. First all your Ornaments must be exactly regular, and perfectly distinct, and without Confusion: Your Embellishments must not be too much crowded together or scattered as it were under Foot, or thrown on in Heaps, but so aptly and neatly distributed, that whoever should go about to alter their Situation, should be sensible that he destroyed the whole Beauty and Delicacy of the Work. There is no Part whatsoever but what the Artist ought to adorn; but there is no Occasion that all should be adorned equally, or that every thing should be enriched with equal Expence; for indeed I would not have the Merit of the Work consist so much in Plenty as in Variety. Let the Builder fix his richest Ornaments in the principal Places; those of a middling Sort, in Places of less Note, and the meanest in the meanest. And here he should be particularly careful, not to mix what is rich with any thing trifling, nothing little with what is great, nor to set any thing too large or high in narrow or close Places; tho' things which are not equal to each other in Dignity, nor alike even in Species, may very well be placed together, so it be done artfully and ingeniously, and in such a Manner, that as the one appears solemn and majestick, the other may shew chearful and pleasant, and that they may not only unite their different Beauties for the Embellishment of the Structure, but also seem as if the one without the other had been imperfect; nor may it be amiss in some certain Places to intermix somewhat even of a coarse Sort, that what is noble may receive a yet further Addition from the Comparison: Always be sure never to make a Confusion of the Orders, which will happen if you mix the *Doric* Members with the *Corinthian*, as I observed before, or the *Corinthian* with the *Ionic*, or the like. Let every Order have its own regular Members, and those all in their proper Places, that nothing may appear perplexed or broken. Let such Ornaments as are proper to the Middle be placed in the Middle, and let those which are at equal Distances on each Side, be proportioned exactly alike. In short, let every thing be measured, and put together with the greatest Exactness of Lines and Angles, that the Beholder's Eye may have a clear and distinct View along the Cornices, between the Columns on the Inside and without, receiving every Moment fresh Delight from the Variety he meets with, insomuch, that after the most careful and even repeated Views, he shall not be able to depart without once more turning back to take another Look, nor, upon the most critical Examination, be able in any Part of the whole Structure to find one Thing unequal,

equal, incongruous, out of Proportion, or not conducive to the general Beauty of the Whole. All these Particulars you must provide for by means of your Model; and from thence too you should before-hand consider not only what the Building is that you are to erect, but also get together all the Materials you shall want for the Execution, that when you have begun your Work you may not be at a Loss, or change or supersede your Design: but having before-hand made Provision of every Thing that you shall want, you may be able to keep your Workmen constantly supplied with all their Materials. These are the Things which the Architect is to take care of with the greatest Diligence and Judgement. The Errors which may happen in the manual Execution of the Work, need not be repeated here; but only the Workmen should be well looked after, to see that they work exactly by their Square, Level and Plumb-line; that they do their Business at the proper Seasons, take proper Seasons to let their Work rest, and at proper Seasons go to it again; that they use good Stuff, sound, unmixed, solid, strong, and suitable to the Work, and that they use it in proper Places, and finish every Thing according to their Model.

CHAP. X.

What it is that an Architect ought principally to consider, and what Sciences he ought to be acquainted with.

BUT to the Intent that the Architect may come off worthily and honourably in preparing, ordering and accomplishing all these Things, there are some necessary Admonitions, which he should by no means neglect. And first he ought to consider well what Weight he is going to take upon his Shoulders, what it is that he professes, what Manner of Man he would be thought, how great a Business he undertakes, how much Applause, Profit, Favour and Fame among Posterity he will gain when he executes his Work as he ought, and on the contrary, if he goes about any thing ignorantly, unadvisedly, or inconsiderately, to how much Disgrace, to how much Indignation he exposes himself, what a clear, manifest and everlasting Testimony he gives Mankind of his Folly and Indiscretion. Doubtless Architecture is a very noble Science, not fit for every Head. He ought to be a Man of a fine Genius, of a great Application, of the best Education, of thorough Experience, and especially of strong Sense and sound Judgement, that presumes to declare himself an Architect. It is the Business of Architecture, and indeed its highest Praise, to judge rightly what is fit and decent: For though Building is a Matter of Necessity, yet convenient Building is both of Necessity and Utility too: But to build in such a Manner, that the Generous shall commend you, and the Frugal not blame you, is the Work only of a prudent, wise and learned Architect. To run up any thing that is immediately necessary for any particular Purpose, and about which there is no doubt of what Sort it should be, or of the Ability of the Owner to afford it, is not so much the Business of an Architect, as of a common Workman: But to raise an Edifice which is to be compleat in every Part, and to consider and provide before-hand every Thing necessary for such a Work, is the Business only of that extensive Genius which I have described above: For indeed his Invention must be owing to his Wit, his Knowledge, to Experience, his Choice to Judgment, his Composition to Study, and the Completion of his Work to his Perfection in his Art; of all which Qualifications I take the Foundation to be Prudence and mature Deliberation. As to the other Virtues, Humanity, Benevolence, Modesty, Probity; I do not require them more in the Architect, than I do in every other Man, let him profess what Art he will: For indeed without them I do not think any one worthy to be deemed a Man: But above all Things he should avoid Levity, Obstinacy, Ostentation, Intemperance, and all those other Vices which may lose him the good Will of his Fellow-Citizens, and make him odious to the World. Lastly, in the Study of his Art I would have him follow the Example of those that apply themselves to Letters: For no Man thinks himself sufficiently learned in any Science, unless he has read and examined all the Authors, as well bad as good that have wrote in that Science which he is pursuing. In the

the same Manner I would have the Architect diligently consider all the Buildings that have any tolerable Reputation; and not only so, but take them down in Lines and Numbers, nay, make Designs and Models of them, and by means of those, consider and examine the Order, Situation, Sort and Number of every Part which others have employed, especially such as have done any thing very great and excellent, whom we may reasonably suppose to have been Men of very great Note, when they were intrusted with the Direction of so great an Expence. Not that I would have him admire a Structure merely for being huge, and imagine that to be a sufficient Beauty; but let him principally enquire in every Building what there is particularly artful and excellent for Contrivance or Invention, and gain a Habit of being pleased with nothing but what is really elegant and praise-worthy for the Design: And where-ever he finds any thing noble, let him make use of it, or imitate it in his own Performances; and when he sees any thing well done, that is capable of being still further improved and made delicate, let him study to bring it to Perfection in his own Works; and when he meets with any Design that is only not absolutely bad, let him try in his own Things to work it if possible into something excellent. Thus by a continued and nice Examination of the best Productions, still considering what Improvements might be made in every thing that he sees, he may so exercise and sharpen his own Invention, as to collect into his own Works not only all the Beauties which are dispersed up and down in those of other Men, but even those which lie in a Manner concealed in the most hidden Recesses of Nature, to his own immortal Reputation. Not satisfied with this, he should also have an Ambition to produce something admirable, which may be entirely of his own Invention; like him, for Instance, who built a Temple without using one iron Tool in it; or him that brought the *Colossus* to *Rome*, suspended all the Way upright, in which Work we may just mention that he employed no less than four-and-twenty Elephants; or like an Artist that in only seemingly working a common Quarry of Stone, should cut it out into a Labyrinth, a Temple, or some other useful Structure, to the Surprise of all Mankind. We are told that *Nero* used to employ miraculous Architects, who never thought of any Invention, but what it was almost impossible for the Skill of Man to reduce to practice. Such Geniusses I can by no means approve of; for, indeed, I would have the Architect always appear to have consulted Necessity and Convenience in the first Place, even tho' at the very same Time his principal Care has been Ornament. If he can make a handsome Mixture of the noble Orders of the Ancients, with any of the new Inventions of the Moderns, he may deserve Commendation. In this Manner he should be continually improving his Genius by Use and Exercise in such Things as may conduce to make him Excellent in this Science; and indeed, he should think it becomes him to have not only that Knowledge, without which he would not really be what he professed himself; but he should also adorn his Mind with such a Tincture of all the liberal Arts, as may be of Service to make him more ready and ingenious at his own, and that he may never be at a Loss for any Helps in it which Learning can furnish him with. In short, he ought still to be persevering in his Study and Application, till he finds himself equal to those great Men, whose Praises are capable of no further Addition: Nor let him ever be satisfied with himself, if there is that Thing any where that can possibly be of Use to him, and that can be obtained either by Diligence or Thought, which he is not thoroughly Master of, till he is arrived at the Summit of Perfection in the Art which he professes. The Arts which are useful, and indeed absolutely necessary to the Architect, are Painting and Mathematicks. I do not require him to be deeply learned in the rest; for I think it ridiculous, like a certain Author, to expect that an Architect should be a profound Lawyer, in order to know the Right of conveying Water or placing Limits between Neighbours, and to avoid falling into Controversies and Lawsuits as in Building is often the Case: Nor need he be a perfect Astronomer, to know that Libraries ought to be situated to the North, and Stoves to the South; nor a very great Musician, to place the Vases of Copper or Brass in a Theatre for assisting the Voice: Neither do I require that he should be an Orator, in order to be able to display to any Person that would employ him, the Services which he is capable of doing him; for Knowledge, Experience and perfect Mastery in what he is to speak of, will never fail to help him to Words to explain his Sense sufficiently, which indeed is the first and main End of Eloquence. Not that I would have him Tongue-tied, or so deficient

deficient in his Ears, as to have no Taſte for Harmony: It may ſuffice if he does not build a private Man's Houſe upon the publick Ground, or upon another Man's: If he does not annoy the Neighbours, either by his Lights, his Spou s, his Gutters, his Drains, or by obſtructing their Paſſage contrary to Law: If he knows the ſeveral Winds that blows from the different Points of the Compaſs, and their Names; in all which Sciences there is no Harm indeed in his being more expert; but Painting and Mathematicks are what he can no more be without, than a Poet can be without the Knowledge of Feet and Syllables; neither do I know whether it be enough for him to be only moderately tinctured with them. This I can ſay of myſelf, that I have often ſtarted in my Mind Ideas of Buildings, which have given me wonderful Delight: Wherein when I have come to reduce them into Lines, I have found in thoſe very Parts which moſt pleaſed me, many groſs Errors that required great Correction; and upon a ſecond Review of ſuch a Draught, and meaſuring every Part by Numbers, I have been ſenſible and aſhamed of my own Inaccuracy. Laſtly, when I have made my Draught into a Model, and then proceeded to examine the ſeveral Parts over again, I have ſometimes found myſelf miſtaken, even in my Numbers. Not that I expected my Architect to be a *Zeuxis* in Painting, nor a *Nicomachus* at Numbers, nor an *Archimedes* in the Knowledge of Lines and Angles: It may ſerve his Purpoſe if he is a thorough Maſter of thoſe Elements of Painting which I have wrote; and if he is skilled in ſo much practical Mathematicks, and in ſuch a Knowledge of mixed Lines, Angles and Numbers, as is neceſſary for the Meaſuring of Weights, Superficies and Solids, which Part of Geometry the *Greeks* call *Podiſmata* and *Emboda.* With theſe Arts, joined to Study and Application, the Architect may be ſure to obtain Favour and Riches, and to deliver his Name with Reputation down to Poſterity.

Chap. XI.

To what Sort of Perſons the Architect ought to offer his Service.

THERE is one Thing that I muſt not omit here, which relates perſonally to the Architect. It is, that you ſhould not immediately run and offer your Service to every Man that gives out he is going to build; a Fault which the inconſiderate and vain-glorious are too apt to be guilty of. I know not whether you ought not to wait till you are more than once importuned to be concerned. Certainly they ought to repoſe a free and voluntary Confidence in you, that want to make uſe of your Labours and Advice. Why ſhould I offer thoſe Inventions which have coſt me ſo much Study and Pains, to gain perhaps no other Recompence, but the Confidence of a few Perſons of no Taſte or Skill? If by my Advice in the Execution of your intended Work, I either ſave you from an unneceſſary Expence, or procure you ſome great Convenience or Pleaſure; ſurely ſuch a Service deſerves a ſuitable Recompence. For this Reaſon a prudent Man ſhould take care to maintain his Reputation; and certainly it is enough if you give honeſt Advice, and correct Draughts to ſuch as apply themſelves to you. If afterwards you undertake to ſuperviſe and compleat the Work, you will find it very difficult to avoid being made anſwerable for all the Faults and Miſtakes committed either by the Ignorance or Negligence of other Men: Upon which Account you muſt take care to have the Aſſiſtance of honeſt, diligent, and ſevere Overſeers to look after the Workmen under you. I would alſo have you, if poſſible, concern yourſelf for none but Perſons of the higheſt Rank and Quality, and thoſe too ſuch as are truly Lovers of theſe Arts: Becauſe your Work loſes of its Dignity by being done for mean Perſons. Do you not ſee what Weight the Authority of great Men is to advance the Reputation of thoſe who are employed by them? And, indeed, I inſiſt the more upon this Piece of Advice, not only becauſe the World has generally a higher Opinion of the Taſte and Judgment of great Men, than for the moſt Part they deſerve, but alſo becauſe I would have the Architect always readily and plentifully ſupplied with every thing that is neceſſary for compleating his Edifice; which thoſe of lower Degree are commonly not ſo able, and therefore not ſo willing to do: to which add, what we find very frequent Inſtances of, that where the Deſign and Invention has been perfectly equal in two different Works, one has been much more esteemed than the other, for the Sake of the Superiority of the Materials. Lastly, I advise you not to be so far carried away by the Desire of Glory, as rashly to attempt any thing entirely new and unusual: Therefore be sure to examine and consider thoroughly what you are going to undertake, even in its minutest Parts; and remember how difficult it is to find Workmen that shall exactly execute any extraordinary Idea which you may form, and with how much Grudging and Unwillingness People will spend their Money in making Trial of your Fancies. Lastly, beware of that very common Fault, by means of which there are so few great Structures but what have some unpardonable Blemishes. We always find People very ready to criticize, and fond of being thought Counsellors and Directors. Now as, by reason of the Shortness of Man's Life, few great Works are compleated by the first Undertaker, we that succeed him, either out of Envy or Officiousness, are vain of making some Alteration in his original Design. By this means what was well begun is spoiled in the finishing. For this Reason I think we should adhere to the original Design of the Inventor, who we are to suppose had maturely weighed and considered it. It is possible he might have some wise Inducement to do what he did, which upon a more diligent and attentive Examination, you may at length discover yourself. If however you do make any Alteration, never do it without the Advice, or rather absolute Direction of the most approved and experienced Masters: By which means you will both provide for the Necessities of the Structure, and secure yourself against the Malice of envious Tongues. We have now treated of publick Buildings, and of private; of sacred, and of profane; of those which relate to Dignity, and those of Pleasure. What remains is to shew how any Defects in an Edifice, which have arisen either from Ignorance or Negligence, from the Violence of Men or Times, or from unfortunate and unforeseen Accidents, may be repaired and amended: Still hoping that these Arts will meet with the Favour and Protection of the Learned.

The End of Book IX.

THE

THE

ARCHITECTURE

OF

Leone Batista Alberti.

BOOK X. CHAP. I.

Of the Defects in Buildings, whence they proceed, and their different Sorts; which of them can be corrected by the Architect, and which cannot; and the various Causes of a bad Air.

SINCE in the Remainder of this Work we are to treat of the correcting the several Defects in Building, it is necessary first to consider what those Defects are which are capable of Emendation by the Hand of Man: As the Physicians think that the Knowledge of the Patient's Distemper, is the greatest Step towards his Cure. Of the Defects in Buildings, as well publick as private, some are innate and owing to the Architect, and others proceed from foreign Causes: And again, of these some are capable of being repaired by Art and Contrivance, and others will not possibly admit of any Remedy. What those are which are owing to the Architect, we have pointed out so plainly in the last Book, that a Repetition of them here is not necessary, having there shewn that some are the Errors of the Mind, some of the Hand; that those of the Mind are an injudicious Election, an inconvenient Compartition, an improper Distribution, or confused Proportions; whereas those of the Hand are an inaccurate or inconsiderate Preparation, Collection, Working, and putting together the Materials: Faults which the Negligent and Unadvised easily fall into. But the Defects which proceed from foreign Causes are scarcely to be numbered for their Multiplicity and Variety: Of which Causes the first is that which is said to overcome all Things, Time, whose Violence is no less deceitful than it is powerful, nor can any Sort of Bodies elude that great Law of Nature, of Feeling the Decays of old Age; insomuch that some are of Opinion, the very Heavens themselves are corruptible only for this Reason, because they are Bodies. We all know the Power of the Sun, of Damps, of Frosts and of Storms. Battered by these Engines, we see the hardest Flints shiver and fall to Pieces, and huge Pieces of Rock broken down from the Mountains, with Parts of the Hill itself along with them. To these add the Violence or Negligence of Men. I call Heaven to Witness, that I am often filled with the highest Indignation when I see Buildings demolished and going to Ruin by the Carelessness, not to say abominable Avarice of the Owners, Buildings whose Majesty has saved them from the Fury of the most barbarous and enraged Enemies, and which Time himself, that perverse and obstinate Destroyer, seems to have destined to Eternity. To these again add the sudden Accidents of Fire, Lightening, Earthquakes, Inundations, and those many surprizing, unheard of and incredible Phænomena which the miraculous Power of Nature so frequently produces, and which are capable of over-turning the best finished Structure of the wisest Architect. *Plato* says, that the whole *Atlantick* Island, which was not less than *Epirus*, vanished away at once into Smoke. History informs us, that the Cities of *Helice* and *Bura* were both swallowed up, one by the Sea and the other by an Earthquake: That the Lake *Tritonis* disappeared in an Instant, and on the contrary, that of *Stymphalis* in *Argos*, appeared as suddenly: That at *Teramene* an Island started up at once, with hot Springs in it; and that between the two Islands of *Therasia* and *Thera* a Flame burst out of the Sea, which made it foam and boil four whole Days successively, and at last appeared an Island twelve Furlongs in Length, wherein the *Rhodians* built a Temple to *Neptune* their Protector. In other Places we are told of such numerous Swarms of Mice, that they bred an Infection, and that the *Spaniards* sent Ambassadors to the *Roman* Senate to implore their Assistance against infinite Numbers of Hares which eat up their Country; and many other wonderful Accidents of the same Nature, whereof we have made a Collection in our little Treatise, entitled *Theogenius*. But all the Defects which proceed from foreign Causes are not uncapable of being corrected: Neither will those which are owing to the Architect, always admit of Amendment; for where every thing is wrong and out of Order, no Improvement is practicable. Where the Building cannot be any ways altered for the better, but by changing almost every Line and Angle, it is much better to pull the Whole quite down, and begin upon a new Foundation. But that is not our Business now: We are here to shew what may be amended or improved by Art. And first we shall speak of Buildings of a publick Nature. Of these the greatest and most important is the City, or rather, if we may so call it, the Region of the City. The Region wherein an inconsiderable Architect has placed his City, may perhaps have those Defects which will admit of Amendment. Either it may be unsecure against sudden Incursions of Enemies, or it may stand in a bad unhealthy Air, or it may not be well supplied with all Necessaries. Of these therefore we shall now treat. The Way from *Lydia* into *Cilicia* lies through a narrow Pass cut by Nature among the Hills, in such a Manner that you would think she designed it as a Gate to that Province. At *Thermopylæ*, now called the *Bocca de Lupo*, is a Pass which three armed Men may defend, being a broken Way interrupted by numberless Rills of Water on every Side, which rise from the very Root of the Mountain. Much like this are the broken Rocks in the Mark of *Ancona*, called by the Vulgar *Fosso ombrone*, and many others in other Places. But such Passes, so fortified by Nature, are not to be found every where: However, they seem in a great Measure, to be capable of being imitated by Art; and accordingly we find it to have been very often prudently done by the Ancients, who in order to secure their Country from the Inroads of their Enemies, used the following Methods, which we shall briefly gather from as many of the great Works of the old Heroes, as may serve to illustrate our present Subject. *Artaxerxes* near the River *Euphrates*, cut a Trench between himself and the Enemy, threescore Foot broad, and ten Miles long. The *Cæsars* (and particularly *Adrian*) built a Wall across *Britain* forescore Miles in Length, by which they divided the Lands of the *Barbarians* from those of the *Romans*. *Antoninus Pius* made another of Turf across the same Island. After him *Severus* threw up a Trench an hundred and twenty-two Miles long, which divided the Island clear from Sea to Sea. *Antiochus Soter* encompassed *Margiana* a Province of *India*, where he built *Antiochia*, with a Wall fifteen hundred Furlongs in Length; and *Seososis* carried a Wall of the same Length from the Borders of *Ægypt* towards *Arabia*, thro' a Desart quite from the City of the Sun, which was called *Thebes*. The *Neritones*, whose Country formerly joined to *Leucadia*, cutting away the Neck of Land, and letting in the Sea, made it an Island: On the contrary, the *Chalcidians* and the *Boeotians* raised a Dike over the Straits, called the *Euripus*, to join *Euboia* to *Boeotia*, that they might be able to succour each other. *Alexander* the Great built six Towns near the River *Oxus*, not far distant from each other, that upon any sudden Attack from the Enemy, they might have Assistance at Hand. The Ancients frequently made use of little Redoubts, which they called *Tyrses*, fortified with very high Ramparts, like Castles, to put a Stop to Incursions from their Enemies. The *Persians* stopt up the *Tygris* with Sluices, that none of the Enemy's Vessels might get up the River: But *Alexander* took them away and opened the Stream, alledging that it was a mean and cowardly Defence, and exhorting them rather to trust to their own Valour for their Security. Some have overflowed their Country and made

made it a perfect Marsh, like *Arabia*, which by means of a Number of Lakes and Bogs occasioned by the River *Euphrates*, was not to be approached by an Enemy. Thus by such Fortifications they both secured their own Country against the Attacks of an Enemy, and at the same Time made their Enemy's Country weaker and more defenceless. What are the Causes which make the Air unhealthy, we have already shewn sufficiently at Length in the proper Place. We may only observe here in general, that for the most Part those Causes are either the too great Power of the Sun, or too much Shade; some infectious Winds from neighbouring Parts, or pestilent Vapours from the Soil itself, or else something in the very Climate itself that is noxious. To mend the Air when it is unhealthy or corrupted, is a Work scarce thought possible to be done by any human Contrivance; unless by appeasing the Wrath of Heaven by Prayers and Supplications, which, like the Nail driven by the Consul, have sometimes, as we read, put a Stop to the most destructive Contagions. Against the Inconveniencies of the Sun or Wind to the Inhabitants of some little Town or Villa, perhaps some Remedy may be found: But to alter the Climate of a whole Region or Province, is a Task too great; not that I deny the Possibility of amending a great many of those Defects which proceed from the Air, by curing the Earth of exhaling noxious Vapours. In order to shew how this may be done, it is not necessary that I should here spend Time in debating whether it is by means of the Power of the Sun, or by some natural inward Heat, that the Earth emits those two Vapours, of which one mounting up into the Air is condensed by the Cold, into Rain and Snow; and the other, which is a dry Vapour, is supposed to be the Cause of Winds: It is enough that we are assured, that both these arise out of the Earth; and as we find that those Steams which proceed from the Bodies of Animals, partake of the Nature of the Bodies from which they arise, pestiferous from pestilentious Bodies, and sweet from wholesome and cleanly ones, and that sometimes where the Sweat or Vapour is not bad in itself, it is rendered offensive by the Nastiness of the Garment through which it passes; so it is with the Earth: For when the Ground is neither well covered with Water, nor perfectly dry, but lies like a Marsh or Bog, it must for several Reasons emit noxious and unwholesome Vapours. Thus we find, that where the Sea is deep, the Water is cold, and warm where it is shallow; the Reason of which, we are told, is because the Rays of the Sun cannot strike to the Bottom of a deep Water: As if you plunge a red-hot Iron into Oil, if the Oil be but a small Quantity, it will raise a strong thick Smoke, but if there is Oil enough to cover it quite over, it will presently quench the Iron, and make no Smoke at all. But to proceed briefly with the Subject which we have begun to take in Hand. *Servius* tells us, that a Marsh near a certain Town being almost dried up, and a Plague succeeding, the Inhabitants went for Counsel to *Apollo*, who commanded them to dry it up entirely. Near *Tempe*, there was a large standing Lake, which *Hercules* made dry Ground, by cutting a Trench to let out the Water, and he is said to have burnt the Serpent *Hydra* in a Place from whence frequent Eruptions of Water used to ravage the neighbouring City; by which means the superfluous Moisture being consumed, and the Soil rendered firm and dry, those over-abounding Channels of Water were entirely stopt. In ancient Times the *Nile* having once swelled higher than usual, when the Waters went off, besides the Mud, they left a great Number of different Animals, which as the Ground became dry, rotted and infected the Air with a dreadful Plague. *Strabo* says, that the City *Mazaca*, near the Hill *Argæus*, abounds in good Water; but if in Summer it has not a Way made for it to run off, it renders the Air unwholesome and infectious. Moreover, towards the northern Parts of *Africa*, and also in *Æthiopia*, it never Rains; so that the Lakes are often dried up, and left like Bogs of Mud, abounding with infinite Numbers of Animals that breed by Corruption, and particularly with great Swarms of Locusts. Against these Inconveniencies, both the Remedies used by *Hercules* are very proper, namely, cutting a Trench that the Water may not stagnate and make a Bog, and then laying the Ground open to the Sun, which I take to be the Fire used by *Hercules* for burning the *Hydra*. It may also be of Service to fill up the Place with Stones, Earth or Sand: And in what Manner you may fill up a standing Water with River-sand, we shall shew in the proper Place. *Strabo* says, that in his Time the Country about the City of *Ravenna*, being continually overflowed by the Sea, used to be incommoded with noisome Vapours, which yet did not make the Air unwholesome, and it seems strange how this should happen, unless

unleſs it be as it is at *Venice*, that the Lakes being kept in conſtant Agitation by the Winds and Tides, never ſubſide, and ſo cannot corrupt. The Country of *Alexandria* is ſaid to have been much of the ſame Nature; but the conſtant overflowing of the *Nile* in Summer, cured it of that Defect. Thus we are inſtructed by Nature what is proper to be done, and that where the Ground is marſhy, we ought either to dry it up entirely, or elſe to bring a conſtant Supply of running Water into it, either from ſome Stream or River, or from the Sea; or laſtly, to dig it ſo deep as to come to ſome living Spring. Of which we ſhall ſay no more in this Place.

Chap. II.

That Water is the moſt neceſſary Thing of all, and of its various Sorts.

WE are now to take care that nothing be wanting, which may be neceſſary for our Uſe. What Things are neceſſary I ſhall not waſte much Time in recounting, becauſe they are manifeſt, as Food, Raiment, Shelter, and, above all Things, Water. *Thales* the *Mileſian* affirmed, that Water was the firſt Principle of all Things, and even of Communities among Men. *Ariſtobulus* ſays, that he ſaw above a thouſand Towns left quite deſart, becauſe the River *Indus* had turned his Courſe another Way. I own it to be my Opinion, that Water is to Animals the Source of natural Heat and the Nouriſher of Life; not to mention its Conſequence to Plants, and to every Thing elſe which is intended for the Uſe of Mankind; to all which I imagine it to be ſo abſolutely neceſſary, that, without Water, nothing which grows or is nouriſhed in the Earth would be capable even of exiſting. In the Country, along the River *Euphrates*, the People do not ſuffer their Cattle to feed as long as they would, for fear of their growing too fat in Paſtures too luxurious, occaſioned, as is ſuppoſed, by the Exuberance of Moiſture: And ſome believe, that ſuch huge Bodies as Whales are produced in the Sea, becauſe of the great Abundance of Nouriſhment which is afforded by Water. *Xenophon* tells us, that the Kings of *Sparta* were allowed, by way of Dignity, to have a Lake of Water before the Doors of their Houſes. Water is uſed by us in the Ceremonies of our Nuptials, Sacrifices, and almoſt all other ſacred Rites, according to the Practice of our Fore-fathers; all which ſhews what a high Eſteem ancient Times had of Water. But indeed who can deny the great Uſe and Service which it is of to Mankind, inſomuch that it is always thought to be deficient, where there is not a very large Abundance of it for all Manner of Occaſions. With this great Neceſſary therefore, we ſhall here begin, ſince, according to the old Saying, we want it whether ſick or well. The *Meſſagetæ*, a Nation of *Scythia*, made their Country abound in Water by opening the River *Aragus* in ſeveral Places. The *Tygris* and *Euphrates* were brought by Labour to *Babylon*, which was built originally in a dry Place. Queen *Semiramis* cut a Paſſage through a high Hill for the Space of five-and-twenty Furlongs to make Way for a Canal, fifteen Foot broad, by which ſhe brought Water to the City of *Ecbatana*. An *Arabian* King brought Water from the *Chorus*, a River of *Arabia*, into that droughty Deſart where he waited for *Cambyſes*, in an Aqueduct made of the Hides of Bulls, if we may believe every thing that we read in *Herodotus*. In the Country of the *Samians*, among other ſurprizing Works, the moſt extraordinary of all was a Trench ſeventy Furlongs in Length, made through a Mountain which was an hundred and fifty Paces high. *Megareus*'s Conduct was alſo mightily admired, which brought the Water of a Spring to the City in a Frame twenty Foot high. But in my Judgment the ancient City of *Rome* far excelled all the Cities in the World in the Grandeur and Contrivance of her Aqueducts, and the great Plenty of Water conveyed in them. But you are not every where ſure to find Springs or Rivers from whence Water can be brought. *Alexander*, to ſupply his Fleet with Water, dug a Number of Wells along the Sea Shore of *Perſia*. *Appian* tells us, that *Hannibal*, when he was cloſe preſſed by *Scipio*, near the Town of *Cilla*, not being able to find Water in the Field where he was encamped, provided for the Neceſſities of his Troops by digging Wells. Beſides, it is not all Waters which you find, that are good and proper for the Uſe of Men; for beſides that, ſome are hot, ſome cold, ſome ſweet, ſome

ſome ſharp, ſome bitter, ſome perfectly clear, others muddy, viſcous, oily, tinctured with Pitch, or of a petrifying Quality; ſome running partly clear, and partly foul, and ſometimes in the ſame Place part ſweet, and part ſalt or bitter: There are alſo ſeveral other Particulars, well worth Note, which make Waters very different from one another, as well in Nature as in Effect, and of no ſmall Conſequence to the Preſervation or Prejudice of the Health. And here let us be allowed juſt to mention ſome miraculous Properties of Water, by Way of Amuſement. The River *Arſione* in *Armenia*, rots the Cloaths which are waſhed in it. The Water of *Diana*'s Fountain, near *Camerinum*, will mix with nothing Male. At *Debri*, a Town of the *Garamanthes*, is a Spring which is cold in the Day, and warm in the Night. The *Helbeſus*, a River in the Country of the *Segeſtani* in *Sicily*, in the Middle of its Courſe grows of a ſudden hot. There is a ſacred Well in *Epirus*, which extinguiſhes any Thing which is put into it burning, and lights that which is extinguiſhed. In *Eleuſina* near *Athens*, is a Spring which leaps and rejoices at the Sound of a Flute. Foreign Animals that drink at the River *Indus*, change their Colour: And upon the Shore of the *Red Sea* there is a Spring, at which if Sheep drink, their Wool preſently turns Black. At *Laodicea* in *Aſia*, there are Springs, near which all the fourfooted Animals that are conceived are of a yellow Hue. In the Country of *Gadara*, is a Water, of which if the Cattle drink, they loſe their Hair and Nails. Near the *Hyrcanian* Sea, is a Lake, wherein all that bathe grow ſcabby, and can be cured with nothing but Oil. At *Suſa*, is a Water which makes the Teeth fall out of the Head. Near the Lake *Zelonium*, is a Spring which makes Women barren, and another which makes them fruitful. In the Iſland of *Chios*, there is one which makes thoſe that drink of it fooliſh: And in ſome other Place, which I do not now recollect, is one which not only upon drinking, but upon the bare Taſting makes the Perſon die laughing, and there is another wherein only Batheing is immediate Death. And near *Nonacris* in *Arcadia*, is a Water perfectly clear to the View, but of ſo poiſonous a Quality, that it cannot be contained in any Metal whatſoever. On the contrary, there are others which are admirable for reſtoring the Health, ſuch as the Waters of *Pozzuolo*, *Siena*, *Volterra*, *Bologna*, and many others of great Fame all over *Italy*. But it is yet more extraordinary which we are told of a Water in *Corſica*, namely, that it will reconſolidate broken Bones, and prevent the Effect of the moſt dangerous Poiſons. In other Places there are Waters which mend the Wit and even inſpire Divination. In *Corſica*, alſo there is another Spring very good for the Eyes, which if a Thief dares to deny a Theft with an Oath, and to waſh his Eyes with its Water, immediately makes him blind. Of theſe we have ſaid enough. Laſtly, in ſome Places no Water at all is to be found, neither good nor bad. To remedy this, it was the Cuſtom all over the Country of *Apulia* to receive and preſerve the Rain-water in Ciſterns.

CHAP. III.

Four Things to be conſidered with Relation to Water; alſo whence it is engendered or ariſes, and its Courſe.

THERE are four Things therefore which are to our Purpoſe with Relation to Water; namely, the finding, the conveying, the chuſing, and the preſerving. Of theſe we are to treat: But we may firſt premiſe ſome few Things concerning the Nature of Water in general. I am of Opinion that Water cannot be contained in any Thing but a Veſſel, and therefore I agree with thoſe, who upon that Account, affirm the Sea itſelf to be nothing but a Veſſel of vaſt Capacity, and Rivers to be great oblong Veſſels too. But there is this Difference between the Waters of the Sea and thoſe of Rivers, that theſe latter have a Current and Motion by their own Nature, whereas the former would eaſily ſubſide and be at Reſt, if they were not put in Agitation by the Force of the Winds. I ſhall not here diſcuſs thoſe philoſophical Queſtions, whether all Waters make their Way to the Sea, as to a Place of Reſt, and whether the regular Flux and Reflux of the Ocean be owing to the Impulſe of the Moon: Thoſe Points not being to our Purpoſe: but we muſt not omit to take Notice of what we

 ſee

see with our Eyes, that Water naturally tends downwards; that it cannot suffer the Air to be any where beneath it; that it hates all Mixture with any Body that is either lighter or heavier than itself; that it loves to fill up every Concavity into which it runs; that the more you endeavour to force it, the more obstinately it strives against you, nor is ever satisfied till it obtains the Rest which it desires, and that when it is got to its Place of Repose, it is contented only with itself, and despises all other Mixtures; lastly, that its Surface is always an exact Level. There is another Enquiry relating to Water, which I remember to have read in *Plutarch*; namely, whether upon digging a Hole in the Earth, the Water springs up like Blood out of a Wound; or whether it distills out like Milk engendering by Degrees in the Breast of a Nurse. Some are of Opinion, that perpetual Springs do not run from any full Vessel from whence they have their supply, but that in the Places from whence they flow, the Water is continually engendering of Air, and not of all Sorts of Air, but only of such as is most apt to be formed into Vapour, and that the Earth, and especially the Hills, are like Spunges, full of Pores, through which the Air is sucked in and condensed and so turned into Water by the Cold: For Proof of which they alledge, that the greatest Rivers spring from the greatest Hills. Others do not agree with this Opinion, observing that several Rivers, and particularly the *Pyramus*, one of no small Note, being navigable, does not take its Rise from any Hill, but from the Middle of a Plain. For this Reason, he who supposes that the Ground imbibes the Moisture of the Rain, which by its Weight and Subtilty penetrates through the Veins and so distills into the Cavities of the Earth, may perhaps be not much mistaken in his Conjecture: For we may observe, that those Countries which have least Rain, have the greatest Scarcity of Springs. *Libya* is said to have been so called *quasi Lipygia*, as wanting Rain, by which means it is scantily supplied with Water. And, indeed, who can deny, that where it Rains much, there is the greatest Plenty of it? It is also to our present Purpose to observe, that a Man who digs a Well never meets with Water, till he has sunk it to the Level of the next River. At *Volsconio*, a Town standing upon a Hill in *Tuscany*, they dug a Well no less then two hundred and twenty Foot deep before they came to any Vein of Water, not meeting with any till they came to the Level of the Springs which rise from the Side of the Hill; and you will generally find the same Observation hold good of all Wells dug upon Hills. We find by Experiment that a Spunge will grow wet by the Humidity of the Air, upon which I have made a Pair of Scales to determine the Heaviness or Dryness of the Air and Winds. I cannot indeed deny that the Moisture of the nocturnal Air is attracted from the Superficies of the Earth, and so consequently may return again into its Pores, and be easily converted once more into Humour; but I cannot pretend to determine any thing certain with Relation to this Question, finding so much Variety among Authors upon the Subject, and so many different Considerations offering themselves to the Mind when we think upon it. Thus it is certain that in many Places, either by some Earthquake, or even from no apparent Cause, Springs have burst out of a sudden, and continued a great While, and again, that others have failed in different Seasons, some growing dry in Summer, others in Winter, and that those which have dried up have afterwards again afforded great Plenty of Water: Nay, and that Springs of fresh Water not only arise from the Earth, but have been found even in the Middle of the Sea; and it has been affirmed, that Water also issues from the Plants themselves. In one of those Islands which are called Fortunate, we are told there grows a Sort of Cane as high as a Tree, some black, some white; from the black comes a bitter Juice, and from the white distills a fine clear Water, very beautiful to the Eye and good to drink. *Strabo*, a very grave Author, says that in the Mountains of *Armenia*, they find a Sort of Worms bred in the Snow, which are full of a Water excellent to drink. At *Fiezole* and *Urbino*, though both Towns standing upon Hills, there is Plenty of Water to be had for the least digging, which is because those Hills are formed of a stony Soil mixed with a Chalk. We are told further, that there are certain Clods of Earth which within their Coats contain a Quantity of the finest Water. Amidst all this wonderful Variety, the Knowledge of the Nature of Springs cannot be otherwise than extremely difficult and obscure.

Chap.

Chap. IV.

By what Marks to find any hidden Water.

LET us now return to our Subject. Hidden Waters are to be found out by certain Marks. These Marks are the Form and Face of the Spot of Ground, and the Nature of the Soil where you are to search for the Water, and some other Methods discovered by the Industry and Diligence of Men. According to the ordinary Course of Nature, a Place which is sunk down into a Hollow, or into a Sort of concave Pit, seems to be a Kind of Vessel ready prepared for the retaining of Water. In those Places where the Sun has much Power, all Humidity is so much dried up by the Force of his Rays, that few or no Veins of Water are to be found; or if any are discovered in a very open Place, they are heavy, thick and brackish. On the north Side of Hills, and where-ever there is a very thick Shade, you may very soon meet with Water. Hills whose Tops are used to be long covered with Snow, afford great Plenty of Springs. I have observed, that Hills which have a flat Meadow at the Top, never want Water; and you will find almost all Rivers have their Rise from some such Place. I have also observed, that their Springs seldom flow from any other Spot of Ground, but where the Soil beneath or about them is sound and firm, with either an even Slope over them, or soft loose Earth: So that if you consider the Matter, you will be of Opinion with me, that the Water which has been gathered there, runs out as from the Side of a broken Bason. Hence it happens that the closest Soil has the least Water, and what there is, lies very near the Surface: But the loosest Earth has the most Humidity; but then the Water generally lies pretty deep. *Pliny* writes, that in some Places, upon cutting down the Woods, Springs burst out: And *Tacitus* says, that when *Moses* journeyed through the Desart, and his Followers were fainting with Thirst, he discovered Springs of Water, only by taking Notice where there were fresh Spots of Grass. *Æmilius*, when his Army suffered a Dearth of Water near Mount *Olympus*, found out a Supply by the fresh Verdure of the Woods. Some Soldiers who were in quest of Water were directed to some little Veins by a young Girl in the *Via Collatina*, where, upon digging they found a very plentiful Spring, over which they built a little Chapel, and in it left the Memory of the Accident described in Painting. If the Earth easily gives Way to the Tread, or cleaves to the Foot, it shews that there is Water under it. One of the most certain Marks of concealed Water, is the Growth and Flourishing of those Plants which love Water, or are used to be produced by it, such as Willows, Rushes, Withes, Ivy, or any others which without Plenty of Moisture could never have attained the Perfection in which we find them. *Columella* tells us, that the Ground which produces Vines very thick of Leaves, and especially that which bears Dwarf-elder, Trefoil and wild Plumbs is a good Soil, and does not want Veins of sweet Water. Moreover great Quantities of Frogs, Earth-worms, with Gnats and other small Flies swarming together in the Air, are Tokens of Water concealed beneath. The Methods for finding Water invented by the Diligence of Men are as follows: The curious Searchers into Nature have observed, that the Earth, and especially the Hills, consist of different Coats or Layers, some closer, some looser, and others thinner; and they have found, that the Hills were composed of these Coates placed one above the other, in such a Manner that towards the Surface or outside these Layers or Coats, and their several Junctures lie level from the Right to Left: But on the Inside, towards the Center of the Hill the Layers incline downwards in an oblique Line, with all their upper Superficies inclining equally, but then the same Line does not continue on, quite to the Center of the Hill, for, suppose at the Distance of every hundred Foot the Line is broken off by a Kind of transverse Step, which makes a Discontinuance in the Layer; and so with these Breaks and Slopes the Coats run from each Side to the Center of the Hill. From an Observation of these Particulars, Men of acute Understanding soon perceived that the Waters were either engendered, or rather that the Rains gathered between these Strata, and in the Junctures of the several Coats, by which means the Middle of the Hill must needs have Water in it. Hence they concluded that in order to come at that

that concealed Water, they muſt pierce into the Body of the Hill, and eſpecially in one of thoſe Parts where the Lines or Junctures of the ſeveral Strata met together, which was likely to be the moſt proper Place for what they wanted, becauſe the Muſcles of the Hill meeting together muſt in all Probability form a natural Reſervoir. Beſides the ſeveral Coats themſelves ſeemed to be of different Natures, ſome likely to imbibe, others to retain the Water. Thus the reddiſh Stone is hardly ever without Water; but then it is apt to deceive you, for it often runs out through the Veins with which that Stone abounds. The moiſt and living Flint which lies about the Roots of the Hill, broken and very ſharp, ſoon affords Water. The light Soil too gives you an eaſy Opportunity of finding Plenty of Water; but then it is of a bad Savour. But the Male-ſand and the hard Grit are ſure to afford the beſt of Water, and with the leaſt Danger of being exhauſted. It is quite the contrary with Chalk, which being too cloſe, yields no Water; but it is very good for retaining that which diſtills into it. In common Sand we find but very ſmall Veins, and thoſe foul, and apt to have a Sediment. From white Clay we have but ſmall Veins, but thoſe ſweeter than any other. The ſoft Stone yields a very cold Water; the black Earth a very clear one. In Gravel, if it is looſe, we cannot dig with any very great Hope; but if it grows cloſer as we come deeper, there is no Danger of finding Water, and when found, in either of them, there is no doubt of its being well taſted. It is alſo certain, that by the Help of Art there is no great Difficulty in finding out the Spot under which the Vein lies: * And the Method by which we are taught to do it, is as follows. In the Morning extremely early, when the Air is perfectly clear and ſerene, lay yourſelf flat with your Chin reſting upon the Ground: Then take a careful Survey of the Country all round you, and where-ever you ſee a Vapour riſing out of the Earth, and curling up into the Air like a Man's Breath in a clear Froſt, there you may be pretty certain of finding Water. But in order to be ſtill more ſure of it, dig a Pit four Cubits deep and as many broad, and in this Pit, about the Time of Sun-ſet, put either an earthen Pot juſt freſh taken out of the Furnace, or a ſmall Quantity of unwaſhed Wool, or an earthen Pot unbaked, or a braſs Pot with the Mouth downwards and rubbed over with Oil; then make up the Mouth of the Pit with Boards and cover it with Earth: If next Morning the baked Pot be much heavier than it was over Night; if the Wool be moiſtened; if the unbaked Pot be wet; if the braſs Pot have Drops hanging upon it, and if a Lamp left in the ſame Pit have not conſumed much Oil, or if upon making a Fire in it, the Earth emits a good deal of Smoke, you may be very ſure that there are Veins of Water concealed. In what Seaſon it is beſt to make theſe Trials has not been ſo clearly declared; but in ſome Writers I find the following Obſervations. In the Dog-days, not only the Earth, but alſo the Bodies of Animals are very full of Humidity: Whence it happens, that in this Seaſon the Trees grow very moiſt under the Bark with Exceſs of Humour; about this Time alſo Men are very ſubject to Fluxes of the Belly, and through exceſſive Humectation, fall into frequent Fevers; and the Waters ſpring out more abundantly at this Time of the Year, than any other. *Theophraſtus* thinks the Reaſon of this to be, that about this Time we have generally ſoutherly Winds, which in their Nature are moiſt and cloudy. *Ariſtotle* affirms, that in this Seaſon the Ground is forced to emit Vapours by means of the natural Fire which lies mixed in the Bowels of the Earth. If this be true, thoſe Times muſt be beſt for the above-mentioned Trials, when thoſe Fires are moſt potent, or leaſt oppreſſed with Exuberance of Humour, as alſo when the Earth is not too much burnt up and too dry. The Seaſon therefore which I would recommend for this Purpoſe, ſhould be the Spring in dry Places, and Autumn in Places of more Shade. When your Hopes of not being diſappointed are confirmed in the Manner before ſhewn, you may begin to dig.

Chap. V.

Of the digging and walling of Walls and Conduits.

THE Work of Digging is performed in two Manners; for either we dig a Well perpendicularly down, or we dig a Conduit horizontally. The Workmen in digging are ſometimes expoſed to Danger, either from unwholeſome Vapours, or from the falling in of the

* *See Plate 65, facing.*

PLATE 65. *(Page 216)*

B. Picart del. 1727.

the Sides of the Pit. The Ancients used to send their Slaves, upon their being convicted of some Crime, to dig in their Mines, where the noisome Air soon dispatched them. Against such Vapours we are taught to secure ourselves, by keeping the Air in continual Motion, and by the Burning of Lamps, to the Intent, that if the Vapour be very subtile, it may be consumed by the Flame, or if it be more gross, the Workmen may know when to get out of Harm's Way, because such a heavy Vapour will give them Notice by extinguishing the Light. But if these Damps multiply upon you, and continue for any Time, we are advised to dig Vents on each Side, to give the Vapour a free Passage to exhaust itself. To prevent the falling in of the Sides, work your Well in the following Manner. Upon the Level of the Ground where you resolve to make your Well, lay a circular Course of Work, either of Marble, or some other stout Material, of the Diameter which you intend for the Breadth of your Well. This will be the Basis or Foundation of your whole Work. Upon this build the Sides of your Well to the Height of three Cubits, and let it stand till it is thoroughly dry. When this is dry, go to digging your Well, and remove the Earth from the Inside of it; by which means, as you dig away the Earth, the Sides already raised will sink by Degrees, and make their own Way downwards; and thus adding to the Sides as you go deeper, you may sink your Work to what Depth you please. Some are for Building the Sides of the Well without Mortar, that the Veins of Water may not be stopt from getting through them. Others are for inclosing it with no less than three different Walls, that the Water rising all up from the Bottom, may be the clearer. But the main Point is the Nature of the Place where you dig; for as the Earth consists of different Strata placed one above the other, it sometimes happens, that the Rain-water, soaking thro' the upper soft Coat, lodges in the first hard Bed; and this never being pure, is unfit for Use: At other Times, on the contrary, it happens, that after you have actually found Water, upon digging deeper, it slips away and is lost. The Reason of this is, that you have dug thro' the Bottom of the Vessel which contained it. Upon this Account I very much approve of those who make their Well in the following Manner. They encompass the Sides of the Well, which is ready dug, with two Circles of Wood or Plank, as if they were making a great Tub, leaving the Space of about a Cubit between the two Circles. This Interspace between the Planks, they fill up with coarse Gravel, or rather with broken Fragments of Flint or Marble, swimming in Mortar, and then leave this Work to dry and harden for six Months. This forms so entire a Vessel, that the Water can get in no other Way but by bubbling up from the Bottom, by which Means it must be thoroughly purged and be perfectly clear and light. If you are to make an horizontal Conduit under Ground, let the Diggers observe the before-mentioned Precautions against noxious Vapours; and in order to keep the Ground from falling down upon them, let them make use of Props, and afterwards support it with a regular Arch. The Conduit should have frequent Vents, some perpendicular, others oblique, not only for the exhaling of unwholesome Vapours, but chiefly for the more convenient bringing out the Earth as it is dug, and any Obstruction which may get in. When we are digging for Water, if we do not, the lower we go, meet with moister Clods of Earth, and if our Tools do not find more and more easy Entrance, we shall certainly be disappointed of our Hopes of finding what we dig for.

CHAP. VI.

Of the Uses of Water; which is best and most wholesome; and the contrary.

WHEN Water is found, it ought not to be rashly applied to the Uses of Men. But as the City requires a very great Plenty of Water, not only for drinking, but also for washing, for supplying the Gardens, for Tanners, and Fullers; for the Drains, and for extinguishing sudden Fires: The best is to be chosen for drinking, and the others are to be allotted to the other Uses, according as they are found to be respectively proper for them. *Theophrastus* was of Opinion, that the colder the Water, the more serviceable to Plants; and it is certain, that the foul and muddy, especially if it takes its Thickness from a fruitful Soil, enriches the Ground. Horſes do not love a very clear Water, but grow fat with any that is moſſy and warm. The hardeſt is beſt for Fullers. The Phyſicians ſay, that the Neceſſity of Water to the Health and Life of Man is of two Sorts; one for quenching the Thirſt, and the other, to ſerve as a Vehicle to carry the Nutriment extracted from the Food into the Veins, that being there purified and digeſted it may ſupply the Members with their proper Juices. Thirſt they tell us is an Appetite of Moiſture, and chiefly of a cold one; and therefore they think that cold Water, eſpecially after Meals, fortifies the Stomach of thoſe that are in good Health; but if it be exceſſively cold it will throw the moſt robuſt into a Numbneſs, occaſion Gripes in the Bowels, ſhake the Nerves, and by its Rawneſs extinguiſh the digeſtive Faculty of the Stomach. The Water of the River *Oxus* being always turbid, is very unwholeſome to drink. The Inhabitants of *Rome*, from the frequent Changes of the Air, and the nocturnal Vapours which ariſe from the River, as alſo from the Winds which commonly blow in the Afternoon, are very ſubject to dangerous Fevers; for theſe Winds generally blow very cold about three o' Clock in Summer, at which Time Mens Bodies are extreamly heated, and even contract the very Veins. But in my Opinion theſe Fevers, and indeed moſt of the worſt Diſtempers there proceed, in a great Meaſure, from the Water of the *Tyber*, which is commonly drank when it is foul; to which Purpoſe it may not be amiſs to obſerve, that the ancient Phyſicians, for the Cure of theſe *Roman* Fevers, order the Uſe of the Juice of Squills and of Inciſives. But to return. We are upon the Search of the beſt Water. *Celſus* the Phyſician, ſays of Waters, that of all the different Sorts the Rain-water is the lighteſt; the ſecond is that of the Spring; in the third Place is the River-water; in the fourth, that of a Well; in the fifth and laſt, that which diſſolves from Snow or Ice. The Lake-water is heavier than any of theſe, and that of a Marſh is the worſt of all. The *Mazaca*, which ſtands under the Hill *Argæus*, abounds with good Water; but having no Way to run off in Summer, it grows unwholeſome and peſtiferous. The Definition which the beſt Philoſophers give us of Water, is, that it is naturally a Body ſimple and unmixed, whereof Coldneſs and Humidity are two Properties. We may therefore conclude that to be the beſt, which deviates the leaſt from its own Nature; becauſe, if it be not perfectly pure, and entirely free from Mixture, Taſte, or Smell, it will certainly very much endanger the Health, by loading the inward Paſſages of the Lungs, choaking up the Veins, and clogging the Spirits, the Miniſters of Life, For this Reaſon we are told that the Rain-water, as it conſiſts of the lighteſt Vapours, is the beſt of all, provided it be not of ſuch a Sort as eaſily corrupts and ſtinks, which when it grows foul is very apt to harden the Belly. Some believe that the Occaſion of this is, that it falls from Clouds formed of a Mixture of too many different Vapours compounded together, drawn, for Inſtance, from the Sea, which is the great Receptacle of all the different Sorts of Springs; becauſe indeed nothing can be more liable to Corruption, than a confuſed Medley of Things in their Nature diſſimilar. Thus the Juice of different Sorts of Grapes mixed together, will never keep.

It was an ancient Law among the *Hebrews*, that no Man ſhould ſow any Seed but what was pick'd and unmixed; it being their Notion, that Nature totally abhorred a Medley of different Particles. Thoſe who follow *Ariſtotle*, thinking that the Vapours which are extracted from the Earth, when they are raiſed up to the cold Region of the Air, are by the Cold compreſſed into Clouds, and afterwards diſſolve in Rain, are of quite a different Opinion. Thus *Theophraſtus* ſays, that cultivated and Garden Fruits fall more eaſily into Diſtempers than wild ones, which being of a tough Contexture never tamed, more vigorouſly reſiſt any Injury from without; whereas the other being made tender by Culture, have not the ſame hardy Conſtitution. The ſame he tells us will hold good as to Waters, and the more tender we make them (to uſe his own Words) the more liable they will be to ſuffer Alteration. For this Reaſon ſome ſay, that Water which has been boyled and ſoften'd by the Fire will ſooneſt grow cold, and ſo be ſooneſt made hot again. Thus much of Rain-water. Next to this the Spring-water is certainly the beſt. Thoſe who prefer the River to the Spring, ſay, what elſe is a River, but an Abundance and Concourſe of many different Springs united together, and maturated by the Sun, Winds and Motion? So they tell us too, that a Well is nothing but a Spring lying very deep: from whence they infer, if we will allow the Rays of the Sun to be of any Service to Water, that it is no hard matter to judge which of theſe Springs muſt be the moſt

moſt undigeſted: unleſs we will ſuppoſe, that there is a fiery Spirit in the Bowels of the earth, by which ſubterraneous Waters are concocted. *Ariſtotle* ſays that the Water in Wells grows warm in the Summer in the Afternoon. Accordingly ſome will have it that Well-water ſeems cold in Summer, only by compariſon with the hot Air which ſurrounds us. Accordingly we find, contrary to the old received Opinion, that Water juſt freſh drawn, does not bedew the Glaſs into which it is put, if the Glaſs be perfectly clean and not greaſy. But as of the firſt Principles whereof all Things conſiſt, eſpecially according to the *Pythagorean* Notion, there are two which may be called male, which are Heat and Cold; and it being the Property of Heat to penetrate, diſſolve, break, attract and ſuck up all Moiſture, as it is that of Cold to compreſs, contract, harden and conſolidate: both theſe have in a great Meaſure the ſame Effects, and particularly upon Water, provided they are exceſſive and of too long Continuance; becauſe they both equally conſume the more ſubtile Parts, which occaſions exactly the ſame aduſt Dryneſs. Thus we ſay, that Plants are burnt up, not only by extreme Heat but alſo by extreme Cold; becauſe when the more tender Parts of the Subſtance of the Wood are conſumed and dried up either by Froſt or Sun, we ſee the Tree look ruſty and chapt as by Fire. From the ſame Cauſes Water grows viſcous by the Sun's Heat, and looks as if it were full of Aſhes in extreme Froſt. But there is another Difference even among Waters allowed to be good; for particularly as to Rain-water, it is of great Importance in what Seaſon of the Year, at what Time of the Day, and in what Winds you collect it, as alſo in what Place you preſerve it, and what Time it has been kept. The Rain which falls after the Middle of Winter is thought to afford the heavieſt Water; and that which is collected in the Winter is ſaid to be ſweeter than that collected in the Summer. The firſt Rains after the Dog-days are bitter and unwholeſome, being corrupted with a Mixture of ſome of the aduſt Particles of the Earth, and we are told that the Earth itſelf has a bitter ſavour at that Time of the Year, from being burnt up by the Heat of the Sun. Hence we are adviſed, that the Rain-water gathered from the Houſe-top, is better than that which is collected in the Ground; and of that which is gathered from the Houſe-top, the moſt wholeſome is ſaid to be that which is got after the Roof has been well waſhed by the firſt Rain. The *African* Phyſicians tell us, that the Rain which falls in Summer, eſpecially when it thunders, is not pure, and is unwholſome from its Saltneſs. *Theophraſtus* thinks, that the Night Rains are better than thoſe in the Day. Hence that is accounted the moſt wholeſome which falls in a North Wind. *Columella* is of Opinion, that Rain-water would not be bad if it were carried through earthen Pipes into covered Ciſterns, becauſe it eaſily corrupts when it ſtands uncovered to the Sun, and ſoon ſpoils, if it is kept in any Veſſel made of Wood. Springs alſo are very different from one another. *Hippocrates* judged thoſe which riſe from the Roots of Hills to be the beſt. The Opinion of the Ancients concerning Springs was as follows. They thought the very beſt of all were thoſe which lay either to the North, or fronting the Sun-riſe about the Equinox; and the worſt they ſuppoſed to be thoſe which lay to the South. The next beſt they thought were thoſe which fronted the Sun-riſe in Winter, nor did they diſapprove of thoſe on the Weſt Side of the Hill, which generally is very moiſt with a great Abundance of light Dew, and conſequently muſt afford a very ſweet Water, becauſe the Dew does not fall but in quiet, clear Places, and where there is a temperate Air. *Theophraſtus* thinks that Water gets a Taſte from the Earth, as in Fruits, Vines, and other Trees, which all have a Savour of the Earth from which they draw their Juices, and from whatever happens to lie near their Roots. The Ancients uſed to ſay, that there were as many different Sorts of Wines, as there were of different Soils wherein the Vineyards were planted. Thus *Pliny* tells us, that the Wines of *Padua* taſted of the Willows to which the Inhabitants of that Country uſed to bind their Vines. *Cato* teaches to medicate the Vines with the Herb *Hellebore*, by laying Bundles of it at the Roots, at the ſame Time that you open them, in order to make them looſen the Belly without Danger. For theſe Reaſons the Ancients thought, that the Water which iſſued out of the living Rock, was better than that which roſe from the Ground. But the beſt of all was thought to be that which diſtilled from ſuch an Earth, which being put into a Baſon with Water, and ſtirr'd together with it, would the ſooneſt ſubſide and leave the Water the leaſt tainted either in Colour, Smell, or Taſte. For the ſame Reaſons *Columella* was of Opinion, that Water which ran down ſtony Precipices muſt

must be the best, being less likely to be spoil'd by any foreign Mixture. But it is not every Water which runs among Stones that is to be approved of, because if it runs in a deep Bed under a dark Shade, it will be too crude; and on the contrary, if its Channel be too open, I should be inclined to subscribe to *Aristole*'s Opinion, that the too great Heat of the Sun consuming the more subtle Parts, would make it viscous. Authors prefer the *Nile* to all other Rivers, because it descends with a very extensive Course; because it cuts through the finest Sorts of Soil which are not either infected with Corruption by Damps, nor tainted with Contagion by being burnt up; because it flows towards the North: And lastly, because its Channel is always full and clear. And indeed it cannot be denied, that Waters which have the longest and the gentlest Current, are the least crude, and are most refined and purged by their easy Motion, leaving all the Weight of their Sediment behind them in their long Course. Moreover, all the Ancients agree in this, that Waters not only receive a Tincture, as we observed before, from the Ground in which they lie as in their Mother's Lap, but also borrow somewhat from the Soils thro' which they flow, and from the Juices of the different Plants which they wash; not merely because they lick those Plants in their Course, but rather because any pestiferous Plant will taint them with the Mixture of the Steams of the unwholsome Soil in which they grow. This is the Reason that unwholsome Plants are said to yield unwholesome Water. You shall sometimes observe the Rain itself to have an ill Smell, and perhaps a bitter Taste. This we are told proceeds from the Infection of the Place from whence the Steam or Vapour first arose. Thus it is affirmed, that the Juices of the Earth, when sufficiently maturated and concocted by Nature, produce every Thing sweet, and on the contrary, when they are crude and undigested, they make every Thing bitter with which they mix. Those Waters which run towards the North may perhaps be supposed to be the most useful, because they are the coldest, as flying from the Rays of the Sun, and being rather visited than scorched by him; and those which flow towards the South the contrary, as throwing themselves into the very Mouth of the Flame. *Aristotle* taught, that the fiery Spirit which was mixed up by Nature in all Bodies, was repelled by the Coldness of the North Wind, and confined within, from evaporating, and that this gave the Water its due Concoction: And it is certain, that this Spirit is exhausted and dissipated by the Heat of the Sun. *Servius*, upon the Authority of experienced Persons, says, that Wells and Springs which lie under a Roof, do not emit any Vapour: That light subtle Breath rising from the Well, not being able to penetrate or make its Way through the dense and gross Air which the Roof compresses together over it; whereas, when it lies under the clear and open Sky, it has free Play, and extends and purges itself without Obstruction: For which Reason, Wells under the open Air are accounted more wholesome than those under Cover. In other respects, all the same Properties are to be wished for in a Well that are required in a Spring; for both seem to have a very near Relation to each other, and hardly differ in any Thing but in Point of Current; though you shall very frequently meet even with Wells which run with a very large Vein of Water; and we are told, that no Water can possibly be perpetual which is absolutely without Motion; and Water without Motion, let it lie in what Soil it will, cannot be wholesome. If a great deal of Water is continually and constantly drawn out of a Well, that Well may be looked upon rather as a deep Spring; and on the other hand, if a Spring does not run over its Sides, but stands quiet and still, it may be accounted a shallow Well rather than a Spring. Some are of Opinion, that no Water can be perpetual, or of very long Duration, which does does not move with the rising and falling of the next River or Torrent; and I believe the same. The ancient Lawyers made this Distinction between a Lake and a Marsh, that the Lake has a perpetual Water, whereas that of the Marsh is only temporary, and what it gathers in the Winter. Lakes are of three Sorts. One, if we may so call it, stationary, content with its own Waters, always keeping within its Bed, and never overflowing. The second, which is as it were the Father of the River, discharges its Waters at some Passage; and the last receives some Stream from abroad, and sends it out again into some River. The first partakes somewhat of the Nature of a Marsh: the second is a direct Spring: and the third, if I mistake not, is only a River spreading out into Breadth in that particular Place. We need not therefore upon this Occasion repeat what we have already said of the Spring and the River. We may only add, that all Water that is covered with

with a Shade, is colder and clearer, but more undigested, than those warmed by the Sun; and, on the contrary, Waters too much heated by the Sun, are brackish and viscous. The being deep is of Service to either Sort, because it prevents the latter from being made too hot, and the former from being too easily affected by Frost. Lastly it is thought that even the Marsh is not always to be despised: because where-ever Eels are found, the Water is reckoned to be not very bad. Of all Marsh-water that is accounted the very worst which breeds Horse-leeches, which is so absolutely without Motion that it contracts a Scurf on the Top, which has an offensive Smell, which is of a black or livid Colour, which being put into a Vessel will continue foul a great while, which is heavy and clammy with a mossy Slime, and which being used in washing your Hands, they are a long Time before they dry. But as a short Summary of what has been said of Water, it should be extremely light, clear, thin and transparent, to which must be added those Particulars which we have slightly touched in the first Book. Lastly it will be a strong Confirmation to you of the Goodness of your Water, if you find that the Cattle which have washed and drank in it for several Months together, are in good Condition and perfectly healthy; and you have a sure Way to judge whether they are sound or not by inspecting their Livers; for what is noxious injures with Time, and the Injury which is latest felt is of the worst Consequence.

CHAP. VII.

Of the Method of conveying Water and accommodating it to the Uses of Men.

HAVING found Water and approved it to be good, the next Work is to convey it artfully and accommodate it properly to the Uses of Men. There are two Ways of conveying Water, either by a Trench or Canal, or by Pipes or Conduits. In either of these Methods, the Water will not move, unless the Place to which you would convey it be lower than that from which it is to be brought. But then there is this Difference, that the Water which is brought by a Canal must descend all the Way with a continued Slope, whereas that which is conveyed in Pipes may ascend in some Part of the Way. Of these two Methods we are now to treat. But first we must premise some Things for the clearer Explication of our Subject. The Searchers into Nature tell us, that the Earth is Spherical, tho' in many Places it rises into Hills, and in many others sinks into Seas: but in so vast a Globe this Roughness is not perceptible; as in an Egg, which tho' it is far from being of a smooth Superficies, yet its little Inequalities bearing but an inconsiderable Proportion to its whole Circumference, they are scarce observed. *Eratosthenes* tells us, that the Compass of this great Globe is two hundred and fifty two thousand Furlongs, or about thirty one thousand five hundred Miles, and that there is no Hill so high or Water so deep as to be above fifteen thousand Cubits perpendicular; not even Mount *Caucasus*, whose Top enjoys the Sun three Hours in the Night. There is a prodigious high Mountain in *Arcadia* called *Cyllene*; and yet those who have measured its perpendicular, affirm, that it does not exceed twenty Furlongs. Even the Sea itself is thought to be no more upon this Globe of Earth, than the Summer's Dew is upon the Body of an Apple. Some have wittily said, that the Creator of the World made use of the Concavity of the Sea as of a Seal with the Impression whereof he stampt the Hills. What the Geometers teach us upon this Head is very much to our present Purpose. They say, that if a straight Line touching the Globe of the Earth at one End were to be drawn on exactly horizontal a Mile in Length, the Space between the other End and the Surface of the Globe would not be above ten Inches. For this Reason Water will never move on in a Canal, but stand still like a Lake, unless every eight Furlongs the Trench has a Slope of one whole Foot from the Place where the Water was first found and its Bed cut; which Place the ancient Lawyers called Incile, from the Incision which is made either in the Rock or Bank for conveying the Water: But if in this Space of eight Furlongs it had a Slope of more than six Foot, it is supposed that the Rapidity of its Current would make it inconvenient for Boats. In order to find whether the Trench which is to convey the Water be lower than this

this Incile or Sluice or no, and what the Slope is, certain Rules and Inſtruments have been invented, which are of excellent Uſe. Ignorant Workmen try their Slope by laying a Ball in the Trench, and if this Ball rowls forwards they think the Slope is right for their Water. The Inſtruments of dexterous Artiſts are the Square, Level, Plumb-line, and, in a Word, all ſuch as are terminated with a right Angle. This Art is a little more abſtruſe; but however I ſhall open no more of it than is neceſſary for the Purpoſe in Hand. * The Practice is performed by means of the Sight and of the Object, which we ſhall call the Points. If the Place through which we are to convey our Water be an even Plain, there are two Ways of directing our Sight: For we muſt ſet up certain Marks or Objects, which we may place either nearer or at a greater Diſtance from each other. The nearer the Points of the Sight and the Mark or Object are to each other, the leſs the ſtraight Line of the Direction of the Sight will depart from the Superficies of the Globe; the further thoſe Points are from each other, the lower the Superficies of the Globe will fall from the Level of the Sight. In both theſe you muſt obſerve to allow ten Inches ſlope for every Mile of Diſtance. But if you have not a clear Plain, and ſome Hill interferes, then again you have two Ways of Proceeding: One by taking the Height from the Incile or Sluice, on the one Side, and the Height of the Slope from the Head on the other. The Head I call that appointed Place to which you would bring the Water, in order to let it run from thence free, or to appropriate it to ſome particular Uſes. We find theſe Heights by taking different Steps of Meaſurement. I call them Steps becauſe they are like thoſe Steps by which we aſcend to a Temple. One Line of theſe Steps is the Ray of Sight which goes from the Beholder's Eye along the ſame Level with his Eye; which is made by the Square, the Level and the Plumb-line; and the other Line is that which falls from the Beholder's Eye down to his Feet, in a Perpendicular. By means of theſe Steps you note how much one Line exceeds the other, by caſting up the Amount of their Perpendiculars, and ſo find which is the Higheſt, that which riſes from the Sluice to the Top of the Eminence, or that which riſes from the Head. The other Method, is by drawing one Line from the Sluice to the Top of the Hill which interferes, and another Lime from thence to the Head, and by computing the Proportions of their Angles, according to the Rules of Geometry. But this Method is difficult in Practice, and not extremely ſure, becauſe in a large Diſtance the leaſt Error occaſioned by the Eye of the Meaſurer is of very great Conſequence. But there are ſome Things which ſeem to bear ſome Relation to this Method, as we ſhall ſhew by and by, which, if we have occaſion to cut a Paſſage through a Hill to bring Water to a Town, may be of great Uſe for obtaining the right Directions. The Practice is as follows: On the Summit of the Hill, in a Place where you can have a View both of the Sluice on one Side and of the Head on the other, having laid the Ground exactly level, deſcribe a Circle ten Foot in Diameter. This Circle we ſhall call the Horizon. In the Center of the Circle ſtick up a Pike exactly perpendicular. Having made this Preparation, the Artiſt goes round the Outſide of the Circle, in order to find in what Part of its Circumference his Eye being directed to one of the Points of the Water which is to be conveyed, touches the lower Part of the Pike which ſtands in the Center. Having found out and marked this exact Place in the Circumference of his Horizon, he draws a Line for this Direction from that Mark quite to the oppoſite Side of his Circle. Thus this Line will be the Diameter of that Circle, as it will paſs through the Center, and cut through both Sides of the Circumference. If this Line, upon taking oppoſite Views leads the Eye on one Side directly to the Sluice, and on the other directly to the Head of our Water, it affords us a ſtraight Direction for our Channel. But if the two Lines of Direction do not happen to meet in this Manner, and the Diameter which leads to the Sluice, falls on one Part of the Circumference, and that which leads to the Head, on another; then from the mutual Interſection of theſe Lines at the Pike in the Center of the Circle, we ſhall find the Difference between the two Directions. I uſe the Help of ſuch a Circle to make Platforms and draw Maps of Towns and Provinces, as alſo for the digging ſubterraneous Conduits, and that with very good Effect. But of that in another Place. Whatever Canal we make, whether for bringing only a ſmaller Quantity of Water for Drinking, or a larger for Navigation, we may follow the Directions which we have here taught. But the Preparation of our Canal muſt not be the ſame for a large Quantity of Water, as for a ſmall. We ſhall firſt go on with the Subject which we have

* *See Plates 66 and 67, facing and following this page.*

PLATE 66. *(Page 222)*

B. Picart del. 1727.

PLATE 67. *(Page 222)*

B. Picart del. 1727.

have begun concerning Water only for Drinking, and proceed afterwards to Canals for Navigation. Canals are either worked up with Masonry, or else are only Trenches dug. Trenches are of two Sorts, cut either through an open Country, or through the Bowels of a Hill, which is called a Mine or subterraneous Conduit. In both these, when you meet with either Stone, Chalk, or compact Earth that does not imbibe the Water, you will have no Occasion for Masonry; but where the Bottom or Sides of the Canal are not sound, then you must fortify them. If you are obliged to carry your Canal through the Heart of a Hill, you must observe the Rules above laid down. In subterraneous Conduits, at the Distance of every hundred Foot, you should open Ventiges like Wells fortified according as the Nature of the Earth through which you dig requires. I have seen such Ventiges in the Country of the *Marsi* near *Rome*, where the Water falls into the ancient Lake *Fucinus* (now called the *Pie di Luco*) built very finely with burnt Brick, and of an incredible Depth. 'Till the four hundred and forty-first year after the building of the City, there was no such thing as an Aqueduct built at *Rome*; but afterwards those Works were brought to such a Pitch, that whole Rivers were conveyed to it through the Air, and we are told, that there were so many of them, that every single House was abundantly supplied with Water. At first they began with subterraneous Conduits; which indeed had a great many Conveniencies. This hidden Work was less subject to Injuries and being exposed neither to the Severity of Frosts, nor to the scorching Dog-day Sun brought the Water fresher and cooler, nor could easily be destroyed or turned away by Enemies that might happen to make Inroads into the Country. These Works were afterwards brought to such a Magnificence, that in order to have high Jets of Water in their Gardens and in their Bathes, they built vaulted Aqueducts, in some Places above an hundred and twenty Foot high, and carried on for above threescore Miles together. From these too they reaped Conveniencies. In several Places, and particularly beyond the *Tyber*, the Water of these Aqueducts served to grind their Corn, and upon their being destroyed by the Enemy, they were forced to make Mills for that Purpose in Ships. To this add, that by means of this Plenty of Water the City was kept cleaner and the Air made fresher and more wholesome. The Architects also added some ingenious Inventions to shew the Hours of the Day to the great Recreation of the Beholders, by the Contrivance of some little moving Statues of Brass, placed in the Front of the Head of the Aqueduct, which represented the publick Games and the Ceremony of the Triumph. At the same Time, the Sound of musical Instruments and sweet Voices was heard, which were caused by the Motion of the Water. These Aqueducts were covered in with an Arch of a good Thickness, to prevent the Water from being heated by the Sun; and this Vault was plaistered on the Inside with such a Composition as we have formerly in this Book recommended for Floors, to the Thickness of at least six Inches. The Parts of the ancient Aqueduct were these. Joining to the Incile was the *Septum*; along the Course of the Conduit were the *Castella*; where any higher Ground interfered the *Specus* was dug; lastly, to the Head was annexed the *Calix*. An ancient Lawyer gives us the following Description of these several Parts. An Aqueduct is a Conduit for conveying Water to a certain Place by means of a gentle Slope. The *Septum* is a Flood-gate or Water-stop made at the Sluice for letting the Water into the Aqueduct. The *Castella* are Water-houses or Conduit-heads for the Reception of the publick Water. The *Specus* is a Kind of Mill-dam dug in the Earth. The *Calix* is the End or Mouth of the Aqueduct, which discharges the Water. All these must be made of very stout Work, the Bottom as strong as possible, the Plaistering tight and by no means subject to crack. The Mouth of the Sluice must be stopt with a Flood-gate, with which you may shut out the Water when it happens to be turbid, and by means whereof you may have an Opportunity to mend any Part of the Aqueduct which is decayed, without being prevented by the Water; and this Flood-gate must have a Grate of Brass to it, that Water may flow into the Aqueduct clearer and more refined, leaving behind it the Leaves, Boughs and other Trash that fall into it. At every hundred Cubits must be either a Conduit-head, or a Mill-dam twenty Foot broad, thirty long, and fifteen deep below the Bottom of the Channel; and these are made to the Intent that those Waters which either fall into the Aqueduct from the Earth, or are thrown into it too violently, may have a Place to subside below the other Stream, which by that means will have room to flow on more refined and clear. The Mouth of the Aqueduct for discharging the

the Water, muſt vary according to the Quantity of the Stream, and the Situation of the Pipe by which it makes it diſcharge. The greater and more rapid the Stream is from whence the Water is brought, the more direct Way it is brought, and the more it has been confined, the more the Mouth of the Conduit muſt be enlarged. If the diſcharging Pipe be placed direct to the Stream and Level, it will maintain an equal Diſcharge. It has been found by Experience, that this Pipe is waſted away by the continual Spray of the Water, and that no Metals ſtand it ſo well as Gold. Thus much of Conduits and Aqueducts. Water may alſo be brought in leaden Pipes, or rather in earthen ones, becauſe the Phyſicians tell us, that thoſe of Lead occaſion an Excoriation of the Bowels, and ſo too will Braſs.

The Learned tell us, that whatever we either drink or eat, is beſt preſerved in Veſſels of baked Earth, which the leaſt alters their Taſte; alledging that the Earth is the natural Place of Repoſe, as well of Water as of every Thing elſe which is produced by the Earth. Wooden Pipes give Water in Time an ill Colour, and an unpleaſant Taſte. Whatever Material they are made of, the Pipes ought to be as ſtrong as poſſible. Veſſels of Braſs are apt to give the Epilepſy, Canker, and ſo breed Diſorders in the Liver and Spleen. The Sides of the Pipes muſt be in Thickneſs at leaſt one fourth Part of the Diameter of the Hollow, and the Joints of the Bricks of which they are made be mortiſed into one another, and cemented with unſlaked Lime mixed with Oil; they ſhould alſo be fortified all round with ſtrong Brick Work, and ſtrengthened a good Weight of Work over them, eſpecially where you bring the Water about winding, or where after a Deſcent it is to riſe upwards again, or where the Pipe upon a ſhort Turn is ſtraitened and made narrower. For the Weight and continual Preſſure of the Water, with the Force and Impetuoſity of its Current, would eaſily carry away or break the Bricks. Experienced Workmen, in order to guard againſt this Danger, and eſpecially about the Windings, made uſe of a living Stone, and particularly of the red Sort, bored through for the Purpoſe. I have ſeen Pieces of Marble above twelve Foot long bored through from one End to the other with a Bore of four Inches Diameter, which by plain Marks in the Stone itſelf appeared to have been made with an Inſtrument of Braſs turned with a Wheel and with Sand. In order to prevent the Effects of this Impetuoſity, you may ſlacken the Current of the Water, by making it run winding, not indeed with a ſharp Elbow, but with an eaſy Sweep, turning ſometimes to the Right, ſometimes to the Left, ſometimes riſing, ſometimes deſcending with a frequent Variety. To this you may add ſomewhat in the Nature of a Conduit-head or Mill-dam, in order for the Water to purify there, and alſo if any Defect ſhould happen, that you may the more eaſily come to ſee how and where it muſt be repaired. But theſe Heads ſhould not be placed in the Bottom of the Sweep of a Valley, nor where the Water is forced upwards, but where it keeps on its Courſe more equally and gently. If you are obliged to carry your Conduit-pipes through a Lake or Marſh, you may do it with a very ſmall Expence, in the following Manner. Provide ſome good Timbers of Scarlet Oak, and in them Lengthways cut a Gutter in Breadth and Depth in Proportion to your Pipes, which you muſt lay into this Gutter well cemented with Mortar, and bound down with good Cramps of Braſs. Then having laid theſe Timbers upon a Float acroſs the Lake, faſten the Ends of them together as follows. You muſt have Pipes of Lead of the ſame Diameter as thoſe upon your Timbers, and of ſuch a Length as to allow for bending as much as may be neceſſary. Theſe leaden Pipes, you muſt inſert into your earthen ones, and cement their Joints with Lime ſlacked with Oil, and fortified with Plates of Braſs. Thus join the Ends of the Timber together, as they hang over your Float, till you bring them from one Shore quite to the other, and their Heads reſt upon the dry Ground on each Side. Then withdraw your Float, and having ſecured the whole Work with good Ropes, where the Lake is deepeſt, let it go down by little and little to the Bottom, as equally as poſſible, all the reſt ſinking by proper Degrees along with it, by which Means the leaden Pipe will bend according to the Occaſion, and the whole will place itſelf conveniently at the Bottom of the Lake. When the Conduit is prepared in this Manner with the firſt Water which you ſend into it throw in ſome Aſhes, that if any of the Joints ſhould happen not to be perfectly cloſe, they may ſtop them up, and help to cement them. You ſhould alſo let in the Water by gentle Degrees, leſt ruſhing in too precipitately, it ſhould ſtruggle with the Wind which is in the Pipe.

It

It is incredible the Violence and Impetuosity of Nature when the Wind in ſuch a Pipe is reſtrained and compreſſed too cloſe. I have read in the Works of the Phyſicians, that the Bone of a Man's Leg has been broken by the ſudden Irruption of a Vapour ſo confined. The Artiſts in Hydraulics can force Water to leap up out of a Veſſel, by confining a Quantity of Air between two Waters.

CHAP. VIII.

Of Ciſterns, their Uſes and Conveniencies.

I Now come to ſpeak of Ciſterns. A Ciſtern is a large Veſſel for holding Water, not unlike the Water-houſe or Conduit-head. Its Bottom and Sides therefore muſt be perfectly ſtrong and well compacted. There are two Sorts, one for containing Water for Drinking, and the other for preſerving it for other Uſes, as particularly againſt ſudden Fires. The firſt we ſhall call a Drinking-ciſtern, the other a Reſervoir. The Drinking-ciſtern out to preſerve its Water in the greateſt Purity; becauſe when it is impure it is the Cauſe of a great many Inconveniencies. In both we are to take care that the Water is properly admitted, preſerved and diſpenſed. Water is brought into the Ciſtern by Pipes from the River or Spring, and ſometimes Rain-water from the Houſe-top or from the Ground. I was extremely pleaſed with the Invention of an Architect, who in a large bare Rock on the Summit of a Hill cut a round Baſon ten Foot deep, which received all the Rain-water which ran into it from that naked Rock. Then in the Plain under the Hill he erected a Water-houſe, open on every Side, and built of Brick and Mortar, thirty Foot high, forty long and forty broad. Into this Water-houſe he brought the Rain-water from the upper Reſervoir by a ſubterraneous Conduit of brick Pipe; that Reſervoir lying much higher than the Top of the Water-houſe. If you ſtrew the Bottom of your Ciſtern with good round Pebbles, or large Gravel from the River very well waſhed, or rather fill it with it to a certain Height, ſuppoſe of three Foot, it will make your Water clear, cool and pure; and the Higher you make this Strewing, your Water will be the more limpid. The Water ſometimes runs out at the Joints and Cracks of the Ciſtern if it is ill made; and ſometimes the Water is ſpoiled by Filth. And indeed it is no eaſy Matter to keep Water impriſoned, unleſs the Reſervoir be ſtrongly built, and even of good ſquare Stone. It is alſo particularly neceſſary, that the Work ſhould be perfectly dry before you let the Water into it, which preſſing hard upon it with its Weight, and Sweating through it by means of its Humidity, if it can but make a ſmall Crack, will be continually working its Way till it has opened itſelf a large Paſſage. The Ancients guarded againſt this Inconvenience, and eſpecially in the Corners of their Reſervoirs, by ſeveral Coats of ſtrong Plaiſtering, and ſometimes by Incruſtations of Marbles. But nothing better prevents this oozing out of the Water, than Chalk cloſe rammed in between the Wall of the Ciſtern and the Side of the Trench in which it is made. We order the Chalk which we uſe for this Purpoſe to be thoroughly dried and beat into Powder. Some think, that if you fill a Glaſs Veſſel with Salt, and ſtop it up cloſe with a Plaiſter of Mortar tempered with Oil, that no Water may get in, and then hang it down in the Middle of the Ciſtern, it will prevent the Water from corrupting, let it be kept ever ſo long. Some add Quick-ſilver to the Compoſition. Others ſay, that if you take a new earthen Veſſel full of ſharp Vinegar, ſtopt up as above, and ſet it in the Water, it will entirely clear it from all Slime. They tell us too, that either a Ciſtern or a Well are purified by putting ſome ſmall Fiſh into them, thinking that the Fiſh feed upon the Slime of the Water and of the Earth. We are told of an old Saying of *Epigenes*, that Water which has been once corrupted, will in Time recover and purify itſelf, and after that never ſpoil any more. Water which is beginning to corrupt, if it is ſtirred about, and poured often out of one Veſſel into another, will loſe its ill Smell, which will alſo hold good of Wine and Oil that is mothery. *Joſephus* relates, that when *Moſes* came to a dry Place, where there was only one Spring of Water, and that foul and bitter, he commanded the Soldiers to draw it; and upon their beating and ſtirring it about heartily, it became drinkable. It is certain that Water may be purified by boiling and ſtraining; and we are told that Water which is nitrous and bitter, by throwing Barley-flower into it may be ſo ſweetened, as to be fit to drink in two Hours Time. But in order to refine the Water of your Drinking-ciſterns more effectually, make a little Well cloſe to your Ciſtern encloſed with its own proper Wall, and its Bottom a ſmall matter lower than the Bottom of the Ciſtern. This Well on the Side next the Ciſtern muſt have ſome ſmall Openings filled up either with Spunge or with Pumice-ſtone, that the Water which gets out of the Ciſtern into the Well may be thoroughly ſtrained and leave all its coarſe Mixture behind it. In the Territory of *Tarragona* in *Spain*, is found a white Pumice-ſtone very full of ſmall Pores, through which Water is preſently ſtrained to the greateſt Clearneſs. It will alſo come out extremely limpid if you fill up the Aperture, through which the Water muſt paſs, with a Pot bored full of Holes on every Side, and filled with River-ſand, in order for the Water to make its Way through this fine Strainer. At *Bologna*, they have a ſoft ſandy Stone of a yellow Colour, through which the Water diſtills Drop by Drop till it is wonderfully refined. Some make Bread of Sea-water; than which nothing can be more unwholeſome. But yet thoſe Strainers which we have mentioned are ſo effectual that they will make even Sea-water wholeſome and ſweet. *Solinus* ſays, that if Sea-water is paſſed through a white Clay it will become ſweet; and we find by Experience that when it has been often ſtrained through a fine Sand, it loſes its Saltneſs. If you ſink an earthen Pot cloſe ſtopped, into the Sea, it will be filled with freſh Water. Nor is it foreign to our Purpoſe what we are told, that when the Water of the *Nile* is taken up into any Veſſel proves foul, if you rub the Veſſel juſt about the Edge of the Water with an Almond, it will preſently make it clear. When your Conduit Pipes begin to be ſtopt with Slime or Dirt, take a Gall-nut, or a Ball made of the Bark of Cork, tied to a long thin Packthread. When the Current of the Water has carried this Ball to the other End of the Pipe, tie to the Pack-thread another ſtronger Cord with a Wiſp of Broom faſtened to it, which being drawn backwards and forwards in the Pipe, will clear away the Dirt that ſtopt it up.

Chap. IX.

Of planting a Vineyard in a Meadow, or a Wood in a Marſh; and how we may amend a Region which is moleſted with too much Water.

I Now proceed to other Conveniencies. We obſerved that Food and Rayment was to provided for the Inhabitants. With theſe we are to be ſupplied by Agriculture, an Art which it is not our Buſineſs to treat of here. Yet there are ſome Caſes wherein the Architect may be of Service to the Husbandman: As particularly when a Piece of Ground being either too dry or too wet, is not in a good Condition for Tillage. A Vineyard may be planted in a moiſt Meadow in the following Manner: Dig Trenches running from Eaſt to Weſt in ſtraight Lines, at equal Diſtances from each other, and as deep as may be, each nine Foot broad and fifteen Foot diſtant from one another, and throw up the Earth which you dig out of the Trenches on the Intervals between them, in ſuch a Manner, that the Slope may lie open to the Mid-day Sun: and theſe little artificial Hills will be very proper for Vines and very fruitful. On the contrary, upon a dry Hill you may make a Meadow by the following Method: Dig a long ſquare Trench in the upper Part of the Hill, with its Sides all equally high and exactly level. Into this Trench bring Water from the next Springs above it, which running over on the lower Side will equally and continually water the Ground beneath. In the Country of *Verona*, a Soil full of round Stones, very naked and barren, the Inhabitants in ſome Places, by continual watering it, have raiſed very fine Graſs and ſo turned it into a beautiful Meadow. If you deſire to have a Wood grow in a Marſh, turn up the Ground with the Plough, and entirely grub up all Brambles, and then ſow it with Acorns about the Time of Sun-riſe. This Plantation will grow up into a thick Wood, and the Trees will draw to themſelves moſt of the ſuperfluous Moiſture: And the ſpreading of the Roots together with the falling of the Leaves and Sprigs, will raiſe the Ground higher. Afterwards if you bring

down

down ſome Land-flood upon it, which may ſubſide there, it will make a Cruſt over the whole. But of this in another Place. If the Region is ſubject to Inundations, as *Lombardy* along the Banks of the *Po*; *Venice*, and ſome other Place; in that Caſe, ſeveral Particulars are to be conſidered: For the Water is troubleſome either from its over-abundance, or from its Motion, or from both theſe. Upon theſe we ſhall make ſome brief Obſervations. The Emperor *Claudius* bored through a Hill near the Lake *Fucinus*, and ſo carried away the ſuperfluous Water into the River; and perhaps it was for the ſame Reaſon, that *M. Curius* opened a Way for the Lake *Velinus* to diſcharge itſelf into the Sea. Thus we ſee the Lake *Nemorenſis*, carried into the Lake *Laurentina* through a Hill bored on purpoſe; to which we owe thoſe pleaſant Gardens and that fruitful Grove which lie below the Former of thoſe Lakes.

Cæſar had Thoughts of cutting a Number of Trenches near *Herda* in *Spain*, in order to diſcharge ſome Part of the Water of the River *Sicoris*. The *Erymanthus*, a River of *Arcadia*, very full of Windings, is almoſt exhauſted by the Inhabitants in watering their Lands, by which means his Remains fall into the Sea without ſo much as preſerving his Name. *Cyrus* cut the *Ganges* into a vaſt Number of Canals, *Eutropius* ſays, no leſs than four hundred and ſixty, by which he ſo ſunk that River, that it might eaſily be forded, and ſometimes even driſhod. Near the Tomb of King *Halyattes*, in the Country of the *Sardes*, built chiefly by the female Slaves, is the Lake *Coloe*, dug by Art on purpoſe to receive Inundations. *Myris* dug a Lake in *Meſopotamia* above the City, three hundred and forty Furlongs in Circumference, and threeſcore Cubits deep, to receive the *Nile* whenever it roſe higher than uſual. Beſides the ſtrong Banks made for keeping in the *Euphrates*, that it might not overflow and waſh away the Houſes, ſome Lakes were alſo dug, together with ſome vaſt hollow Caves, that the ſtanding Water in thoſe might receive and break the Fury of Inundations. Thus much may ſuffice of Waters which are apt to overflow, or to do Miſchief by the Impetuoſity of their Motion. If any thing is wanting to this Head, we ſhall inſert it immediately, when we come to ſpeak of Rivers and the Sea.

CHAP. X.

Of Roads; of Paſſages by Water, and of artificial Banks to Rivers.

THE next Buſineſs is to get as conveniently as is poſſible from abroad, thoſe Neceſſaries which we cannot be ſupplied with at home. To this Purpoſe are Roads and Highways, which are to be made ſuch, that whatever is wanting may be eaſily brought, in its proper Seaſon. There are two Sorts of Highways, one by Land, the other by Water, as we hinted in the formar Part of this Work. Care is to be taken that the Highway by Land is not too deep, nor too much broke by Carriages; and beſides thoſe Cauſeways which we have ſpoken of formerly, we ſhould be ſure to let them be open to a good deal of Sun and to a free Air, and that they be not covered with too much Shade. In our Days, near the Wood by *Ravenna*, the Road which uſed to be very bad, has been made extremely convenient by cutting down the Trees, and admitting the Sun to it. We may generally obſerve little Puddles under Trees which ſtand by the Side of the Road, occaſioned by the Tread of Cattle, and the Shade preventing the Ground from drying ſo faſt as it otherwiſe would do, ſo that the Rain always ſettles and lies there. Highways (if we may ſo call them) by Water are of two Sorts: One which may be corrected and forced; as Rivers or Canals; the other which cannot; as the Sea. We may venture to ſay, that there happen the ſame Faults in a River as we find in a ſmaller Veſſel for containing Water; that is, that perhaps either the Sides, or the Bottom are defective or not ſound and convenient. For as a large Quantity of Water is neceſſary for the carrying of Ships, if it is not contained in ſtout Banks, it may break its Way through them and drown all the Country, and ſo even ſpoil the Highways on Shore. If the Bottom be very ſteep, how can we imagine that a Ship can make its Way up againſt the Rapidity of the Stream? and if it riſes into Shelves, it will ſpoil the Navigation. Upon bringing the famous Obelisk from *Ægypt* to *Rome*, it was found that the *Tyber* was a more convenient River for Navigation than the *Nile*. The latter indeed was much broader, but the former

former was of a more convenient Depth: For it is not ſo much a great Plenty as a good Depth of Water that is neceſſary for Navigation. Though a handſome Breadth is very convenient too, becauſe by that means the Streams comes ſlower againſt the Banks. A River that has not a ſound Bottom, will ſcarce have ſtrong Banks; and ſcarce any Bottom can be called ſound, which has not ſuch a Strength as we have formerly required in the Foundations of Buildings, namely, to be ſo ſolid as in a Manner to defy even Tools of Iron. Thus the Bottom will be uncertain if the Banks are chalky, or if the River runs along a flat Plain, or if the Soil is covered with looſe round Stones. When the Banks of a River are unfirm, its Channel will be ſtopt up with Shelves, Ruins, broken Trunks of Trees, and ſoft Stones. The weakeſt Sides of all, and the moſt variable, are thoſe thrown up by ſome ſudden Inundation. From this Weakneſs of the Sides follows what is ſaid of the *Meander* and the *Euphrates*, the former of which we are told, uſed eaſily to cut through his ſoft Banks and be daily running into new Windings, and the *Euphrates* on the other Hand was continually ſtopping up the Canals, through which he was conveyed, with the Ruins of his Shore. Theſe Defects in the natural Banks the Ancients uſed to remedy with artificial ones; the Rules for which are much the ſame with thoſe for other Kinds of Structures; for we are to conſider well with what Lines we erect it, and with what Kind of Work. If the artificial Bank is built in a parallel Line with the Current of the River, the Force of the Stream will never bear againſt it: But if it is built ſo as to ſtand againſt the Current, if it is not very ſtrong it will be overthrown by it; or if it be too low the Water will overflow it. If ſuch a Bank be not overthrown, it will be continually growing higher and higher at the Bottom, becauſe there every Thing which the Stream brings along with it will ſtop, till at laſt having made a Hill againſt it which it can remove no further, it will be apt to turn its Courſe another Way. If the Force of the Water throws down the Bank, then it will have thoſe Effects natural to it, which we obſerved before, by filling all the Hollows, driving out the Air, and ſweeping away every Thing that it meets in its Paſſage: But ſtill leaving behind it by Degrees as it ſlackens the Violence of its own Courſe, ſuch heavy Things as are not eaſily carried far. Thus in the Mouth of the Breach which the River makes in its Banks, the Inundation will leave a Shelf of coarſe Sand of a conſiderable Height; but as it goes further it will only cover the Ground with a ſmall Slime. If the River does not immediately break down its Bank, but only overflows the Top of it, the Violence with which it falls upon the Ground on the other Side of it will waſh away the Earth, till by Degrees it undermines and brings down the whole Bank itſelf. If the Current neither is parallel with the Bank, nor ſets againſt it directly, but only ſtrikes it obliquely, it will bear no leſs, in Proportion to the Angle of its Obliquity, againſt the Sides to which it is thrown off, than againſt that which it meets with firſt. And indeed this Flexion will give it ſomewhat of the Nature of a Bank that fronts the Current directly; ſo that it will be liable to the very ſame Injuries as the latter. Thus the Bank will be waſhed away ſo much the ſooner, as the Eddies of the Water will be more vehement and furious, foaming, and in a Manner boiling with Violence: For theſe Whirls and Eddies in a River ſeem to have ſomewhat of the Nature and Force of a Screw, which no Strength or Solidity can long reſiſt. We may obſerve as well under Stone Bridges, how deep the Channel is dug by the Fall of the Water; as in thoſe Part of the River where after having been ſome Time confined within narrower Banks, it finds a broader Channel to extend itſelf in, with what Fury it breaks out, rowling into Variety of Eddies, and tearing away every Thing that it meets with, either from the Banks or from the Bottom. I dare venture to affirm, that *Hadrian*'s Bridge at *Rome*, is one of the ſtouteſt Pieces of Work that perhaps ever was performed; and yet the Fury of the Water has ſo decay'd it, that I dread its Deſtruction: For the Land-floods every Year load its Piers with Boughs and Trunks of Trees which they bring down along with them, and in a great Meaſure ſtop up the Arches. This makes the Water riſe ſtill higher, and then it falls down percipitately into wild Eddies, which undermine the Back of the Piers and endanger the whole Structure. Thus much of the Banks: Let us now ſay ſomething of the Bottom of the River. *Herodotus* relates, that *Nitocris*, King of the *Aſſyrians*, ſlackened the Courſe of the River *Euphrates* near *Meſopotamia*, which before was too impetuous, by making its Channel wind about more than it uſed to do. It is alſo reaſonable to ſuppoſe that the Water which has the

the floweft Current will be the moft lafting: Which may be fomewhat illuftrated by the Comparifon of a Man that defcends from a fteep Hill, and who comes down not direct and as faft as he can, but fetching different Compaffes about the Sides, fometimes to the right Hand, and fometimes to the Left. The Rapidity of the Stream proceeds from the Steepnefs of the Channel. A Current either too fwift or too flow, is inconvenient. The former demolifhes the Banks; the latter produces Weeds, and is eafily frozen. Making the River narrower may perhaps force the Water to rife higher, and another Way to make it deeper is digging the Channel, lower. Deepening the Channel, removing Impediments, and clearing the River are all done by the fame Methods and for the fame Purpofes, whereof we fhall fpeak prefently: But deepening the Bottom of a River will be in vain, unlefs we go on to do it quite away to the Sea, in order to give the Stream its due Slope all the Way.

CHAP. XI.

Of Canals; how they are to be kept well fupplied with Water, and the Ufes of them not obftructed.

WE now proceed to fpeak of Canals. What we are to provide for in thefe, is that they be well fupplied with Water, and that the Ufes for which they are intended be not obftructed. There are two Ways of preventing their failing. The firft is to have a large Quantity of Water conftantly running into them from fome other Stream; the fecond is to contrive that they keep what does come into them as long as can be. The Water is to be brought into Canals in the manner above fet down: and our Diligence muft prevent their Ufes from being obftructed, by often cleaning them, and removing whatever Incumbrances may be brought into them. A Canal is faid to be a fleeping River; and it fhould therefore have all the fame Properties which a River has, and efpecially its Bottom and Sides fhould be perfectly found, that the Water may neither be fucked up, nor run out at any Cracks. It fhould be more deep than broad, as well for the better carrying off all Sorts of Veffels, as that it may be lefs exhaufted by the Sun and breed the fewer Weeds. A great many Canals were cut from the *Euphrates* to the *Tygris*, becaufe the Channel of the former lay higher than that of the Latter. *Lombardy* lying between the *Po* and the *Adige*, is every where navigable by Canals; an Advantage which it gains by lying all upon a Flat. *Diodorus* tells us, that when *Ptolomey* went out of the Mouth of the *Nile*, he opened a Canal on Purpofe, and had it ftopp'd up as foon as he was got through it. The Remedies for the feveral Faults of either Canals or Rivers are confining, clearing and ftopping them. Rivers are confined by artificial Banks. The Line of fuch Banks fhould not reftrain the River at once, but by degrees, by means of an eafy Slope. When you would fet it at Liberty again from a narrow Channel into a wider Breadth, you muft obferve the fame Method, not let it out at once, but gently, left upon too fudden an Enlargment it does Mifchief by Eddies and Whirlpools. The River *Melas* ufed of old to run into the *Euphrates*; but King *Artanatrix*, perhaps out of a Defire to make his Name famous, ftopp'd it up and overflowed the Country all round: but foon afterwards the Waters return'd with fuch Eddies and fo much Fury that they tore up all that refifted them, wafhed away a great many Eftates, and laid Wafte a great Part of *Phrygia* and *Galatia*. The *Roman Senate* fined the King for this audacious Attempt, in thirty Talents. Nor is it foreign to our Purpofe juft to mention what we read of *Iphicrates* the *Athenian*, that when he was befieging *Stymphalus* in *Arcadia* he attempted with a vaft Quantity of Spunge to ftop up the River *Erafinus* which enters into the Hill and rifes up again in the Country of *Arges*; but by the Admonition of *Jupiter* he laid afide the Defign. I advife therefore, that your artificial Bank be made as ftrong as poffible. This Strength muft be owing to the Solidity of your Materials, your Method of putting them together, and the Breadth of the whole Work. Where it is neceffary that the Water fhould run over this Bank, do not let the Outfide of it be a Perpendicular, but fall in an eafy Slope, that the Water may run down it eafily and not form any Eddies. If in its Fall it begins to dig up the Bank, fill up the Holes immediately, not with trifling Materials, but with large, ſolid, ſquare Stone. It may alſo be of Service to lay Bundles of Bruſhwood underneath the Fall of the Water, to break its Force before it comes to the Bottom. We ſee that the *Tyber* at *Rome* is for the moſt Part confined with ſolid Maſonry. *Semiramis*, not contented with a ſtrong Bank of Brick, covered it with a Coat of Plaiſter made of Bitumen, no leſs than four Cubits in Thickneſs, with Walls for many Furlongs together equally high with thoſe of the City. But theſe are Royal Works. For us, we may be contented with a Bank of Earth, like that of *Nitocris* in *Aſſyria*, which was of Mud, or like thoſe Banks in *France* which confine ſome very great Rivers, in ſuch a Manner that they ſeem to hang in the Air, the Water in ſome Places being above the Level of the Tops of the Cottages: and we may be ſatisfied if we can have our Bridges of Stone. Some commend the Graſs Turfs cut out of a Meadow for making up of Banks: and I think they will do very well, becauſe the interweaving of their Roots will fortify the Work, provided they be rammed very cloſe together: for the whole Bank, and eſpecially that Part of it which is waſhed by the Water, ought to be ſo ſolid as not to be penetrated or diſunited. Some interlace Rods of Ozier in the Bank; and this makes a very firm Bank, but then it will laſt but for a Time, for as ſuch Rods eaſily rot, little Rills of Water will penetrate into the Places of the Twigs which are decayed, and working their Way onwards, will be apt to enlarge their Paſſage till the whole River may break through in great Streams. There will not indeed be ſo much Danger of this if we take the Oziers when they are green. Others plant Willows, Elder, Poplars and ſuch other Trees as love the Water along the Shores in cloſe Rows. This has ſome Advantages; but then it is attended with the ſame Inconvenience which we juſt now mentioned; for when the Roots decay, the Water will work its Way into their Cavities. Others (which I am very well pleaſed with) plant the Shore with all Manner of Shrubs that flouriſh in the Water, and ſtrike out more Root than Branches, ſuch as Lavender, Bulruſh, Reeds, and eſpecially Withes; the laſt of which puſhes out a great deal of Root, and pierces down into the Earth with very long Fibres, which are continually making new Shoots, while at the ſame Time its Head is but ſmall, is very pliant, and does not reſiſt the Stream; and which adds to the Advantage, this Plant, out of its particular Love to Water, advances on continually even into the Current. But where the Bank runs on parallel with the ſtrong Current of the River, the Shore ought to be entirely naked and clear, that nothing may diſturb or enrage the Stream, but that it may run on peaceably. Where the Bank winding about ſtands againſt the Set of the Current, that it may make the ſtouter Reſiſtance, let it be fortified with good Plank. But if the whole Force of the River is to be withſtood and oppoſed; then, in the Summer, when the Water is loweſt, and the Shore is left dry, make Hurdles bound about ſtrong Stakes of a good Length, and faſtened to them very tight with ſtout Braces; lay theſe Hurdles with the Heads of the Stakes againſt the Current of the Stream, and drive Piles through them, by Holes made in them before-hand for that Purpoſe, as deep as the Nature of the Bottom will permit. When this is knit together, join other Beams to them croſſways, and fill up this Frame with large Stones cemented together with Mortar; or where the Expence of Mortar cannot be afforded, you may knit them together by throwing Bavins of Juniper in amongſt them. This great Weight will prevent the Water from ſtirring the Frame; and if any Eddies ſhould get within it, they will do rather Good than Harm, for by endeavouring to work downwards they will make the whole Weight of Stone ſink ſtill lower, and ſo ſtrengthen the Foundation ſtill more. But if the River always keeps at ſuch a Height, that there is no Opportunity to make ſuch a Frame, then we muſt make uſe of thoſe Methods which we formerly taught for erecting the Piers of a Bridge.

Chap. XII.

Of the Sea Wall; of ſtrengthening the Port; and of Locks for confining the Water of a River.

THE Sea-ſhore alſo is to be fortified with artificial Banks, but not in the ſame Manner as the River, whoſe Streams does Miſchief in a different Manner from the Waves of the Sea. We are told, that the Sea in its own Nature is quiet and peaceable, but it is agitated

tated and drove about by the Winds, which push on the Waves in great Rows to the Shore, where if they meet with Opposition, especially from any hard rugged Body they beat against them with their whole Strength, and being dashed back again they break, and falling from on high with continual Repetition dig up and demolish whatever resists their Fury. A full Proof of this is the great Depth of Water which we constantly find under high Rocks by the Sea-side. But when the Shore runs off with an easy Descent, the raging Sea not finding any Thing to exert its Force against, grows quiet, and falls back less furious upon itself; and if it has brought any Sand along with it, leaves it there; by which Means we see such Shores growing higher and higher into the Sea every Day. But when the Sea meets with a Promontory, and afterwards with a Bay, the Current runs impetuously along the Shore, and turns back again upon itself; which is the Reason that in such Places we frequently meet with deep Channels cut under the Shore. Others maintain, that the Sea hath a Breath and Respiration of its own, and pretend to observe, that no Man ever dies naturally but when the Tide is going off, whence they would infer, that our Life has some Connection and Relation with the Motion and Life of the Sea: but this is not worth Dwelling upon. It is certain, that the Tides rise and fall variously in different Places. The *Negropont* has no less than six Tides every Day. At *Constantinople* it has no other Change but by flowing into the *Pontus*. In the *Propontis* the Sea naturally throws upon the Shore every Thing that is brought down into it by the Rivers: because every Thing which is put into an unnatural Agitation rests of Course where-ever it finds a Place which is not disturbed. But as upon almost all Shores we see Heaps of Sand or Stones thrown up, it may not be a miss just to mention the Conjectures of the Philosophers upon this Occasion. I have said elsewhere, that Sand is form'd of Mud dried by the Sun, and separated by the Heat into very minute Particles. Stones are supposed to be engendered by the Sea-water; for they tell us, that by Means of the Sun's Heat and of Motion, the Water grows warm, dries, and its lighter Parts evaporating hardens into a Consistence, which grows to have so much Solidity, that if the Sea is but a little while at rest, it by degrees contracts a slimy Crust, of a bituminous Nature; this Crust in Time is afterwards broken, and by new Motion and Collision the new-made Substance becomes globular, and grows somewhat like a Spunge: These globular Spunges are carried to the Shore, where by their Sliminess they lick up the Sand which is put into Agitation, which again is dried and concocted by the Heat of the Sun, and by the Salts, till by Length of Time it hardens into Stone. This is the Conjecture of the Philosophers. We frequently see the Shore grow higher and higher towards the Mouth of Rivers, especially if they flow through loose Grounds, and are much subject to Land-floods; for such Rivers throw up vast Quantities of Sand and Stones before their Mouths into the Sea, and so lengthen out the Shore. This manifestly appears from the *Danube*, the *Phasis* in *Colchis*, and others, and especially in the *Nile*. The Ancients called *Ægypt* the *Nile*'s House, and tell us, that it was formerly covered by the Sea quite as far as the *Pelusian* Marshes. So it is related, that a great Part of *Cilicia* was added to it by the River. *Aristotle* says, that all Things are in perpetual Motion, and that in length of Time the Sea and the Hills will change Places with one another. Hence the Saying of the Poet:

All that the Earth in her dark Womb conceals,
Time shall dig up and drag to open Light.

BUT to return. The Waves have this particular Property, that when they meet with any Bank which resists them, they dash against it with the more Fury; and being beaten back, according to the Height they fall from, the more Sand they root up. This appears from the great Depth of the Sea under the Rocks, against which they beat with much more Violence, than they fall upon a soft and sloping Sand. This being the Case, it requires great Diligence and the most careful Contrivance to restrain the Rage and Strength of the Sea, which will many Times defeat all our Art and Ability, and is not easily subdued by the Power of Man. However, the Sort of Work which we formerly recommended for the Foundations of a Bridge may be of some Service in this Case. But if it is necessary for us to carry out a Pier into the Sea in order to fortify a Port, we must begin our Work upon the dry Ground, and so by Additions work it forwards into the Sea. Our first and greatest Care must be to chuse a firm Soil for this Structure; and where-ever you raise it, raise it up with a Slope of the lightest Stones that can be got, in order

order to break the Fury of the Waves, that not finding any Thing to beat against with their whole Strength, they may fall back gently and not with too violent a Precipitation. Thus the Wave which is upon Return will meet that which is coming on, and deaden its Force. The Mouths of Rivers seem to be of the same Nature with the Port, as they afford Shelter to Vessels against Storms. They ought therefore to be fortified and made narrower to exclude the Fury of the Sea. *Propertius* says,

Resolve to conquer or be o'ercome,
This is the Wheel of Love ——

It is the same in this Case; for the Mouths of Rivers by the incessant Attacks of the Sea are either overcome and filled up with Sand; or else by a constant and obstinate Resistance, they conquer and keep their Passages clear. For this Reason it is an admirable Method to open the River a double Discharge into the Sea by two different Branches, if you have but Water enough to supply them; not only that Ships may be able to get in at one of them, though the Wind be contrary for the other; but also that if one of them be stopt up, either by some Storm at Sea, or by some strong Wind blowing into it, in such a Manner that the Land-floods would be driven back again into the Country, they may have another Passage open to discharge themselves into the Sea. But of this enough. The next Point is how to clean a River. *Cæsar* took a great deal of Care about cleaning the *Tyber*, which was stopt up with Rubbish, and there are vast Heaps of the Stuff that was taken out still to be seen not far from the River, as well within the City as without. By what Methods he got so much Rubbish out of so swift a River, I do not remember to have read: But I suppose he made use of Frames to shut out the River and then emptying the Water out of them, he might easily take out the Rubbish. These Frames are made in the following Manner: Prepare some strong Timbers cut square, with Grooves cut in the Sides of them from Top to Bottom four Inches deep, and in Breadth equal to the Thickness of the Planks which you intend to use in this Work; and prepare your Planks also of equal Length and Thickness with one another. Having got these Things ready, drive down your Timbers so as they may stand perpendicular, at Distances from each other equal to the Length of your Planks. When your Timbers are well fixed, let your Planks into the Grooves and drive them down to the Bottom. Our Workmen call these Frames Cataracts. Go on in the same Manner to fill up the Spaces between the Timbers with Planks and drive them as close together as possible. Then go to work immediately with your Pumps, Syphons, Buckets and all your other Implements for emptying out the Water, putting on as many Hands as you can, and labouring without Intermission till you have thrown out all the Water within your Inclosure. If it leaks in any Part, stop up the Crack with any old Rags: And thus the Business may be done. Between this Frame and that which we mentioned as necessary in the Building of Bridges, there is this Difference; that the latter must be stable and lasting, being to stand not only till the Piers are built, but even till the Superstructure is settled; whereas this is only temporary, and as soon as the Dirt is got out to be presently removed to another Place. But I advise you, whether you clean your River by the Help of this Frame, or by turning the Course of the Water, that you do not pretend to strive against the whole Force of the Stream at a Time in any one Place, but go on Step by Step and by Degrees. All Works raised against the Violence of Waters, if they are made in the Form of Arches, with their Backs turned against the Weight of the Water, they will be able to make the stouter Resistance. You may level a Torrent or Water-fall by laying a Barrier across the Stream in such a Manner that the Water is obliged to rise a good deal higher than usual: For the Water running over from the Top of this Barrier, will dig up the Ridge in the Channel by its fall; and then even the Channel above the Torrent, quite to the Spring will be levelled in Proportion to the lower Part of the Channel; for the Water in its Descent will be continually moving and carrying away the Earth. You may clean your Channel by turning Oxen into it in the following Manner: Stop it up that the Water may swell; then drive your Cattle about in it so that they may disturb all the Mud, and then opening the Stream that the Water may pour in rapidly, it will wash and carry away all the Dirt. If any thing lies buried and fixed in the Stream so as to spoil the Navigation, besides the common Machines used by Workmen for removing such Obstructions, it is a very good Method to load a Barge deep, and to it fasten with Ropes the Impediment which you would pull up: Then unload

unload the Barge, which by that Means rising higher in the Water, will pull up what is tyed to it. It will be a Help to the Operation, if you keep the Vessel stirring about by moving the Rudder backwards and forwards while you are unloading it; to shew the Use of which, I shall just mention, that in the Country of *Præneste* I have seen a moist Sort of Clay into which if you run a Stick or a Sword but the Depth of a single Cubit, it was not by the Force of a Man's Arm to be got out again by pulling; but if as you pulled you wriggled your Arm backwards and forwards as Men do that are turning a Skrew, it would easily come forth. At *Genoa* there was a Rock lying under the Surface of the Water so as to stop up the Entrance into the Port. A Man was found in our Age, endued with surprizing Qualifications both of Art and Nature, who broke it away, and laid the Passage very wide. It is said, that this Man used to stay under Water many Hours together, without ever coming up to take Breath. You may take up the Mud from the Bottom by means of an Oyster-net covered with Tarpawlins; for as you draw it along it will fill itself. You may also fetch it up from the Bottom, where the Sea is shallow, with the following Contrivance. You must have two Smacks, like those of Fishermen; in the Stern of one of these you must have an Axis upon which a very long Pole must swing like the Beam of a Balance; to that End of the Pole which lies out from the Stern must be fasten'd a Shovel three Foot broad and six long. By lowering down this Shovel to the Bottom you scoop up the Mud, and so throw it into the other Smack which lies by for that Purpose. From these Principles many other Engines yet more useful may be contrived; but to speak of them here would be too tedious. And thus much may suffice for cleaning any Channel. The Locks in a River are made either by Sluices or Flood-gates. For either of these the Sides must be made full as strong as the Piers of a Bridge. We may draw up the heaviest Sluice without Danger to our Men, by applying to the Spindle or Windless which is to draw up the Sluice Wheels notch'd with Teeth like the Wheels in a Clock, which must take hold of the Teeth of the other Spindle which is to be put in Motion by them. But the most convenient of all is the Flood-gate, which in the Middle has a Spindle that turns upon a perpendicular Axis; to this Spindle is fastened a broad square Valve, like the square Sail of a Barge which may be easily turned about to which Side of the Vessel the Master pleases; but the two Sides of this Valve shall not be exactly equal to one another in Breadth, but let one be above three Inches narrower than the other; by which means it may be opened by a Child, and will shut again of itself; because the Weight of the broader Side will exceed that of the Narrower. To each Lock you ought to make two Stops, cutting the River in two Places, and leaving a Space between them equal to the Length of a Vessel, to the Intent, that if the Vessel is to ascend, when it comes to the Stop the lower Sluice may be shut the upper one opened; or if it be to descend, the upper one may be shut and the lower opened; for by this means the Vessel will run down with the lower Part of the Stream, while the rest of the Water is stopp'd by the upper Sluice. There is one Thing which I must not omit concerning publick Ways, that I may have no Occasion for Repetition; namely, that the Streets of a Town ought never to be heaped up with any Sort of Rubbish, as it is grown a bad Custom to do under the Notion of mending them, which should rather be done by removing and carrying away all the Superfluities; lest the Houses come in Time to be buried, and the Level of the Town to be sunk under Rubbish.

Chap. XIII.

Of the Remedies for some other Inconveniencies.

I Shall now proceed to the Remedies for some other Inconveniencies of smaller Moment; in which I shall be as brief as possible. In some Places, upon bringing Water to them, the Country has been made warmer; in others, colder. Near *Larissa* in *Thessaly* there was a Field covered with a standing Water, which made the Air heavy and hot. Upon carrying off this Water, and laying the Field dry, the Country became cooler. The contrary happened at *Philippi*, where, as we are informed by *Theophrastus*, upon drawing off the Water and drying up a Lake, the Country was made warmer. The Cauſe of theſe Alterations is ſuppoſed to have lain in the Purity or Groſſneſs of the Air; for a thick Air is more difficultly moved, and longer retains either the Heat or the Cold than a thin one, which is ſoon apt to be frozen with Cold, or on a Change of Weather, to be warmed again with the Sun's Heat. A Country which lies uncultivated and neglected is ſaid to afford a thick and unhealthy Air; and in Places ſo much covered with Wood, that neither Sun nor Wind can eaſily get through, the Air is generally crude. The Caves about the Lake *Avernus* were ſo ſurrounded with thick Woods that the Sulphur which exhaled from them uſed to kill the Birds which flew over them: But *Cæſar*, by cutting down thoſe Woods, made that peſtilential Spot of Ground very healthy. At *Leghorn* a Sea-port Town in *Tuſcany*, the Inhabitants uſed always to be afflicted with ſevere Fevers in the Dog-days: By banking off the Sea with a good Wall, the Town was freed from thoſe Diſtempers; but afterwards, when they let the Water again into their Ditches, for the better Fortification of the Place, their Fevers return'd. *Varro* writes, that when his Camp lay in the Iſland of *Corcyra* (now *Corfu*) and his Soldiers died apace of Peſtilence; by keeping all the Windows towards the South cloſe ſhut, he preſerved his Army. At *Murano*, a famous Town belonging to the *Venetians*, they are very ſeldom touched with the Plague, though, their neighbouring Metropolis, *Venice*, is frequently and ſeverely afflicted with it. The Reaſon of this is ſuppoſed to be the great Number of Glaſs-houſes there; for it is very certain that the Air is wonderfully purged by Fire. And for a Proof that all Manner of Poiſons hate the Fire, it is obſerved, that the dead Bodies of poiſonous Animals do not breed Worms, like others; becauſe it is the Nature of Poiſon to deſtroy and totally to extinguiſh the Principles of Life: But if ſuch Bodies are touched by Lightening they will engender Worms, becauſe then their Poiſon is deſtroyed by Fire; for Worms are bred in the dead Bodies of Animals from no other Cauſe than a certain fiery Power in Nature working upon a Humidity which is apt to be put in Motion by a Heat which it is the Property of Poiſon to extinguiſh, where it prevails, as it is itſelf extinguiſhed by it, where that Heat is the moſt powerful. If you root out poiſonous Herbs, and eſpecially Squills, the good Plants will draw to themſelves the bad Nouriſhment which they uſed to imbibe from the Earth, by which means our Food will be corrupted. It may be of Service to ſhelter your Houſe from unwholeſome Winds by a Grove and eſpecially of Apple-trees; for it is of a good deal of Conſequence out of the Shade of what Leaves you receive your Air. Pitch-trees are ſaid to be very good for Phthyſical Folks, or for thoſe who are recovering their Health ſlowly after long Sickneſs. It is contrary with Trees which have a bitter Leaf, for they yield an unwholeſome Air. Thus where-ever the Country is low, cloſe and maſhy, it will be of Service to lay it quite open to the Sun and Air; becauſe the Damps and noxious Animals which ariſe from ſuch Places will be preſently deſtroyed by Dryneſs and Winds. At *Alexandria* is a publick Place to which the Filth and Rubbiſh of the Town is carried, and it is now grown up to ſuch a Hill, that it ſerves as a Land-mark to Mariners to find their Way into the Port. How much more convenient would it not be to fill up low hollow Places with ſuch Stuff? Thus at *Venice*, (for which I highly applaud them) they have in my Time filled up ſeveral of their Marſhes with the Rubbiſh of the Town. *Herodotus* tells us, that the People who live among the Marſhes in *Ægypt*, in order to avoid the Gnats, lie a Nights in very high Towers. At *Ferrara* by the *Po* few or no Gnats appear within the City; but out of Town, to thoſe who are not uſed to them, they are execrable. It is ſuppoſed that they are driven from the Town by the great Quantity of Smoke and Fire. Flies do not haunt Places which are cold or expoſed to much Wind, and eſpecially where the Windows are very high. Some ſay that Flies will not enter where the Tail of a Wolf is buried, and that a Squill hung up will alſo drive away venomous Animals. The Ancients made uſe of a great many Defences againſt the violent Heats; among which I am very well pleaſed with their Crypts or ſubterraneous Porticoes, Vaults, which received Light no where but from the Top. They were alſo fond of Halls with large Windows turned away from the South, open to a cool Air, and ſhaded by ſome neighbouring Edifice. *Metellus*, the Son of *Octavia*, *Auguſtus*'s Siſter, made an Awning over the Forum with Sails, that the People might follow their Cauſes without prejudicing their Healths. But Air is more effectual

effectual to cooling any Place than Shade, as you may find by hanging a Sail upright before that Place to keep out the Air. *Pliny* tells us, that they used to make Places in their Houses on purpose for Shade; but in what Manner they were contrived he does not describe. Whatever they were, Nature must be the best Pattern to imitate. We find, that when we gape with our Mouths wide open, our Breath issues out warm; but when we blow with our Lips pretty close together, the Air comes out cool. Thus in an Edifice, when the Air comes through a very wide Aperture, especially if the Sun lies upon that Aperture, it is warm; but if it passes through a straiter and more shady Passage, it comes quicker and cooler. If warm Water be carryed in a Tube through cold Water, it will be refrigerated. The same will hold good of Air. It is a Question what is the Reason that those that walk in the Sun do not tan so soon as those that sit in it; but the Answer is easy: For by our Motion the Air too is moved, whereby the Sun's Rays are thrown aside. Moreover, in order to make the Shade the Cooler, we may add Roof to Roof, and Wall to Wall, and the greater Space that is left between these, the Cooler, will be our Shade and the more impenetrable to the Heat; for this Interval between has almost the same Effect for this Purpose as a Wall of the same Thickness would have; and in one Respect it is better, because a Wall would retain either the Heat of the Sun or the Cold that had once penetrated it much longer; whereas these double Walls will preserve an equal Temperature of the Air. In Places where the Sun is excessively scorching, a Wall built of Pumice Stone will admit the least Heat and retain it the least Time. If the Doors to the private Apartments are double, that is to say, if there be two Doors, one opening inwards and the other outwards, with a Space of about two Foot between them, what is said within cannot be over-heard by those who are without.

CHAP. XIV.

Some more minute Particulars relating to the Use of Fire.

IF we build in a very cold Place, we shall be obliged to make use of Fire, which is done several Ways, but the most convenient of all is to have it in an open Place, where we can see it shine while we feel its Warmth; for when it is enclosed, as in Stoves, the Smoke is apt to affect the Eyes and injure the Sight. To this add, that the very Sight of the Flame and Light of a Brick Fire, is a chearful Companion to the old Men that are chatting together in the Chimney Corner. But then up towards the Middle of the Funnel of the Chimney there ought to be a transverse Iron Door, which you may shut when all the Smoke is exhausted, and the Fire burns perfectly bright, and so stop up the Tunnel, in order to prevent any Wind from getting down that Way into the Room. Walls built of Flint or Marble are both cold and damp; for by their Chilness they compress the Air into Moisture. Soft Stone and Brick are more convenient, when they are thoroughly dried. Those who venture to sleep between Walls that are new and wet, especially if the Cieling be arched, are sure to catch some very dangerous Illness, Pains, Fevers, or Rheums. Some by that Folly have lost their Eye-sight, others the Use of their Limbs, some their Senses. In order that they may dry the sooner, the Windows and Doors should be left open to give the Winds a thorough Passage. The best Walls for the Health of the Inhabitants are those built of Brick not burnt but dried in the Sun two Years before. Incrustations of Stuc thicken the Air and make it unwholsome and prejudicial to the Lungs and Brain. If you wainscot your Walls with Fir or even Poplar, it will make the House the wholsomer, warmer in Winter, and not very hot in Summer; but then you will be troubled with Mice and Bugs. This you may prevent by stuffing the Interspace with Reeds, or stopping up all the Holes and Retreats of those Vermin with Chalk and Hair tempered together with Lees of Oil: for all Sorts of Oil are mortal Enemies to those Vermin which breed of Corruption.

Chap. XV.

By what Methods to deſtroy or drive away Serpents, Gnats, Bugs, Flies, Mice, Fleas, Moths, and the like troubleſome Vermin.

SINCE we are fallen upon this Subject, I ſhall venture to ſet down ſome Things which we find in very grave Authors. It were certainly to be wiſhed, that a Building could be free from all Manner of Inconveniencies. The Inhabitants of Mount *Ætna* inſtituted a Sacrifice to *Hercules*, becauſe he delivered them from the Gnats; as did alſo the *Mileſians* for clearing their Vineyards from the Caterpillars. The *Æolians* ſacrificed to *Apollo* for deſtroying their Swarms of Mice. Theſe were doubtleſs great Benefits; but by what Means they were done, has not been recorded. However, in ſome Authors I find what follows: The *Aſſyrians* by means of a burnt Liver, together with an Onion and a Squill hanging over the Tranſom of the Door, drove away all poiſonous Animals. *Ariſtotle* ſays, that Serpents may be driven from a Houſe by the Smell of Rue, and that by laying ſome Fleſh in a Pot you will draw great Numbers of Waſps into it, where you may ſhut them in, and that by laying Sulphur and Baſtard-marjoram upon the Holes of Ants-neſts, you may exterminate the Ants, *Sabinus Tyro* wrote to *Mæcenas*, that if their Holes were ſtopt up with Sea-mud, or Aſhes, it would deſtroy them. *Pliny* ſays, that the Herb Wart-wort will effectually do it. Others think that pouring in Water where unbaked Brick has been ſteept, is a great Enemy to them. The Ancients affirm, that Nature has made mortal Enmities between certain Animals and certain Things, inſomuch, that the one is ſure Deſtruction to the other. Hence the Weaſel flies from the Smell of a roaſted Cat, and Serpents from that of a Leopard. Thus they tell us, that when a Leech ſticks the moſt obſtinately to a Man's Fleſh, if you apply a Bug to its Head, it will immediately quit its Hold, and fall off languid; as, on the other hand, the Smoke of a burning Leech will drive the Bug out of his moſt private lurking Places. *Solinus* ſays, that ſtrewing a Place with ſome of the Duſt of the Iſle of *Thanet*, in *Britain*, will preſently drive away Serpents: And Hiſtorians relate, that the ſame may be done by the Earth of ſeveral other Places, and particularly of the Iſland *Ebuſus*. The Earth of the Iſland *Galeon* belonging to the *Garamanthes* kills both Serpents and Scorpions. *Strabo* ſays, that the *Africans*, when they went to reſt, uſed to rub the Feet of their Beds with Garlick, to keep off the Scorpions. *Saſernas* tells us how to kill Bugs, in the following Words. Boil a wild Cucumber in Water; then pour it where-ever you think fit; they will never come near the Place; or elſe rub your Bedſtead with an Ox's Gall mixed with Vinegar. Others direct us to fill up all the Cracks with Lees of Wine. The Root of the Holm-oak, ſays *Pliny*, is an Enemy to Scorpions, and the Aſh too is excellent againſt ſuch noxious Animals and eſpecially Serpents; which alſo will never retire under Fern. Serpents are likewiſe driven away by the Burning of a Woman's Hair or of a Goat's Horn, or of that of a Stag, or of the Sawduſt of Cedar, or of ſome Drops of *Galbanum*, or of Oſier, green Ivy or Juniper; and thoſe who are rubbed with Juniper-ſeed are perfectly ſecure from Hurt by Serpents. The Smell of the Herb *Haxus* inebriates Aſpics, and lays them ſo faſt aſleep that they are quite benumbed. Againſt Canker-worms we are directed only to ſtick the Skeleton of a Mare's Head upon a Poſt in the Garden. The Palm-tree is an Enemy to Bats. Where-ever you ſprinkle Water wherein Elder-flowers have been boiled, you will kill all the Flies; but this is ſooner done with Hellebore, eſpecially with the black Sort. Burying a Dog's Tooth, together with his Tail and Feet in the Hill, will they ſay rid you of Flies. The *Tarantula* cannot endure the Smell of Saffron. The Smoke of burning Hops will kill the Gnats. Mice are killed by the Smell of Wolf-bane, though it be at a Diſtance. So both Mice and Bugs are deſtroyed by the Smoke of Vitriol. Fleas, if you ſprinkle the Place with a Decoction of Coloquintida or of the Caltrop-thiſtle, will all vaniſh. If you ſprinkle a Place with Goat's-blood, they will march to it in whole Swarms; but they are driven away by the Smell of Colewort, and yet more effectually

ally by that of Oleander. Broad flat Veſſels full of Water ſet about the Floor are dangerous Traps for Fleas that take their Leaps too daringly. Moths are driven away by Wormwood, Aniſe-ſeed, or the Smell of the Herb Savin: Nay we are told, that Cloaths are ſafe from them ſo long as they hang upon Ropes. But upon this Subject we have dwelt long enough, and perhaps longer than a very grave Reader may like; but he will pardon it, if he conſiders, that what we have ſaid may be of ſome Service for ridding a Situation of Inconveniencies, and that all is little enough againſt the inceſſant Plague of theſe intolerable Vermin.

Chap. XVI.

Of making a Room either warmer or cooler, as alſo of amending Defects in the Walls.

I NOW return to my Subject. It is a wonderful Thing, that if you cover a Wall with Hangings woven of Wool it will make the Room warmer, and if they are of Flax, colder. If the Platform be damp, dig Pits and Drains under it, and fill them up either with Pumice-ſtone or Gravel, to prevent the Water from rotting in them. Then ſtrew the Ground with Coal to the Height of one Foot, and cover that with Sand or rather with Tiles, and over all this lay your Floor. It will be all to no Purpoſe if there is Room for the Air to paſs under the firſt Pavement or Floor. But againſt the Heat of the Sun in Summer, and the Severity of the Cold in Winter, it will be of very great Service, if the Soil thereabouts in general is not damp but dry. Under the Area of your Parlour dig away the Earth to the Depth of twelve Foot, and then floor it with nothing but naked Boards; the Space beneath which is floored only with Plaiſter will make the Air in your Parlour much cooler than you would imagine, inſomuch that you ſhall find it make your Feet cold even when your Shoes are on, nothing being over the ſubterraneous Pavement but plain Boards. The Ceiling of this Parlour ſhould be arched; and then you will be ſurprized how warm it will be in Winter and how cold in Summer. If you are troubled with the Inconvenience which the Satyriſt complains of the Noiſe of Carriages paſſing through a narrow Street, together with that of the rough Language of their bruitiſh Drivers, ſo dreadful to the poor Man in his ſick Bed; *Pliny* the younger tells us, in one of his Epiſtles, how to prevent this Diſturbance, in the following Words. Next to this Room lies the Chamber of Night and of Repoſe, in which was never heard the Voice of Servants, nor the hollow Murmur of the Sea, nor the Crack of Tempeſt, nor can you here perceive the Gleam of Lightening, nor even the Light of the Sun, unleſs you open the Windows, ſo retired is the Place. The Reaſon is, that there is a Lobby between this Chamber and the Garden, in which intermediate Space all the Sounds are loſt, let us now come to the Walls. The Defects in theſe are as follows; either they ſcale off, or they crack, or the Ribs give Way, or they lean from their Perpendicular. The Cauſes of theſe Defects are various, and ſo are their Remedies. Some of the Cauſes indeed are manifeſt, others more concealed, ſo that often we know not what Remedies to apply, till we have ſeverely felt the Miſchief. Others are not in the leaſt obſcure; but then perhaps the Negligence of Men makes them inclined to hope that they may not do ſo much Hurt as they certainly will do. The manifeſt Cauſes of Defects in the Wall are, when it is too thin, when it is not well knit together, when it is full of improper dangerous Apertures, or laſtly, when it is not ſufficiently ſtrengthened with Ribs againſt the Violence of Storms. Thoſe Cauſes which happen unexpected or unforeſeen, are Earthquakes, Lightening, the Inconſtancy of the Foundation, and indeed of Nature itſelf. But in ſhort, the greateſt Injury to all Parts of a Building is the Negligence and Heedleſſneſs of Men. A certain Author ſays, that a Weed is a ſecret Battering-ram againſt a Wall; nor is it to be believed what vaſt Stones I have myſelf ſeen removed and puſhed out of their Places by the Force, or indeed by the Wedge of a little Root that grew between the Joints; which if you had only pulled out while it was young, the Work would have been preſerved from that Injury. I greatly commend the Ancients, who kept a Number of People in

Pay, only to preserve and look after the publick Buildings. *Agrippa* left Pay for two hundred and fifty for this Purpose, and *Cæsar* for no less than four hundred and sixty; and they dedicated the next fifteen Feet to the Structure to lie quite clear by their Aqueducts, that their Sides or Arches might not breed any Weeds to demolish them. The same seems to have been done even by private Persons, with relation to those Edifices which they were desirous to have eternal; for we find, that the Inscription upon their Sepulchres generally mentioned how many Foot of Ground was consecrated to Religion in that Structure; sometimes it was fifteen, sometimes twenty. But not to fall into a Repetition of these Things, the Ancients thought, that you might entirely destroy a Tree even after it was pretty well grown, if in some Part of the Dog-days you cut it down to the Height of one Foot, and boring a Hole through the Heart, pour into it Oil of Vitriol mixed with Powder of Brimstone, or else sprinkling it plentifully with a Decoction of burnt Bean-shells. *Columella* says, that you may destroy a Wood with the Flower of Hops steept one Day in Juice of Hemlock, strewed about the Roots. *Solinus* says, that a Tree touched with the Menstrua will lose its Leaves, and some affirm, that it will even kill the Tree. *Pliny* says, that a Tree may be killed by touching the Root with a wild Carrot. But to return to the Defects of a Wall. If a Wall be thinner than it ought to be, we must either apply a new Wall to the old one, in such a Manner that they may make but one; or, to avoid the Expence of this, we may only strengthen it with Ribs, that is to say, with Pilasters or Columns. A new Wall may be superinduced to an old one, as follows. In several Parts of the old Wall fix strong Catches made of the soundest Stone, sticking out in such a Manner as to enter into the Wall which you are going to join to the other, and to be in the Nature of Bands between the two Walls; and your Wall in this Case should always be built of square Stone. You may fortify an old Wall with a new Pilaster, in the following Manner. First mark out its future Breadth upon the Wall with red Oker. Then open a Break in the Bottom of the Wall quite down below the Foundation, in Breadth some small Matter more than your Pilaster, but not very high. Then immediately fill up this Break with square Stone worked together strong and even. By this Means that Part of the Wall which is between the red Marks will be shored up by the Thickness of the Pilaster, and so the whole will be made stronger. Then in the same Manner that you have laid the Bottom of this Pilaster you must go on to work up the Body of it quite to the Top. Thus much of a Wall that is too thin. Where the Wall has not made good Bond, we must use Cramps or Spars of Iron, or rather of Brass; but you must take great Care that you do not weaken the Ribs by boring the Holes from them. If the Weight of any crumbling Earth pushes against some Part of the Wall, and threatens Injury to it by its Humidity, dig a Trench along the Wall as broad as you find it necessary, and in this Trench build some Arches to support the Weight of the Earth which is falling in, with a Current or Drain through these Arches for the Humidity to purge off by; ot else lay some Girders along the Ground with the Heads setting against the Wall which is shoved out by the Weight of the Earth, and let the Heads of these Girders into Summers, which you may cover over with new Earth. This will strengthen the Foundation, because this new Earth will consolidate, and grow compact, before the Strength of the Girders will give Way.

Chap. XVII.

Of some Defects which cannot be provided against, but which may be repaired after they have happened.

I NOW proceed to those Defects which cannot be foreseen, but which when they have happened may be repaired. Cracks in the Wall and Inclination from the Perpendicular, are sometimes occasioned by the Arches over it, which push out the Wall, or because it is not sufficiently strong to bear the Weight which is laid upon it. But the greatest Defects of this Sort almost constantly proceed from some Faults in the Foundation; however we may easily discover

discover whether they are from thence, or from some other Cause by certain Symptoms. Thus to begin with Cracks in the Wall; to which soever Side the Crack runs in its Ascent, on that Side you may be sure the Cause of the Defect lies somewhere in the Foundation. If it does not verge to either Side, but runs up in a direct Line, and grows wider at the Top, then let us take a careful View of the Courses of Stonework on each Side; for on which ever Side they sink from their Level, on that Side we may be sure the Foundation has failed. But if the upper Part of the Wall is entire, and there are Cracks in several Places towards the Bottom, which in their Ascent run together close at Top; then we may be satisfied that the Corners of the Building stand firm, and that the Defect is somewhere about the Middle in the Foundation. If there is but one Crack of this Sort, the higher up it goes, the the more it shews the Corners to have given Way. In order to strengthen the Foundations in any of these Cases, according to the Magnitude of the Structure and the Solidity of the Ground, dig a narrow Pit near the Wall, but so deep as to come to a firm Soil, and there breaking through the Bottom of the Wall, immediately work up to it with square Stone, and then leave it to settle. When that is settled, dig another Pit in another Part, and underprop it in the same Manner, and in the same Manner give it Time to settle. By this Means you will make a Kind of new Foundation to the whole Wall. But if even by digging you cannot come at any firm Ground, then make Holes in certain Places not too near the Corners, but pretty close to the Foundation of the Wall, on both Sides, that is to say, as well under the Roof as under the open Air, and into those Holes drive Piles as close as they will stick, and over them lay the stoutest Summers you can get lengthways, with the Sides of the Wall. Then across these Summers lay the strongest Girders running under the Bottom of the Foundation, which must rest with their whole Weight upon these Girders, as it were upon a Bridge. In all these Reparations great Care must be taken that no Part of the new Work be too weak to support the Weight which is to bear upon it, and that for ever so long Time: because the whole Pile bearing towards that weaker Part, would immediately fall to Ruins. But where the Foundation has given Way somewhere about the Middle of the Wall, and the upper Part does not appear to be affected by the Crack, then upon the Face of the Wall mark out with your Oker an Arch as large as the Case requires, or, in other Words, so big as to take in all that Part of the Wall which is sunk. Then beginning at one End of this Arch, break into the Wall with an Opening not bigger than one Stone of your intended Arch will fill up; which Stones in an Arch we formerly called Wedges, and immediately insert one of these Wedges in such a Manner that its Lines may exactly answer to the Center to which you have described your Arch. Then make another Break close above it, and fill it up with another such Wedge; and so continuing the Work successively, compleat your whole Arch: and thus you may fortify your Wall without Danger. If a Column or any other of the Ribs of the Building is weakened, you may restore it in the following Manner. Underprop the Architrave with a strong Arch of Tile and Plaister beat together, as also with Piers of Plaister rais'd for this Purpose, in such a Manner that this new Arch may quite fill up the old Intercolumnation, or Aperture between the Ribs: and let this underproping be run up as fast as possible, and without the least Intermission. It is the Nature of Plaister to swell as it dries: so that this new Work, though quite fresh, will be able to take upon itself and sustain the Weight of the old Wall Vault. Then, having before got ready all your Materials, take out the defective Column, and supply its Place with a sound one. If you chuse rather to rest the old Wall upon Timbers, then undershore it with Levers made of strong Beams, and load the longer Ends of those Levers with Baskets filled with Sand, which will raise up the Weight by degrees equally and without any Shocks. If the Wall is swerved from its Perpendicular, fix Planks or Timbers upright against it, and against each of these set a strong Timber by Way of Shore, with its Foot stretching at some Distance from the Wall. Then either with Levers or with Wedges, drive forwards the Feet of the Shores by degrees, so as they may press against the Wall, and so by distributing this Force equally in all Parts, you will raise the Wall again to its perpendicular. If this cannot be done, prop it up with Shores of Timber fixed well in the Ground, with their Ends well daubed over with Pitch and Oil to prevent their being corroded by the Touch of Mortar; then erect Buttresses of square Stone, built so as to enclose those Shores of Timber.

Perhaps

Perhaps a Coloſſus or ſome ſmall Church is ſunk to one Side in its whole Foundation. In this Caſe, you muſt either raiſe that Part which is ſunk, or take away that Part which is too high; both very bold Attempts. The firſt Thing you are to do, is to bind and faſten together, as ſtrongly as poſſible, the Foundation and thoſe Parts which will be in Danger of being ſeparated by Motion, with good Timbers and the ſtrongeſt Braces. There are no better Sort of Braces than ſtrong Hoops of Iron with Wedges drove in between them to keep them tight. Then we raiſe up the Side of the Wall which is ſunk with ſtrong Timbers put under it after the Manner of Levers, as above. If you would rather rectify the Fault by taking away from the Side which is too high, you may do it in the following Manner: Dig away the Ground about the Middle of that Side quite below the Foundation, in the Bottom of which you muſt there open a Break, not very wide, but high enough for you to make it good with ſtrong ſquare Stone. In making good this Break you muſt not work it up quite to the reſt of the Building, but leave ſome Inches ſpace between the new Work and the Old; and this Space you muſt fill up with Wedges of the tougheſt Oak drove in at very ſmall Diſtances from each other. In this Manner you muſt go on to ſhore up all that Side which you want to let down lower. When the whole Weight is thus ſupported, knock out the Wedges by degrees, as gently and cautiouſly as poſſible, till the Wall is ſunk to its juſt Perpendicular. Then fill up the Spaces between the Wedges which are left, with other Wedges of the ſtrongeſt Stone that can be got. In the great Baſilique of St. *Peter* at *Rome*, ſome Parts of the Wall which were over the Columns being ſwerved from their Uprights, ſo as to threaten even the Fall of the whole Roof; I contrived how the Defect might be remedied as follows. Every one of thoſe Parts of the Wall which had given Way, let it reſt upon what Column it would, I determined ſhould be taken clear out, and made good again with ſquare Stone which ſhould be worked true to its Perpendicular, only leaving in the old Wall ſtrong Catches of Stone to unite the additional Work to the former. Laſtly, I would have ſupported the Beam under which thoſe uneven Parts of the Wall were to be taken out, by means of Engines, called *Capra*'s, erected upon the Roof, ſetting the Feet of thoſe Engines upon the ſtrongeſt Parts of the Roof and of the Wall. This I would have done at different Times over the ſeveral Columns where theſe Defects appear. The *Capra* is a naval Engine conſiſting of three Timbers, the Heads of which meet and are ſtrongly braced or bound together, and the Feet ſtretch out to a Triangle. This Engine, with the Addition of Pullies and a Capſtern is very uſeful for raiſing great Weights. If you are to lay a new Coat over an old Wall or an old plaiſtered Floor, firſt waſh it well with clean Water, and then with a Bruſh whiten it over with Whiting diſſolved and mixed with marble Duſt; and this will prepare it for holding the new Coat of Plaiſter or Stuc. If a Pavement which is expoſed to the open Air has any Cracks in it, you may ſtop them up with Aſhes ſifted fine, and tempered Oil, eſpecially of Linſeed. But the beſt Material for this Sort of Reparation is Chalk mixed with quick Lime well beat together and thoroughly burnt in the Kiln, and then ſlaked immediately with Oil; taking Care before you fill up the Cracks with it to clean them from all manner of Duſt, which you may do with Feathers, or by blowing it out with Bellows. Nor let us under this Article of Amendments, quite forget all Ornament. If any Wall looks unhandſome from being too high, embelliſh it either by faſtening on a Cornice of Stuc-work, or by Painting it like Pannels, in order to divide its Height into more decent Proportions. If a Wall be too long, adorn it with Columns reaching from the Top to the Bottom, not ſet too cloſe to each other, which will be a kind of Reſting-places to the Eye, and make the exceſſive Length appear leſs offenſive. There is another Thing not foreign to our preſent Purpoſe. Many Parts of a Building, from being either placed too low or encompaſſed with Walls not high enough, ſeem leſs, and more contracted than they really are; whereas when they are either raiſed upon a higher Platfom, or have ſome Addition made to the Height of their Walls, they ſeem at a Diſtance much larger than they did before. It is alſo certain, that a handſome Diſpoſition of the Apertures, and placing the Door and Windows gracefully, gives all the Aparments a greater Share both of Dignity and Elegance than is to be imagined.

The End of Book X.